Written by one of the UK's leading scholars of welfare law, this book analyses the current child support legislation in its broader historical and social context, synthesising both doctrinal and socio-legal approaches to legal research and scholarship. It draws on the historical and legal literature on the Poor Law and the development of both the public and private law obligation of child maintenance. Modern child support law must also be considered in the context of both social and demographic changes and in the light of popular norms about child maintenance liabilities. The main part of the book is devoted to an analysis of the modern child support scheme. The following key issues are addressed: the distinction between applications in 'private' and 'benefit' cases and the extent to which the courts retain a role in child maintenance matters; the basis and justification for the exception from the obligation for parents with care on benefit to co-operate with the Child Support Agency where they fear 'undue harm or distress'; the assessment of income for the purposes of the formula and the evidential difficulties this entails; the tension between the formula, which ignores the parent with care's income, and the demands of distributive justice; the further conflict between the formula, under which liability is capped only for the very wealthy, and the traditional approach of private law, which is premised on children being entitled to maintenance rather than a share in family wealth; the treatment of special cases under the formula by way of 'variations' (formerly 'departures'); the nature of Agency decision-making and the scope for appeals; and the efficacy of the provisions relating to collection and enforcement. The final chapter explores the factors which impact on child support compliance and considers various models for redesigning the child support scheme.

Child Support
Law and Policy

Nick Wikeley

·H A R T·
PUBLISHING

OXFORD – PORTLAND OREGON
2006

Published in North America (US and Canada) by
Hart Publishing
c/o International Specialized Book Services
920 NE 58th Avenue, Suite 300
Portland, OR 97213-3786
USA
Tel: +1 503 287 3093 or toll-free: (1) 800 944 6190
Fax: +1 503 280 8832
E-mail: orders@isbs.com
Web Site: www.isbs.com

© Nick Wikeley, 2006

Hart Publishing, 16c Worcester Place,
Oxford OX1 2JW
Telephone: +44 (0)1865 517530 or Fax: +44 (0)1865 510710
e-mail: mail@hartpub.co.uk
WEBSITE: http//www.hartpub.co.uk

British Library Cataloguing in Publication Data
Data Available
ISBN-13: 978–1–84113–532–8 (paperback)
ISBN-10: 1–84113–532–1 (paperback)

Typeset by Hope Services (Abingdon) Ltd.
Printed and bound in Great Britain on acid-free paper by
TJ International, Padstow, Cornwall

FOREWORD

No child asks to be born, though few regret it for long. It ought to be self-evident that every child has the right to be cared for and brought up to adult self-sufficiency. It also ought to be self-evident that the corresponding obligation should rest primarily upon the two people responsible for bringing the child into the world. The child has the right to expect what they collectively are able to provide for him. If they are living together, they take it for granted that they should share this task and that the child should share their standard of living. Most parents take great pride and pleasure in doing this. They work out between themselves how to manage their shared responsibilities. One may do more of the actual caring and the other do more to find the money necessary to fund it. As their circumstances change, so will their arrangements change. Little negotiations about who does what happen every day; larger negotiations happen every so often, usually when milestones in the child's or the adults' lives are reached.

But if the parents are living apart, all that sense of a shared enterprise can quickly disappear. If they have never lived together, it may never have developed at all. Everything becomes at once more rigid, more complicated and more formal. The easy interaction which a father had with his children when he came home from work now has to be planned. The shared bank account is wound up, the bills no longer routinely paid, the house-keeping allowance a thing of the past. The caring and financing roles are more sharply divided. Small wonder that, even with the best will in the world, endless opportunities arise for misunderstanding and disagreement. And the best will in the world is not always to be found between parents who no longer live together. Yet the child still has exactly the same needs, and the same rights, as he had before. He also has some new ones. Two households cannot live as cheaply as one. Nor should he be made to suffer because of his parents' differences.

The moral and legal case for parents to go on looking after their children after they separate is taken for granted. Why then have we been so slow to recognise the moral and legal case for parents to go on financing that care after they have separated? We in the courts have not always helped. Perhaps this is because the power to order parents to make meaningful financial payments for the benefit of their children is of remarkably recent origin. Even when we had that power, the courts were for some time content to allow the State to take over or underwrite the main financial burden. We preferred to promote a clean break and preserve the family home for the children and their carer. When we made an order for support, we left it up to the recipient parent to enforce. We cannot be surprised that the State stepped in to nationalise the assessment and enforcement of this basic obligation. Much reviled though it has been and continues to be, the child support scheme has made a difference. It could make a much bigger difference if it became as effective as similar schemes elsewhere in the common law world.

All this is made very clear by Professor Wikeley's penetrating and scholarly analysis. The days before the Child Support Act 1991 were not a golden age for children and their carers. Nor have the days since then been such a dark age for the parents with whom they no longer live, if they ever did. But there is a great deal to be done in order that the vision of the scheme can be properly recognised and achieved. There is still a great deal to learn from the comparative successes of Australia and the United States. We can still hope that the latest review will lead to a scheme which, if not universally liked, is at least generally thought to be sensible, fair and efficient.

I certainly look forward to the day when the appellate committee of the House of Lords does not have to consider four cases about child support in less than a year.[1] Only one of those concerned a point of universal principle, the treatment of same sex couples in the calculation of child support. The others all arose, one way or another, from frustration with the inefficiency and occasional absurdity of the current system. This is not a conventional legal text book with a little commentary thrown in. In laying bare the precursors, the principles, the practice and the policy, Professor Wikeley has done lawyers, policy-makers, parents and children a great service. It is also timely. He almost makes me believe that we could make things better for the children we are there to serve.

Brenda Hale
House of Lords
30 May 2006

---

[1] *R v Secretary of State for Work and Pensions ex p Kehoe* [2005] UKHL 48; *Secretary of State for Work and Pensions v M* [2006] UKHL 11, *Farley v Child Support Agency* [2006] UKHL 31 and *Smith v Secretary of State for Work and Pensions* [2006] UKHL 35.

PREFACE

This book examines the law and policy relating to child support. It is widely acknowledged that the Child Support Agency in the United Kingdom, which started operations in such difficulties in 1993, remains in a state of crisis. At the time of writing, the Government is awaiting the recommendations of Sir David Henshaw, who is undertaking a further 'root and branch' review of the child support system. This book offers no easy solutions; rather, it takes a step back and seeks to address a number of fundamental questions—what is the purpose of child support? How did we get where we are today? What is the legal framework of the child support system? What are (and should be) the principles underpinning the current and any redesigned scheme?

At the outset, however, I should make three points about the coverage of child support issues in this book. The first is that this is principally a book about the 'new scheme' which operates under the Child Support Act 1991 as amended, especially by the Child Support, Pensions and Social Security Act 2000. Accordingly, the detailed analysis that follows is centred on the law which has applied since 3 March 2003. As well as the legislation itself, this includes consideration of the jurisprudence developed by the Child Support Commissioners (on the numbering system used in this branch of case law, see pages 431–32 below). It is true that the Child Support Agency's caseload today includes many 'old scheme' cases under the original 1991 Act, which are therefore still governed by the law that applied to child support applications made between 5 April 1993 and 2 March 2003. However, this book is long enough as it is, and time and space do not permit a full account of the finer points of the old scheme legislation. Subject to that rather large proviso, I have sought to state the law as it stands at 1 June 2006. It follows that this book has been written before the publication of the Henshaw Report, as well as before the delivery of the opinions of the House of Lords in *Smith v Secretary of State for Work and Pensions* (discussed at page 353 below).

The second point is that there are in fact two child support jurisdictions in the United Kingdom—one in Great Britain and a parallel system in Northern Ireland. Although the primary focus of the discussion in this book is on Great Britain, there are references to the Northern Ireland case law as the child support regimes are effectively identical. I have also drawn attention in appropriate places to the differences that exist within Great Britain, not least as Scotland has its own legal system and so the child support scheme there operates in the context of a distinctive family law jurisdiction.

The third matter relates to questions of style. I have adopted the usage of referring to the non-resident parent as 'he' and the person with care (or parent with care) as 'she'. Obviously this does not apply in every case, but it reflects the overwhelming majority of arrangements in practice, a point recognised by the terms of the legislation itself (see Child Support Act 1991, section 6(7)). For the avoidance of doubt I should add that I have used 'CSA' throughout as the standard abbreviation for the Child Support Act, rather than for the Child Support Agency (unless an original quote describes the Agency as the 'CSA').

The chapters of this book are divided into three main sections. Part I of the book explores the basis for the child support obligation (chapter 1) and traces its evolution in both public law and private law in the United Kingdom (chapters 2 to 5). Chapter 6 examines the international experience of formula-based child support schemes, principally in the United States of America and in Australia. I would hope that all those interested in child support law and policy, lawyers and non-lawyers alike, would find Part I of interest.

Part II is the heart of the book and consists of a detailed analysis of the 'new scheme' which has been in place since 3 March 2003. Chapter 7 explores the boundaries between the statutory child support scheme and the role of the courts, while chapter 8 defines the personal scope of the 1991 Act—so it considers who is a 'non-resident parent', a 'parent with care' and a 'qualifying child' respectively for the purposes of the legislation. Chapter 9 examines the ways in which an application for a child support maintenance calculation may be made and the role, and information-gathering powers, of the Child Support Agency. Chapters 10 to 12 explain the principles governing the child support formula, the assessment of income and the circumstances in which a variation from the formula may be sought. Chapter 13 analyses the arrangements for complaints, reviews of Agency decisions and appeals, while chapter 14 deals with the collection and enforcement of child support liabilities. Overall, Part II has been designed to provide an authoritative and comprehensive account of the legislative framework, as elaborated by the relevant case law. It may be that only a true 'child support techie' (ie a person who displays an enthusiastic, if not obsessive, interest in the detailed minutiae of child support law) will wish to read Part II from beginning to end. On the other hand, the doctrinal analysis of child support law has been developed with an eye to the policy issues underpinning child support law, and so it is hoped that non-lawyers (and indeed non-techie lawyers) will also find it illuminating.

Part III of the book, which comprises the concluding chapter 15, seeks to bring together the main themes of the book, and to explore ways in which compliance with the child support scheme might be increased in the light of the Government's current review and projected redesign of the child support system. If this book goes into a second edition, it is safe to assume that there will be rather more to say in this final section.

I must also express my sincere thanks to all those institutions and individuals who have made this book possible. First and foremost, I am indebted to the Leverhulme Trust for the award of a Major Research Fellowship to carry out the research for this book, as a result of which I was relieved of teaching and (more importantly) University management responsibilities for two years. Without that very generous assistance, this book simply would not have been written. I am especially grateful to Baroness Hale of Richmond for kindly agreeing to write the Foreword. My thanks must also go to Lisa Young of Murdoch University in Perth, Western Australia, for being such a brilliant research collaborator, correspondent and sabbatical exchange partner. I am also grateful to Murdoch Law School and to Lisa's colleagues for providing such a congenial environment to conduct my comparative research during an extended stay there in 2004.

Many other individuals have helped me in various ways in the course of this project. For their insightful comments on drafts of various chapters, I would like to thank, as well as Lisa Young, the following: Lorie Charlesworth, Ira Ellman, Andrew Halpin, Bernard Harris, Caroline Jones, Emma Laurie, James Pirrie, Rebecca Probert, Allan Shephard, Sally Sheldon and John Stewart. I have also learnt much from conversations with Janet Allbeson, Ed Bates, Natalie Lee, Jonathan Montgomery and Gywnn Davis (although he may doubt this). In addition, I have benefited from discussions with many judicial colleagues, but especially Edward Jacobs, John Mesher and David Williams amongst the Child Support Commissioners and Godfrey Cole, Martha Street, David Teagle, Robin Weare and Penny Wood in the Appeals Service. I should emphasise that none of the views expressed in this book should be associated with any of my judicial colleagues; in my own capacity as a deputy Child Support Commissioner, I must also reserve the right to disagree, on further reflection and in the light of parties' submissions, with any propositions found in this book. I wish to thank those DWP civil servants who have helped me with my various enquiries.

From other parts of the British Isles I am indebted to Conall MacLynn and Kenneth Mullan (Northern Ireland) and David Nichols, Kenneth Norrie, Christopher Smith and Tanya Parker (Scotland). Farther afield, in Australia I had assistance from Karyn Bartholomew, Peter Bath, Peter Cane, Terry Carney, Nick Gye (and his colleagues in the Perth CSA office), John McMillan, Patrick Parkinson, Ruth Pilkinton, Allan Shephard, David Sippel, Mike Spivak and Justice Stephen Thackray. Bill Atkin and Graham Hill helpfully answered queries about New Zealand and Ira Ellman and Tom Oldham about the United States. Paula Cogan provided outstanding research assistance and Miranda Bayliss always managed to find even the most obscure Commissioner's decision. My library and archiving queries were always efficiently answered by Joy Caisley in Southampton, Anne Greenshields at Murdoch and the Public Record Office staff at Kew. Richard Hart and his efficient team at Hart Publishing have been, as ever, a delight to work with. Several cohorts of Southampton University students have enthusiastically acted as guinea-pigs for testing some of the ideas in this book in the course of the Law School's final year specialist child support law option.

Above all, I would like to thank Clare for her support, not least as at times she must have felt that I was due some first-hand experience of the child support system, and Nigel and Olga Wikeley for all their very practical and personal child support over the years. Finally, as one of the themes of this book is that the child's voice has been absent from child support law and policy, I have been left in absolutely no doubt whatsoever that I must thank Sarah (IT support), Jem (Tottenham support) and Carl (percussion support).

Nick Wikeley
School of Law
University of Southampton
1 June 2006

TABLE OF CONTENTS

Part I

Part II

Part III

LIST OF ABBREVIATIONS

AAR	Administrative Appeals Reports
AAT	Administrative Appeals Tribunal
AATA	Administrative Appeal Tribunal of Australia
AFDC	Aid to Families with Dependant Children
AGPS	Australian Government Publishing Service
AIFS	Australian Institute of Family Studies
ALD	Administrative Law Decisions
AMP/NATSEM	Australian Mutual Provident/ National Centre for Social and Economic Modelling
ANAO	Australian National Audit Office
ATO	Australian Tax Office
CCSO	Chief Child Support Officer
CFLQ	Child and Family Law Quarterly
CPAG	Child Poverty Action Group
CSPSSA	Child Support, Pensions and Social Security Act
CSA	Child Support Act
CSCS	Child Support Computer System
CSEAG	Child Support Evaluation Advisory Group
CTC	Child Tax Credit
DEO	Deduction from Earnings Order
DHSS	Department of Health and Social Security
DLA	Disability Living Allowance
DMA	Decision Making and Appeals
DPMCA	Domestic Proceedings and Magistrates' Courts Act
DPO	Departure Prohibition Order
DPTC	Disabled Person's Tax Credit
DVLA	Driver and Vehicle Licensing Agency
DWA	Disability Working Allowance
DWP	Department for Work and Pensions
DSS	Department of Social Security
ECHR	European Convention on Human Rights
EU	European Union
EWCA	England and Wales Court of Appeal
EWHC	England and Wales High Court
FLA	Family Law Act
FLR	Family Law Reports

FLRA	Family Law Reform Act
FPSC	Family Policy Studies Centre
GMA	Guaranteed Maintenance Allowance
HC	House of Commons
HL	House of Lords
HMRC	Her Majesty's Revenue and Customs
ICE	Independant Case Examiner
IRS	Internal Revenue System
IRLR	Industrial Relations Law Reports
IS	Income Support
ITEPA	Income Tax (Earnings and Pensions) Act
JSA	Jobseeker's Allowance
LCD	Lord Chancellor's Department
LRO	Liable Relative Officer
MAF	Maintenance Application Form
MASC	Maintenance Assessments and Special Cases
MCA	Matrimonial Causes Act
MEF	Maintenance Enquiry Form
MSS	Ministry of Social Security
NAPs	Non-Agency Payments
NAO	National Audit Office
NACRO	National Association for the Care and Resettlement of Offenders
NCSEM	National Centre for Social and Economic Modelling
NICA	Northern Ireland Court of Appeal
NINo	National Insurance Number
NLJ	New Law Journal
NRP	Non-Resident Parent
NZFLR	New Zealand Family Law Reports
OECD	Organisation for Economic Co-operation and Development
ONS	Office for National Statistics
OSCE	Office of Child Support Enforcement
PAYE	Pay As You Earn
PRWORA	Personal Responsibility and Work Opportunity Reconciliation Act
PWC	Person With Care
QBD	Queen's Bench Division
RPC	Regular Payment Condition
SBC	Supplementary Benefits Commission
SLFA	Solictors Family Law Association
SLT	Scots Law Times
SSA	Social Security Act
SSAA	Social Security Administration Act
SSCBA	Social Security Contributions and Benefits Act
TANF	Temporary Aid to Needy Families

UIFSA	Uniform Interstate Family Support Act
VSCA	Victoria Court of Appeal
WFTC	Working Families' Tax Credit
WTC	Working Tax Credit

LIST OF TABLES

LIST OF FIGURES

TABLE OF CASES

UK cases are at the beginning, followed by Practice Directions, Commissioners' Decisions, and then international legislation

Practice Directions

Commissioners, Great Britain

TABLE OF STATUTES

UK legislation is followed by international instruments and then international legislation

Bills

TABLE OF STATUTORY INSTRUMENTS

European Union

Part I

1

The Moral and Legal Basis for Child Support

Introduction

Three fundamental questions are explored in the course of this chapter in order to provide a theoretical context for this book's analysis of child support law and policy.[1] First, as a matter of principle, do children have a *right* to child support? It follows that the focus of the first main section of this chapter, having highlighted some definitional difficulties, is on the underlying moral basis for child support, reviewing some of the philosophical issues underpinning this debate. Secondly, and assuming that children do enjoy such a right, who has the *duty* of providing child support? This necessarily raises fundamental questions about the respective roles of private and public responsibility for supporting children. Thirdly, and on the further assumption that the duty is owed primarily (but not exclusively) by a child's parents, how might one construct a model of such a parental obligation? In this context we explore societal attitudes towards the principles that should govern the construction of the parental child support obligation, before considering a number of different models for determining the allocation and quantification of such liabilities. The penultimate part of the chapter examines the potential significance of international human rights norms in the field of child support law. It also considers the declared goals of the various statutory schemes which operate in the United Kingdom, Australia, New Zealand and across the United States of America. Clearly the nature and form of such child support schemes will be strongly influenced by economic, demographic, historical, political and social factors in each of the countries concerned. As we shall see later, some of these considerations—for example, a growing concern about the welfare costs of supporting children living in lone parent households—have been common across jurisdictions, albeit that they have emerged at different times.[2] The impact of such

---

[1] I am especially indebted to Andrew Halpin for his invaluable insights as I struggled with this chapter. He should not, of course, be associated with any of the views expressed or any errors which remain.

[2] Other factors, however, have influenced the debate in one country but have been largely absent in others—for example, race has long cast its shadow over child support issues in the United States, but has been of little (or no) significance elsewhere: see ch 6 below.

broader factors is summarised in subsequent chapters as regards the United Kingdom (chapters 2–5) and, more briefly, for other common law systems (chapter 6). The analysis in this chapter is more concerned with issues of principle, which are also summarised in the final section below. At the outset, however, we need to address two definitional issues: what do we mean by a 'child' and a 'parent' respectively?

Questions of Definition: 'Children' and 'Parents'

Logically, we cannot meaningfully debate whether children have a right to child support, and (or indeed or) whether parents have a duty to provide child support, without some common understanding of the terms 'child' and 'parent'. The former is relatively unproblematic in this context: for the purposes of this discussion, it is simplest to adopt the formal legal definition of a 'child' as a minor, in other words a young person who has yet to attain the age of 18 years.[3] It follows that this book is not concerned with any rights that adult children may or may not have (or expectations or hopes that they may harbour) in respect of their parents.[4]

The meaning of 'parent' is more contentious. In everyday speech, if we ask whether parents should be liable to pay child support, the usual underlying assumption is that by 'parents' we mean the child's 'biological' parents. Moreover, given both the inviolability of the private sphere of the family—which means that there is no effective public regulation of the allocation of resources within subsisting relationships, however unstable[5]—and the social reality of life after divorce and separation, the question 'should (biological) parents be liable to pay child support?' is usually understood in popular discourse to mean 'should (biological) fathers living apart from their children pay child support?' In this context, given the semantic uncertainty which attaches to the term 'biological', it might be more accurate to refer to the child's genetic father.[6] So who then is a 'father'? As recently as 1997, the European Court of Human Rights expounded the 'commonsense' view that, as characterised (and perhaps not unfairly caricatured) by Bainham, 'we all know a father when we see one—it is the man who has the genetic link with the child—the man whose sperm brings about the child's conception'.[7] Yet there are

---

[3] Family Law Reform Act 1969, s 1. This is not quite the definition adopted for the purposes of child support law (see ch 8 below) but will suffice for the present.
[4] See further J Finch and J Mason, *Passing On: Kinship and Inheritance in England* (Routledge, London, 2000).
[5] On the dynamics of which see J Pahl, *Money and Marriage* (Macmillan, Basingstoke, 1989) and C Vogler and J Pahl, 'Money, power and inequality within marriage' (1994) 42 *Sociological Review* 263.
[6] For mothers the position is less clear, in that the law may prioritise a gestational mother over a genetic mother (eg in surrogacy cases).
[7] Commenting on *X, Y and Z v United Kingdom* (1997) EHRR 143: see A Bainham, 'Parentage, Parenthood and Parental Responsibility: Subtle, Elusive Yet Important Distinctions' in A Bainham, S Day Sclater and M Richards (eds), *What is a Parent? A Socio-Legal Analysis* (Hart Publishing, Oxford, 1999), ch 2 at 25.

at least three difficulties with this overly simplistic conceptualisation of what it means to be a parent, and especially a father.

First, we should note that, although United Kingdom law regularly uses the concept of 'being a parent', Bainham has helpfully argued that it is more instructive to think in terms of the triad of concepts of parentage, parenthood and parental responsibility.[8] On his analysis, the focus of parentage is on the 'one-off' issue of the actual or presumed genetic link between the parent and child; parenthood is concerned with the ongoing status that an adult has in relation to a child; whilst parental responsibility is 'really a sort of trusteeship over the child'.[9] The linkages between these three notions are not always self-evident—for example, the history of the law governing children born outside marriage demonstrates that 'even being a genetic parent does not, of itself, imply legal parenthood'.[10]

Secondly, the focus on a genetic nexus between parent and child necessarily takes us no further than parentage; it necessarily excludes social parenthood, such as step-parenting. Whereas modern private law has made provision for step-children and other 'children of the family' to be maintained by a non-biologically related parent, the insistence of the Child Support Act 1991 on genetic parentage[11] as the exclusive basis for financial liabilities in relation to children reflects, in an atavistic way, the concerns of both the poor law and bastardy law.[12]

The third difficulty with defining 'parent' exclusively in terms of the genetic link between parent and child is that it ignores advances in the science and technology of assisted reproduction. These developments have 'wreaked havoc on conventional and legal notions of parenthood',[13] not least where couples experiencing infertility, or same-sex couples, have accessed such procedures to bring a child into the world. The potential for the creation of new family forms is such that the traditional assumption that every child must have two parents (and no more or no less) may well be misleading:

> In such families, more than two adults will have been involved in the creation of the child. These may be any combination of genetic parents, their partners, an egg donor, a sperm donor and a surrogate mother.[14]

Clearly assisted reproduction is far less common in practice than social (but non-genetic) parenthood, but both phenomena present challenges to conventional understandings of what is meant by a parent.

---

[8] *Ibid*, ch 2.

[9] *Ibid*, at 35.

[10] G Douglas and N Lowe, 'Becoming a Parent in English Law' (1992) 108 *Law Quarterly Review* 414 at 414.

[11] Or, in some cases, *presumed* genetic parentage: see ch 8 below.

[12] See further ch 2 below.

[13] JL Hill, 'What does it mean to be a "parent"? The claims of biology as the basis for parental rights' (1991) 66 *New York University Law Review* 353 at 353.

[14] New Zealand Law Commission, *New Issues in Legal Parenthood* (Report 88, Wellington, April 2005), at para 1.6. Note that it is also possible for a child to be 'fatherless' under the Human Fertilisation and Embryology Act 1990.

There is a rich philosophical literature on what it is that makes someone a parent. For some, the genetic link is paramount,[15] for others the intention to be a parent is crucial.[16] Others have adopted a more pluralist approach with a focus on causation: 'being causally implicated in the creation of a child is the key basis for being its parent'.[17] Much of this discussion has centred on the meaning of being a parent in the context of surrogacy. However, for the purposes of the present discussion, it is sufficient at this stage simply to highlight these definitional difficulties. We will return to some of these issues later in the book,[18] but for the time being the discussion here focuses on the arguments for linking 'straightforward' genetic parentage with the duty to provide child support. Before doing so, we need to consider whether children themselves have a right to child support.

The Child's Right to Child Support

Do children have a right to child support? Such a rhetorical question may be thought to be inviting an affirmative response. Yet the answer is by no means self-evident. Notwithstanding the burgeoning literature on children's rights, moral and legal philosophers continue to debate whether it is meaningful to speak of children as having rights at all.

One school of thought, adherents of the 'will' or 'choice' theory, predicate that only fully autonomous human beings with the capacity to exercise choice can be right-holders, in that they can decide for themselves whether to enforce a duty incumbent upon another, or to waive performance of that duty. If this view is accepted, a 'right' represents 'the protected exercise of choice'.[19] On this analysis, to assert that children, and especially young children, have 'rights' is inherently problematic; indeed, Hart modified the 'will' theory with an exception for children—although they cannot exercise choice, appropriate adults may do so on

---

[15] B Hall, 'The Origin of Parental Rights' (1999) 13 *Public Affairs Quarterly* 73.

[16] Hill, n 13 above. For an argument that the basis of paternity should be contract, see KK Baker, 'Bargaining or Biology? The History and Future of Paternity Law and Parental Status' (2004) 14 *Cornell Journal of Law and Public Policy* 1.

[17] T Bayne and A Kolers, 'Towards a Pluralist Account of Parenthood' (2003) 17 *Bioethics* 221 at 241. See also A Kolers and T Bayne, '"Are You My Mommy?" On the Genetic Basis of Parenthood' (2001) 18 *Journal of Applied Philosophy* 274 and G Fuscaldo, 'Genetic Ties: Are They Morally Binding?' (2006) 20 *Bioethics* 64.

[18] See ch 8 below.

[19] DW Archard, *Children, Family and the State* (Ashgate, Aldershot, 2003) at 9, who usefully summarises the competing views. For an example of the 'choice' theory of rights in this context, see J Griffin, 'Do Children Have Rights?' in D Archard and CM Macleod, *The Moral and Political Status of Children* (Oxford University Press, Oxford, 2002), ch 2. See also MDA Freeman, *The Rights and Wrongs of Children* (Frances Pinter, London, 1983), chs 2 and 3, P Alston, S Parker and J Seymour (eds), *Children, Rights and the Law* (Clarendon Press, Oxford, 1992) and J Fortin, *Children's Rights and the Developing Law* (LexisNexis Butterworths, London, 2nd edn, 2003) ch 1. For the argument that the children's rights agenda has been used to serve adults' interests, see M Guggenheim, *What's Wrong with Children's Rights?* (Harvard University Press, Cambridge Massachusetts, 2005).

their behalf.[20] There are, however, conceptual difficulties with the notion of waiver in the context of inalienable rights.[21] Even so, and although not articulated in such terms, we might argue that the 'will' theory lay behind the decision of the majority in *R (Kehoe) v Secretary of State for Work and Pensions*[22] (the first case under the Child Support Act 1991 to reach the House of Lords). In that case the majority of the House held that neither the parent with care of the children, nor the children themselves, had any 'civil right'[23] in enforcement proceedings brought under the 1991 Act.

The alternative school of thought, advanced by proponents of the 'interest' or 'welfare' theory, is that rights exist to protect certain important interests with a view to ensuring that others are under an enforceable duty to respect them. Adherents of the 'interest' theory take the view that the capacity of those whose interests are at issue to exercise a degree of choice for themselves is irrelevant.[24] For MacCormick, the difficulties faced by the 'will' theory in accommodating children's rights is proof enough of the intrinsic merits of the 'interest' theory as an explanation for the nature of rights.[25] Similarly, and returning to our opening rhetorical question—do children have a right to child support?—MacCormick asserts that it would be 'a plain case of moral blindness' if one failed to recognise that 'at least from birth, every child has a right to be nurtured, cared for, and, if possible, loved, until such time as he or she is capable of caring for himself or herself'.[26] MacCormick shows how this proposition is saying more than simply children *ought* to be cared for, nurtured and loved—on his analysis, children have that *right*, as human beings deserving of respect, and irrespective of whether there may be strong utilitarian arguments for their support (such as the wider needs of society).[27] This type of analysis, again by implication, underpinned the dissenting opinion in *Kehoe*, in which Baroness Hale argued that children have a fundamental right to child support. In her view, echoing MacCormick:

---

[20] HLA Hart, 'Bentham on Legal Rights' in AWB Simpson (ed) *Oxford Essays in Jurisprudence* (Oxford University Press, Oxford, 1973), ch VII at 192 n 86.

[21] See eg G Sreenivasan, 'A Hybrid Theory of Claim-Rights' (2005) 25 *Oxford Journal of Legal Studies* 257 at 259. Note that the right to bring a private law action for maintenance cannot be bargained away, given the public interest involved: see *Hyman v Hyman* [1929] A C 601 and *Bennett v Bennett* [1952] 1 K B 249.

[22] [2005] UKHL 48; [2006] 1 AC 42; see further N Wikeley 'A duty but not a right: child support after *R (Kehoe) v Secretary of State for Work and Pensions*' (2006) 18 *Child and Family Law Quarterly* 287.

[23] In the sense that this term is used in Article 6 of the ECHR.

[24] For an analysis of rights that seeks to reconcile the 'will' and 'interest' theories, see Sreenivasan n 21 above.

[25] N MacCormick, 'Children's Rights: A Test-Case for Theories of Right' in N MacCormick, *Legal Right and Social Democracy: Essays in Legal and Political Philosophy* (Clarendon Press, Oxford, 1982) ch 8. For a contrary view, see C Wellman *An Approach to Rights: Studies in the Philosophy of Law and Morals* (Kluwer, Dordrecht, 1997), ch 8.

[26] MacCormick, n 25 above, at 154–55. See further H Brighouse, 'What Rights (if Any) do Children Have?' and S Brennan, 'Children's Choices or Children's Interests: Which do their Rights Protect?' in Archard and Macleod, n 19 above, chs 3 and 4 respectively.

[27] MacCormick, n 25 above, at 159–61.

It is difficult to think of anything more important for the present and future good of society than that our children should be properly cared for and brought up. We who are nearing the end of our productive lives will depend more than most upon the health, strength and productivity of the following generations. The human infant has a long period of dependency in any event. But we have added to that by our requirements that they be educated up to the age of 16 and disabled from earning their own living until then. Someone must therefore provide for them.[28]

The moral justification for children's rights more generally has also been explored by Eekelaar, who has advanced a threefold taxonomy of the types of claims that children might make (or might wish to make if they could).[29] First, he argues, children have rights which revolve around their 'basic' interests to physical, emotional and intellectual care. Secondly, children have 'developmental' interests, such that their potential should be developed so that, as far as is possible, they enter adulthood without disadvantage. Thirdly, children have 'autonomy' interests, namely the freedom to choose and pursue their own life-styles. Eekelaar's contention is that children's rights which flow from their 'basic' interests are pre-eminent, whereas there may well be circumstances in which their 'developmental' and 'autonomy' interests must be compromised.[30]

The remainder of this chapter seeks to develop a theoretical model for child support based on the notion of children's rights. Applying the insights of MacCormick and Eekelaar, we may argue that children's basic interests mean that children have a right that their essential needs for food, shelter and clothing are satisfied. This right may be conceptualised in two parallel and complementary ways. First, it might be characterised as a fundamental human right, which is vested in children by virtue of their membership of the wider community and irrespective of their own parents' particular circumstances. In the United Kingdom, the availability of child benefit as a universal social security benefit may be seen as a tangible manifestation of this principle, in that it reflects a (modest) contribution by society at large to assist all parents (for the most part) in meeting the costs of raising their children. The resource implications for the state of the child's fundamental human right to support may be more extensive in some circumstances: so, for example, we might argue that orphans are absolutely entitled to adequate publicly-funded support in the absence of proper provision by their parents. Secondly, the child's right to support might be construed as a correlative claim-right, in the sense that the failure to satisfy those needs would amount to a breach of duty by an individual subject to a corresponding obligation. The decision to

---

[28] n 22 above at para 50.

[29] J Eekelaar, 'The Emergence of Children's Rights' (1986) 6 *Oxford Journal of Legal Studies* 161. For an earlier exploration of these issues, see J Eekelaar, 'Parents and children—Rights, Responsibilities and Needs: An English Perspective' (1984) 2 *New York Law School Human Rights Annual* 81.

[30] See also Archard, n 19 above at 10, noting the common view amongst moral theorists that children should have 'welfare' rights, to protect core interests (such as their health and upbringing), but not 'liberty' rights involving the exercise of choice (such as the right to vote). Whether a rights discourse is the best way to advance children's interests is explored by B Arneil, 'Becoming versus Being: A Critical Analysis of the Child in Liberal Theory' in Archard and Macleod, n 19 above, ch 5.

impose such a duty on a particular individual—for example, the child's parent(s)—will be the outcome of a process of weighing up a range of considerations drawn from the realms of moral insight and social policy. These factors will also influence the priority which is accorded within society to the child's correlative right to (private) child support, as against the contribution made by (public) child support.[31]

One undoubted benefit of such a twin-track approach to understanding the child's right to support is that it would appear to command widespread popular support.[32] A further advantage of this framework is its universality in that it is not predicated on family breakdown; in principle it applies just as much to children who live in intact families as to those whose parents have separated (or indeed whose parents have never lived together at all). Yet in practice, as has already been noted, the state is inhibited from seeking to regulate the distribution of resources within the private domain of the intact family. For this reason, the problems of identifying and quantifying a child's basic needs remain largely hidden from view.[33] It is the public fact of separation that throws these questions into sharp relief: even if we assume that child support is first and foremost a call on parental income, how do we define a child's basic needs? One answer would be to limit such needs to the bare minimum necessary in terms of the provision of a subsistence lifestyle (which might, for convenience, be defined in terms of the rates payable in respect of children for families living on benefit[34]). This solution would at least be consistent with the notion that it is the child's basic interests that are at stake, although it might be difficult to justify in terms of both elementary fairness or social policy (for example, as between the treatment of the children living in a first and second family respectively). An alternative view would be that, to take the case of formerly intact families, the children's needs should, so far as is possible, reflect the standard of living enjoyed to date—so in this sense, and in crude terms, children's needs will be defined in the first instance by their social class.[35] If so, we must accept that the categories of children's needs are open, and thereby necessarily contentious. Does the child of now separated middle-class parents really *need* private music lessons?[36] We are also, inevitably, moving further away from the concept that there is direct linkage between children's fundamental human right to have their basic needs satisfied and the correlative duties imposed on others, notably parents.

---

[31] This will, of course, vary over time with implications for the vocabulary used—eg see J Bradshaw and D Piachaud, *Child support in the European Community* (Bedford Square Press, London, 1980, Occasional Papers in Social Administration 66), which is a study purely of *public* systems of assistance with the costs of raising children.

[32] See pp 16–21 below.

[33] This is not to deny, for example, the importance of research into the adequacy of social security rates for children living in families reliant on mean-tested benefits.

[34] The original formula in the Child Support Act 1991 adopted this approach.

[35] The new formula, inserted by the Child Support, Pensions and Social Security Act 2000, with its use of percentage of income rates, reflects a more relativist methodology.

[36] At its most extreme, this thinking has led the US courts to conclude that a cap on child support is appropriate as 'no child needs three ponies': see p 334 below.

In concluding this section, it may be possible to resolve this dilemma by returning to Eekelaar's analysis of children's rights in terms of basic, developmental and autonomy interests. Applying this taxonomy, we might argue that children enjoy a fundamental human right to child support in terms of having their basic living needs met, and that these are to be satisfied by a combination of public and private resources (the precise balance between those two sources to be determined by both value judgments and social policy considerations). On top of this, we might also contend that children have at the very least a legitimate expectation that they will benefit from the standard of living enjoyed by both their parents, irrespective of with which parent they actually happen to reside. This is, admittedly, a question of values and political choices rather than fundamental human rights. Obviously, the state itself cannot fund such expectations, not least given other and more pressing demands on public expenditure. One may, however, suggest that it is not unreasonable for the state to create the legal structures within which such expectations may be realised. The nomenclature of legitimate expectations, rather than rights, is deliberate, in that it implies that such expectations may be subject to compromise where there are other compelling interests to take into account. Its importance, however, lies in the message that child support is not simply a question of ensuring that food is put on the table and clothes on the child's back. Rather, child support is about improving the child's overall life chances—a matter in which society at large has a considerable interest and investment.[37] Admittedly, the concerns of the parent with care will inevitably be more pressing, as Baroness Hale explained in her dissenting opinion in *Kehoe*:

> The children's carer has a direct and personal interest in enforcement which the Agency, however good its intentions, does not. Even in benefit cases, where the state does have a direct interest in enforcement, it is not the sort of interest which stems from needing enough money to feed, clothe and house the children on a day to day basis. Only a parent who is worrying about where the money is to be found for the school dinners, the school trips, the school uniform, sports gear or musical instruments, or to visit the 'absent' parent, not only this week but the next and the next for many years to come, has that sort of interest.[38]

We may note here how Baroness Hale moves seamlessly from the child's basic interests (the need for money 'to feed, clothe and house the children') to the child's broader interests (school trips, sports gear etc). The lesson is that private child support has the potential to play a role in furthering the child's developmental and autonomy interests, albeit that such provision may be conditional rather than absolute. In this way, child support may be seen as a twin-track right (of public and private support, however 'basic needs' are defined) allied with a second tier expectation that the child will continue to benefit—at least until adulthood—from the prosperity of both parents.

---

[37] The research evidence is reviewed in SE Mayer, *The Influence of Parental Income on Children's Outcomes* (Ministry of Social Development, New Zealand, 2005).

[38] n 22 above at para 72.

Figure 1.1 seeks to represent this theoretical approach diagrammatically and to relate it to the arrangements prevailing in the United Kingdom.[39] The *x* axis measures weekly parental income and the *y* axis the weekly sum of money required to satisfy a child's needs. In the latter context, *A* is the sum contributed by the state by way of universal child benefit and *B* is the amount which the state determines as the minimum necessary to feed, clothe and house a child. The balance of *B* – *A* is met either by public funds (in the form of means-tested benefits or tax credits) or from the family's private resources or from a combination of the two. There will come a point (*P*), which the state determines to be the poverty line, above which the parents no longer qualify for further cash assistance in supporting their child from public funds. The child, however, will continue to have a legitimate expectation to receive support in excess of *B*. A moot point, which need not be resolved here, is whether there is a higher figure, *C*, being a cap on the child's legitimate expectations.[40] We may then regard the child as having a basic right to receive support (from whatever source) in the amount of *B*, supplemented by an expectation to benefit from such further support as may be appropriate in the light of parental income (which sum may be limited to *C* – *B*). The advantage of such an approach is that, as a matter of principle, it applies to children who live with both their parents as much as those who do not. It also provides a rational basis for integrating public and private support for children.[41]

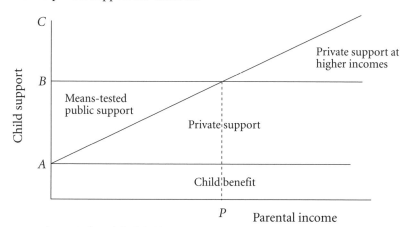

FIG. 1.1 A theoretical model of child support

But is it reasonable to regard the support of children as primarily the responsibility of their parents?

[39] As should be evident elsewhere in this chapter, I am indebted to the pioneering discussion of child support by John Eekelaar—see eg *Regulating Divorce* (Clarendon Press, Oxford, 1991) ch 5.
[40] See further pp 332–334 below for discussion of this point.
[41] Figure 1.1 is, of course, a simplified representation—for example, the introduction of Child Tax Credit (CTC) in 2003 means that the (near) universal element of publicly-funded child support goes much further up the income scale than point *P*, and the means-tested component also exceeds *P*.

The Parental Duty of Child Support

The discussion so far has been in terms of children having a basic right to child support at a certain level, supplemented by a legitimate expectation to receive support beyond that point. If this is correct, how can one make the step (or perhaps the leap) from a child having such a right (let alone a legitimate expectation) to the child's parent having a correlative duty? Alternatively, even if we accept the 'will' theory and conclude that children are not rights-holders, is it possible to argue that parents have an obligation to support their children in any event?

There is, of course, an extensive theoretical literature on the nature of parental rights and duties.[42] For some philosophers, the parental obligation of child support 'is a basic moral duty that does not require further justification'.[43] Traditionally lawyers too have tended to make the same assumption; as one now dated American study declared, 'The existence of the duty to support arises from the biological parent-child relationship'.[44] Contemporary legal scholarship is more questioning: for example, Sheldon argues that 'to state the existence of a genetic link is to make an empirical rather than a normative claim: it does not in itself provide any moral argument'.[45] So, according to Altman, 'we need a theory of child support to answer questions about the level of public duty and the allocation of private responsibility'.[46] Although MacCormick's principal concern was to test competing conceptions of rights, he also discussed the correlative issue of duties. In MacCormick's view, rather than assuming that a duty imposed on another is a logical prerequisite to recognising children's rights—as dictated by the 'will' theory—it makes more sense to hold that:

> it is because children have the right, and because their parents stand in a particular natural relationship to their own children, that it is the parents upon whom in the first instance the duty of care and nurture is incumbent.[47]

MacCormick's analysis, as an exercise in analytical jurisprudence, may provide us with a justification for the existence of a duty of child support, but is necessarily of

---

[42] For recent contributions see Hall, n 15 above, arguing that the genetic tie establishes a moral presumption that the 'natural' parent has parental rights (and so presumably duties). For an alternative view, see P Montague, 'The Myth of Parental Rights' (2000) 26 *Social Theory and Practice* 47.

[43] S Altman, 'A Theory of Child Support' (2003) 17 *International Journal of Law Policy and the Family* 173 at 174, n 4, citing LD Houlgate, 'Ethical Theory and the Family' in DT Meyers, K Kipnis and CF Murphy (eds), *Kindred Matters: Rethinking the Philosophy of the Family* (Cornell University Press, Ithaca, 1993), ch 3 (see esp at 63–69).

[44] MA Goodman, IA Oberman and PL Wheat, 'Rights and Obligations of Child Support' (1975) 7 *Southwestern University Law Review* 36.

[45] S Sheldon, ' "Sperm bandits", birth control and the battle of the sexes' (2001) 21 *Legal Studies* 460 at 480.

[46] Altman, n 43 above, at 174.

[47] MacCormick, n 25 above, at 163. Moreover, the uncertainty as to who may be subject to some such duties—eg children have a right to education, but who is subject to the duty: the parent, the local authority or the state?—is a further reason for insisting that the starting point is that children have rights: *ibid*, at 163.

less assistance in determining how that obligation should be quantified. One view, of course, is that the duty is simply confined to meeting the child's basic needs (however those are defined). For example, Vallentyne has argued that the only special duty which those who procreate children owe their offspring is to ensure that their life chances are 'non-negative', in the sense of being 'worth living'. In particular, 'there is no special procreative duty . . . to ensure that one's offspring have life prospects that are as high as reasonably possible'.[48] This has resonance in the traditional (English) common law view that children have a right to reasonable maintenance, but not to any share in their parents' wealth.[49]

Eekelaar's work suggests that this may be an unduly restrictive approach. He has argued that contractarian and quasi-contractarian theories of morality, grounded ultimately in enlightened self-interest, fail to explain why parents should owe their children duties.[50] Instead, drawing on both the natural law tradition and human-ist principles, Eekelaar contends that 'cardinal moral principles ordain the nurturing and promotion of every individual human life'.[51] His conclusion is similar to that of MacCormick:

> The duty to care for children is embedded in the *conjunction* of two sources. One is the *a priori* duty to promote human flourishing, which exists independently of the actual organization of any society. That moral duty binds everyone and is not specifically directed towards parents (although it will fall primarily on them for no other reason than their physical proximity to children). The other is derivative from society itself, for social practice determines the application of that duty within its structure . . . while social practice does not itself create the duties towards children, it may place a particular responsibility on some people rather than others to discharge them with respect to particular children.[52]

The notion that the parental obligation is grounded in both moral and social norms is consistent with the twin-track and two-tier model of child support advocated in the previous section. In social policy terms, Eekelaar identifies several reasons which justify the attachment of the support obligation to parents: it coincides with most parents' instincts, contributes to the parent/child bonding process and is economically efficient.[53] Writing at the time that the proposals which led to the Child Support Act 1991 were under discussion, Eekelaar also addressed the implications of such an approach for the way in which society handles cases in which one

---

[48] P Vallentyne, 'Equality and the Duties of Procreators' in Archard and Macleod, n 19 above, ch 11 at 208. See also P Vallentyne, 'Rights and Duties of Childbearing' (2002–2003) 11 *William and Mary Bill of Rights Journal* 991.

[49] See the discussion at p 69 below.

[50] J Eekelaar, 'Are Parents Morally Obliged to Care for Their Children?' (1991) 11 *Oxford Journal of Legal Studies* 340 at 343–7; see also P Smith, 'Family Responsibility and the Nature of Obligation' in Meyers *et al*, n 43 above, ch 2.

[51] Eekelaar, n 50 above, at 353.

[52] *Ibid*, at 351 (original emphasis).

[53] *Ibid*, at 352.

parent—in his example, the father—'abandons his children'.[54] In particular, he identified three objectives which might justify coercive action against a parent who defaults on child maintenance. These are that such action may represent an attempt; (1) to maintain the responsibility (by continued payment for the children's support); (2) to reinforce that responsibility (by contributing towards the costs incurred by others, especially the state); and (3) to redress the imbalance which would otherwise arise between the parents in the discharge of that responsibility when the father leaves the family.[55]

As Eekelaar argues, although 'these purposes might combine in a single financial order, they nevertheless remain distinguishable objectives'.[56] This analysis helpfully highlights the multifaceted nature of the child support obligation.

Regardless of whether or not children have rights, and whether or not one can construct, or simply assume, a moral or ethical basis for the child support obligation, there may be other ways to justify the imposition of such a duty of support. Altman, in a somewhat iconoclastic review of the arguments, explores a range of possible justifications for imposing a child support obligation on parents.[57] Altman first considers, but dismisses, what he describes as three 'traditional' theories, based on causation, children's vulnerability and parental consent. Whilst relevant, causation—put simply, parents cause children to exist, so they should support them—is not, he argues, a sufficient justification for imposing duties on parents, rather than society as a whole.[58] In his view the other two 'traditional' theories are essentially circular: 'children's vulnerability and parental consent explain why parents may reasonably be asked to pay support only if one assumes the current child-support regime'.[59] Likewise, although writing from a feminist perspective, Sheldon questions whether private child support obligations can be grounded in the voluntary creation of needs and suggests that meeting children's needs should be seen as a collective responsibility.[60] Altman also examines a range of further social policy arguments for the child support obligation—for example, as a means of communal intergenerational insurance, furthering gender equality, or providing family planning incentives.[61] Each of these, in his view, is found

---

[54] Eekelaar, *ibid, at* 352. The perhaps now dated use of the language of abandonment is unfortunate, as it brings in questions of fault. Surely Eekelaar's objectives apply equally where a parent, for whatever reason, lives apart from his or her children?

[55] *Ibid*, at 352–3.

[56] *Ibid*, at 353.

[57] Altman n 43 above.

[58] *Ibid*, at 176.

[59] *Ibid*, at 199.

[60] S Sheldon, 'Unwilling Fathers and Abortion: Terminating Men's Child Support Obligations?' (2003) 66 *Modern Law Review* 175.

[61] There is some evidence from the USA that stricter child support enforcement deters non-marital births: see A Case, 'The Effects of Stronger Child Support Enforcement on Nonmarital Fertility', ch 7 in I Garfinkel, SS McLanahan, DR Meyer and JA Seltzer (eds), *Families under Fire: the Revolution in Child Support Enforcement* (Russell Sage Foundation, New York, 1998) and I Garfinkel, C-C Huang, SS McLanahan and DS Gaylin, 'The roles of child support enforcement and welfare in non-marital childbearing' (2003) 16 *Journal of Population Economics* 55.

wanting as a justification for the imposition of the child support duty. Altman also considers distributive justice arguments, but concludes that they 'demean' children in that they effectively treat child support as a 'users' fee'. However, the difficulty with this reasoning is that it views distributive justice norms primarily in economic terms.[62]

Altman's own conclusion is that child support should be seen primarily as a remedy for a parental wrong: 'child support seeks to deter and punish certain behaviour, and to mitigate consequential harm to children'.[63] He therefore perceives the obligation to pay child support in quasi-tortious terms: 'parents who do not pay support wrong their children by failing to demonstrate love, and by failing to establish and maintain a loving relationship with each other'.[64] Putting to one side Altman's failure to explore the distributive justice arguments more fully, there are several obvious problems with such a harm-based analysis. In the first place it simply fails to address the argument that children have an inherent right to support, irrespective of any 'harm' done to them by one or other parent. It is also arguably as circular as the traditional theories which he discards—it can only be a wrong to fail to provide love and support if there is a right to receive such goods; either the right and the duty co-exist or they do not.[65] Moreover, Altman's preferred theory is undesirable from a social policy standpoint, in that it seemingly re-introduces issues of fault into the disposition of family assets on divorce and separation. Likewise, his approach has an avowedly punitive aspect, whereas pragmatically there are strong reasons to think that such a 'universal assumption of knavery' will do little to encourage separated parents to meet their child support obligations.[66] It is axiomatic that a child support system which reflects the values held by the majority of the population is more likely to be perceived as fair by all those concerned, and so achieve better compliance.[67] This is, therefore, an appropriate juncture at which to consider attitudes within society at large to the issue of child support.

---

[62] For a broader conception of distributive justice in the context of child support, see the work by Garrison, discussed below at pp 23–25.

[63] Altman, n 43 above, at 175.

[64] *Ibid*, at 200.

[65] See further A Halpin, *Rights and Law—Analysis and Theory* (Hart Publishing, Oxford, 1997) at 262.

[66] S Uttley, 'Child Support: the Limits of Social Policy Based on Assumptions of Knavery' (1999) 33 *Social Policy & Administration* 552 at 558. See further J Le Grand, 'Knights, Knaves or Pawns? Human Behaviour and Social Policy' (1997) 26 *Journal of Social Policy* 149.

[67] NC Schaeffer, 'Principles of Justice in Judgments About Child Support' (1990) 69(1) *Social Forces* 157 at 158. See further ch 15 below.

Societal Attitudes Towards the Obligation of Child Support

This section reviews a number of studies that have been undertaken, in various jurisdictions, which cast light on societal attitudes towards supporting children. But perceptions of the parental obligation to support children are simply one facet of views held within society about the nature and extent of family responsibilities more generally, for example towards partners, parents and other relatives. For example, Finch has shown that family obligations are not simply 'a set of ready-made moral rules which all right-thinking people accept and put into practice'.[68] Rather, family obligations are negotiated over time, and are influenced by the parties' gender, ethnicity, generation and economic position.[69] Similarly, in subsequent work, Finch and Mason concluded that parents' sense of obligation towards their adult children was related more to the development of that commitment than to the fact of a genetic link.[70] Intuitively, however, one might anticipate—at least in the culture of western societies—that the primary obligation to support one's own children, at least until they reach adulthood, is widely accepted. For present purposes, it is social attitudes towards the nature of that obligation in the context of separated families (or, as it is more accurately described, 'cross-household parenting') which is of more interest. This section therefore reviews studies of attitudes to child support responsibilities which have been undertaken in the United Kingdom, Australia and the United States. We may note at the outset that there has been relatively little research into children's own views on such matters. It seems, however, that children hold a strong commitment to the principle of equality of treatment and share their mothers' views on the dominant role for genetic parentage as the source of the child support obligation.[71]

The pioneering work in the United Kingdom was the qualitative study by Maclean and Eekelaar[72] which examined attitudes towards parental obligations held by adults who shared parenthood across households (whether they were formerly married, cohabiting, or indeed had never lived together). A majority of both mothers (73 per cent) and fathers (59 per cent) agreed that, as a matter of principle, a person's own children should take priority over step-children in terms

---

[68] J Finch, *Family Obligations and Social Change* (Polity Press, Oxford, 1989) at 242.

[69] See further M Maclean and J Eekelaar, 'The Obligations and Expectations of Couples Within Families: Three Modes of Interaction' (2004) 26 *Journal of Social Welfare and Family Law* 117.

[70] J Finch and J Mason, *Negotiating Family Responsibilities* (Routledge, London, 1993) at 168–69. See also Finch and Mason, n 4 above.

[71] The available UK research is summarised in A Diduck, *Law's Families* (LexisNexis UK, London, 2003) at 178. The most detailed study is probably from Australia: P Parkinson, J Cashmore and J Single, 'Adolescents' Views on the Fairness of Parenting and Financial Arrangements after Separation' (2005) 43 *Family Court Review* 429, which highlighted the 'acute sense of injustice' felt by young people 'if a parent spent more money on the children in a new family than on themselves': *ibid*, at 441.

[72] M Maclean and J Eekelaar, *The Parental Obligation: A study of parenthood across households* (Hart Publishing, Oxford, 1997) at 141. This research was undertaken about a year after the implementation of the Child Support Act 1991.

of the support obligation,[73] although substantially more men (22 per cent) than women (10 per cent) believed that natural children and step-children should be treated equally. Similarly, significantly more fathers (66 per cent) than mothers (37 per cent) took the view that step-children should affect the level of financial support for the first family. In the same way, fathers (42 per cent) were more likely than mothers (28 per cent) to say that a later natural child should affect one's liabilities to the first family. Moreover, when presented with a range of five possible options as regards child and spousal support following the first wife's remarriage, fathers were almost three times as likely as mothers to believe that payments for the children of the first marriage should cease.

Overall, therefore, the evidence points one way—mothers tended to view *natural* parenthood as the basis for an unconditional support obligation, whereas fathers regarded that obligation as mediated by *social* parenthood.[74] As Maclean and Eekelaar concluded, 'fathers adjust the extent of the obligation which they feel they owe towards their natural children by reference to subsequent social parenthood whereas mothers do not think that they should do this'.[75] As we shall see in chapter 4, fathers' attitudes were reflected in the policy and practice of the social security authorities before the Child Support Act 1991, whereas the approach of that legislation is much more in accord with the views expressed by mothers. Maclean, writing elsewhere, has reminded us that

> The link between financial responsibility and biological parenthood rather than established social parenthood is a harsh one, but we should remember that in practice it is only men who have the choice to distinguish between the two. For women, biological parenthood is almost always coterminous with social parenthood.[76]

Interestingly, Maclean and Eekelaar's findings in this context contrast with their later conclusions about the broader family obligations derived from being a member of a couple;[77] thus it appears that men are inclined to view their obligations to their wider kin in prescriptive and static terms, whereas the specifically monetary

---

[73] Interestingly, this approach may not last into adulthood: Finch and Mason's study of inheritance practices identified a strong commitment amongst those interviewed to 'equality of treatment' for all adult children, regardless of status, with step-children often being treated in the same way as natural children: n 4 above at 42–53 and 175.

[74] See also C Burgoyne and J Millar, 'Enforcing Child Support Obligations: the attitudes of separated fathers' (1994) 22 *Policy and Politics* 95. For an argument that there is a class dimension to child support, and that the 1991 Act represents 'an attempt to impose a particular normative order', see R Edwards, V Gillies and JR McCarthy, 'Biological Parents and Social Families: Legal Discourses and Everyday Understandings of the Position of Step-Parents' (1999) 13 *International Journal of Law, Policy and the Family* 78.

[75] n 72 above, at 142.

[76] M Maclean, 'The Origins of Child Support in Britain and the Case for a Strong Child Support System' in R Ford and J Millar, *Private Lives and Public Responses*, ch 13 at 230. See also Sheldon n 60 above at 185, pointing out that father's rights groups assume that 'men's and women's relationships to reproduction are equivalent, when clearly they are not'.

[77] In their study of couples, men tended to view family responsibility in a static way, based on prescribed norms and expectations, whilst 'women spoke in more interactive terms, about needs and responses': n 69 above at 128. See also J Eekelaar and M Maclean, 'Marriage and the Moral Bases of Personal Relationships (2004) 31 *Journal of Law and Society* 510.

child support obligation is seen in more fluid terms. Conversely, women are more likely to regard the parental support obligation as immutable, but their wider family ties as being more flexible and open to change.

One of the particular strengths of Maclean and Eekelaar's study was that it explored the nuances of attitudes towards financial support of children in the context of different forms of parenting across households. Its focus, however, was necessarily on the views of parents who had themselves had personal experience of separation. So what do we know of the views of society as a whole? Quantitative surveys of social attitudes in the United Kingdom have demonstrated strong support from the community at large for the principle of parental responsibility for child support following separation. For example, the 2000 British Social Attitudes Survey found that 88 per cent of respondents supported the proposition that unmarried non-resident parents of primary school age children should 'always' pay child maintenance, as compared with 84 per cent in 1994.[78] This suggests that the Child Support Act 1991 (which came into force in April 1993) may have had some marginal impact on changing social mores in terms of reinforcing the child support obligation.[79] More recently, the Office for National Statistics (ONS) Omnibus Survey in 2004 reported that nearly three-quarters of respondents felt that parents were solely responsible for maintaining their children following separation, whilst a quarter believed that this responsibility should be shared between the parents and government.[80] The same survey showed that 81 per cent of those interviewed thought that non-resident parents should *always* be liable to make child maintenance payments.[81] In the same vein, some two-thirds of respondents to both the British Social Attitudes and the ONS Omnibus Surveys stated that fathers with second families should not expect any reduction in their liability for the financial support of their children who do not live with them.[82] A related question is whether there should be any reduction in child support liabilities if the parent with care remarries. In 1994 only 38 per cent of those interviewed felt that child maintenance should continue regardless, but by 2000 this proportion had risen to 50 per cent,[83] again suggesting that the child support legislation has had some impact on moulding attitudes. In addition, however, this indicates the lack of a clear consensus within society as to the way in which second families should be accommodated within the child support regime.[84]

---

[78] D White, *Attitudes toward child support and the Child Support Agency* (Department for Work and Pensions (DWP) In-house report 100, 2002) at 12; see *ibid*, at 10 on the nature of the BSA Survey questions.

[79] The percentage of respondents supporting this proposition peaked at 90% in 1999.

[80] V Peacey and L Rainford, *Attitudes towards child support and knowledge of the Child Support Agency, 2004* (DWP Research Report No 226 (2004)) at 16.

[81] *Ibid*, at 13.

[82] White, n 78 above, at 21; Peacey and Rainford, n 80 above, at 14.

[83] *Ibid*, at 22; see also J Hills, 'Poverty and social security: What rights? Whose responsibilities?' in A Park *et al* (eds), *British Social Attitudes: The 18th Report* (Sage, London, 2001) at 21.

[84] See to similar effect W O'Connor and J Kelly, *Public Attitudes to Child Support Issues* (DWP In-house report 46, 1998), ch 4 and T Williams, M Hill and R Davies, *Attitudes to the Welfare State and the Response to Reform* (Department of Social Security (DSS) Research Report No 88, 1999) at 124–26.

The 2000 British Social Attitudes Survey, confirming Maclean and Eekelaar's findings, also showed that support for the general principle of unconditional parental responsibility for maintaining children on separation was not so firm amongst those respondents who were themselves subject to the operations of the Agency—while 80 per cent of parents with care expressed this view, it was shared by only 54 per cent of non-resident parents.[85] This gender differential in attitudes to child support was likewise reflected in a major survey of the Agency's own clientele, which explored their views on the impact of new relationships and other factors on child support liabilities. Thus, in stark contrast to the majority view amongst the general population, some 44 per cent of non-resident parents believed that a father should indeed pay less in child support if he had another child with a new partner, a view shared by just 17 per cent of parents with care.[86] This study also identified significant differences of view *amongst* non-resident parents. Those non-resident parents on below average incomes were much less likely to subscribe to an unconditional view of the parental obligation of child support than those who were better off.[87] Self-employed non-resident parents and those with a child aged under 16 living in their own household were also more likely to assert that the father's child support liability should 'depend on the circumstances', rather than being unconditional.[88]

A large-scale Australian study, undertaken after its new child support system had been introduced, reported similar findings to the United Kingdom's quantitative surveys. The Australian study demonstrated very strong popular backing for the principle that parents should always, or nearly always, 'share' the financial support of their children after divorce or separation.[89] The principle of shared responsibility in the context of parents who had divorced or separated was affirmed by 91 per cent of respondents; similarly, 87 per cent of respondents believed that parents who had never been married should share financial responsibility for their children once they ceased living together. Even where the child's parents had never cohabited, a clear majority of those questioned (76 per cent) still thought that financial responsibility should be shared.[90] Respondents who had been divorced themselves shared very similar views on this question to those who had never experienced divorce.[91] The researchers comment that 'this degree of commonality may be revealing and comforting', given the assumptions underpinning the child support scheme.[92]

---

[85] White, n 78 above, at 12. The same pattern was identified by N Wikeley *et al*, *National Survey of Child Support Agency Clients* (DWP Research Report No 152, 2001) at 151.

[86] *Ibid*, at 154–55.

[87] *Ibid*, at 151.

[88] *Ibid*, at 152.

[89] K Funder and B Smyth, *Family Law Evaluation Project 1996: Parental responsibilities: Two national surveys (Part One: Report)* (Melbourne, Australian Institute of Family Studies, 1996).

[90] *Ibid*, at 28.

[91] *Ibid*, at 30.

[92] *Ibid*, at 30. They also report, consistent with fathers' rights campaigns in both Australia and the United Kingdom, that divorced men expressed firmer views about the importance of shared contact following divorce or separation.

Subsequent research conducted on behalf of the Australian Child Support Agency reported that more than 95 per cent of respondents agreed with the proposition that, in the event of separation, both parents were responsible for the financial support of their children.[93] Although all those interviewed expressed high levels of agreement with this statement, views on other aspects of the scheme demonstrated marked contrasts in opinion as between payers and payees (for example, as to whether child support liabilities were too high and whether the money paid actually supported the children in question).[94] However, this type of quantitative study casts only limited light on respondents' views as to the *extent* that this responsibility should be shared, or indeed how (if at all) it might be affected by subsequent events.

Several American studies have explored attitudes to child support by presenting survey populations with more detailed hypothetical vignettes, and with the added dimension of asking respondents for concrete assessments as to the actual dollar amounts of child support that should be payable as the parties' circumstances change. Schaeffer's survey, conducted in Wisconsin, demonstrated strong support for the principle of proportional contributions, dependent on parental incomes and the needs of both the adults and children concerned. Increases in the father's earnings tended to result in higher suggested awards, but the proposed amounts were lower where either parent had remarried or the mother had an independent income.[95] The range of suggested awards also supported the proposition that children's needs were perceived to decrease somewhat as a proportion of parental income as one went further up the income scale. In addition, female respondents to the survey proposed larger child support awards than men.[96]

Schaeffer's study was conducted as long ago as 1985, before the introduction of the most important American reforms in this area, and so did not map proposed awards against the state guidelines as to appropriate levels of child support in order to determine the degree of congruence between popular beliefs and official norms.[97] This further step was taken in two later studies, but it is difficult to generalise from the results; one, in Maryland, reported that most respondents suggested higher award levels than those mandated by state guidelines,[98] whereas a later survey in Missouri reported that the majority of respondents proposed child support awards which were below those set by the state's guidelines.[99] Such dis-

---

[93] Child Support Agency, *CSA Community Perceptions Survey: Results and Analysis* (Research & Policy Unit, Child Support Agency, Australia, Paper 2/99) at 7.

[94] *Ibid*, at 11 and 17.

[95] Schaeffer, n 67 above, at 171.

[96] *Ibid*, at 167.

[97] Moreover, the prime purpose of Schaeffer's study was to test models of child support against public perceptions of fairness.

[98] BR Bergmann and S Wetchler, 'Child Support Awards: State Guidelines vs. Public Opinion' (1995) 29 *Family Law Quarterly* 483 at 488–89. Whereas the state guidelines predicated awards based on 17% of the father's net income, suggested awards averaged 24% of net income.

[99] M Coleman, LH Ganong, T Killian and AK McDaniel, 'Child Support Obligations: Attitudes and Rationale' (1999) 20 *Journal of Family Issues* 46.

crepancies may simply reflect sampling and other methodological differences between the two studies.[100] The Maryland study reported strong popular support for child support awards to be automatically adjusted upwards to reflect inflation, with a substantial majority of respondents also supporting the notion that awards should be increased to reflect growth in the non-custodial parent's income.[101] As with the Wisconsin study, this survey also found that female respondents on average selected higher child support award levels than the men who were surveyed,[102] although this was not replicated in the Missouri research.[103] A related survey in Missouri demonstrated strong popular support for the notion that stepfathers should assume some financial responsibility for their stepchildren, at least whilst their relationship with the children's mother subsists.[104] As the authors note, this contradicts the assumption underpinning the child support legislation and may explain difficulties in enforcing official norms.[105] In contrast to Maclean and Eekelaar, this study, conducted in Missouri, found no gender difference in attitudes towards the respective responsibilities of natural parents and step-parents.[106] It is a moot point whether these divergent findings simply reflect methodological differences between the two studies[107] or cultural variations between the United Kingdom and the United States.[108]

Models for Allocating and Quantifying Child Support Liabilities

We have seen that there is a growing body of scholarship on the principles which might underpin child support law and policy. There is also a much more extensive literature, especially in the United States, on the technical issues of implementation, but this work tends to sidestep or even ignore the more basic policy questions about the structure of any scheme.[109] In particular, relatively little attention has been devoted to how one might translate any statements of general principle about the child support obligation into the design of a model for quantifying and

---

[100] *Ibid*, at 64.

[101] Bergmann and Wetchler, n 98 above, at 491.

[102] *Ibid*, at 490.

[103] Coleman *et al*, n 99 above, at 65.

[104] LG Ganong, M Coleman and D Mistina, 'Normative Beliefs about Parents' and Stepparents' Financial Obligations to Children following Divorce and Remarriage' (1995) 44 *Family Relations* 306.

[105] *Ibid*, at 314.

[106] The authors do not expressly address this question, but they do report that demographic variables revealed no significant differences (other than the marital status of respondents' parents when they were growing up).

[107] It may well be significant that the primary focus of the Missouri study was whether the natural parent or step-parent should pay for extra tutoring, rather than whether the former should pay *any* child support. This makes it difficult to assess the wider relevance of the study.

[108] See further in this context R Edwards *et al* n 74 above for a class-based analysis.

[109] M Garrison, 'Autonomy or Community? An Evaluation of Two Models of Parental Obligation' (1998) 86 *California Law Review* 41 at 59; her comments relate to the USA in the 1980s but are of wider application.

allocating such liabilities. Necessarily, decisions on how the financial responsibility for raising children is to be shared following divorce or separation raise fundamental policy questions. It inevitably costs more to run two households than one intact family, and so one or both parties will experience a reduction in their standard of living. More often than not, according to the research evidence, the economic well-being of the parent with care (typically the mother) and children, falls sharply, whilst that of the non-resident parent may actually rise.[110] As Eekelaar has explained, 'the evidence is overwhelming that the families of children broken by divorce suffer economic hardship which is likely to be significantly relieved only if the lone parent remarries'.[111] One reason for such outcomes is that the private family law system in common law jurisdictions has 'patently produced results which benefited men at the expense of children, women and the state'.[112]

At the outset, therefore, policy makers must determine the extent to which the state is prepared to contribute additional resources to supporting children, typically by way of social security benefits. The balance between private obligations and public responsibility for the support of children following separation will inevitably reflect the values of the individual society.[113] In the United Kingdom, the report of the Finer Committee in 1974 represented the highpoint of the belief—expressed in the language of the time—that 'the community has to bear much of the cost of broken homes and unmarried motherhood'.[114] The Finer Committee's principal proposals were never implemented, and official policy since has been to place greater emphasis on private responsibility, although—in the United Kingdom at least—we have not reached the ultimate libertarian position that 'children are the financial responsibility of their parents, and of no one else'.[115] The public policy choices made in respect of the support of children generally have an undeniable impact on the arrangements for maintaining children whose parents live in different households. For example, the United States lacks any system of universal and tax-funded child benefits; whilst this may reflect a willingness to tolerate higher levels of child poverty,[116] it also means that

---

[110] D Betson, E Evenhouse, S Reilly and E Smolensky, 'Trade-Offs Implicit in Child-Support Guidelines' (1992) 11 *Journal of Policy Analysis and Management* 1 at 4. The most well-known study is probably L Weitzman, *The Divorce Revolution: the unexpected social and economic consequences for women and children in America* (Free Press, New York, 1985); although criticized, the underlying trend seems well-established. For recent evidence of this phenomenon, see S Kelly and A Harding, *The Financial Impact of Divorce in Australia* (AMP/NATSEM, Sydney, 2005).

[111] J Eekelaar, 'Family Law and Social Control' in J Eekelaar and J Bell (eds), *Oxford Essays in Jurisprudence—Third Series* (Clarendon Press, Oxford, 1987) ch 6 at 141. The same applies to unmarried cohabiting couples who separate: see A Avellar and PJ Smock, 'The Economic Consequences of the Dissolution of Cohabiting Unions' (2005) 67 *Journal of Marriage and Family* 315.

[112] S Parker, 'Rights and Utility in Anglo-Australian Family Law' (1992) 55 *Modern Law Review* 311 at 314.

[113] J Millar and A Warman, *Family Obligations in Europe* (FPSC, 1996) ch 1.

[114] *Report of the Committee on One-Parent Families* (1974, Cmnd 5629); see further ch 4.

[115] R George, 'Who should bear the cost of children?' (1987) *Public Affairs Quarterly* 1 at 11.

[116] S Danziger, 'After welfare reform and economic boon: why is child poverty still so much higher in the U.S. than in Europe?' in J Bradshaw (ed), *Children and Social Security* (Ashgate, Aldershot, 2003), ch 1.1.

payment (and non-payment) of private child support assumes much greater significance.[117]

Once the appropriate level of public support has been identified, the next question is to determine which 'parent should bear what portion of the economic loss?'[118] Phrasing the question in financial terms is in itself telling—policy makers typically overlook the fact that raising children involves significant non-monetary costs, 'which tend to be borne disproportionately by one parent and which in many cases may exceed monetary expenditures on children'.[119] Bradbury, applying an econometric analysis, puts the case even more strongly, concluding that cash outlays 'are only a small part of the cost of children'.[120] In particular, the parent with care's opportunity costs—caring for children undeniably affects educational and career choices, which in turn affects future earning capacity—tend not to be factored into the equation. It follows, as Schaeffer observes, that defining the problem as one of apportioning economic loss (in a narrow sense) involves issues of fairness: 'suggesting a child support award involves more than an allocation; it requires an initial qualitative decision about what is to be allocated and a decision about how its amount should be set'.[121] Hence policy conclusions about the design of a child support regime are not value-free; they necessarily involve issues of fairness and justice on a number of levels. Indeed, Schaeffer helpfully identifies three stages at which such considerations will impinge.[122]

The first order issue is to decide what it actually is that is to be the subject matter of the child support allocation—what is the pie being divided up, to use Schaeffer's analogy: is it the amount that the children 'need' to live on, or is it the parental income? The answer to this question will be determined by our perception of both the moral justification and policy rationale for child support. If the function of child support is merely to ensure that children's rights to have their 'basic interests' are satisfied, then the 'pie' is defined by those needs. If, however, child support is seen as having a wider role in giving effect to children's fundamental rights and legitimate expectations, then the 'pie' must be parental income. Garrison's analysis is an important contribution to the wider debate as to the principles which should govern this choice. Having provided a compelling critique of the way in which state guidelines are used in the United States to fix child support levels,[123] she characterises child support policy as a question of distributive justice, but one that should be informed by a policy science approach.[124] In her view, the

---

[117] MA Glendon, *The Transformation of Family Law* (University of Chicago Press, Chicago, 1989) at 236–37.

[118] A Giampetro, 'Mathematical Approaches to Calculating Child Support Payments: Stated Objectives, Practical Results and Hidden Policies' (1986–87) 20 *Family Law Quarterly* 373 at 389.

[119] D Betson *et al*, n 110 above, at 18.

[120] R Bradbury, *The Price, Cost, Consumption and Value of Children* SPRC Discussion Paper No 132 (UNSW, Sydney, June 2004) at 17.

[121] Schaeffer, n 67 above, at 171.

[122] *Ibid*, at 159–60.

[123] Garrison, n 109 above, at 57–72.

[124] ie, one that proceeds by 'articulating and critiquing goals, assumptions, expected outcomes and implementational problems': *ibid*, at 72.

problem of child support is a paradigm example of a distributive justice dilemma, being 'a question of fair allocation: a finite resource, family income, must be divided between two households'.[125] She then explores several theories of distributive justice which might inform the development of child support principles, describing these as the consequentialist,[126] contractarian, communitarian, feminist and libertarian perspectives. With the notable exception of libertarianism, all these approaches share 'a common emphasis on group membership as the primary determinant of a distributional principle'.[127] It follows that four of the perspectives adopt 'a sharing norm as a governing principle and some variant of the equal outcomes model . . . as a decision-making rule'.[128] The libertarian approach stands apart; its overriding premise is that individuals are entitled to retain or dispose of their assets as they see fit, assuming that they were acquired without violation of the principles of justice.[129] Thus 'a libertarian child support law would intrude minimally upon the non-custodial parent's prerogatives',[130] subject only to ensuring that the community was properly reimbursed for any support that it provided in the event of parental default. As Garrison explains, modern (American) child support law is closest to this libertarian approach—'it is the only perspective that views child support as a taking which demands justification; it is the only perspective that measures the child support obligation based on public expense and private contractual obligation'.[131]

Drawing on these theories of distributive justice, Garrison postulates two principal models of child support; a 'community model', founding the obligation on family membership and mandating income sharing as the basic approach,[132] and an 'autonomy model', derived from the libertarian perspective, with a focus on the economic costs of raising children.[133] She also refines these two basic approaches to include two variants of each, depending on whether a restrictive or broader view is taken of the underlying purpose.[134] These four models are then applied to different factual scenarios (such as different levels of parental incomes and changes in relationship status) to establish the outcomes in terms of cash child support liabilities. On Garrison's analysis, all the models have similar effects in terms of keeping families off welfare and preventing poverty. Thus the fundamental question as to the choice of model 'will depend on whether we want the additional

---

[125] Garrison, n 109 above, at 74.

[126] A consequentialist theory might involve a utilitarian or egalitarian approach: *ibid*, at 76–80.

[127] *Ibid*, at 84.

[128] *Ibid*, at 83.

[129] *Ibid*, at 83–84.

[130] *Ibid*, at 85.

[131] *Ibid*, at 86, and see further 87–89, emphasizing the Lockean influence on child support law.

[132] For a similar argument in the context of spousal support, see J Carbone, 'Income Sharing: Redefining the family in terms of community' (1994) 31 *Houston Law Review* 359.

[133] Garrison, n 109 above, at 92ff.

[134] Thus the 'Narrow Autonomy Model' assumes that welfare avoidance is the primary goal and the 'Broad Autonomy Model' focuses on poverty prevention, while the 'Limited Community Model' and the 'Full Community Model' aim at equality of basic resources and in living standards respectively.

sharing that the community models demand'.[135] Garrison's conclusion is that a community model for child support is more effective at meeting public policy goals and is more consistent with trends in the development of family law. She also argues that such an approach fits better with what we know about public attitudes towards child support.[136]

We must now return to Shaeffer's initial question as to the nature of the pie—is our vision for child support one that allocates financial responsibility for the child's needs or one that encompasses a child's legitimate expectation to a share in parental income? To sum up the discussion so far, those who prefer Garrison's community-based approach believe that children are entitled to a share of both parents' financial resources, irrespective of which parent they happen to be living with. Conversely, those who adopt a libertarian perspective assert that the primary purpose of child support transfers is simply to assist in meeting children's economic needs.

A secondary question, according to Schaeffer, once the nature of the pie has been identified, is to decide on the type of rule to be applied in dividing it up. If the decision is taken to use children's economic needs as the appropriate basis of allocation, then these needs must obviously be quantified. However, as we have seen, defining what is meant by a child's 'needs' may be highly contentious. Is it possible to specify a child's needs in terms of a fixed amount, or do children's needs vary according to parental income and social status? If the latter, by definition 'a middle-class child "needs" more than a poor child'.[137] Again, issues of fairness and justice cannot be sidestepped. Once the child's 'needs' are ascertained, a number of different methods might be employed to divide this amount between the parents. For example, the parents may be equally obligated in cash terms, or their obligation may be based on some principle of proportionality, according to their level of income.[138] Whichever of these various approaches is adopted, they all lend themselves to a formulaic approach—as Dewar observes, child support schemes are 'notoriously rule-bound', in contrast to the traditional approach of legislatures in developed states, which has been to vest the judiciary with a very broad discretion to make such orders for financial provision as they saw fit, so as to do justice (or perhaps injustice) to the intrinsic or perceived merits of the case.[139] This is a classic instance of the rules/discretion dichotomy:

> rules may delimit entitlement precisely, but in doing so they frustrate the need for flexible responses to individual circumstances. Discretion may seem to provide individualised justice, but at the price of uncertainty and high legal costs.[140]

---

[135] Garrison, n 109 above, at 98.

[136] *Ibid*, at 117. On societal attitudes, see above.

[137] n 67 above, at 161.

[138] As Schaeffer indicates, there is a third, albeit unattractive, possibility: a 'remainder' rule under which the non-resident parent simply pays the balance of expenses which the parent with care cannot meet: *ibid*, at 161.

[139] J Dewar, 'The Normal Chaos of Family Law' (1998) 61 *Modern Law Review* 467 at 471.

[140] E Jackson, F Wasoff with M Maclean and RE Dobash, 'Financial Support on Divorce: The Right Mixture of Rules and Discretion?' (1993) 7 *International Journal of Law and the Family* 230 at 233—but

If, however, the view is taken that children may expect to benefit from a share in their parents' financial resources, Schaeffer identifies two types of rule that might be applied.[141] The most radical is 'income-equalization', namely that child support transfers should ensure that income per person is roughly equal in both households. An avowedly egalitarian approach such as this is unlikely to command overwhelming public support and would be inconsistent with widely accepted social policy objectives (such as the desirability of minimising labour market disincentives). A more modest and politically acceptable approach is 'income-sharing', which allocates a percentage share of parental income to an individual's child or children living in another household.

Once these first and second order issues (namely, what is the pie and what type of rule do we apply for dividing it up?) have been resolved, a host of further or third-level issues present themselves for determination; in Schaeffer's terms, 'what characteristics, resources, or inputs of the parents, if any, should be considered in making the allocation and how should they be weighted'?[142] For example, should the income of both parents enter into the equation, or only that of the non-resident parent? Regardless of the answer to that question, should there be a cap on the non-resident parent's income, beyond which the child support obligation does not attach? In addition, what impact should shared care have on the allocation? Furthermore, what effect (if any) should the parent with care's remarriage (or repartnering) have? And what should be the implications if the paying parent re-partners and acquires new dependants? Logically, the choice of answer to the central question as to the subject-matter of the allocation (child's needs or parental income) should have a significant impact on resolving these more detailed aspects of the scheme's design. For example, if the child's needs are the determining factor, then the case for a cap on the amount of the non-resident parent's income which is taken into account is compelling, if not overwhelming. On the other hand, if the governing principle is that children should presumptively share in the economic prosperity of *both* parents, then an assessment based on some percentage of the non-resident parent's income is a rational starting point.[143] Yet it does not necessarily follow that the parent with care's income needs to be factored into this equation, as the child living with her will share in her standard of living in any event. Indeed, disregarding the parent with care's income is justifiable on the basis that she will in any event shoulder the burden of the hidden economic costs of childcare (such as loss of earning capacity and less generous pension provision).

Designing a child support scheme thus raises fairness issues at every level. The lesson at the heart of the analyses by both Schaeffer and Garrison is simple:

---

note also their finding that clients were surprised and disappointed that lawyers could not give them 'a clear and definite indication of the levels of support which they could expect': *ibid*, at 252.

[141]   Schaeffer, n 67 above, at 161–62.

[142]   *Ibid*, at 160.

[143]   Principle, of course, does not mandate a particular percentage 'take'.

the fundamental question of principle is to identify what is being divided up—children's needs or parental income. The decision on this fundamental issue will then have implications for the details of the scheme, but the multi-dimensional nature of the problems raised is such that the answers to subsequent policy questions are not pre-determined. Instead, it is important to recognise that there are trade-offs to be made between competing considerations, such as between protecting children's economic interests whilst also preserving the work incentives for both parents.[144] In this way both principle and pragmatism will combine to contribute to the design of a child support scheme.

International Norms and National Objectives for Child Support

The discussion so far has been at a somewhat abstract level; do children have a right to child support, or a right allied with a legitimate expectation? In so far as children do have a claim-right to child support, who is subject to any correlative duty and how might that responsibility (whether public or private) be framed in a way that accords with societal norms? Furthermore, how might those principles be translated into the actual structure of a child support scheme, depending on whether one adopts the purely needs-based right or a conception of child support comprising a right in conjunction with a legitimate expectation? In this section we examine legal instruments at both supra-national and national level to see whether these texts give us any clues as to the fundamental principles being adopted. This discussion also maps out the background to the analysis of the statutory child support schemes in the United Kingdom and elsewhere that follows later in this book.

International Norms Governing Child Support

The United Nations Convention on the Rights of the Child, which came into force in 1990, is the pre-eminent global legal instrument in terms of children's social and economic rights.[145] Its framework is very much one of children's rights, rather than the duties owed to children by others: 'the strength of the rights formulation is its recognition of humans as individuals worthy of development and fulfilment'.[146] However, the Convention advances children's rights within the context of an express recognition that the family is 'the fundamental group of society and the natural environment for the growth and well-being of all its members

---

[144] Betson *et al*, n 110 above.

[145] See further G Van Bueren, *The International Law on the Rights of the Child* (Dordrecht: Martinus Nijhoff, 1995), D Fottrell (ed), *Revisiting Children's Rights: 10 years of the UN Convention on the Rights of the Child* (Kluwer, The Hague, 2000); Fortin, n 19 above, ch 2 and P Alston and J Tobin, *Laying the Foundations for Children's Rights* (Unicef, Florence, 2005).

[146] J Eekelaar, 'The importance of thinking that children have rights' (1992) 6 *International Journal of Law and the Family* 221 at 234.

and particularly children'.[147] Article 6(2) then declares that 'States Parties shall ensure to the maximum extent possible the survival and development of the child', a right which has been described as 'more well-meaning than well-conceived'.[148] Similarly, Article 27(1) requires contracting states to recognise 'the right of every child to a standard of living adequate for the child's physical, mental, spiritual, moral and social development'.[149] As Fortin observes, it is difficult to see how this can be translated into a genuine legal right and its 'extreme vagueness' makes enforcement problematic.[150] In any event, Article 27(2) specifies that the child's parents (or others responsible for the child) 'have the primary responsibility to secure, within their abilities and financial capacities, the conditions of living necessary for the child's development'. Other provisions reinforce the notion that the role of the state is secondary and supportive to that of the child's parents.[151] Indeed, Article 27(4) stipulates that:

> State Parties shall take all appropriate measures to secure the recovery of maintenance for the child from the parents or other persons having financial responsibility for the child.

This provides express authority for a system of child support (although not necessarily one based on an official assessment, collection and enforcement agency). Overall, however, it is difficult to escape the conclusion that the Convention embodies 'liberal values about the virtues of the family as a sphere to be kept separate from, and privileged over, that of the state . . . and about the rights and responsibilities which parents have in priority to those of the state'.[152] Other international treaties at a global level do not take the matter much further: for example, the International Covenant on Civil and Political Rights similarly affirms that 'the family is the natural and fundamental group unit of society and is entitled to protection by society and the State', but then adds, rather lamely, that in the event of divorce 'provision shall be made for the necessary protection of any children'.[153]

European law provides little more by way of assistance to articulating a theory of child support law. Child support issues have arisen in the context of both

---

[147] See UN Convention on the Rights of the Child UN Doc A/44/736 (1989), Preamble ¶ 5. See also Preamble ¶ 6 and Art 5.

[148] Griffin, n 19 above, at 24.

[149] For a discussion of Art 27 in the context of New Labour policy, see C Hamilton and M Roberts, 'State Responsibility and Parental Responsibility: New Labour and the Implementation of the United Nations Convention on the Rights of the Child in the United Kingdom' in Fottrell, n 145 above, ch 9.

[150] Fortin n 19 above at 12 and 44.

[151] See, eg, Art 27(3) and also Art 26 on the right to social security; see further N Harris, 'Social security and the UN Convention on the Rights of the Child in Great Britain' (2000) 7 *Journal of Social Security Law* 9.

[152] S Parker, 'Child Support: Rights and Consequences' (1992) 6 *International Journal of Law and the Family* 148 at 166. See further S Parker, 'Child Support in Australia: Children's Rights or Public Interest?' (1991) 5 *International Journal of Law and the Family* 24.

[153] U.N. Doc. A/6316 (1966), Art 23(1) and (4). See also International Covenant on Economic, Social and Cultural Rights, U.N. Doc. A/6316 (1966), Art 10. International Covenant on Economic, Social and Cultural Rights, G.A. res. 2200A (XXI), 21 U.N.GAOR Supp. (No 16) at 49, U.N. Doc. A/6316 (1966),

European human rights law and also, although rather less obviously, European Union law. In broad terms, the focus of the European Convention on Human Rights (ECHR) is on civil and political rights, rather than economic and social rights. Consequently the ECHR does not, in so many terms, guarantee children a right to child support, let alone to any particular level of support. The experience to date is that the ECHR has primarily been invoked as a way of *challenging* the duty to pay child support, rather than as a means of *reinforcing* that obligation. The one notable exception to date has been *Kehoe*,[154] in which the parent with care, rather than the non-resident parent, was challenging the Child Support Act 1991 on the basis that her exclusion from the enforcement process constituted a breach of her Article 6 rights to a fair trial. However, the majority of the House of Lords held that neither the parent with care nor the children enjoyed any 'civil right' within the meaning of Article 6 of the Convention so as to give them a voice in the child support enforcement process. Challenges to the 1991 Act by non-resident parents have typically been based on Article 8 of the Convention, guaranteeing the right to respect for 'private and family life', and Article 1 of the Protocol 1, which protects property rights.

Article 8 sets out the presumption that there should be no state interference in family life, although public authorities are entitled to act in the furtherance of the various objectives set out in Article 8(2), namely where interference is 'necessary in a democratic society in the interests of . . . the economic well-being of the country . . . [and] for the protection of the tights and freedoms of others'. A series of cases have ruled that the scheme established by the Child Support Act 1991 is compliant with Article 8 of the Convention. In *Logan v United Kingdom*,[155] the first such challenge to reach Strasbourg, the European Commission of Human Rights ruled that the non-resident parent's complaint about the child support legislation was inadmissible. The father's argument that the level of his child support assessment restricted his ability to have contact with his children did not get past first base; in the Commission's view, the applicant had not shown 'that the effect of the operation of the legislation in his case is of such a nature and degree as to disclose any lack of respect for his rights under Article 8'. There was, therefore, no need to consider whether interference was justified under Article 8(2).[156] A subsequent complaint (by a male non-resident parent in receipt of income support) that the provisions governing reduced benefit directions involved a breach of Article 8 was also ruled inadmissible, the Court holding that any interference with those rights was justified.[157]

---

[154] n 22 above.

[155] Application no 00024875/94; (1994) 22 EHRR CD 178.

[156] The Commission also ruled inadmissible complaints in *Logan* based on the right to a fair trial (Art 6) and freedom of religion (Art 9)—the latter based on the ingenious (if not ingenuous) argument that he was less able to practice his faith of Zen Buddhism, given the financial costs incurred in visiting his nearest place of worship.

[157] *Stacey v United Kingdom*, Application no 00040432/98.

The domestic courts have been little more receptive to human rights challenges to child support law based on Article 8. In the very first such case before the domestic courts, following the coming into force of the Human Rights Act 1998,[158] Munby J, in dismissing the non-resident parent's complaint, applied the Strasbourg jurisprudence in holding that Article 8 was not engaged by the process of applying for a liability order, which was a necessary, reasonable and proportionate part of the overall statutory scheme.[159] Similarly, the majority of the House of Lords in *Secretary of State for Work and Pensions v M*[160] ruled that the child support formula's differential treatment of the housing costs of a non-resident parent in a same-sex relationship was too tenuous to engage Article 8 at all.[161] Several other complaints about the statutory scheme have likewise failed, although the courts have expressed their sympathy for the position of those perceived to be meritorious non-resident parents. For example, the Administrative Court has held that, where a non-resident parent is on benefit, the standard child support deduction from his weekly jobseeker's allowance was not an interference with the right to family life, and was in any event justified.[162] Similarly, the rules governing the treatment of contact costs for the purposes of departure directions have been held to be justified, given the 'pressing social need' to which the child support regime is a response.[163]

Some non-resident parents have sought to argue that the child support system constitutes an unwarranted interference with the individual's peaceful enjoyment of his possessions, a freedom guaranteed by Article 1 of Protocol 1 to the Convention. This approach was given short shrift by the European Commission of Human Rights in *Burrows v United Kingdom*,[164] in which it was ruled that the 'aims of reducing taxation and increasing parental responsibility must be considered as in the public interest' for the purposes of Article 1 of Protocol 1. On the facts of that case, the child assessment liability of 20 per cent of the applicant's gross earnings did not represent a disproportionate legislative response. The domestic courts been similarly robust in rejecting arguments based on Article 1 of Protocol 1. As Sedley LJ observed in *Secretary of State for Work and Pensions v M*, 'child support is neither a tax nor a form of expropriation: it is an allocation of

---

[158] The Human Rights Act 1998 came fully into force on 2 October 2000; on implementation in context of the Child Support Act 1991, see *R(CS) 6/03*.

[159] *R (on the application of Denson) v Child Support Agency* [2002] EWHC 154 (Admin); [2002] 1 FLR 938. A subsequent complaint by the same non-resident parent about the statutory time limits for appealing, based on Art 6, was dismissed in *Denson v Secretary of State for Work and Pensions* [2004] EWCA Civ 462, reported as *R(CS) 4/04*.

[160] [2006] UKHL 11.

[161] Note that this was an old scheme case; the discrimination has since been removed as a result of the Civil Partnership Act 2004.

[162] *R (on the application of Plumb) v Secretary of State for Work and Pensions* [2002] EWHC 1125 (Admin).

[163] *R (on the application of Qazi) v Secretary of State for Work and Pensions* [2004] EWHC 1331 (Admin), reported as *R(CS) 5/04*.

[164] Application no 00027558/95.

private financial responsibility'.[165] The House of Lords agreed with this aspect of the Court of Appeal's decision in *M*; according to Lord Nicholls, the machinery of the 1991 Act 'is far outside the scope of Article 1 of the first protocol'.[166]

Nor does European Union (EU) law take us very much further in terms of defining the right to child support or the extent of any correlative duty. In the same way as with human rights law, to date EU law has only been used to challenge the legality of the statutory child support scheme, albeit unsuccessfully so far. Thus an early Tribunal of Child Support Commissioners[167] held that the obligation to pay child support and the imposition of a deduction from earnings order (DEO) could not found a sex discrimination complaint under what was then Article 119 of the EC Treaty, guaranteeing equal pay for equal work, even though far more men than women were affected.[168] Similarly, although EU Directive 79/7 on equal treatment has been invoked successfully on a number of occasions in the field of social security law, it has no application in the context of child support law.[169] There may, however, still be some circumstances in which the scheme established by the Child Support Act 1991 might be found to be in breach of EU law.[170] In truth, the principal significance of European law in the context of child support is in the cross-border enforcement of maintenance liabilities, a subject that falls outside the scope of this book.

Statutory Objectives of National Child Support Schemes

Clearly the philosophy underpinning child support schemes in different jurisdictions cannot simply be ascertained by examining the legislation applicable in the respective countries. Even so, a comparison of the declared statutory objectives of the child support schemes operating in the United Kingdom, Australia, New Zealand and the United States of America may be instructive in itself.

The Child Support Act 1991 is typical of much British parliamentary drafting; long on detail and short on principle. Obviously one can arrive at an understanding of the aims of the 1991 Act by examining its genesis,[171] but the casual reader is given no real clue as to the philosophy which underpins this most contentious of social legislation. According to the long title of the 1991 Act, it was designed:

---

[165] [2004] EWCA Civ 1343 at para 53. See also *Department for Social Development v MacGeagh* [2005] NICA 28, reported as *R 2/05 (CS)* at para 28.

[166] n 160 above at para 33.

[167] Child Support Commissioners usually sit alone; this was a very rare example of a Tribunal of three Commissioners being convened: see further p 430 below.

[168] *R(CS) 2/95*; the Tribunal of Commissioners ruled that child support did not fall within the meaning of 'pay' for the purposes of what was then Art 119, now Art 141, of the EU Treaty.

[169] As the Directive is confined to the various risks enumerated, which do not include family breakdown: *R(CS) 3/96*.

[170] See the ingenious argument advanced in E Jacobs and G Douglas, *Child Support: The Legislation* (Sweet & Maxwell, London, Edition Seven, 2005/2006) at 17–18 in relation to EU Regulation 1612/68.

[171] See further chs 4 and 5 below.

to make provision for the assessment, collection and enforcement of periodical maintenance payable by certain parents with respect to children of theirs who are not in their
care; for the collection and enforcement of certain other kinds of maintenance; and for
connected purposes.

The first ten sections of the Act, although grandiosely described by their heading
as 'The basic principles', are likewise more about the machinery of child support
than its underlying rationale. The closest we get to a statement of principle is the
bald declaration in section 1(1) that 'each parent of a qualifying child is responsible for maintaining him'. Beyond this bare assertion, the Act is remarkably reticent
about the actual purposes of the legislation. The statutory omission to spell out
precisely to whom this responsibility is owed was cited by the majority of the
House of Lords in *Kehoe* to justify their decision that neither a parent with care nor
a child's Convention rights are engaged in the enforcement process.[172] It is true
that section 2 to the Act is grandiosely entitled 'Welfare of children: the general
principle', but the apparent breadth of this description is then betrayed by the
terms of the provision:

> Where, in any case which falls to be dealt with under this Act, the Secretary of State is
> considering the exercise of any discretionary power conferred by this Act, he shall have
> regard to the welfare of any child likely to be affected by his decision.

It follows that the children's welfare comes into play only in the context of *discretionary* decisions, which are those involving a genuine power of choice: for example, whether to make a reduced benefit decision, whether to agree a variation to
the standard formula assessment and whether, and if so how, to enforce an award.
So the children's welfare is not a relevant consideration in questions of
judgment—such as whether there is shared care, or whether a person is habitually
resident.[173] The application of the formula itself, once the relevant facts are established, involves neither discretion nor judgment. Consequently, the wording of
the heading to section 2 may 'seem hollow indeed' as 'it is manifest that it has no
influence on the quantification of liability'.[174] Moreover, although the concepts
are not coterminous, the residual role allotted to children's *welfare* arguably
undermines any claims that the child support scheme is at heart concerned with
children's *rights*. Certainly the absence of any clearly articulated statutory goals has
made it more difficult for the British scheme to achieve widespread public acceptance. It is noteworthy that legislatures in other jurisdictions have been much more
explicit about the objectives of their child support schemes. We shall consider
Australia, New Zealand and the United States briefly in turn.

The principal Australian child support statute, the Child Support (Assessment)
Act 1989, declares that the child's parents (in contradistinction to the state) have

---

[172] n 22 above.

[173] See F Bennion, 'Distinguishing judgment and discretion' [2000] *Public Law* 368 for an invaluable discussion.

[174] *R v Secretary of State for Social Security, ex parte Biggin* [1995] 1 FLR 851 at 855 *per* Thorpe J.

'the primary duty to maintain the child'.[175] As we have seen, the United Kingdom legislation does not even go this far, as it makes the primacy of the parental support obligation at best implicit. Moreover, the Australian statute asserts that the parental duty 'is not of lower priority than the duty of the parent to maintain any other child or another person' but 'has priority over all commitments of the parent other than commitments necessary' to enable parents to support themselves or others (including other children) to whom they owe a duty of maintenance.[176] This highlights the legislative priority attached to the parental child support obligation. Section 4 of the 1989 Act then builds on this by providing that 'the principal object of this Act is to ensure that children receive a proper level of financial support from their parents'.[177] Furthermore, the same section itemises the following non-exhaustive but 'particular' goals of the legislation, namely to ensure:

(a) that the level of financial support to be provided by parents for their children is determined according to their capacity to provide financial support and, in particular, that parents with a like capacity to provide financial support for their children should provide like amounts of financial support; and

(b) that the level of financial support to be provided by parents for their children should be determined in accordance with the legislatively fixed standards; and

(c) that persons who provide ongoing daily care for children should be able to have the level of financial support to be provided for the children readily determined without the need to resort to court proceedings; and

(d) that children share in changes in the standard of living of both their parents, whether or not they are living with both or either of them; and

(e) that Australia is in a position to give effect to its obligations under international agreements or arrangements relating to maintenance obligations arising from family relationship, parentage or marriage.

In addition, the 1989 Act expresses the parliamentary intent that, so far as possible, the child support legislation should be interpreted so as to encourage private ordering and a respect for individuals' right to privacy.[178]

It should be noted that these statutory objectives do not mirror exactly the policy objectives for the child support scheme as originally announced by the Australian government.[179] Thus section 4 of the 1989 Act makes no reference to the goal of ensuring that public expenditure is limited to the minimum necessary for supporting children not living with both parents, nor to the desirability of

---

[175] Child Support Assessment Act 1989 (Cth), s 3(1).

[176] *Ibid*, s 3(2)(a) and (b). The parental duty is also not affected by the duty of anyone else to maintain the child (typically the other parent) or the fact that the child or another (eg the carer) is entitled to a means-tested benefit: *ibid*, s 3(2)(c).

[177] *Ibid*, s 4(1). See, to similar effect, the principal objects of the Child Support (Registration and Collection) Act (Cth) 1988, s 3(1).

[178] Child Support Assessment Act 1989 (Cth), s 4(3).

[179] Cabinet Sub-Committee on Maintenance, *Child Support: A discussion paper on child maintenance* (AGPS, Canberra, 1986) at 14.

protecting work incentives.[180] In 1994 a parliamentary Joint Select Committee criticised the drafting of section 4 for failing to prioritise the statutory (and indeed implicit policy) objectives. The Committee recommended that the legislation be amended to reflect the following order of priorities: (1) adequate support should be available to all children not living with both parents; (2) non custodial parents should share in the cost of child support according to their capacity to pay; and (3) public expenditure should thereby be kept to the minimum necessary.[181] The Australian government has not adopted this proposal. The more recent independent review of the Australian child support system also involved no reassessment of the scheme's fundamental principles.[182]

New Zealand has adopted a similar, but not identical, approach to its neighbour across the Tasman Sea; its own Child Support Act 1991 does not list any one 'principal object', but details a total of 11 statutory objects. Although these aims are not expressly stated in any hierarchy, the first three were presumably regarded as being of overriding importance, being expressed in terms of *affirming* certain *rights* as well as the parental obligation: (a) the right of children to be maintained by their parents; (b) the obligation of parents to maintain their children; and (c) the right of caregivers of children to receive financial support in respect of those children from non-custodial parents of the children.[183]

Objects (a) and (b) are simple correlatives—children have a claim-right to support and their parents owe them a corresponding duty. Object (c) is less straightforward. In the first place the right is enjoyed by 'caregivers', given that the adult with day to day responsibility for the child may not be the other parent.[184] Furthermore, the reference to 'a right . . . to receive financial support' is ambiguous. This expression may just be a synonym for 'maintenance', a term which would be inappropriate in the context of a non-parent caregiver. But it may also reflect a conception of child support that goes beyond basic needs and encompasses broader standard of living issues. Whichever it is, object (c) is seen as a right enjoyed by adults, not children. Be that as it may, the New Zealand statute is the only one of those reviewed in this chapter which explicitly articulates its objectives in terms of a rights discourse. The remaining objectives in the 1991 Act, which to a great extent reflect and expand upon the five 'particular' objects in the Australian statute, are in the form of goals which should underpin the assessment process.[185] There are, however, some potentially telling differences; the New Zealand statute lacks any explicit commitment that children should share in any changes in their

---

[180] The policy objective of ensuring minimum intrusion into personal privacy was reflected in Child Support (Assessment) Act 1989 (Cth) s 4(3), along with the encouragement of private ordering.

[181] Joint Select Committee on Certain Family Law Issues, *Child Support Scheme: An examination of the operation and effectiveness of the scheme* (AGPS, Canberra, 1994) at 59–61.

[182] Report of the Ministerial Taskforce on Child Support, *In the Best Interests of Children* (Canberra, May 2005) at 102.

[183] Child Support Act 1991 (NZ), s 3(a)–(c).

[184] Similarly the UK legislation usually refers to a 'person with care' rather than a 'parent with care': see below p 248.

[185] Thus *ibid*, s 3(d)–(g) reflect Child Support (Assessment) Act 1989 (Cth) s 4(1)(a)–(c).

parents' standard of living[186] but, unlike its Australian predecessor, it includes an express reference to the need 'to ensure that the costs to the State of providing an adequate level of financial support for children and their custodians is offset by the collection of a fair contribution from non-custodial parents'.[187] This may well reflect the rather different political environment in New Zealand at the inception of the child support scheme as compared with that in Australia.[188]

Modern child support regimes were first established in the United States of America, where every state has its own child support scheme, making a comprehensive comparison of statutory objectives impracticable. These state-based systems have also developed incrementally over time, and inevitably a range of political factors have been to the fore at different stages.[189] What is beyond dispute is that there has been an increasing federal influence on the development of state child support schemes—for example, in 1984 Congress required states to lay down formulaic guidelines for advising on the assessment of child support liabilities, and four years later federal legislation gave such guidelines presumptive force.[190] Following a recommendation by a congressional committee, a national Advisory Panel on Child Support Guidelines was established. The Advisory Panel set out a number of principles for states to consider in devising their own guidelines.[191] These were that: (1) parents should share responsibility for supporting their children according to their income; (2) parents' subsistence needs should be recognised, but the child support obligation should rarely be set at zero; (3) children should share in the above-subsistence level standard of living of higher income parents; (4) each child of a given parent has an equal right to share in that parent's income; (5) children have an equal right to child support, irrespective of their parents' marital status; (6) child support guidelines should be sexually non-discriminatory; (7) guidelines should avoid creating marriage or work disincentives; (8) guidelines should encourage the involvement of both parents in a child's upbringing and recognise shared care arrangements. The adoption of these principles suggests that the United States is not committed to a purely needs-based vision of child support. In particular, principles (2) to (4) envisage a system of child support that combines both the child's fundamental right to support and, beyond that, the legitimate expectation to share in parental affluence. However, the weight to be accorded to each of these principles is a matter for individual states to determine, resulting in the diversity of child support arrangements evident today in the United States.

---

[186] However, Child Support Act 1991 (NZ), s 4(h) provides that one of its objects is 'to ensure that equity exists between custodial and non-custodial parents, in respect of the costs of supporting children'.

[187] *Ibid*, s 4(j).

[188] See p 176 below.

[189] See JE Crowley, *The Politics of Child Support in America* (Cambridge University Press, Cambridge, 2003).

[190] Child Support Enforcement Amendments 1984 and Family Support Act 1988; see further ch 6 below.

[191] See HD Krause, 'Child Support Reassessed: Limits of private responsibility and the public interest' (1989) *University of Illinois Law Review* 367 at 375.

Conclusion

This chapter has explored the moral and legal arguments that may be used to underpin a child support system. The hypothesis of this chapter is that children have a fundamental human right, simply by virtue of their status as children, to a level of child support which meets their essential needs. There are strong reasons, grounded in both moral philosophy and social policy, why this claim-right should give rise to a duty on behalf of both society as a whole as well as the individual child's parents. The respective levels of the contributions made by public and private responsibility towards meeting this fundamental right will reflect contemporary political values. More contentiously, however, this chapter argues that, beyond the satisfaction of their basic needs, children also enjoy a legitimate expectation that they will benefit from their parents' prosperity. One advantage of this approach is that it ensures that children are entitled to an irreducible minimum level of support, based on public or private responsibility or a combination of both, and may then continue to benefit from both parents' standard of living beyond this point. A further advantage is that this twin-track and two-tier model of child support means that the very real difficulties in defining precisely what are a child's basic needs become a second-order issue. Above all, however, this is a child-centred perspective which places the emphasis on the child's basic, developmental and autonomy interests—in this way, the child is the subject of child support, as an individual with the potential to grow rather than merely an object who needs to be housed, fed and clothed. There will, of course, be very real problems in weighing those interests against the interests of others, but the point is that the child's rights and legitimate expectations should be the starting point for that debate—child support is not, and should not be, a gift. Historically, however, child support in the United Kingdom has not matched these aspirations, for the reasons explored in the following chapters.

2

The Child Maintenance Obligation and the Poor Law

Introduction

State agencies in Britain have been involved in arrangements for the financial support of children for more than 400 years. The Child Support Agency, operating at a national level, performs one of the functions of the parishes under the former poor law regime, namely seeking to recoup from parents the cost borne by the state in supporting children. In many cases the Agency has also taken over the role previously played by the courts in adjudicating on private disputes between separated parents in relation to the support of their children. In this way 'the child support system has elements of private and public law but fundamentally it is a nationalised system for assessing and enforcing an obligation which each parent owes primarily to the child'.[1] However, the development of the child maintenance obligation looks very different according to whether one views it through the prism of public law or private law. TenBroek emphasised how:

> the family law of the poor, which evolved as an integral part of the labor and poor law systems, was the creation of Parliament and was then as today primarily statutory. The family law of the rest of the community was created by the common law courts.[2]

Finer and McGregor, in their historical review for the Finer Report, took this analysis a stage further and demonstrated how, on the private law side, the development of canon law and the common law had created two systems of family law—'one to meet the needs of the rich and powerful, and another which regulated the family life of the rest of the community'.[3] But Finer and McGregor, echoing tenBroek, also identified a third system of family law, the poor law, which demarcated the boundary between the merely poor (included for this purpose in 'the rest of the community') and the positively destitute. The poor law:

---

[1] *Huxley v Child Support Officer* [2000] 1 FLR 898 at 908 *per* Hale LJ.

[2] J tenBroek, 'California's Dual System of Family Law: Its Origins, Development, and Present Status' (1964) 16 *Stanford Law Review* 257 at 261.

[3] M Finer and OR McGregor, 'The History of the Obligation to Maintain' in *Report of the Committee on One-Parent Families* (Cmnd 5629, 1974: the 'Finer Report'), vol 2, Appendix 5, at 111.

comprised the imposition of support obligations upon relatives; the denial and subordination of their parental rights to the control of custody of children and the determination of their education or occupational training; as well as a general regulation of
familial relationships.[4]

This chapter explores the evolution of the parental obligation to maintain a
child in the sphere of public law. The approach is broadly chronological, with the
'old poor law' of 1601 and the 'new poor law' of 1834 being taken as major landmarks, together with the Royal Commissions which reported on the operation of
the poor law in 1834 and 1909. The time line of this chapter closes with the end of
the Second World War. This is a convenient watershed as 1948 saw the final repeal
of the last vestiges of the poor law and the creation of the late twentieth century
welfare state presaged in the Beveridge Report.[5] Chapter 3 examines the development of parents' private law duty to maintain their children over a similar time-
frame, whether at common law or under statute. The inter-relationship between
parents' public and private law duties to maintain their children in the decades
between 1948 and the passage of the Child Support Act 1991 is then considered in
chapter 4. At the outset, however, there are three preliminary points that should
be borne in mind when considering the history of the poor law.

The first is that historians have generated an immensely rich literature on the
poor law which can only be touched upon in this study. There have also been
significant shifts in the theoretical approaches of historians in recent generations.
Early histories of the poor law were written as case studies in the administrative
reform of social policy. Accounts written in the 1950s and 1960s tended to adopt
a 'Whiggish' reformist perspective, which mapped out a natural and linear road
from the harshness of the poor law to the promised land of the post-Beveridge
Welfare State.[6] More recent studies have emphasised that the relationship of poor
people and the parish was one of negotiation, rather than simply the imposition of
social controls from above, and hence have characterised paupers as 'active agents
rather than simply victims'.[7] Furthermore, Charlesworth has argued that it was
meaningful to speak of a right to relief under the old poor law,[8] at least for those
with ties to particular localities, a right which became much more difficult to

---

[4] M Finer and OR McGregor, 'The History of the Obligation to Maintain' in *Report of the Committee
on One-Parent Families* (Cmnd 5629, 1974: the 'Finer Report'), vol 2, Appendix 5,, at 112.

[5] *Social Insurance and Allied Services* (Cmd 6404, 1942). There were, of course, important differences between Beveridge's vision and the reality of the post-war welfare state, not least in the role of
means-tested benefits.

[6] Or, as Lynn Hollen Lees graphically describes, 'In both popular and scholarly lore, the poor laws
have taken on the role of the ugly stepmother who oppressed her virtuous, needy children until the
good fairy of the welfare state banished her forever': *The Solidarities of Strangers* (Cambridge University
Press, Cambridge, 1998) at 7. For introductions to the historiography of the poor law, see A Brundage,
The English Poor Laws, 1700–1930 (Palgrave Macmillan, Basingstoke, 2002), ch 1 and S King and
A Tomkins (eds), *The poor in England 1700–1850: An economy of makeshifts* (Manchester University
Press, Manchester, 2003) ch 1.

[7] A Blaikie, 'Nuclear hardship or variant dependency? Households and the Scottish Poor Law'
(2002) 17 *Continuity and Change* 253 at 275.

[8] See L Charlesworth, 'The Poor Law: a legal analysis' (1999) 6 *Journal of Social Security Law* 79.

realise after 1834.[9] However, the historical orthodoxy seems to be rather that parishes had a duty to relieve the deserving poor, rather than that the poor had a right to relief as such.[10]

Secondly, there are obvious dangers in treating legislative landmarks such as the 1601 and 1834 statutes as defining moments in the evolution of the poor law. Although these are convenient staging posts, the extent to which they each involved a significant change in direction is easily exaggerated. Rather, as we shall see, there were important continuities in legislative policy and administrative practice before and after both 1601 and 1834. Moreover, throughout the history of the old and the new poor law there have been important differences between the rhetoric of the legislation and its application on the ground. As Poynter explained:

> only by courtesy could poor relief be described as a system before 1834, being rather a multitude of practices within (and sometimes without) the framework of a complicated aggregation of law.[11]

Thus factors other than legal reform itself may well be more significant; for example, changes forced by social and economic circumstances meant that the operation of the 1834 new poor law was markedly different after the 1860s.[12] It follows that any legislative chronology of the poor law must be seen in the context of Holdsworth's observation that 'it is one thing to adopt principles, and quite another to carry them into effect and to secure their smooth working'.[13] In addition, there were marked regional divergences in the administration of the poor law throughout its history.[14]

Thirdly, and subject indeed to the last caveat, it must be emphasised that the focus of this chapter is on the *English* poor law.[15] The development of the old poor law in Scotland, for example, was very different, with the Church playing a much

---

[9] L Charlesworth, 'How poor law rights were lost but Victorian values survived: a reconsideration of some of the hidden values of welfare provision' in A Hudson (ed), *New Perspectives on Property Law, Human Rights and the Home* (Cavendish Publishing Ltd, London, 2004), ch 14.

[10] See below at p 44.

[11] JR Poynter, *Society and Pauperism: English Ideas on Poor Relief, 1795–1834* (Routledge & Kegan Paul, London, 1969) at 1.

[12] See ME Rose, 'The Crisis of Poor Relief in England, 1860–1890' in WJ Mommsen (ed), *The emergence of the welfare state in Britain and Germany 1850–1950* (Croom Helm, London, 1981) and Lees n 6 above at 16.

[13] WS Holdsworth, *A History of English Law*, vol IV (Methuen & Co, London, 1924) at 396. 'Administration and not legislation has always been the difficulty in laws concerning the poor': EM Leonard, *The Early History of English Poor Relief* (Frank Cass & Co Ltd, London, 1965, second impression of book first published by Cambridge University Press, 1900) at ix.

[14] S King, *Poverty and Welfare in England, 1750–1850: A regional perspective* (Manchester University Press, Manchester, 2000). See also S Hindle, *On the Parish? The Micro-Politics of Poor Relief in Rural England c. 1550–1750* (Clarendon Press, Oxford, 2004).

[15] There appears to be no uniquely Welsh jurisprudence on the poor law, presumably because the Law in Wales Act 1535 (27 Hen 8 c 26), which formally assimilated England and Wales for legal purposes, predates the main poor law legislation. See further SA King and J Stewart, 'The history of the poor law in Wales: Under-researched, full of potential' (2001) 36 *Archives* 134 and, on the broader legal aspects, TH Jones and JM Williams, 'Wales as a Jurisdiction' [2004] *Public Law* 78.

more important role in the absence of effective local government.[16] Secularization of the poor law did not arrive in Scotland until the 1845 Act which, in structural terms, was markedly less radical than its English and Welsh counterpart of 1834.[17] Ireland too has its own poor law history, the Irish Poor Law Act of 1838 introducing a public relief regime that was both more centralised and far harsher than the equivalent system under the 1834 Act.[18]

The Origins of the Old Poor Law

TenBroek has demonstrated that the poor law was 'not only a law *about* the poor but a law *of* the poor', and so 'it dealt with a condition, and it governed a class'.[19] For centuries, starting with the Statute of Labourers 1349,[20] the English poor law regulated both the working and the non-working poor,[21] along with their dependants. The main features of the early legislation were the regulation of the labour market through wage controls and restrictions on the mobility of labour, together with penalties for able-bodied beggars and vagrants.[22] Legislation in 1388 decreed that the 'impotent poor' were to remain where they were resident, or to be sent to their place of birth.[23] As Holdsworth dryly observed, 'presumably the legislature expected that they would there get relief from existing charitable agencies, as it made no provision for raising funds for this relief, or for creating funds to administer it'.[24] Relief of poverty was a matter for the Church, local guilds and private charitable foundations.[25]

The beginnings of the first comprehensive English system of poor relief are to be found in the Tudor Poor Law Acts of 1530 and 1535,[26] enacted at a time when

---

[16] See generally Finer Report, n 3 above, vol 2 Appendix 6 at 253–7 and R Mitchison, *The Old Poor Law in Scotland* (Edinburgh University Press, Edinburgh, 2000).

[17] Poor Law (Scotland) Act 1845 (8 & 9 Vic (1845) c 83). See further A Paterson, 'The Poor Law in Nineteenth-Century Scotland' in D Fraser (ed), *The New Poor Law in the Nineteenth Century* (Macmillan, London, 1976) ch 8 and D Englander, *Poverty and Poor Law Reform in Britain: From Chadwick to Booth, 1834–1914* (Addison Wesley Longman Ltd, London, 1998) ch 4.

[18] Brundage, n 3 above, at 7. On the export of the poor law to the then colonies, see the sources cited by R Cranston, *Legal Foundations of the Welfare State* (Weidenfeld and Nicolson, London, 1985) at 342 n 11.

[19] tenBroek, n 2 above, at 286 (original emphasis).

[20] 23 Edw III (1349) c 7. See K de Schweinitz, *England's Road to Social Security* (University of Pennsylvania Press, Philadelphia, 1947) ch I.

[21] See WP Quigley, 'Five hundred years of English poor laws, 1349–1834: regulating the working and nonworking poor' (1996) 30 *Akron Law Rev* 73, a useful modern review of the legal history of the old poor law.

[22] See generally Leonard, n 13 above, ch 1.

[23] 12 Rich II cc 3 and 7 (1388). The language of all the older statutes cited in this chapter has been modernised, eg by substituting 's' for 'f' and putting capital letters into lower case where appropriate.

[24] Holdsworth, n 13 above, at 390.

[25] See Charlesworth, n 9 above, at 273–76.

[26] 22 Hen VIII c 12 (1530) and 27 Hen VIII c 25 (1535). See de Schweinitz, n 20 above, ch III and Quigley, n 21 above, at 92.

the existing forms of charitable provision were under considerable strain.[27] Whilst these statutes reinforced existing legislative sanctions for those who were able to work but neglected to do so, they also started the process of establishing a local government responsibility to identify, assess and maintain the destitute,[28] based on a system of local taxation. The 1530 Act, a one clause statute, was essentially a repressive measure, which prohibited all begging except under licence from the justices, and so was designed to restrict the number of beggars rather than to provide relief.[29] The 1535 Act was the first to stipulate that the poor should be provided for in their own neighbourhood and that the state should have a role in raising funds and administering relief (principally through the collection of alms every Sunday). The 1535 Act also authorised justices of the peace and parish officials to remove children aged between the ages of 5 and 14, who lived 'in idleness' and were found begging, in order to put them 'to service . . . to husbandry, or other crafts or labours'.[30] A little over a decade later, legislation dispensed with the need for any parental consent to such action.[31] According to Kahn-Freund, the conditions in which such children worked were 'hardly distinguishable from the slave trade'.[32]

Throughout the greater part of the sixteenth century there was no national system of poor relief, but rather 'isolated municipal attempts' to tackle the problems associated with destitution.[33] Subject to his reservation about the disparity between principle and practice, Holdsworth concluded that by 1576 the legislature had adopted the essential principles of the later poor law.[34] The Poor Law Act 1572[35] provided justices with more extensive powers, enabling parishes to institute compulsory taxation for the relief of the destitute.[36] The 1572 Act also provided for the registration of the 'impotent poor' in the parish of their settlement,[37] and prohibited the removal from their parish of those who were so settled. The Poor Act

---

[27] However, recent research suggests that the pre-Reformation Church provided a greater amount of poor relief than historians had previously thought: NS Rushton, 'Monastic charitable provision in Tudor England: quantifying and qualifying poor relief in the early sixteenth century' (2001) 16 *Continuity and Change* 9.

[28] See P Slack, *From Reformation to Improvement: Public Welfare in Early Modern England* (Clarendon Press, Oxford, 1999) at 16–17.

[29] Leonard, n 13 above, at 53–54. The 1530 Act provided furthermore that 'if any do beg without such licence, or without his precinct, he shall be whipped, or else be set in the stocks three days and three nights, with bread and water only'.

[30] 27 Hen VIII c 25 (1536) s 2. See Quigley, n 21 above, at 97.

[31] 3 & 4 Edw VI c 16 (1549), s 10: see Holdsworth, n 13 above, at 394.

[32] O Kahn-Freund, 'Blackstone's Neglected Child: the Contract of Employment' (1977) 93 *Law Quarterly Review* 508 at 518.

[33] Leonard, n 13 above, at 45.

[34] Holdsworth, n 13 above, at 396.

[35] 14 Eliz I c 5 (1572).

[36] As was typical of the era, legislative action followed local initiative: compulsory taxes for the levying relief for the poor began in London in 1547: Leonard, n 13 above, at 29.

[37] Thus beggars were surveyed; those incapable of work were licensed to beg whilst others were forbidden to seek relief: *ibid*, at 45.

1575[38] was the first statute to make express provision for the position of illegitimate children.[39] The rationale for the 1575 Act was evident from its preamble:

> Concerning bastards begotten and born out of lawful matrimony (an offence against God's law and man's law), the said bastards being now left to be kept at the charges of the parish where they be born, to the great burden of the same parish, and in defrauding of the relief of the impotent and aged true poor of the same parish, and to the evil example and encouragement of lewd life.

It followed that the prime purpose of the legislation was 'to indemnify the parish for the cost of maintenance and incidentally to discourage vice'.[40] The 1575 Act provided that, where a child had become a charge on the parish, two justices of the peace could punish both the mother and the reputed father, and charge either parent for the costs of the child's maintenance, as well as committing them to jail in the event of non-payment.[41] That said:

> it was found to be easier to pass an [A]ct of this character than to enforce its provision, for the reputed father, with the intention of evading his legal responsibilities, often absconded, leaving the parish to bear all the charges in connection with the child.[42]

Consequently the majority of punishment orders under the 1575 Act were made against women,[43] reflecting society's double standards about sexual morality.[44]

The Principles of the 1601 Act

These early statutes were consolidated in the Poor Law Act 1597,[45] which 'reached its definitive form' in the Poor Relief Act 1601,[46] traditionally seen as the starting

---

[38] 18 Eliz I c 3, s 1, described by Slack as 'portmanteau legislation put together by committees': n 28 above at 38. This statute is commonly described as the 1576 Act, but formally it is listed in the *Chronological Table of Statutes* as the Poor Act 1575.

[39] I Pinchbeck and M Hewitt, *Children in English Society* (Routledge & Kegan Paul, London, 1969) vol 1 at 206; see also H Elisofon, 'A Historical and Comparative Study of Bastardy' (1973) 2 *Anglo-American Law Review* 306 at 318–19.

[40] HH Robbins and F Deák, 'The Familial Property Right of Illegitimate Children: A Comparative Study' (1930) 30 *Columbia Law Review* 308 at 317; see also M Jackson, *New-Born Child Murder: women, illegitimacy and the courts in eighteenth-century Britain* (Manchester University Press, Manchester, 1996) at 30.

[41] Even today imprisonment remains the ultimate sanction for non-payment of child support: see ch 14.

[42] D Marshall, *The English Poor in the Eighteenth Century* (George Routledge & Sons Ltd, London, 1926) at 207.

[43] GR Quaife, *Wanton Wenches and Wayward Wives: Peasants and Illicit Sex in Early Seventeenth Century England* (Croom Helm, London, 1979) at 216–17.

[44] Jackson, n 40 above, at 30.

[45] 39 Eliz I c 3 (1597).

[46] 43 Eliz I c 2 (1601). See Hindle, n 14 above, at 12. The expression 'consolidated' is used here somewhat loosely in its ordinary sense rather than in its technical legal meaning. In fact the 1601 Act overlaid previous legislation; for example, the Poor Act 1575 was not fully repealed until the Statute Law Revision Act 1863.

point for the old (or Elizabethan) poor law. In fact the 1601 Act differed only at the level of detail from its 1597 predecessor.[47] Whatever its statutory source, the Elizabethan poor law was not concerned with solving the underlying causes and problems of destitution; rather, it was designed to deal with the immediate symptoms of poverty and, in doing so, sought to minimise the cost to the public purse (in this case, local property taxes).[48] The old poor law was characterised by three fundamental principles: (1) the concept of local responsibility for the organisation of poor relief; (2) the doctrine of settlement (and, conversely, the possibility of removal);[49] (3) the notion that the primary responsibility for maintenance lay with the family.[50]

The role of the parish was fundamental to the operation of the 1601 Act.[51] Responsibility for the organisation of poor relief was to be discharged by the churchwardens along with overseers of the poor, who were to be appointed by the justices of the peace. In practice, the poor who sought relief had to demonstrate that they had acquired a settlement in the parish. Indeed, 'in legal terms, poor law was largely settlement law'.[52] In the Elizabethan period it was relatively easy to establish settlement simply by residence. In 1662, statute[53] defined the modes of obtaining this status more restrictively, so that an individual acquired settlement by apprenticeship, by being hired for a year, by paying local taxes, by owning or renting local property or by holding a local office. A woman acquired her husband's settlement on marriage and legitimate children inherited settlement rights from their father. The settlement of illegitimate children was determined by their place of birth.

The 1662 Act allowed parishes to eject new arrivals who were 'likely to be chargeable', and who had no right of settlement, in the first 40 days of their stay. The consequences of a pauper acquiring settlement were such that parishes were like 'warring principalities'.[54] As one eighteenth century account remarked, 'every parish is in a state of expensive war with the rest of the nation; regards the poor of all other places as aliens; and cares not what becomes of them if it can but banish

---

[47] See tenBroek, n 2 above, at 268; see further Leonard, n 13 above, at 78 and 133–35, including a useful table of the main differences between the 1597 and 1601 Acts. The 1597 Act itself, originally designed as a temporary measure, was the product of a committee of the House of Commons, involving Sir Francis Bacon and Sir Edward Coke; Sir Walter Raleigh later played an important part: *ibid*, at 74–76.

[48] tenBroek, n 2 above, at 286.

[49] See de Schweinitz, n 20 above, ch V.

[50] Quigley, n 21 above, at 100 and see SA Riesenfeld, 'The Formative Era of American Public Assistance Law' (1955) 43 *California Law Review* 175 at 199.

[51] The legislation 'declared *local* public responsibility for the relief of poverty in the form of a mandatory directive which the localities were legally obligated to effectuate': tenBroek, n 2 above, at 264 (original emphasis).

[52] Charlesworth, n 8 above, at 80, who also notes (at 90–91) that M Nolan, *A Treatise of the Laws for the Relief and Settlement of the Poor*, first published in 1805, comprised 400 pages on settlement but only 14 pages on relief payments. See also the specialist volumes of law reports, Burrow's *Settlement Cases*. See further Hindle, n 14 above, ch 5.

[53] 13 & 14 Cha II c 12 (1662).

[54] de Schweinitz, n 20 above, at 46.

them from its own society'.[55] The 1662 Act meant, as Cranston notes, that 'persons could be removed not only if they applied for relief but also if it *appeared* that they *might* apply for relief'.[56] This remained the position until the Poor Removal Act 1795, which made an application for relief a precondition of removal[57]—but this statute retained an exemption for unmarried mothers, who were presumed to be chargeable to the poor rates, even if they had not applied for relief.[58] Public concern at the cost involved in supporting illegitimate children meant that the relevant legal niceties were not always observed, leading to:

> The removal of [unmarried] mothers before birth (at times by gangs of local men without the warrant of a removal order), sometimes during labour itself, to ensure that birth took place across parish boundaries.[59]

There was, however, a more positive aspect to the doctrine of settlement, as it meant that the old poor law established a form of localised social citizenship as early as the seventeenth century.[60] Historians have contended that the poor regarded parish settlement and the consequential right to relief as part of their birthright.[61] Hindle argues that the evidence suggests that 'the Elizabethan statutes did not in themselves confer entitlement. The "right to relief", rather, was negotiated in the course of local practice'.[62] Certainly scrutiny of parish records has shown that poor people used both informal and legal processes to assert their right to a settlement (and hence to poor relief).[63] As Lees observes, the parishes:

> gave the familiar destitute a secure place at the very bottom of the social ladder, whereas they denied a space and status to those without a settlement. The poor laws ratified this distinction between low status and no status.[64]

The old poor law made specific provision for dealing with the children of the poor. Following earlier legislation, churchwardens and overseers enjoyed the power under the 1601 Act to remove children from parents whom they considered unable to keep and maintain them, regardless of whether the parents were in receipt of poor relief.[65] The principal means of providing for the maintenance of the children of the poor was apprenticeship; hence the churchwardens and overseers were empowered to bind children to be apprentices 'where they shall see

---

[55] W Hay, *Remarks on the Laws Relating to the Poor with Proposals for Their Better Relief and Employment* (London, 1951), Preface VI, quoted in de Schweinitz, n 20 above, at 39. See further KDM Snell, 'The culture of local xenophobia' (2003) 28 *Social History* 1.

[56] Cranston, n 18 above, at 22–23 (original emphasis).

[57] 35 Geo III c 101 (1795), Preamble.

[58] *Ibid* s 6.

[59] KDM Snell, *Annals of the labouring poor: social change and agrarian England, 1660–1900* (Cambridge University Press, Cambridge, 1985) at 107. For examples of contemporary criticism of such practices by local magistrates, see Hindle, n 14 above, at 412.

[60] Lees, n 6 above, at 11 and Charlesworth, nn 8 and 9 above.

[61] Snell, n 59 above, at 107 and 112.

[62] Hindle, n 14 above, at 446; see further *ibid*, at 398–405 for a penetrating analysis of this issue.

[63] Lees, n 6 above, ch 1.

[64] *Ibid*, at 39.

[65] 43 Eliz I c 2 (1601) s 1.

convenient'.[66] Parish officials could therefore require merchants, masters and other men of property to take an apprentice as part of their contribution to the support of the local poor.[67] Formally the consent of the justices was required but, as Kahn-Freund notes, this was 'often given perfunctorily'.[68]

Yet not all children were both of an age and in satisfactory health to be apprenticed. Some of these children were accommodated in charitable schools, training homes and orphanages.[69] For those who did not die in the 'care' of the poor law,[70] the cost of relief could not be readily externalised in the same way as for apprenticed children. As a result, some other form of mechanism had to be devised to limit the parish's liability. This was achieved through the imposition of a legal liability to maintain on members of the immediate family.[71] The drafting of the 1601 Act itself has been characterised as 'rambling, imprecise and inartistic'.[72] Section 6 of the 1601 Act[73] declared that:

> the father and grandfather, and the mother and grandmother, and the children of every poor, old, blind, lame and impotent person, or other poor person not able to work, being of a sufficient ability, shall, at their own charges, relieve and maintain every such poor person, in that manner and according to that rate, as by the Justices of the Peace of that county where such sufficient persons dwell, or the greater number of them, at their general Quarter-Sessions shall be assessed; upon pain that every one of them shall forfeit twenty shillings for every month which they shall fail therein.

Accordingly, the test for indemnification of the parish was one of direct lineal consanguinity.[74] Consequently, either the father or mother of a legitimate child[75] who

---

[66] *Ibid* s 5. Leonard, n 13 above at 215–16, explains how this was one of the most important duties of the overseers.

[67] tenBroek, n 2 above, at 280–81. The power to compel masters to take on a pauper apprentice was eventually repealed by the Poor Law Amendment Act 1844 (7 & 8 Vict c 101), s 13.

[68] Kahn-Freund, n 32 above at 512, citing *R v Hamstall Ridware* (1789) 3 T R 380. See also Hindle, n 14 above, at 193, who argues that 'the binding out of pauper children was arguably the most controversial issue in the judicial interpretation of the Elizabethan poor laws'.

[69] Leonard, n 13 above, at 215–20.

[70] See n 99 below.

[71] tenBroek, n 2 above, at 283. On the importance of kinship as a source of material assistance for the poor, see S Barrett, 'Kinship, poor relief and the welfare process in early modern England' in King and Tomkins (eds), n 6 above, ch 7.

[72] tenBroek, n 2 above, at 262.

[73] Re-enacting a provision first found in Poor Law Act 1597 (see *ibid*, at 283), and extending its scope to include grandparents: Leonard, n 13 above, at 134. This provision is referred to variously as s 6 or s 7 of the 1601 Act, depending on the source consulted. Although the original statute labels this rule as VII, this is premised on that what we would now regard as s 1 being numbered II, with the preamble being (implicitly) para I. Section 6 is therefore the preferred numbering.

[74] tenBroek, n 2 above, at 284. As L Neville Brown observed, the Act made no mention of any liability imposed on *husbands* as they were in any event subject to a common law duty to maintain their wives: 'National Assistance and the Liability to Maintain one's Family' (1955) 18 *Modern Law Review* 110, at 113. See further ch 3 below. The precise scope of the Elizabethan liable relative rule was defined by later case law; thus a man was not liable to maintain his mother in law (*R v Munden* [1719] 1 Stra 190), his daughter-in-law (*R v Dempson* [1734] 2 Stra 955) or his step-children (*Tubb v Harrison* 4 Term Rep 118 (1790)). Nor, in a judicial response to Genesis 4;9, was he his brother's keeper: *R v Smith* 2 Car & P 449 (1826).

[75] For the position as regards illegitimate children, see n 85 below.

could not work might be required to maintain that child at a rate determined by the justices, subject to the stated penalty for defaulting on this obligation. So, according to the Finer Report:

> the essence of the poor law system was that it was the means through which the public supported those who were unable to support themselves, but sought reimbursement by imposing a legal liability upon their relatives in accordance with early seventeenth century notions of kinship.[76]

This assessment may not give sufficient weight to the goal of deterrence; arguably the real purpose of section 6 was to prevent the poor becoming chargeable to the parish in the first place, rather than providing a mechanism for reimbursement.[77] We should also note that the 1601 Act imposed what we would now characterise as an exclusively public law obligation—the right to apply for reimbursement was not that of the mother or, to use the modern terminology, the parent with care. Rather, the ratepayers of the parish in which the maintained person was resident had the right to lodge a complaint with the justices under this provision. In practice, however, as the Webbs explained, the activity of parish officers in seeking recovery of such costs was:

> confined to the case of illegitimate children, the family connections of ordinary paupers being themselves usually too nearly destitute to be worth proceeding against for contribution towards their support.[78]

Amendments to the Old Poor Law

The Poor Relief Act 1601 proved to be remarkably enduring. As Poynter remarks, it survived 'because it was adaptable, permitting diversity of practice in time as well as place'.[79] Throughout this period there were no changes to the fundamental principle of liability derived from kinship, notwithstanding the considerable social and economic changes that took place.[80] Instead, much of the poor law legislation enacted between 1601 and 1834 dealt with reforms to the administrative structure of the scheme. Other legislative changes were designed to improve the enforcement of the public law maintenance obligation, especially in relation to the children of deserted wives and unmarried mothers respectively.

As to the former, the Poor Relief (Deserted Wives and Children) Act 1718 permitted the justices to seize both the land and chattels of an absconding father who

---

[76] Finer Report, n 3 above, vol 1, para 4.19. On the relationship between s 6 and contemporary conceptions of kinship, see Hindle, n 14 above, at 48–58.

[77] *Arrowsmith v Dickinson* (1888) 20 QBD 252 at 256 *per* Willis J.

[78] S Webb and B Webb, *English Poor Law History—Part 1: The Old Poor Law* (Longmans, Green & Co, London, 1927, repr Frank Cass & Co Ltd, London, 1963) at 308. This involved a separate procedure (see n 85 below).

[79] Poynter, n 11 above, at 2.

[80] Lees, n 6 above, at 171.

had abandoned his family for them to become a charge on the parish.[81] The legislation enabled such chattels to be sold and the proceeds to be applied, along with the rent from the land, to meeting the costs of the family's maintenance. A century later, the Poor Law Act 1819, amongst many other provisions concerned with the administration of poor relief, allowed the justices to deduct the costs of maintenance from the wages of merchant seamen and from military and naval pensions, the forerunner of the system of direct deductions from salary that remains in operation today for those in the armed services and the merchant navy.[82] Ten years before the inception of the new poor law, the Vagrancy Act 1824[83] increased criminal penalties against husbands who absconded and left their families chargeable to the parish.[84]

Bastardy, rather than desertion, was seen by legislators as the more pressing social and economic problem. It is worth noting that conceptually the bastardy legislation was a distinct body of law, apart from the main corpus of the poor law,[85] which outlived the abolition of the poor law itself, surviving in the form of affiliation proceedings. Between 1601 and 1834 a series of measures were enacted with the twin goals of seeking to discourage procreation outside wedlock and to ensure that the parents, and not the parish, bore financial responsibility for illegitimate children. Legislation during the early part of this period tended to be directed primarily towards punishing promiscuous women. For example, a 1609 statute provided that 'every lewd woman, which shall have any bastard which may be chargeable to the parish' should be sentenced to one year in a house of correction,[86] but appears to have been little used.[87] In practice officials invoked the bastardy jurisdiction only where private arrangements for support of the children in

---

[81] 5 Geo I c 8 (1718).

[82] 59 Geo III c 12 (1819) s 30. See now Naval Forces (Enforcement of Maintenance Liabilities) Act 1947, s 1(1)(aaa), Army Act 1955, s 150A, Air Force Act 1955, s 150A and Merchant Shipping Act 1970, s 11(4), all as inserted by the Child Support Act 1991 (Consequential Amendments) Order 1993 (SI 1993/785).

[83] 5 Geo IV c 83 (1824). See L Charlesworth, 'Why is it a crime to be poor?' (1999) 21 *Liverpool Law Review* 149.

[84] *Ibid*, ss 3, 4, 5 and 10: first offenders were designated as 'idle and disorderly persons', liable to one month's imprisonment; second offenders as 'rogues and vagabonds', subject to three months' imprisonment with hard labour; offenders were 'incorrigible rogues', liable to 12 months' such imprisonment and whipping (at the justices' discretion): G Nicholls, *A History of the English Poor Law Vol II 1714–1853* (PS King & Son, London, new edn, 1898) at 196–97. According to Neville Brown, this 'triptych of villainy' originated in 13 Geo II c 24 (1739): n 74 above at 114, n 14. Section 4 of the 1824 Act, making it an offence to be in 'any enclosed . . . area, for any unlawful purpose', and deeming the offender to be a 'rogue and vagabond', remains in force today: see *Talbot v DPP* [2000] 1 WLR 1102.

[85] As there was no legal relationship between a reputed father and his illegitimate child, it followed that the usual kinship rule enshrined in s 6 of the Poor Relief Act 1601 did not apply: *City of Westminster v Gerrard* (1621) 2 Bulst 346: 'If the childe to be relieved be a bastard-childe, this is clearly out of the statute of 43 Eliz cap 2' *per* Whitlock and Croke JJ.

[86] 7 Ja I c 4 (1609) s 7. On a repeat offence, she was 'to be committed to the said house of correction as aforesaid, and there to remain until she can put in good sureties for her good behaviour, not to offend so again'.

[87] Marshall, n 42 above, at 221. The punitive approach to illegitimacy was also demonstrated by the 1623 legislation on concealment of the birth of bastards, on which see Jackson, n 40 above.

question had broken down.[88] In the same way, subsequent legislative reforms were driven more by financial rather than moral concerns. For example, although the main purpose of the 1662 Act was to define the grounds on which settlement could be acquired, it also gave the churchwardens and overseers the power to seize the goods and chattels of an absconding putative father (or indeed those of the 'lewd mother' of an illegitimate child) and receive rents from any lands in order to meet the cost of raising a child.[89] Similarly, the Bastard Children Act 1732[90] enabled a man to be apprehended on warrant and committed to jail unless he provided security to guarantee his appearance at the next quarter sessions.[91] The more punitive aspects of the bastardy legislation were further emphasised in 1809, with a measure authorising the justices to sentence parents of either sex who neglected or refused to meet their liabilities under affiliation or maintenance orders to three months' hard labour.[92] In the following year, justices were empowered to commit to a house of correction any unmarried mother whose illegitimate child was a charge on the parish, for a period of between 6 weeks and 12 months.[93]

The fact that the law imposed sanctions on the fathers of illegitimate children only where their offspring became a charge on the community confirms that financial considerations predominated over moral concerns. Records of the activities of parish officials demonstrate that 'determination to protect the ratepayer frequently overbore a zeal for justice',[94] not least as (until 1834 at least) illegitimate children derived their settlement from their place of birth rather than the residence of either parent.[95] As we have seen, the authorities resorted to various tactics to deal with this problem: 'overseers would export pregnant women to their home parishes when they could, pay them to marry their lovers or seducers, or if all else failed, sue the fathers of their children for support payments'.[96]

---

[88]   Quaife, n 43 above, at 206.

[89]   13 & 14 Cha II c 12 (1662) s 29.

[90]   6 Geo II c 31 (1733).

[91]   For an illuminating account of justices' enquiries into paupers' settlement and the paternity of illegitimate children, using original records, see T Hitchcock and J Black, *Chelsea Settlement and Bastardy Examinations 1733–1766* (London Record Society, London, 1999).

[92]   49 Geo III c 68 (1809).

[93]   50 Geo III c 51 (1810). This repealed the more penal provision which mandated one year's imprisonment with hard labour for such conduct: 7 Ja I c 4 (1609) s 7. To that extent these reforms worked to the advantage of unmarried mothers and against the interests of putative fathers, a trend criticised by Victorian writers on the poor law: see Nicholls, n 84 above, at 140–41 and PF Aschrott, *The English Poor Law System* (Knight & Co, London, 1902) at 19.

[94]   Pinchbeck and Hewitt, n 39 above, at 210. See also the detailed account in Marshall, n 42 above, at 207–24.

[95]   Thus 'many women were turned adrift when the time of their delivery drew near': *ibid*, at 211. See above at p 44.

[96]   Lees, n 6 above, at 58.

The Birth of the New Poor Law

The fundamental principles of the 1601 poor law—local administration, the doctrine of settlement and the liability of family members to support one another—remained in place at the start of the nineteenth century. But this disguised considerable diversity at local level. As Poynter argues:

> the pattern of eighteenth-century practice was not one of law determining methods of relief, but of fashions in relief receiving the sanction of law, the statutory framework providing an ever-increasing number of alternative procedures which could be adopted.[97]

The poor law continued to develop incrementally; in the eighteenth century workhouses were introduced[98] and overseers were given the power to refuse relief to paupers who declined to enter such institutions.[99] The problems thrown up by the agrarian crisis of the late eighteenth century, allied with wartime inflation, prompted local justices to seek other solutions, such as the Speenhamland system, established in 1795, under which agricultural labourers' wages were supplemented with allowances from the poor relief funds, according to a set scale.[100] Parishes increasingly had resort to various forms of 'outdoor relief', and the perception developed that the Elizabethan poor law was proving both costly and ineffective.[101] In 1802–03 over one million people received poor relief, representing 11.4 per cent of the population.[102] By 1818, the overall cost of poor relief was more than five times that of 1760, although the population had only doubled in size.[103] Theorists such as Malthus[104] and Ricardo[105] challenged the rationale for the poor

---

[97] Poynter, n 11 above, at 13.

[98] The precise origins of the workhouse test are unclear, but seem to predate the Poor Relief Act 1722 (9 Geo 1, c 7): see Slack, n 28 above, at 134. See more generally N Longmate, *The Workhouse: A Social History* (Pimlico, London, 2003) and for an architectural and social study, see K Morrison, *The Workhouse: A Study of Poor-Law Buildings in England* (English Heritage, Swindon, 1999), especially ch 8 'Poor-Law Buildings for Children'.

[99] The workhouse test appeared in the Poor Relief Act 1722 (9 Geo I c 7): see Brundage, n 6 above, at 12. From the outset conditions were very poor: one survey in 1760 established that four-fifths of children born in London workhouses died within the first year: Webb and Webb, n 78 above, at 298. By the end of the eighteenth century children accounted for well over half the number of workhouse inmates: Morrison, n 98 above, at 132.

[100] See M Neuman, *The Speenhamland County: poverty and the poor law in Berkshire 1782–1834* (Garland, New York, 1982). The Speenhamland system, associated with the southern agrarian counties, was just one of a number of different devices used to raise the incomes of the poor: see Lees, n 6 above, at 66–67.

[101] Industrialisation and the consequent rural–urban migration added to the problems. However, for a powerful argument that the English poor law system had facilitated economic growth in the seventeenth and eighteenth centuries, see PM Solar, 'Poor Relief and English Economic Development before the Industrial Revolution' (1995) 48 *Economic History Review* 1.

[102] Lees, n 6 above, at 44.

[103] de Schweinitz, n 20 above, at 114. One nineteenth century source estimates that the cost of relief in 1817 (nearly £8 million) was about the same sum as in 1871, by which date the size of the population had doubled again: TW Fowle, *The Poor Law* (Macmillan and Co, London, 2nd edn, 1890, repr 1893) at 72.

[104] See eg T Malthus, *An Essay on the Principle of Population* (1798) at para V.14.

[105] See eg D Ricardo, *On the Principles of Political Economy and Taxation* (1817) at para 5.35.

law, arguing that it created perverse incentives (eg that allowances for children simply depressed wages, encouraged larger families and generated more pauperism).[106] The association between the poor law and moral decay became part of contemporary political discourse.[107] According to one Victorian commentator, 'in some districts out-door relief was granted to the able-bodied upon so liberal a scale that pauperism became a very remunerative employment'.[108] Historians have argued that the growing ideology of the free market resulted in a reassessment of public responsibility for poor relief and a transformation in attitudes to the poor. In this way the legitimacy of parish support for the destitute was increasingly brought into question as the ethos of individualism became all pervasive. The consequence was that 'work, confinement and discipline became central to the evolving political economy of welfare long before the passage of the New Poor Law'.[109]

This classical economic thinking influenced the Report of the Royal Commission on the poor law which reported in 1834 after two years' study,[110] led by Bentham's disciple Edwin Chadwick and the economist Nassau Senior.[111] As Poynter wryly observed, 'The Commissioners found the evils they expected to find, and documented them at great length'.[112] The Royal Commission asserted that the principle of 'less eligibility' should be central to reform of the poor law. This meant that the position of the pauper 'on the whole shall not be made really or apparently so eligible as the situation of the independent labourer of the lowest class',[113] in order to avoid the perverse incentives which were regarded as inherent in the operation of the old poor law. In the view of the Royal Commission:

> Throughout the evidence it is shown, that in proportion as the condition of any pauper class is elevated above the condition of the independent labourers, the condition of the independent class is depressed; their industry is impaired, their employment becomes unsteady, and its remuneration in wages is diminished. Such persons, therefore, are under the strongest inducements to quit the less eligible class of labourers and enter the more eligible class of paupers.[114]

---

[106] Lees, n 6 above, at 88–93.

[107] See also FM Eden, *The State of the Poor: A History of the Labouring Classes in England* (first published 1797, abridged version, AGL Rogers (ed), George Routledge & Sons Ltd, London, 1928) and the discussion in Poynter, n 11 above, ch IV. For a late twentieth century resonance of these ideas, see C Murray, *Losing Ground: American Social Policy 1950–1980* (Basic Books, New York, 1984).

[108] H Fawcett, *Pauperism: Its Causes and Remedies* (Macmillan and Co, London, 1871) at 18.

[109] Lees, n 6 above, at 83. As she explains pithily, 'in the public eye, the poor had lost their moral entitlement to what was seen as a free lunch': *ibid*, at 111.

[110] *Report from HM Commissioners for Inquiring into the Administration and Practical Operation of the Poor Laws* (London, 1834). This Report (the 'Poor Law Commissioners' Report 1834'), was reissued as Cd 2728 in 1905, to which the references below refer. See further A Brundage, *The Making of the New Poor Law* (Hutchinson & Co, London, 1978).

[111] Classical economic liberalism and Benthamism were by no means the only influences: for a compelling argument that liberal toryism was a major factor in the reform process, see P Mandler, 'Tories and Paupers: Christian Political Economy and the Making of the New Poor Law' (1990) 33 *Historical Journal* 81.

[112] Poynter, n 11 above, at 318.

[113] Poor Law Commissioners' Report 1834, n 110 above, at 228.

[114] *Ibid*, at 228.

Consequently, it was argued, relief for the able-bodied should only be made available through the grim and repressive institution of the workhouse.

Given that the Royal Commission viewed pauperism as the consequence of inadequate work incentives for the able-bodied labourer, it followed that relatively little attention was paid to the status of women and children under the poor law. So, according to the Webbs:

> with regard to the really baffling problems presented by the widow, the deserted wife, the wife of the absentee soldier or sailor, the wife of a husband resident in another parish or another country—in each case whether with or without dependent children—the Report is silent.[115]

As Thane notes, the 1834 policy makers assumed 'the universality of the stable two-parent family, primarily dependent upon the father's wage, and the primacy of the family as a source of welfare'.[116] As a result, 'the wife is throughout treated exactly as is the child; and it is assumed that she follows her husband'.[117] For the most part the social problems experienced by women were simply ignored by the authors of the 1834 Report. Although widows were numerically far more important, the only group of women discussed in any detail in the Royal Commission's Report were unmarried mothers,[118] reflecting contemporary concerns about the 'allegedly immoral, socially irresponsible, and even predatory sexual behaviour of working-class women'.[119] These concerns had been 'fuelled by Malthusian concerns over population growth and Evangelical fears of moral collapse'.[120] It may be no coincidence that the illegitimacy rate had been rising since the 1750s, as it had been in the late sixteenth century when the Elizabethan poor law was established.[121] The authors of the 1834 Report concluded that the existing provisions were both ineffective and vulnerable to abuse.[122] Anticipating the concerns of Conservative governments in the late twentieth century, they reported that 'not one-half of the money paid by parishes to the mothers of bastards is recovered from the putative fathers, and that the portion so recovered is generally recovered at an enormous expense'.[123] They found that 'in almost every case the parish pays

---

[115] Webb and Webb, n 117 above, at 6.

[116] P Thane, 'Women and the Poor Law in Victorian and Edwardian England' (1978) 6 *History Workshop* 29 at 29.

[117] S Webb and B Webb, *English Poor Law Policy* (Longmans, Green and Co, London, 1910) at 6.

[118] *Ibid*, at 30. Whilst it may not be correct to suggest, following the Webbs, that the 1834 Report *ignored* women workers, there are certainly few references in the Report to women as workers: A Clark, 'The New Poor Law and the Breadwinner Wage: Contrasting Assumptions' (2000) 34 *Journal of Social History* 261 at 266–67.

[119] Brundage, n 6 above, at 69.

[120] *Ibid*, at 68–69. See further G Reekie, *Measuring Immorality: Social Inquiry and the Problem of Illegitimacy* (Cambridge University Press, Cambridge, 1998) chs 2 and 3.

[121] See further P Laslett, *Family life and illicit love in earlier generations: essays in historical sociology* (Cambridge University Press, Cambridge, 1977) ch 3.

[122] Poor Law Commissioners' Report 1834, n 110 above, at 165–78. See further URQ Henriques, 'Bastardy and the new poor law' (1967) 37 *Past and Present* 103 and LF Cody, 'The Politics of Illegitimacy in an Age of Reform: Women, Reproduction, and Political Economy in England's New Poor Law of 1834' (2000) 11 *Journal of Women's History* 131.

[123] Poor Law Commissioners' Report 1834, n 110 above, at 177.

to the woman the sum, whatever it may be, that has been *charged* on the man, whether paid by him or not'.[124] Amongst various other evils, the bastardy laws were also perceived as an inducement to perjury and blackmail, as 'loose women would swear not to the real father of the child, but to the wealthiest man against whom the charge could stick'.[125] According to one German observer, writing in the late Victorian period, 'debauchery became a lucrative trade'.[126]

The 1834 Report made a series of recommendations designed to tackle these perceived problems.[127] In an attempt at social engineering no less ambitious than the philosophy underpinning the Child Support Act 1991, the Royal Commission concluded that the most effective means of discouraging bastardy was to throw the burden of illegitimacy on the mother. Its proposals relating to illegitimate children were thus directed towards liability (or, as it was known under the poor law, chargeability) rather than the methods of relief.[128] The 1834 Report therefore proposed placing the primary duty for support of an illegitimate child upon the mother (and hence often, in practice, upon her parents) and exempting the putative father from any liability for the child's maintenance.[129] It followed that the settlement of an illegitimate child became that of the mother, rather than the child's place of birth, until the child reached 16 or acquired his or her own settlement.[130] As Finer and McGregor describe:

> the principle of less eligibility visited the assumed moral delinquency of a mother upon her child in the supposed interest of preserving the parental responsibilities of the independent poor and the integrity of lawful wedlock.[131]

Somewhat disingenuously, the authors of the 1834 Report argued that the mother's private law remedies remained open to her.[132] Failing that, 'if a mother really could not support her illegitimate child, the place for both was in a new Union workhouse'.[133]

The original Bill accordingly made no provision for the parish (or indeed the mother) to bring an action in order to recover the costs of poor relief against an

---

[124] *Ibid*, at 167–68. 'To the woman, therefore, a single illegitimate child is seldom any expense, and two or three are a source of positive profit': *ibid*, at 168.

[125] Henriques, n 122 above, at 106; see also at 104. See further Fowle, n 103 above, at 90–92 and also Webb and Webb n 117 above, at 309: 'What perjury and extortion, what oppression and petty tyranny, this system produced can only be faintly estimated'. But financial corruption was not, in their view, the worst evil: 'More revolting, and more socially disastrous, was the direct premium which the system placed upon female unchastity' (*ibid*, at 311).

[126] Aschrott, n 93 above, at 30. Lees states that 'the image of women producing multiple bastards for profit haunted the commissioners': n 6 above at 141.

[127] Poor Law Commissioners' Report 1834, n 110 above, at 346–51.

[128] Webb and Webb, n 117 above, at 7.

[129] Henriques, n 122 above, at 108. See Poor Law Amendment Act 1834 ss 69–76.

[130] *Ibid* s 71.

[131] Finer Report, n 3 above, vol 2 Appendix 5 at 121.

[132] 'It must be remembered too, that we do not propose to deprive either the woman or her parents of their direct means of redress; she may still bring her action for breach of promise of marriage, and her parents may still bring theirs for the loss of their daughter's service': Poor Law Commissioners' Report 1834, n 110 above, at 351. Such private law rights were more apparent than real: see ch 3 below.

[133] Henriques, n 122 above, at 109.

alleged father of a child born outside marriage. This proposal did not survive scrutiny in the Parliament, and the government agreed to an amendment restoring the parish's right to seek recoupment, providing nothing was paid to the mother.[134] However, in keeping with the original policy intention, those responsible for the 1834 Act sought to make the process of such recovery as difficult as possible. In particular, these affiliation proceedings were transferred from the justices to the Quarter Sessions and made subject to a requirement of independent corroboration of the mother's evidence, reflecting contemporary concerns that unscrupulous women typically brought unfounded charges as a means of securing financial support for their offspring. Maintenance orders were limited in amount to the cost to the parish of supporting the child and were in any event to cease when the child reached the age of seven. Finally, the power to imprison putative fathers for failing to pay was repealed.[135] Given the difficulties associated with proceedings at Quarter Sessions, the result was that 'the burden, cost and obloquy fell solely and squarely upon the women'.[136]

The Operation of the New Poor Law

Given the principal focus of this chapter, the preceding discussion has centred on the way in which the Royal Commission dealt with the position of women with dependent children. At the organisational level, the Royal Commission recommended sweeping changes to the administrative machinery of the poor law, designed to increase central control over the system. The Poor Law Amendment Act 1834, described by one historian as 'the single most important piece of social legislation ever enacted',[137] established a central supervisory body in the Poor Law Commissioners, who were empowered to merge the thousands of parishes into larger unions, each governed by an elected board of guardians.[138] Although the

---

[134] *Ibid*, at 113.

[135] According to the Poor Law Commissioners' Report 1834, n 110 above, 'In affirming the inefficiency of human legislation to enforce the restraints placed on licentiousness by Providence, we have implied our belief, that all punishment of the supposed father is useless. We believe that it is worse than useless' (at 350).

[136] Finer Report, n 3 above, vol 2 Appendix 5 at 116. For a Victorian (and rather different) perspective, see Fowle, n 103 above, at 91–92 on the mischief at which the 1834 reforms were aimed:

> The consequences of this interference with nature's law, that the shame and burden of illegitimacy shall devolve mainly upon the woman, are too shocking to be detailed in these pages: suffice it to say, that it was another example of the ruin which human folly, trying to be wise above what is written in nature's book, can bring upon the class or sex it seeks to benefit.

[137] Englander, n 17 above, at 1. The scope of the 1834 Act was confined to England and Wales. Special legislation followed for Ireland in 1838 (see p 40 above). The new poor law began in Scotland in 1845 with the secularization of the old parish system. The 1845 Act appeared to be sterner than its English counterpart, enshrining the basic principle that the able-bodied had no right to relief of any kind: see Blaikie, n 7 above, at 254.

[138] The status of the overseers was little different after 1834: according to Fowle (n 103 above, at 77), 'the office was disagreeable, unpopular and unpaid . . . against partiality, favouritism, and jobbing there was no check; against embezzlement, very little'. To some extent their functions were taken over by

central authorities made considerable progress in rationalising the many disparate parishes into unions, the application of the substantive principles of the new poor law was not so straightforward.

The reality was that whereas the 1834 reforms had been devised to deal with the problems of rural poverty, the challenge for the future was urban, industrial poverty exacerbated by cyclical mass joblessness.[139] Some historians emphasise that the 1834 changes did not revolutionize the administration of poor relief; rather, change was gradual, incremental and pragmatic.[140] True, increasing numbers of workhouses were built, but their inmates were not the able-bodied jobless. As Patricia Hollis[141] has observed of the period after 1834:

> Much of the history of poor law work, and especially of women's work, over the next half century, was the attempt to modify and reform a punitive institution that was misconceived and misbegotten: designed for idle able-bodied men, but occupied by the very young, the very old, and women.[142]

Indeed, throughout the Victorian period most of the poor were relieved outside the workhouse,[143] despite central edicts[144] and notwithstanding periodic efforts to restrict the availability of such outdoor relief (most notably in the 1870s, led by the Charity Organisation Society,[145] which emphasised individuals' moral responsibility for their own economic welfare).[146] It was, of course, much cheaper for

---

relieving officers, whose responsibilities covered the wider area of the union, thus minimising the scope for personal negotiation that had been a feature of the old poor law: Snell, n 59 above, at 119–20.

[139] ME Rose, *The Relief of Poverty 1834–1914* (Macmillan, Basingstoke, 2nd edn, 1986) at 14.

[140] See Mandler, n 111 above, at 82, A Digby, *Pauper Palaces* (Routledge & Kegan Paul, London, 1978) and Brundage, n 6 above. But see B Harris, *The Origins of the British Welfare State: Social Welfare in England and Wales 1800–1945* (Palgrave Macmillan, Basingstoke, 2004) at 47–53 on the 1834 'watershed' argument.

[141] Writing in her then academic capacity; later Minister for Children and the Family and Parliamentary Under Secretary of State in the DWP with responsibility for child support (1997–2005).

[142] P Hollis, *Ladies Elect: Women in English Local Government 1865–1914* (Clarendon Press, Oxford, 1987) at 197.

[143] See generally Webb and Webb, n 117 above. By 1854 some 84% of recipients were on outdoor relief: WR Cornish and G de N Clark, *Law and Society in England 1750–1950* (Sweet & Maxwell, London, 1989) at 432. However, the proportion of the population as a whole on poor relief fell steadily in the second half of the nineteenth century, and by 1900 the proportion of those subject to the poor law but on outdoor relief had dropped to 73%: Lees, n 6 above, at 180 and 264. Welsh poor law unions were 'the most notorious' in their opposition to workhouses and their commitment to the widespread use of outdoor relief: AM McBriar, *An Edwardian Mixed Doubles: The Bosanquets versus the Webbs* (Clarendon Press, Oxford, 1987) at 40.

[144] eg the 1844 Outdoor Relief Prohibitory Order and the 1852 Outdoor Relief Regulation Order.

[145] Or, to give it its full title, The Society for Organising Charitable Relief and Repressing Mendicity; see further R Humphreys, *Sin, Organized Charity and the Poor Law in Victorian England* (Macmillan, Basingstoke, 1995) and J Lewis, *The voluntary sector, the state and social work in Britain* (Edward Elgar, Aldershot, 1995).

[146] See M MacKinnon, 'English Poor Law Policy and the Crusade against Outrelief' (1987) 47 *Journal of Economic History* 603. For a contemporary account, see Fawcett, n 108 above, complaining that 'out-door relief is regarded by a considerable section of our population as a fund from which they are perfectly justified in obtaining as much as possible', and is seen as 'a gift which carries with it no onerous conditions' (at 29).

guardians to provide outdoor relief than to take families into the workhouse.[147] Moreover, just as the 1834 Report stigmatised unmarried mothers, so too did the practice of the poor law authorities throughout the remainder of the nineteenth century and beyond. By 1872 nearly half of all adults on outdoor relief were widows, 4 per cent were deserted wives and just 1 per cent were mothers of illegitimate children.[148] Conversely, whilst widows[149] (and often deserted wives[150]) with dependent children tended to be seen as 'deserving', it was expected that the unmarried mothers would have to enter the workhouse in return for relief.

Although the position of separated women was largely ignored in the 1834 Report, five years later the Poor Law Commissioners issued a circular to boards of guardians providing advice on how to deal with cases of desertion.[151] The circular indicated that the appropriate course of action was to prosecute the defaulting husband under the Vagrancy Act 1824 for failure to maintain, but it acknowledged that such proceedings were rarely brought as the costs of the prosecution usually fell on the parish officers. Accordingly, boards of guardians were advised to grant relief by way of a loan in such cases,[152] reflecting official concerns about collusion.[153] Central directives also prohibited the granting of outdoor relief to able-bodied men and women, but 'deserving' categories, such as deserted wives with dependent children, were exempt.[154] Although there were differences in both national and local policy, such women typically received a weekly allowance as a form of income supplement, paid through outdoor relief.[155] This sort of minimal protection was denied to men.[156] Married women were seen as mothers first and workers second. The married woman's dependency was reinforced by the continuing law of settlement, which assumed that she acquired settlement in her

---

[147] See Clark, n 117 above, at 265.

[148] Statistics calculated from Table 2.1 in Humphreys, n 145 above, at 23.

[149] However, the rule in the Poor Removal Act 1846 (9 & 10 Vic c 66) that a widow could not be removed from the parish of her husband's death during the following year actually led to the forcible ejection of some men who had dependents and were thought to be at death's door: Snell, n 59 above, at 107 n 9.

[150] But see n 153 below.

[151] Circular No 6 in *Fifth Annual Report of the Poor Law Commissioners* (London, 1839) Appendix A at 83.

[152] On the use of loans under the new poor law, see Cranston, n 18 above, at 33–34. The modern manifestation is in the social fund.

[153] Suspicions were from time to time expressed that deserted wives were receiving undeclared payments from 'absent' husbands: Clark, n 117 above, at 266. This is a recurrent theme of those responsible for public relief systems: see also H Bosanquet, *The Poor Law Report of 1909* (Macmillan and Co Ltd, London, 1909) at 192. Similar concerns lay behind the 1996 changes to the rules governing reduced benefit directions in the modern child support scheme (see p 272 below).

[154] Lees, n 6 above, at 142.

[155] *Ibid*, at 196–210; Digby, n 140 above, at 150; see also M Levine-Clark, 'Engendering relief: Women, Ablebodiedness, and the New Poor Law in Early Victorian England' (2000) 14 *Journal of Women's History* 107 at 113. Official policy after 1871 was that deserted wives should not receive outdoor relief during the first 12 months after the desertion: Webb and Webb, n 117 above, at 175.

[156] Lees, n 6 above, at 210.

husband's place of birth.[157] As a result, deserted women who sought relief in another locality remained at risk of removal to their husband's place of settlement,[158] although generally 'settlement law became increasingly redundant as and because England and Wales moved gradually towards a national welfare system'.[159] Throughout the remainder of the Victorian era there was relatively little legislative activity in the context of the poor law in relation to husbands who deserted their wives. However, the poor law authorities were empowered to recover the costs of relief for a wife from her husband by virtue of the Poor Law Amendment Act 1868,[160] and married women with separate property were made subject to an equivalent liability by the Married Women's Property Act 1870.[161] It was not until 1927 that husbands were finally added to the list of relatives who were subject to the formal statutory duty to maintain.[162]

The position of unmarried mothers was the subject of much more statutory intervention. The provisions in the 1834 Act, known as the 'Bastardy Clauses', restricting the powers of the authorities to recover the costs of poor relief for illegitimate children, were deeply unpopular with officials in the new unions.[163] The years immediately following 1834 saw marked reductions in both the numbers of illegitimate children charged to parishes and of affiliation orders,[164] although these may not be primarily attributable to the effects of the Act itself.[165] Following lobbying of Parliament, however, amending legislation in 1839 returned affiliation proceedings to Petty Sessions whilst retaining the other principal features of the Bastardy Clauses.[166] This limited concession was followed by a *volte-face* with the

---

[157] The 1834 Act retained a modified version of the law of settlement. Despite this, litigation between parishes over settlement disputes became a regular feature, generating an increasingly complex body of case law: see Cranston, n 18 above, at 345 n 61.

[158] This humiliating practice continued right into the early twentieth century: Thane, n 116 above, at 30.

[159] KDM Snell, 'Pauper settlement and the right to poor relief in England and Wales' (1991) 6 *Continuity and Change* 375 at 378. The Union Chargeability Act 1865 (28 & 29 Victoria c 79) transferred the cost of poor relief from the parish to the union, so putting a stop to *intra*-Union removals, but *inter*-Union removals persisted: URQ Henriques, *Before the Welfare State* (Longman, London, 1979) at 58. See generally ME Rose, 'Settlement, Removal and the New Poor Law' in Fraser, n 17 above, ch 1.

[160] Section 33. The Poor Law Amendment Act 1850, s 5 had imposed such a liability in the special case where a wife was admitted to an asylum or registered hospital as a 'lunatic'.

[161] Section 13. But a married woman could not be required to support her father under the poor law: *Guardians of Pontypool v Buck* [1906] 2 KB 896.

[162] Poor Law Act 1927, s 41(1). The reason for the delay was presumably that a husband was in any event subject to a common law duty to maintain his wife. The account here is indebted to the analysis by Neville Brown, n 74 above, at 115–16.

[163] eg in the Easingwold union the board of guardians resigned, on being informed by the Poor Law Commissioners that they could not pay outdoor relief to an unmarried mother whom they regarded as of 'deserving character', and only resumed their duties when reminded that they would be personally liable for any neglect caused by their actions in renouncing office: T Mackay, *A History of the English Poor Law* vol III (PS King & Son, London, 1899) at 307–8 (this volume supplemented Nicholls n 84 above).

[164] The number of chargeable illegitimate children fell by 13% from 71,298 in 1835 to 61,826 in 1836, and the number of affiliation orders by 38% from 12,381 to 7,686: Nicholls, n 84 above, at 317.

[165] The reasons may well have been demographic: see Reekie, n 120 above, at 34.

[166] Bastard Children Act 1839 (2 & 3 Vict 85); see Mackay, n 163 above, at 315–18.

Poor Law Amendment Act 1844, which, for the first time, provided the mother of an illegitimate child, regardless of whether or not she herself was on poor relief, with a direct civil remedy against the reputed father.[167] Local officials were barred from bringing maintenance actions so long as the mother was alive and capable of doing so. Instead, the mother could—in theory at least—bring an action against the alleged father in Petty Sessions, subject still to the requirement that her assertion as to the child's paternity be corroborated by independent evidence.[168] Not surprisingly, few women were willing to bring such proceedings of their own initiative,[169] not least as putative fathers could abscond with relative ease.[170] In practice 'mothers came on the parish, and the poor law authorities exerted pressure on her to retrieve money from the father through either an informal approach or a legal action'.[171]

The right of the poor law authorities to recover the costs of maintenance from the putative father was not restored until 1868.[172] Further reforms were made by the Bastardy Laws Amendment Act 1872, which increased the limit on the amount of child maintenance that could be awarded and extended the duration of payment for children up to the age of 16.[173] The 1872 Act also enabled a mother to obtain an order for the maintenance of an illegitimate child against the putative father before the child was born.[174] The fundamental principles and procedures underpinning the bastardy jurisdiction, established in the mid-Victorian period, were still firmly in place when the Finer Committee reported just over 100 years later.[175] Indeed, they remained part of the regular diet of the magistrates' court civil jurisdiction until the Family Law Reform Act 1987 repealed the Affiliation Proceedings Act 1957.

The Royal Commission on the Poor Laws of 1909

At the start of the twentieth century, the poor law was still very much part of the fabric of the nascent British welfare state. When a further Royal Commission was

[167] For the first time South of the border, in any event: the action for aliment in Scotland goes back at least to medieval times: Finer Report, n 3 above, vol 2 Appendix 6 at 173.

[168] Henriques, n 122 above, at 119. The legislation prescribed maximum amounts for child maintenance and stipulated that such payments could continue until the child was 13.

[169] For example, in one parish in Scotland there were 295 illegitimate births recorded in 1858; paternity was not acknowledged at registration in 211 cases, and was established by court decree in just 20 cases: A Blaikie, *Illegitimacy, Sex, and Society: Northeast Scotland, 1750–1900* (Clarendon Press, Oxford, 1993) at 173.

[170] *Ibid*, ch 7.

[171] Digby, n 140 above, at 154.

[172] Poor Law Amendment Act 1868, s 41.

[173] The 1872 Act replaced the Poor Law Amendment Act 1844; see further Finer Report, n 3 above, vol 2 Appendix 5 at 119.

[174] See TE James, 'The Illegitimate and Deprived Child' in RH Graveson and FR Crane (eds), *A Century of Family Law 1857–1957* (Sweet & Maxwell, London, 1957) ch 3 at 40 n 6.

[175] Finer Report, n 3 above, vol 2 Appendix 5 at 119.

established in 1905 to review its operation, the poor law was 'the sole statutory cash-paying social service in Britain'.[176] The Royal Commission, which was divided principally on the nature and extent of the necessary administrative reforms of the poor law,[177] produced a majority and minority report in 1909.[178] The authors of the majority report, which was compiled by senior poor law officials and luminaries of the Charity Organisation Society, such as Helen Bosanquet, 'aimed at improvements in administration rather than changes in principle'.[179] As such, they proposed the transformation of the poor law into public assistance, to be overseen by committees at county level.[180] They also envisaged more intensive scrutiny of individual applications for relief,[181] not least as they remained convinced that 'the causes of distress are not only economic and industrial; in their origin and character they are largely moral'.[182] Or, as Bosanquet herself asserted more bluntly, 'It is difficult for anyone not intimately acquainted with Poor Law administration to realise that many of those who claim relief are suffering from sheer laziness'.[183] The minority report, in which Beatrice Webb played a leading part, adopted a more radical approach as regards organisational reform. It recommended the abolition of the poor law and the transfer of those functions previously carried out by the poor law authorities to other government agencies (for example, under the minority's plans, unemployment relief was to become the responsibility of the Ministry of Labour).

The Royal Commission's combined reports represent a monumental survey and analysis of the poor law at the start of the twentieth century.[184] At this time, there were 234,792 children in receipt of poor law relief,[185] most of whom were children living at home[186] with their widowed mothers, who subsisted on low earnings supplemented by outdoor relief,[187] while unmarried mothers were still more likely to end up in the workhouse. In the limited space available here, this discussion of the 1909 Royal Commission is confined to four issues of relevance to the future development of public policy on maintenance for children. These are the treatment of widows and deserted wives respectively, the principles governing recovery of the cost of poor relief and the rules governing support for illegitimate children.

---

[176] J Fulbrook, *Administrative Justice and the Unemployed* (Mansell, London, 1978) at 107.

[177] MA Crowther, *The Workhouse System 1834–1929* (University of Georgia Press, Athens, Georgia, 1981) at 55.

[178] *Report of the Royal Commission on the Poor Laws and Relief of Distress* (Cd 4499, 1909).

[179] McBriar, n 143 above, at 304.

[180] The majority report's full recommendations are summarised in n 178 above, pt IX, at 595–670.

[181] A concern shared by the minority: minority report, n 178 above, at 754.

[182] Majority report, n 178 above, pt IX, at 643, para 168.

[183] n 153 above (her summary version of the Report) at 4.

[184] Taken together, the majority and minority reports ran to a total of 1,238 printed foolscap pages.

[185] For developments in methods of poor law relief for children during the nineteenth century, under the Poor Law Commissioners, the Poor Law Board and the Local Government Board respectively, see Webb and Webb, n 117 above, at 43–46, 104–15 and 179–206.

[186] Only 62,426 were in institutions, of whom just 16,221 were in workhouses (statistics as at January 1, 1908): Bosanquet, n 153 above, at 65; see also at 77.

[187] *Ibid*, at 189–92.

The majority report expressed reservations about the indiscriminate granting of outdoor relief to widows with children,[188] not least as this was perceived to lower wages and encourage dependency. There was, however, no clear solution: the majority report proposed no more than that all such cases should receive 'special and individual attention'.[189] The position of deserted wives was regarded as analogous but in some ways more difficult, given the concerns about collusion with the other partner. The majority report accordingly reaffirmed the Local Government Board's longstanding policy that, save in exceptional cases, deserted wives should not receive outdoor relief in the first 12 months of their separation.[190] A more radical solution was proposed by the minority members of the Royal Commission, who regarded it as unrealistic to expect widows and deserted wives with dependent children to be self-supporting in the labour market. They noted that in England and Wales the official policy of not paying outdoor relief to the able-bodied was widely ignored for women with dependent children.[191] Their broader recommendations for labour market reform envisaged that the male industrial wage would be sufficient to support a man's wife and children. In the absence of the wage-earner—through widowhood or desertion—the mother should not be encouraged to seek work; rather, she should remain at home to care for her children, supported by an adequate Home Aliment,[192] in some ways presaging the Finer Report's proposal for a guaranteed maintenance allowance.[193] In the case of deserted wives, the payment of Home Aliment was to be without prejudice to the right of the authorities to seek an appropriate contribution from the errant husband. In the minority's view, for policy makers

> deliberately to punish a deserted wife, and deliberately to injure deserted children, by compelling them to enter the admittedly demoralising General Mixed Workhouse, because we fail to apprehend the scoundrel himself, and because we do not know how to prevent collusion, is, in our opinion, wholly unjustifiable.[194]

On the issue of the liability to maintain, the majority report expressed concern at the wide varieties in local practices.[195] It recommended that the authorities should pursue the policy of recovery from liable relatives 'uniformly and with

---

[188] As at January 1, 1907, there were 34,749 widows with 96,342 children on outdoor relief and just 1,240 widows with 2,998 children in the workhouse: majority report, n 178 above, pt VI, at 154, para 273.

[189] *Ibid*, at 157, para 285. On the different approaches of Bosanquet and Webb, see McBriar, n 143 above, at 295.

[190] Majority report, n 178 above, at 157–58, para 286.

[191] They approved as 'more logical' the policy of the Scottish poor law, which prohibited outdoor relief to the able-bodied whilst excluding all women with the care of children from the category of able-bodied for this purpose: minority report, n 178 above, at 1045–46.

[192] *Ibid*; see also at 1194. Such Home Aliment was to be conditional on the woman maintaining the home to minimum standards and not having been adjudged unworthy to have the care of children entrusted to her: *ibid*, at 1217.

[193] See ch 4.

[194] Minority report, n 178 above, at 1046 n §.

[195] Majority report, n 178 above, pt VIII at 548–57, paras 69–122.

firmness and discretion'. They also proposed that individual paupers should be able to bring maintenance proceedings against liable relatives in their own right.[196] In addition, the majority members proposed various procedural reforms in an attempt to simplify the legal process of recovery.[197] The minority members, while disagreeing with a number of the majority's specific proposals, also argued for greater uniformity of principle and practice with regard to the recovery of poor law expenditure across a range of services. The existing arrangements, they complained, revealed 'a chaos of careless laxity and arbitrary oppression'.[198]

As regards the operation of the bastardy laws, the majority report's proposals were partly procedural and partly institutional in nature. The first was that the authorities should have the power to apply for an increase in the amount payable under such order where the original order had been obtained by the woman. They also recommended that payments under affiliation orders should be made via some third party, rather than directly to the mother herself, in order to avoid the stigma and moral danger associated with her having direct contact with the putative father.[199] The majority report included proposals for the accommodation of unmarried mothers, in appropriate cases away from the morally contaminating environment of the workhouse, advocating that such women be categorised into one of three types: 'the feeble-minded or irresponsible, the young mothers who are responsible but have fallen for the first time, and the women who have no desire to lead a respectable life'.[200] Whilst highly judgmental, this was at least a shift from the position of the 1834 Royal Commission, which had sought to stigmatise all unmarried mothers without distinction.

Public Assistance in the Early Twentieth Century

In practice the work of the 1909 Royal Commission was overtaken by events. Its appointment was one of the last acts of the 1905 Conservative administration[201]

---

[196] Majority report, n 178 above, pt VIII, at 555, para 110 (which the minority report opposed: at 932). The majority were much exercised by the failure of adult children to provide any contribution towards the support of their aged parents: at 550–52, paras 83–95. The majority also proposed that grandchildren should be made liable relatives: at 555, para 112 (which would have reversed *Maund v Mason* LR 9 QB 254 (1874)); again the minority argued against any extension of the scope of liability originally established in 1601: at 935.

[197] Such as enabling the authorities to institute proceedings before or after the person concerned was actually chargeable: majority report, n 178 above, at 555, para 111.

[198] Minority report, n 178 above, at 944.

[199] 'It is not right that the terms of a legal order should serve as a pretext for periodical visits by a man to the woman he has seduced, and the position is even worse when, through failure of the payments, the women is induced to frequent the man's house with a view to obtaining her money', majority report, pt VII, para 144 at 562. See also Bosanquet, n 153 above, at 253–54.

[200] Majority report, n 178 above, pt VII, at 563, para 152. The minority report gave no detailed consideration to bastardy orders, focussing instead on questions of accommodation and treatment: ch III, at 772–800.

[201] The warrant for the Royal Commission was issued on the same day that the Conservative government resigned: de Schweinitz, n 20 above, at 199.

and by the time it had reported the Liberal government had won a landslide general election victory. The Liberal administrations led by Campbell-Bannerman, Asquith and then Lloyd George effectively bypassed the Royal Commission of 1909[202] by implementing a series of reforms which indirectly paved the way for the modern welfare state, using different funding mechanisms. In one sense, their first initiative—the Provision of Meals Act 1906—was a modest enough measure, making provision for free school meals.[203] Symbolically, however, it marked a reversal of the principles of 1834—it involved a system of public relief entirely independent of the poor law, and the parents of those children retained their civic rights.[204] Even more important was the Old Age Pensions Act of 1908, which introduced a small non-contributory weekly pension for those aged 70 or over. Paid through the post office and out of general taxation, this avoided the stigma of the poor law and resulted in a significant fall in the numbers of elderly in receipt of outdoor relief.[205] This was followed by the National Insurance Act 1911 which brought in contributory sickness and unemployment insurance for men in certain industries. The extension of unemployment insurance to most of the workforce after the First World War, and the inclusion of allowances for dependants, demonstrated a state commitment to supporting the jobless outside of the poor law. This contributory principle was later extended to include widows' pensions.[206]

The developments of these new schemes, funded by social insurance or taxation, meant that the poor law moved from the centre to the margins of welfare policy. In keeping with this trend, the Local Government Act 1929 was designed 'to rationalize local administration and curb the uncoordinated policies of social relief which had prevailed since the war'.[207] It abolished boards of guardians[208] and transferred their functions to county councils and borough councils. The 1929 Act also enabled local authorities to take designated categories out of the poor law,[209] paving the way for the break-up of the poor law itself.[210] The inability of time-limited unemployment insurance to accommodate mass joblessness eventually resulted in the Unemployment Act of 1934, which introduced unemployment assistance, a national scheme for those who had exhausted their right to the insurance-based benefit.[211] The new scheme was administered by the Unemployment

---

[202] A process doubtless made easier by the lack of unanimity in the 1909 Report; McBriar, n 143 above, at 374.

[203] See further Harris, n 140 above, at 157–58.

[204] de Schweinitz, n 20 above, at 202.

[205] D Vincent, *Poor Citizens—The State and the Poor in Twentieth Century Britain* (Longman, London, 1991) at 27 and 40. See further M Pugh, 'Working-Class Experience and State Social Welfare, 1908–1914: Old Age Pensions Reconsidered' (2002) 45 *The Historical Journal* 775.

[206] Widows' Orphans and Old Age Contributory Pensions Act 1925.

[207] McBriar, n 143 above, at 365.

[208] Thus finally implementing a unanimous proposal of the 1909 Royal Commission: see Bosanquet, n 153 above, ch VI for criticisms of boards of guardians. McBriar, n 143 above, at 374 argues that abolition in 1909 would have been politically controversial for no immediate gain.

[209] Section 5.

[210] McBriar, n 143 above, at 367.

[211] See further Harris, n 140 above, at 204–7.

Assistance Board rather than the poor law authorities. The Board operated the controversial household means-test, which equated the household with the family when assessing entitlement to assistance, with the result that all earning members of the household were assumed to share in its financial support, and not just those who were legally liable under the poor law definition.[212] By the end of the Second World War the Board had dropped the 'Unemployment' prefix, having assumed responsibility for pensioners, evacuees and refugees, amongst others. It was then a small step for that body to transmute into the National Assistance Board under Beveridge's proposals.

The legislative developments of the first half of the twentieth century had paved the way for Beveridge's wider reforms in other respects too. The contributory principle necessarily favoured those with established work histories amongst the male working class. The structures of the new welfare state thus reinforced conventional notions of the dependency of women and children on male earners. This was also reflected in the signal lack of success of the campaign for family endowment in the inter-war period;[213] it was only in the changed economic and social circumstances of the Second World War that public (and trade union) support shifted in favour of a family allowance.[214]

All these changes meant that during the first part of the twentieth century the poor law remained a reality for those without access to the new social insurance benefits.[215] As for this group, in 1920 widows with children were still, in numerical terms, a far larger category of poor law recipients than unmarried mothers (see Table 2.1[216]). There was also little change in the way in which women with dependent children were categorised within the poor law according to their moral deservingness. Widows were almost invariably accorded outdoor relief, as were (usually) deserted wives, whereas unmarried mothers typically faced the workhouse.

In addition, throughout the first half of the twentieth century, there was a steady stream of what was essentially state-sponsored maintenance litigation before the magistrates' courts. For example, between 1900 and 1939 the authorities made some 3,000–5,000 applications annually under the poor law for failure to support, with a success rate of 90 per cent or more. Over the same period the number of applications made each year in bastardy and affiliation proceedings (where the success rate was about 80 per cent) fell from some 8,000 annually before the First

---

[212] See MA Crowther, 'Family Responsibility and State Responsibility in Britain before the Welfare State' (1982) 25 *Historical Journal* 131–45. For a contemporary analysis of the use of means-testing, see P Ford, *Incomes, Means Tests and Personal Responsibility* (PS King & Son Ltd, London, 1939).

[213] Vincent, n 205 above, at 116.

[214] See generally J Macnicol, *The Movement for Family Allowances, 1918–45: A Study in Social Policy Development* (Heinemann, London, 1980) and S Pedersen, *Family Dependence, and the Origins of the Welfare State* (Cambridge University Press, Cambridge, 1993).

[215] See Crowther, n 177 above, for an account of the twentieth century history of the poor law. The poor law also acted as a supplement to other forms of income: Harris, n 140 above, at 202–4.

[216] Adapted from Crowther, n 177 at 100, citing 1st Report Ministry of Health PP 1920 (932) xvii at 328 (workhouses were renamed 'institutions' in 1913: *ibid*, at 87).

Table 2.1 Women with dependent children in receipt of poor relief on 1 January 1920

Categories of women with dependent children	% of all women with children on poor relief	Number in receipt of outdoor relief	Number in receipt of indoor relief	% on indoor relief
Widows	81.6	35,061	892	2.5
Deserted wives	6.4	2,356	470	16.6
Other separated wives	4.0	1,306	451	25.6
Unmarried mothers	8.0	731	2,783	79.2
Total	100.0	39,454	4,596	

World War to about half that number by 1939.[217] In contrast, the number of private law matrimonial applications (where the success rate was some 70 per cent) rose from about 10,000 per annum at the turn of the century to 14,000 in the inter-war years. Across all three jurisdictions—the poor law, bastardy law and private law—imprisonment was routinely used as a penalty for non-payment of maintenance, resulting in several thousand committals each year.[218] As the next chapter demonstrates, this was to change radically after the Second World War. The National Assistance Act 1948 abolished the last vestiges of the poor law. In policy terms this led to what was effectively the privatisation of the enforcement of public law maintenance obligations; arguably, the perceived failure of that process in turn led to the decision to introduce the child support scheme in 1993.

Conclusion

The obligation of parents to maintain their children was first established under the poor law. This early public law of child support reflected contemporary views on the importance of kinship as the source of intra-familial financial responsibilities. Widowhood was the prime cause of child poverty throughout the period reviewed in this chapter; realistically, in the absence of a male breadwinner, outdoor relief was the most cost-effective form of public assistance in such cases. Although the dependent children of deserted wives and unmarried mothers were far less

[217] O McGregor, L Blom-Cooper and C Gibson, *Separated spouses: a study of the matrimonial jurisdiction of magistrates' courts* (Duckworth, London, 1970) at 33, Table 1. The peak for bastardy orders was 1919 (11,862), reflecting the well-established demographic correlation between wars and illegitimacy rates.
[218] *Ibid*, at 34, Table 2. See further chs 3 and 4.

significant in numerical terms, the legal and practical ramifications of such lone parenthood were far more complex. In theory, husbands who deserted their wives and children could be required to reimburse the parish authorities, applying the principle in the Poor Relief Act 1601, although in practice enforcement was notoriously difficult. Men who fathered illegitimate children were separately liable under the bastardy legislation, but again enforcement was problematic. In both instances, however, public law intervened only if the children in question became a charge on the rates. The public policy imperative of minimising the cost of poor law relief expended on children who had liable relatives was paramount, although there were periods when moral concerns also came to the fore (for example, in the first half of the nineteenth century). These financial and moral factors were both to resonate strongly in the debates over the Child Support Act 1991.

3

The Child Maintenance Obligation in Private Law

Introduction

The previous chapter examined the development of the child maintenance obligation in the arena of public law, from the earliest days of the poor law through to the mid-twentieth century. This chapter considers the treatment of child maintenance under English private law over the same period. A convenient starting point for an analysis of the position at common law is Blackstone's *Commentaries on the Laws of England*; this chapter then examines the early case law on child maintenance and how this came to be modified over time by the intervention of statute, and in particular by the development of the separate matrimonial jurisdictions vested in the High Court and magistrates' courts respectively. There are, however, three preliminary qualifications which should be noted about the discussion that follows.

First, the purpose of this chapter is to provide no more than a panoramic view of the development of the law governing child maintenance in a private law context, not least as the history of these provisions is examined in much greater depth elsewhere.[1] So the treatment here is necessarily selective, bearing in mind that, as Neville Brown wrote in 1968, 'the law of maintenance has become a treacherous quagmire through which textbook writers vainly essay to chart a path for bewildered students and harassed practitioners'.[2] The emphasis, accordingly, is on the 'bigger picture', at the risk of some lack of detail.

Secondly although the primary emphasis of this chapter is on child maintenance, it is somewhat artificial to view this form of support in isolation. Historically, for the most part at least, the law has drawn a clear conceptual distinction between support for children and spousal maintenance. However, in terms of the development of legal practice, and especially in the twentieth century, it was always difficult to disentangle the issue of support for children from private law rights to spousal maintenance. This perception still bedevils child support law and policy in the

---

[1] See, most notably and magisterially, S Cretney, *Family Law in the Twentieth Century: A History* (Oxford University Press, Oxford, 2003).
[2] L Neville Brown, 'Maintenance and Esoterism' (1968) 31 *Modern Law Review* 121 at 121.

twenty-first century. In strict private law terms this has perhaps been less of an issue as regards children born outside marriage, where maintenance has traditionally been seen as matter for the law of bastardy, discussed in the previous chapter.[3]

Thirdly, as with the previous chapter, the discussion below is irredeemably Anglocentric. The private law position of child maintenance in Scots Law has always been very different to that in England and Wales. For example, whilst the English common law,[4] as we shall see, has long struggled with the notion of a child's right to maintenance, the Scots common law obligation of aliment required a father to provide his children with support even into adulthood, if they were unable to earn their own livelihood.[5] This parental obligation was founded in natural law and enacted in civil law, and also extended to the parents of illegitimate children.[6] The Family Law (Scotland) Act 1985, which now governs aliment in those cases to which the child support legislation does not apply, specifically declares that both a father and mother owe an obligation of aliment to their children.[7] Surprisingly, the House of Lords, in its decision in *Kehoe*,[8] attached no weight to this very different legal heritage north of the border.

Blackstone's *Commentaries on the Laws of England*

Blackstone's *Commentaries on the Laws of England*, first published in 1765, identified the relationship between parent and child as 'the most universal relation in nature'.[9] In keeping with his times, he distinguished, when discussing the support of children, between those who were legitimate and those who were 'spurious, or bastards'.[10]

The parents of legitimate children, according to Blackstone, owed three duties to their offspring, the obligations to maintain, protect and educate. This triumvirate of parental obligations reflected social norms which were well established by the early modern period.[11] So far as maintenance was concerned, Blackstone declared that:

---

[3] On which see G Lushington, *The law of affiliation and bastardy*, first published in 1897 and finally in its 7th edn by AJ Chislett as *Lushington's Law of affiliation and bastardy* (Butterworths, London, 1951).

[4] There appears to be no uniquely Welsh dimension to the private law of child maintenance.

[5] K McK Norrie, *The Law Relating to Parent and Child in Scotland* (W Green, Edinburgh, 1999, 2nd edn) at 411 and see *Coldingham Parish Council v Smith* [1918] 2 KB 90.

[6] *Laws of Scotland* (Law Society of Scotland, Edinburgh, 1987), vol 10, paras 1230 and 1235, citing Stair, *Institutions* I, 5,1,7 and Erskine, *Institute*, I, 6, 56.

[7] Family Law (Scotland) Act 1985, s 1(1)(c); see also s 1(1)(d) and (5).

[8] *R (Kehoe) v Secretary of State for Work and Pensions* [2005] UKHL 48; [2006] 1 AC 42.

[9] W Morrison (ed), *Blackstone's Commentaries on the Laws of England* vol I (Cavendish Publishing, London, 2001) ch 16 at 343.

[10] *loc cit.*

[11] See LA Pollock, 'Parent-Child Relations' in DI Kertzer and M Barbagli (eds), *Family Life in Early Modern Times 1500–1789* (Yale University Press, New Haven, 2001) ch 7 at 191, citing William Gouge's treatise *Of Domesticall Duties* (London, 1622), which declared that parents had a threefold task: to nourish, nurture and instruct their children.

The duty of parents to provide for the maintenance of their children, is a principle of natural law; an obligation, says Puffendorf, laid on them not only by nature herself, but by their own proper act, in bringing them into the world: for they would be in the highest manner injurious to their issue, if they only gave their children life, that they might afterwards see them perish. By begetting them therefore, they have entered into a voluntary obligation, to endeavour, as far as in them lies, that the life which they have bestowed shall be supported and preserved. And thus the children will have a perfect right of receiving maintenance from their parents.[12]

Blackstone cites Montesquieu with approval for the proposition that 'the establishment of marriage in all civilized states is built on this natural obligation of the father to provide for his children'.[13] The reason for this is that the institution of marriage:

ascertains and makes known the person who is bound to fulfil this obligation: whereas, in promiscuous and illicit conjunctions, the father is unknown; and the mother finds a thousand obstacles in her way;—shame, remorse, the constraint of her sex, and the rigour of laws;—that stifle her inclinations to perform this duty: and beside she generally wants ability.[14]

As regards the substance of the common law obligation, Blackstone observed that the duty to maintain is a limited one, being confined to 'necessaries':

For the policy of our laws, which are ever watchful to promote industry, did not mean to compel a father to maintain his idle and lazy children in ease and indolence: but thought it unjust to oblige the parent, against his will, to provide them with superfluities, and other indulgences of fortune; imaging they might trust to the impulse of nature, if the children were deserving of such favours.[15]

After reviewing the provision made in civil law systems, Blackstone explains that the natural duty of parents to maintain their children is translated into law in the obligations imposed under the poor law.[16] Tellingly, he makes no reference to any private law procedures to enforce this duty. Rather, in cases of default, where the burden would otherwise fall wholly on the parish, the enforcement of the child maintenance obligation was seen as a public law matter. Three further observations may be made about Blackstone's treatment of child maintenance for legitimate children, which even today casts its long shadow over modern thinking on child support.

First, Blackstone's discussion must be seen in its broader social context. While the nature of childhood is the subject of much scholarly debate amongst historians,[17] what is beyond doubt is that in previous centuries children were expected to

[12] *Blackstone's Commentaries* n 9 above (footnote omitted).
[13] *loc cit.*
[14] *loc cit.*
[15] *Ibid*, at 345.
[16] *Ibid*, at 344.
[17] See eg P Aries *Centuries of childhood: a social history of family life* (Jonathan Cape, New York, 1962) and LA Pollock, *Forgotten children* (Cambridge University Press, Cambridge, 1983); see also

be self-sufficient at a much earlier age. Indeed, in the early modern period most children worked from about the age of seven. In pre-industrial society children in poor families were a valuable economic resource: 'either they made it possible for other family members to work, or they supplied unpaid labor, or they earned and thereby supplemented the family finances'.[18] In wealthy families, children—for which essentially read *male* children—were the means by which property was handed down through the generations.[19] In this way aristocratic settlements were a way of both 'giving legal form to legitimate family expectations' and to satisfying a 'natural' obligation.[20] Either way, children were 'of significant actual or potential economic value to their parents, either as collaborators in family production or as agents for the transmission of family wealth'.[21] These social differences were reflected in evolving legal norms. For example, Holdsworth notes that as late as the twelfth century there was no fixed rule as to the age of majority, with the tendency being 'to fix different ages for different classes of society'.[22] Thus a knight came of age at 21 and the heir to a socman at 15, whilst the age of majority for 'the burgess's son [was] when he was of age to count pence, measure cloth, and conduct his father's business'.[23] Gradually, however, the age of majority for knights came to be accepted as 'the general rule for all classes of society'.[24]

Secondly, the analysis in *Commentaries on the Laws of England* is explicitly framed in terms of the father's *obligation*. This perspective reflects the patriarchal nature of common law thinking; as we shall see, a wife had no independent legal status as a result of the doctrine of unity; fathers were regarded as the natural guardians of their legitimate children; and the right to custody and the obligation to maintain were seen as correlative. To Blackstone and his contemporaries it would have been nonsensical to talk of a mother's *right* to child maintenance.

The third point to note is that Blackstone's notion that the paternal duty to maintain is limited to 'the bare necessities of life' reflects the common law's traditional adherence to strict respect for private property rights. The entrenched hostility of the legal system to any interference with such rights was also exemplified by the principle of testamentary freedom which, as Blackstone acknowledged, meant that 'our law has made no provision to prevent the disinheriting of children

---

H Hendrick, 'Constructions and Reconstructions of British Childhood: An Interpretative Survey, 1800 to the Present' in A James and A Prout, *Constructing and Reconstructing Childhood* (Falmer Press, London, 1997, 2nd edn), ch 2.

[18] Pollock, n 11 above, at 206.

[19] A Pottage, 'Proprietary Strategies: The Legal Fabric of Aristocratic Settlements' (1998) 61 *Modern Law Review* 162.

[20] *Ibid*, at 171.

[21] J Eekelaar, 'Family Law and Social Control' in J Eekelaar and J Bell (ed), *Oxford Essays in Jurisprudence; Third Series* (Clarendon Press, Oxford, 1987), ch 6 at 136.

[22] WS Holdsworth, *A History of English Law*, vol III (Methuen & Co, London, 1923, 3rd edn) at 510.

[23] *loc cit*. See also F Pollock and FW Maitland, *The History of English Law* (Cambridge University Press, Cambridge, 1898, 2nd edn) at 438.

[24] Holdsworth, n 22 above, at 510.

by will'.[25] His suggestion that 'it had not been amiss, if the parent had been bound to leave them at least a necessary subsistence'[26] was not reflected in law until 1938.[27] In that year legislation provided that, where a testator had failed to make reasonable provision for his dependants, the court might order such provision to be made out of the estate for the surviving spouse and certain classes of children.[28] Yet Blackstone's restricted view of the content of the maintenance obligation must be viewed through the prism of eighteenth century thinking. As we have seen children, and especially older children, were regarded as economic agents, and the provision of overly generous financial support might have unwanted behavioural effects—in effect, a moral hazard problem. Yet the adoption of 'the bare necessities of life' as the benchmark for child maintenance has proved remarkably enduring, notwithstanding shifts in the perception of childhood and the other radical social changes which have taken place since the late eighteenth century. For example, during the passage of the Child Support, Pensions and Social Security Act 2000, several parliamentarians and commentators criticised the notion that child support liabilities should be based on a percentage slice of the non-resident parent's income, irrespective of the child's actual day-to-day needs and without any maximum cap being set.[29]

In contrast to the treatment accorded to the support of legitimate children, the position of illegitimate children and their financial support was dealt with somewhat peremptorily in *Commentaries on the Laws of England*. Blackstone's analysis acknowledged the traditional common law position that an illegitimate child was a 'fillius nullius', or a child of no-one;[30] 'for, though bastards are not looked upon as children to any civil purposes, yet the ties of nature, of which maintenance is one, are not so easily dissolved'.[31] As private law had little to say on the matter, it followed, even more so than with legitimate children, that the incorporation of this maintenance obligation into English law was exclusively a matter for the (public) poor law.[32] We now turn to review the early case law on the scope of the child and spousal maintenance obligations in the realm of private law.

---

[25] Blackstone, n 9 above, at 345. It was not always so: as late as the Tudor era, the common law entitled widows and children a fixed proportion of the deceased husband/father's personalty, but this notion of community of property had disappeared by the eighteenth century: WR Cornish and G de N Clark, *Law and Society in England 1750–1950* (Sweet & Maxwell, London, 1989) at 366—'The power to cut off without a penny was the ultimate sanction of Victorian respectability' (*ibid*). As the courts were to comment, this meant that a child could be thrown on to the poor law without the parish having any recourse to the deceased parent's estate: see p 71 below.

[26] *loc cit.*

[27] Inheritance (Family Provision) Act 1938.

[28] See N Lowe and G Douglas, *Bromley's Family Law* (Butterworths, London, 1998, 9th edn) at 885. See also now the court's more extensive powers in the Inheritance (Provision for Family and Dependants) Act 1975.

[29] See further ch 1, pp 9–11 and ch 11, pp 332–34.

[30] See *Barnardo v McHugh* [1891] A C 388 at 398 *per* Lord Herschell.

[31] Blackstone, n 9 above, at 351. This passage 'is usually quoted out of context: it is a particularly humane and sympathetic one', O Stone, *Family Law* (Macmillan, London, 1977) at 14.

[32] Blackstone, n 9 above, at 352 (see statutes cited at note c).

The Child Maintenance Obligation and the Early Case Law

The common law orthodoxy (in England and Wales at least) was that married parents owed their legitimate children no positive duty of maintenance. As early as 1662, in *Manby v Scott*, the courts declared that 'It is clear the father is not chargeable at the common law to maintain his children, otherwise than as the late statutes of the poor have provided' (a reference to the Poor Relief Act 1601).[33] Similarly, a judge in the late Victorian era, echoing Blackstone's analysis, explained that 'as regards maintenance, the parents' obligations were measured both at law and in equity by the Poor Laws'.[34] The sole exception to this principle was if the parent had contracted to provide support for his or her child, reflecting the importance attached by the courts to the sanctity of contracts. According to Baron Abinger in *Mortimore v Wright* (1840), 'In point of law, a father who gives no authority, and enters into no contract, is no more liable for goods supplied to his son, than a brother, or an uncle, or a mere stranger would be'.[35] So far as the common law was concerned, it followed that parents were at best under a moral duty to provide such support. In extreme cases, where a child died of starvation or neglect, the criminal law might find a parent guilty of manslaughter, but the civil law could not be invoked at any earlier stage to enforce any duty to maintain.[36]

Arguably, it would have been unrealistic to have expected the early common law to have taken any other approach. After all, the father of a legitimate child effectively enjoyed absolute authority over his wife and children.[37] In the event of the couple's separation, the presumption was that the father was entitled to custody. Given both the prevailing social circumstances and the contemporary legal framework, very few women had the independent means such that they could even begin to think about living apart from their husband, let alone bringing up their children in a separate household. In the Victorian period societal norms were such that the notion that husbands should be subject to an enforceable private law duty to support their legitimate children would simply have been fanciful. The position was, naturally, no better for illegitimate children; neither their fathers[38] nor

---

[33] (1662) Bridg 0 229 at 257 *per* Lord Bridgman CJ, with the caveat in a footnote that 'Except inasmuch as by the law of nature, which is part of the common law, maintenance is due to the child from his father'. See also n 52 below.

[34] *Thomasset v Thomasset* [1894] P 295 at 299 *per* Lindley LJ.

[35] (1840) 6 M & W 482 at 486; see also *Seaborne v Maddy* (1840) 9 Car & P 497 at 497–98 *per* Parke B; *Shelton v Springett* (1851) 11 C B 452; and *Coldingham Parish Council v Smith* [1918] 2 KB 90 at 96 *per* Salter J.

[36] *National Assistance Board v Wilkinson* [1952] 2 QB 648 at 657, *per* Lord Goddard CJ.

[37] Subject always to the rare possibility of supervision by the courts: for the argument that the judicial supervision of testamentary guardianship dates back to the Tenure Abolitions Act 1660, see S Abramowicz, 'English Child Custody law, 1660–1839: The Origins of Judicial Intervention in Paternal Custody' (1999) 99 *Columbia Law Review* 1344.

[38] *Seaborne v Maddy* (1840) 9 C & P 497. But there was case law to suggest that if a father of an illegitimate child provided support for the child (in the absence of an affiliation order), then at the very least due notice must be given of any intention to withdraw such support: see PRH Webb and HK Bevan, *Source Book on Family Law* (Butterworths, London, 1964) at 424.

mothers[39] were under any common law duty to support them, accounting for the development of the separate bastardy jurisdiction alongside the poor law. Consequently, the parental duty to maintain a child continued to evolve exclusively in the context of the poor law. Moreover, just as the father was under no legally enforceable obligation to support his children during his lifetime, so too on death:

> If the father had thought fit, he might, I am afraid, by the law of this country leave his children upon the parish. I am surprised, that should be the law of any country: but, I am afraid, it is the law of this . . . Not even the parish in such a case can come against the executor.[40]

As a result, the traditional understanding of family lawyers was that 'there was no civil obligation to maintain one's child at common law or in equity, but statute has imposed a duty'.[41] In summary, as one of today's senior family judges has observed, 'the strange state of our law is that there may be a so-called common law duty to maintain, but when one analyses what that duty is it seems effectively to come to nothing'.[42]

A powerful challenge to this orthodoxy was launched by Baroness Hale in her dissenting opinion in *Kehoe*.[43] In her view, this was a case 'which has been presented to us largely as a case about adults' rights when in reality it is a case about children's rights'.[44] In summary, her conclusion was that children have a civil right to be maintained by their parents, as the common law, drawing on Blackstone, 'has always recognised the right of a child who is too young to fend for herself to be provided for by her parents. The problem has always been to find an effective method of enforcement'.[45] This underlying common law right was:

> reinforced and expanded by two kinds of statutory obligation: a private law obligation to make the payments ordered by a court under the various statutes listed earlier; and a public law obligation to reimburse the state for benefits paid for the children.[46]

This is undoubtedly an attractive analysis, which certainly finds support in both the common law and legislation of Scotland[47] and in the jurisprudence and philosophy of children's rights.[48] Yet Baroness Hale's child-centred approach is not

---

[39] *Ruttinger v Temple* (1863) 4 B & S 491, holding that the mother's duty to maintain her illegitimate child was a purely personal liability created by statute (Poor Law Amendment Act 1834, s 71: see p 52 above).

[40] *Rawlins v Goldfrap* (1800) 5 Ves 440 at 444 *per* Sir Richard Arden, MR.

[41] JC Hall, *Sources of Family Law* (Cambridge University Press, 1966) at 271 (footnotes omitted). See, to similar effect, JL Barton, 'The Enforcement of Financial Provisions' in RH Graveson and FR Crane, *A Century of Family Law* (Sweet & Maxwell, London, 1957) ch 14 at 355 and Webb and Bevan, n 38 above, at 403.

[42] *Re C (A Minor) (Contribution Notice)* [1994] 1 FLR 111 at 116, *per* Ward J.

[43] [2005] UKHL 48; [2006] 1 AC 42.

[44] *Ibid*, at para 49.

[45] *Ibid*, at para 51.

[46] *Ibid*, at para 65; see further below for a discussion of the private law statutes referred to here.

[47] See p 66 above.

[48] See ch 1 above.

without its own problems. It sidesteps authorities such as *Manby v Scott*[49] and the refusal of the common law to countenance any parental obligation towards non-marital children.[50] It also assumes that the problem of enforcing children's maintenance rights should be constructed as one of a lack of legal capacity, whereas the weight of authority would suggest that the problem is rather the absence of an underlying legal right.[51]

Whether or not the Hale hypothesis is correct, there is no doubt that the common law failed to accommodate child maintenance obligations in any meaningful way. Private law, however, gradually became more receptive to the concept of spousal (and later child) maintenance, although this required the intervention of statute before it began to be properly acknowledged. But first we need to consider the question of spousal maintenance at common law.

The Spousal Maintenance Obligation at Common Law

Wives, at common law, were little better off than children in so far as maintenance was concerned. As we have seen, the husband was under a legal duty to maintain his wife—but this duty was unenforceable in the common law courts. The explanation for this paradox lay in the traditional doctrine of matrimonial unity. As husband and wife were one in the eyes of the common law, and a man owed a duty to the community to support himself, so it followed in principle that, if married, he was necessarily under an obligation to support his wife.[52] However, until the mid-nineteenth century this obligation was unenforceable in the civil courts as marriage and related issues lay within the exclusive province of the ecclesiastical courts. Yet married women had no effective remedy under canon law. In principle, the ecclesiastical courts could make an award of alimony on granting a decree of divorce *a mensa et thoro*,[53] but the means of enforcement were 'of more theoretical than practical utility'.[54] Until 1813 the only sanction was excommunication or

---

[49] n 33 above.

[50] n 38 and n 39 above.

[51] See by analogy *Stevens (Inspector of Taxes) v Tirard* [1940] 1 KB 204 and *Supplementary Benefits Commission v Jull* [1981] AC 1025 and the further discussion in N Wikeley, 'A duty but not a right: child support after *R (Kehoe) v Secretary of State for Work and Pensions*' (2006) 18 *Child and Family Law Quarterly* 287.

[52] *Manby v Scott* (1663) 1 Mod 124 at 128 *per* Hyde J. See the detailed account of the arguments in this case in OR McGregor, L Blom-Cooper and C Gibson, *Separated spouses: A study of the matrimonial jurisdiction of magistrates' courts* (Gerald Duckworth & Co Ltd, London, 1970) at 3–7.

[53] This was effectively a decree of judicial separation rather than a divorce proper, and so the parties were not free to remarry. By the early seventeenth century the Church of England and the ecclesiastical courts had affirmed the indissolubility of marriage, subject only to divorce divorce *a mensa et thoro*; full divorce *a vinculo* was rejected: M Finer and OR McGregor, 'The History of the Obligation to Maintain' in *Report of the Committee on One-Parent Families* (1974, Cmnd 5629: the 'Finer Report'), vol 2 Appendix 5, at 87.

[54] *Ibid*, at 99. Similarly, as Lindley LJ observed in *Thomasset v Thomasset* [1894] P 295, at 297, 'it is so long since [the Ecclesiastical] Courts have interfered between parent and child, that it is needless to refer further to them'.

other ecclesiastical censure; imprisonment then became an option, but there is no record that this was ever invoked in the ecclesiastical courts.[55] The refusal of the common law to engage with issues of spousal maintenance was subject to one narrow exception, in that a wife was able to pledge her husband's credit, based on the notion of agency,[56] again demonstrating the sanctity of contract. Yet the reality was that, for most married women, 'the common law obligation of maintenance was of no great consequence'.[57]

The Development of Two Systems of Private Family Law in the Victorian Era

The history of the Divorce Court and the magistrates' matrimonial jurisdiction has received considerable scholarly treatment and needs only to be summarised in this chapter.[58] Accordingly, the discussion that follows sketches the principal developments in both jurisdictions and provides an overview of the law and practice relating to maintenance liabilities during this period. It will be apparent from the preceding discussion that neither the common law nor the ecclesiastical courts provided any effective redress to a married woman whose husband had failed to maintain her or her children. The first tentative steps to tackle this indifference occurred with a series of legislative reforms in the mid-Victorian period. In time these developments led to the creation of the two systems of (private) family law identified by Finer and McGregor and foreshadowed in the introduction to chapter two above: 'one to meet the needs of the rich and powerful, and another which regulated the family life of the rest of the community'.[59]

So far as the former was concerned, the canon law monopoly on the law of divorce was finally broken with the Matrimonial Causes Act 1857, which introduced the possibility of judicial divorce.[60] Before this, given the refusal of the ecclesiastical courts to grant full divorce, the only alternative was a private Act of Parliament to effect divorce,[61] an option necessarily available only to the very wealthy.[62] But as Dicey observed, although in principle the 1857 Act represented

---

[55] McGregor *et al*, n 52 above, at 2.

[56] This exception can be traced back to *Manby v Scott* (1663) itself, n 52 above.

[57] Finer and McGregor, n 53 above, at 99.

[58] Finer and McGregor provides a 'learned but far from dispassionate account', according to Cretney's own magisterial account, n 1 above, at 376, n 367.

[59] Finer and McGregor, n 53 above, at 111.

[60] See Cretney n 1 above, ch 5.

[61] See *ibid*, at 161 n 4 on the series of procedural hurdles to be overcome. See also L Stone, *Road to Divorce: England 1530–1987* (Oxford University Press, Oxford, 1990) ch X.

[62] Moreover, 'For practical purposes the Private Act procedure could be invoked only by men whose wives were adulterous', OR McGregor, *Divorce in England: A Centenary Study* (Heinemann, London, 1957) at 11. There were 317 such private acts in the period before 1857, dating back to at least 1551: Finer and McGregor, n 53 above, at 91–92. Only four were ever granted to women: *ibid*, at 94. On related maintenance issues, see *ibid*, at 100.

'a triumph of individualistic liberalism and of common justice' in abolishing the bar on divorce, in reality it 'conceded to the rich a right denied to the poor'.[63] Divorce proceedings had to be launched before the Divorce Court in London with the all the associated formality and expense, and so by 1900 there were still only some 500 decrees of divorce each year.[64] As well as being socially exclusive, the 1857 Act was also inherently discriminatory; whereas a husband could secure a divorce on the grounds of his wife's adultery, a wife had to demonstrate some aggravating factor in addition to adultery.[65] However, the grounds for an order of judicial separation—relieving spouses of the duty to cohabit, although not freeing them for remarriage—were gender-neutral, but access to court remained the preserve of the rich.[66]

The courts had no general power under the 1857 Act to award periodic spousal maintenance on divorce; post-divorce financial support could only be ordered indirectly, by requiring a husband to use his capital to secure maintenance for his wife's benefit.[67] As Cretney observes, the legislation was 'framed primarily in the context of the wealthier families who had at least some capital', whilst also reflecting 'the Victorian belief that capital was to be used to provide income and not to be spent'.[68] Even so, the judiciary were initially divided over whether the new statutory power could be invoked by a wife petitioning on the basis of her husband's (aggravated) adultery.[69] Subsequently, the Matrimonial Causes Act 1866 empowered the Divorce Court to order a husband to make unsecured periodical payments of maintenance to his former wife during their joint lives.[70] Yet this provision too was not without difficulty.[71]

There was a marked contrast between the narrow range of orders available to the Divorce Court and the very broad discretion granted to the court as regards the terms of any such order. The court could make an order for secured payments under the 1857 Act in favour of a wife 'having regard to her fortune (if any), to the ability of the husband, and to the conduct of the parties, [as] it shall deem reasonable'.[72]

---

[63] AV Dicey, *Law and Public Opinion in England during the Nineteenth Century* (Macmillan & Co, London, 1914, 2nd edn, reissued 1962), Lecture X, at 347.

[64] Cretney, n 1 above, at 195.

[65] eg cruelty, sodomy or bestiality: see Matrimonial Causes Act 1857, s 27 and *Dodd v Dodd* [1906] P 189. Parity for wives as regards the grounds of divorce had to wait until the Matrimonial Causes Act 1923.

[66] Matrimonial Causes Act 1857, s 16 (adultery, cruelty or two years' desertion).

[67] *Ibid*, s 32; in addition, *ibid* s 45 granted a limited power to order settlements for children of the marriage if the wife was found to have committed adultery.

[68] Cretney, n 1 above, at 397.

[69] See *Fisher v Fisher* (1861) 2 Sw & Tr 410 (*per* Sir Cresswell Cresswell) and *Sidney v Sidney* (1865) 4 Sw & Tr 178 (*per* Sir James Wilde), discussed by Cretney, n 1 above, at 396 n 12.

[70] Matrimonial Causes Act 1866, s 1.

[71] As Cretney notes, n 1 above at 397, n 15, the courts held it was restricted to cases in which the husband had no capital on which payments could be secured: *Medley v Medley* (1882) 7 PD 122. Moreover, according to Lord Jessel MR, 'it was not intended by [the 1857 Act] that an order should be made for payment of the allowance directly by the husband to the wife' (at 125).

[72] Matrimonial Causes Act 1857, s 32. Likewise, orders under the s 1 of 1866 Act were for such amounts 'as the court may think reasonable'.

Given the fault-based nature of divorce, it might be supposed that a wife who had committed adultery would thereby forfeit any right to maintenance. Yet whilst judges might well be reluctant to exercise their discretion in favour of the 'guilty' party, the courts recognised that they enjoyed an 'absolute discretion'.[73] This largely untrammelled discretion has remained an enduring feature of the law governing financial provision on divorce (known by family lawyers as ancillary relief) through to the present day.

The absence of any clear guidance in the legislation led the Victorian judiciary to look elsewhere for a principle to govern the allocation of maintenance such cases. In particular, the Divorce Court drew on the traditional practice of the ecclesiastical courts in making orders for alimony. In so far as orders for maintenance were made, the court would make an order for maintenance representing one-third of the joint income, at least where an 'innocent' wife was concerned, together with an amount for any children in respect of whom she was granted custody.[74] As a result, during this period when maintenance obligations were first established by statute, financial support for children was treated as parasitic upon the spousal right to maintenance. Furthermore, as a matter of principle, and reflecting Blackstone's *Commentaries*, child maintenance was limited to meeting the *necessary* costs of supporting the child as part the mother's own necessary expenses.[75] This secondary status of child maintenance was to persist as child support became at best a second class obligation in the context of the development of private family law.

Divorce itself, of course, was to remain a matter of social stigma for more than a century after the 1857 reforms. Moreover, the patriarchal nature of private family law was firmly established. The doctrine of matrimonial unity also meant that married women had no independent right to own property, a fiction which remained firmly in place until the Married Women's Property Act 1882 adopted a regime of separate property for married women.[76] Just as husbands had absolute authority over their wives, so too they enjoyed complete dominion over their children. This was reflected in the fact that, at common law, the father of a legitimate child was that child's natural guardian, a status which, nominally at least, he continued to enjoy until the passage of the Children Act 1989.[77] Thus, 'to

[73] *Ashcroft v Ashcroft and Roberts* [1902] P 270 at 275 *per* Vaughan Williams LJ.

[74] See generally Cretney, n 1 above, at 400–1 (noting the absence of empirical data on awards made) and 409–11 and Barton, n 41 above.

[75] *Bazeley v Forder* (1868) LR 3 QB 559 (Lord Cockburn CJ dissenting), a case decided under the Custody of Infants Act 1839 (also known as Talfourd's Act), under which the Court of Chancery was permitted to grant a mother custody of her child under the age of 7, providing she had not committed adultery.

[76] Married women from wealthy backgrounds had long been able to circumvent the common law doctrine and so retain control of their own (often their family's) property through various conveyancing devices: see Finer and McGregor, n 53 above, at 96–97.

[77] The first statutory challenge to this orthodoxy was the Custody of Infants Act 1839 (see n 75 above). The Guardianship of Infants Act 1925 granted married mothers 'like powers' to apply to court, and the Guardianship of Minors Act 1973 asserted that the mother's rights and authority were the same as the fathers, but without actually making her a guardian: see SM Cretney, JM Masson and R Bailey-Harris, *Principles of Family Law* (Sweet & Maxwell, London, 2002, 7th edn) at 521. The Children Act 1989 now confines the status of guardian to non-parents.

mid-Victorian England it appeared unthinkable under any circumstances to infringe the common law right of the father to the sole and exclusive control and guardianship of his children'.[78] Indeed, historically the absolute nature of the father's right over his legitimate children was such that the courts had no jurisdiction even to grant the mother a right of access to the children.[79] In this context it was inevitable that the parental—effectively, in this context, the paternal—duty to maintain one's child remained at best a moral rather than legal responsibility, with no effective method of enforcement.[80]

In any event, for the great majority of the population in the Victorian era, the Divorce Court remained out of reach, resulting in the development of the summary matrimonial jurisdiction exercised by the magistrates' courts. This process began with the enactment of the Matrimonial Causes Act 1878 but without any consideration of the long-term implications.[81] The 1878 Act granted the magistrates' courts the power to make a separation order on the application of a wife whose husband had been convicted of aggravated assault upon her.[82] The Act also enabled the magistrates in such cases to grant the mother custody of children of the marriage under the age of 10 and to make an order for maintenance. This measure in the 1878 Act was primarily designed as an early response to domestic violence,[83] but the utility of the associated financial provision developed a momentum of its own.[84] The Married Women (Maintenance in Case of Desertion) Act 1886 enabled deserted wives to summons their errant husbands for non-payment of maintenance. Although the 1878 Act itself had contained no cap on the amount of maintenance that the court could order,[85] the 1886 Act restricted maintenance awards to a maximum of £2 a week.[86] There was no independent element within this figure for children; any such award was clearly designed to provide support for the wife and any children of which she secured

---

[78] RH Graveson, 'The Background of the Century' in Graveson and Crane, n 41 above, ch 1 at 17 (see further PH Pettitt 'Parental Control and Guardianship' in *ibid*, ch 4). In this context Graveson refers to Bentham's proposal for a 'somewhat mechanical rule' that fathers should retain custody of their sons but that custody of girls should be awarded to their mothers: J Bentham, *Theory of Legislation* (Trübner & Co, London, 1871, 2nd edn) at 228.

[79] Pettitt, n 78 above, at 58. The position as regards illegitimate children 'was, of course, quite different', in that in so far as anyone had custody of a *fillius nullius*, it was the mother rather than the putative father: *ibid*, at 58 n 12.

[80] However, the fact that the father could not provide for his child was one of the rare grounds upon which the Court of Chancery was prepared to interfere with his right to custody: *ibid*, at 65–66 and see *Lyons v Blenkin* (1821) Jac 245.

[81] GK Behlmer, *Friends of the Family: The English Home and Its Guardians, 1850–1940* (Stanford University Press, Stanford, 1998) at 192. The 1878 Act was principally concerned with the costs of the Queen's Proctor.

[82] Matrimonial Causes Act 1878, s 4.

[83] See McGregor *et al*, n 52 above, at 12–14; it should be recalled that the husband's common law 'right' to chastise or imprison his wife was not ended until *R v Jackson* [1891] 1 QB 671, and indeed it was not until *R v R* [1992] 1 AC 599 that it became possible to convict a husband of the rape of his wife.

[84] Cornish and Clark, n 25 above, at 391–92.

[85] See *Grove v Grove* (1878) 39 LT 546 (order for £3 p/w not manifestly excessive).

[86] Married Women (Maintenance in Case of Desertion) Act 1886, s 1.

custody.[87] However, as Cretney observes, this provided deserted wives with a 'direct financial remedy' against their husbands, without any need to invoke the poor law.[88] In the same year the Guardianship of Infants Act 1886 re-enacted provisions in the Custody of Infants Act 1873 enabling magistrates to grant wives custody of their children under the age of 16.[89] The utility of these provisions may have been lessened by contemporary attitudes; outside of the middle classes, women were seen as workers first and mothers second. As one senior judge stated, 'When a working man who has married a washerwoman obtains a divorce, she can very well go to washing again'.[90]

The justices' powers in matrimonial matters were consolidated in the Summary Jurisdiction (Married Women) Act 1895,[91] which also empowered magistrates to make separation and maintenance orders against a husband who had wilfully neglected to maintain his wife and family.[92] This code 'remained the basis for the magistrates' matrimonial jurisdiction for more than 70 years'.[93] In practice, although maintenance orders were routinely made alongside orders for judicial separation, effective enforcement of the former was as problematic as under the poor law; the typical working-class wife applying to court 'might have learned the hard lesson that winning the right to weekly maintenance payments was one thing, and actually receiving the stipulated sum was quite another'.[94] As one senior judge of the time commented, 'rather than pay the allowance ordered, the man goes else-where, either to another town, or to America, or to the Colonies, and forms other ties almost as a matter of course'.[95]

The Two Systems of Private Family Law in the First Half of the Twentieth Century

The Matrimonial Causes Act 1857 was essentially a procedural reform; it did not 'significantly alter the substance . . . of the law governing the availability of divorce'.[96] Parliament rejected several bills designed to reform the grounds for

---

[87] Brown, n 2 above, at 130.

[88] Cretney n 1 above, at 200.

[89] The Custody of Infants Act 1839 limited this power to children under the age of 7; the Guardianship of Infants Act 1886 also allowed mothers to gain custody of children up to the age of 21.

[90] *Robertson v Robertson and Favagrossa* (1883) 8 P 94 at 96–97 *per* Lord Jessel MR—although whether a 'working man' or a 'washerwoman' would have the funds to petition for divorce is a moot point.

[91] See generally Finer and McGregor, n 53 above, at 107.

[92] As McGregor *et al* observe (n 52 above, at 15), this power was not conferred upon the High Court until 1949. For contemporary judicial criticism of the 1895 Act, see *Dodd v Dodd* [1906] P 189: 'I am convinced that the result of the Act has been to cause women in numerous cases to rush off to the Court on slight provocation and to endeavour to make a case sufficient to obtain an order' *per* Sir Gorrell Barnes, P at 203.

[93] Cretney, n 1 above, at 201.

[94] Behlmer, n 81 above, at 206.

[95] *Dodd v Dodd* [1906] P 189 at 206 *per* Sir Gorrell Barnes P.

[96] Cretney, n 1 above, at 202.

divorce in the late nineteenth and early years of the twentieth centuries.[97] In 1909, however, the Liberal government established a Royal Commission on Divorce and Matrimonial Causes (the Gorrell Commission), which reported three years later.[98] The Commission was unable to produce a consensus report; the majority advocated the extension of the ground for divorce from adultery to include other serious causes, such as desertion and cruelty. This proposal was opposed by the minority members on the basis that it was the 'thin end of the wedge' which would inevitably result in divorce by consent or on the basis of mutual incompatibility.

A Bill to implement some of the proposals on which the Commission was unanimous fell with the outbreak of the First World War,[99] and it was not until 1937 that the majority's recommendations were implemented, extending the ground for divorce to include desertion for three years and cruelty.[100] In the meantime, a degree of equality had been attained in 1923 by legislation giving a wife the right to divorce her husband on the ground of his adultery, without proof of any aggravating factors.[101] By then, however, an important procedural change had already quietly taken place—the Administration of Justice Act 1920 had broken the High Court monopoly in dealing with divorce petitions. Assizes judges—a portmanteau term covering High Court judges, county court judges and special commissioners—were empowered to process undefended divorce petitions.[102] As Cretney notes, the 1920 Act was 'far more significant in the development of divorce law than is often realised'.[103] In particular, 'the notion that the trial of divorce cases required the special expertise of a small and select priesthood became increasingly difficult to sustain'.[104]

Throughout this period there was little change to the court's limited powers to make financial orders on divorce. One exception was the Matrimonial Causes Act 1907, which invested the court with the power to make unsecured maintenance orders, untrammelled by the difficulties associated with the 1857 and 1866 measures.[105] It followed that, 'in theory at least, the divorced but property-less artisan or clerk could thenceforth be made to support the wife he had betrayed'.[106] The extent to which the courts still followed the 'one-third rule' in practice is by no means clear,[107] and certainly competing approaches to the exercise of the courts'

---

[97] The Hunter Bill of 1892 and Russell Bills of 1902 and 1903: *ibid*, at 202–5.

[98] The Gorrell Report was published as Cd 6478 (1912); see further Cretney, n 1 above, at 209–14.

[99] *Ibid*, at 213–14.

[100] Matrimonial Causes Act 1937 (the 'Herbert' Bill); see Cretney, n 1 above, at 214–73.

[101] Matrimonial Causes Act 1923; see further R Probert, 'The controversy of equality and the Matrimonial Causes Act 1923' (1999) 11 *Child and Family Law Quarterly* 33.

[102] This reform was prompted by a combination of pressure on judicial time in the High Court and the need to provide a more localised service: Cretney, n 1 above, at 277–78. The 1920 Act went further than the Gorrell Commission proposal that Assize courts be allowed to process only divorce petitions brought by the poorest members of the community.

[103] *Ibid*, at 280.

[104] *Ibid*, at 279.

[105] Matrimonial Causes Act 1907, s 1; *ibid*, s 2 accordingly repealed s 32 of the 1857 Act and s 1 of the 1866 Act.

[106] Cretney, n 1 above, at 397.

[107] *Ibid*, at 411, especially n 101.

discretion emerged in the case law. For example, in some cases the emphasis was on a needs-based perspective; in others, the court articulated its goal as being to put the 'innocent' party in the financial position she would have enjoyed had the marriage not broken down.[108] For most of the population, however, divorce remained out of reach. We therefore need to consider the expansion of the magistrates' matrimonial jurisdiction in the first half of the twentieth century.

By 1909, when the Gorrell Commission was appointed, the magistrates' courts were dealing with some 10,000 matrimonial applications annually, as compared with just 800 petitions for divorce or judicial separation in the High Court.[109] So, in the period before the First World War, 'nine out of ten matrimonial complaints received summary treatment',[110] although the incidence of marital conflict was undoubtedly much higher.[111] The Gorrell Report expressed serious reservations as to the desirability of the 'police courts', as magistrates' courts were traditionally known, having a jurisdiction in matrimonial matters. However, the Royal Commission viewed the abolition of this jurisdiction as impracticable, given that such courts were 'the only remedy within the reach of the very poor'. The Gorrell Report instead proposed that magistrates should lose their power to make a permanent decree of judicial separation, as this was a matter more properly reserved to a superior court.[112] This central recommendation was not implemented.

Instead, rather than being curtailed, the magistrates' matrimonial jurisdiction steadily, if slowly, expanded during the first half of the twentieth century. For example, the grounds on which magistrates could make separation orders were gradually extended,[113] as were their powers to make orders in relation to the maintenance of children independently of spousal maintenance.[114] The £2 a week limit on orders for spousal maintenance in the magistrates' courts remained in place until 1949.[115] In practice orders were for much more modest amounts, reflecting

---

[108] *Ibid*, at 411–14.

[109] Finer and McGregor, n 53 above, at 108, where the figure of 15,000 applications before the justices is cited. The correct figure seems to be closer to 10,000: see McGregor *et al*, n 52 above, at 33, Table 1. In the same period magistrates' courts were dealing with some 4,000 applications under the poor law and a further 8,500 or so under the bastardy and affiliation jurisdiction: see p 62 above.

[110] Behlmer, n 81 above, at 190.

[111] *Ibid*, at 190, observing that for every registered action 'perhaps three more sought relief of some kind without invoking the formal machinery of justice'; see also S Cretney *Law, Law Reform and the Family* (Clarendon Press, Oxford, 1998) at 116. The techniques used to divert such applicants are considered further in Cretney, n 1 above, at 292–93.

[112] Finer and McGregor, n 53 above at 109.

[113] See Licensing Act 1902, Summary Jurisdiction (Separation and Maintenance) Act 1925 (see McGregor *et al* n 52 above at 21) and the Matrimonial Causes Act 1937 which, as Cornish and Clark note (n 25 above at 392, n 29) finally added the husband's adultery as a ground.

[114] The Married Women (Maintenance) Act 1920 enabled magistrates' courts to make an order for up to 10s (now 50 pence) a week for any child aged under 16.

[115] The financial limits were increased to £5 (with £1 10s. for a child) in 1949 and to £7 10s and £2 10s respectively by the Matrimonial Proceedings (Magistrates' Courts) Act 1960, limits described as 'arbitrarily chosen, since there was no statistical or other evidence available to indicate the amounts in fact awarded by the courts' (McGregor *et al* n 52 above at 28). The upper limits were finally abolished by the Maintenance Orders Act 1968, following the recommendation of the *Report of the Departmental Committee on Statutory Maintenance Limits* (the 'Graham Hall Committee') (Cmnd 3587, 1968).

the low incomes experienced by the magistrates' courts' clientele. Faced with the reality of working-class life, magistrates had little option but to eschew consideration of any principle for a firmly pragmatic approach: 'overwhelmingly, the question was simply how much could, somehow, be extracted from a husband'.[116] An important procedural reform, recommended by the Gorrell Report, was instigated by the Criminal Justice Administration Act 1914. This allowed magistrates' courts to order that payments should be made via an officer of the court, rather than placing responsibility for enforcement wholly with the wife.[117] For the first time outside the realm of the poor law, an element of bureaucracy was interposed between husband and wife as regards the payment of maintenance.[118]

Enforcement, however, remained problematic. Early attempts to provide for attachment of wages for maintenance debts were unsuccessful. The Summary Jurisdiction (Married Women) Bill of 1911 would have conferred on a wife an independent right to apply to the magistrates' court for an order requiring the deduction of maintenance at source from the husband's wages but made no progress. In the following year the Gorrell Report advocated a permissive power of attachment, with employers retaining the right not to implement the order.[119] This recommendation was not taken forward. Throughout the inter-war years the focus was on the machinery of enforcement rather than the capacity of men to meet their obligations under court orders.[120] The enforcement of maintenance orders became a matter of increasing public concern; for example, in 1930 alone there were nearly 16,000 maintenance applications, leading to 11,296 orders and 4,274 imprisonments for non-payment.[121] The Fischer Williams Committee, which reported in 1934, recommended that courts should inquire into the debtor's means and only commit to prison if default was due to wilful refusal or culpable neglect.[122] This proposal was embodied in the Money Payments (Justices' Procedure) Act 1935. But again, the one notable omission was the Committee's proposal that attachment of wages be instituted for maintenance debtors,[123] which attracted considerable opposition from organised labour. This particular reform was not finally enacted until the passage of the Maintenance Orders Act 1958.[124]

---

[116] Cretney, n 1 above, at 450.

[117] *Ibid*, at 453 and McGregor *et al*, n 52 above, at 21. See also Affiliation Orders Act 1914.

[118] The significance of this measure should not be overstated—the role of the court officer was no more than a conduit for payment. Hence the initiative for instituting proceedings remained very much a private matter.

[119] Gorrell Report, n 98 above, at para 174.

[120] OR McGregor, *Family Breakdown and Social Policy* (British Academy, London, 1974) at 12.

[121] McGregor *et al*, n 52 above, at 22. See also Cretney, n 1 above, at 456.

[122] See *Report of the Departmental Committee on Imprisonment by Courts of Summary Jurisdiction in Default of Payment of Fines and Other Sums of Money* (the Fischer Williams Committee) (Cd 4649, 1934) and the discussion in Cretney, n 1 above, at 456–58.

[123] McGregor *et al*, n 52 above, at 23.

[124] See generally *ibid*, at 96-102 for a useful historical account of the development of attachment of earnings.

Conclusion

The previous chapter demonstrated that for centuries Parliament regarded children's maintenance as an issue to be addressed only in the context of the indemnification of the public purse for the costs of poor relief. Similarly, this chapter has shown how the courts declined to impose any general legal liability on parents to maintain their children, being content to refer to parents' natural duty or moral responsibility to do so. In addition, we have seen how the intervention of statute did little to enhance the status of child maintenance. Instead, whether in the Divorce Court or in the magistrates' matrimonial jurisdiction, parents' liability to support their children was viewed as parasitic upon the question of spousal support. Divorce and separation were seen in adult-centred terms, relegating the interests of children to a second-class status. True, the welfare principle, acknowledging the paramountcy of children's interests, however they were to be defined, became increasingly important in the discourse of family law, but this was largely confined to custody disputes and failed to spill over into the field of financial support in the wake of relationship breakdown. Contemporary legal texts exemplify this approach. For example, the fourth edition of *Lush on the Law of Husband and Wife*,[125] published in 1933, mentions the financial support of children in just two places and then only in passing, in the context of the magistrates' jurisdiction and the poor law respectively.[126] Similarly, Barton's post-war account of the enforcement of financial provisions in family law devotes just one short paragraph to the rights of children to support, noting that the history of the child maintenance obligation is 'rather curious'.[127]

As McGregor noted, by the time of the Second World War:

> the situation remained for divorced, separated, and deserted wives what it had always been. They could secure maintenance from their husbands either by agreement or by a court order and, if such means of support failed, they had to seek their subsistence from the poor law.[128]

In the previous chapter the final demise of the poor law in 1948 formed a natural watershed in considering the development of the obligation to maintain one's spouse and children in the field of public law. The development of the private law of maintenance does not lend itself so easily to the identification of a definite turning point. However, the dislocation caused by the Second World War led to a steep

---

[125] SN Grant-Bailey, *Lush on the Law of Husband and Wife* (4th edn, Stevens and Sons Ltd, London, 1933), ch XII, 'Liability to support'.

[126] *Ibid*, at 398–99 and 414–15. It is telling that although the principal public law provisions were contained in the Poor Law Act 1930, *Lush* also refers to liabilities under the then still in force Poor Relief (Deserted Wives and Children) Act 1718, the Vagrancy Act 1824 and the Divided Parishes and Poor Law Amendment Act 1876 (at 419–20). The relevant provisions were not finally repealed until the National Assistance Act 1948, s 62(3) and sch 7, pt I.

[127] Barton, n 41 above, at 373.

[128] n 120 above at 13–14.

rise in the number of divorce petitions being presented.[129] The work of the Rushcliffe Committee in 1945 (on legal aid), resulting in the introduction of legal aid for divorce proceedings in 1950,[130] and the Denning Committee (on matrimonial procedure) more conveniently form part of the backdrop for the post-war era. The next chapter therefore explores the shifting nature of the inter-relationship between the public and private laws of child maintenance from the late 1940s until the enactment of the Child Support Act 1991.

---

[129] From 8,517 in 1939 to 24,857 in 1945: Cretney, n 1 above, at 281.
[130] *Ibid*, at 317.

4

The Child Maintenance Obligation in the Post-War Period

Introduction

This chapter examines the treatment of the child maintenance obligation in the four decades after the end of the Second World War from the perspectives of both public and private law. The first part of this chapter explores the public law dimension of maintenance in terms of the work of the National Assistance Board and its successors, both in providing financial support to families after relationship breakdown and in seeking to recover at least part of that expenditure from liable relatives. The second part considers the private law aspects relating to the assessment and enforcement of maintenance obligations during this period, and especially those relating to children. The third section reviews the interrelationship between these public and private law aspects of maintenance in the period immediately before the Child Support Act 1991.[1]

At the outset, however, it is important to bear in mind the significant social and demographic developments which took place during this period. Lone parenthood itself is not a new phenomenon; the number of widowed and divorced women, as a proportion of all widowed, divorced and married women of childbearing age, was virtually the same in 1981 as in 1861.[2] But, as Lewis has explained, there have been two major changes in the marriage system in the post-war period.[3] First, there has been 'a widespread separation of sex and marriage',[4] resulting in a marked increase in the extra-marital birth rate.[5] This, together with the rising divorce rate,[6] led to the second important shift, being the separation of marriage

---

[1] The following chapter charts the birth and early years of the Child Support Agency.

[2] The respective rates were 8.1% (1861) and 8.9% (1981), although there were fluctuations in between: J Millar, *Poverty and the lone parent: the challenge to social policy* (Avebury, Aldershot, 1989) at 13–14.

[3] J Lewis, 'Lone Mothers: the British case' in J Lewis (ed), *Lone Mothers in European Welfare Regimes* (Jessica Kingsley, London, 1997) ch 2.

[4] *Ibid*, at 52.

[5] From 10.2 per 1,000 single, divorced and widowed women in 1950 to 42.4 per 1,000 in 1992; *ibid*, at 53.

[6] From 2.8 per 1,000 married population in 1950 to 13.0 in 1990: *ibid*, at 54.

and parenthood,[7] characterised by a resurgence of lone parenthood, especially since the early 1970s. However, lone parenthood is an extremely dynamic social phenomenon; it is not simply that there were far more lone parents in 1991 than there had been in 1951—there were also significant shifts in the composition of the lone parent population.[8] In the early 1950s the two largest groups were widows and separated wives, who had relatively high levels of labour market participation, so minimising the extent to which they needed to call on other sources of financial support.[9] Between 1971 (when the 1969 divorce law reforms came into effect) and 1991 both the number and the percentage of lone mother households (as a pro-portion of all families with children) more than doubled, and the two biggest groups had become those who were either single or divorced.[10] Over the same period the employment rates of married women increased, while those for unmar-ried lone parents and for those who were either divorced or separated fell.[11] These changes had major implications for the benefits system, as is shown by Figure 4.1—in particular, during the 1980s there was a dramatic increase in the number of female lone parents (especially single women) in receipt of supplementary benefit (and later income support).

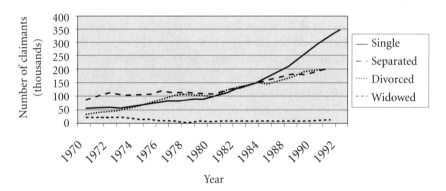

Fɪɢ. 4.1 Categories of female lone parents on SB/IS 1970–1990

[7] J Lewis, 'Lone Mothers: the British case' in J Lewis (ed), *Lone Mothers in European Welfare Regimes* (Jessica Kingsley, London, 1997) ch 2, at 55.

[8] See Millar, above n 2, at 8–9.

[9] Although the comparison is not quite like for like, the 1951 Census showed that 45% of widows and divorced women were working full-time and 7% part-time; the rates for married women were just 19% and 8% respectively: K Kiernan, H Land and J Lewis, *Lone Motherhood in Twentieth-Century Britain* (Clarendon Press, Oxford, 1998) Table 6.1, at 158.

[10] Lewis, n 3 above, Tables 2.5 and 2.6, at 55 and 59. See further J Haskey, 'One-parent families—and the dependent children living in them—in Great Britain' (2002) 109 *Population Trends* 46, Figure 6 at 53. Northern Ireland appears to be a special case with much higher rates of separated women, as divorce remains unacceptable to a large proportion of the population for religious reasons: JC Brown, *Why don't they go to work? Mothers on benefit* (SSAC Research Paper 2, HMSO, 1989) at 11 and 13.

[11] Lewis, n 3 above, Table 2.8 at 62. See further on this phenomenon Brown n 10 above, Millar, n 2 above, ch 8 and K Rowlingson and S McKay, *Lone Parent Families: Gender, Class and State* (Prentice Hall, Harlow, 2002) chs 1 and 2.

The Public Law Dimension of Maintenance After 1948

As we saw in chapter 2, the poor law survived for more than four centuries before its abolition in 1948. The following four decades saw the introduction of three successor benefits, national assistance (1948–1966), supplementary benefit (1966–1988) and income support (1988 to date). The names of the official agencies charged with policy or operational responsibility (or both) for such subsistence benefits have changed even more frequently.[12] However, as with *la longue durée*[13] of the poor law, the continuities in policy and practice in the post-war period are as significant, if not more so, as the differences in details between the various benefit regimes. With this in mind, the discussion below is divided into two sections. The first is an overview of the national assistance, supplementary benefit and income support schemes, which also explores policy responses to the needs of those who have experienced family breakdown. The second is a more detailed review of the legal measures designed to secure the payment of maintenance from liable relatives over this period and how these provisions were operated in practice.

Benefits and Family Breakdown

The new post-1948 structure of contributory benefits made no provision for separated, divorced or unmarried mothers. Instead, Beveridge's national insurance scheme covered those risks which were, at that time, the most common reasons for loss of earnings—principally sickness, unemployment, widowhood and retirement. There were two main reasons for Beveridge's failure to accommodate the social risks associated with relationship breakdown within the new scheme. The first was structural—the national insurance scheme was premised on the notion that the typical contributor was a full-time male employee who was the head of a household comprising himself, a dependant wife and their child or children.[14] Most married women 'made marriage their sole occupation'[15] and so 'social policy had to be geared to the needs of the majority and not to the needs of an atypical minority'.[16] Indeed, the dependency of married women was institutionalised through their liability to pay a lower rate of contributions with correspondingly

---

[12] The National Assistance Board (NAB), the SBC, the Ministry of Social Security (MSS), the Department of Health and Social Security (DHSS), the DSS and now the DWP.

[13] Or, perhaps more accurately, *la moyenne durée*; see further the work of Fernand Braudel and the Annales School of historiography, eg F Braudel, *Capitalism and material life, 1400–1800* (Weidenfeld & Nicolson, London, 1973).

[14] See generally E Wilson, *Women and the welfare state* (Tavistock, London, 1977).

[15] *Social Insurance and Allied Services* (Cmd 6404, 1942; 'the Beveridge Report') at para 108. This assumption was, of course, based on pre-war perceptions of both the labour market and family structures.

[16] J Harris, *William Beveridge: A Biography* (Clarendon Press, Oxford, 1997, revd edn) at 395.

reduced individual benefit entitlements.[17] The second reason was practical—although Beveridge had actively explored the feasibility of providing an insurance benefit payable to married women in the event of relationship breakdown,[18] no effective means of verifying the fact of separation was identified,[19] or of avoiding intrusive inquiries into the parties' conduct in cases of desertion.[20] Ultimately, neither marriage breakdown nor unmarried motherhood were perceived to be major social ills on a par with Beveridge's 'Five Giants',[21] and so the need for special provision was not regarded as sufficiently pressing. Instead, separated, divorced or unmarried mothers, where they had no other means of support, could turn to means-tested national assistance, which replaced poor relief.[22]

National assistance provided a subsistence level of support for those with no other sources of income, or by way of a 'top up' to those whose incomes[23] were otherwise below the official 'poverty line'.[24] Although a person's 'needs' were defined by reference to scales laid down by Parliament, the National Assistance Board's officers enjoyed considerable discretion at the margins in deciding on the appropriate level of allowance payable.[25] From the outset, given the gendered nature of the national *insurance* scheme, the majority of national *assistance* claimants were women. For example, in 1950 a total of 1.28 million people received national assistance, of whom 62 per cent were women (typically pensioners).[26] In the same year, women of working age (other than those who were sick or disabled) accounted for at most 15 per cent of the caseload, of whom the great majority were widows.[27] It followed that relatively few national assistance claimants were separated, divorced or unmarried mothers, although there had been a modest increase in their numbers in the immediate aftermath of the

---

[17] See further the Beveridge Report, n 15 above, at paras 107–17.

[18] Harris, n 16 above, at 394.

[19] Beveridge's civil service advisers warned him of 'the dangers of "collusive desertion" and of "exploitation by the anti-social elements in the community"', *ibid*, at 394.

[20] *Ibid*, at 398.

[21] Namely Want, Disease, Ignorance, Squalor and Idleness—see generally N Timmins, *The Five Giants: A Biography of the Welfare State* (Harper Collins, London, 2001, revised edn).

[22] Moreover, Beveridge's proposal for a separate family allowance scheme 'perhaps made it easier to consign these mothers to social assistance', J Lewis, 'The problem of lone-mother families in twentieth-century Britain' [1998] *Journal of Social Welfare and Family Law* 251 at 260.

[23] Including earnings, maintenance, family allowances or national insurance benefits.

[24] National Assistance Act 1948, s 4.

[25] DC Marsh, *National Insurance and National Assistance in Great Britain* (Pitman & Sons Ltd, London, 1950) at 150. See further MJ Hill, 'The Exercise of Discretion in the National Assistance Board' (1969) 47 *Public Administration* 75 and, for a fuller account, see D Marsden, *Mothers Alone* (Allen Lane, London, 1969), esp chs 10 and 11.

[26] If the caseload was differentiated by age rather than gender, a similar proportion of the total caseload were pensioners: NAB, *Annual Report of the National Assistance Board for 1950* (Cmd 8276, 1951) at 6.

[27] See Table, *ibid*, at 6, giving the following figures for claimants of working age: widows—97,760 (7.6%), separated or deserted wives—34,860 (2.7%) and 'others' (including divorced mothers, unmarried mothers and carers)—43,500 (3.4%). Not all of these claimants were lone parents—the early NAB data do not differentiate between those with and without dependent children.

transition from poor relief to national assistance in 1948,[28] in part because claiming national assistance did not carry the same degree of stigma as applying for poor relief. Indeed, the Board acknowledged that they were dealing 'only with the exceptional cases' amongst those women experiencing the breakdown of a relationship.[29] In most such cases the women supported themselves without resort to benefit.[30]

By 1966, the final year of the national assistance scheme, the Board's total case-load had increased to some 2 million claimants. Whilst pensioners still constituted the great majority of the caseload, the characteristics of female claimants of work-ing age had begun to shift—in particular, there were now twice as many non-widowed women with dependent children (118,000) as there were widows under the age of 60 (53,000).[31] Moreover, it was not just that the former were numeri-cally more important, as the detailed data for the new supplementary benefit scheme made plain. Individually, women with children who were claiming because of relationship breakdown received much more by way of supplementary benefit than widows, who could usually rely on widows' allowances paid under the national insurance scheme, and so only needed a modest top-up from the means-tested scheme.[32]

The transition from national assistance to supplementary benefit, as with the replacement of the poor law by national assistance in 1948, represented both change and continuity in terms of social security provision. Decisions on eligibil-ity for national assistance involved the exercise of discretion at all levels.[33] Entitlement to supplementary benefit, on the other hand, was clearly a matter of right.[34] Decisions on benefit claims under the new scheme were made by depart-mental officers in the name of the Supplementary Benefits Commission (SBC), the independent body charged with responsibility for the new arrangements. In practice, however, the administration of supplementary benefit, as with national

---

[28] In July 1948 the NAB had responsibility for 15,890 separated wives and 4,495 unmarried moth-ers (most of whom had been 'inherited' from the poor law); a year later these figures had more than doubled to 33,810 and 9,131 respectively: NAB, *Annual Report of the National Assistance Board for 1949* (Cmd 8030, 1950) at 21.

[29] *Ibid*, at 21.

[30] See p 84 above on labour market participation rates.

[31] MSS, *Report of the Ministry of Social Security for the year 1967* (Cmnd 3693, 1968) Table 28, at 100.

[32] Marsden, n 25 above, at 33. See also MSS, n 31 above, Table 30, at 102: in 1967 non-widowed women with dependent children qualified for the highest average weekly payment of supplementary benefit, 149s 3d (approx £7.46), whereas the average payment to widows aged under 60 was just 38s 10d (approx £1.94). A further reason for the disparity was that widows had fewer dependents (and indeed some were childless); non-widowed women with dependent children had an average of 1.9 dependents each, whereas the ratio for widows was only 0.4 dependents each: *ibid* Table 31, at 103.

[33] National Assistance Act 1948, s 4 placed the Board under a duty to assist persons in need; more-over, the question 'whether a person is in need of assistance, and the nature and extent of any assistance to be given' was for the Board: *ibid*, s 5(1); see also n 25 above.

[34] Ministry of Social Security Act 1966, s 4, declaring that those in need 'shall be entitled' to benefit. The 1966 Act was subsequently renamed the Supplementary Benefit Act 1966: Social Security Act 1971, s 11(1)(c).

assistance, was subject to detailed internal (and at that time unpublished) guidelines.[35]

So far as lone parent families were concerned, the number of women with dependent children who had no access to national insurance benefits, and so were reliant on supplementary benefit, continued to grow relentlessly.[36] At the same time there was an increasing awareness that the post-war welfare state had not eradicated poverty; on the contrary, social research 'rediscovered' poverty, especially in families with children.[37] This became the impetus for the development of an influential voluntary sector lobby on behalf of low income families.[38] Meanwhile, in the decade after 1966, the number of supplementary benefit claimants increased by about one-fifth, whilst the number of lone parent families on benefit more than doubled,[39] with the SBC predicting that the numbers would continue to rise with demographic changes.[40]

The particular problems faced by lone parent families, and the associated policy issues which they raised, were given greater prominence by the publication of the Finer Committee's report in 1974.[41] The report, 'an outstanding piece of social and historical analysis',[42] highlighted the 'disorderly and anomalous tangle of relationship between the three systems of family law'[43]—English private family law was in the 'habit of dispensing two brands of matrimonial justice',[44] neither of which sat easily with the third system of means-tested benefits. As well as advocating the abolition of the magistrates' matrimonial jurisdiction and the creation of a system of family courts, the Finer Committee set out radical proposals for the administrative rather than judicial assessment of liable relative orders.[45] In short, instead of the existing parallel and poorly co-ordinated arrangements operated by the benefit offices and courts, it recommended that the SBC should have the

---

[35] Arguably a more important watershed was 1980, when the loose framework established by the original 1966 legislation was replaced by a much more detailed statutory scheme, underpinned by a dense body of secondary legislation in the form of regulations: see N Wikeley and A Ogus, *The Law of Social Security* (Butterworths, London, 2002, 5th edn) at 275.

[36] DHSS, *Annual Report of the Department of Health and Social Security* (Cmnd 6150, 1975) at 29.

[37] See eg B Abel-Smith and P Townsend, *The poor and the poorest* (Occasional papers on social administration 17: Bell, London, 1965).

[38] Notably the Child Poverty Action Group (CPAG); see M McCarthy, *Campaigning for the Poor* (Croom Helm, London, 1986).

[39] SBC, *Supplementary Benefits Commission Annual Report 1976* (Cmnd 6910, 1977) at 20, para 2.6.

[40] *Ibid*, at 26 para 2.16.

[41] *Report of the Committee on One-Parent Families* (1974, Cmnd 5629: the 'Finer Report').

[42] S Cretney, *Family Law in the Twentieth Century: A History* (Oxford University Press, Oxford, 2003) at 468. As Cretney notes (*ibid*, at 467), Professor McGregor was instrumental in the work of the Finer Committee—many of the themes in its Report were presaged in his earlier work (see eg n 167 below and his 'sociological broadside' to a paper delivered by Professor Bromley to an SPTL Colloquium on Family Law: (1964–65) 8 *Journal of Society of Public Teachers of Law* 166 at 206–7).

[43] Finer Report, n 41 above, vol 1 at para 4.190.

[44] ie in the higher courts and magistrates' courts respectively; *ibid*, at para 4.68.

[45] As Cretney explains, n 42 above, at 458–70, this idea surfaced (albeit in passing) in the earlier Graham Hall and Payne reports: *Committee on Statutory Maintenance Limits* (Cmnd 3587, 1968) and *Committee on the Enforcement of Judgment Debts* (Cmnd 3909, 1969). See further p 91 below on the scope of the liable relative rules.

primary responsibility for assessing the means of liable relatives, according to published criteria, and making an 'administrative order' requiring the payment of the relevant amount.[46] Women would then have no need to use the court system, except in the small minority of cases where they might have a claim to maintenance at a rate above their supplementary benefit entitlement. This proposal was never implemented,[47] although the idea was subsequently revived and remodelled to form the basis for the Child Support Agency.

The Finer Committee also recommended the creation of a generous new non-contributory social security benefit, or 'Guaranteed Maintenance Allowance' (GMA), designed to lift lone parents off supplementary benefit.[48] This proposal was doomed, given the economic crisis of the mid-1970s and the tight fiscal controls imposed to secure assistance from the International Monetary Fund.[49] The introduction of a modest one parent benefit,[50] as a supplement to the new child benefit, was but a pale shadow of the Finer Committee's grandiose plans for a GMA.[51] This was followed by the 1980 changes to the supplementary benefit system, which included a number of modest measures beneficial to lone parents.[52] Governmental reluctance to implement the proposal for a GMA was doubtless influenced by the SBC's own research, which suggested that whilst lone parents on benefit were 'hard-pressed', there was no evidence that they had 'any special expenses or greater needs than comparable two-parent families on benefit'.[53] The Commission's own conclusion was that it was families with children, irrespective of whether they were intact or separated, 'who are the hardest hit of all groups on supplementary benefit', and that the unemployed faced the greatest difficulties.[54]

During this period supplementary benefit expenditure on lone parents increased apace—in 1975 the total cost of benefits attributable to family breakdown was £370 million,[55] nearly a ten-fold increase on the amount in 1965. By 1976 there were 303,000 lone parent families in receipt of supplementary benefit,

---

[46] See generally Finer Report, n 41 above, vol 1 at paras 4.224–4.277.

[47] Although, following the publication of the Finer Report, the courts demonstrated greater awareness of the need to align the principles governing the assessment of maintenance liabilities: see eg *Williams v Williams* [1974] Fam 55 (Finer J himself) and *Smethurst v Smethurst* [1977] 3 WLR 472, Fam D.

[48] Finer Report, n 41 above, at paras 5.111–5.249.

[49] Cretney, n 42 above, at 469.

[50] See Wikeley and Ogus, n 35 above, at 658.

[51] A point acknowledged by the late Lady Castle, then Secretary of State for Social Services: see B Castle, *The Castle Diaries 1974–1976* (Weidenfeld & Nicolson, London, 1980) at 170 (diary entry for 23 August 1973).

[52] Notably lone parents became eligible to the (higher) long-term rate of SB after one year (instead of two), the SB rates for children were restructured, increasing the amounts for younger children, and an increased earnings disregard introduced for lone parents: see Millar, n 2 above, at 174–75.

[53] SBC, *Supplementary Benefits Commission Annual Report 1978* (Cmnd 7725, 1979), paras 4.30–4.43 at 42–46, esp para 4.38 at 45. If anything, two-parent families on benefit 'appeared in general to be having a marginally harder time', *ibid* para 4.33 at 43.

[54] *Ibid* para 4.40 at 45.

[55] This global figure relates to separated wives, divorced women and unmarried mothers, not all of whom, of course, will have been responsible for children, so the figure does not correlate precisely to expenditure on lone parent families.

amounting to only 10 per cent of the total caseload but accounting for 21 per cent of all supplementary benefit expenditure.[56] Two years later, children in lone parent families accounted for 60 per cent of all children living on supplementary benefit; furthermore, nearly half of lone parent families relied on supplementary benefit compared with about one in ten of the general population.[57]

The dependency of lone parents on supplementary benefit became still more pronounced in the period of high unemployment in the early 1980s.[58] In the mid-1980s the Conservative government instituted the Fowler Reviews of social security, which concluded that supplementary benefit was no longer sustainable in its then form.[59] As well as the growing costs of welfare, a fundamental structural problem was identified—the supplementary benefits scheme sought to combine general income maintenance on a weekly basis with lump sum assistance for occasional one-off needs. As a result of the Social Security Act 1986, the structure of the means-tested benefits system looked very different from April 1988.[60] In terms of weekly allowances, supplementary benefit was replaced by a new 'simpler' benefit,[61] income support. Income support payments were to be calculated on the basis of personal allowances and premiums, payable for claimants in particular categories (eg pensioners and disabled people), supplemented by housing costs for those who were owner occupiers with mortgages.[62] Premiums were also payable for families, and an extra premium was payable for lone parents. So, at the inception of the income support scheme, there was at least some degree of official recognition for the special needs of lone parents.[63] However, during the 1980s lone parent families, and especially those on benefit for prolonged periods, had become increasingly reliant on single payments, and this aspect of the supplementary benefits scheme was replaced by a new cash-limited discretionary social fund. The 1988 changes also saw the replacement of family income supplement (FIS)[64] with family credit. FIS had been designed as a benefit to support those in low paid work; whilst popular with working lone parents, it had been bedevilled with problems associated with low take-up in intact families. Family credit proved to be a more

[56] SBC, *Supplementary Benefits Commission Annual Report 1976* (Cmnd 6910, 1977), Table 2.1, at 23. The principal reason, of course, was that they (usually) had no access to national insurance benefits.

[57] SBC, *Supplementary Benefits Commission Annual Report 1978* (Cmnd 7725, 1979) at 41–42 para 4.28.

[58] Between November 1979 and February 1986 the total number of lone parents grew by 20%, whereas the proportion reliant on SB increased from 38% to 60%: National Audit Office (NAO), *Department of Social Security: Support for Lone Parent Families* (HC 328, Session 1989–1990) at para 2.3.

[59] DSS, *The Reform of Social Security* (Cmnd 9691, 1985).

[60] The relevant provisions of the Social Security Act (SSA) 1986 were consolidated in the Social Security Contributions and Benefits Act (SSCBA) 1992.

[61] The term 'simpler' is used advisedly.

[62] Tenants received help with the costs of renting through housing benefit.

[63] The preceding Green and White Papers had not suggested that lone parents as a group were seen as particularly problematic: Kiernan, Land and Lewis, n 9 above, at 188–89.

[64] FIS was introduced in 1970, initially as a stop-gap measure.

successful benefit than its predecessor, and was modified in various ways to provide yet further encouragement to lone parents to take up part-time employment.[65]

In summary, the four decades after the end of the Second World War saw a series of fundamental changes to the structure of the benefits system. The next section observes how the liable relative rules were operated during this period in the context of the national assistance, supplementary benefit and income support schemes.[66]

Means-tested Benefits and the Enforcement of the Liable Relative Rules

This section considers the enforcement of the liable relative rules in the context of the principal means-tested benefit schemes throughout the post-war period under review. In order to gain a proper understanding of the issues, two questions will be addressed in turn. First, what was the legal framework for recovery of benefit expenditure from liable relatives? Secondly, how were those rules actually operated in practice by the benefit authorities, and to what effect?

The Legal Framework for the Enforcement of the Liable Relative Rules

At one level the changes made by the National Assistance Act 1948 represented a radical break with the past.[67] Section 1 of the National Assistance Act 1948 declared that 'The existing poor law shall cease to have effect'. Yet, so far as liable relatives were concerned, the Board inherited much (if not quite all) of the legal architecture of the poor law in terms of both the attribution and enforcement of maintenance obligations. The cardinal principle of familial responsibility for the support of kin, albeit in an attenuated form, focussing on the nuclear family,[68] was enshrined in the National Assistance Act 1948,[69] which declared that spouses[70] were liable to maintain each other and parents were liable to maintain their

---

[65] eg in April 1992 the minimum hours threshold of 24 hours p/w was reduced to 16 hours p/w for lone parents and a maintenance disregard introduced (none applied for income support claimants). In October 1994 a child care disregard was added to the family credit scheme.

[66] Although the liable relative rules appeared in the original Bill governing FIS, they were later withdrawn by government: Kiernan, Land and Lewis, n 9 above, at 172. They never applied to family credit (or indeed to other means-tested benefits such as housing benefit).

[67] According to Birkett LJ, the change made by the 1948 Act 'was really quite revolutionary', *National Assistance Board v Parkes* [1955] 2 QB 506, CA, at 519.

[68] G Douglas, *An Introduction to Family Law* (Clarendon Press, Oxford, 2004, 2nd edn) at 74.

[69] National Assistance Act 1948, s 42.

[70] Section 42 did not deprive a husband of any defence he would enjoy at common law as regards spousal maintenance, eg where his wife had committed adultery or deserted him: *National Assistance Board v Wilkinson* [1952] 2 QB 648 (on which see L Neville Brown, 'National Assistance and the Liability to Maintain One's Family' (1955) 18 *Modern Law Review* 110). *Wilkinson* was a test case brought by the Board to clarify the law, following *obiter dicta* in the unreported decision of *Aldritt v Aldritt* (12 June 1951, Div Ct), suggesting that s 42 imposed an absolute duty: NAB, *Annual Report of the National Assistance Board for 1952* (Cmd 8900, 1953), at 18. The decision in *Wilkinson* reflected the Board's own understanding of the position and so 'was not unexpected, or indeed unwelcome', NAB *Items of Interest—June 1952* PRO file AST 7/1132 (11 July 1952).

children, whether legitimate or not.[71] It followed that on divorce there could be no public law liability to maintain one's *former* spouse, in contrast to the position under private law.[72]

In terms of enforcing the public law duty of support through legal proceedings, there were three options available to the Board, each of which was based on well-established poor law principles. First, where a person received national assistance, the Board could seek to recover the expenditure incurred by bringing civil proceedings in the magistrates' court against 'any other person who . . . is liable to maintain the person assisted'.[73] Secondly, and under a separate civil procedure, but one with overtones of criminality,[74] the Board had a parallel right of recovery against the fathers of illegitimate children.[75] Finally, the Board could bring criminal proceedings against the man concerned for persistently refusing or neglecting to maintain his wife and/or children (whether legitimate or not).[76]

There was effectively no change in this legal framework for the enforcement of the maintenance obligation through public law proceedings in the entire period from 1948 to 1988. Thus in 1966, when supplementary benefit replaced national assistance, the statutory provisions relating to the recovery of benefit expenditure from liable relatives were re-enacted without any significant amendments.[77] In the same way, and in marked contrast to the major structural changes to the landscape of the welfare system following the Fowler Reviews, the Social Security Act 1986 re-enacted the supplementary benefit liable relative provisions largely

---

[71] 'Child' in this context meant a person under the age of 16: National Assistance Act 1948 s 64(1).

[72] Furthermore, s 42 (and its successors) imposed no obligation of support in respect of other members of one's family, eg one's mother or mother-in-law—see *R v West London SBAT ex parte Clarke* [1975] 1 WLR 1396.

[73] National Assistance Act 1948, s 43(1). In fixing the amount recoverable, the court was required to have regard to all the circumstances, including the liable person's resources, and make such order as it considered appropriate: *ibid*, s 43(2). A private agreement between the parties could not oust the Board's right of recovery under s 43: *National Assistance Board v Prisk* [1954] 1 WLR 443 and *Stopher v National Assistance Board* [1955] 1 QB 486, confirmed on appeal in *National Assistance Board v Parkes* [1955] 2 QB 506; see further L Neville Brown, 'Separation Agreements and National Assistance' (1956) 19 *Modern Law Review* 623.

[74] As the successor to the bastardy jurisdiction.

[75] National Assistance Act 1948, s 44. This right was independent of the mother's right to apply in affiliation proceedings for support (*Clapham v National Assistance Board* [1961] 2 QB 77); moreover, the Board was not subject to the same time limit as the mother (*National Assistance Board v Mitchell* [1956] 1 QB 53), nor did it have to prove that she was a 'single woman', as required in affiliation proceedings (*National Assistance Board v Tugby* [1957] 1 QB 506: see L Neville Brown, 'Bastardy and the National Assistance Board' (1957) 20 *Modern Law Review* 401). If the woman later came off benefit, she could apply for payments under the order originally obtained by the Board to be paid to her: *Payne v Critchley and National Assistance Board* [1962] 2 QB 83.

[76] National Assistance Act 1948, s 51. This provision was phrased in gender neutral terms but was used almost exclusively against men.

[77] Supplementary Benefit Act 1966 (on which see n 34 above), ss 22 (liability to maintain), 23 (recovery from liable relatives), 24 (affiliation orders) and 30 (failure to maintain); these provisions were in turn later re-enacted, with some minor drafting amendments, in Supplementary Benefits Act 1976, ss 17–19 and 25.

unchanged.[78] The relevant provisions have since been consolidated in the 1992 legislation governing the benefits system.[79]

However, in the period immediately before the enactment of the Child Support Act 1991 there were two important sets of statutory changes to the framework of liable relative legislation. First, the old affiliation jurisdiction was abolished by the Family Law Reform Act 1987,[80] which sought to eradicate the last vestiges of legal discrimination against children born outside marriage. One consequence of these changes was the abolition of the separate public law procedure by which the authorities sought to recover benefit expenditure from those alleged to be the fathers of illegitimate children.[81] Instead, as from 1 April 1989, such cases were dealt with through the ordinary liable relative proceedings. Whilst this was change largely a matter of form, as it effected no modification to either the principle or method of assessment of liability, the second set of reforms, enshrined in the Social Security Act 1990, was much more significant. Indeed, the 1990 Act anticipated one of the most controversial aspects of the subsequent child support legislation. As we have seen, the post-1948 liable relative rules confined the support obligation to spouses and parents; in public law terms, regardless of any private law agreement or order, there was no obligation to maintain a former spouse.[82] This longstanding principle was breached by the 1990 Act.[83] The new provision[84] applied to cases in which one parent (typically the mother) was claiming income support for herself and her children, and the father was liable only to maintain the children.[85] It allowed the courts, in liable relative proceedings, to take into account sums payable by way of income support to the lone parent in calculating the amount to be paid for the children.[86] The 1990 Act also introduced two further reforms, enabling the Department to transfer an order it had obtained against a liable relative to the lone parent, if she came off benefit,[87] and to enforce directly a private law maintenance order previously obtained by a lone parent who was now in receipt of income support.[88] Thus, to recap, and aside from these changes made

---

[78] SSA 1986, ss 24 (recovery from liable relatives), 25 (affiliation orders) and 26 (criminal offence of failure to maintain). See J Webb, 'Maintenance Payments, Social Security and the Liable Relative' (1988) 18 *Family Law* 267 and 307 for a detailed analysis of the position before and after the 1986 Act.

[79] See Social Security Administration Act (SSAA) 1992, ss 105 (criminal offence of failure to maintain) and 106 (recovery from liable relatives).

[80] Implementing the recommendations of the Law Commission report *Family Law: Illegitimacy* (Law Com No 118, 1982).

[81] *Ibid* para 6.50 and Family Law Reform Act (FLRA) 1987, s 33, sch 2 para 92 and sch 4.

[82] See p 92 above.

[83] As Mesher's commentary notes in *Current Law Statutes Annotated* (vol 2, at 27-21), there was relatively little Parliamentary debate owing to the operation of the guillotine.

[84] SSA 1986, s 24A(1)–(2), inserted by SSA 1990, s 8(1). See now SSAA 1992, s 107(1)–(2).

[85] ie because he had never been, or was no longer, married to the mother. Only children under 16 were affected: SSA 1986, s 24A(11) inserted by SSA 1990, s 8(1); see now SSAA 1992, s 107(15).

[86] See further Income Support (Liable Relatives) Regulations 1990 (SI 1990/1777).

[87] SSA 1986, s 24A(3)–(10), inserted by SSA 1990, s 8(1); these provisions were supplemented by provisions added by the Maintenance Enforcement Act 1991, s 9; see now SSAA 1992, s 107(3)–(14).

[88] SSA 1986, s 24B, inserted by SSA 1990, s 8(1); see now SSAA 1992, s 108.

in the 1987 and 1990 Acts, the benefit authorities had three options by way of instituting legal action—civil proceedings for recovery against a liable relative, or against a reputed father, or prosecution for failure to maintain. But what actually happened in practice? In answering this question we first consider the operation of the liable relative provisions in the national assistance scheme, before turning to examine how they worked in the context of the supplementary benefit and income support schemes.

The Operation of the Liable Relative Rules in Practice

The very first annual report of the National Assistance Board indicated that the enforcement of maintenance responsibilities had not been a priority for the nascent organisation.[89] This admission was to typify the departmental failure to prioritise liable relative work for much of the next four decades. The Board noted that before 1948 the public assistance authorities had advised and helped deserted wives in receipt of poor relief to bring proceedings on their own behalf, if they were unable to arrive at a satisfactory private arrangement for the payment of maintenance. The Board declared its intention to pursue the same approach, 'as it seemed preferable in her own interests for the woman to exercise her own legal rights'.[90] Hence the Board's formal position was that its statutory powers would only be invoked in those cases 'which could not be dealt with satisfactorily' through private law proceedings.[91] Instead, the Board's practice was for an officer to negotiate with the liable relative with a view to him making voluntary payments to meet his maintenance responsibility.[92] In this way the existence of the statutory powers was primarily employed as a lever by the Board's officers in informal negotiations, as a means of reminding a defaulting husband or father of his legal responsibilities to support his wife and children. In the event that voluntary payments were not forthcoming, typically the Board would not then exercise its own powers to institute civil proceedings; rather, officials would encourage the woman to apply for a court order in her own name. Indeed, in the absence of legal aid during the early part of this period, the Board actively facilitated the bringing of private law proceedings by underwriting the costs involved.[93]

Once the amount of financial support had been resolved, the Board often played a continuing role as a collector of maintenance payments, whether made by

---

[89] 'In view of other demands on their time as a result of the extension of their duties, it was not until towards the end of the year that the Board and their local officers were able to give full attention to this work', NAB, *Annual Report of the National Assistance Board for 1948* (Cmd 7767, 1949) at 22–23.

[90] *Ibid*, at 22. One justification for this approach was that a private law order automatically remained in force if the woman came off benefit.

[91] *Ibid*, at 22. See also NAB, n 28 above, at 23.

[92] *Ibid*, at 23.

[93] Thus before May 1961, when the legal aid scheme in England and Wales was extended to civil proceedings in the magistrates' courts, the Board frequently paid for the costs of the woman's legal representation—800 such cases in 1960 compared with just 16 in 1962: NAB, *Annual Report of the National Assistance Board for 1962* (Cmnd 2078, 1962) at 36. In Scotland, legal aid for proceedings in the sheriffs' courts had been made available since the Legal Aid and Solicitors (Scotland) Act 1949.

voluntary contributions or under a court order.[94] Typically the amount of maintenance payable was insufficient to lift the woman off benefit; in addition, default was common on the part of the men ordered to pay. Accordingly the Board quickly adopted a practice known as the 'diversion procedure', whereby it paid the woman her national assistance in full and arranged with the parties concerned for maintenance payments to be directed to the Board.[95] The chief advantage of this procedure, described by the Finer Committee as 'a victory of realism over bureaucracy',[96] was that it avoided the need for the women concerned to shuttle to and fro between the respective offices of the magistrates' court and the Board when the payer defaulted,[97] 'in harassed pursuit of the subsistence which each expected the other to produce'.[98] Although the diversion procedure minimised unnecessary stress on the women concerned, it created other problems: claimants might well be unaware whether or not maintenance was actually in payment, and moreover had little incentive to institute enforcement action in their own name.[99]

The official statistics reveal a marked contrast in the volume of maintenance enforcement activity by public authorities through formal legal channels before and after the Second World War. Before the war, the poor relief authorities actively pursued recalcitrant husbands and fathers in public law proceedings, bringing some 4,000 civil actions a year.[100] The National Assistance Board, however, whilst declaring that the existence of its powers to institute such civil proceedings was a matter of 'great importance', conceded that in practice these powers were rarely used.[101] There was also little change in this approach over the lifetime of the Board, as shown by Figure 4.2.[102] In the early 1950s, the number of new civil proceedings[103] instituted each year by the Board in the liable relative and affiliation jurisdictions could be counted in the tens; a decade later, it was still only in the low hundreds. The highest figure was in 1966, the year of transition from national assistance to supplementary benefit, when a total of 336 new civil

---

[94] In some cases such payments were made direct by the liable relative to his ex-partner.

[95] Diversion came to be the norm in England and Wales (77% of all cases in 1970) but the exception in Scotland (32%), where court structures did not lend themselves to this arrangement: Finer Report, n 41 above, vol 1 para 4.469 and Table 4.18 at 239.

[96] *Ibid*, at para 4.209.

[97] 'This course saves work but what is more important it avoids much inconvenience and anxiety to the woman. She is assured of a regular income, is not worried by uncertainty whether the contributions will be paid regularly, and does not have to make a further application to the Board every time payment is not made or is delayed': NAB, *Annual Report 1949*, n 28 above, at 24. For one mother's graphic description of the problems when diversion was *not* in operation, see Marsden, n 25 above, at 157–58.

[98] Finer Report, n 41 above, vol 1 at para 4.206.

[99] Although the Board noted that it was 'in a strong position to oblige her to take such action', NAB, *Annual Report of the National Assistance Board for 1953* (Cmd 9210, 1954) at 22.

[100] *Excluding* their involvement in bastardy actions.

[101] NAB, n 28 above, at 23.

[102] Pre-1966 data are based on statistics in the NAB *Annual Reports*; post-1966 data are based on annual reports of MSS, SBC and DHSS.

[103] Figure 4.2 includes only new applications, and so omits proceedings to vary or enforce an existing order, but the picture would be little different were they also counted.

proceedings were brought, resulting in 294 orders.[104] Yet the Board's infrequent use of its own statutory powers to bring civil proceedings tells only a part of the story. Over the same period there was a significant increase in the number of private law proceedings for maintenance.[105] Some of this latter increase may be attributable to extraneous factors such as increased rates of relationship breakdown or to demographic changes—but at least part of the explanation must lie in the Board's policy of encouraging, and indeed in many cases underwriting, private law proceedings.[106]

In contrast to its reluctance to initiate civil proceedings in its own name, the Board made increasing use of its power to prosecute liable relatives for failure to maintain,[107] as demonstrated by Figure 4.3.[108] In 1950 just 40 prosecutions were brought,[109] but by the early 1960s there were over 400 prosecutions annually, almost all of which were successful, resulting in some 200 or more committals to

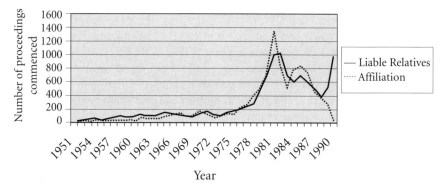

FIG. 4.2 Civil proceedings against liable relatives 1951–1991

[104] In 1966 there were a further 117 proceedings for enforcement or variation of existing orders: MSS, *Report of the Ministry of Social Security for the year 1966* (Cmnd 3338, 1967) at 76.

[105] In the inter-war period there were some 14,000 applications annually in the magistrates' courts for matrimonial orders; in the 1950s the average number nearly doubled to some 25,000 applications a year; in addition, in the 1950s there were some 7,000 applications annually under the Guardianship of Infants Acts, as compared with less than 1,000 p/a before the war: OR McGregor, L Blom-Cooper and C Gibson, *Separated spouses* (Gerald Duckworth & Co Ltd, London, 1970) at 33, Table 1.

[106] For example, in 1960 the Board itself instituted 139 new proceedings against liable relatives and reputed fathers; but we also know that it paid the legal costs of some 800 women who brought their own actions: n 93 above.

[107] This was reflected in the increased staffing devoted to prosecution work: in 1954 the NAB employed just 16 special investigators into suspected benefit abuse; by 1964 this number had risen to 97: Kiernan, Land and Lewis, n 9 above, at 164.

[108] These figures exclude prosecutions for failure to maintain based on a refusal to work, as this was primarily a labour market sanction. All pre-1966 data are based on statistics contained in the NAB *Annual Reports.*

[109] In 15 of these cases prosecutions were brought because of the jurisdictional difficulties in enforcing English court orders for maintenance in Scotland (and vice versa) through civil proceedings: NAB, n 26 above, at 19; see also Maintenance Orders Act 1950.

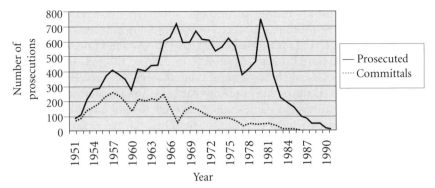

FIG. 4.3 Prosecutions and committals for failure to maintain 1951–1991

prison each year.[110] For example, in 1966 the authorities brought a total of 635 pros-ecutions for failure to maintain,[111] almost twice the number of civil proceedings instituted by the Board in the same year. The Board evidently valued the symbolic significance of such criminal proceedings, describing their purpose as being 'to impress on the offender himself—and upon others who may be tempted to default on their liabilities—the importance of maintaining his wife and children regularly in the future'.[112] However, the Board's apparent eagerness to resort to criminal prosecutions resulting in imprisonment for defaulters needs to be seen in its proper context in two respects. First, committal to prison was at that time regarded in private law proceedings as an appropriate sanction for maintenance debtors—in the 1960s, more than 2,000 men a year were imprisoned for non-payment of mainten-ance in family proceedings.[113] Secondly, it would be wrong to assume that the adop-tion of a more punitive approach to maintenance defaulters simply represented a return to the harsh inter-war policy of the poor law authorities. In fact, the reality was rather more prosaic—criminal prosecutions for failure to maintain were both predominantly and disproportionately a Scottish phenomenon, reflecting the pecu-liar inadequacies of the private law remedies for aliment in that jurisdiction.[114]

What then was the effect of the Board's enforcement activity, whether dir-ectly through instituting its own legal proceedings or indirectly, either through

---

[110] Although the proportion of those convicted who were then sentenced to imprisonment fell from 84% in 1951 to around 50% in the early 1960s.

[111] MSS, n 104 above, at 75.

[112] NAB, *Report of the National Assistance Board for 1961* (Cmnd 1730, 1961) at 28.

[113] O R McGregor *et al*, n 105 above, at 34, Table 2.

[114] Over half of all prosecutions between 1968 and 1970 were brought in Scotland: Finer Report, n 41 above vol 1 at para 4.467 and Table 4.17 at 238. The NAB's *Annual Reports* do not provide a break-down by jurisdiction, but there is no reason to believe that the position before 1966 was any different. See also n 109 above.

negotiations with liable relatives or through encouraging women to take legal action? This can be measured in at least two ways: (1) how many women on benefit were in receipt of maintenance?; (2) what proportion of benefit expenditure was recovered from liable relatives? As to the former, throughout the history of national assistance only a minority of claimants regularly received adequate maintenance payments from their previous partners. An early study of long-term recipients of national assistance revealed that 'only about a fifth were receiving from the liable relative regular payments of amounts accepted as sufficient in the circumstances'.[115] By 1965 the position was little better—about half of all separated wives had neither a court order nor a voluntary agreement for the payment of maintenance. Although 40 per cent of these women had a court order, only half of these were being regularly complied with; the remaining 10 per cent had out-of-court agreements (although with markedly better compliance rates).[116] Viewed another way, overall in 1965 'almost two thirds of husbands paid nothing and only between one quarter and one third of them paid regularly'.[117]

Successive annual reports by the Board identified two principal reasons for the shortfall in maintenance payments—the difficulty in tracing husbands and the inability of many husbands, even if located, to support both their original family and their new household.[118] As to the former, up to half of all liable relatives simply 'disappeared'.[119] According to a later report:

> The very way of life of some of these men—moving about the country, frequently changing jobs, and evolving ingenious ways of covering their tracks—calls for prolonged and time-consuming enquiries on the part of the Board's officers.[120]

As regards the latter, the Board coyly referred to 'the delicate problem of deciding whether the assistance is to be given to the wife or to the paramour'.[121] As we have seen, its pragmatic solution was usually[122] to pay national assistance to the deserted wife in full and, where feasible, to seek to recover an appropriate contribution from the husband after the event. The basis of assessment used by the Board's officers in judging whether contributions were sufficient was never publicly articulated, with the result that staff exercised a considerable degree of discretion in liable relative work. Moreover, the Board's dealings with liable relatives were characterised by a strong sense of realism:

---

[115] NAB, n 28 above, at 22. There is no hint as to the criterion used to judge whether maintenance was 'sufficient'.

[116] NAB, *Annual Report of the National Assistance Board for 1965* (Cmnd 3042, 1966) at 27.

[117] Finer Report, n 41 above, vol 1 at para 4.84.

[118] NAB, n 99 above, at 18.

[119] *Ibid*, at 19—in a sample of 57,700 separated wives on national assistance for more than two years, 2,750 husbands had left the country 'often, no doubt, in order to escape liability for his wife's maintenance' and the Board had been unable to trace a further 24,000 men, thought to be in the country.

[120] NAB, n 93 above, at 35.

[121] NAB, n 99 above at 19.

[122] As under the poor law, there was the ever present concern of collusion between 'deserted' wives or unmarried mothers and their partners: see Hill, n 25 above, at 82, describing various 'mucking around' techniques used by staff to deter suspected fraudulent claims on the part of such women.

extracting money from husbands to maintain wives is at best an uncertain business; it is easier to enforce the maintenance of those with whom the man is living than of those from whom he is parted, and the man is more likely to exert himself to maintain the former.[123]

To this end the Board actively enforced the cohabitation rule, whereby a man was assumed for benefit purposes to be financially supporting the woman (and her children) with whom he was living, even though they were not married (and so owed each other no private law obligation of support). The zealous application of the cohabitation rule by officials, which was to become the subject of intense criticism in the 1970s, taken together with the pragmatic approach to the liable relative provisions, can be seen as reflecting an element of give-and-take in the treatment by the welfare state of the financial consequences of relationship break-down. In effect, a man was required by the cohabitation rule to support his second family, irrespective of the position in private law; in the event of any spare capa-city, he was also expected to provide a modest contribution to the costs of main-taining his first family. The unwritten understanding was that this latter obligation would not be enforced too vigorously.[124]

The other way of measuring the effectiveness of the Board's liable relative activ-ity is in terms of overall recovery rates. Expenditure under the national assistance scheme on supporting separated and divorced wives and their children, along with mothers of illegitimate children, rose slowly but steadily in the immediate post-war period, if only because the numbers of claimants in these categories increased with the demographic and social changes outlined above. In 1955 the gross cost to the Board of supporting such claimants was £11.1 million, in respect of whom liable relatives made voluntary contributions totalling £960,000[125] and the Board recovered some £900,000 through legal proceedings.[126] By 1965, the total cost had increased to £42.7 million; voluntary payments made directly to claimants were estimated at £4.4 million and the Board recovered just over £3 million from liable relatives.[127] Figure 4.4 confirms that the Board made little progress either in encouraging voluntary contributions or in improving collection rates from liable

---

[123] NAB, n 99 above, at 19, a view echoed two decades later by the Finer Report: 'When a man is put in such a dilemma the solution he will lean towards is tolerably clear. He will feed, clothe and house those with whom he is living, knowing that the State will provide for the others', n 41 above, vol 1 at para 4.182.

[124] Moreover, if the first wife was not reliant on benefit, the state had no direct interest in ensuring maintenance was paid; even if she was, but the man's *new* partner had herself previously been on benefit, then the failure to take enforcement action against him could be rationalised on the basis that the cost of public support for the first family was (in broad terms) balanced by the benefit savings secured by the operation of the cohabitation rule in respect of the new partner.

[125] Sums paid by liable relatives direct to their ex-partners were taken into account in assessing national assistance payments, although the Board seems to have operated a disregard for child main-tenance: Lewis, n 22 above, at 269.

[126] NAB, n 99 above, at 21.

[127] NAB, n 116 above, at 27.

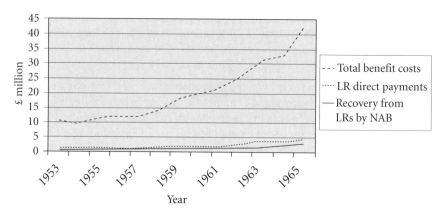

F$_{IG}$. 4.4 Recovery of benefit expenditure from liable relatives 1953–1965

relatives, which remained stubbornly at about 10 per cent and 8 per cent respectively of the Board's gross expenditure in such cases throughout this period. Following this inauspicious start, we now turn to consider the operation of the liable relative rules in the period after the abolition of national assistance.

In 1967 the new Ministry of Social Security's first report noted wearily that whilst only 7 per cent of supplementary benefit claimants were separated wives or lone parents, 'the work necessary to persuade the man to meet his liability often involves disproportionate time and effort'.[128] Such claimants also experienced frequent changes in their circumstances,[129] so generating further work for local offices, and the rise in the number of lone parent claimants fuelled officials' ever-present concerns about suspected abuse.[130] When negotiating with liable relatives, the SBC's staff relied on a formula, inherited from the Board, the existence of which first became public knowledge in the report of the Finer Committee.[131] The Commission's liable relative formula differed from that adopted in the subsequent child support scheme in three important respects. First, it was relatively simple. A liable relative was assumed to need a weekly amount to live on calculated by aggregating three figures: the sum payable had he been in receipt of supplementary benefit himself, his actual rent and a 'disregard' of the higher of £5 or a quarter of his take-home earnings.[132] Any income above that level was regarded as available to meet his liable relative obligation. Secondly, the liable relative formula institutionalised the custom and practice of the Board and then the Commission in

---

[128] MSS, n 104 above, at 62.

[129] In contrast to pensioners, whose circumstances tended to be static: O Stevenson, *Claimant or client?* (George Allen & Unwin Ltd, London, 1973) at 129.

[130] *Ibid*, at 130.

[131] n 41 above, vol 1 at paras 4.188–4.189.

[132] 'The effect of this is to discriminate against the claimant in so far as it allows the payer to subsidise his new family at the expense of the old', Webb, n 78 above, at 267. In practice, as Ormrod LJ observed, this means 'transferring part of his liability to the taxpayer', *Shallow v Shallow* [1979] Fam 1 at 7.

acknowledging the reality of second families—thus the man's notional supplementary benefit entitlement was based on the rates payable for himself and any dependants with whom he was now living, regardless of whether or not he was married to his new partner.[133] Finally the formula was always only a starting point: in terms of its application, the Commission's staff enjoyed the same broad discretion as their predecessors in the National Assistance Board in deciding whether the sum being offered by a liable relative was a 'reasonable' contribution.[134]

At the outset, the SBC followed the same policy as its predecessor Board in terms of encouraging women to take out maintenance proceedings in their own name,[135] only rarely invoking its own statutory recovery powers (see Figure 4.2). However, from the mid-1960s onwards concerns were expressed in various quarters that the official policy of 'encouraging' female claimants to apply to court for maintenance resulted in practice at best in misunderstandings and at worst in staff 'bullying' women.[136] Reviewing the evidence, the Finer Committee expressed its concern that the Commission 'frequently urge proceedings on women who have no desire to engage in them',[137] a policy which in its view caused 'pain and anxiety, for no tangible advantage, to far more claimants than those upon whom it may confer some advantage'.[138] It followed, in the Committee's view, that officials should desist from encouraging women to bring their own legal proceedings against the liable relative.[139]

In 1975, in response to this recommendation, the Commission changed its formal stance on private law applications to one of simply explaining the options available, and leaving the woman to decide for herself.[140] This change in policy appears to have had a marked impact in practice, as is evident in Figure 4.2—as

---

[133] As we have seen, if he was *not* married to her, then he owed her no public or private law maintenance obligation; equally, he owed his step-children no such duty, unless in private law (after 1958) he was found to have treated them as 'children of the family'.

[134] Many, of course, were the same individuals as before but working in the new structures.

[135] The impact of this policy seems to have been confined to England and Wales: in Scotland, the problems in securing and enforcing orders for aliment were such that 'the statement of policy [was] more honoured in the breach than in the observance', Finer Report, n 41 above, vol 1 at para 4.466. Just 7 liable relative proceedings were brought in Scotland in 1968 as against 189 in England: *ibid*, Table 4.17 at 238.

[136] P Morris, *Prisoners and their Families* (Allen and Unwin, London, 1965) at 269, Marsden, n 25 above, at 152 and J Streather and S Weir, *Social Insecurity: Single Mothers on Benefit* Poverty Pamphlet 16 (CPAG, London, 1974) at 14.

[137] Finer Report, n 41 above, vol 1 at para 4.192 (although they found that 'pressure' was applied in only 'a very small proportion of the whole', *ibid*, at para 4.197).

[138] *Ibid*, at para 4.202.

[139] *Ibid*, at para 4.228. County court registrars, however, strongly supported the SBC's policy of encouraging women to bring maintenance proceedings: W Barrington Baker, J Eekelaar, C Gibson and S Raikes, *The Matrimonial Jurisdiction of Registrars* (Centre for Socio-Legal Studies, Oxford, 1977) at para 5.14.

[140] SBC, *Supplementary Benefits Commission Annual Report 1975* (Cmnd 6615, 1976) at 79. A copy of the Commission's explanatory leaflet for separated women, setting out its policy ('the decision whether or not to take your own proceedings is entirely for you') was reproduced in SBC, *Supplementary Benefits Commission Annual Report 1976* (Cmnd 6910, 1977) at 249–50 (App G).

more women elected not to take proceedings in their own name,[141] so it seems departmental officials became more willing to bring recovery proceedings on the Commission's behalf. Indeed, the rate of increase in enforcement activity became even more marked with the election of Mrs Thatcher's first administration in 1979 and the subsequent abolition of the SBC in 1980. From that date onwards the then Department of Health and Social Security assumed direct responsibility for instituting civil proceedings to enforce public law maintenance obligations. Initially, at least, the Department attached some priority to liable relative work as part of its wider drive against fraud and abuse in the benefits system.[142] In 1981, and for the first time since the Second World War, the total numbers of new proceedings brought in the liable relative and affiliation jurisdictions exceeded 1,000 in both instances. However, this burst in enforcement activity was short-lived, and the amount of liable relative work, at least as measured by the volume of new court proceedings, fell away during the rest of the 1980s. By 1989 the number of new applications to court had fallen back below the level recorded ten years previously.

What were the main reasons for this decline in enforcement activity during the 1980s? In response to a National Audit Office investigation, the Department itself suggested several reasons, including the fact that since 1982 its own internal guidance had placed greater emphasis on the need for action against liable relatives to be cost-effective.[143] Other factors included increasing unemployment amongst liable relatives and the formation of second families,[144] as well as the approach of the courts (which typically made low orders). The National Audit Office also pointed out that there had been a significant reduction in staff resources devoted to such work during the 1980s.[145] Moreover, even if staff were nominally designated as liable relative officers, the pressure on local offices in the mid to late-1980s was such that they were frequently re-assigned to other duties on a daily basis, as civil service staffing levels were reined back at the same time as benefit caseloads increased.[146]

---

[141] Although the absence of hard data on the numbers of applications in the magistrates' courts makes it difficult to demonstrate this point empirically, the literature certainly suggests that prior to 1975 many women only brought private law proceedings as a result of SBC 'encouragement'. That said, there were also clearly cases of 'encouragement' after 1975: see eg *Titheradge v Titheradge* (1983) 4 FLR 552, in which the ex-wife on benefit 'said, quite fairly, that an increase in maintenance would not affect her; that the Department of Health and Social Security had asked her to get the order increased, it was their idea' (at 553). See also C Smart, *The Ties that Bind* (Routledge & Kegan Paul, London, 1984) at 198.

[142] See R Smith, 'Who's fiddling? Fraud and abuse' in S Ward (ed), *DHSS in Crisis* (CPAG Report No 66, London, 1985), ch 9; see further D Cook, *Rich Law, Poor Law* (Open University Press, Milton Keynes, 1989).

[143] Smith, n 142 above, at 114–15 and NAO, n 58 above, at para 4.4.

[144] *Ibid*, at para 4.11, both factors which impinged on cost-effectiveness: *ibid*, at para 4.4.

[145] Officially, the total number of 'staff years' devoted to such work fell from 2,356 in 1981 to 1,578 in 1988: *ibid*, at para 4.19. However, in 1986 there were about 900 LROs: NACRO, *Enforcement of the Law Relating to Social Security* (NACRO, December 1986, London) at para 8.10.

[146] NAO, n 58 above, at paras 4.15–4.17; see also J Bradshaw and J Millar, *Lone Parent Families in the UK* (DSS Research Report No 6, London, 1991) at 79. The warning from NACRO in 1986 ('it is essential to keep staffing levels and the competence of staff adequate for the tasks involved'; original emphasis) was clearly not heeded: n 145 above, at para 8.11.

Furthermore, up until the early 1970s at least, lone parents were automatically subject to home visits once every 13 weeks.[147] However, during the 1980s infrequent home visits were replaced by postal review procedures, making it much more likely that liable relative issues would go undetected and not be pursued.[148] For example, one major study in 1989 revealed that a third of lone parents who were or had been on income support had never been asked by the Department for the name and address of the absent parent.[149] One inevitable consequence was that the proportion of lone parents on benefit who received maintenance plummeted,[150] fuelling concerns about welfare dependency. However, even allowing for the impact of abolition of affiliation proceedings in respect of illegitimate children under the 1987 Act,[151] enforcement activity started picking up again after 1989, as shown by Figure 4.2. This reflects the measures contained in the Social Security Act 1990 and the greater political (and hence policy) interest in the enforcement of maintenance liabilities following the publication of *Children Come First* in 1990,[152] the White Paper that preceded the Child Support Act 1991.

As regards criminal proceedings, the SBC at first followed the practice of the National Assistance Board in using prosecutions as a means of enforcing maintenance obligations (principally against husbands in desertion). Furthermore, the criminal offence of failure to maintain with the possibility of committal to prison survived the Finer Committee's recommendation for its abolition.[153] Indeed, it was not until 1977[154] that the total number of civil proceedings instigated by the Commission exceeded the number of prosecutions for failure to maintain.[155] The conviction rate for such prosecutions remained at 94 per cent or more throughout this period,[156] although the courts tended to use the sanction of immediate imprisonment more and more sparingly from the 1970s onwards (see Figure 4.3).[157] However, the 1980s was marked by a dramatic decline in the Department's use of

---

[147] Stevenson, n 129 above, at 134.

[148] Kiernan, Land and Lewis, n 9 above, at 187.

[149] Bradshaw and Millar, n 146 above, at 85.

[150] From 50% in 1981 to 23% in 1988: NAO, n 58 above, at para 4.10.

[151] Those cases which formerly would have been dealt with via affiliation proceedings were subsumed within the ordinary liable relative rules as from 1 April 1989.

[152] Cm 1263, 1990.

[153] Finer Report, n 41 above, vol 1 at para 4.211. Indeed, the offence still remains on the statute book today (SSAA 1992, s 105), although it appears to have fallen into desuetude.

[154] By which time, as we have seen, the Department had begun to take a more proactive stance towards invoking its civil recovery powers.

[155] SBC instructions at the time advised that cases of deliberate desertion to an unknown address or refusal to pay maintenance, knowing the SBC would have to pay benefits, should be considered for prosecution: Streather and Weir, n 136 above, at 57.

[156] As the Finer Report was later dryly to observe: 'We have no means of telling whether success of this order represents supreme caution in selecting cases for prosecution or abnormal incompetence on the part of those prosecuted in defending themselves': n 41 above vol I, at para 4.211.

[157] There is some doubt as to the figures for committals; much higher figures are cited for the period 1967–1972 (typically 200 or more p/a) in DHSS *Social Security Statistics* 1972 (1973) Table 34.93, at 162, but Figure 4.3 uses the (presumably corrected) data from the 1981 report.

criminal proceedings: in 1980, there were some 700 proceedings instituted in each of the liable relative, affiliation and criminal jurisdictions—by 1990, when there were nearly 1,000 new civil proceedings in total, there were just 11 prosecutions.

Notwithstanding these shifts in official policy and practice, the one statistic that changed very little throughout most of this period was the proportion of benefit expenditure which was recovered from liable relatives. We have seen that during the last decade of the National Assistance Board, the authorities managed to recover at most 8 per cent of benefit outlays from liable relatives.[158] There was no improvement on this in subsequent years—compare Figure 4.5 with Figure 4.4.[159] In the 1970s and 1980s the recovery rate was typically about 6 per cent until 1987,[160] when it started falling even lower. At its low point, in 1990—coinciding with the publication of *Children Come First*—just 1.9 per cent of the amount of benefit spent on separated, divorced and unmarried mothers (and their children) was recovered by the Department from liable relatives.

The Private Law Dimension of Child Maintenance After 1945

In the previous chapter we saw how English family law developed a 'twin track' model of dispute resolution. In short, the matrimonial disputes of the well-to-do were regulated through the Divorce Court, as a division of the High Court, whilst relationship breakdown in working class families was processed through the

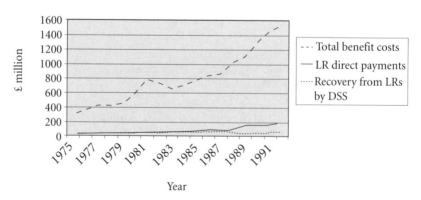

FIG. 4.5 Recovery of benefit expenditure from liable relatives 1975–1992

[158] p 100 above.

[159] The sums involved in Figure 4.5 are of a different order, given the passage of time, but the overall trend is remarkably similar to that in Figure 4.4.

[160] Note that the figures for totals recovered by the Department from liable relatives until 1983 in Figures 4.4 and 4.5 *include* recoveries from sponsored immigrants etc (these are only disaggregated in the official data from 1984), but this has only a marginal impact on the overall picture.

domestic jurisdiction of the magistrates' courts (assuming, that is, that the parties resorted to law at all). The Finer Committee's powerful critique demonstrated how firmly entrenched this dichotomy had become within the family justice system. The development of this bifurcated private law jurisdiction in the latter half of the twentieth century is fully documented elsewhere,[161] and so this section need only highlight the most important staging posts en route to the enactment of the child support legislation in 1991. Despite their very different paths,[162] there is one common theme in the post-war evolution of the two court-based jurisdictions: little if any importance was attached to the child maintenance obligation, in terms of periodical payments between parents after separation or divorce, within the wider context of resolving disputes following relationship breakdown.[163] Indeed, although the legislative framework suggested that Parliament had always thought in terms of a 'distinction between child's maintenance and wife's maintenance',[164] in practice the common law tradition reflected 'a tendency to mix all the economic questions together in one pot'.[165]

The law and practice relating to divorce was fundamentally recast in the second half of the twentieth century. Although the extension of legal aid in 1950 increased the accessibility of the Divorce Court, the long-running campaign for divorce law reform itself appeared to have suffered a major setback in 1956 with the publication of the report of the Royal Commission on Marriage and Divorce,[166] which was 'hopelessly divided'[167] on the issue. Yet, as the Finer Report was to observe nearly 20 years later, the Royal Commission's report was 'little more than a ripple on the surface of a tide that was moving strongly in the other direction'.[168] The breakthrough[169] finally came with the Divorce Reform Act 1969,[170] which

---

[161]   Most notably in Cretney, n 42 above.

[162]   For example, a wife had no independent right to obtain a maintenance order in the High Court, without instituting some other matrimonial proceedings, until the Law Reform (Miscellaneous Provisions) Act 1949, s 5—whereas this facility had been available in the magistrates' courts since 1878.

[163]   This is not to say that the interests of children were ignored—as we shall see, the 1984 reforms required the divorce court to give first consideration to the children's interests when considering ancillary relief applications.

[164]   L Neville Brown, 'Maintenance and Esoterism' (1968) 31 *Modern Law Review* 121 at 129 and 131 (although this was not the case with the original 1878 legislation—see p 76 above).

[165]   A Agell, 'Grounds and Procedures Reviewed' in L Weitzman and M Maclean (eds), *Economic Consequences of Divorce* (Clarendon Press, Oxford, 1992) ch 3 at 62; see eg *Stevens (Inspector of Taxes) v Tirard* [1940] 1 KB 204, CA, and *Supplementary Benefits Commission v Jull* [1981] AC 1025, HL.

[166]   *Royal Commission on Marriage and Divorce, Report 1951–1955* (Cmd 9678, 1956).

[167]   Cretney, n 42 above, at 336–37. For a stinging contemporary critique of the Morton report, see OR McGregor, *Divorce in England: A Centenary Study* (Heinemann, London, 1957): 'It is a matter of opinion whether the Morton Commission is intellectually the worst Royal Commission of the twentieth century, but there can be no dispute that its Report is the most unreadable and confused' (at 193). In McGregor's damning indictment, 'the Morton Commission joined the Jumblies and went to sea in a sieve' in the absence of any understanding of the research evidence (*ibid*, at 181).

[168]   Finer Report, n 41 above, vol 1 at para 4.32.

[169]   See further Cretney, n 42 above, ch 9 for a comprehensive and authoritative analysis of the reform process. See also S Cretney, *Law, Law Reform and the Family* (Clarendon Press, Oxford, 1998) ch 2.

[170]   The 1969 Act came into force in 1971; the relevant provisions were then re-enacted in the Matrimonial Causes Act 1973, which remains in force (as amended) today.

provided for just one 'ground' for divorce—the irretrievable breakdown of marriage—but one which could only be proved by one or more of five facts, three being fault-based and the remaining two depending on separation, consensual or otherwise.[171] Independently of reforms to the substantive law, divorce law procedure underwent a series of even more radical, if much less-publicised, changes over this period. For example, whereas in 1945 divorce petitions required the full panoply of a court hearing with representation of the parties by counsel,[172] by the 1980s 'do-it-yourself' divorce had become a reality. Furthermore, much of the real business of the divorce jurisdiction—in particular, ancillary relief work—was handled by district judges (formerly registrars).[173]

For most of the twentieth century the courts had at their disposal a relatively limited number of mechanisms for awarding financial provision on divorce, but enjoyed a wide discretion with regard to the basis for actually making such orders. The Divorce Court adopted various approaches—for example, the 'one-third' rule, the desirability of meeting the wife's 'reasonable needs' or the goal of putting the parties in the position they would have been in had the marriage not broken down—whilst official bodies largely neglected to articulate any underpinning principles.[174] The law of ancillary relief took a significant step forward in 1963, when courts were given the power to order payment of a lump sum on divorce.[175] As Cretney observes:

> The long-term significance of this provision on perceptions of the nature of the divorce process is considerable; the courts and the legislature began to move away from thinking solely in terms of income maintenance, and towards making provision by way of capital adjustment.[176]

Initially the courts adopted a guarded policy to the exercise of this power,[177] but the landscape changed dramatically with the implementation of a new code on ancillary relief in the wake of the 1969 Act.[178] This enabled the court 'to redistrib-

---

[171] The weaknesses of the current divorce law are well-known, and this is not the place to dwell on the fate of the subsequent attempt to provide for further reform of divorce law and procedure, leading to the government's decision in 2000 not to implement pt II of the Family Law Act 1996: see SM Cretney, JM Masson and R Bailey-Harris, *Principles of Family Law* (Sweet & Maxwell, London, 2002, 7th edn), discussing 'the reform which never was' (at 297–309) and see further H Reece, *Divorcing responsibly* (Hart Publishing, Oxford, 2003).

[172] Formally, until 1967 only the High Court could hear divorce petitions; in practice, the volume of business after the Second World War made this unsustainable, and Special Commissioners in Divorce (typically county court judges) exercised this jurisdiction from 1946: see Cretney, n 42 above, at 281–86.

[173] *Ibid*, at 403–5.

[174] *Ibid*, at 415.

[175] Matrimonial Causes Act 1963, s 5, implementing one of the Morton Commission's proposals: *ibid*, n 166 at paras 515–21.

[176] Cretney, n 42 above, at 416 (footnote omitted).

[177] *Ibid*, at 416–19.

[178] Matrimonial Proceedings and Property Act 1970, the relevant provisions of which were re-enacted in the Matrimonial Causes Act 1973 (which in turn was substantially amended by the Matrimonial and Family Proceedings Act 1984).

ute virtually all the parties' economically valuable resources, whether capital or income, if it considered it appropriate to do so'.[179] The statutory goal, building on the previous practice of the courts,[180] was the so-called 'minimal loss' principle. In the convoluted language of the legislation, the court, having considered 'all the circumstances' was:

> so to exercise its powers as to place the parties, so far as it is practicable and, having regard to their conduct, just to do so, in the financial position in which they would have been if the marriage had not broken down and each had properly discharged his or her financial obligations and responsibilities towards the other.[181]

The leading case on this provision, *Wachtel v Wachtel*,[182] whilst indicating that in practice the parties' (mis)conduct was usually to be disregarded, was less instructive on elucidating the underlying principle governing the exercise of the court's wide powers.[183] Indeed, the legislation required 'the court to take account of almost every conceivable factor',[184] without any indication as to their respective weighting. In practice, in cases in which there were children involved, the courts looked for solutions which would ensure that the custodial parent[185] and any children were adequately housed. In this context, the breadth of the courts' new powers became even more significant as owner-occupation developed as the dominant tenure in the post-war period.[186] This became even more important after the 'right to buy' was introduced for council tenants in 1980. It also rapidly became apparent that in many (if not nearly all) cases the 'minimal loss' objective was simply unattainable.[187] Following the Law Commission's recommendations,[188] and intense pressure from fathers' rights pressure groups,[189] this statutory goal was

---

[179] Cretney, n 42 above, at 422. This must be read subject to the caveat that the courts' powers to reallocate pension rights were at that stage very limited.

[180] See eg *Kershaw v Kershaw* [1966] P 13 at 17, *per* Sir Jocelyn Simon P, on hearing an appeal from the magistrates' court: 'the wife's maintenance should be so assessed that her standard of living does not suffer more than is inherent in the circumstances of separation . . . in general the wife should not be relegated to a lower standard of living than that which her husband enjoys'. See also *Attwood v Attwood* [1968] P 591.

[181] Matrimonial Proceedings and Property Act 1970, s 5, later re-enacted as Matrimonial Causes Act 1973, s 25(1).

[182] [1973] Fam 72.

[183] Cretney, n 42 above, at 430.

[184] *Mortimer v Mortimer-Griffin* [1986] 2 FLR 315, CA, at 318 *per* Sir John Donaldson MR. For a feminist critique of the courts' exercise of this broad discretion, see Smart, n 141 above.

[185] To use the pre-Children Act 1989 terminology.

[186] The number of owner occupiers more than trebled between 1951 and 1985 (from just over 4 million to nearly 14 million), increasing that tenure's share of the housing sector from 30% to 62%: *Social Trends 17* (Central Statistical Office, London, 1987) at 137.

[187] Registrars (now district judges) reported that they were 'constantly dealing with low income families' Barrington Baker *et al*, n 139 above, at para 2.3; see also para 2.26.

[188] Law Commission, *Family Law: The Financial Consequences of Divorce* (Law Com No 112, HC 68, Session 1981–82). The Law Commission noted the Finer Committee's proposals but observed that the balance between public and private support raised 'essentially matters for political decision' (para 5).

[189] Notably the Campaign for Justice in Divorce.

repealed by the Matrimonial and Family Proceedings Act 1984. Instead, courts were charged with having 'regard to all the circumstances of the case' but giving 'first consideration' to the welfare of any minor children.[190] Again, building on the experience of the post-1971 case law,[191] courts were also required to have regard to the desirability of a financial 'clean break' as between the parties.[192] In tabloid terms, this measure was designed to end maintenance based on a 'meal ticket for life'.[193] However, this particular aspect of the 1984 Act was a good example of 'evidence-free' legislative reform; there was precious little empirical evidence to suggest that the 'alimony drone' was a problem in practice.[194] Rather, research suggested that the receipt of maintenance acted as an incentive for lone parents to leave benefit and take up employment.[195] The considerable public attention devoted to *spousal* support in the debates surrounding the 1984 Act meant that the issue of *child* support was largely neglected.

Indeed, the impact of the 1984 amendments was to reinforce practitioners' negotiating goals in the case of a divorcing couple with children, modest joint incomes and one substantial asset (the matrimonial home)—typically to engineer an outcome whereby the man would transfer his equity in the home to his ex-spouse in return for at best nominal periodical payments for both her and the children.[196] Such a solution met the twin goals of securing an almost complete financial 'clean break' between the parties and giving 'first consideration' to the children's needs (at least in terms of their housing), whilst also enabling both parents to 'start again' by rebuilding their lives (albeit that the man might be left with minimal, if any, capital assets and the woman little by way of income). This practice was facilitated by the fact that supplementary benefit (later income support) would meet the interest payments (if not the capital repayments) in respect of the mortgage on the former family home.[197] Although in principle the man's child maintenance obligation survived the divorce settlement,[198] the reality was that its already low status was diminished still further. The Chancellor's decision

---

[190] Matrimonial Causes Act 1973, s 25, as amended by Matrimonial and Family Proceedings Act 1984, s 3.

[191] *Minton v Minton* [1979] AC 593, HL.

[192] Matrimonial Causes Act 1973, s 25A, inserted by Matrimonial and Family Proceedings Act 1984, s 3A.

[193] See further Smart, n 141 above, esp ch 8.

[194] Indeed, quite the contrary; see eg Millar, n 2 above, at 178–79.

[195] J Eekelaar, *Regulating Divorce* (Clarendon Press, Oxford, 1991) at 36.

[196] See generally G Davis, S Cretney, K Bader and J Collins, 'The Relationship between Public and Private Financial Support following Divorce in England and Wales' in LJ Weitzman and M Maclean (eds), *Economic Consequences of Divorce* (Clarendon Press, Oxford, 1992), ch 17.

[197] A 'welfare benefit clean break', as described by G Davis, S Cretney and J Collins, *Simple Quarrels* (Clarendon Press, Oxford, 1994) at 31. These rules were tightened up in the 1990s: see Wikeley and Ogus, n 35 above, at 306–12.

[198] See eg *Hully v Thompson* (1981) 2 FLR 53 and *Griffiths v Griffiths* [1984] FLR 662, CA.

to abolish tax relief on child maintenance in 1988[199] further weakened the incentive to pay child maintenance, at least amongst middle class fathers.[200]

In sharp contrast to the fundamental reshaping of the county courts' divorce jurisdiction, the magistrates' courts experienced only incremental change in this area of their work. Confusingly, orders for financial provision on family breakdown could be achieved through three principal and quite separate types of private law proceedings before the justices: the domestic, guardianship and affiliation jurisdictions.

First, in the domestic jurisdiction, which was available exclusively to married couples, there were no significant reforms to the substantive law governing maintenance orders in the half century between the Summary Jurisdiction (Separation and Maintenance) Act 1925 and the Domestic Proceedings and Magistrates' Courts Act 1978.[201] As in the divorce jurisdiction, there was precious little statutory guidance on the principles of assessment for maintenance orders, whether for spouses or for children.[202] The amounts awarded by way of maintenance were typically low, reflecting both the predominantly working class clientele of the magistrates' courts[203] and the pragmatic view that men's second family responsibilities should be recognised.[204] The substantive basis for the magistrates' maintenance jurisdiction was finally overhauled by legislation in 1978,[205] with the underlying policy goal of harmonising the law administered in the magistrates' courts with the post-1969 divorce law operated by the higher courts.[206] Given this relatively modest objective, the statutory changes were equally limited in scope—the grounds on which relief could be obtained were rationalised,[207] broad guidelines on the exercise of the court's discretion, akin to those in the divorce jurisdiction, were introduced and magistrates' courts were given the power to

---

[199] Finance Act 1988, ss 36–40.

[200] Tax relief was highly regressive in at least three senses. First, it only benefited taxpayers. Secondly, it provided the most support to higher rate tax payers. Finally, it applied only to child maintenance payments enforceable through private law; no relief was available where the father paid maintenance as a result of a public law order under SBA 1976, s 18: *McBurnie (HM Inspector of Taxes) v Tacey* [1984] FLR 730.

[201] Cretney, n 42 above, at 449. The Matrimonial Proceedings (Magistrates' Courts) Act 1960 increased the weekly amounts for spousal and child maintenance (from £5 to £7 10s a week and from £1 10s to £2 10s respectively; the latter increase was also applied to orders made in affiliation and guardianship proceedings), as well as empowering the courts to make maintenance orders in respect of a 'child of the family'. Orders for these maximum amounts (eg as in *Kershaw v Kershaw* [1966] P 13) were very much the exception rather than the rule: see McGregor *et al*, n 105 above, at 81.

[202] Thus magistrates' courts were directed to make such orders as they considered 'reasonable in all the circumstances of the case', Matrimonial Proceedings (Magistrates' Courts) Act 1960, s 2.

[203] Cretney, n 42 above, at 451–52; see further Smart, n 141 above, ch 9.

[204] WE Cavanagh, 'The Broken Home and Illegitimacy' (1966–67) 9 *Journal of Society of Public Teachers of Law* 232.

[205] The 1978 Act implemented the recommendations of the Law Commission in *Report on Matrimonial Proceedings in Magistrates' Courts* (Law Com No 77, 1976).

[206] Cretney, n 42 above, at 471.

[207] DPMCA 1978, s 1 sets out three grounds for making an order: failure to provide reasonable maintenance; desertion; and behaviour such that the applicant cannot reasonably be expected to live with the respondent.

make small lump sum orders.[208] The 1978 Act remains in force today, but the jurisdiction appears to be little used;[209] in any event, in most (but not all) cases the courts' role has been supplanted by the Child Support Agency.[210]

Secondly, financial support might be claimed in magistrates' courts through guardianship proceedings. For most of this period only the parents of legitimate children could avail themselves of this jurisdiction.[211] Although there was no need for the applicant to prove any matrimonial fault on the part of the other parent, an order for custody was essentially a prerequisite to a financial order.[212] In practice the weaknesses of the magistrates' domestic or matrimonial jurisdiction were mirrored in guardianship proceedings, whatever the technical differences between the two jurisdictions.

Thirdly, where the parents were not married to each other, the former bastardy jurisdiction lingered on under the guise of affiliation proceedings,[213] but again with little change to the substantive law for most of the twentieth century.[214] This was arguably the one area of law in which illegitimate children encountered 'the most serious discrimination'.[215] Affiliation proceedings were unsatisfactory in four principal respects.[216] First, reflecting their history, affiliation proceedings were widely regarded as 'humiliating and distressing'[217] for those concerned, given that they were 'tainted with the aura of "criminality"'.[218] Secondly, applications were subject to a series of restrictive conditions,[219] generating some notoriously arcane case law.[220] Thirdly, the court's powers on making orders were severely limited.[221] Finally, such orders as were made were typically for very low amounts,

[208] *Ibid*, s 2; originally subject to a £500 limit, now £1,000.

[209] Douglas n 68 above, at 74. On the absence of adequate (or indeed any) statistics, see Cretney, n 42 above, at 472–3.

[210] CSA 1991, s 8: see further ch 7 below. Of course, orders may still be made under the 1978 Act in respect of spousal support or for children not subject to the 1991 Act (eg 'children of the family' rather than biological children).

[211] Guardianship of Minors Act 1971, ss 9(2) and 14(2); this only changed when the FLRA 1987 came into force.

[212] Although, perversely, in the infrequent cases where it was relevant, the father awarded custody of a minor child could not obtain a maintenance order against the mother, given the wording of the original Guardianship of Minors Act 1971, s 9(2).

[213] The Affiliation Proceedings Act 1957 consolidated legislation going back to the Poor Law Amendment Act 1844.

[214] See Cretney, n 42 above, at 556–60 on the history of affiliation proceedings.

[215] Law Commission, n 80 above, at para 3.23.

[216] See further V Wimperis, *The Unmarried Mother and Her Child* (George Allen & Unwin Ld, London, 1960), ch 6.

[217] Law Commission, n 80 above, at para 6.1.

[218] *Ibid*, at para 3.23. Some appeals even went to the Crown Court: see eg *R v Hereford City Justices* [1982] 1 WLR 1252.

[219] An application could only be brought by a mother, who had to be a 'single woman'; her evidence had to be corroborated; and the application had to be brought within three years of the child's birth, subject to certain exceptions.

[220] eg did the gift of a jumper and trousers constitute the payment of maintenance for a child?—see *Willett v Wells* [1985] FLR 514 (in short, yes). Similarly, and counter-intuitively, a 'single woman' could be a married woman: see Law Commission, n 80 above, at paras 6.23–6.24.

[221] There was no power to make secured orders or property adjustment orders; moreover lump sum orders (limited to £500) only became available in 1978.

rarely varied and frequently fell into arrears, arguably even more so than in the domestic and guardianship jurisdictions.[222] As we have seen, this ancient jurisdiction was finally abolished by the Family Law Reform Act 1987.[223]

So far as the collection and enforcement of maintenance (and affiliation) payments ordered by the justices were concerned, a series of modest changes were made over the years. For example, in 1949 justices' clerks were charged with the formal duty of acting as collecting officers and instituting enforcement proceedings in cases of arrears, but practice was at best patchy.[224] More significantly, the Maintenance Orders Act 1958 provided for Divorce Court maintenance orders to be registered (and both varied and enforced) in magistrates' courts. This amounted to an official recognition that 'the magistrates' courts had become the usual form for dealing with default in the making of orders for periodical payments'.[225] The 1958 Act also enabled the courts to make attachment of earnings orders where payments under maintenance or affiliation orders were in arrears. Subsequent official reports revealed that there were a number of practical problems which limited the effectiveness of this enforcement tool.[226]

Benefits and Child Maintenance in the 1980s

This chapter has so far charted how the means-tested benefit system and the private law of maintenance treated the child support obligation in the post-war era. The purpose of this section, by way of drawing these threads together, is to focus on the interplay between the public and private law of child support in the two decades leading up to the enactment of the Child Support Act 1991. In particular, when dealing with individual entitlements, how did the social security system regard the payment of maintenance and, conversely, how did the court system view the actual or potential receipt of benefits by a party to a maintenance application?

So far as the means-tested benefits system was concerned, the position was, on one level at least, straightforward.[227] In crude terms the purpose of such benefits was to provide a basic subsistence income. The minimum income which a person

---

[222] McGregor *et al*, n 105 above, ch 11. The Affiliation Proceedings Act 1957, as originally enacted, contained no guidance at all as to how the magistrates' court should exercise its powers; statutory guidelines were eventually inserted by Domestic Proceedings and Magistrates' Courts Act 1978.

[223] p 93 above.

[224] Cretney, n 42 above, at 454.

[225] *Ibid*, at 455. This was particularly important as it enabled divorced women on national assistance (and later supplementary benefit or income support) to have their court orders 'signed over' to the benefit authorities via the diversion procedure.

[226] Cretney, n 42 above, at 458; see eg *Report of the Committee on the Enforcement of Judgment Debts* (Cmnd 3909, 1969) at paras 594–601.

[227] The rules governing the specific treatment of payments received by claimants from liable relatives were anything but straightforward. See Income Support (General) Regulations 1987 (SI 1987/1967) Chapter VII and, for some of the complexities involved, *Bolstridge v Chief Adjudication Officer* [1993] 2 FLR 657.

needed was calculated according to prescribed rates, depending on such factors as their age, their status (single, member of a couple, etc) and the number of dependants in their household.[228] In broad terms, any other sources of income received by the household were then taken into account and set against that statutory minimum, unless they were either fully or partially 'disregarded', to use the lexicon of social security law. Payments of supplementary benefit, and later income support, filled the gap between the individual's income as assessed under these rules and that person's prescribed minimum income requirement. Most forms of income—including part-time earnings, non-means-tested benefits and maintenance—were taken into account.[229] But whereas part-time earnings have traditionally been subject to a modest disregard, in order to provide some work incentives, maintenance was taken into account in full.[230] The consequence was that every pound received in maintenance meant a pound less by way of supplementary benefit or income support.[231] In short, the lone parent on welfare saw no financial benefit even if maintenance was in payment. Inevitably, this provided little incentive for parents in receipt of means-tested benefits either to pursue the issue of child maintenance or to assist the benefit authorities in doing so. Moreover, the operation of the diversion procedure meant that most benefit claimants simply had no knowledge as to whether or not maintenance was actually in payment in their case.

Viewing the matter from the other way round, how (if at all) did the courts take account of the fact that the beneficiary of a maintenance order was in receipt of benefits, or might be eligible for such benefits? In a series of cases in the late 1960s and early 1970s, the higher courts articulated two doctrines for the guidance of magistrates' courts.[232] First, and as a matter of principle, the court should ignore the fact of the wife's entitlement to benefit, as otherwise the husband would be able 'to throw on to social security the burden which he ought himself to bear'.[233] Secondly, however, and more pragmatically, the court should 'not make such an order as would bring the husband below subsistence level'.[234] As to that latter issue, in broad terms 'subsistence level' was understood to mean the basic supplementary benefit rates, without the more generous leeway allowed by the liable

---

[228] The details of this calculation obviously differed as between supplementary benefit and income support, but the underlying idea remained the same.

[229] Indeed, the law goes further than this: the general rule is that capital payments from liable relatives are almost always commuted into periodical payments for benefit purposes: see n 227 above.

[230] The NAB used to operate a disregard for child maintenance: see n 125 above.

[231] Likewise for family income supplement and family credit during the 1980s. However, a maintenance disregard for family credit (£15 p/w) was introduced in April 1992 and maintenance payments were wholly disregarded from October 1999, when family credit was replaced by working families' tax credit (WFTC), itself now superseded by working tax credit and CTC.

[232] The extent to which magistrates' courts actually applied these principles in practice is discussed by Smart, n 141 above, ch 9.

[233] *Barnes v Barnes* [1972] 1 WLR 1381 at 1386, CA, *per* Russell LJ; see to similar effect *Ashley v Ashley* [1968] P 582 and, rather later, *Peacock v Peacock* [1984] FLR 263.

[234] *Ashley v Ashley* [1968] P 582 at 591 *per* Sir Jocelyn Simon P.

relative formula.[235] The awkward question then arose as to how exactly one assessed the husband's notional supplementary benefit needs, in particular in those cases in which he had acquired new dependants. The courts acknowledged that it was unhelpful to seek to differentiate between 'legal' and 'moral' obligations of support to first and second families,[236] but were much less clear as to what weight should be attached to any second family responsibilities. Rather unhelpfully, the Family Division ruled that a 'mistress's' (moral) claim 'must be taken into account for whatever weight it is held to bear'.[237] At the same time, a green light was given to justices making modest orders on applications for maintenance by an appeal to realism: 'it is little use ordering a man to pay a sum which is beyond his capacity, or on which he will in all probability default'.[238]

As we have seen, the post-1971 legislation vested the higher courts with a very broad discretion in weighing relevant considerations when making a financial order on divorce. Indeed, Parliament's failure to explain whether or not a divorcing parent's benefit entitlement was a relevant 'financial resource' to be considered in determining ancillary relief applications resulted in uncertainty in the courts. In *Barnes v Barnes*,[239] one of the first decisions under the new regime, the Court of Appeal held that, as a general rule, the court should seek to arrive at a 'fair figure' without regard to any benefits that might be payable. However, in cases of 'modest' means, the Court of Appeal held that it was proper to have regard to the fact that social security benefits were available to the wife and children, so as 'to avoid making such an order as would be financially crippling to the husband'.[240] In effect, 'the existence of such benefits enables the court in effect to deal with a larger purse than would otherwise be available'.[241]

In this way the Court of Appeal in *Barnes v Barnes* sought to apply the two doctrines derived from the existing case law on the exercise of the magistrates' maintenance jurisdiction in the context of ancillary relief on divorce. The difficulty with this approach was that like was not being compared with like. In the magistrates' courts, justices were necessarily dealing with subsisting (albeit fractured) marriages, in which the parties owed each other a duty of support, as a matter of both public and private law. In this context there was a strong public interest in ensuring that husbands did not transfer their liabilities to the tax-payer.[242] On divorce,

---

[235] *Shallow v Shallow* [1979] Fam 1, CA; however, SBC rates were not conclusive: *Billington v Billington* [1974] Fam 24 and *Freeman v Swatridge* [1984] FLR 762. On the liable relative formula, see p 100 above and M Hayes 'Supplementary Benefit and Financial Provision Orders' [1978–79] *Journal of Social Welfare Law* 216 at 219–21.

[236] *Roberts v Roberts* [1970] P 1 at 7 *per* Rees J; see, to similar effect in the magistrates' jurisdiction, *Blower v Blower* [1986] 1 FLR 292.

[237] *Roberts v Roberts*, n 236 above, at 10.

[238] *Ibid*, at 10.

[239] [1972] 1 WLR 1381.

[240] *Ibid*, at 1384 *per* Edmund Davies LJ.

[241] *Ibid*, at 1386 *per* Russell LJ, whose judgment, whilst purporting to reaffirm the case law discussed above, is hedged with the qualification that 'social security benefits will provide sufficient addition to his contribution to the wife and children, producing a proper standard of living for them'.

[242] Not least in view of the risk of fraud caused by collusive desertion.

however, the marriage was at an end—and with it the public law obligation on the adults to maintain each other disappeared, although their legal responsibility to support their children survived. The question then was what weight the county courts would attach to the availability of welfare benefits when assessing the continuing and exclusively private law obligation to support a former spouse.

Practice in the county courts varied; some registrars, as a matter of principle, ignored the fact that social security benefits were available to lone parents; others took a more pragmatic stance.[243] As one registrar in the latter camp memorably put it, whilst describing the difficulty of making the husband pay, 'His bread is buttered on the side of the woman he is sleeping with'.[244] These differences reflected the division of opinion in the appellate courts. The trend of the case law during the 1970s tended to adopt the former philosophy,[245] whilst the 1980s saw a shift towards the latter approach.[246] In one sense there was little new in the courts seeking refuge in realism; in evidence to the Morton Commission in 1952, Hodson LJ had pointed out that in cases involving men on modest wages 'there is simply not enough money to go round'.[247] In effect, in the absence of the failure to implement the Finer Report, the courts increasingly gave effect to the view that 'if the community permits divorce it must be prepared to meet the inevitable consequences of divorce'.[248] In practice this meant that the parties' benefit entitlements were regarded as part and parcel of the pot to be divided on divorce.[249]

The courts' pragmatic approach to divorce cases involving parties on low incomes was reinforced by the 1984 amendments to the law governing ancillary relief applications. The courts gradually, albeit implicitly, acknowledged that there was an irreconcilable conflict between the two guiding principles established in the early case law from the magistrates' jurisdiction. In low income cases the courts could not *both* ignore the wife's actual or potential benefit entitlement *and* strive to avoid making an order which would bring the husband below subsistence level. Faced with that dilemma, and given the 'clean break' philosophy, the courts prioritised the latter objective over the former. Thus in *Ashley v Blackman*,[250] in which both parties were on low incomes, the court agreed some 16 years after the

[243] See Eekelaar, n 195 above, ch 5 and Barrington Baker *et al*, n 139 above, at paras 2.3–2.7.

[244] *Ibid*, at para 2.5.

[245] See eg *Tovey v Tovey* (1978) 8 Fam Law 80, CA; *Shallow v Shallow* [1979] Fam 1, CA, and *Clarke v Clarke* (1979) 9 Fam Law 15.

[246] The general approach in later cases was to regard all social security benefits as being financial resources within what was then MCA 1973, s 25(1): see eg *Stockford v Stockford* (1982) 3 FLR 58 and *Walker v Walker* (1983) 4 FLR 44. However, the fact that a mother on benefit saw no personal advantage from a maintenance order could not justify the court making no order at all: *Peacock v Peacock* [1984] FLR 263.

[247] Morton Commission, *Minutes of Evidence* (HMSO, 1953) at 772 (30th day, 18 & 19 November 1952).

[248] McGregor, n 167 above, at 198.

[249] Thus a mother's one parent benefit was to be taken into account as a 'financial resource' (*Stockford v Stockford* and *Walker v Walker*, both n 246 above, disapproving *Moon v Moon* (1980) 1 FLR 115). However, attendance allowance and mobility allowance (now disability living allowance) paid to a man's second wife were excluded from consideration: *Claxton v Claxton* (1982) 3 FLR 415.

[250] [1988] Fam 85.

parties' divorce that the ex-husband should no longer be required to pay mainte-nance to his former wife (which gave her no financial advantage as she was in receipt of benefit). This was, the court said, 'a classic instance for applying the clean break objective'.[251] This conclusion appeared to rest on two considerations. The first revolved around the intrinsic merits of this particular husband's case.[252] In this context the court's confidence in its ability to exercise its discretion appro-priately was clear:

> The devious or feckless husband will be prevented from throwing his proper mainten-ance obligations on the state. The genuine struggler, on the other hand, will be spared the burden of having to pay to his former spouse indefinitely the last few pounds that separate him from total penury.[253]

The second factor was the desirability of bringing a degree of closure to the par-ties' former relationship:

> No human society could tolerate, even in the interests of saving its public purse, the prospect of a divorced couple of acutely limited means remaining manacled to each other indefinitely by the necessity to return at regular intervals to court for no other purposes than to thrash out at public expense the precise figure which the one shall pay the other, not for any benefit to either of them, but solely for the relief of the tax-paying section of the community to which neither of them has sufficient means to belong.[254]

The issue in *Ashley v Blackman* concerned spousal rather than child mainten-ance; but the same approach was applied shortly afterwards by the Court of Appeal in the context of support for children in *Delaney v Delaney*.[255] Here the parties had only just been divorced, but the combination of the limited means of both parties and the fact that the wife could claim family credit to top up her earnings per-suaded the court to impose a 'virtual' clean break by reducing child maintenance payments to a purely nominal amount.[256] Whilst Ward J deprecated 'any notion that a former husband and extant father may sloth off the tight skin of familial responsibility and may slither into and lose himself in the greener grass on the other side', the court had to accept that 'among the realities of life is that there is life after divorce'.[257] In summary, the demands of individualised justice for fathers

---

[251] *Ibid*, at 92 *per* Waite J.

[252] The father had cared for both children throughout virtually all the post-divorce period, given the seriousness of the wife's mental health problems. There is no suggestion that the wife, who was in receipt of disability benefits, was ever required to pay child maintenance.

[253] [1988] Fam 85 at 92.

[254] *Ibid*, at 92–93.

[255] [1990] 2 FLR 457.

[256] The county court had made an order that the ex-husband pay £10 p/w for each of his 3 children (and 5p a year to his ex-wife); the CA reduced the orders for children to a nominal 5p p/a (on the mean-ing of a 'nominal order', see *Freeman v Swatridge* [1984] FLR 762: 50p p/w—as opposed to per annum—*not* nominal).

[257] [1990] 2 FLR 457 at 461. See also Ward LJ's entertaining footnote to *R (Kehoe) v Secretary of State for Work and Pensions* [2004] EWCA Civ 225, [2004] 1 QB 1378, CA, admitting to being 'the villain in the piece' for the decision in *Delaney*, which was said ('I like to think only apocryphally') to have aroused Mrs Thatcher's fury: *ibid*, at para 18.

establishing new families—and so avoiding making orders which would be 'financially crippling to the husband'[258]—trumped both the claims of the mother[259] and the children,[260] as well as the less visible interests of the public purse. The fact that the father still owed a public law duty to maintain his children (albeit not his ex-wife) was to no avail. To use the terminology of *Ashley v Blackman*, the father in *Delaney v Delaney* was a 'genuine struggler' who deserved a (clean) break,[261] reflecting the extent to which the language of the fathers' rights lobby, so influential in the campaign leading up to the 1984 amendments, had been internalised by the courts by the end of that decade.

Conclusion

The increase in the number of lone parents during the second half of the twentieth century was the result of a number of social and demographic developments. At the same time, the composition of the lone parent population altered as widowhood was overtaken by divorce, separation and unmarried parenthood as contributory factors. At the outset of the national assistance scheme in 1948, relatively few single women with dependent children were reliant on the main means-tested benefit. Over the following four decades, and especially during the 1980s, lone parents became increasingly reliant on benefits—and so an issue which was largely invisible in 1948 had become a matter of pressing political concern by 1988. Throughout this same period there was effectively no change whatsoever in the legal framework governing the recovery of benefit expenditure from liable relatives—a modified version of the traditional poor law rules. There were, however, a number of changes in official practice over these years. For example, having barely used its statutory powers to bring civil proceedings for three decades, the Department changed tack in the mid-1970s, only for such direct enforcement activity to tail off again after the early 1980s as local offices sought to cope with other pressures on the benefits system. Similarly, although the pattern of activity was rather more uneven, criminal prosecutions for failure to maintain became a more significant feature of official practice,[262] at least until the early 1980s, after

---

[258] [1990] 2 FLR 457 at 462.

[259] Whilst the mother was 'a hard working lady to whom all credit must be given' (*ibid*, at 458)—she was struggling to support herself and three children on a sales assistant's earnings and income from a part-time evening job and child benefit—the main focus was the father's financial difficulties, although on any basis his financial situation was less pressing.

[260] Contrast the outcome in *Delaney* with Watkins LJ's comment six years earlier (and shortly before MFPA 1984 came into effect): 'I doubt very much whether the doctrine of clean break, so called, can ever apply to applications for periodical payments in respect of children. Their legal rights to be maintained by their father can neither be bought nor compromised away', *Griffiths v Griffiths* [1984] FLR 662, CA, at 671.

[261] Thus, even though the husband had actually been paying £10 p/w in child maintenance, as against £30 p/w actually ordered, Nourse LJ concluded that 'he cannot reasonably afford it', [1990] 2 FLR 457 at 463.

[262] And especially in Scotland; see p 97 above.

which point the Department effectively abandoned all use of penal proceedings. These changes in civil and criminal enforcement policy appear to have had little, if any, impact in terms of the proportion of social security expenditure caused by relationship breakdown which was recovered from liable relatives. The National Assistance Board, operating during a period of relative social stability, was perhaps the most successful agency (a relative term in this context), recovering from liable relatives about 8 per cent of the gross benefit costs of supporting separated families.[263] The official recovery rate fell to 6 per cent under the supplementary benefit regime and even lower in the mid to late 1980s.

By the 1980s both the benefits system and the courts had arrived at a pragmatic consensus on how to deal with the consequences of family breakdown. In practice the Department expected men to support their second families, not least through the operation of the cohabitation rule and the allowance for second families in the liable relative formula. Throughout the post-war period it made at best half-hearted attempts to make them pay a contribution towards the maintenance of their first family. The courts took rather longer to arrive at the same position, not least because of the primacy attached to the marriage vows, as a result of which there was no parallel to the cohabitation rule in private law. However, the divorce courts, encouraged by legislative developments—and especially the 1984 Act—increasingly saw their role as one of providing for the housing needs of the wife and children whilst otherwise facilitating a financial clean break between the parents. Magistrates' courts, predominantly dealing with families on low incomes, had always historically tended to make modest orders for child maintenance. Either way, arguably even less priority was attached to periodical payments for child support in 1988 than had been the case 40 years earlier. It was against this unpromising background that Mrs Thatcher brought forward her radical plans for a Child Support Agency.

---

[263] As well as persuading liable relatives to make contributions direct to their former families amounting to some 10% of overall costs.

5

The Child Support Act 1991 and the Agency's Troubled Early Years

Introduction

This chapter provides an overview of the genesis of the Child Support Act 1991 and the troubled early years of the Child Support Agency in the United Kingdom. It also summarises the principal changes to the legislative structure for child support, culminating in the decision to abandon the complex formula underpinning the original scheme and to introduce a new and purportedly streamlined system with effect from 3 March 2003, under the reforms instituted by the Child Support, Pensions and Social Security Act (CSPSSA) 2000. The chapter also examines the difficulties encountered by the Agency in managing the transition from the old to the new child support schemes, including the problematic 'conversion' and 'migration' of its existing caseload.

The Gestation of the Child Support Act 1991

The public gestation period of the Child Support Act 1991 was remarkably short. In a speech in January 1990 Margaret Thatcher declared that 'no father should be able to escape from his responsibility' and made it clear that the government was examining how to improve arrangements for the recovery of maintenance.[1] Thereafter matters moved swiftly. In May 1990 the Permanent Secretary at the DSS confirmed that a ministerial review was reviewing the whole question of maintenance. He also conceded that any decision to give the Department a central role would have 'considerable resource consequences' and would need 'careful study' before such a strategy was agreed.[2] Yet just two months later the Prime Minister, with the declaration that 'parenthood is for life', announced the government's intention to establish a Child Support Agency with the task of assessing maintenance according to a

---

[1] National Children's Homes Lecture, 17 January 1990.
[2] House of Commons (HC) Committee of Public Accounts, *Department of Social Security: Support for Lone Parent Families*, Thirty-eighth Report (HC 429, Session 1989–90) Minutes of Evidence at 8–9 (16 May 1990).

standard administrative formula.[3] In her memoirs she later recalled that she 'was appalled by the way in which men fathered a child and then absconded, leaving the single mother—and the tax payer—to foot the bill for their irresponsibility and condemning the child to a lower standard of living'.[4] This attitude was to set the tone for much of the public debate that followed. A White Paper with the ringing title *Children Come First* appeared that autumn[5] and almost exactly nine months later, on 25 July 1991, the Child Support Act received the Royal Assent.[6]

Privately, however, the legislation had been rather longer in preparation. Towards the end of 1986 David Willetts's final act as a member of staff in the Downing Street Policy Unit had been to write a paper highlighting the growth in the number of lone parents and commending the child support enforcement programmes he had seen on a visit to the United States.[7] In the late 1980s John Moore, then Secretary of State for Social Services,[8] argued that the welfare state had spawned a culture of dependency.[9] Moore's review of social security provision for lone parents was overtaken by his own departure from office in July 1989.[10] Yet the Conservative Government's preoccupation with reducing welfare dependency and reaffirming traditional family values was by now well-established,[11] reflected in the Prime Minister's public lectures in January and July 1990. In this way, driven by Mrs Thatcher, what had started as 'an intermittent interest in child support had become a concentrated policy activity by the beginning of the 1990s'.[12]

The 1990 White Paper's assessment of the system then in place for child maintenance was that it was 'unnecessarily fragmented, uncertain in its results, slow and ineffective'.[13] The headline figures were compelling: only 30 per cent of lone mothers and 3 per cent of lone fathers regularly received child maintenance; over 750,000 lone parents (some 70 per cent of the total) relied on income support; and the proportion of lone parents on income support who received child maintenance payments had dropped from 50 per cent in 1979 to just 23 per cent in 1989.[14]

---

[3] Pankhurst Lecture, 18 July 1990.

[4] M Thatcher, *The Downing Street years* (Harper Collins, London, 1995) at 630.

[5] DSS, *Children Come First: The Government's Proposals on the Maintenance of Children* (Cm 1264-I and II, October 1990).

[6] The first published version of the Child Support Bill had appeared (with a nice sense of irony) on Valentine's Day 1991: Child Support Bill, HL Bill 29 (14 February 1991).

[7] N Timmins, *The Five Giants: A Biography of the Welfare State* (Harper Collins, London, revised edn, 2001) at 450.

[8] Moore also became the first Secretary of State for Social Security after the old DHSS was divided into the Department of Health and DSS in July 1988.

[9] An idea adopted from the work of Charles Murray: see *Losing Ground: American Social Policy 1950–1980* (Basic Books, New York, 1984).

[10] *The Guardian* reported that 'Moore is planning to crack down on single-parent state benefits', 'Moore urged to blood test errant fathers' (14 May 1989).

[11] See generally M Maclean, 'Child Support in the UK: Making the Move from Court to Agency' (1994) 31 *Houston Law Review* 515 and 'The Making of the Child Support Act of 1991: Policy Making at the Intersection of Law and Social Policy' (1994) 21 *Journal of Law and Society* 505.

[12] H Barnes, P Day and N Cronin, *Trial and error: a review of UK child support policy* (FPSC Occasional paper 24, London, 1998) at 24.

[13] White Paper, n 5 above, vol I at i.

[14] *Ibid*, at para 1.5.

For lone parents as a whole, the most important sources of income were income support (45 per cent), earnings (22 per cent) and child benefit (14 per cent), with maintenance accounting for just 7 per cent of total income.[15] The White Paper identified a number of problems with the current arrangements—the division of responsibilities between the (then) DHSS local offices and the courts; the reliance on discretion, resulting in inconsistent levels of awards; delays in making awards; the lack of automatic reviews; the prevalence of arrears and problems with enforcement. This account was supported by Volume II of the White Paper, which summarised the findings of recent surveys. The emphasis, however, was very much on the undeniably poor outcomes experienced under these maintenance arrangements, which had changed little since the time of the Finer Report.[16] The White Paper singularly failed to explore some of the wider factors that contributed to low and inconsistent awards—such as the reduction in staffing levels for DHSS liable relative work.[17] There was also little discussion of the capacity of non-resident parents to afford to pay more by way of maintenance.[18]

Introducing the White Paper to the House of Commons, Tony Newton—then the Secretary of State for Social Security—emphasised three central elements to the Government's proposals. The first was the use of 'a clear formula for the assessment of maintenance, which can be applied administratively rather than through the courts'.[19] The second was the creation of a 'purpose-built agency' to undertake such assessments. The third comprised reforms to the benefits system designed to encourage lone parents to go out to work. Only the first of these three elements in the package required primary legislation. The Child Support Act 1991, although it provided the statutory basis for the formula, made no mention of the Child Support Agency, which was established as a 'Next Steps' agency, effectively by executive edict.

The social security reforms—making more lone parents eligible for the in-work benefit, family credit, by reducing the entitlement threshold from 24 to 16 hours work a week, and introducing a maintenance disregard of £15 a week for family credit and housing benefit claimants—were brought in by changes to the regulations. Responding to the minister's statement, Michael Meacher reaffirmed the Labour Party's support for the principle of parental responsibility for child maintenance.[20] However, he criticised the apparent emphasis on saving public expenditure rather than tackling child poverty. In a slogan that was to haunt the early

---

[15] J Bradshaw and J Millar, *Lone Parent Families in the UK* (DSS Research Report 6, London, 1991) at 31.

[16] Finer Committee, *Report of the Committee on One-Parent Families* (Cmnd 5629, 1974).

[17] See ch 4 above. Between April and December 1990 only 62% of staff days allocated to liable relative work were actually devoted to that purpose: HC Social Security Committee, *Changes in Maintenance Arrangements, Third Report* (HC 277-II, Session 1990–91) at para 19.

[18] White Paper, n 5 above, vol I at 1.5; see also vol II, paras 3.3.4 and 3.3.5 and Bradshaw and Millar, n 15 above, at 83–5.

[19] *Hansard* HC Debates vol 178 col 729 (29 October 1990).

[20] Labour's own plans shared some common themes with those of the Government: 'Meacher seeks to make all fathers pay maintenance', *The Times* (30 December 1989).

years of the Agency, he argued that readers could be forgiven for thinking that the White Paper should have been entitled 'The Treasury Comes First'.[21] The fiscal objectives of the Act were evident in the fact that parents with care on income support were effectively required to apply for child support and so were denied the choice of opting out which was available to those not on benefit (or at least those not on benefit who could agree child support with their ex-partner).[22] This perception was given greater force by the Government's adamant refusal to countenance any form of maintenance disregard for lone parents in receipt of income support. Indeed, ministers made it clear that the underlying policy was to reverse 'the inadvertent nationalization of fatherhood' that had taken place.[23] In this way the overriding objective of child support policy was characterised as being 'to substitute private transfers for public transfers, rather than augment family income for impoverished lone-parent families'.[24] In fact, however, it seems that the moral agenda was at least as important as financial considerations—Treasury pressure was described by key players as 'about the norm for public policy-making at the time'.[25] Nevertheless, from a feminist perspective, the clear message was that 'economic security for women and children is gained by attachment to a man'.[26] Certainly the failure to prioritise the role of child support as part of a wider strategy to tackle child poverty was to prove highly damaging to public perceptions of the new scheme.

The decision not to issue a Green Paper was itself indicative of the strength of the Government's resolve to push ahead with reform: 'the public response was assumed rather than tested'.[27] According to the White Paper, while 'the main shape of the new system is decided . . . some of the detail is still under consideration'.[28] Similarly, the White Paper's public consultation period of just six weeks demonstrated that the child support juggernaut was well under way. No summary of the responses to this process was ever published, although it appears that views on the proposed formula 'ranged from scepticism to outright opposition'.[29] The

---

[21] *Hansard* HC Debates vol 178 col 732 (29 October 1990). This became a regular refrain amongst critics, and was echoed in one of the first studies of the new scheme: A Garnham and E Knights, *Putting the Treasury First: The truth about child support* (CPAG, Poverty Publication 88, London 1994).

[22] R Boden and M Childs, 'Paying for Procreation: Child Support Arrangements in the UK' (1996) IV *Feminist Legal Studies* 131 at 150 and contrast CSA 1991 ss 4 and 6; see ch 9 below.

[23] Peter Lilley MP, Secretary of State for Social Security, 6 March 1993, quoted in H Land, 'Reversing "the inadvertent nationalization of fatherhood": The British Child Support Act 1991 and its consequences for men, women and children' (1994) 47 *International Social Security Review* 91 at 92.

[24] JJ Rodger, *Family Life and Social Control* (Macmillan, Basingstoke, 1995) at 126. See further, on the reconstruction of fatherhood, R Collier, *Masculinity, law and the family* (Routledge, London, 1995) and 'In Search of the "Good Father": Law, Family Practices and the Normative Reconstruction of Parenthood' in J Dewar and S Parker (eds), *Family Law: Processes, Practices and Pressures* (Hart Publishing, Oxford, 2003), ch 11.

[25] Barnes *et al*, n 12 above, at 25.

[26] A Diduck, 'The Unmodified Family: The Child Support Act and the Construction of Legal Subjects' (1995) 22 *Journal of Law and Society* 527.

[27] C Harlow, 'Accountability, New Public Management, and the Problems of the Child Support Agency' (1999) 26 *Journal of Law and Society* 150 at 158.

[28] White Paper, n 5 above, vol I at iii.

[29] G Davis, N Wikeley and R Young, *Child Support in Action* (Hart Publishing, Oxford, 1998) at 8–9.

objections of the county court judiciary—'these proposals will cause poverty and bitterness among many people who do not deserve it'[30]—appear to have been dismissed as special pleading by vested interests. Indeed, the whole process reflected 'a government largely impervious to constructive criticism',[31] resulting in 'probably one of the worst examples of social policy making in modern history'.[32] Yet the passage of the Child Support Act 1991 itself was swift and relatively trouble-free; much of the Parliamentary time was devoted to processing official amendments to the Bill, rather than debating the merits of the proposals. The cross-party consensus in favour of the Bill was reflected in the fact that, unusually, there was no vote on its Third Reading in the House of Commons.[33] Concerted opposition was evident only in the House of Lords, with peers expressing particular concern at the breadth of the powers to be vested in the new agency.[34] The absence of effective consultation on the White Paper was replicated as the Act was brought into force—in November 1991 the Government issued draft child support regulations with a six-week deadline for comments. Again, these regulations were subject to inadequate scrutiny in Parliament,[35] although one peer warned that they represented 'a bureaucrat's dream and a citizen's nightmare'.[36]

The Original Formula

The original child support formula comprised four key elements: the *maintenance requirement*; the respective parents' *assessable incomes*; the *deduction rate*; the absent parent's *protected income*.[37]

First, the *maintenance requirement*, described as the 'maintenance bill' in the White Paper, represented a figure 'which is to be taken as the minimum amount necessary for the maintenance' of the child or children in question.[38] This amount was calculated by aggregating the income support personal allowances and premiums applicable to the parent with care and the relevant child or children, and deducting the child benefit payable. It followed that the starting point for the assessment of child support liabilities was seen in terms of the costs of supporting a family on income support, whether or not the parent with care was actually on

---

[30] Response by Association of County Court and District Registrars, cited *ibid*, at 9.

[31] Harlow, n 27 above, at 158.

[32] J Bradshaw, C Stimson, C Skinner and J Williams, *Absent fathers?* (Routledge, London, 1999) at 125.

[33] *Hansard* HC Debates vol 195 cols 571–78 (18 July 1991).

[34] The Government lost one vote on the Bill in the upper House, which had defeated the proposed benefit sanction for lone parents who failed to co-operate with the new agency, but this measure was re-inserted in the Commons: Davis *et al*, n 29 above, at 10.

[35] See *Hansard* HC Debates vol 210 cols 755–78 (30 June 1992).

[36] Davis *et al*, n 29 above, at 12, citing Lord Stoddart: *Hansard* HL Debates vol 539 col 351 (16 July 1992).

[37] For an early account, anticipating many of the problems in implementation that duly transpired, see J Eekelaar, 'Child Support—An Evaluation' [1991] Fam Law 511.

[38] Child Support Act (CSA) 1991, sch 1 para 1(1) (before amendment by CSPSSA 2000).

benefit. The justification for this approach was that benefit rates were already used as standard income measures outside the social security system (eg in assessing entitlement to legal aid) and were uprated annually.[39] The most controversial feature of the maintenance requirement was the inclusion of a sum representing the adult rate personal allowance within the income support scheme. In this way the 'maintenance bill' appeared to include a sum for the parent with care as well as the personal allowance rates for the children. While this could be justified,[40] it was soon to be attacked by fathers' rights groups as a form of disguised spousal maintenance, applicable even in cases in which the child's parents had not been married to each other.[41]

Secondly, a parent's *assessable income* was calculated by deducting that individual's 'exempt income' from his or her 'net income'. Net income meant the person's gross weekly income from virtually all sources less tax, national insurance and half of any private pension contributions. The parent's exempt income comprised the adult single person's income support allowance, with added elements for natural and adopted children living with them, along with income support premiums (if applicable) and 'reasonable housing costs'. The underlying idea was that the exempt income represented the first charge on each parent's total income, for their own self-support; as such, it was supposedly confined to 'essential expenditure'.[42] This was reflected in the use of basic income support allowances. As a result, the exempt income made no provision for what many perceived as necessary rather than optional outgoings, such as travel to work expenses.[43] The exempt income calculation also took no account of the presence of a new partner, the rationale being that to do so would not be putting children's interests first—'an adult would be maintained at the expense of the children'.[44] Furthermore, reflecting the primacy of biological parentage in the new scheme, the exempt income was adjusted for subsequent natural children, but not for new stepchildren.[45] On the other hand, the elasticity of the notion of 'reasonable housing costs' provided an incentive for non-resident parents to maximise their mortgage liabilities with a view to reducing their overall child support bill.[46]

---

[39] White Paper, n 5 above, vol I at para 3.3.

[40] On the basis that the parent with care had childcare responsibilities that typically limited her employment opportunities.

[41] Critics overlooked the fact that in affiliation proceedings the courts had accepted that financial support for an illegitimate child could properly include an allowance for the mother, reflecting the services she provided: *Haroutunian v Jennings* (1980) 1 FLR 62 and *Osborn v Sparks* (1982) 3 FLR 90. See also *Northrop v Northrop* [1968] P 74 on 'the close identification of interest between mother and dependent child'.

[42] White Paper, n 5 above, vol I at para 3.2.

[43] Subsequent changes to the regulations and the introduction of the departures scheme made some provision for travel to work costs.

[44] White Paper, n 5 above, vol 1 at para 3.16.

[45] *Ibid*, at para 3.19.

[46] HC Social Security Committee, *The Operation of the Child Support Act: Proposals for Change, Fifth Report* (HC 470, Session 1993–94) at para 55.

The third element of the original formula was the *deduction rate*, represented by the letter P, and gnomically defined by the 1991 Act as 'such number greater than zero but less than 1 as may be prescribed'.[47] Regulations duly gave P the value of 0.5.[48] The starting point for the application of the formula was to add together the parents' respective assessable incomes and then divide the sum by two (or multiply by P). If, as in many low income cases, the resulting figure was less than (or equal to) the maintenance requirement, then the non-resident parent's child support liability was limited to a maximum of 50 per cent of his assessable income. If, on the other hand, the outcome exceeded the maintenance requirement, then the non-resident parent's child support liability was the aggregate of the 'basic' and 'additional' elements.[49] The end result was that non-resident parents on higher incomes paid more in cash terms than those on low incomes, but less as a proportion of their assessable income. In addition, the regulations made provision for various types of special case, such as shared care—assuming that there were at least 104 overnight stays in the preceding year—and imposed a maximum cap on the amount of child support payable by high earners.[50]

Lastly, the amount of child support due under the formula was checked against the non-resident parent's *protected income*, designed to keep payers above the poverty line. The non-resident parent's protected income figure was based on the amount of income support to which his household would be entitled—at this stage, therefore, there was some limited recognition of second family responsibilities, although the 'biological determinism' underpinning the scheme meant that this was secondary to the financial priority accorded to children of the first family.[51] The protected income figure also included further elements for housing costs, council tax, an earnings disregard[52] and an additional allowance based on a proportion[53] of the difference between the parent's basic protected income and his disposable income (including the income of any new partner). To maintain work incentives, the payer's income, after the payment of child support, was not to fall below this protected income level. This safeguard was denied to non-resident parents on benefit; all parents in receipt of income support were defined as having no assessable income, but non-resident parents in this position were still required to make a fixed minimum weekly contribution to their children's support. In this way 'such a person is to be reminded of his responsibilities, even if this means reducing his benefits below subsistence level'.[54]

---

[47] CSA 1991, sch 1 para 2(1).

[48] Child Support (Maintenance Assessment and Special Cases) Regulations 1992 (SI 1992/1815), reg 5(b).

[49] This can be seen as an attempt to reflect the dual purpose of child support discussed in ch 1 above, namely to address both the child's right to basic support and the legitimate expectation to share in parental income above a given threshold.

[50] In practice, of course, this was only relevant if the parties were unable to agree a consent order.

[51] Boden and Childs, n 22 above, at 156.

[52] Initially just £8 p/w, raised to £30 p/w in February 1994.

[53] Initially 10%, increased to 15% from February 1994.

[54] M Maclean and J Eekelaar, 'Child Support: The British Solution' (1993) *International Journal of Law and the Family* 205 at 225.

The simplified account above of the original child support formula, shorn of many of its intricacies, is sufficient to demonstrate its inherent complexity. As Ward J famously remarked, the formula involved 'mathematically obtuse calculations in innumerable unintelligible Schedules to the Act'.[55] Some of its features were clear enough despite the complications. Thus, with the exception of the generous leeway given to housing costs, the formula made no provision for actual living costs, other than those allowed for in the basic benefit rates. This inevitably came as a shock to many men, especially to those who had previously had little if any exposure to the realities of either meeting the full costs of raising children or living on benefit.[56] In addition, child support liabilities were only indirectly related to the number of children for whom a parent was responsible, insofar as the age and number of children affected the calculation of the maintenance requirement at the first stage of the process. Indeed, the operation of the formula in low-income cases meant that non-resident parents paid 50 per cent of their assessable income until the maintenance requirement was met, irrespective of the number of children they had. Moreover, the opacity of the formula fuelled misunderstandings—many non-resident parents strenuously objected to disclosing the earnings of their new partners (as indeed did their partners) on the assumption that such income would be used to increase their child support liabilities. In fact, such earnings only became relevant at the protected income stage, and then only as a means of controlling child support liabilities—if the new partner lacked any independent income, this could reduce the maintenance assessment.

The Early Years of the Agency: A Difficult and Unhappy Birth

The policy decision to impose a formula did not of itself necessitate the creation of the Agency. Although the formula model had been adopted in Australia, in the United States the courts had retained jurisdiction over the assessment of child support, albeit subject to state-specific 'guidelines' (formulae) that were initially presumptive and later mandatory in their effect.[57] However, the 1990 White Paper envisaged the new formula as a discretion-free zone. Accordingly, as 'the rules will mainly require an arithmetical calculation based on the facts provided',[58] they were to be applied by an administrative agency. This solution was seen as having the added advantage of preventing the courts from being overburdened with annual reviews. Such a dual justification, with its naïve assumption that parents would readily supply the required information, simultaneously underestimated

---

[55] *Re C (A Minor) (Contribution Notice)* [1994] 1 FLR 111 at 117.

[56] See A Diduck, *Law's Families* (Lexis Nexis UK, London, 2003) at 167–68 and also J Goode, C Callender and R Lister, *Purse or Wallet?* (Policy Studies Institute, London, 1998) at 46 on the gendered nature of expenditure patterns that 'legitimated men's personal spending and defined women's collective expenditure, for example on children, as personal'.

[57] See ch 6 below.

[58] White Paper, n 5 above, vol 1 at 3.39.

the potential for non-compliance and overestimated the capacity of an agency to cope with the crushing weight of periodic reviews. Nevertheless, the Child Support Agency was duly established as a Next Steps agency within the then Department of Social Security (DSS). The Australian model, locating the agency within the Inland Revenue (now Her Majesty's Revenue and Customs, or HMRC), was not followed. At the time the principal justification for housing the Agency within the DSS was that the Department had extensive experience across its local office network of dealing with the consequences of marriage breakdown and lone parenthood, as against the Revenue's lack of familiarity with social issues and limited personal contact with taxpayers.[59] Moreover, and in contrast to Australia, most United Kingdom taxpayers, given the PAYE system, need not file an income tax return.[60]

The Agency formally started operations on 5 April 1993, although it operated the old liable relative system as a shadow agency for the preceding year.[61] The child support system itself was not subject to any pilot, although the original timetable envisaged a transitional period of four years, with the Agency becoming fully operational as from April 1997.[62] At the outset the Agency employed some 5,000 staff, half of whom were inherited from the DSS and half recruited from the private sector, and who were given just six weeks' training on making assessments.[63] Simultaneously, the Agency introduced a new IT system, the Child Support Computer System (CSCS), based on software used in Florida.[64] The Agency's lack of preparedness was also reflected in its initial and highly optimistic working assumption that maintenance assessments would be issued within 6 to 12 weeks in straightforward cases;[65] subsequently, the Agency's chief executive indicated that 26 weeks was more realistic.[66] The Agency quickly faced widespread and active resistance from non-resident parents (sometimes including organised obstructive tactics), who were faced with the prospect of higher awards, and simultaneously

[59] DSS, *Child Support: Reply by the Government to the Second and Third Reports of the Select Committee on Social Security Session 1990–91* (Cm 1691, 1991) at para 9. In retrospect the argument there that 'the tax office dealing with an employee can be at the other end of the country from the employee's residence' is hardly compelling given the Agency's organisational structure.

[60] In fact the Australian Agency was subsequently moved to the equivalent of the DSS, although it has retained strong operational links with the Australian Tax Office (ATO).

[61] Little has been written on the work of the shadow agency, but see M Speed, C Roberts and K Rudat, *Child Support Unit National Client Survey 1992* (DSS Research Report No 14, 1992).

[62] The Agency assumed responsibility for all new claims from 5 April 1993; existing benefit cases were scheduled to be taken on between April 1993 and April 1996, whilst existing private cases with court orders or written maintenance agreements were due to have access to the Agency between April 1996 and April 1997.

[63] HC Select Committee on the Parliamentary Commissioner for Administration, *The Child Support Agency Third Report* (HC 199, Session 1994–95) at para 23.

[64] Florida's IT system was designed solely for the collection of child support, whereas the United Kingdom scheme had to accommodate assessment as well.

[65] HC Social Security Committee, *The Operation of the Child Support Act, First Report, Minutes of Evidence* (HC 69, Session 1993–94) at 4.

[66] HC Social Security Committee, *The Operation of the Child Support Agency, Minutes of Evidence* (HC 781-I, Session 1994–95) at 20.

from parents with care on benefit, given the absence of any maintenance disregard in the income support scheme.[67] Combined with the complexity of the formula and the associated Byzantine administrative processes, the growing volume of cases swiftly resulted in a catastrophic administrative failure. In short, the Agency 'became a byword for bureaucratic incompetence'.[68] To take just one indicator, the error rate on maintenance assessments in the first year was in the order of 40 per cent.[69]

The early years of the Agency's operations saw repeated initiatives to try and get the Agency back on track and on top of its workload, starting in the summer of 1993 with the 'Closing the Gap' project and in the spring of the following year with the 'Recovery Plan'. The official response was the creation of a culture of constant change at both a legislative[70] and operational[71] level. The legislative changes are considered in more detail in the next section. Operationally, as the Agency fell further and further behind in coping with its caseload in this early period, managers prioritised the throughput of assessments over the quality of decision making. The original objective of having one case officer handling the assessment from the start to the end of the process proved to be unworkable and was abandoned. Instead, the Agency resorted to functionalisation, the traditional DSS conveyor-belt method of working, with each member of staff concentrating on handling one particular stage of the assessment, collection and enforcement process. As a consequence, no one individual took overall responsibility for processing an application for child support, and the Agency's clientele were often unable to speak to someone working on 'their case' when they telephoned (assuming, that is, that they got through the switchboard). The end result was a legacy of inaccurate assessments that continues to plague the system today, along with the frustration and ill-will generated amongst the Agency's clientele.

Somewhat belatedly, politicians recognised that the 1991 Act represented 'the most fundamental change in social policies for 40 years or more'[72] and that the

---

[67] According to one early small-scale study, parents with care 'felt that they knew all they needed to know once they were informed that any maintenance payable by ex-partners would be deducted pound for pound from their benefit', D Abbott, 'The Child Support Act 1991: the lives of parents with care living in Liverpool' [1996] 18 *Journal of Social Welfare and Family Law* 21 at 29. See generally K Clarke, C Glendinning and G Craig, *Losing Support: Children and the Child Support Act* (The Children's Society, London, 1994).

[68] H Davies and H Joshi, 'Who has borne the cost of Britain's children in the 1990s?' in K Vleminickx and TM Smeeding (eds), *Child Well-Being, Child Poverty and Child Policy in Modern Nations* (Policy Press, Bristol, 2001) ch 12 at 303.

[69] Central Adjudication Services, *Annual Report of the Chief Child Support Officer 1993/94* (1994) at 3–4.

[70] Eg in the first three years there were eight separate sets of legislative measures involving 62 changes to the elements within the assessment process: HC Committee of Public Accounts, *Child Support Agency: Client Funds Account 1996–97, Twenty-First Report* (HC 313, Session 1997–98) at para 12.

[71] Eg in April 1996 ministers were reported to have introduced 'no fewer than 112 changes in the past 10 months that are designed to improve the work of the Agency', *Hansard* HC Debates vol 276 col 368 *per* James Pawsey MP (24 April 1996).

[72] HC Social Security Committee, n 65 above, at para 15.

consequence for the Agency was 'a difficult and unhappy birth'.[73] Two common themes were emerging in the press coverage of the Agency's work in its initial six months. The first reflected the concerns of many middle class men who now faced much higher child maintenance liabilities under the new formula than previously,[74] and of men generally, who faced the 'culture shock . . . that money should follow blood, rather than affective ties'.[75] The second, but rather less publicised theme, was the new Agency's failure to deliver increased child maintenance payments to parents with care.[76] These two strands came together in the much-publicised revelation that an Agency directive, in the face of the tough benefits savings target imposed by ministers,[77] had instructed staff to focus their efforts on 'absent parents in work with higher-than-average earnings'. Similarly, an internal memo had reportedly advised that 'the name of the game is maximising the maintenance yield—don't waste a lot of time on non-profitable stuff',[78] reinforcing the widely held view that the Agency's sole purpose was to reduce benefit expenditure,[79] rather than to improve children's welfare. This perception was reinforced by the fact that in the overwhelming majority of cases the Agency was dealing with parents with care who were reliant on benefits.[80] Such press reports also caused considerable damage to the legitimacy of the child support scheme in the eyes of the Government's natural supporters.[81] There were, however, at least two arguable justifications for the Agency's policy. First, given its limited resources, it made obvious business sense for the Agency to focus its attention on securing additional child maintenance in a cost-effective fashion. Secondly, parents with care in cases where child maintenance was already in payment were more likely to be in work themselves, and so increased awards would

---

[73] HC Social Security Committee, *Child Support, Fifth Report* (HC 282, Session 1996–97) at para 17.

[74] A Neustatter, 'Fathers who are reduced to paupers', *The Independent on Sunday*, 19 September 1993.

[75] G Davis, 'Comments on Child Support in the UK: Making the Move from Court to Agency' (1994) 31 *Houston Law Review* 539 at 541.

[76] 'Single parents facing long wait for maintenance cash', *The Independent*, 26 July 1993.

[77] In the first year the benefit savings target was £530 million and actual savings achieved were £418 million: HC Social Security Committee, n 46 above, at para 11. The formal benefit savings target was dropped thereafter, although such savings remained 'a natural by-product' of the Agency's work: HC Social Security Committee, n 73 above, *Minutes of Evidence* at 5 (Ann Chant).

[78] 'Struggling child support agency targets better-off absent fathers', *The Guardian*, 12 September 1993, and 'Child support body targets easy money', *The Guardian*, 13 September 1993.

[79] This perception was fuelled by a series of ministerial speeches in the summer of 1993, deploring the rise in fatherless families and in particular the increase in the number of teenage lone parents: Rodger, n 24 above, at 124.

[80] In the Agency's first year 96% of the new caseload involved PWCs and children on benefit: R Hepplewhite, 'The Child Support Agency' (1994) 11 *Benefits* 2.

[81] As one Conservative MP complained: 'When we debated the Bill that became the Child Support Act 1991, we all thought that its purpose was to chase errant parents who were contributing nothing to their children's welfare; but once the Act was in operation, the priority seemed to be increasing existing payments . . . because they were the easier targets'. *Hansard* HC Debates vol 276 col 380 (24 April 1996) *per* Michael Lord MP.

directly benefit those families, rather than the Exchequer.[82] Yet these nuances were crowded out in the media outcry that engulfed the Agency.

One Conservative backbencher subsequently announced that 'we have created a monstrous bureaucracy'.[83] Members of Parliament referred many of their constituents' grievances to the Ombudsman, who in August 1994 took the unusual step of refusing to take on the investigation of any new child support complaints, unless they involved some new issue or the complainant had suffered actual financial loss. Despite these restrictions, the Agency still accounted for nearly one-third of all cases taken on for investigation by the Ombudsman in 1995.[84] In January of that year the Ombudsman issued a special report on the Agency's customer service problems.[85] These included cases of mistaken identity, inadequate procedures, incorrect or misleading advice and, of course, delays at all stages of the maintenance process.[86] These delays, resulting in many cases in substantial arrears, created 'the unavoidable impression . . . that fathers were being made to pay for the agency's inefficiency'.[87] As Wallbank has tellingly observed, non-resident fathers campaigning against the Act 'successfully portrayed themselves as the victims of an unjust and immoderate law'.[88]

In this context we may note that, within nine months of the Agency commencing operations, the House of Commons Social Security Select Committee had issued a report highlighting the concerns of non-resident parents, especially about the Agency's prioritisation of its caseload and the operation of the formula.[89] The Government responded by introducing amendments to the child support regulations in February 1994.[90] The Select Committee issued a further report in October 1994. Again, this made a series of recommendations for adjustments to the formula, designed to accommodate some of the concerns of non-resident parents, who waged

---

[82] P Bingley, E Symons and I Walker, 'Child Support, Income Support and Lone Mothers' (1994) 15 *Fiscal Studies* 81 at 83. Thus Bradshaw and Millar (n 15 above at 21) had shown that lone parents not on income support (43%) were more likely to be receiving maintenance than those on benefit (22%), and average weekly amounts were higher for the former (£33 as against £21).

[83] *Hansard* HC Debates vol 251 col 1096 (15 December 1994) *per* Sir J Wiggin MP.

[84] Parliamentary Commissioner for Administration, *Investigation of complaints against the Child Support Agency* (Third Report, Session 1995–96, HC 20) p i.

[85] Parliamentary Commissioner for Administration, *Investigation of complaints against the Child Support Agency* (Third Report, Session 1994–95, HC 135). For more general studies, see M Speed, J Crane and K Rubat, *Child Support Agency National Client Satisfaction Survey 1993* (DSS Research Report No 29, 1994), M Speed and J Seddon, *Child Support Agency National Client Satisfaction Survey 1994* (DSS Research Report No 39, 1995) and M Speed and N Kent, *Child Support Agency National Client Satisfaction Survey 1995* (DSS Research Report No 51, 1996),

[86] The Agency's decision to establish the office of Independent Case Examiner was made in response to a recommendation by the Ombudsman: see also p 407 below.

[87] Harlow, n 27 above, at 165.

[88] J Wallbank, 'The Campaign for Change of the Child Support Act 1991: Reconstituting the "Absent" Father' (1997) 6 *Social & Legal Studies* 191 at 210.

[89] HC Social Security Committee, n 65 above, at para 15. See J Eekelaar, 'Third Thoughts on Child Support' [1994] Fam Law 99.

[90] p 133 below.

a vociferous media campaign against the Agency.[91] In both reports the Committee endorsed the underlying principle of a standard formula;[92] thus the answer to the Agency's operational problems was seen as tinkering, not fundamental change.[93] In its October 1994 report the Committee debated whether more radical reform was required, involving a shift to some version of the much simpler Australasian percentage of income formula. The Conservative majority on the Committee opposed a formal recommendation to this effect, and the final report noted the disruption and delay that would be caused by such a major change.[94] The then Government adopted some of the Committee's detailed proposals with modifications to the regulations in April 1995.[95] It also went further than the Committee envisaged with the introduction of a departures scheme in the Child Support Act 1995, providing a very limited degree of flexibility to the formula to accommodate special cases. It was to take another three years, and a change in government, before politicians returned to the percentage of income model as the basis for the new formula.

The Agency's first Chief Executive, Ros Hepplewhite, who had been recruited from the voluntary sector, left in September 1994, to be replaced by Ann Chant, a DSS career civil servant.[96] The appointment of an 'insider' has been seen as an implicit recognition of the need to have a Chief Executive who shared 'an institutionalised "Whitehall" understanding of how to manage a next steps agency under the continued doctrine of ministerial responsibility'.[97] However, it was generally accepted that the Agency had successfully implemented the February 1994 adjustments (under Hepplewhite) and the April 1995 changes (under Chant) to the formula.[98] Certainly by the spring of 1996 official pronouncements started to suggest that the Agency had indeed begun to turn the corner. Yet the performance indicators which were cited merely highlighted the Agency's utterly disastrous performance in its first two years of operations.[99] Even so, the Select Committee,

---

[91] The Agency's Chief Executive was reported as observing that 'whilst the men's campaigning is well organized, women living on social security often can't even afford stamps to write to their MPs' (Abbott, n 67 above, at 31)—or, one might add, the time or energy.

[92] HC Social Security Committee, n 65 above, at para 50 and n 46 above, at para 52.

[93] R Bird, 'Child Support; Reform or Tinkering?' [1995] Fam Law 112.

[94] n 46 above, at para 61 and 'Proceedings of the Committee' at xxxiv.

[95] p 134 below.

[96] Although Ann Chant joined the Agency from the Contributions Agency, she was steeped in DSS culture—indeed, early in her career she had conducted liable relative interviews. Chant was succeeded as Chief Executive by Faith Boardman (April 1997–September 2000), also recruited from the Contributions Agency, Doug Smith (September 2000–April 2005) and now Stephen Geraghty (from April 2005).

[97] F Gains, ' "Hardware, Software or Network Connection?" Theorizing Crisis in the UK Next Steps Agencies' (2004) 82 *Public Administration* 547 at 561. Harlow, noting that no minister resigned, sees this as a failure of accountability: n 27 above at 173–74.

[98] HC Social Security Committee, *The Performance and Operation of the Child Support Agency, Second Report* (HC 50, Session 1995–96) at para 7.

[99] For example, in the month of April 1996 the Agency recovered more maintenance than in the whole of its first year of operations; similarly, in the same month the Agency received fewer than 200 complaints a week, as against 370 a week 18 months earlier. *Hansard* HC Debates vol 276 cols 369 and 386 (24 April 1996).

reporting in 1997 in the closing weeks of the Conservative government, acknowledged that 'significant progress had been made in the development of an efficient
child maintenance system'.[100] Most, if not quite all, of the government's targets
had been met, and 'whereas the Agency was heading for disaster in 1993/94, there
is now no danger that this could occur'.[101] Yet the apparent improvement in the
Agency's performance had been achieved at a considerable price in terms of the
treatment of both its current and potential future caseload. The decision to func-
tionalise the processing of maintenance assessments was followed by the adoption
of a 'post-driven' system—instead of dealing with its existing caseload in date
order, or on some other rational basis, cases were only subject to any action if one
of the parties contacted the Agency. This tactic was described by researchers as the
'complete abandonment of the principle of effective case management'.[102]
The Agency's standard operating mode had become reactive, in the same way as
the much criticised court system that it had supplanted. In addition, the timetable
for taking on the backlog of cases outside the Agency was further delayed. In
December 1994 the Government announced that the phased take-on of some
340,000 pre-April 1993 benefit cases was to be postponed.[103] This was compounded by the Child Support Act 1995, which deferred indefinitely the take-on
of pre-April 1993 private cases in which there was an existing court order or
written maintenance agreement in place.[104] In effect, the objective of a unified
child maintenance system for all had been discarded.[105] The continued exclusion
of these private cases again reinforced the perception that the sole objective of the
scheme was to recoup benefits expenditure.[106]

What impact did this sorry experience have on the actual payment of child
maintenance? According to the White Paper in 1990 the then 'going rate' for child
maintenance was about £18 a week for one child.[107] Bradshaw and Millar reported
that, in those cases in which child maintenance was paid regularly, the mean
weekly payment was £24.[108] The Government's original expectation was that the
new formula would increase such average child maintenance liabilities from £25 a

---

[100] HC Social Security Committee, n 73 above, at para 2.

[101] *Ibid*, at para 3.

[102] Davis *et al*, n 29 above, at 72. As the Committee of Public Accounts confirmed, 'the Agency have
taken the decision to let hundreds of thousands of incorrect assessments hang fire until individual cases
rise to the surface of attention or come up for periodic review': *Twenty-First Report*, n 70 above, at para 4.

[103] *Hansard* HC Debates vol 251 col 1026w (20 December 1994). By March 1997 165,000 of these
deferred cases were still outstanding (Committee of Public Accounts, n 70 above, at para 35). In practice many of these cases were 'resolved' by the parent with care coming off benefit: E Knights and S Cox,
Child support handbook (5th edn 1997/98, CPAG, London, 1997) at 70.

[104] CSA 1995, s 18.

[105] As this author anticipated at the time might be the case (Current Law annotations to CSA 1995,
s 18 at 34–29), these private cases remain outside the CSA today.

[106] M Horton, 'Improving child support—a missed opportunity' (1995) 7 *Child and Family Law
Quarterly* 26 at 32.

[107] White Paper, n 5 above, vol 1 at para 1.5 and vol II at para 4.2.1.

[108] Bradshaw and Millar, n 15 above, at 70, Table 7.8 (this total figure might relate to one or more
children).

week to £40 a week.[109] This was one official prediction that was remarkably accurate—in June 1994 the value of the average full maintenance assessment for non-resident parents who were not on benefit was £40.14.[110] By May 1997 the amount of the average assessment had dipped slightly to £38.99, although those for self-employed non-resident parents were appreciably lower at an average of £23.68 a week.[111] But assessment has to be matched by collection and enforcement, and the Agency was notoriously weak in these aspects of its operations. By May 1997 approximately one third of the Agency's live and fully assessed caseload were the subject of full compliance; a further third of cases were respectively partially compliant and non-compliant.[112] In practice this meant that women continued to bear the greater part of the expense of raising children (including the costs of income forgone because of childcare responsibilities).[113] The following section, however, considers some of the changes made to the child support legislation with a view to placating the demands of non-resident parents and encouraging greater compliance.

Early Legislative Changes to the Child Support Formula

Since the implementation of the 1991 Act in April 1993, successive governments have sought to respond to criticisms of the child support system with a series of legislative reforms of increasing magnitude, and introduced in three main stages.[114] The first and second phases of changes, both instituted by the then Conservative Government, involved amendments to the child support regulations and the enactment of the Child Support Act 1995 respectively. The third phase, examined in the following sections, comprised the more radical reforms initiated by the first Blair administration.

The first phase of changes was implemented in two tranches, with amendments to the regulations in February 1994[115] and April 1995[116] in response to reports from the Select Committee. The 1994 modifications included a reduction in the carer component of the maintenance requirement,[117] at least where older children

---

[109] White Paper, n 5 above, vol 1 at para 3.37.

[110] DSS, *Social Security Statistics 1994* (HMSO, London, 1994) Table G2.08 at 281.

[111] DSS, *Social Security Statistics 1997* (TSO, London, 1997) Table G2.07 at 267.

[112] DSS, *Child Support Agency Quarterly Summary of Statistics May 1997* (DSS, London 1997) Table 4.6 at 40. This was an undoubted improvement on the performance in November 1995: 22% full compliance, 34% partial compliance and 44% nil compliance: *ibid.*

[113] H Davies and H Joshi, n 68 above.

[114] G Douglas, 'The Family, Gender, and Social Security' in N Harris (ed), *Social Security Law in Context* (Oxford University Press, Oxford, 2000), ch 9 at 279.

[115] Child Support (Miscellaneous Amendments and Transitional Provisions) Regulations 1994 (SI 1994/227); see *Hansard* HC Debates vol 236 cols 944–989 (2 February 1994).

[116] Child Support and Income Support (Amendment) Regulations 1995 (SI 1995/1045). These were approved without a debate: *Hansard* HC Debates vol 257 col 1617 (4 April 1995).

[117] ie the adult rate personal allowance for the parent with care which was included in the assessment.

were concerned, and adjustments to the protected income formula, as well as more flexible phasing-in provisions. The April 1995 changes included several further adjustments: an allowance in the formula for high travel-to-work costs; a broad brush allowance in the formula to take account of capital and property settlements; full allowance in exempt income for the housing costs of new partners and step-children; an upper limit for child support maintenance of 30 per cent of net income for current awards; and a reduction in the maximum level of maintenance payable under the formula. These regulations also made various procedural changes, such as the suspension of fees and interest for two years and the introduction of two-yearly (as opposed to annual) periodic reviews of assessments. The April 1995 changes were criticised by Baroness Hollis, then the shadow minister in the House of Lords, as constituting government 'concessions . . . to the sharp-elbowed absent parents'.[118]

The second stage of reforms represented a more significant modification of the original statutory framework with the introduction of the system of departure directions. The Child Support Act 1995, which followed the publication of the White Paper *Improving Child Support*,[119] was designed 'to introduce a degree of flexibility so as to address certain special costs which it would be neither right nor realistic to include in the universal formula'.[120] However, this flexibility had its limits—the 1995 White Paper had made clear the Government's intention that 'the standard formula assessment should be the starting point even when a departure is allowed; and that departures should not be common'.[121] In addition, the revised scheme continued 'to give primacy to biologically determined notions of kinship'.[122] In outline, the 1995 Act provided for three categories of departure directions: cases involving special expenses; property or capital transfers; so-called 'additional cases'.

In principle, these various grounds were made available to non-resident parents and parents with care alike. In practice, applications under the heads of special expenses or property or capital transfers were intended to assist non-resident parents, while applications under the additional cases were more likely to be made by parents with care. Some parents with care on benefit also stood to benefit from the child maintenance bonus, introduced by the 1995 Act as an alternative to a child support disregard.[123]

---

[118] *Hansard* HL Debates, vol 565 col 116 (19 June 1995). For example, the abolition of the apportionment of housing costs represented 'a windfall to the second family, at the expense of the children and the taxpayer', see Horton n 106, above, at 29.

[119] Cm 2745 (January 1995).

[120] Standing Committee E, col 3 (28 March 1995).

[121] n 119 above para 2.4. On CSA 1995 and the departures scheme, see Horton, n 106 above, and JA Priest, 'Departure directions in the Child Support scheme' (1998) 5 *Journal of Social Security Law* 118.

[122] Boden and Childs, n 22 above, at 148.

[123] A child support disregard, as with the child maintenance premium under the new scheme, would simply have allowed benefit claimants to receive some child support (eg £5 p/w) without it affecting their weekly benefit entitlement. The child maintenance bonus involved crediting PWCs on benefit, and in receipt of child support, with a maximum of £5 p/w which was then aggregated and

This is not the place for a detailed analysis of each of these changes. But a recurring and central issue in these initial two phases of modifications to the formula was how the child support system should handle past property settlements entered into as part of a 'clean break' divorce. Although the 1990 White Paper implied that there would be some allowance for equity foregone by a non-resident parent,[124] the original formula made no provision for such settlements. It followed that a non-resident parent was obliged to pay the full maintenance assessment, even in cases where he had, for example, transferred his share in the equity of the matrimonial home to his ex-wife as part of a 'clean break' divorce settlement (typically in return for no spousal maintenance and at most nominal payments of child maintenance).[125] The outrage voiced by non-resident parents (and their new partners) as to the inherent injustice of such an outcome was entirely predictable.[126] Even before the 1991 Act had been enacted, the Select Committee had recommended that special provision be made for such cases.[127] The Conservative government disagreed with that proposal, observing that the policy of the legislation had been to encourage clean breaks as between spouses, and not as between parents and their children.[128] Moreover, as a matter of principle, it argued that it was unfair to expect taxpayers generally to underwrite the costs of relationship breakdown.[129]

In the period immediately after the introduction of the child support scheme, the Select Committee accepted the government's arguments.[130] Instead, the Committee's view was that non-resident parents should return to court to seek a variation of the original court order on the basis of a change in circumstances. However, this potential avenue for redress was blocked, a week after the publication of the Select Committee's December 1993 report, by the decision of the High Court in *Crozier v Crozier*.[131] Here a consent order had been made in divorce proceedings in 1989, under which the father had transferred his share of the equity in the former

payable as a lump sum when they came off benefit. According to Baroness Hollis at the time 'the Government are merely offering a back to work bonus which will take at least four years to be arrived at, and gives the wrong money to the wrong mothers at the wrong time for the wrong reasons', *Hansard* HL Debates vol 564, col 1195 (5 June 1995).

124 White Paper, n 5 above, vol I at para 4.12.

125 See ch 4 above.

126 Even if such cases were not actually common: Bradshaw *et al*, n 32 above at 153–55.

127 HC Social Security Committee, *Changes in Maintenance Arrangements*, Second Report (HC 277-I, Session 1990–1991) at para 14; *Changes in Maintenance Arrangements*, Third Report (HC 277-II, Session 1990–91) at para 72.

128 DSS, *Reply by the Government to the Second and Third Reports of the Select Committee on Social Security*, Session 1990–91 (Cm 1691, 1991), para 14.

129 In practice, in many of these cases, the wife's mortgage interest payments on the former matrimonial home were met by the income support scheme; these rules were changed in 1994.

130 'We can see no sensible way of attempting to place a current value on settlements made in the past in order to give some notional figure for current income which could be taken into account in the formula', HC Social Security Committee, n 65 above, at para 74.

131 [1994] Fam 114. Similarly a NRP's agreement with a DHSS liable relative officer could be overturned by an Agency assessment: *R(CS) 2/97*.

matrimonial home to his ex-wife and had agreed to a nominal[132] maintenance order for the couple's five year old son. Anticipating a child support liability in the order of £29 a week, the father then applied for leave to appeal out of time against the consent order. Booth J, refusing his application, held that the introduction of the child support scheme was not a new event which invalidated the basis of the consent order. In her view:

> The fact that Parliament has chosen a new administrative method by which the State may intervene to compel a parent to contribute towards the maintenance of a child, bypassing the jurisdiction of the courts, does not fundamentally alter the position as it was in law in February 1989. The parties were then unable to achieve a clean financial break in respect of their son. The legal liability to maintain him remained on them both as his parents. While the wife was prepared to assume that responsibility as between herself and the husband, she could not in fact fulfil that obligation without the assistance of State monies. The State was never bound by the agreement or the order. At any time it could have intervened, through the Secretary of State, to seek an order through the courts, and the parties were not entitled to assume for the purposes of their agreement that it would not do so. I consider that it is immaterial for this purpose that that same parental liability will now be enforced through an agency outside the courts. That is a difference only in the means by which the State may proceed to relieve itself of the obligation which it is the duty of the parents to discharge. The fact that the sum required of a parent may be greater under the new procedure than under the old is a consequence of the procedural change and not of any new and unforeseen power vested in the State.[133]

Following the decision in *Crozier v Crozier*,[134] the Select Committee rediscovered its scepticism about the government's stance, noting that in this respect the policy of the 1991 Act 'offends against a sense of fair play and common justice'[135] and calling for the question of the treatment of past property and capital settlements to be revisited as part of any review.

The government subsequently implemented a two-pronged approach to accommodate past property or capital settlements within the child support scheme.[136] In the short term, the April 1995 amendments enabled non-resident parents who had entered into such settlements to claim an allowance as part of their exempt income. This system was both crude (the allowances were based on broad bandings representing settlement values) and restrictive, as the success of a claim depended on the precise terms of the court order or written maintenance

---

[132] The law report does not indicate how nominal, but it was presumably less than the order subsequently obtained by the DSS in March 1993 (under SSAA 1992) for £4 p/w in child maintenance.

[133] [1994] Fam 114 at 123.

[134] n 131 above; but see also *Mawson v Mawson* [1994] 2 FLR 985 and *Smith v McInerney* [1994] 2 FLR 1077 (on which see G Miller, 'The Child Support Act and the clean break' (1995) 3 *Child and Family Law Quarterly* 152).

[135] HC Social Security Committee, n 46 above, at para 49.

[136] *Reply by the Government to the Fifth Report from the Social Security Committee Session 1993–94* (Cm 2743, 1995), paras 32–34.

agreement in question.[137] In the longer term, the Child Support Act 1995 allowed such settlements to be used as the basis of an application for a departure direction. The departures scheme came into force in December 1996, but within five months the Conservative government had left office. Fittingly, the last Adjournment Debate of the Major Government was on the work of the Agency. Ever optimistic, the minister reported that the Agency was now collecting and arranging 'as much each fortnight as it did in the whole of its first year of operations'.[138] The Select Committee's report, published at the same time, echoed this upbeat analysis, concluding that 'ensuring that the Child Support Agency becomes a smooth running and effective feature of British life should be a high priority for the next Government and beyond'.[139] Harlow's more realistic assessment was that 'the child support system bequeathed to the present [Labour] government leaves a legacy of entrenched mistrust and bitterness'.[140]

New Labour and Child Support Reform

New Labour was voted into government with a landslide victory in the General Election of May 1997. Tony Blair's first cabinet included Harriet Harman as Secretary of State for Social Security; amongst her junior ministers, as Minister for Welfare Reform, was Frank Field, with a notable track record as a CPAG campaigner and latterly as Chairman of the House of Commons Social Security Select Committee, with the brief of 'thinking the unthinkable' on welfare reform.[141] They were joined by Baroness Patricia Hollis as Parliamentary Under-Secretary of State, whose portfolio included responsibility for child support matters.[142] In Opposition she had described the Agency as 'an anonymous, bureaucratic, error-ridden and deeply flawed organisation'.[143] In terms of welfare policy, the first year in office was dominated by the new government's insistence on carrying through the Conservatives' plan to abolish one-parent benefit,[144] as part of its commitment to follow the previous administration's spending plans for the two years following

---

[137] See SI 1992/1815, reg 9 and sch 3A, inserted by SI 1995/1045. See *CCS/248/2000* for an indication of the complexities involved.

[138] *Hansard* HC Debates vol 292 col 1112 (20 March 1997) *per* Andrew Mitchell MP, Parliamentary Under-Secretary of State for Social Security.

[139] HC Social Security Committee, n 73 above, at para 25.

[140] Harlow, n 27 above, at 174.

[141] According to Timmins, Field had anticipated being made Secretary of State and very nearly declined to accept the junior post: see n 7 above, at 561–62.

[142] Patricia Hollis was made a life peer in 1990, and has had a distinguished career as an academic historian—her books include *Ladies elect: women in English local government, 1865–1914* (Clarendon Press, Oxford, 1987) and *Jenny Lee—A Life* (Oxford University Press, Oxford, 1998). She left office in the reshuffle following the 2005 General Election.

[143] *Hansard* HL Debates vol 574 col 1246 (22 July 1996).

[144] Timmins describes this as one of two 'elephant traps' left by the outgoing Secretary of State, Peter Lilley—the other being housing benefit cuts. Reportedly Brown gave Harman the choice of dropping one cut or the other, but not both: Timmins n 7 above, at 567–68.

the election. This controversial policy provoked substantial unrest amongst Labour backbenchers; there was also considerable tension within government between Field, with his vision of a modernised universal welfare state based on stakeholder principles, and the Chancellor of the Exchequer, Gordon Brown, whose tax credit policies were, in practice, premised on an extension of means-testing.[145] These disagreements delayed the publication of the DSS's Green Paper on welfare reform until March 1998, a document short on specifics and described by Timmins as looking like 'a building in need of an architect's plan'.[146] Even so, the Green Paper conceded that the Agency had 'failed on a number of counts', promising a 'root and branch review' of its operation.[147] This reflected the damning critique of the House of Commons Committee of Public Accounts, which described the Agency's performance in terms of the accuracy of assessments as 'an unacceptable standard of service in a modern society' and was 'disturbed' that accrued child support debts exceeded £1 billion, of which the Agency expected to recover about one quarter.[148] Meanwhile, the tensions within government culminated in both Harman and Field losing their posts in Blair's first ministerial reshuffle in late July 1998[149]—according to one government insider, Field 'did think the unthinkable, but it was unworkable'.[150]

Shortly before the reshuffle in July 1998,[151] the Department published its Green Paper on child support reform, with yet another upbeat title.[152] In his Foreword, the Prime Minister, acknowledging that the Agency had lost the public's confidence, argued that the system inherited from the previous government was 'a mess' in that it had failed children, parents and taxpayers alike. The old formula 'led to a massively complicated system with the CSA spending 90 per cent of its time assessing maintenance and only 10 per cent of its time collecting it'.[153] The Green Paper accordingly set out a series of proposals for 'a radically more efficient and effective child support service'.[154] The central proposal was to abandon the old formula and to replace it with a new simpler scheme, based on a straight-forward percentage slice of the non-resident parent's income and designed 'to

---

[145] Timmins n 7 above, at 562–70.

[146] *Ibid*, at 570.

[147] DSS, *New Ambitions for our Country: A New Contract for Welfare* (Cm 3805, March 1998) at 60. For a user perspective see S Hutton, J Carlisle and A Corden, *Customer Views on Service Delivery in the Child Support Agency* (DSS Research Report No 74, 1998).

[148] HC Committee of Public Accounts, *Twenty-First Report* n 70 above at paras 4 and 49.

[149] Frank Field announced his resignation outside 10 Downing Street, following two meetings with the Prime Minister on the day of the reshuffle, much to the surprise of the waiting press.

[150] Timmins, n 7 above, at 569.

[151] Timmins reports an 'unseemly hour-long squabble' between Harman and Field in the Cabinet's welfare reform committee which discussed these proposals: *ibid*, at 570.

[152] DSS, *Children First: a new approach to child support* (Cm 3992, July 1998). Barton has wryly observed that this title, along with *Children Come First* (1990) and *Improving Child Support* (1995), was 'optimistic to the point of mendacity', C Barton, 'Third Time Lucky for Child Support?—The 1998 Green Paper' [1998] 28 Fam Law 668 at 668.

[153] DSS, n 152 above, at iii–iv.

[154] *Ibid*, at iii.

strike a fair balance between the needs of children and the reasonable expectation that parents will be left with sufficient money to live on'.[155] This would, the Prime Minister argued, enable the Agency to 'focus on the job of collecting maintenance and provide a more professional service, ending the delays and mistakes that have dogged it'.[156] In making this proposal, the Labour Government concluded that two other potential strategies for reform—incremental change on the one hand, and reverting to the courts on the other—were both unsustainable.[157]

Although the Green Paper proposals were put in the context of the Government's commitment to an 'active family policy which links children's rights and parents' responsibilities',[158] there was actually very little discussion of the fundamental principles which should underpin the child support regime. Indeed, chapter 1 of the Green Paper, entitled 'Our Principles', was just a single page, declaring merely that 'children have a right to care and support from both their parents, wherever they live', and that the Government's belief was that the child support system should ensure that, where they were separated, both parents should contribute to the financial support of their children and that the scheme should be 'fair, efficient and firmly enforced'.[159]

The Green Paper was followed by a consultation period of nearly five months, in the course of which the Department received and analysed over 1,500 responses.[160] This was a marked improvement on the 1990 experience, both in terms of the length of the consultation period and the transparency of the process.[161] A year later, the Government published its White Paper.[162] In broad terms, the White Paper confirmed the approach to reform outlined in the Green Paper, although there were a number of differences of detail[163] as well as some announcements of decisions on issues which had been left open in the consultation paper.[164] The White Paper was followed by an inquiry by the Select Committee[165] and the

---

[155] *Ibid*, at ch 5, para 9.

[156] *Ibid*, at iv.

[157] HC Social Security Committee, *Child Support, Minutes of Evidence* (HC 1031-i, Session 1997–98) at 2 *per* Baroness Hollis.

[158] DSS, n 152 above, ch 3, para 2.

[159] *Ibid*, at ch 1, para 1. For views on the Green Paper, see Barton, n 152 above, and N Mostyn QC 'The Green Paper on Child Support—Children First: a new approach to child support' [1999] 29 Fam Law 95.

[160] House of Commons Library, *Research Paper 99/110* at 18.

[161] A summary of the responses was deposited in the House of Commons Library, *ibid*, at 18, and the minister had many meetings with pressure groups.

[162] DSS, *A new contract for welfare: Children's Rights and Parents' Responsibilities* (Cm 4349, July 1999).

[163] For example, the Green Paper had proposed that all variations (formerly departures) would be determined by tribunals; the White Paper conceded that this would not be feasible in practice. The Green Paper's suggestion that the 'good cause' exemption might be removed was also absent from the White Paper.

[164] Such as the treatment of second families under the formula and how the transition from old to new schemes would be managed.

[165] House of Commons Social Security Committee, *The 1999 Child Support White Paper* (HC 798, Tenth Report, Session 1998–99); see also DSS, *The 1999 Child Support White Paper: Reply by the Government to the Tenth Report* (Cm 4536, November 1999).

introduction of the Bill that became the CSPSSA 2000. The Government stated that the aims of the child support reforms were two-fold—to support families and to tackle child poverty.[166] Whilst supporting families (or at least supporting family responsibilities) might have been an objective of the 1991 Act, this was the first time (in the United Kingdom at least) that child support had been viewed in official quarters as part of the strategy to combat child poverty. This reflected the Prime Minister's announcement earlier in 1999 of the target to eradicate child poverty within a generation.[167]

The main features of the child support reforms outlined in the White Paper, and subsequently embodied in the 2000 Act and associated regulations, were fourfold. First, as indicated above, the old formula was to be replaced by a simpler system of rates that set child support liabilities according to a simple percentage of the non-resident parent's income: 15 per cent for one child, 20 per cent for two and 30 per cent for three or more children, subject to adjustments in the case of those with second families or low incomes. Secondly, parents with care on benefit were to gain from the child maintenance premium: instead of losing income support pound-for-pound where they received child support, those assessed under the new scheme would see the first £10 per week in maintenance payments disregarded in calculating their benefit entitlements. Thirdly, the sanctions regime was to be toughened, for example by the introduction of a new criminal offence of misrepresenting information to the Agency. Finally, the Government promised a new child support service with a customer focus, making greater use of telephone contact with parents. The details of these reforms are covered in subsequent chapters; suffice to say at this stage that the rhetoric has yet to be reflected in the reality, not least because of the continuing saga of endemic problems with the Agency's IT systems.

The Transition From the Old Scheme to the New Scheme

The Government recognised from the outset that the task of managing the transition from the old to the new child support schemes was likely to prove problematic. This change-over involves two distinct processes, 'migration' and 'conversion'. 'Migration' is the transfer of the Agency's existing caseload from its old computer system (CSCS) to its new IT system (CS2). 'Conversion' is the process of changing a child support liability from a 'maintenance assessment' (under the old scheme) to a 'maintenance calculation' (under the new scheme). The reality, however, has been that the operational difficulties involved have probably surpassed policy-makers' worst nightmares. These problems have been exacerbated by continuing high levels of staff turn-over in the Agency. For example, in 1998–99 more than a

---

[166] White Paper, n 162 above, at 57.
[167] See H Sutherland and D Piachaud, 'Reducing Child Poverty in Britain: An Assessment of Government Policy 1997–2001' (2001) 111 *The Economic Journal* F85.

quarter of its staff left, with the Chief Executive acknowledging that some junior employees were paid less than supermarket check-out staff.[168] Indeed, researchers have noted that the combination of high staff turn-over and frequent internal organisational changes has been such that for some years the Agency has not even been able to produce a comprehensive, up-to-date internal staff directory.[169]

As regards the process of transition itself, the 1998 Green Paper made it clear that all 'new cases'—those in which there was no existing assessment, or where the parents separated or a child was born to a lone parent on or after the commencement date—would be dealt with under the reformed child support formula.[170] The more difficult issue, in terms of both principle and practice, concerned existing cases. The Green Paper ruled out keeping such cases within the old scheme indefinitely, as this 'would mean running the current scheme alongside the new scheme for up to 19 years'.[171] Instead, it put forward for consideration two models for handling the change-over for the Agency's current caseload (of over one million cases). Option A would involve transferring the existing assessments in stages, whenever the two-yearly periodic review fell due, and phasing in payment of the revised amounts. Option B envisaged the reassessment of all liabilities in advance of implementation, which would then become payable on a set date, albeit with the possibility of phasing of the amounts to be paid in individual cases. The Green Paper suggested that the implementation date for the transfer might be six months to a year after the start of the new scheme.[172] The arguments for and against each option were reviewed, but no official view was expressed as to which was preferable. The 1999 White Paper explained that the Government's then intention was that the new scheme would be introduced 'towards the end of 2001'.[173] It also confirmed the intention to transfer existing cases to the new arrangements 'as soon as possible' thereafter, and indicated that Option B had been selected.[174]

The subsequent history of the implementation of the 2000 Act has pushed the meaning of 'as soon as possible' beyond the legitimate boundaries of the English language. The reality has been a process of continued and continuing slippage. The 2000 Act received the Royal Assent in July 2000. The original plan had been to launch the new child support scheme in October 2001; this was then put back to

---

[168] HC Committee on Public Accounts, *Child Support Agency: Client Funds Account 1998–99, Fourteenth Report* (HC 184, Session 1999–2000) at paras 20–21.

[169] A Fowler and J Pryke, 'Knowledge management in public service provision: the Child Support Agency' (2003) 14 *International Journal of Service Industry Management* 254 at 273.

[170] DSS, n 152 above, at Annex 2.

[171] *Ibid*, ch 8, para 5. In one sense this would not have been impossible—in Australia the Agency has handled Stage 1 cases (court ordered maintenance) and Stage 2 cases (Agency assessed child support) in parallel for many years. Whether or not operating parallel schemes might be administratively problematic, such a strategy would have been politically unsustainable in the UK given the state of public opinion.

[172] *Ibid*, Annex 2.

[173] n 162 above, at 6.

[174] *Ibid*, at 28.

April 2002,[175] with the expectation that the Agency's existing caseload would be transferred by April 2003.[176] The Agency duly advised its customers of the revised start date, but operational problems with the new computer system compelled the Secretary of State to announce in March 2002, effectively at the eleventh hour, that implementation had been further deferred.[177] The new scheme finally came into force on 3 March 2003,[178] known within the Agency as 'A' Day, but even then only for new cases. The existing caseload was to be transferred to the new system on or after 'C' Day ('C' for conversion); however, ministers refused to commit themselves as to when this date would be, indicating only that conversion would take place once they were satisfied that robust operational arrangements were in place. The prime cause for these delays has lain in problems with the introduction of the Agency's ambitious new IT system, CS2, described by the Select Committee as 'clearly over-spec, over-budget and overdue',[179] compounded by difficulties with the Agency's new telephony system. The Committee observed that 'it is a lucky caller who gets put through to somebody that can actually retrieve the relevant files on to their screen, and extract the necessary information before the computer screen crashes'.[180] The simplification of the formula had meant that the Agency's Business Units were supposed to abandon functionalisation and embrace 'end-to-end' working, with staff seeing a case through from the initial contact to first payment, although this seems not to have been achieved in practice.[181] The parallels between 1993 and 2003 were plain: 'the complicated IT system not ready, staff spending all their time making calculations, and payments not made for months, years or not at all'.[182] In a further report in January 2005, the Select Committee described the Agency's performance over the preceding two years as 'woefully inadequate' and its failure to meet ministerial targets as 'totally unacceptable'.[183] At the end of that year, more than two and a half years after the launch of the new scheme, nearly two-thirds of the Agency's caseload remained old scheme cases.[184]

---

[175] *Hansard* HC Debates vol 343 col 465W (31 January 2000).

[176] A target described by the National Audit Office as early as July 2000 as a 'huge and escalating challenge', NAO, *Child Support Agency Client Funds Account 1999–2000* (HC 658, Session 1999–2000), para 4.11.

[177] *Hansard* HC Debates vol 382 col 315 (20 March 2002).

[178] Child Support, Pensions and Social Security Act 2000 (Commencement No 12) Order 2003 (SI 2003/192) (C 11).

[179] HC Work and Pensions Committee, *DWP's Management of Information Technology Projects: Making IT Deliver for DWP Customers, Third Report of Session 2003–04* (HC 311) at para 183.

[180] *Ibid*, at para 1.

[181] A Atkinson and S McKay, *Child Support Reform: the views and experiences of CSA staff and new clients* (DWP Research Report No 232, 2005) at 48. See also *ibid*, at 51–56 for a catalogue of staff complaints about the poor performance of CS2.

[182] HC Work and Pensions Committee, n 179 above, at para 149. See also the less than convincing *Government Response to the Committee's Third Report, Second Special Report of Session 2003–04* (HC 1125).

[183] HC Work and Pensions Committee, *The Performance of the Child Support Agency, Second Report of Session 2004–05* (HC 44-I, Session 2004–05) at paras 18 and 31.

[184] Some 930,000 of the total caseload of 1,475,000 cases: DWP, *Child Support Agency Quarterly Summary Statistics: December 2005*, Table 1.

Furthermore, there were still 68,000 old scheme cases and 232,000 new scheme cases waiting to be assessed.[185]

The Secretary of State's announcement in February 2006 on the future of the child support scheme also did not mention when 'C' Day would take place.[186] In addition, the Agency's Operational Improvement Plan, issued at the same time, included no commitment to bulk migration and conversion.[187] However, the Agency's Strategic Plan, as put to ministers, indicated that conversion would occur between October 2007 and October 2008.[188] It remains to be seen whether this timetable is viable. Meanwhile, the continuing logjam of work in the Agency has inevitably meant that the rules governing the transfer of individual cases from the old to new schemes have assumed added significance, especially for those parents with care and non-resident parents who anticipate gaining under the new arrangements.[189]

The Transfer of Cases from the Old Scheme to the New Scheme

The transfer of the Agency's existing caseload from the old to the new scheme is governed by some highly complex statutory provisions.[190] The space available here permits only an outline of these rules.[191] The basic rule is that an existing case continues to be subject to the old scheme legislation until either 'C Day' or, if before, the occurrence of an 'early conversion'. Old cases are subject to an early conversion where a maintenance assessment is currently in force and a 'related decision' is made.[192] The relevant Commencement Order sets out a number of scenarios in which a 'related decision' is made—for example, a maintenance calculation under the new scheme falls to be made with respect to the parent with care or non-resident parent, whether or not in relation to a different qualifying child. The implementation of an early conversion of one case may cause a domino effect in terms of other linked old scheme cases, which may result in these associated cases moving onto the new computer system. This phenomenon, known as 'reactive migration', is 'automatic, unplanned and uncontrolled', exacerbating the Agency's operational problems.[193]

---

[185] *Ibid*, Table 1.

[186] DWP Press Release, 'Hutton signals major overhaul of Child Support' (9 February 2006).

[187] Child Support Agency, *Operational Improvement Plan* (February 2006) at 4.

[188] Child Support Agency, *Summary of CSA Strategic Plan* (3 November 2005).

[189] A threatened ECHR challenge to the delays in introducing the new scheme for old cases (see http://news.bbc.co.uk/1/hi/scotland/3931445.stm) has apparently been ruled inadmissible (personal communication).

[190] Child Support (Transitional Provision) Regulations 2000 (SI 2000/3186) and Commencement No 12 Order, n 178 above, made under the authority of CSPSSA 2000 s 29.

[191] For a full account, see R Hadwen and K Pawling, *Child support handbook 2005/2006* (CPAG, London, 2005, 13th edn) ch 9.

[192] Commencement No 12 Order, n 178 above, Art 3.

[193] Independent Case Examiner, *Annual Report 2004/05* (ICE, Chester, 2005) at 25. See further Atkinson and McKay, n 181 above, at 78–80 for problems with migration.

The Agency calculates the child support payable in an early conversion case by reference to the new formula and the information it holds at the calculation date, and in the light of any relevant departure direction or property transfer.[194] The effective date of a conversion decision is usually the start of the first maintenance period on or after the conversion date.[195] The new rate is then payable immediately, unless the transitional phasing rules apply.[196] These operate where the difference between the old and new sums payable (whether that is more or less) exceeds the so-called phasing amount, which acts as a form of buffer—if the difference between the two liabilities is less, parents are expected to cope with that degree of variation; if it is more, then they are granted some protection against too sudden change. The phasing amount thresholds are £10 a week if the non-resident parent's income exceeds £400 p/w, £5 where the income is more than £100 a week but less than £400 weekly, and £2.50 if the weekly income is below £100.[197] As a general rule, where the transitional provisions apply, the child support payable is the old scheme amount, increased or decreased by the phasing amount as appropriate.[198] As each year passes, this figure is then increased (or decreased) by the addition (or subtraction) of the relevant weekly phasing amount.[199] This process continues in a series of annual steps until the sum payable under the new scheme is attained, subject to a maximum transitional period of five years.[200] In those cases which previously had a nil liability but which are now subject to the flat rate (on the basis of receipt of a relevant benefit), the non-resident parent is required to pay £2.50 a week in the first year and the standard flat rate of £5 as from the second year.[201] There are also detailed rules governing the impact on conversion decisions of departure directions or allowances for property transfers.[202] In keeping with the old scheme rules, the maximum transitional amount which a non-resident parent can be required to pay is 30 per cent of his net weekly income.[203] Once made, the conversion decision is itself treated as a maintenance calculation decision, and so is susceptible to revision, supersession, variation and appeal.[204]

Finally, we need to consider the consequences of an old scheme maintenance assessment coming to an end. In principle, once an old scheme assessment ceases to be in force, an application may be made for a maintenance calculation under the new scheme. There are, inevitably, exceptions to this principle, governed by

---

[194] SI 2000/3186, reg 16(1). On the notification requirements, see *ibid* reg 3(3).

[195] *Ibid*, reg 15(1).

[196] *Ibid*, reg 9(1). For cases in which the new rate is always applicable, see *ibid* reg 14.

[197] *Ibid*, reg 24(1). The 'relevant income' is typically the NRP's net weekly income under the new scheme: *ibid*, reg 24(2).

[198] *Ibid*, reg 11(1).

[199] *Ibid*, reg 24(1).

[200] *Ibid*, reg 2(1).

[201] *Ibid*, reg 13.

[202] *Ibid*, regs 17–23A.

[203] *Ibid*, reg 25.

[204] *Ibid*, reg 16(2). For a detailed discussion of the relevant provisions, see Hadwen and Pawling, n 191 above, at 203–208.

the so-called 'linking rules', a concept borrowed from social security law. There are two main linking rules. First, where an application for a new scheme calculation is made after 3 March 2003 but before C Day, the case will continue to be governed by the old scheme if the new application is made within 13 weeks of an old scheme assessment being in force which itself also relates to the same parent with care, non-resident parent and qualifying child.[205] Secondly, where an application for a new scheme calculation is made after C Day, the case will be dealt with by way of a conversion decision, again assuming the new application is made within 13 weeks of the existing assessment being in force, involving the same three parties.[206] These two rules apply irrespective of whether an application is actually made or one is treated as made (as in a benefit case[207]). However, the rules do not apply if, before the new application in question, an application is made (or treated as made) for a new-style calculation that includes one, but not both, of the parents in question.[208] For example, assume that A (the parent with care) and B (the non-resident parent), who separated five years ago, are subject to an old scheme assessment. If A ends the assessment and reapplies 10 weeks later, she will normally be barred from access to the new scheme by the 13 week linking rule. If, on the other hand, B has separated from his new partner C, and C makes her own new scheme application before A does likewise, then A's case is handled under the new scheme (even though it falls within 13 weeks of the currency of the previous assessment).

These linking rules are designed to discourage parents from opting out of the old scheme by 'artificially' ending the existing assessment and then applying for a new scheme calculation, so bypassing the phasing rules. The linking rules apply to applications made by parents with care and non-resident parents alike, not least as, depending on the circumstances, either parent may stand to gain from their case being dealt with under the new scheme. Notwithstanding the disincentive effect of the 13 week rule, there remains considerable potential for some private clients[209] to institute tactical withdrawals of old scheme applications followed by later applications for maintenance calculations. If the other parent is sufficiently well-informed and astute, he or she can stymie this tactic by making their own application within 13 weeks, so ensuring the case remains governed by the old scheme.[210]

---

[205] SI 2000/3186, reg 28(1) and (3).

[206] *Ibid*, reg 28(2) and (3).

[207] See further ch 9 below.

[208] *Ibid*, reg 28(2A).

[209] PWCs on benefit cannot avail themselves of this tactic as they have no right to withdraw from the old scheme assessment.

[210] See eg *R(CS) 1/06*. But note that the new scheme formula cannot be applied via the 'back door', the hypothetical new scheme outcome cannot be used in assessing what is 'just and equitable' in terms of an old scheme departure direction: *CCS/3078/2004*.

6

Child Support—The International Perspective

Introduction

This chapter provides an overview of both the historical development and the main features of the child support systems which operate in the United States of America and in Australia. There is also a brief discussion of the schemes which apply in the respective neighbouring jurisdictions of Canada and New Zealand. There are, inevitably, constraints on the international perspective which this chapter can offer.[1] In particular, there is no discussion here of the child support systems operated closer to home, for example in the rest of the European Union. The primary focus in this chapter on the United States and Australia can be justified for three reasons. First, in terms of its demographic characteristics, and especially rates of marriage, divorce, absent fatherhood and lone parenting, the United Kingdom is closer to both countries than the rest of Europe.[2] Secondly, the American and Australian child support systems have been established within a common law framework that is much more familiar to most readers than the civilian tradition of mainland Europe.[3] Thirdly, the United States and Australia child support reforms predated those in the United Kingdom, and were influential on the Conservative government which developed the proposals enacted in the Child Support Act 1991. This chapter is therefore intended to provide a comparative context for the analysis of the United Kingdom's child support scheme in the rest of this book, and so concludes with a brief overview of some of the reasons for the different performances of the various child support regimes.

---

[1] This book is also not concerned with the very real problems in enforcing child support obligations across international borders; see further W Duncan, 'The Development of the New Hague Convention on International Recovery of Child Support and Other Forms of Family Maintenance' (2004) 38 *Family Law Quarterly* 663.

[2] L Clarke, EC Cooksey and G Verropoulou, 'Fathers and Absent Fathers: Sociodemographic Similarities in Britain and the United States' (1998) 35 *Demography* 217 and Child Support Agency *Child Support Schemes: Australia and Comparisons* (Child Support Agency, Canberra, Australia, 2001), at 9 n 4.

[3] See generally A Corden, *Making child maintenance regimes work* (Family Policies Study Centre, London, 1999). For a French study of the advantages and disadvantages of using a more formulaic approach to child maintenance, see I Sayn (ed), *Un barème pour les pensions alimentaires?* (La documentation Française, Paris, 2002).

Child Support in the United States

The Federal Context

The default position in the American constitutional framework is that legislation is a matter for the states unless the constitution confers authority on the federal government to regulate. As a result, family law is seen as the exclusive province of the individual states, rather than the domain of federal law.[4] On this basis federal legislation in the field of family law is seen as an exception to the general rule that the states have exclusive jurisdiction in such matters.[5] It follows that the role of the federal courts in family matters is likewise restricted, for example to ensuring that a citizen's individual constitutional rights are protected. For example, in *Zablocki v Redhail*[6] the Supreme Court struck down as unconstitutional a Wisconsin statute which had required those already subject to a child support order to obtain a court's permission to marry. Under this law, marriages contracted in violation of its provisions were both void and punishable as criminal offences. The Supreme Court ruled that this infringed the fundamental right to marry; any countervailing state interest had to be sufficiently important to justify the restriction and the law had to be narrowly tailored to accomplish those interests.[7]

Recent years have seen several critiques of this traditional framework for federal-state relations. Resnick has challenged what she describes as 'categorical federalism', with its associated presumption of exclusive control for the states in family law matters.[8] Whilst federal law has become increasingly significant in the development of child support law in the USA, it remains the case that there are no uniform federal guidelines as to the appropriate amount of child support in any case. The starting point, therefore, for understanding American child support law is to appreciate that, just as there are 50 states in the USA, it follows there are—in principle—50 child support systems,[9] although enforcement in all states is heavily

---

[4]   For a justification of this approach, see AC Dailey, 'Federalism and Families' (1995) 143 *University of Pennsylvania Law Review* 1787 at 1790.

[5]   What Adler calls 'exceptionalization', LS Adler, 'Federalism and Family' (1999) *Columbia Journal of Gender and Law* 197 at 200.

[6]   434 US 374 (Supreme Court, 1978). See also *Loving v Virginia* 388 US 1 (1967), in which the US Supreme Court ruled the state's antimiscegenation statute to be unconstitutional.

[7]   See the discussion in JA Barron, 'The Constitutionalization of American Family Law: The Case of the Right to Marry' in SN Katz, J Eekelaar and M Maclean, *Cross Currents* (Oxford University Press, Oxford, 2000) ch 12 at 266.

[8]   J Resnick, 'Categorical Federalism: Jurisdiction, Gender, and the Globe' (2001) 111 *Yale Law Journal* 619; see also Adler, n 5 above; NR Cahn, 'Family Law, Federalism, and the Federal Courts' (1994) 79 *Iowa Law Review* 1073; JE Hasday, 'Federalism and the Family Reconstructed' (1998) 45 *UCLA Law Review* 1297 and JE Hasday, 'The Canon of Family Law' (2004) 57 *Stanford Law Review* 825 at 870–92.

[9]   To be precise, there are 50 state schemes with separate systems for DC, Guam, Puerto Rico and the Virgin Islands. In practice, as we shall see, these systems are to a large extent variants on two or three standard models. However, the system is further fragmented by differences within the justice system at county level within states. To complicate matters further, there are also differences across states in terms of welfare provision: see further n 57 below.

influenced by federal legislative requirements. To overseas observers, child support in the United States is commonly associated with the state of Wisconsin, not least because this jurisdiction was to the fore in terms of developing a child support formula in the 1980s.[10] This led to politicians and policymakers from other countries visiting Wisconsin to investigate how a modern child support scheme operates. But, as we shall see, only a minority of American states have adopted the Wisconsin model for determining child support liabilities. The following sections examine the evolution of American child support law and analyse the different types of guidelines employed by state courts and administrative agencies in assessing child maintenance liabilities, before considering the specific problems of interstate enforcement of child support orders within the United States.

The Early History of Child Support in the United States

The first British settlers in America brought with them the Elizabethan poor law;[11] in particular, 'English bastardy law was imported more or less intact to the colonies . . . to impose social control on a mobile and diverse population'.[12] As was the case in Britain, enforcement of this legislation in practice was at best patchy.[13] However, during the early nineteenth century, the American courts, unlike their English counterparts, began to assert that a father had a legal (and not simply a moral) obligation to maintain his natural children.[14] By the end of the nineteenth century most states recognised that this private child support obligation was enforceable in law.[15] The imposition of such a duty was premised on public policy considerations, and in particular the need to avoid dependency—'in the dual sense of wanting to prevent poverty and wanting to prevent unnecessary drains on the public treasury'.[16] Given this public interest, state legislation increasingly provided that those who defaulted

---

[10] Indeed, in the early twentieth century Wisconsin had become the first state to establish collection services for child maintenance payments: D Schuele, 'Origins and Development of the Law of Parental Child Support' (1988–89) 27 *Journal of Family Law* 807 at 838.

[11] See SA Riesenfeld, 'The Formative Era Of American Public Assistance Law' (1955) 43 *Californian Law Review* 175.

[12] MA Mason, *From Father's Property to Children's Rights: The History of Child Custody in the United States* (Columbia University Press, New York, 1994) at 25. The principal difference was that unmarried mothers in the colonies (and later the states) could bring actions for the support of their children against fathers in their own right: *ibid*, at 98.

[13] *Ibid*, at 70 and 94. However, poor law officials made extensive use of their powers to apprentice or 'place out' poor children to work in farming communities: *ibid*, at 76–80.

[14] See *Stanton v Wilson* 3 Day 37 (Conn 1808) and *Van Valkinburgh v Watson* 13 Johns 480 (NY 1816), cited by DD Hansen, 'The American Invention of Child Support: dependency and punishment in early American child support law' (1999) 108 *Yale Law Journal* 1123 at 1134. See further Schuele, n 10 above, but note also that during the colonial period children were divided into four classes: natural children, apprentices, illegitimate children and slaves, each with a different status: MA Mason, 'The US and the International Children's Rights Crusade: Leader or Laggard?' (2005) 38 *Journal of Social History* 955 at 957.

[15] Hansen, n 14 above, at 1142, citing WR Vance, 'The Parent's Liability for Necessaries Furnished His Minor Child' (1901) 6 *Virginia Law Register* 585.

[16] Hansen, n 14 above, at 1135.

on their child support obligations should be subject to criminal sanctions.[17] As a result, non-payment of child support is still an offence in most states and non-payment across state lines is also now a federal offence,[18] although in practice criminal proceedings are very rarely instituted today.[19] Instead, a range of other enforcement tools have been developed, including most notably the automatic deduction of child support payments from liable parents' salaries.[20]

In the course of the twentieth century, welfare in the United States became synonymous with Aid to Families with Dependent Children (AFDC), established in 1935 as part of the New Deal, at a time when (as in the United Kingdom) bereavement was the principal cause of lone parenthood.[21] The AFDC programme provided a minimum subsistence income 'administered through a social work paradigm . . . focused on the professional judgment of administrators'.[22] In the post-war years, welfare, and in particular AFDC, came to be increasingly associated with illegitimacy in the black community. The first federal initiative in the arena of child support came in 1950, when state AFDC agencies were required, as a condition of receiving federal funding for their welfare programmes, to report to the law enforcement authorities any cases in which claimants had been abandoned or deserted by their partners.[23] Subsequently legislation required each state to establish a single organizational unit to establish paternity and to collect child support for deserted children in families receiving AFDC.[24] This approach confined the role of state agencies to the collection and enforcement of child support in welfare cases; in practice, however, social service agencies 'attempted only spotty and desultory efforts at collecting child support from absent fathers (and occasionally mothers)'.[25] In practice, therefore, 'fathers could simply walk away from their children with impunity'.[26] The position in non-AFDC cases was little different; the assessment of liability remained firmly the exclusive preserve of the courts, to

---

[17] *Ibid*, at 1149. See also Mason, n 12 above, at 87.

[18] See p 153 below.

[19] For a remarkable exception, see *State of Wisconsin v Oakley* 629 NW 2d 200 (Supreme Court of Wisconsin, 2001) in which the court upheld a condition of probation, imposed following conviction for non-payment of child support, requiring the offender to avoid having further children unless he could afford to maintain all his offspring. See further AF Epps, 'Unacceptable Collateral Damage: The danger of probation conditions restricting the right to have children' (2005) 38 *Creighton Law Review* 611. For a contrary view, see *State of Ohio v Talty* 814 NE 2d 1201 (Supreme Court of Ohio, 2004).

[20] See further below.

[21] AFDC was originally known as Aid to Dependent Children (ADC), emphasising the primary focus of the programme. On the earlier 'mothers' pensions', see Mason, n 12 above, at 92–100.

[22] M Diller, 'The revolution in welfare administration: rules, discretion, and entrepreneurial government' (2000) 75 *New York University Law Review* 1121 at 1135. See further JE Crowley, *The Politics of Child Support in America* (Cambridge University Press, Cambridge, 2003), ch 4.

[23] Social Security Act 1935, §402(a)(11) (42 USC 602(a)(11)). The most detailed account of the development of federal child support legislation is to be found in Office of Child Support Enforcement (OSCE), *Child Support Enforcement, Twenty-Third Annual Report to Congress*, Appendix G.

[24] Social Security Amendments 1967.

[25] Mason, n 12 above, at 148.

[26] Crowley, n 22 above, at 104.

which state legislatures had granted an unfettered discretion.[27] Moreover, the enforcement of child support in private cases was at best uneven, and especially across state lines; in effect 'the absent father could all but choose not to pay'.[28]

The Social Security Amendments of 1974

By the early 1970s the social work philosophy underpinning the AFDC programme had been replaced by a legal-bureaucratic model, with the welfare system 'reconceived as a hierarchically ordered legal system, rather than a platform for thousands of individualised professional judgments'.[29] At the same time, Congress championed stricter enforcement of child support liabilities as a means of recouping the growing federal expenditure on AFDC.[30] Thus the Social Security Amendments of 1974, which constituted the first major federal initiative in the field of child support, reflected Congress's conclusion that the problem of welfare was 'to a considerable extent, a problem of the non-support of children by their absent parents'.[31] The 1974 Amendments inserted Title IV-D into the Social Security Act and established the framework for the division of responsibility between state and federal agencies in child support matters. The legislation placed the primary responsibility on states, which were required to develop a child support enforcement plan, to be implemented on a state-wide basis. The child support enforcement agency in each state was required to establish paternity and secure child support orders for both AFDC claimants and private clients, although in practice these services were designed primarily for the former. Agencies had to provide a parent locator service and to liaise with agencies in other states in enforcing child support liabilities.[32] The role of the federal government[33] was partly operational (eg establishing a federal parent locator service) but principally supervisory, providing advice to, and auditing the work of, state child support enforcement agencies. Writing in 1981, Krause referred to this as the 'federalization of child support enforcement'.[34] The 1974 Amendments also required all AFDC claimants to co-operate with the state authorities as a condition of receiving welfare payments; however, this was relaxed by the provision of a 'good cause'

---

[27] Schuele, n 10 above, at 834–35.

[28] HD Krause, 'Child Support Reassessed: Limits of Private Responsibility and the Public Interest' (1989) *University of Illinois Law Review* 367 at 370.

[29] Diller, n 22 above, at 1137.

[30] See generally Crowley, n 22 above, ch 5: the number of families in receipt of AFDC more than tripled from 984,000 in 1964 to 3.17 million in 1974: *ibid*, at 104, Table 5.4.

[31] Congressional record as cited in AL Estin, 'Federalism and Child Support' (1998) 5 *Virginia Journal of Social Policy & Law* 541 at 549.

[32] For a fuller account, see J Cassetty, *Child Support and Public Policy* (Lexington Books, Massachusetts, 1978) at 11–12.

[33] Through what was then the DoH, Education and Welfare, now the Department of Health & Human Services.

[34] HD Krause, *Child Support in America: the legal perspective* (Charlottesville, Michie & Co, 1981) at 307–11.

exemption in a further amendment in 1975.[35] As part of this package of measures, the Uniform Parentage Act of 1973 established a series of presumptions for attributing paternity. According to Mason, this statute 'changed the focus of child support, shifting the right from the mother to the child'.[36]

Legislative Developments in the 1980s

The two principal federal initiatives in the 1980s were the Child Support Enforcement Amendments of 1984 and the Family Support Act of 1988. These reforms, implemented during the Reagan years, reflected the coalescence of two very different political forces in the United States—the New Right, concerned to reduce public spending on welfare and to reinforce traditional family values, and women's groups, which were also pressing for more effective child support enforcement, but as a means of increasing women's economic independence.[37] A comparison of the 1984 and 1988 measures demonstrates the growing federal influence in the assessment, collection and enforcement of child support in the United States.

The 1984 Amendments required states to formulate guidelines for the assessment of child support liabilities and to circulate those benchmarks to the judiciary, although courts retained the discretion to fix child support at whatever level they deemed appropriate in the light of state law and practice.[38] The new legislation also meant that state child support agencies had to provide the full range of their services to families who were not on welfare, as well as to AFDC claimants.[39] As a result, 'both clientele groups were suddenly subject to the same intake, implementation, and enforcement procedures',[40] so that child support suddenly became a major issue for the American middle class. However, the 1984 reforms were principally concerned with improving the enforcement of existing orders; in particular, in cases in which child support was in arrears for at least one month, state agencies were required to implement mandatory income withholding procedures (under which child support liabilities were deducted at source direct from salaries), as well as introducing new enforcement measures (such as liens against property).[41] Changes were also made to the federal audit process, with

---

[35] See further the discussion in ch 9 below.

[36] Mason, n 12 above, at 148.

[37] Crowley, n 22 above, ch 6. On the impact of women's groups, see also L Keiser, 'The Influence of Women's Political Power on Bureaucratic Output: The Case of Child Support Enforcement' (1997) 27 *British Journal of Political Science* 136.

[38] DH Bell, 'Child Support Orders: The Federal State Partnership—Part I' (1999) 69 *Mississippi Law Journal* 597 at 599.

[39] LW Morgan, 'The federalization of child support a shift in the ruling paradigm: child support as outside the contours of "family law"' (1999) 16 *Journal of the American Academy of Matrimonial Lawyers* 195 at 203.

[40] JE Crowley, 'The Gentrification of Child Support Enforcement Services, 1950–1984' (2003) 77 *Social Service Review* 585 at 586; see further Crowley, n 22 above ch 6.

[41] For a detailed account of these changes, see RG Kreuger, *Analyzing the Development of the American Child Support System* (Writers Club Press, Lincoln, NE, 2001) at 125–28.

federal subsidies adjusted in an effort to provide incentives for state child support agencies to improve their performance.[42] Other legislation in 1984 affected the interface between child support and welfare; in particular, states were now obliged to disregard the first $50 a month a claimant received by way of child support when calculating entitlement to welfare.[43]

The Family Support Act of 1988 tightened up federal requirements in a number of respects. In particular, and as discussed in more detail below, state child support guidelines were now accorded presumptive force. This marked a decisive shift away from the reliance on judicial discretion, which had been the traditional hall-mark of the common law system for settling child support awards.[44] Moreover, the 1988 Act specified detailed targets for improving paternity establishment rates for Title IV-D (welfare) cases which state agencies had to meet in order to qualify for federal funding. The 1988 Act also required states to review and adjust indi-vidual child support orders in AFDC cases every three years.[45] In addition, each state was required to initiate wage withholding from the outset of the order for the collection of all child support payments.[46] In summary, 'by the end of the 1980s, child support enforcement had become the first line of defense in the govern-ment's long-running war on poverty and welfare dependency'.[47]

Legislative Developments in the 1990s

This decade also saw two main federal initiatives in child support law—the Child Support Recovery Act of 1992[48] and, most importantly, the Personal Responsibility and Work Opportunity Reconciliation Act 1996. The 1992 Act was specifically directed at the problem of non-payment of child support where the non-resident parent lives in a different state (within the United States) to the child concerned. Thus the 1992 Act applies solely to non-payment which is *inter*-state rather than purely *intra*-state in nature. It made the wilful failure to pay child support in such circumstances a federal crime[49] and, as subsequently honed by the Deadbeat

---

[42] For an assessment of the impact of federal incentives, see JH Cassetty and R Hutson, 'Effectiveness of federal incentives in shaping child support enforcement outcomes' (2005) 27 *Children and Youth Services Review* 271.

[43] AH Beller and JW Graham, *Small Change: The Economics of Child Support* (Yale University Press, New Haven, 1993) at 26. In US parlance this is known as a 'pass through' rather than a 'maintenance disregard'.

[44] JC Murphy, 'Eroding the myth of discretionary justice in family law: the child support experi-ment' (1991) 70 *North Carolina Law Review* 209.

[45] This requirement was subsequently relaxed by PRWORA 1996.

[46] With effect from 1990 for Title IV-D (welfare) cases and by 1994 for all cases: I Garfinkel and MM Klawitter, 'The Effect of Routine Income Withholding of Child Support Collections' (1990) 9 *Journal of Policy Analysis & Management* 155 at 158.

[47] Beller and Graham, n 43 above, at 2.

[48] 18 USCA § 228. See Kreuger, n 41 above, at 218–24.

[49] State laws typically make non-payment of child support a state crime: see RS Kornreich, 'The con-stitutionality of punishing deadbeat parents: the Child Support Recovery Act of 1992 after *United States v Lopez*' (1995) 64 *Fordham Law Review* 1089 at 1097.

Parents Punishment Act of 1998, provides for three categories of offence.[50] The US appellate courts have rejected arguments that the 1992 Act is unconstitutional.[51] However, the significance of the Child Support Recovery Act 1992 appears to be at best symbolic rather than practical. The federal authorities regard prosecution as a last resort,[52] as demonstrated by the fact that by 1999 a total of just 109 convictions had been recorded, mostly in high profile cases where wealthy non-resident parents had significant child support debts.[53]

The Personal Responsibility and Work Opportunity Reconciliation Act (PRWORA) 1996 was the principal welfare reform measure of the Clinton years. This reflected bipartisan concern amongst politicians and policy makers about the perceived growth of the 'dependency culture'.[54] Indeed, the goal of the first version of the (Republican-sponsored) Personal Responsibility Bill of 1995 was declared to be to 'restore the American family, reduce illegitimacy, control welfare spending and reduce welfare dependence'.[55] The PRWORA represented a fundamental shift away from the legal-bureaucratic model of welfare; instead of claimants having rights, state agencies were vested with a broad discretion to deliver welfare as they saw fit. Thus the 1996 Act itself abolished AFDC and replaced it with a new system of Temporary Need to Needy Families (TANF). In summary, AFDC was a federal welfare programme delivered by state agencies which guaranteed a certain level of financial assistance. In the new regime, the federal government provides TANF block grants to the states, which then set their own criteria for the payment of benefits, subject to certain federal conditions[56] such as the imposition of welfare to work requirements and the introduction of

---

[50] Codified as amended as 18 USCA § 228. The first comprises cases in which the arrears have been outstanding for more than a year or exceed $5,000 (the penalty is a fine and/or imprisonment for no more than six months), which applies even if it is the child (and parent with care) who has moved to another state. The second is where the arrears have been outstanding for more than a year or exceed $5,000 *and* the non-resident parent has travelled to another state intending to avoid his child support liability. The third category consists of parents who are at least two years in arrears or have child support debts in excess of $10,000 (the penalty for the second and third categories is a fine and/or imprisonment for up to two years).

[51] See eg *US v Faasse* 265 F3d 475 (6th Cir, 2001). See further Kornreich, n 49 above, at 1099–113, KA Kemper, 'Validity, Construction, and Application of Child Support Recovery Act of 1992' 147 ALR Fed 1 (1998) and DR Zmijewski, 'The Child Support Recovery Act and its Constitutionality after *US v Morrison*' (2003) 12 *Kansas Journal of Law and Public Policy* 289.

[52] Kornreich, n 49 above, at 1097–98.

[53] C Wimberly, 'Deadbeat Dads, Welfare Moms, and Uncle Sam: How the Child Support Recovery Act Punishes Single-Mother Families' (2000) 45 *Stanford Law Review* 729 at 740, 743. Although the 1992 Act sets the floor for arrears at $5,000, in practice guidance to federal prosecutors refers to a $20,000 limit; *ibid*, at 745.

[54] The AFDC caseload increased by 25% between 1988 and 1992: R Levesque, 'Looking to Unwed Dads to Fill the Public Purse: A Disturbing Wave in Welfare Reform' (1993–94) 32 *Journal of Family Law* 1 at 1, n 3.

[55] DL Chambers, 'Fathers, the Welfare System, and the Virtues and Perils of Child-Support Enforcement' (1995) 81 *Virginia Law Review* 2575 at 2579, n 15.

[56] For an unsuccessful challenge to these conditions, see *Kansas v United States* 214 F3d 1196 (US Court of Appeals, Tenth Circuit, 2000).

time-limited welfare payments.[57] Furthermore, the 1996 Act specifically declared that the provisions governing TANF 'shall not be interpreted to entitle any individual or family to assistance under any State program funded under this part'.[58] The block grant system also abandoned the federal requirement for states to 'pass through' the maintenance disregard of $50 a month that had been in place since 1984. Moreover, claimants' procedural rights are now undermined by states using the private sector to deliver welfare programmes.[59] Czapanskiy also argues that the deletion of 'children' from the title of the programme as the AFDC programme transmuted into TANF was in no way accidental: 'welfare reform is viewed as the story of getting single women to become self-sufficient, whether by work, marriage, or child support, or through some combination of the three'.[60]

Whilst the PRWORA 1996 marked the dismantling of a national welfare programme, it saw increased federal intervention in the child support system, with the emphasis on collection and enforcement.[61] The introduction of time-limited welfare necessarily made child support even more important to low income lone parent households.[62] The PRWORA 1996 streamlined the legal process for establishing paternity; in particular, schemes for in-hospital paternity establishment were encouraged[63] and states were required to have in place administrative procedures for ordering genetic testing without prior judicial approval.[64] Brito has characterised these changes as representing the 'welfarization of family law', with the overriding goal of reducing welfare costs trumping the legitimate privacy

---

[57] The general rule (to which there are exceptions) is that claimants are limited to five years' receipt of TANF in their lifetime: 42 USC § 608(a)(7). Even before TANF there were substantial differences across states in the provision of public support for children: see MK Meyers, JC Gornick, LR Peck and AJ Lockshin, 'Public policies that support families with young children: variation across US states' in K Vleminickx and TM Smeeding (eds), *Child Well-Being, Child Poverty and Child Policy in Modern Nations* (Policy Press, Bristol, 2001), ch 17.

[58] 42 USC § 601(b).

[59] ME Gilman, 'Legal Accountability in an Era of Privatised Welfare' (2001) 89 *California Law Review* 571.

[60] K Czapanskiy, 'Parents, Children, and Work-First Welfare Reform: where is the C in TANF?' (2002) 61 *Maryland Law Review* 308 at 310 and 328. See also S Hays, *Flat Broke with Children* (Oxford University Press, Oxford, 2003) at 76–84. For a more positive account of PRWORA 1996 see AM Rotondo, 'Helping families help themselves: using child support enforcement to reform our welfare system' (1997) 33 *Californian Western Law Review* 281.

[61] See Kreuger, n 41 above, at 295–96 for a discussion of the reasons for the different federal roles in welfare and child support respectively. See further PK Legler, 'The Coming Revolution in Child Support Policy: Implications of the 1996 Welfare Act' (1996) 30 *Family Law Quarterly* 519 and, on federal audits, see US House of Representatives Committee of Ways and Means, *2004 Green Book* (WMCP: 108–6, US Congress, April 2004) at 8–56.

[62] PK Legler, 'The Impact of Welfare Reform on the Child Support Enforcement System' in JT Oldham and MS Melli (eds), *Child Support—The Next Frontier* (Michigan, University of Michigan Press, 2000) at 46.

[63] See further R Mincy, I Garkinkel and L Nepomnyaschy, 'In-Hospital Paternity Establishment and Father Involvement in Fragile Families' (2005) 67 *Journal of Marriage and Family* 611.

[64] States must provide that a voluntary signed acknowledgment of paternity constitutes a legal finding of paternity, subject to rescission within 60 days: 42 USC § 666(a)(5) (2000).

concerns of both parents with care and non-resident parents alike.[65] States became subject to a duty to establish computerised registries of child support orders. As a further reform, designed to improve the systems for locating non-resident parents, employers were placed under a duty to report the details of all newly employed workers, or 'new hires', to the relevant state agency, which in turn transmits that information to the (federal) National Directory of New Hires.[66] Innovative enforcement tools were also introduced, such as the revocation of driving licences and professional licences.[67] According to one commentator, the 'only possible stronger measures would be turning the entire enforcement process over to the federal government'.[68] However, proposals to make the Internal Revenue Service (IRS) responsible for collecting and enforcing child support orders alongside the recovery of tax revenues have yet to find favour with Congress.[69] Even so, income withholding at source has become more and more prevalent—by 2002 65 per cent of all child support payments were collected in this way in the United States.[70]

The PRWORA 1996 was also significant for other measures it omitted to include. Most notably, there was no role for a child support assurance system, developed by Professor Irwin Garfinkel and others in Wisconsin.[71] The idea behind this proposal was that in principle there would be a guaranteed level of publicly-funded child support available to all children with an absent parent. If that parent could afford to pay child support, no assured benefit would be payable. But if he could not meet that liability in part or in full, the assured benefit would meet the gap between the private maintenance and the state guaranteed level of support. In broad terms, this represented an American equivalent to the proposal for a Guaranteed Maintenance Allowance developed earlier in the United Kingdom by the Finer Committee.[72] As with its British counterpart, the idea failed to find favour with politicians who were more concerned with controlling welfare expenditure than extending the potential scope of such schemes.[73]

We now focus on two specific issues relating to child support in the United States; the problem of inter-state enforcement and the use of formulaic guidelines in assessing child support awards.

---

[65] TL Birito, 'The Welfarization of Family Law' (2000) 48 *University of Kansas Law Review* 229.

[66] Over 4 million NRPs were located through the National Directory in 2001: *2004 Green Book*, n 61 above, at 8–14.

[67] See further ch 14 below.

[68] LD Elrod, 'Child Support Reassessed: Federalization of Enforcement nears Completion' (1997) *University of Illinois Law Review* 695 at 703.

[69] See the 'Downey-Hyde Proposal' of 1992 (discussed by Levesque, n 54 above, at 11) and the 'Hyde-Woolsey Bill' of 1998 (discussed by JS Jemison, 'Collecting and Enforcing Child Support Orders with the IRS: An analysis of a novel idea' (1999) 20 *Women's Rights Law Reporter* 137 at 141).

[70] *2004 Green Book*, n 61 above, at 8–34.

[71] See eg I Garfinkel, *Assuring child support: An extension of social security* (Russell Sage Foundation, New York, 1992).

[72] See p 89 above.

[73] On the failure of these proposals, see Crowley, n 22 above, at 194–99 and Kreuger, n 41 above, at 266–68.

The Problem of Inter-state Enforcement

A peculiar feature of the arrangements in the United States is the difficulty of enforcing child support orders across state lines,[74] which was the first child support issue to come before Congress.[75] Early measures were singularly ineffective in addressing the problems of inter-state enforcement. The first such attempt, the Uniform Reciprocal Enforcement of Support Act of 1950,[76] was not implemented consistently across the USA. There were also serious procedural problems in securing orders in the courts of one state and then seeking to enforce them in the courts of another state. On top of this, the Title IV-D provisions introduced in 1975 meant that state child support authorities had every financial incentive to focus efforts on recovering payments in their own AFDC cases, rather than pursuing inter-state cases.[77] Following amendments to the Uniform Reciprocal Enforcement of Support Act in 1958 and 1968, the next major initiative, prompted by the passage of the Family Support Act of 1988,[78] was the Uniform Interstate Family Support Act (UIFSA). This code established the principle that the original state in which the child support order is obtained retains control throughout, and its jurisdiction can be extended under the 'long arm' provisions.[79] However, states were slow to adopt the new code,[80] and it was estimated in 1992 that about a third of all child support cases in arrears involved non-resident parents living out-of-state, with recovery rates as low as 10 per cent.[81] This prompted Congress to try a different tack with the criminalisation of inter-state child support arrears in the 1992 legislation, as discussed above. The PRWORA 1996 subsequently required all states to adopt UIFSA by 1 January 1998, or face cuts in federal funding.[82] While inter-state enforcement has been important in the domestic context, of much greater significance for other common law jurisdictions has been the development of the use of guidelines for assessing child support awards in the United States.

---

[74] There have, historically at least, been serious difficulties in enforcing child maintenance orders as between the various jurisdictions in the UK (especially as between England & Wales and Scotland), but this appears to be much less problematic now.

[75] Kreuger, n 41 above, at 94; the first moves to make this a federal crime were in 1941: *ibid*, at 49. For a contemporary discussion, see *2004 Green Book*, n 61 above, at 8.43–8.50.

[76] This measure, known as the 'Runaway Pappy Act', was not passed by Congress, but rather as a model statute by the National Conference of Commissioners on Uniform State Laws: see JT Calhoun, 'Interstate child support enforcement system: juggernaut of bureaucracy' (1995) 46 *Mercer Law Review* 921 at 927.

[77] *Ibid*, at 943.

[78] The 1988 Act established the US Commission on Interstate Child Support.

[79] A 'long arm statute' is a law which permits one state to 'reach out' and claim personal jurisdiction over someone who lives in another state.

[80] By February 1996 just 12 states had done so (AE Watkins, 'The Child Support Recovery Act of 1992: Squeezing Blood from a Stone' (1996) 6 *Seton Hall Constitutional Law Journal* 845 at 857) although this increased to 34 by autumn of the same year (Elrod, n 68 above, at 699–700).

[81] Calhoun, n 76 above, at 924.

[82] 42 USC § 666(f).

Child Support Guidelines in the American Courts

By the 1970s, as was later argued in the United Kingdom, 'the traditional case-by-case method for setting amounts of child support orders was archaic and was widely perceived as resulting in the inequitable treatment of cases with similar circumstances'.[83] Although some individual judges might be consistent in applying their own criteria, there were marked variations across the judiciary as whole.[84] Child support awards, as well as being unpredictable, also bore little relation to children's needs; indeed, most fathers paid more in monthly car purchase payments than they did in child support.[85] The initial moves away from the traditional discretionary approach took place at state level. For example, the courts in Michigan began to use a simple numerical standard for establishing child support liabilities, based on a percentage of the non-resident parent's income.[86] In 1978 just six states used child support guidelines, a number that had doubled by 1983, but by 1985 the total had risen to 34 states.[87]

The principal impetus lay in the Child Support Enforcement Amendments of 1984, which required all states to develop advisory guidelines for child support awards or face loss of federal funding for their AFDC programmes.[88] Such guidelines were intended to remedy the three principal weaknesses in the case-by-case method: the shortfalls as between the amounts ordered and the costs of raising children, inconsistent orders in cases with similar circumstances and long time delays in processing awards.[89] Guidelines were also seen as 'the single most important step towards stemming the decline in the real value of expected child support

---

[83] JC Venohr and RG Williams, 'The Implementation and Periodic Review of State Child Support Guidelines' (1999) 33 *Family Law Quarterly* 7 at 9. For an empirical study of the extent of non-payment in one state, see J Pearson, N Thoennes and J Anhalt, 'Child Support in the United States: The Experience in Colorado' (1992) 6 *International Journal of Law and the Family* 321.

[84] See KR White and RT Stone, 'A Study of Alimony and Child Support Rulings with Some Recommendations' (1976) 10 *Family Law Quarterly* 75.

[85] DM Yee, 'What really happens in child support cases: An empirical study of establishment and enforcement of child support orders in the Denver District Court' (1979) 57 *Denver Law Journal* 21 at 36. For an econometric analysis, concluding that the courts prioritised the welfare of non-custodial fathers over the interests of mothers and children, see D Del Boca and CJ Flinn, 'Rationalizing Child Support Decisions' (1995) 85 *American Economic Review* 1241.

[86] D Chambers, *Making Fathers Pay: The Enforcement of Child Support* (University of Chicago Press, Chicago, 1979), at 39. The first states to use guidelines were Illinois and Maine in 1975: Beller and Graham, n 43 above, at 165. See further *Smith v Smith* 626 P2d 342 (Supreme Court of Oregon, 1981). For a critique of these early types of formula, see A Giampetro, 'Mathematical Approaches to Calculating Child Support Payments: Stated Objectives, Practical Results, and Hidden Policies' (1986) 20 *Family Law Quarterly* 373.

[87] Beller and Graham, n 43 above, at 169, Table 6.1.

[88] The actual mechanism by which guidelines are laid down is for states to determine (42 USC § 667(a)): 27 states have incorporated their guidelines in statutes; 18 have implemented them through court rules and six through administrative regulations: Venohr and Williams, n 83 above, at 11 (Table 1). These data refer to the 50 US states and the District of Columbia.

[89] N Thoennes, P Tjaden and J Pearson, 'The Impact of Child Support Guidelines on Award Adequacy, Award Variability, and Case Processing Efficiency' (1991) 25 *Family Law Quarterly* 325 at 326.

payments' caused by inflation.[90] The resulting guidelines were then accorded presumptive force by the Family Support Act of 1988, which declared that 'the amount of the award which would result from the application of the guidelines is the correct amount of child support to be awarded'.[91] States were given until 1994 to implement such a rebuttable presumption; the various guidelines have since successfully withstood constitutional challenges in a series of cases.[92]

Federal regulations specify that state guidelines must conform to certain requirements: they must be based on numeric criteria (ie a formula); they must take into account all earnings and income of the *non-residential* parent;[93] and they must provide for the child's health care needs to be covered.[94] States were also required to review their guidelines every four years,[95] although not all states have adhered to this federal directive.[96] In conducting such reviews, states must have regard both to the 'economic data on the cost of raising children' and to the range of awards in their caseloads, bearing in mind the Congressional mandate to promote consistency in like cases.[97] Courts may only depart from the guidelines—producing an outcome known as a 'deviation'—if they make a specific written finding that the application of the guidelines would be inappropriate or unjust on the particular facts of the case.[98] This does not provide the courts with a licence to ignore the guidelines; the courts have recognised, in the light of the Congressional mandate, that deviations should be limited so that their presumptive force is not diluted.[99]

It is important, however, to recognise the limits of federal intervention in the setting of child support awards. The 1988 Act did not stipulate that states should adopt any particular type of guideline or formula, nor did it require that the guidelines be set at any particular level.[100] Key terms—such as what is meant by

---

[90] Beller and Graham, n 43 above, at 122.

[91] 42 USC § 667(2)(b).

[92] See the authorities cited in Morgan, n 39 above, at 205–6 and especially n 52.

[93] As we shall see, some (but not all) state guidelines also have regard to the PWC's income.

[94] 45 CFR § 302.56, cited in Venohr and Williams, n 83 above, at 10.

[95] For critiques see MS Melli, 'Guideline Review: The Search for an Equitable Child Support Formula' in Oldham and Melli, n 62 above, 112–27 and M Garrison, 'Child Support Guideline Review: Problems and Prospects' in A Bainham (ed), *The International Survey of Family Law* (Family Law, Bristol, 2001) at 437–48.

[96] eg Louisiana failed to undertake a review of its guidelines between their enactment in 1989 and 2001: KS Spaht, 'The Two "ICS" of the 2001 Louisiana Child Support Guidelines: Economics and Politics' (2002) 62 *Louisiana Law Review* 709 at 713. See further JC Venohr and TE Griffith, 'Child Support Guidelines: Issues and Reviews' (2005) 43 *Family Court Review* 415.

[97] 45 CFR § 302.56(e) and (h); see Melli, n 95 above, and JM Beld and L Biernat, 'Federal Intent for State Child Support Guidelines: Income Shares, Costs Shares, and the Realities of Shared Parenting' (2003) 37 *Family Law Quarterly* 165 at 168–73.

[98] This must be determined in accordance with criteria laid down at state level, which must take into account the child's best interests: see 42 USC § 667(b)(2) and 45 CFR § 302.56(g).

[99] See eg *Guillot v Munn* 756 So 2d 290 (Louisiana 2000), discussed by D Cross, 'Preserving continuity and fairness: the Louisiana Supreme Court limits deviation from child support guidelines' (2001) 47 *Loyola Law Review* 885.

[100] Venohr and Williams, n 83 above, at 8.

'income'—are left undefined by federal law.[101] It is therefore no surprise to find that the levels of child support awards, given the same factual circumstances, vary considerably across the USA.[102] According to Krause, 'more consistent and coherent results would be achieved if federal (not state-by-state) standards would set a national standard, with adjustments for regional variations in the cost of living'.[103] States also vary considerably in the processes through which their guidelines are implemented in individual cases: some adhere to the traditional court-based model, whereas others have established administrative systems for establishing, modifying and enforcing child support orders, especially in welfare cases.[104] In practice, whatever the structures in place, nearly all states have adopted one or other of two main types of guidelines, known as the 'percentage of obligor income' and the 'income shares' models. Some 13 states have implemented a 'percentage of obligor income' scheme, whilst 33 have opted for an 'income shares' basis to their guidelines and five states have variants on these two principal models.[105]

The simplest type of guideline is the 'percentage of obligor income' model, which was pioneered in Wisconsin and has since become the basis for the reformed United Kingdom scheme. Such a scheme applies a percentage slice to the non-resident parent's income[106] in order to arrive at the appropriate child support award. In Wisconsin the standard rates are 17 per cent for one child, 25 per cent for two children, 29 per cent for three children, 31 per cent for four children and 34 per cent for five or more. However, these rates are modified for those on very low or higher incomes,[107] and in some states the percentage rates also vary by locality.[108] Usually the appropriate award is translated into an actual dollar amount, although in some cases awards are expressed in terms of a specific percentage of monthly income. The latter approach is designed to be self-adjusting,

---

[101] Melli, n 95 above, at 116.

[102] See LW Morgan and MC Lino, 'A Comparison of Child Support Awards Calculated Under States' Child Support Guidelines with Expenditures on Children Calculated by the U.S. Department of Agriculture' (1999) 33 *Family Law Quarterly* 191 and T Graves, 'Comparing Child Support Guidelines' (2000) 34 *Family Law Quarterly* 149.

[103] Krause, n 28 above, at 376. For a more recent argument that there should be federal guidelines, see Morgan, n 39 above, at 216–21.

[104] See the discussion in M MacDonald, *Expedited Child Support* (Department of Justice, Ottawa, 1997).

[105] Venohr and Williams, n 83 above, at 11 (Table 1). Perhaps the most detailed and most readily available account (running to over 100 pages) is PW Faerber, 'Empirical Study: A Guide to the Guidelines: A Longitudinal Study of Child Support Guidelines in the United States' (1999) 1 *Journal of Law & Family Studies* 151. For an early but authoritative account see RG Williams, 'Guidelines for Setting Levels of Child Support Orders' (1987) 21 *Family Law Quarterly* 281.

[106] Wisconsin, in using the NRP's *gross* income, is even in the minority of percentage of obligor income states, as most calculate awards on the basis of *net* income, and so apply higher percentages to allow for the effect of taxes; eg Minnesota (one child: 25%; two children: 30%; three children: 35%): Venohr and Williams, n 83 above, at 12.

[107] For example, since January 1, 2004, the rates drop to 14%, 20%, 23%, 25% and 27% respectively on income above $84,000 a year, with further reductions when the NRP's income exceeds $150,000: see D Rossmiller, 'New child support guidelines effective Jan 1, 2004' (2003) 76 *Wisconsin Lawyer* 26 (November) at 27.

[108] Thoennes, Tjaden and Pearson, n 89 above, at 329.

so avoiding the need to return to court if the non-resident parent's income increases or decreases significantly, but is not without its difficulties.[109]

Most states, however, have adopted an income shares model.[110] This form of guideline is premised on the notion that children should receive the same proportion of parental income following the couple's separation as if they had continued living together. Accordingly the incomes of both parents are aggregated to replicate the joint income of an intact family. The guidelines then employ economists' estimates of how much a family of the same size and with the same income would devote to child-related expenditure. The resulting figure (a fixed dollar amount, being less than their total income) is then pro-rated for each parent, according to their relative incomes. For example, guidelines might specify that an intact family earning $6,000 a month would typically spend $1,500 in child-related expenditure on say two children (and assume the non-residential parent earns $4,000 and the parent with care $2,000). The non-resident parent would then be required to pay $1,000 a month in child support (being ⅔ of the overall cost, reflecting his share of the joint incomes). As with the percentage of income model, some states base their income share guidelines on gross income, others on net income. One criticism of such a scheme is that it fails to acknowledge 'the nonmonetary contribution of the custodial parent in directly caring for the children'.[111]

A minority of states operate some form of variant on either of the main schemes. Three states (Delaware, Hawaii and Montana) use the so-called Melson formula,[112] a more complex version of the income shares model involving three stages.[113] First, each parent's income is reduced by a self-support reserve, which serves broadly the same purpose as the exempt income in the original British scheme. According to one study, this means that the Melson formula 'results in a more realistic determination of actual ability to pay child support' when compared with the other two models.[114] Secondly, the children's 'primary support needs' are met by prorating the relevant guideline dollar figure (which obviously depends on the number of children) to each parent in line with their share of the joint incomes. Thirdly, any remaining parental income is subject to a percentage slice, reflecting a standard of living allowance to ensure that children enjoy the benefits of any higher incomes. The non-resident parent's child support liability is assessed by adding together the figures calculated in the second and third stages of this process.[115] Two jurisdictions (Massachusetts and the District of Columbia) use a hybrid of the two main schemes, under which a percentage of obligor income

---

[109] JT Oldham, 'New Methods to Update Child Support' in Oldham and Melli, n 62 above, at 131–34.

[110] Indeed, two states which originally opted for percentage of obligor income schemes subsequently switched to income share models.

[111] Beller and Graham, n 43 above, at 201.

[112] Named after Judge Elwood F Melson, Jr, who developed this formula in Delaware Family Court.

[113] See further Venohr and Williams, n 83 above, at 15–16.

[114] M Takas, 'Improving Child Support Guidelines: Can Simple Fomulas Address Complex Families?' (1992) 26 *Family Law Quarterly* 171 at 178.

[115] For a worked example, see Venohr and Williams, n 83 above, at 17 (Figure 3).

model applies where the non-resident parent's income is below a specified threshold, but an income shares system operates above that limit.[116]

The diversity of child support regimes in the United States is further compounded by the very many different arrangements for handling special factors in the guidelines. The four main areas relate to the treatment of shared parenting, work-related child care costs, children's health insurance premiums and extraordinary medical expenses (ie beyond those covered by insurance). Some states deal with some special costs as part of the formula calculation, typically by prorating them[117], others treat them as grounds for a deviation from the formula figure or for a separate order, some use different mechanisms for different types of special cost and in a handful of cases no special provision is made at all for particular types of expense.[118]

There have been several studies of the impact of the different types of guidelines in operation in the USA. One early but comprehensive study[119] undertook an analysis of formula outcomes based on a comparison of three states using the percentage of income, shared incomes and Melson models respectively. The percentage of income approach produced the highest awards in upper income families, the income shares model resulted in the highest awards amongst low income households, whilst the Melson formula generated the highest awards in middle income families.[120] The same study concluded that the Congressional objectives for guidelines had been achieved, but that the resultant gains were modest,[121] in part because in many instances the non-resident parent had only limited resources.[122] Later reviews have similarly concluded that the introduction of state guidelines has achieved at best a marginal improvement in terms of outcomes for child support orders.[123] The reasons for this include the failure of guidelines to prioritise the prevention of poverty amongst children and the continued reliance of the American system on individualised case processing and private bargaining.[124]

Ellman has delivered the most powerful critique of the methods used by the various consultants to advise state legislatures and others on their child support guidelines.[125] He notes that those charged with developing such guidelines

---

[116] Venohr and Williams, n 83 above, at 16–18.

[117] Or, in the case of shared parenting, cross-crediting within the formula: see ch 11 below.

[118] Eg all states bar Illinois, Mississippi and Tennessee make some adjustment for work-related child care costs within their guidelines: Venohr and Williams, n 83 above, at 18–21.

[119] Thoennes, Tjaden and Pearson, n 89 above; Marsha Garrison describes it as 'the largest and most detailed study to date', see M Garrison, 'The Goals and Limits of Child Support Policy' in Oldham and Melli, n 62 above, at 33, n 7. See also D Betson, E Evenhouse, S Reilly and E Smolensky, 'Trade-Offs Implicit in Child-Support Guidelines' (1992) 11 *Journal of Policy Analysis and Management* 1.

[120] Thoennes, Tjaden and Pearson, n 89 above, at 344.

[121] *Ibid*, at 345.

[122] See also the concerns expressed by Krause, n 28 above, at 380–82.

[123] See eg Beller and Graham, n 43 above, ch 6.

[124] Garrison, n 119 above, at 17–22.

[125] IM Ellman, 'Fudging Failure: The Economic Analysis Used to Construct Child Support Guidelines' (2004) *University of Chicago Legal Forum* 167. For a rather different critique of child support guidelines in the USA, written from a law and economics perspective, see several of the chapters in WS Comanor (ed), *The Law and Economics of Child Support Payments* (Edward Elgar, Cheltenham, 2004).

typically rely on the 'continuity of expenditure model', which is based on how much intact families spend on their children. This model, however, is based on the notion of an equivalence scale, which seeks to assess how much more a couple with (for example) one child would have to spend to maintain the same standard of living as a childless couple. Ellman argues that conceptually this approach is highly problematic, given that it has been 'appropriately criticized in the economic literature as theoretically suspect and empirically unverifiable'.[126] The end result, according to Ellman, is that both:

> income and expenditures are underreported, but it appears that income is disproportionately underreported in the low-income groups, while expenditures are disproportionately underreported in the high-income groups, so that guideline recommendations are distorted at both ends of the scale, but in opposite directions.[127]

In his view, reliance on neutral technocrats adopting purportedly value-free methodologies simply obscures the policy choices and trade-offs that are inevitable in constructing child support guidelines.

Child Support in Canada

We have seen that family law in the United States is primarily a matter for the states, although federal law has increasingly driven changes in the area of child support. The position in Canada has always been more complex. The division of powers is such that child support (and spousal support) in the wake of divorce is governed by federal law, whilst provincial law deals with child support where married or unmarried couples separate.[128] Enforcement, however, is a provincial responsibility in all cases.[129] Historically, in the same way as in the USA and in the United Kingdom, child maintenance liabilities were determined on a case-by-case basis, resulting in 'inadequate, inconsistent and arbitrary' awards.[130] As one distinguished Supreme Court judge noted, these low child support orders were 'generally inextricably linked to the societal assumption that women should bear primary responsibility for children'.[131] By the late 1980s the pressure for reform came from a combination of advocates for women's rights, arguing for a better

---

[126] Ellman, n 125 above, at 168. In addition, the continuity of expenditure model, he contends, is based on compromised data from the US Consumer Expenditure Survey.

[127] *Ibid*, at 214.

[128] T Maisonneuve, 'Child Support under the Federal and Quebec Guidelines: A Step Forward or Behind?' (1999) 16 *Canadian Journal of Family Law* 284 at 305.

[129] N Bala, 'A Report from Canada's "Gender War Zone": Reforming the Child-Related Provisions of the Divorce Act' (1999) 16 *Canadian Journal of Family Law* 163 at 170.

[130] Maisonneuve, n 128 above, at 287 and 300. See further A Bissett-Johnson, 'Reform of the law of Child Support: by judicial decision or by legislation?' (1995) 74 *Canadian Bar Review* 585 and (1996) 75 *Canadian Bar Review* 1.

[131] C L'Heureux-Dubé, 'Economic Consequences of Divorce: a view from Canada' (1994–1995) 31 *Houston Law Review* 451 at 470–71.

financial deal for lone parents, and provincial governments, which in Canada bear the main cost of welfare payments.[132] Statutory child support guidelines, enacted in the form of regulations rather than primary legislation, came into force in Canada with effect from 1 May 1997, some ten years after their introduction in the United States.[133] The Canadian guidelines, unlike the USA's, were issued by the federal government. The federal guidelines use a 'percentage of income model' and so exclude consideration of the non-custodial parent's income. They apply to all provinces with the exception of Quebec, which has adopted its own guidelines, based on the income shares model (and so which takes into account both parents' incomes).[134] Subsequently the majority of provinces have adopted identical or very similar guidelines for assessing child support under provincial family maintenance legislation.[135]

The percentage of income approach in the federal guidelines is based on a formula which takes into account average expenditures on children at various income levels.[136] As with the American state guidelines, the Canadian guidelines make no attempt to factor in the hidden or indirect costs of child-rearing,[137] which fall predominantly on women. Instead, the standard methodology for calculating child support liabilities under the federal guidelines involves two steps. The first is to identify the formula amount of child support based on the non-resident parent's income and the number of children; this produces a figure known as the 'Table amount'. The second is to make any adjustments or 'add ons' to the Table amount for prescribed special expenses. The guidelines are binding on the courts, although deviations are permitted in special cases (eg high income families[138] or step-parents) or where there would otherwise be 'undue hardship'.[139] There is some evidence that the Canadian courts are more willing than their American counterparts to invoke this procedure.[140] Parents are also able to reach their own private agreements on child support levels.

---

[132] Bala, n 129 above, at 169–70.

[133] Federal Child Support Guidelines SOR/97-175. This was the outcome of a process of consultation which started in 1990. For a comprehensive review of the early case law, see N Bala, 'The Child Support Guidelines: Highlights and Insights' (Family Law Institute of the Canadian Bar Association, January 1999).

[134] Maisonneuve, n 128 above, at 305–18. For a review of the Quebec scheme, see *Report of the Follow-up Committee on the Quebec Model for the Determination of Child Support Payments* (Ministère de la Justice du Québec, 2000, English translation July 2004).

[135] C Rogerson, 'Child support under the guidelines in cases of split and shared custody' (1998) 15 *Canadian Journal of Law & Society* 11 at 12, n 2.

[136] Maisonneuve, n 128 above, at 303–4.

[137] DAR Thompson, 'Who Wants to Avoid the Guidelines? Contracting Out and Around' (2001) 19 *Canadian Family Law Quarterly* 1 at 47.

[138] See eg *Simon v Simon* (1999) 182 DLR (4th) 670 discussed in S Buhler, 'Case Comment: *Simon v Simon* and *Penner v Penner*' (2001) 18 *Canadian Journal of Family Law* 183.

[139] Federal Child Support Guidelines, s 10(2).

[140] According to one Canadian practitioner, 'Practically speaking, I see many deviations and little record-keeping', M Gordon, 'Spousal Support Guidelines and the American Experience: Moving Beyond Discretion' (2002) 19 *Canadian Journal of Family Law* 247 at 263. See also Masionneuve, n 128 above, at 320 to similar effect.

The Canadian Divorce Act provided for a comprehensive review of the use of child support guidelines once they had been in place for five years. The resulting report concluded that the guidelines were working well, delivering predictable and consistent child support awards which were higher than those before 1997.[141] Across all types of cases, and across the whole period under review, the award was equal to the Table amount in 58 per cent of cases, indicating 'a high degree of predictability of child support amounts for cases in similar circumstances'.[142] Furthermore, the proportion of orders in which the sum awarded was equal to the Table amount increased steadily from 50 per cent in 1998 to 63 per cent in 2003. Over the same period the proportion of contested cases fell from 19 per cent to just 6 per cent.[143] Overall, in 31 per cent of cases the amount ordered was higher than the formula figure, suggesting that the Canadian judiciary are viewing the Table amount 'as a "floor" that needs to be increased if warranted by the circumstances of a particular case, frequently by ordering special or extraordinary expenses'.[144]

Child Support in Australia

The Federal Context

Family law in Australia has adopted a very different route to that of the United States in terms of the constitutional division of responsibilities at national and state level. The remit of the federal (or Commonwealth[145]) parliament is defined by the 1901 Constitution, which grants the Canberra legislature the power to 'make laws for the peace, order and good government of the Commonwealth' with respect to various matters, most of which lie in the domain of public law. However, the Constitution also empowers the federal parliament to legislate in respect of marriage, divorce and matrimonial causes, together with incidental matters relating to children.[146] The justification for the inclusion of these private law matters has been seen as two-fold. First, they are matters of 'public concern' to the (national) state and, secondly, those responsible for drafting the Constitution were alive to the need for uniformity of legislation across the Commonwealth.[147]

---

[141] Department of Justice, *Children Come First: A Report to Parliament Reviewing the Provisions and Operation of the Federal Child Support Guidelines* vol I (Ottawa, 2002) at 9. For criticism of the federal guidelines, see P Millar and AH Gauthier, 'What were they thinking? The Development of Child Support Guidelines in Canada' (2002) 17 *Canadian Journal of Law & Society* 139.

[142] LD Bertrand, JP Horncik, JJ Paetsch and N Bala, *Phase 2 of the Survey of Child Support Awards: Final Report* (Department of Justice, 2005) at 22 and 38.

[143] *Ibid*, at 11.

[144] *Ibid*, at 38; see further *ibid*, at 25–28. 'Undue hardship' was an issue in only 0.5% of cases: *ibid*, at 31.

[145] All references in this chapter to the 'Commonwealth' (Cth) are to the Australian sense of the term (the federal Australian state), and not the British usage (the successor to the Empire).

[146] Constitution of the Commonwealth of Australia, s 51(xxi) and (xxii).

[147] *Russell v Russell; Farrelly v Farrelly* (1976) 134 CLR 495 at 546–47 per Jacobs J.

This appears to have been a conscious decision by those framing the Constitution to adopt a different path to that of the United States.[148] More generally, Commonwealth legislation prevails over any inconsistent state law.[149] In addition, the Constitution enables states to refer matters to the federal parliament for legislative action at national level.[150] Between 1986 and 1990 all states (with the exception of Western Australia) exercised this power to refer most matters relating to children—including child maintenance—to the federal parliament.[151] An important consequence of this very different history of federal-state relations in family law matters, as contrasted with the United States, is that Australia was able to develop a national and more far-reaching child support regime.

The Early History of Child Support in Australia

Historically at least, Australian law largely followed the approach of the United Kingdom in defining the scope of the maintenance obligation. A husband's common law duty to maintain his wife was 'more theoretical than real' and a father's obligation to support his children was 'poorer still'.[152] Thus, following the English authorities, a father was under no obligation to support his legitimate children 'save to the extent that neglect to do so would constitute a criminal offence'.[153] Similarly, a man was under no common law obligation at all to support his illegitimate children.[154] Moreover, in contrast to the position in the United States, the English poor law was not transplanted to Australia.[155] However, early state legislation made provision for a destitute person to seek maintenance directly from eg a husband or father of an illegitimate child.[156] Subsequent legislation extended the courts' powers to encompass the award of financial provision more generally to deserted wives and their children. The enforcement of awards remained very much a matter of private initiative, although in the early twentieth century official collection facilities were established in two states.[157]

In the latter half of the twentieth century maintenance increasingly became the province of Commonwealth as opposed to state law. In 1961 federal law assumed responsibility for laying down the principles governing financial relief on

---

[148] A Dickey, *Family Law* (Lawbook Co, Sydney, 2002, 4th edn) at 14.

[149] Constitution of the Commonwealth of Australia, s 109.

[150] *Ibid*, s 51(xxxvii).

[151] Dickey, n 148 above, at 14–15.

[152] *Ibid*, at 461.

[153] *Ibid*, citing *Chantler v Chantler* (1906) 6 SR (NSW) 412 at 413 as well as UK authorities.

[154] *Cekulis v Beard* [1970] SASR 32.

[155] Dickey, n 148 above, at 463. As a result, Australia never had any equivalent to the United Kingdom's liable relative procedures: S Parker, 'Rights and Utility in Anglo-Australian Family Law' (1992) 55 *Modern Law Review* 311 at 327.

[156] Maintenance Act 1837 (Tasmania) and Deserted Wives and Children Act 1840 (NSW).

[157] In South Australia the state's Department for Family and Community Services established a maintenance collection programme in the 1930s; Western Australia developed a similar scheme based on the state Family Court.

divorce;[158] subsequently the Family Law Act 1975 (Cth) covered most maintenance issues relating to married couples and their children.[159] Later legislation, enacted following the referrals by state parliaments described in the previous section, meant that the Family Law Act came to apply to virtually all child maintenance issues for both legitimate and illegitimate children.[160] In making such decisions, the Australian courts, as elsewhere, enjoyed a wide discretion in fixing the level of child maintenance, taking into account a range of factors with no one consideration being conclusive.[161] In 1987 the legislature amended the 1975 Act to reinforce the child maintenance obligation,[162] at the same time setting out three priorities to be applied in determining child maintenance liabilities.[163] First, a parent should not accord lower priority to the maintenance of one child as against another (eg to support a child of a second marriage).[164] Secondly, the duty of child maintenance should prevail over all other commitments, save the obligation to support oneself and any other person to whom a parent owes a duty of support.[165] Finally, the duty of child maintenance is not affected by the duty of any other person to support the child or, in marked contrast to the development of the English case law, the entitlement of the child or any other person (typically the parent with care) to any means-tested benefit. These were, however, no more than general statements of principle to be applied within a highly discretionary framework. They were also rapidly overtaken by the government's decision to implement more radical child support reforms, as a result of which today the Family Law Act only applies to the assessment of child maintenance in exceptional cases.[166]

The Introduction of the Australian Child Support Scheme

The origins of the Australian Child Support Agency can be traced back to 1978, when a parliamentary joint select committee was established to monitor the operation of the Family Law Act.[167] Two years later that committee recommended that a national agency be established to collect and enforce maintenance along the

---

[158] The Matrimonial Causes Act 1959 (Cth) came into force in 1961.

[159] The Family Law Act 1975 (Cth) came into force in 1976.

[160] Or, as they are known rather quaintly in Australian usage, nuptial and ex-nuptial children. Western Australia, however, remains a special case to this day: see n 239 below.

[161] See generally *In the Marriage of Mee and Ferguson* (1986) 10 Fam LR 971.

[162] 'The parents of a child have . . . the primary duty to maintain the child', Family Law Act 1975 (Cth), s 66C(1).

[163] *Ibid*, s 66C(2).

[164] See *Ganter v Grimshaw* [1998] FLC 92-810.

[165] See further GT Riethmuller, 'Conflicting duties: child support and Australia's maintenance quagmire' (1997) 71 *Australian Law Journal* 190.

[166] eg where the child is aged over 18, the application is against a step-parent or the child or liable parent lacks the requisite connection with Australia: P Parkinson and J Behrens, *Australian Family Law in Context: Commentary and Materials* (Lawbook Co, Sydney, 2004, 3rd edn) at 506–7.

[167] See generally Child Support Evaluation Advisory Group, *Child Support in Australia: Final report of the evaluation of the Child Support Scheme* vol one—main report (AGPS, Canberra, 1992) ch 4.

lines of the state agencies which operated in South Australia and Western Australia.[168] A report from the Attorney-General's Department reached the same conclusion in 1984.[169] Subsequent research confirmed that the weaknesses of the private law system for determining child maintenance were similar to those identified in both the United States and the United Kingdom. Orders were not always applied for, and those that were made were typically for low amounts; furthermore, maintenance orders failed to keep pace with inflation over time and enforcement was at best sporadic.[170]

In 1986 a Cabinet Sub-Committee report, having observed that 'the payment of maintenance is effectively a voluntary act',[171] noted that the existing court-based system meant that growing numbers of parents with care were dependent on welfare benefits, with obvious consequences for the public purse.[172] Moreover, as in the United Kingdom, the official perception was that judges and practitioners were structuring divorce settlements so as to maximise the caring parent's social security entitlements.[173] Furthermore, in the majority of cases the financial circumstances of parents with care worsened following separation, whereas most men living alone after relationship breakdown were found to be better off.[174] The consequential greater capacity to pay maintenance in many cases was 'camouflaged by poor assessment procedures and almost non-existent enforcement mechanisms'.[175] Anticipating an argument which the Blair government was later to adopt, the Australian prime minister emphasised that child maintenance reforms were central to tackling the problems of child poverty.[176]

Given the systemic weaknesses in the existing system, the Cabinet Sub-Committee report concluded that modest reforms of the court-based arrangements for assessing maintenance would not deliver the desired objectives.[177] Instead, the report declared that a reformed scheme would be based on a legislative formula, rather than judicial discretion, with collection arranged through the tax system.[178] The decision in principle to adopt a formula-based regime having been taken, the details of the new scheme were worked out by a Child Support Consultative Group,

---

[168] See n 157 above.

[169] The National Maintenance Inquiry's report *A Maintenance Agency for Australia* (Attorney-General's Department, 1984) preferred the South Australian model.

[170] The available evidence base was reviewed more fully, albeit from a reformist perspective, in M Harrison, P McDonald and R Weston, 'Payment of Child Maintenance in Australia: The Current Position, Research Findings and Reform Proposals' (1987) *International Journal of Law and the Family* 92.

[171] Cabinet Sub-Committee on Maintenance, *Child Support: A discussion paper on child maintenance* (AGPS, Canberra, October 1986) at 6.

[172] *Ibid*, at 7–9.

[173] *Ibid*, at 11 and 12.

[174] *Ibid*, at 13.

[175] See Harrison, McDonald and Weston, n 170 above, at 100.

[176] See the speech of former premier Bob Hawke, quoted in R Ingleby, *Family Law and Society* (Butterworths, Sydney, 1993) at 207–8.

[177] Cabinet Sub-Committee on Maintenance, n 171 above, at 14.

[178] *Ibid*, at 14–15.

chaired by a federal Family Court judge.[179] The Group's declared objective was 'to design a system that is predictable, accessible, simple, inexpensive and readily understood'[180]—all features which were absent from the court-based scheme. However, given the limitations of the available research base, Parker has characterised the Group's ultimate proposals for the formula as having 'all the hallmarks of an educated stab in the dark'.[181] That said, the Group's recommendations were accepted by government with three main exceptions.[182] First, the government opted to use taxable income as the basis for formula assessments, rather than the Group's definition of 'income for child support purposes'. Secondly, the final scheme applied a different formula for cases involving substantial contact and shared care. Finally, the government rejected the Group's proposal that existing cases be permitted to apply to court for an administrative assessment; in doing so, Australian policy makers avoided the retrospectivity problem which has beset both the New Zealand and United Kingdom schemes.

In March 1987 the federal government announced its decision to introduce the child support scheme in two stages. Stage 1 was launched on 1 June 1988,[183] when existing court orders for child maintenance were registered with the new Agency, but solely for the purposes of collection and enforcement under the Child Support (Registration and Collection) Act 1988.[184] Stage 2, which began a little over a year later, involved the more ambitious project of the Agency assuming responsibility for the assessment of child support liabilities under the new formula. Stage 2 was not retrospective: the new formula, introduced by the Child Support (Assessment) Act 1989, applied to children born on or after 1 October 1989[185] or whose parents separated after that date.[186] As a result, for the last decade and more, the Australian child support scheme has had two cohorts: a diminishing (and soon to disappear) Stage 1 group,[187] whose maintenance liabilities are still determined by the courts

---

[179] Fogarty J who, as Ingleby (n 176 above at 216) notes, had sat on the bench which heard *the Marriage of Mee and Ferguson* (n 161 above), in which the Family Court had grappled with the uncertainties created by the discretionary regime under the Family Law Act 1975. He later chaired the post-implementation CSEAG.

[180] DSS (Child Support Consultative Group), *Child Support: Formula for Australia* (AGPS, Canberra, May 1988) at 7.

[181] With the important caveat that 'the previous system of child maintenance was a highly uneducated stab in the dark', S Parker, 'Child Support in Australia: Children's Rights or Public Interest?' (1991) 5 *International Journal of Law and the Family* 24 at 50. For an attempt to calculate the costs of children, see R Percival and A Harding, 'The public and private costs of children in Australia, 1993–94' in Vleminickx and Smeeding, n 57 above, ch 13.

[182] CSEAG, n 167 above, at 57.

[183] For an evaluation of Stage 1 see M Harrison, G Snider, R Merlo and V Lucchesi, *Paying for the children: parent and employer experience of stage one of Australia's Child Support Scheme* (AIFS, Melbourne, 1991).

[184] Originally known just as the Child Support Act 1988. Related Stage 1 reforms were implemented by the Family Law (Amendment) Act 1987 (Cth) and the Social Security and Veterans' Entitlements (Maintenance Income Test) Amendment Act 1988 (Cth).

[185] Or children who had a sibling born on or after that date.

[186] See generally Child Support (Assessment) Act 1989, ss 18–21 and 24.

[187] The last Stage 1 cases will drop out of the system in 2007.

under the Family Law Act, and a steadily growing Stage 2 caseload. Following the implementation of Stage 2, the Child Support Evaluation Advisory Group, echoing the earlier proposal of the Consultative Group, recommended that all parents, whatever the date of their separation, be given access to Stage 2,[188] but this proposal was not endorsed by the subsequent Parliamentary Joint Select Committee report.[189] Therefore, in Australia at least, the argument against retrospectivity trumped the case for increasing maintenance levels in existing cases determined under the court-based discretionary regime.[190] In practice, however, orders in Stage 1 cases gradually increased in any event, as the courts had close regard to formula assessments as a guideline.[191]

The Principal Features of the Australian Child Support Scheme

The following section can only summarise the principal features of the Australian scheme; subsequent chapters will highlight particular points of comparison or contrast between this system and the United Kingdom regime. Organizationally, the new Child Support Agency was originally located within the ATO, enabling the Agency both to rely on income tax data in making assessments and also to arrange for the deduction of child support liabilities at source from wages, alongside tax dues (at least for non-resident parents who were employed rather than self-employed). In 1998 the Agency moved out of the ATO and became a freestanding part of the Department of Family and Community Services, the Australian equivalent of the DWP. In 2004, as part of a wider reorganisation within the federal government, the Agency became part of the new Department of Human Services. These transfers principally affected lines of departmental accountability—in terms of its daily operations, the Agency remains closely integrated with the tax system. Constitutionally, however, the child support legislation is not a taxing statute, and nor does it involve the usurpation by the executive of judicial power.[192]

As in the United Kingdom, if the Agency has jurisdiction to make an assessment, then an Australian court is barred from making an order for child maintenance, whether or not an application has been made to the Agency.[193] Parents (and indeed others caring for a child) may apply to the Child Support Registrar[194]

---

[188] CSEAG, *The Child Support Scheme* (AGPS, Canberra, October 1990) at 73–75 and *Child Support in Australia* (AGPS, Canberra, 1992) at 57–59 and 153–60.

[189] Joint Select Committee on Certain Family Law Issues, *The Operation and Effectiveness of the Child Support Scheme* (AGPS, Canberra, November 1994).

[190] R Bailey-Harris, 'Child Support: is the Right the Wrong One? A Comment on Parker' (1992) 6 *International Journal of Law and the Family* 169 at 170.

[191] H Rhoades, 'Australia's Child Support Scheme—is it working?' (1995) 7 *Journal of Child Law* 26 at 29; see further *Beck v Sliwka* (1992) 15 Fam LR 520.

[192] *Luton v Lessels* (2002) 187 ALR 529.

[193] Family Law Act 1975 (Cth), s 66E (for the UK, see in similar terms CSA 1991, s 8).

[194] An office established by Child Support (Registration and Collection) Act 1988 (Cth), s 10.

for a child support determination based on the statutory formula.[195] The Australian formula is essentially a modified 'percentage of income' scheme—a liable parent is required to pay a set percentage of his income once an allowance is made for basic living expenses.[196] Unlike in the United Kingdom, most Australians have to complete an annual tax return, and in the typical case the starting point for the calculation is the liable parent's taxable income for the last relevant year.[197] In appropriate cases, in order to arrive at a more accurate reflection of that parent's true income, various further sums may be brought into the equation (eg foreign income which is exempt for tax purposes and the value of reportable fringe benefits).[198] The aggregated gross amount is known as the 'child support income amount', from which is deducted an 'exempted income amount', based on social security rates, to provide an element of protected earnings for the liable parent's self-support.[199] The resulting net figure is described as the 'adjusted income amount', to which the relevant child support percentage is applied (ranging from 18 per cent for one child to 36 per cent for five or more children).[200]

Special rules apply for those who are high or low earners. So far as the former are concerned, the liable parent's gross income is capped at two-and-a-half-times average earnings for the purpose of the application of the formula.[201] On the other side of the equation, the carer's gross income is effectively disregarded unless it exceeds the official average weekly earnings figure.[202] In addition, carers who are on welfare qualify for a maintenance disregard, enabling them to receive at least Aus$20 a week in child support before their benefit is affected.[203] At the other end of the scale, there is provision for liable parents who have suffered a drop in earnings to have their current rather than past income used as the basis of the assessment in certain circumstances.[204] For those on even lower incomes, there is a standard liability of Aus$260 a year (Aus$5 a week).[205] The figure produced by the child support formula is the annual child support award, which is then apportioned at a daily rate and collected as a monthly liability.[206] The child support liability is reassessed whenever a new income tax assessment is made in respect of

---

[195] Child Support (Assessment) Act 1989 (Cth), ss 25 and 25A.
[196] *Ibid*, s 36.
[197] *Ibid*, s 38.
[198] *Ibid*, s 38A.
[199] *Ibid*, s 39.
[200] *Ibid*, s 37.
[201] *Ibid*, s 42.
[202] *Ibid*, ss 43–46.
[203] Under the Maintenance Income Test a maintenance recipient who is a lone parent is entitled to an annual disregard of Aus$1,150 (in 2005), plus Aus$383 for each child after the first. In addition, any child support received above this threshold has the effect of reducing entitlement to Family Tax Benefit (Part A) by 50 cents in the dollar: A New Tax System (Family Assistance) Act 1999 (Cth), s 58(1) and sch 1, cls 20 and 22.
[204] Child Support (Assessment) Act 1989 (Cth), ss 59–64A.
[205] *Ibid*, s 66.
[206] Child Support (Assessment) Act 1989 (Cth), ss 36(1) and 78; see also Child Support (Registration and Collection) Act 1988 (Cth), s 66.

the liable parent or parent with care, or at the very latest after a period of fifteen months has elapsed.[207]

As under the United Kingdom scheme, there are further statutory variations on the standard formula to deal with more complex family arrangements, such as shared care.[208] In addition, the standard outcome may be changed if the Child Support Registrar decides to make a determination for a departure from the normal formula where exceptional circumstances are shown to exist.[209] Unlike in the United Kingdom—where the possibility of a departure was not introduced until five years after the start of the scheme—this type of adjustment has been a feature of the Australian system since the outset. Originally departure decisions were taken by the Agency with a right of appeal to the Family Court, but this right was only rarely exercised. Since 1992 there has been an intermediate stage in that the Agency employs 'senior case officers' (formerly 'child support review officers') to conduct informal hearings and to make departure decisions.

Once made, the effect of the Agency's assessment is to create a debt due by the liable parent to the carer.[210] Carers may also elect either to operate private arrangements for the payment of child support ('Private Collect') or for the Agency to assume responsibility for collection ('CSA Collect').[211] If the latter course is chosen, the child support liability transmutes into a debt payable to and enforceable by the Commonwealth, not the other parent.[212] In the normal course of events, the Agency will then recover the child support due by direct deduction from salary,[213] although it also enjoys an extensive range of other collection and enforcement powers.[214]

Notwithstanding the Agency's machinery, the Australian child support legislation still reflects a degree of commitment to private ordering. True, where the family's circumstances fall within the Agency's jurisdiction, parents have no right to apply to court for child maintenance under the Family Law Act 1975.[215] In addition, in contrast to the position in the United Kingdom, the Australian courts have no power to make consent orders in relation to child maintenance for children who fall within the Agency's potential ambit. As a result, it is estimated that about 90 per cent of Australian children affected by divorce or separation are covered by the Agency.[216] Nor can parents make an agreement to oust the Agency's jurisdiction.[217] However, the legislation specifically provides that it

---

[207] Child Support (Assessment) Act 1989 (Cth), s 34A.

[208] On shared care see *ibid*, ss 47–49 and below pp 319–21.

[209] Child Support (Assessment) Act 1989 (Cth), pt 6A (ss 98A–98R).

[210] *Ibid*, s 79.

[211] Child Support (Registration and Collection) Act 1988 (Cth), s 24A.

[212] *Ibid*, s 30.

[213] *Ibid*, s 43: thus in Australia (as in the USA) deduction from salary is a normal collection method, whereas in the UK it is primarily an enforcement tool.

[214] See generally ch 14 below. See further A Shephard, 'The Australian Child Support Agency: Debt Study and Follow-Up on Intensive Debt Collection Process' (2005) 43 *Family Court Review* 387.

[215] Family Law Act 1975, s 66E, which formed the model for CSA 1991, s 8 in the UK.

[216] A Burgess, 'Bringing fathers back in' (2005) 12 *Public Policy Research* 49 at 50.

[217] *In the Marriage of Sloan* (1994) FLC 92-507 and *B v J* (1996) FLC ¶92-716.

should be construed so as 'to permit parents to make private arrangements for the financial support of their children', so long as this accords with the underlying objectives of the scheme.[218] In practice, private ordering is facilitated in four principal ways. First, where the parent with care is not on benefit,[219] parties are at liberty to reach an informal private agreement as to both the amount and the method of paying child support—although, of course, there is nothing to stop the parent with care later reneging on the agreement and applying to the Agency. Secondly, parents may enter into a more formal arrangement known as a 'child support agreement',[220] specifying the agreed amount of periodic child support or providing that child support is to be paid in some other form, such as a lump sum.[221] A child support agreement has no effect until lodged with the Child Support Registrar, who then issues a child support assessment in accordance with the agreement and without further scrutiny.[222] The exception is where the carer is in receipt of benefit, in which case the social security authorities must be satisfied with the terms of the agreement.[223] Thirdly, whereas the United Kingdom scheme insists on cash transfers in discharge of child support liabilities, the Australian system provides for a degree of flexibility as regards the method of payment in that it permits 'non-agency payments' (NAPs). Parents may agree that certain payments made to third parties or the provision of goods and services count as the payment of child support.[224] In addition, even where the parties do not agree, a non-resident parent may meet up to 25 per cent of his child support liability in NAPs, for example payment of the child's school fees or medical costs, providing he is otherwise in full compliance with the assessment.[225] Finally, once an Agency assessment is in place, either party is entitled to apply to court for a 'substitution order', for example capitalising a periodic child support liability into a lump sum payment.[226]

Review and Reform of Australian Child Support

In the period since 1989 the Australian child support scheme has been subject both to intense public scrutiny and to frequent amendment. Within the first five years of the scheme, two substantial official reviews had been published, one by the Child Support Evaluation Advisory Group (CSEAG)[227] and the other by a parliamentary

---

[218] Child Support (Assessment) Act 1989 (Cth), s 4(3)(a).

[219] If the PWC receives social security as a lone parent, the benefit authorities may require her to apply to the Agency: A New Tax System (Family Assistance) Act 1999 (Cth) sch 1, cl 10.

[220] Child Support (Assessment) Act 1989 (Cth), ss 80–98.

[221] *Ibid*, s 84.

[222] *Ibid*, ss 91 and 92.

[223] *Ibid*, s 91A.

[224] *Ibid*, ss 71–71B. In certain circumstances the Agency can decline to credit such NAPs against a child support liability: *ibid*, s 71D.

[225] *Ibid*, s 71C.

[226] *Ibid*, ss 121–131.

[227] CSEAG, n 167 above, running to 462 pages.

joint select committee.[228] The CSEAG report concluded that the new scheme had succeeded in increasing both the levels of child support orders and the collection rate for awards in its first three years of operation. However, it also identified a number of deficiencies in the scheme, especially in operational matters—for example, parents found it difficult to communicate with the Agency, there were delays in passing on payments and enforcement rates were low in cases of default.[229] The high level of public dissatisfaction with the Agency's performance was evidenced by the fact that the subsequent parliamentary joint select committee received a total of 6,197 submissions, the largest number ever received by such a committee.[230] Despite this, the joint select committee concluded that the scheme 'had been a qualified success', not least in engineering a change in societal attitudes to the importance of child support.[231] However, the committee's report was damning in its assessment of the Agency's performance to date,[232] and devoted the bulk of its 163 detailed recommendations to administrative and operational issues. A subsequent report by the Australian National Audit Office concluded that the Agency had improved the way in which it handled its workload, but also identified a number of areas in which further reforms were needed (especially debt management).[233] The Agency's work continues to generate a large number of complaints to the Commonwealth Ombudsman,[234] whose office has also produced major reports on particular aspects of the Agency's operations such as the recovery of overpayments,[235] the complaints service[236] and the departures system.[237]

The steady flow of official reviews, allied with continued public pressure, particularly from non-resident fathers,[238] has resulted in the federal parliament passing a series of amendments to the already complex body of primary legislation.[239]

---

[228] n 189 above (687 pages).

[229] CSEAG, n 167 above at iv–v.

[230] n 189 above, at 1.

[231] *Ibid*, at 3.

[232] The Agency's: 'inaction or lack of service is inexcusable . . . The end result is an often appalling client service delivery by the Child Support Registrar and the CSA which often appears to reflect an expectation that the problems clients have, and the clients, will go away if their rights are not explained', *ibid*, at 8.

[233] Australian National Audit Office (ANAO), *Management of Selected Functions of the Child Support Agency* (ANAO, Canberra, 1998). See also ANAO, *Client Service in the Child Support Agency Follow-up Audit* (Report No 7 2002–03).

[234] See eg Commonwealth Ombudsman, *Annual Report 2002–2003*, ch 4.

[235] Commonwealth Ombudsman, *Child Support Overpayments: A case of give and take?* (January 1998).

[236] Commonwealth Ombudsman, *Review of the Child Support Agency's Complaint Service* (July 2001).

[237] Commonwealth Ombudsman, *Child Support Agency change of assessment decisions* (Report No 01/2004, May 2004).

[238] See eg RA Cruickshank, *Child Support: The Financial Cost to the Taxpayer* (PIR, Melbourne, 2004). The voice of parents with care and children seems to be largely absent from this debate: K Funder, 'Changes in Child Support' (1997) 48 *Family Matters* 36.

[239] This creates special problems in Western Australia (WA), which has not referred its powers to legislate in respect of ex-nuptial children to the Commonwealth. Federal legislation which amends child support law must be separately implemented by the WA legislature in order to apply to ex-nuptial children. Such state legislation does not always follow expeditiously, presenting the Agency with some operational problems.

The first significant post-implementation reform measure was the Child Support Legislation Amendment (No 2) Act 1992, which modified the formula for shared care cases and adjusted the provisions governing taxable income for assessment purposes. Following a series of other relatively minor statutory amendments in the early to mid-1990s,[240] some of the joint select committee's recommendations from 1994 were finally enacted in 1998,[241] including the introduction of a minimum rate of child support (eg for non-resident parents on benefit) and various adjustments to the formula, principally to the benefit of non-resident parents.[242] Further amending legislation, enacted in 2001, provided a new ground for departure from the standard formula for non-resident parents with second family responsibilities.[243] The 2001 Act also added departure prohibition orders to the Agency's armoury of enforcement measures.[244] However, government proposals to lower the formula percentage rate in cases where the non-resident parent had some contact (but not shared care) and to lower the cap on the liable parent's assessable income did not survive scrutiny in the Senate.

One consequence of these developments is that the original aspirations for 'a system that is predictable, accessible, simple, inexpensive and readily understood' have clearly not been met in full. Indeed, one commentator has claimed that Australian child support law is 'incomprehensible to all but an elite of child support officers and specialist family lawyers'.[245] There is no immediate prospect of a halt to this culture of constant change. A further child support amendment bill, introduced in 2004, failed to make progress before that year's federal election was called,[246] but entirely separately a new review of aspects of the child support scheme had been launched. In December 2003 the parliamentary Family and Community Affairs Committee, in its report on post-separation arrangements for children, proposed further changes to child support law.[247] In particular, the committee recommended various modifications to the formula, most of which would have the effect of reducing the amounts paid by non-resident parents, whilst also advocating that the Agency be granted wider enforcement powers. In response, the government

---

[240] Child Support Legislation Amendment Acts 1990, 1992 and 1995 (Cth); see also Child Support Legislation Amendment (No 1) Act 1997.

[241] The original Bill, announced in 1997, failed to complete its parliamentary passage before the 1998 federal election.

[242] Child Support Legislation Amendment Act 1998 (Cth); for a summary, see D Bryant, 'Amendments to Child Support Legislation' (1997) 12 *Australian Family Lawyer* 19.

[243] Child Support Legislation Amendment Act 2001 (Cth). The Child Support Legislation Amendment Act 2000 (Cth) dealt with international child support issues.

[244] See further pp 466–67 below.

[245] J Wade, *Child Support Handbook* (CCH, Sydney, 1998) para 90,104, quoted in T Altobelli, *Family Law in Australia—Principles & Practice* (LexisNexis Butterworths, Australia, 2003).

[246] The Child Support Legislation Amendment Bill 2004, a largely technical measure, sought to clarify the reciprocal provisions governing child support orders with an overseas dimension, as well as including minor procedural and policy changes. It received its Second Reading on 31 March 2004 but further parliamentary time was not available before the general election.

[247] House of Representatives Family and Community Affairs Committee, *Every picture tells a story* (Canberra, December 2003), ch 6.

appointed an independent Taskforce to advise on the committee's short-term proposals and to evaluate the existing formula in the context of research evidence on the
costs of supporting children.[248] The Taskforce's substantial report, published in
May 2005, concluded that the scheme 'has been a success in a great many ways' and
had 'certainly led to a cultural change in community attitudes' about parental
responsibility for child support.[249] Yet the Taskforce report also identified a number of problems with the existing arrangements and made proposals for sweeping
changes to the Australian scheme. Its principal recommendation was that the existing percentage of income formula should be replaced a by a new formula, based on
research on the 'real cost' of raising children, which would take into account both
parents' incomes. The overall effect of the reform package, given the parallel recommendation to increase the minimum payment, is expected to be that in future
better off non-resident parents will pay less by way of child support whereas those
on low incomes will pay more. The changes, widely regarded as at least a partial
victory for father's rights groups,[250] were adopted by the federal cabinet in October
2005 and will be phased in between 2006 and 2008.

Child Support in New Zealand

The structure of New Zealand's child support system owes much to the reforms
initiated by its larger neighbour across the Tasman Sea, but the factors leading to
these changes and the details of the two schemes are by no means identical.

So far as the background is concerned, the political context of the New Zealand
reforms was much closer to that in the United Kingdom than in Australia.[251]
Indeed, the election in New Zealand of a conservative National government in
November 1990 resulted in a 'rapid move from a mature welfare state to a neo-
liberal testbed' for radical changes in the field of social policy.[252] Domestic purposes benefit had been payable to lone parents on a statutory basis since 1973,[253]
and by 1991 New Zealand had the highest proportion of lone parents solely reliant
on social security benefits, as well as the second highest rate of lone parenthood, in
the Organisation for Economic Co-operation and Development (OECD).[254] The

[248] Statement of Minister for Children and Youth Affairs, 16 August 2004.
[249] FaCS, Report of the Ministerial Taskforce on Child Support, *In the Best Interests of Children—
Reforming the Child Support Scheme* (Canberra, May 2005) at 76.
[250] 'Child support changes "a win for dads"', *The Australian*, 13 October 2005.
[251] See S Uttley, 'Child Support: The Limits of Social Policy Based on Assumptions of Knavery'
(1999) 33 *Social Policy and Administration* 552 at 556 and generally M McClure, *A Civilised
Community: A History of Social Security in New Zealand 1898–1998* (Auckland University Press,
Auckland, 1998).
[252] J Veit-Wilson, 'States of Welfare: A Conceptual Challenge' (2000) 34 *Social Policy and
Administration* 1 at 6.
[253] Previously domestic purposes benefit (DPB) had been paid to lone parents on a discretionary
basis; see McClure, n 251 above, at 158 and generally on DPB see *ibid*, at 179–89.
[254] S Uttley, 'Lone Mothers and Policy Discourse in New Zealand' (2000) 29 *Journal of Social Policy*
441 at 450.

incoming administration in 1990 was especially concerned at the rising cost of domestic purposes benefit, given that the existing liable parent scheme, operated by the Department of Social Welfare, had proven to be singularly unsuccessful in recouping contributions from separated fathers.[255] The New Zealand Child Support Act 1991, which came into force on 1 July 1992, was thus primarily a revenue reimbursement measure. As Atkin commented at the time, 'the reform is motivated by fiscal exigencies rather than the needs of women and children'.[256] This was implicitly acknowledged by the High Court's observation that the philosophy underpinning the legislation was that a lesser proportion of the financial responsibility for supporting the children of non-custodial parents should fall on taxpayers: 'or, to put the point another way, one of the objectives is to induce parents to alter their priorities'.[257] The new scheme was, moreover, accompanied by reductions in the value of the domestic purposes benefit as part of the National government's strategy to 'arrest new Zealand's drift from work to welfare'.[258]

As regards the scheme's overall structure, the New Zealand arrangements were certainly modelled on those introduced in Australia, with a new Agency housed within the Inland Revenue being made responsible for conducting administrative assessments of child support liabilities.[259] This was also more radical than the country's previous liable parent scheme in that it applied to all separated parents, not just to cases in which the parent with care was on benefit.[260] The statutory nexus between biological parenthood and the imposition of child support liability likewise follows the Australian model.[261] The structure of the New Zealand child support formula is broadly similar to that in Australia, in that awards are calculated by applying a child support percentage (slightly lower than in Australia) to the liable parent's taxable income, having deducted a living allowance based on

---

[255] See GJ Thomas, 'New Zealand's Nonjudicial Parental Income Attachment Scheme' in JM Eekelaar and SN Katz (eds), *The Resolution of Family Conflict* (Butterworths, Toronto, 1984) ch 33 for a summary of the scheme. However, it was estimated that only about one-third of liable parents were making contributions: JD Howman, 'New Zealand Child Support System', First World Congress on Family Law and Children's Rights, *Congress Papers* (Sydney, 1994), at 686.

[256] B Atkin, 'Financial Support: The Bureaucratization of Personal Responsibility' in M Henaghan and B Atkin (eds) *Family Law Policy in New Zealand* (Auckland OUP, 1992).

[257] *Re M* [1993] NZFLR 74 at 85 *per* Eichelbaum CJ.

[258] McClure, n 251 above, at 234; see further R Stephens, 'Re-orienting support for children in New Zealand' in J Bradshaw (ed) *Children and Social Security* (Ashgate, Aldershot, 2003) ch 2.3.

[259] The New Zealand Agency was subsequently retitled Inland Revenue Child Support: B Atkin and A Black, 'Child Support—Supporting Whom?' (1999) 30 *Victoria University of Wellington Law Review* 221 at 222 n 5.

[260] WR Atkin, 'Child support in New Zealand runs into strife' (1994–95) 31 *Houston Law Review* 631 at 634.

[261] Thus the New Zealand scheme effectively ignores the fact that the 'whanau', or extended family, is much more important in the Mâori community: *ibid*, at 632 and see further J Ruru, 'Indigenous Peoples and Family Law: Issues in Aotearoa/New Zeland' (2005) 19 *International Journal of Law, Policy and the Family* 327. Note that Mâoris constitute about 15% of the New Zealand population (2001 census, New Zealand Statistics), whereas the Aboriginal and Torres Strait Islander communities make up only about 2% of the total population of Australia: *Australian Social Trends* (2000).

social security rates.[262] The New Zealand scheme has also provided for departures from the standard formula in special cases since its inception.[263]

There are, however, a number of significant differences between the New Zealand scheme and that introduced in Australia.[264] First, the New Zealand scheme was retrospective in that in principle it applied to all cases, regardless of the date of separation. As a result, as was also to happen in the United Kingdom, many pre-existing court-ordered or negotiated matrimonial settlements were effectively overturned. Secondly, the New Zealand formula takes no account of the carer's income, although this may constitute a ground for seeking a departure. Thirdly, the New Zealand scheme makes some allowance for the liable parent's step-children in applying the formula;[265] conversely, and in contrast to both the Australian and United Kingdom statutory child support schemes, a step-parent may exceptionally be made liable for child support.[266] Finally, there is no main-tenance disregard for social security claimants in New Zealand.[267]

The New Zealand child support scheme has proven to be no less controversial than its Australian or British counterparts. Atkin, writing shortly after its intro-duction, described how 'its history has been a legal, social and political night-mare'.[268] In 1994 the New Zealand scheme was subject to a major review, chaired by a retired judge, which led to the publication of the Trapksi report.[269] This made a number of recommendations for reform—including several proposals to adjust the formula, such as abolishing the living allowance deduction and simply dividing a proportion of the liable parent's income between all his dependent children—as well as rejecting other ideas for change (such as introducing a child support disregard for welfare claimants).[270] However, most of the Trapski pro-posals for reform have been shelved.[271]

---

[262] See CSEAG, n 167 above, at 110–11 for a summary of the similarities between the two schemes.

[263] Initially this required an application direct to the Family Court, but an internal review system was introduced in New Zealand in 1994, two years after the Australian procedural reforms. Nevertheless, child support cases still account for a significant proportion of the New Zealand Family Court's caseload: see P Tapp, N Taylor and M Henaghan, 'Agents or Dependants: Children and the Family Law System' in J Dewar and S Parker (eds), *Family Law Processes Practices and Pressures*, ch 14, at 309.

[264] *Ibid*, at 111 and Joint Select Committee, n 189 above, App 9 at para 1.36.

[265] Child Support Act 1991 (NZ), s 30.

[266] *Ibid*, s 99, but only on application to the Family Court: see *BPS v MNS* [1998] NZFLR 289 and *A v R* [1999] NZFLR 249.

[267] A proposal for a disregard was dropped from the original draft legislation: see Uttley, n 251 above, at 560. Historically the New Zealand scheme has also operated one of the narrowest 'good cause' exemptions for welfare claimants: see further p 275 below.

[268] Atkin, n 260 above, at 642.

[269] P Trapski *et al, Child Support Review 1994: Report of the Working Party* (November 1994).

[270] The Trapski proposals were critically reviewed by B Atkin, 'New Zealand Family Law 1994—More promise than achievement' in A Bainham (ed) *International Survey of Family Law 1994* at 378–82.

[271] Atkin and Black, n 259 above, at 222.

Conclusion

This chapter has provided an overview of the principal features of the child support schemes which operate in other common law jurisdictions, and especially in Australia and the United States. It is very difficult to make a meaningful comparison of the effectiveness of these different regimes, given the limitations of the available data. A direct comparison between the effectiveness of the American and British schemes is especially difficult because of the diversity of arrangements in the United States, and the very different structures in place in the two countries.[272] A more instructive approach may be to compare the Australian and United Kingdom schemes, given that in both countries a national agency has primary responsibility for the assessment, collection and enforcement of child support liabilities, operating a formula-based assessment with relatively restricted grounds for departures from that formula. Moreover, unlike in the United States, in both countries the role of the courts in setting child support is at best residual.

In terms of administrative cost-effectiveness, the Australian Agency has made a tentative attempt to analyse the performance of the various schemes,[273] which suggests that its own scheme compares favourably with overseas organizations. On this analysis, the Australian agency recovers Aus$7 in child support for every Aus$1 spent on administration, compared with Aus$4 and Aus$2.9 collected by the American and British authorities respectively.[274] Put another way, it costs the Australians 14 cents to collect one Australian dollar in child support, as against outlays of 25 cents and 35 cents respectively in the United States and the United Kingdom. The Australian scheme also appears to perform well in terms of its compliance rates. Independent researchers concluded that the percentage of those potentially eligible for child support in Australia who actually received payments rose from 24 per cent in 1981 to 41 per cent in 1994.[275] Using a rather different measure, the Australian Agency's own data suggests that its overall recovery rate for all liabilities in Agency collect cases has increased from 65 per cent in 1991 to 89 per cent by 2004,[276] a compliance rate which is well beyond that achieved to date in the United Kingdom. Other research in Australia has tended to confirm

---

[272] But see A Benson, 'Child support reforms in the United Kingdom and the United States' in J Bradshaw (ed), *Children and Social Security* (Ashgate, Aldershot, 2003), ch 3.2.

[273] Child Support Agency, *Child Support Scheme: Facts and Figures 2003–04* (Canberra, 2004), Table 7.3, at 39. There are, of course, significant variations in performance across the USA: see *2004 Green Book*, n 61 above, at 8–65.

[274] The latter figure may be an over-estimate, as UK data suggests that the ratio of administrative costs to maintenance paid is actually 1:1.8: *Hansard* HC Debates vol 440 col 72W (28 November 2005).

[275] J Kunz, P Villeneuve and I Garfinkel, 'Child support among selected OECD countries: a comparative analysis' in Vleminickx and Smeeding, n 57 above, ch 19 at 492.

[276] Child Support Agency, n 273 above, Table 5.5, at 28. But note the Taskforce's doubts about the robustness of the official data on compliance in Australia: n 249 above at 85.

that the scheme there has gone some way to meeting its goals, especially in terms of tackling poverty in lone parent households,[277] although women's disposable incomes still drop more sharply than men's on separation.[278]

What then are the reasons for the relative success of the Australian agency? In an early study Millar identified two main groups of factors which might explain the greater legitimacy enjoyed by the Australian scheme, which relate to the way in which the respective schemes were developed and structured.[279] First, as we have seen, in terms of development there was extensive and prolonged consultation in Australia about the principles underpinning the scheme before its introduction, since when there has been detailed monitoring and evaluation. In the United Kingdom, by contrast, the legislation was rushed through, with minimal public debate, and there has been only limited independent evaluation since implementation. Secondly, there were also important differences in the structures of the two schemes. Although fiscal concerns were a factor in both schemes, their influence was much stronger in the United Kingdom—thus the original British formula was based on benefit rates, and did not vary directly with family size, unlike its Australian counterpart.[280] In addition, in the absence of a maintenance disregard, the original British scheme provided no financial incentive for lone parents on benefit (or their former partners) to co-operate with the Agency. Furthermore, the legitimacy of the United Kingdom scheme, both amongst the Agency's clients and the wider public, was undermined by its retrospective nature.[281] We might also add that the hideous complexity of the original formula under the 1991 Act, allied with the absence of access to income tax data and the potential for almost endless reviews of liability on changes of circumstances, presented the United Kingdom's Agency with an almost insuperable administrative task. These systemic problems in fixing child support assessments at the outset (and periodically thereafter) inevitably meant that the prospects for effective enforcement disappeared. The net result of these various differences is that the Australian scheme 'had a relatively solid base on which to build' whereas the United Kingdom scheme, 'starting badly as it did, has remained constantly in survival mode'.[282]

---

[277] A Harding and A Szukalska, *Trends in child poverty in Australia: 1982 to 1995–96* (NCSEM Discussion Paper No 42, Canberra, 1999).

[278] S Kelly and A Harding, *Love can hurt, divorce will cost* (AMP/NATSEM Income and Wealth Report Issue 10, 2005).

[279] J Millar, 'Poor mothers and absent fathers: Support for lone parents in a comparative perspective' in H Jones and J Millar (eds), *The Politics of the Family* (Avebury, 1996).

[280] The Australian targets for public expenditure savings were also much more modest: P Whiteford, 'Implementing Child Support—Are There Lessons From Australia?' (1994) 11 *Benefits* at 3.

[281] See further J Millar and P Whiteford, 'Child Support in Lone-Parent Families: Policies in Australia and the UK' (1993) 21 *Policy and Politics* 59 and for a more recent comparison T Ridge, 'Supporting Children? The Impact of Child Support Policies on Children's Wellbeing in the UK and Australia' (2005) 34 *Journal of Social Policy* 121.

[282] Burgess, n 216 above, at 53.

Dolowitz identifies a similar constellation of factors in his analysis of the reasons why the policy transfer process from the United States and Australia led to implementation failure in the United Kingdom.[283] Moreover:

> in the US and Australia the prime groups targeted were individuals who had fallen into arrears or who were not making any child support payments. In Britain, the primary target group became those who could make the biggest contribution to reducing the PSBR [Public Sector Borrowing Requirement].[284]

Other comparative research suggests that weaknesses in enforcement policy in both the United Kingdom and the United States may account for the relative success of the Australian scheme.[285] Somewhat belatedly, many of these lessons had been heeded by the time that the Blair government introduced its child support reforms in 2003—for example, the new scheme formula varies according to the number of children, breaking the linkage with benefit rates, and a child support premium or disregard has been belatedly introduced.[286] There remain, however, several significant differences between the two schemes, most notably in the arrangements for collection and enforcement.[287]

---

[283] DP Dolowitz, 'Welfare: the Child Support Agency' in DP Dolowitz (ed) *Policy Transfer and British Social Policy* (Open University Press, Milton Keynes, 2000), ch 2.

[284] *Ibid*, at 56.

[285] Kunz *et al*, n 275 above, at 496.

[286] See further ch 15.

[287] See further ch 14.

Part II

7

Private Ordering, Child Maintenance and the Courts

Introduction

The clear policy of the law today is to encourage couples to resolve between themselves, perhaps with the assistance of lawyers and mediators, the problems which arise on the breakdown of a relationship.[1] This principle is known as 'private ordering'.[2] As one senior family law judge has observed:

> As a matter of general policy I think it is very important that what the parties themselves agree at the time of separation should be upheld by the courts unless there are overwhelmingly strong considerations for interference.[3]

Initially, this policy developed in ancillary relief proceedings concerned with financial matters, but it is also now fundamental to the private law framework for determining the residence and related arrangements for the children of the relationship, especially since the Children Act 1989. There are a number of sound reasons for adopting such an approach, not least the argument that parties may feel more inclined to adhere to an agreement which has been negotiated rather than imposed. Such private ordering may also help to avoid the costs associated with protracted litigation, which can increase exponentially once the parties are actually in court. Consequently, family law practice has developed a strong 'settlement culture', which is seen in operation most clearly in negotiated agreements being struck at or before 'the door of the court' and is such that 'many practitioners regard a contested hearing on a divorce matter as tantamount to an admission of professional failure'.[4]

Yet an inevitable danger of private ordering is that it may simply reinforce the inequality of bargaining power which often exists. This may be one explanation for

---

[1] S Cretney, JM Masson and R Bailey-Harris, *Principles of Family Law* (Sweet & Maxwell, London, 7th edn, 2002) at 320.

[2] See further S Cretney, 'Private Ordering and Divorce—How far can we go?' [2003] Fam Law 399.

[3] *Smith v McInerney* [1994] 2 FCR 1086 at 1090E *per* Thorpe J.

[4] G Davis, S Cretney and J Collins, *Simple Quarrels* (Clarendon Press, Oxford, 1994) at 212. This process has now been institutionalised through the system of Financial Dispute Resolution appointments, introduced nationally in 2000: see Cretney *et al*, n 1 above, at 327–28.

the fact that in general men prefer to negotiate maintenance issues directly with their former partner, whereas women's preference is for such matters to be resolved at arm's length, through an external agency.[5] One potential consequence of such inequality is that women may feel compelled to settle disputes on terms which do not properly reflect their interests (or those of the children).[6] It follows that there is a tension between the official policy of encouraging private settlements and the state's interest in ensuring that such settlements are fair to the parties, their children and the wider community.[7] Indeed, those responsible for the introduction of the Child Support Act were concerned that courts and practitioners had become too focussed on reaching outcomes that suited the interests of the immediate parties and had neglected this broader public interest.

As we have seen in chapter 5, the policy intention underpinning the 1991 Act was that the Agency would take over responsibility for assessing, reviewing and enforcing nearly all child maintenance claims. The central provision is section 8 of the 1991 Act. As Ward LJ has observed, 'A firm purpose of the Act which many family lawyers have found so unattractive is to remove from the courts the power to make periodical payments in respect to the children'.[8] The original thinking was that once the initial transitional period had come to an end in April 1997, the powers of the courts would be confined to making orders in very exceptional cases (such as those involving very high earning non-resident parents, or where there were extra costs associated with the child's disability or education). True, for the time being, at least in non-benefit cases, the parties' right to reach a private settlement with the court's approval by the mechanism of a consent order was preserved. In all other cases, the expectation was that child maintenance would be exclusively a matter for the Agency. Yet acute operational problems and the systemic failure of the Agency in its early years meant that this aspiration soon had to be abandoned.

Instead, the Child Support Act 1995 amended the 1991 Act so that many pre-1993 private cases were left indefinitely outside the ambit of the Agency.[9] Accordingly, parents with care in these cases have, from the outset of the scheme, been barred from applying to the Agency and so have had to rely on private negotiation or court adjudication and enforcement,[10] the very system which had been condemned as unsatisfactory by policy makers in 1991. No change was made to this state of affairs by the 2000 Act—so, for better or worse, these cases remain outside the Agency's jurisdiction. However, much more controversially, the 2000 Act enables a parent with care in a (new) private case to apply to the Agency for a

---

[5] In the baseline study 68% of NRPs (and 88% of self-employed NRPs) preferred to arrange child maintenance privately, whereas nearly half of all PWCs preferred to use the Agency: N Wikeley *et al, National Survey of Child Support Agency Clients* (DWP Research Report No 152, 2001) at 148–50.

[6] See F Wasoff, 'Mutual Consent: Separation Agreements and the Outcomes of Private Ordering in Divorce' [2005] *Journal of Social Welfare and Family Law* 237.

[7] Cretney *et al*, n 1 above, at 320.

[8] *Secretary of State for Social Security v Foster* [2001] 1 FCR 376 (CA) at para 7 *per* Ward LJ.

[9] On the background to this, see p 132 above.

[10] As Sheriff JT Fitzsimons observed, 'The transitional period is still continuing, with no end in sight', *McGilchrist v McGilchrist* 1998 SLT (Sh Ct) 2 at 5.

maintenance calculation, despite having previously agreed to a consent order. The only restriction is that such an application must not be made within a year of such a consent order. The principal justification for the rule in the 2000 Act was that it would encourage parties to negotiate child support in the shadow of the Agency, and so avoid a 'two-tier' child maintenance service.[11] The one year delay was designed to give the parties (and their lawyers) sufficient time to renegotiate a new voluntary agreement in appropriate circumstances.[12]

The legislation governing the jurisdiction of the Agency and the relationship between private ordering, child maintenance and the courts is hideously complex, even by the usual standards of child support law. This chapter starts by setting out the general rule that the Agency's role ousts the jurisdiction of the courts. The next section explores the various special circumstances in which the courts still retain jurisdiction, notwithstanding the general rule. We then examine how the 1991 Act provides some recognition for the role of past and present private ordering, in terms of the ways in which the existence of court orders or maintenance agreements may limit the Agency's jurisdiction. Finally, we see how maintenance calculations impinge on court orders and private maintenance agreements in individual cases.

The Courts and the Child Support Agency: The General Rule

The statutory presumption in section 8(3) of the 1991 Act is deceptively simple:

> no court shall exercise any power which it would otherwise have to make, vary or revive any maintenance order in relation to the child and non-resident parent concerned.[13]

This rule applies:

> in any case where the Secretary of State would have jurisdiction to make a maintenance calculation with respect to a qualifying child and a non-resident parent of his on an application duly made (or treated as made) by a person entitled to apply for such a calculation with respect to that child.[14]

This qualification has important implications—if the parties are still living in the same household, although estranged, then there is no non-resident parent and so by definition their child cannot be a 'qualifying child'. It follows that the court is perfectly at liberty to make a private law child maintenance order if its involvement is sought at this early stage,[15] whether or not in the form of a consent order.[16]

---

[11] DSS, *A new contract for welfare: Children's Rights and Parents' Responsibilities* (Cm 4349, 1999) at 54–55.

[12] For criticism of this provision, see below at p 208.

[13] This is based on the Australian precedent enshrined in Family Law Act 1975 (Cth), s 66E.

[14] CSA 1991, s 8(1).

[15] See J Pirrie, 'The Courts and Child Maintenance' [2003] Fam Law 431 at 432, asking rhetorically whether token interim periodical payments should be part of the standard agenda for the court at first appointments.

[16] As this chapter will explain, a consent order is the principal way in which the rule in CSA 1991, s 8(3) can legitimately be avoided, at least in old scheme cases.

In addition, the general exclusionary principle takes effect 'even though the circumstances of the case are such that the Secretary of State would not make a calculation if it were applied for'.[17] The purpose of this last provision is by no means clear. On one view, it means that the parent with care is barred from applying to court for an order in a case in which the Secretary of State declines to make a calculation because of the non-resident parent's low income.[18] This scenario appears less likely now given that one of the principles underpinning the 2000 Act is that non-resident parents should make a contribution, however modest, in virtually all cases.

The concept of a 'maintenance order' is central to the operation of the general exclusionary rule in section 8(3). The 1991 Act defines this as 'an order which requires the making or securing of periodical payments to or for the benefit of the child' and which is made under one of the following enactments:

— Part II of the Matrimonial Causes Act 1973;[19]
— the Domestic Proceedings and Magistrates' Courts Act 1978;[20]
— Part III of the Matrimonial and Family Proceedings Act 1984;[21]
— the Family Law (Scotland) Act 1985;[22]
— Schedule 1 to the Children Act 1989;[23]
— Schedules 5 to 7 of the Civil Partnership Act 2004 and 'any other prescribed enactment'.[24]

The statutory definition also includes any order under these disparate statutory schemes which varies or revives such an order.

As the expression 'maintenance order' is defined in terms of one which involves the 'making or securing of periodical payments to or for the benefit of the child', it necessarily follows that the courts retain their jurisdiction to make orders for

---

[17] CSA 1991, s 8(2).

[18] R Bird, *Child Support—The New Law* (Family Law, Bristol, 2002) at 108.

[19] The 1973 Act governs financial relief for parties to marriage and children of the family (in divorce or nullity proceedings): see Matrimonial Causes Act 1973, s 23(1)(d) and (e).

[20] This concerns matrimonial proceedings in magistrates' courts.

[21] This deals with financial relief in England and Wales after an overseas divorce (or annulment).

[22] This governs financial relief in Scotland: see further JM Thomson, *Family Law in Scotland* (Butterworths, London, 4th edn, 2002) ch 7.

[23] This makes provision for financial provision for children, and superseded the powers previously found in a motley collection of statutes relating to children, eg the Guardianship of Minors Act 1971 and the FLRA 1987.

[24] There are a total of 18 statutes so prescribed, most of which are now no longer in force: see the full list in the Child Support (Maintenance Arrangements and Jurisdiction) Regulations 1992 (SI 1992/2645), reg 2. Originally reg 2 prescribed only the Affiliation Proceedings Act 1957, the successor to the traditional bastardy jurisdiction. As the Guardianship of Minors Act 1971 and Guardianship Act 1973 were not initially prescribed, it followed that an order made under those powers could not qualify, initially at least, as being made under 'any other prescribed enactment', see *A M-S v Child Support Officer* [1998] 1 FLR 955 (CA). The full list of prescribed enactments, including the 1971 and 1973 Acts, was substituted by the Child Support and Income Support (Amendment) Regulations 1995 (SI 1995/1045), reg 26.

spousal maintenance under the Matrimonial Causes Act 1973.[25] In practice, however, and given the statutory presumption in favour of a clean break in divorce proceedings, such orders are uncommon.[26] In those cases where they are made, the amount of any such order will inevitably be affected by any child support maintenance calculation that is operative. A spouse may also apply for maintenance for herself under the Domestic Proceedings and Magistrates' Courts Act 1978, without instituting divorce proceedings.[27] Property adjustment or lump sum orders in respect of divorcing spouses are much more common. The difficulty, however, is that the absence of any power to make orders of periodical payments for children in contested proceedings may impinge on other aspects of the overall package of ancillary relief. In *V v V (Child Maintenance)*[28] Wilson J made this plea:

> For a judge to rail against the statutory block placed upon his jurisdiction to order child maintenance is not a knee-jerk reaction to loss of power; nor yet is it the product of perceived deficiencies in the working of the statutory system. Its basis is . . . that the level of child maintenance bears upon the content of the other orders for capital and/or income provision which it is for the court to make; and that its hard-won possession of all the relevant material makes it absurd that its resolution of that one issue has to be foregone. But, until parliament looks again at the interface between the jurisdictions, judges have to tread an awkward path between the provision of a sensible dispute-resolution service for the benefit of children and their parents and loyalty to the existing statutory provisions.[29]

The statutory definition of 'maintenance order' also means that the courts' powers to make lump sum orders or property adjustment orders in favour of children are unaffected.[30] In practice such orders are unusual, but may be particularly

---

[25] This provides some scope for circumventing the s 8(3) bar, eg by the ingenious Segal order, discussed below, pp 210–11.

[26] As Baroness Hale explained in *R v Secretary of State for Work and Pensions (ex parte Kehoe)* [2005] UKHL 48, at para 64, the effect of the Matrimonial and Family Proceedings Act 1984 in most cases was 'the ending of private maintenance for divorced wives'.

[27] Cretney *et al* in a footnote (n 1 above at 79, nn 66–8) develop the ingenious argument that a spouse may secure an order *for herself* where the other party has failed to provide, or make a proper contribution towards, reasonable maintenance *for a child of the family*, citing *Northrop v Northrop* [1968] P 74. They suggest that such an order would not be 'to or for the benefit of the child' within the definition of 'maintenance order' in CSA 1991, s 8(11). Whilst evidently not 'to' the child, the order is surely 'for the benefit of the child', given that is the neglect of the child which forms the basis for granting the order in the first place (cf by analogy *CCS/8328/95*, in which Commissioner Rowland held (at paras 15–17) that an undertaking to court was 'for the benefit of the child' even though (i) the child was not named in the agreement and (ii) the amount for the child was not expressly identified). A court might well take the view that such an application was in effect an order for child maintenance, but designed so as to escape the s 8(3) embargo—see further *Phillips v Peace* below.

[28] [2001] 2 FLR 799.

[29] *Ibid*, at para 11.

[30] Thus an order for the payment of a lump sum, even in two instalments, is not within CSA 1991, s 8(11): *A M-S v Child Support Officer* [1998] 1 FLR 955, upholding *CCS/4741/1995*. Such powers exist under the Matrimonial Causes Act 1973, ss 23(1)(f) and 24(1) and the Children Act 1989, sch 1 para 1(2)(c)–(e). The magistrates' jurisdiction under the Domestic Proceedings and Magistrates' Courts Act 1978, s 2(1)(d) is less significant given the £1,000 limit on orders; *ibid* s 2(3).

appropriate where the non-resident parent is very wealthy. The case law also demonstrates that the courts will not accede to applications designed to circumvent the section 8(3) embargo by seeking a lump sum order as a form of capitalised periodic maintenance.[31] In *Phillips v Peace* Johnson J held that in exercising its residual jurisdiction 'a court should do so only in order to meet the need of a child in respect of a particular item of capital expenditure'.[32] That said, the Court of Appeal has indicated that in 'big money' cases the court should arrive at a 'broad assessment' of the child's needs, bearing in mind that a child is entitled to be raised 'in circumstances which bore some sort of relationship to her father's current resources and his present standard of living'.[33] These issues are discussed further below in the context of 'top-up orders'.[34]

Circumstances in Which the Courts Retain Jurisdiction

There are a number of situations in which the courts retain their jurisdiction to make orders for child maintenance, notwithstanding the general rule that the courts' role is secondary to that of the Secretary of State.[35] Some of these exceptions to the general rule are consequential upon, or implicit in, other provisions in the 1991 Act, whilst others are expressly spelt out (more or less clearly)[36] in section 8 of the Act itself. The consequential or implicit exceptions are threefold and will be considered first; in each of these the Agency simply has no jurisdiction to act, irrespective of section 8. The remaining four express exceptions deal with circumstances in which the courts' jurisdiction is either instead of or supplementary to that of the Agency.[37]

---

[31] In *P v T* [2003] EWCA 837, [2003] 2 FCR 481 the Court of Appeal also acknowledged the 'inevitable tension' between the propositions that the mother of an unmarried child has no personal entitlement to maintenance but is entitled to an allowance as the child's primary carer: para 48, *per* Thorpe LJ.

[32] [1996] 2 FLR 230 at 235. On the facts this led to an order that the father settle £90,000 on trustees for the provision of a home for the child until she completed her education and a lump sum order of nearly £25,000 for the provision of furniture and the payment of private maternity hospital costs. For the subsequent history of this case see *Phillips v Peace* [2004] EWHC 3180 (Fam); [2005] 1 WLR 3246 and n 79 below. See further *Re L M (a minor)*, unreported, 9 July 1997 (CA), where Sir Stephen Brown P indicated that Johnson J perhaps 'went too far . . . it might be that one could find items of capital expenditure which were not restricted to particular items'.

[33] *P v T* n 31 above at para 74 *per* May LJ.

[34] pp 194–96 below.

[35] Applications to court are checked to ensure that the court has jurisdiction; in the event of a dispute, the matter is referred to a district judge for a decision on admissibility: see Family Proceedings Rules 1991 (SI 1991/1247), r 10.24 (and Family Proceedings Courts (child support act 1991) Rules 1993 (SI 1993/627 (L8)) r 6 for the equivalent procedure in magistrates' courts). If the court has jurisdiction and proceeds to make an order, a court officer is required to notify the Secretary of State if the order is likely to affect the maintenance calculation: Child Support (Maintenance Arrangements and Jurisdiction) Regulations 1992 (SI 1992/2645), reg 6.

[36] The lack of clarity in CSA 1991, s 8 reflects the limited scrutiny this provision received during its Parliamentary passage: see eg *Hansard* HL Debates vol 527 cols 554–6 (19 March 1991) and Standing Committee A, cols 67–88 (13 June 1991).

[37] If the Secretary of State is collecting child support, collection of maintenance under a court order may be made alongside payments under the 1991 Act: see p 441 below.

In those cases in which the courts retain jurisdiction, judges and magistrates are expected to take what would be the child support liability as the starting point for determining the appropriate level of child maintenance. For example, in the context of variation proceedings, the courts have indicated that the likely level of a formula-based child support assessment is a very relevant consideration when determining the level of maintenance to be paid in those cases in which the court retains jurisdiction.[38] This suggests that whilst the probable formula assessment should be an influential factor, it cannot be determinative, not least as the courts—and so the parties in their negotiations—are directed to consider a range of matters in the exercise of their discretion.[39] However, the impact of the 2000 Act has been to reinforce the significance in other proceedings of the amount of any likely liability under the 1991 Act. As Nicholas Mostyn QC, sitting as a Deputy High Court judge, has observed:

> If a child maintenance order, whether made by consent or after a contest, is markedly at variance with the calculation under the new regime then there will be a high temptation for one or other party after the order has been in force for a year, and after giving two-months notice, to approach the CSA for a calculation. Quite apart from the obvious acrimony that this would engender, a calculation in a different amount to the figure originally negotiated or awarded may cast doubt on the fairness of the original ancillary relief settlement between the parties, leading to further litigation. These spectres should be avoided at all costs.[40]

1 Child is Not a 'child' for Child Support Purposes

The Agency's jurisdiction is confined by the definition of 'child' for the purposes of the 1991 Act,[41] especially as this relates to older teenagers. Not all 17 and 18 year olds are covered by the 1991 Act: they have to be in full-time education (not being university level education), or have recently left such education, or be aged under 18 and registered for work or youth training.[42] Those who are 17 and 18 years old and who fall outside these categories are necessarily excluded from the scope of the Agency. Similarly, young people who have reached their 19th birthday will always be outside the scope of the 1991 Act. This means that applications for maintenance in respect of all such older children and young persons have to be brought instead in the courts. Although there is no mention of any upper age limit in the context of the statutory definition of a 'child' for the purposes of proceedings ancillary to divorce,[43] the usual rule is that financial provision orders generally should not be

---

[38] *E v C (Calculation of Child Maintenance)* [1996] FLR 472 (unemployed NRP; magistrates should have considered that—under the then rules—he would have had a nil liability under the 1991 Act).

[39] Bird, n 18 above, at 113. See also J Pirrie, 'Time for the Courts to stand up to the Child Support Act?—An address to District Judges' [2002] Fam Law 114.

[40] *GW v RW* [2003] EWHC 611(Fam), [2003] 2 FLR 108 at para 74.

[41] CSA 1991, s 55.

[42] See ch 8 below.

[43] Matrimonial Causes Act 1973, s 52(1).

made for children who have reached the age of 18, and that orders for periodical maintenance payments should not extend beyond that age.[44] However, this restriction does not apply in two exceptional types of case which may come before the courts.

The first is where the child is 'receiving instruction at an educational establishment or undergoing training for a trade, profession or vocation'. The most likely scenario in which this power may be invoked is in respect of an adult child studying at college or university.[45] This power may become more significant with the increased costs of tertiary education at a time when students' access to social security benefits has been drastically curtailed.[46] Thus a court order has the potential to provide some support for students who might otherwise be disadvantaged by the failure of policies relating to child support, higher education and social security to dovetail neatly.[47] It is well-established that a child can intervene in the parents' matrimonial proceedings to seek a financial order,[48] but there is little evidence that this power is invoked other than rarely.[49]

The second exceptional situation is where there are 'special circumstances which justify the making of an order' in any event.[50] This might include, for example, cases of grown-up children with severe disabilities who are unable to establish themselves independently.[51] In principle, in such cases, a maintenance order could continue indefinitely.[52] There are effectively identical provisions in the other two principal statutes governing maintenance for children aged 18 and over in the private law context in England and Wales.[53]

---

[44] Matrimonial Causes Act 1973, s 29(1) and (2). Indeed, the (weak) statutory presumption is that periodical orders should not extend beyond school leaving age, but this can be overridden and payments ordered to the age of 18 if the child's welfare so requires: *ibid*, s 29(2)(a).

[45] See M Letts, 'Children: The Continuing Duty to Maintain' [2001] Fam Law 839. For an Australian perspective, see B Smyth, 'Child support for young adult children in Australia' (2002) 16 *International Journal of Law, Policy and the Family* 22.

[46] For example, most university students are excluded from entitlement to both income support and jobseeker's allowance; the only exceptions relate to those who are also lone parents or are disabled. See further NJ Wikeley and AI Ogus, *The Law of Social Security* (Butterworths, London, 5th edn, 2002) at 288–90 and 331.

[47] For an early study of the general 'lack of fit' in such policies regarding young adults, see NS Harris, *Social Security for Young People* (Avebury, Aldershot, 1989).

[48] *Downing v Downing (Downing intervening)* [1976] Fam 288; see now Family Proceedings Rules 1991 (SI 1991/1247) r 2.54.

[49] Evidence from Australia also suggests that support in such cases is the exception rather than the norm, and that many parents are unaware that their children may be eligible for such support (eg from the other parent): Smyth, n 45 above, at 32.

[50] Matrimonial Causes Act 1973, s 29(3)(b).

[51] See eg *C v F (Disabled Child: Maintenance Orders)* [1998] 2 FLR 1, CA.

[52] N Lowe and G Douglas, *Bromley's Family Law* (Butterworths, London, 9th edn, 1998) at 766. Such an order ceases to have effect (other than as regards arrears) in the event of the payer's death: Matrimonial Causes Act 1973, s 29(4).

[53] Domestic Proceedings and Magistrates' Courts Act 1978, s 5 and the Children Act 1989, sch 1 paras 2 and 16(1). The position in Scotland, of course, is different: see Thomson, n 22 above.

2 Child is Not a 'Qualifying Child' for Child Support Purposes

As is discussed in detail in chapter 8 below, a maintenance calculation may only be made under the 1991 Act if the child in question is a 'qualifying child', meaning a natural or adoptive child of both parents.[54] It follows that other children who have lived with both parents—for example, step-children[55]—are not within the ambit of the Agency. However, the jurisdiction of the courts is more extensive in this regard, in that it encompasses any child who is a 'child of the family',[56] defined as either a child of both parties or any child who has been treated by them as a child of their family.[57] The statutory definition excludes children who have been placed with the couple under a fostering arrangement organised by a local authority or voluntary body, but a child who has been privately fostered may well qualify, on the facts, as a 'child of the family'. This definition involves an objective, factual test,[58] which is concerned with social rather than biological parenthood. It is therefore entirely possible for a court to order that a step-parent should pay child maintenance in respect of a step-child, even though an earlier maintenance order against the natural parent in respect of the same child remains in force.[59]

The concept of a 'qualifying child' also requires that at least one of the child's natural or adoptive parents is a non-resident parent.[60] A parent cannot be a non-resident parent if he lives in the same household as the child or the child does not have her home with a person with care.[61] Hence if the relationship between the parents (but not the household) has broken up, the child cannot be a 'qualifying child', however inadequate the level of support being provided by the parent who is the primary earner.[62]

---

[54] CSA 1991, ss 3(1) and 54: see further pp 217–24 below.

[55] See further S Ramsey and J Masson, 'Stepparent support of stepchildren: a comparative analysis of policies and problems in the American and English experience' (1985) 36 *Syracuse Law Review* 659. Step-children were likewise outside the scope of the rules governing recovery of poor law relief: *Tubb v Harrison* 4 Term Rep 118 (1790).

[56] See Domestic Proceedings and Magistrates' Courts Act 1978, s 1, Matrimonial Causes Act 1973, s 21(1) and Children Act 1989, sch 1, para 16(2).

[57] Domestic Proceedings and Magistrates' Courts Act 1978, s 88(1), Matrimonial Causes Act 1973, s 52(1) and Children Act 1989, s 105(1).

[58] See eg *Teeling v Teeling* [1984] FLR 808, CA and generally the discussion in Lowe and Douglas, n 52 above, at 288–90.

[59] As indeed happened in *Carron v Carron* [1984] FLR 805, CA. Applying the same principles, it should now be no bar to an order against a step-parent that eg the child's natural father is subject to a child support liability for the same child under the 1991 Act. However, the amount of child support in payment might well be a factor in determining the amount of any court order against the step-parent: see the considerations listed in Matrimonial Causes Act 1973, s 25(3).

[60] CSA 1991, s 3(1).

[61] *Ibid*, s 3(2).

[62] See eg *CCS/14625/96* and *R(CS) 8/99*.

3 One or more Parties not Habitually Resident in the United Kingdom

The Secretary of State only has jurisdiction to make an assessment where all three relevant parties—the qualifying child, the person with care and the non-resident parent—are habitually resident in the United Kingdom.[63] If any one of those three individuals is not habitually resident within the jurisdiction, then the Secretary of State has no power to act.[64] It follows that in such a case an application for child maintenance may be made to the ordinary courts. This assumes, of course, that the court itself has jurisdiction, although the qualifying conditions are less onerous than under the 1991 Act.[65] If the non-resident parent lives abroad, then there may be severe practical problems in enforcing any court order for maintenance.[66] We now turn to examine the four situations in which section 8 expressly preserves the courts' jurisdiction to make private law maintenance orders.

4 Top-up Orders

There will be some cases involving very wealthy non-resident parents in which the application of the normal child support formula will not necessarily produce an appropriate or just outcome. To deal with this eventuality, section 8(6) of the 1991 Act makes provision for so-called 'top-up' orders. The court's jurisdiction may be invoked so long as three conditions are satisfied. The first is that a maintenance calculation under the 1991 Act is in force (hence the court's role here is necessarily supplementary to, rather than in substitution for, that of the Agency).[67] The Agency calculation is therefore a 'necessary gateway to a judicial determination'.[68]

---

[63] CSA 1991, s 44; see further pp 250–54 below.

[64] See eg *G W v R W* [2003] EWCA 611 (Fam), [2003] 2 FLR 108.

[65] Typically these requirements are expressed in the alternative, rather than cumulatively. If the application is under Matrimonial Causes Act 1973, s 27 (financial provision in case of failure to maintain), then *either* the applicant or respondent must be domiciled in England and Wales at the date of the application *or* the applicant must have been habitually resident for the previous year *or* the respondent must be resident on the date of the application (*ibid*, s 27(2)). For divorce and related proceedings, *either* the court must have jurisdiction under Council Regulation (EC) No 1347/2000 *or* no court of a Contracting State has such jurisdiction and either spouse is domiciled in England and Wales on the date when proceedings are begun (Domicile and Matrimonial Proceedings Act 1973, s 5(2)). For maintenance proceedings under Children Act 1989, see sch 1 para 14.

[66] See Cretney *et al*, n 1 above, at 480–82. For example, if one of the parties is habitually resident abroad, thus excluding the case from the ambit of the Agency, the courts may still have jurisdiction to make maintenance and property orders for a child: see *A v A (A Minor) (Financial Provision)* [1994] 1 FLR 657.

[67] CSA 1991, s 8(6)(a). Any court order can be backdated to the date of the maintenance calculation, providing the application to court is made within six months of the Agency's assessment: Matrimonial Causes Act 1973, s 29(5), Domestic Proceedings and Magistrates' Court Act 1978, s 5(5) and Children Act 1989, sch 1 para 3(5).

[68] *P v T* [2003] EWCA 837, [2003] 2 FCR 481 (CA) at para 6, *per* Thorpe LJ.

Rather unhelpfully, however, any subsequent Agency calculation after the top-up order is made has the effect of discharging the latter order.[69] The second is that the non-resident parent's income exceeds the statutory cap for the purposes of child support.[70] In practice, of course, most of these cases are unlikely to find their way into the Agency—it is far more probable that it will be in both parties' interests to arrive at a private resolution of the matter by consent,[71] thus sidestepping the Agency's jurisdiction altogether.[72] Finally, the court must be

> satisfied that the circumstances of the case make it appropriate for the non-resident parent to make or secure the making of periodical payments under a maintenance order in addition to the child support maintenance payable by him in accordance with the maintenance calculation.[73]

Where these conditions are met, the court will then determine the appropriate level for a top-up order, having taken into account the various considerations which are enumerated in the legislation under which the court is acting.[74] Unlike the 1991 Act, each of these private law statutes requires the court to have regard to the financial circumstances of both parties, not just the income of the non-resident parent.[75] The courts' concern is whether provision is required for the child's maintenance during his or her dependency,[76] and at a standard of living which bears some relationship to the non-resident parent's resources.[77] Thus the provision of a home for the child is more appropriately achieved by way of settlement of property rather than outright transfer to the parent with care.[78] Any such order is a

---

[69] CSA 1991, s 10 and Child Support (Maintenance Arrangements and Jurisdiction) Regulations 1992 (SI 1992/2645), reg 3: note that reg 3(3) exempts only courts orders made under CSA 1991, s 8(7) and (8).

[70] *Ibid*, s 8(6)(b), on which see *Flood v Flood* [2002] EWHC 1898. Charles J held that there was no jurisdiction to make a top-up order in a case where the Agency had (mistakenly) originally informed the parties that the ceiling on child support had been reached under the 1991 Act.

[71] Conversely, as Thorpe LJ argued in *P v T*, n 68 above, at para 45, cases where 'one or both of the parents lie somewhere on the spectrum from affluent to fabulously rich . . . may be more likely to be litigated . . . because the affluent and very rich may be less deterred by the costs of litigation'.

[72] True, in such a case the PWC, if she is or becomes dissatisfied, would be able to apply under the new scheme for an Agency calculation a year after the making of the consent order. But the very existence of the cap on the NRP income means that there is little incentive for her to apply to the Agency as regards issues of assessment. If enforcement is the problem, is it really likely that the Agency will succeed where the courts' powers have failed?

[73] CSA 1991, s 8(6)(c).

[74] ie the Matrimonial Causes Act 1973, the Domestic Proceedings and Magistrates' Courts Act 1978 or the Children Act 1989. For guidance on the exercise of the 'highly discretionary jurisdiction' in sch 1 of the latter, see *P v T* n 68 above.

[75] See eg Matrimonial Causes Act 1973, s 25(2)(a), (b) and (3). Thus the courts consider the income *and* capital of *both* parties.

[76] *Kiely v Kiely* [1988] FLR 288. Dependency may extend to 21 rather than 18: see *J v C (Child: Financial Provision)* [1999] 1 FLR 152 and *V v V (Child Maintenance)* [2001] 2 FLR 799. If the child is disabled dependency might continue into full adulthood.

[77] *J v C (Child: Financial Provision)* [1999] 1 FLR 152; see also *F v G (Child: Financial Provision)* [2004] EWHC 1848 (Fam); [2005] 1 FLR 261.

[78] *A v A (Minor: Financial Provision)* [1994] 1 FLR 657, where Ward J made an order for periodical payments of £20,000 per annum in addition to private school fees, in a case in which the then child support standard formula would have produced a maximum assessment of some £7,500 a year. The precise amount of the maintenance calculation is not cited in the law report, but see Cretney *et al*, n 1 above, at 451 n 94. The periodical payments were secured as the father was domiciled outside the jurisdiction.

'once and for all' solution; the court has no power to make a further order where one has been made in the past.[79] In the leading case, *P v T*,[80] the father acknowledged to the court that his wealth was such that he could, 'without financial embarrassment',[81] meet a lump sum order in excess of £10 million, if ordered to do so. He had been initially assessed by the Agency to pay child support of approximately £115 a week, increased on appeal to the grand sum of £152.53 weekly. Thorpe LJ observed that 'these assessments under the Child Support Acts appear to be absurd given that the father was voluntarily paying £1,200 per month' in child maintenance.[82] Allowing the mother's appeal against the trial judge's overall solution (awarding, in particular, a house at £450,000 and payments of some £35,000 p/a), the order of the Court of Appeal included provision for a home valued at £1 million and annual payments of £70,000.[83]

5 Additional Educational Expenses

The court retains its jurisdiction to make orders in respect of children who have educational or other training expenses, providing any such order is made solely for the purpose of meeting 'some or all of the expenses incurred in connection with the provision of the instruction or training'.[84] This exception adopts the same formulation for educational or other training provision as that used in the legislation governing private law applications for maintenance orders to meet the educational costs of children who are over the age of 18.[85] Typically, this provision enables a court to make an order for payment of private school fees, whether or not a maintenance calculation is also in place.[86] Furthermore, the fact that there is a pre-existing court order in place which makes provision for the payment of school fees (but no other form of maintenance) does not preclude a private application to the

---

[79] *Phillips v Peace* [2004] EWHC 3180 (Fam), [2005] 1 WLR 3246; and see n 32 above.

[80] *P v T* n 68 above; see further S Gilmore 'Case Commentary' [2004] 16 CFLQ 103.

[81] According to May LJ, *ibid* para 74, the father 'will pay whatever the court orders without blinking'. The father owned a house in Mayfair worth more than £10 million, a house in South Africa, a Rolls Royce, a Bentley, an Aston Martin and employed household staff and retinue including bodyguards and two chauffeurs.

[82] *Ibid*, at para 6.

[83] The mother's application included claims for funds for a home in the region of £1.2 to £2.3 million and child maintenance of £170,000 p/a. The father's proposals included a home for £350,000 and periodical payments of £25,000.

[84] CSA 1991, s 8(7).

[85] ie 'the child is, will be or (if the order were to be made) would be receiving instruction at an educational establishment or undergoing training for a trade, profession or vocation (whether or not while in gainful employment)', *ibid*, s 8(7)(a). The term 'educational establishment' is not defined—contra 'recognised educational establishment' in *ibid*, s 55(3).

[86] An order for payment of part or all of a child's school fees may be combined with a relatively modest child support order: see [1994] NLJ 702, reporting a district judge's order that a father with a declared income of £26,000, who was subject to a CSA assessment of £25 p/w, pay half of the child's school fees of £4,200 p/a.

Agency.[87] However, in the context of this exception, the child in question must not have reached their nineteenth birthday.[88] If the young person has already reached that age, then of course he or she will no longer be a 'qualifying child' under the 1991 Act, and so the court potentially has jurisdiction in any event.[89] At the other end of the age spectrum, it seems that this exception 'quite plainly' does not permit a court to make an order for the payment of nursery school fees for a 15-month old baby.[90] If this is right, it may leave those parents with care who do not qualify for assistance with childcare costs under the tax credits scheme in some difficulty, given that such expenditure is not one of the statutory grounds for seeking a variation.[91]

6 Disabled Children

The court also retains its jurisdiction to make orders in respect of disabled children, providing any such order is made solely for the purpose of meeting 'some or all of any expenses attributable to the child's disability'.[92] Such an order may continue into the child's adulthood where appropriate.[93] The justification for this exception is that the original formula-based method of assessment could not be fine-tuned with sufficient sensitivity to accommodate the special needs of disabled children.[94] The court may entertain such an application in any case in which either disability living allowance (DLA) is paid in respect of the child or the child is otherwise 'disabled'. DLA is a non-contributory and non-means-tested social security benefit which is paid to adults and children who have personal care and/or mobility needs.[95] The use of entitlement to DLA as a convenient proxy test for disability is itself a technique that has been borrowed from social security law.[96] Even if DLA

---

[87] CSA 1995, s 18(6). In *Secretary of State for Social Security v Foster* [2001] 1 FCR 376 (also reported as *R(CS) 1/01*) the Court of Appeal held that a pre-existing court order for school fees barred a private application to the Agency, but that decision was based on the law as it stood before the 1995 Act.

[88] Given the definition of 'child' in *ibid*, s 55(1). As Bird observes (n 18 above at 111), children aged between 16 and 18 and not receiving full-time education will be outside the scope of the Agency in any event, and the court will already have jurisdiction.

[89] And so recourse may be had to the powers under the Matrimonial Causes Act 1973 and Children Act 1989 sch 1, which, as Letts observes (n 45 above), have no upper limit in age terms. The Family Law (Scotland) Act 1985, s 1(5) has a maximum age of 25 for bringing applications.

[90] *Re L M (a minor)*, unreported, 9 July 1997 (CA).

[91] In contrast to the position in Australia.

[92] CSA 1991, s 8(8).

[93] See *C v F (Disabled Child: Maintenance Orders)* [1998] 2 FLR 1 (CA), holding that the age limit in CSA 1991, s 55(1) does not constrain the exercise of the court's discretion when using s 8(8) to make an order under CA 1989, sch 1.

[94] This argument is all the stronger as a result of the reforms to the formula in the 2000 Act.

[95] The principal rules governing entitlement to DLA are contained in Social Security Contributions and Benefits Act 1992, ss 71–73. See further Wikeley and Ogus, n 46 above, at 682–705 and also N Wikeley, 'Children and Social Security Law' in J Fionda (ed), *Legal Concepts of Childhood* (Hart Publishing, Oxford, 2001) ch 13 at 226–29.

[96] See eg Income Support (General) Regulations 1987 (SI 1987/1967) sch 2 para 12, where DLA entitlement is used as one of the routes for qualifying for the disability premium in income support.

is not in payment,[97] the court still has jurisdiction if the child is 'disabled' within the rather dated meaning ascribed to that term in the 1991 Act.[98]

As with orders for additional educational expenses, the fact that there is a pre-existing court order in place which makes special provision for a disabled child (but no other form of maintenance) does not preclude a private application to the Agency.[99]

7 Orders against the person with care

The general bar in cases where the Secretary of State has jurisdiction stipulates that 'no court shall exercise any power which it would otherwise have to make, vary or revive any maintenance order in relation to the child and *the non-resident parent* concerned'.[100] There is, therefore, in terms, no rule precluding a court from making an order in relation to the child and the *person with care*, typically but not necessarily the parent with care. Indeed, the legislation expressly admits this possibility.[101] The policy underlying the relevant statutory provision has been described as 'not altogether clear',[102] although the supposition is that it was designed to fill the gap left by the Secretary of State's inability to make an assessment against the parent with care where the parents are equally responsible for the child's support. It is undoubtedly the case that some non-resident parents express the view that the shared care provisions, even following the amendments made by the 2000 Act, fail to achieve an equitable outcome in terms of the parties' respective financial contributions to the child's upkeep.[103] However, there are no reported cases in which a non-resident parent has pursued this grievance to the extent of seeking a private law maintenance order against the parent with care.[104] Indeed, it may be that this supposed rationale reflects an unduly Anglo-centric perspective on child support law. An alternative explanation, but one which can only apply to Scotland, is that section 8(10) is designed to deal with the situation where a child may seek an order for aliment against the person caring for her or him even in circumstances where a maintenance calculation might otherwise be made against the non-resident parent.[105]

---

[97] This may be for a reason unconnected with the child's disability, eg in relation to the residence requirement for DLA eligibility: see Social Security Contributions and Benefits Act 1992, s 71(6) and Social Security (DLA) Regulations 1991 (SI 1991/2890), reg 2.

[98] For this purpose, 'a child is disabled if he is blind, deaf or dumb or is substantially and permanently handicapped by illness, injury, mental disorder or congenital deformity or such other disability as may be prescribed', CSA 1991, s 8(9). The terminology reflects its origins in the National Assistance Act 1948, s 29(1); see now also Children Act 1989, s 17(11) as regards (disabled) children in need. No regulations have been made under CSA 1991, s 8(9).

[99] CSA 1995, s 18(6).

[100] CSA 1991, s 8(3).

[101] See *ibid*, s 8(10).

[102] Cretney *et al*, n 1 above, at 452. See also Bird, n 18 above, at 112.

[103] See below p 318.

[104] In any event a subsequent maintenance calculation would presumably have the effect of discharging any such order.

[105] *McGilchrist v McGilchrist* 1998 SLT (Sh Ct) 2 at 3 *per* Sheriff JT Fitzsimons.

Private Ordering and the Child Support Agency

The previous section explored the circumstances in which the courts retain jurisdiction to make child maintenance orders. This section examines the interrelationship between private ordering (including, where available, court-ordered resolution of a dispute over child maintenance) and the ambit of the Agency. Two preliminary issues must be discussed at the outset: the meaning of 'maintenance' and the significance of the dates of any court order or private agreement.

First, what is 'maintenance' (as in a 'maintenance agreement' or 'maintenance order')? The Child Support Act 1991 does not purport to offer any definition of maintenance[106] as such, although it does define 'maintenance order'.[107] As we have seen, statute merely asserts that 'each parent of a qualifying child is responsible for maintaining him' and declares that this duty is fulfilled by making periodical payments of maintenance in accordance with the Act.[108] Nor do the regulations contain any all-purpose definition of maintenance.[109] In other statutory contexts 'maintenance' means recurring payments of an income nature to meet the costs of daily living,[110] but maintenance is not limited to daily living 'in its most literal and restrictive sense'.[111] So a consent order which made provision solely for the payment of private school fees qualifies as a maintenance order.[112]

Secondly, the rules governing the extent to which existing court orders and maintenance agreements may limit the jurisdiction of the Agency are exceedingly complex. In part this reflects the process of phasing in the Agency's operations after 1993 as well as subsequent legislative amendments. As a result, the operation of the rules differs in important respects, depending upon the date of the order or agreement in question. For maintenance agreements, the critical issue is whether or not the agreement was made before 5 April 1993, the date that the 1991 Act came into force. The position for court orders is more complicated. In summary, the 5 April 1993 date is still significant in that before that date court orders could be made following contested child maintenance applications in all cases. Since that date, and subject to the special cases discussed in the previous section, the courts'

---

[106] Or its Scottish equivalent, aliment. See further pp 215–16 below.

[107] See above p 188.

[108] CSA 1991, s 1(1) and (2).

[109] As Jacobs and Douglas observe (*Child Support: The Legislation*, Sweet & Maxwell, London, Edition Seven, 2005/2006, at 203), the closest is reg 17(4) of the Child Support (Variation) Regulations 2000 (SI 2001/156), which defines maintenance—but only for the purpose of regs 16 and 17 of those regulations—as 'the normal day-to-day living expenses of the qualifying child'.

[110] See *Re Dennis (decd)* [1981] 2 All ER 140 at 145 *per* Browne-Wilkinson J, in the context of the Inheritance (Provision for Family and Dependants) Act 1975.

[111] *A v A (Maintenance Pending Suit: Provision for Legal Fees)* [2001] 1 FLR 377 at 382 per Holman J. It was recognised in the former affiliation jurisdiction that child maintenance might include an allowance for the mother if she was unable to work because she was caring for the child: *Haroutunian v Jennings* (1980) 1 FLR 62; see also *Osborn v Parks* (1982) 3 FLR 90.

[112] *Secretary of State for Social Security v Foster* [2001] 1 FCR 376 (CA) at para 22 *per* Ward LJ, also reported as *R(CS) 1/01*. See also *R(CS) 10/99* at paras 22–23 *per* Mr Commissioner Howell QC.

powers have been limited to making consent orders. Until 3 March 2003, being the material date under the reforms introduced by the 2000 Act, any court order could effectively lock out the Agency indefinitely (unless, and until, the parent with care claimed a relevant benefit). Court orders made since 3 March 2003 only have this effect for 12 months. These rules are now explored in more detail.

1 Maintenance Agreements made before 5 April 1993

According to section 4(10)(a) of the 1991 Act, and assuming that the parent with care is not on benefit, the Agency has no jurisdiction to act on a private application with respect to a qualifying child or children where:

> there is in force a written maintenance agreement made before 5th April 1993 . . . in respect of that child or those children and the person who is, at that time, the non-resident parent.[113]

The practical significance of this exception will naturally diminish over time,[114] but it inevitably attracted attention in the early years of the child support scheme as a potential means of escaping the Agency's clutches.

There is no statutory definition of a 'written maintenance agreement', but a 'maintenance agreement' is defined for the purposes of the 1991 Act as:

> any agreement for the making, or for securing the making, of periodical payments by way of maintenance, or in Scotland aliment, to or for the benefit of any child.[115]

Applying normal contractual principles,[116] it follows that there must actually be an agreement—hence by definition a written maintenance agreement cannot exist where the parent with care has not accepted the financial arrangement offered by the non-resident parent, even if the offer itself is in writing.[117] Moreover, it is not sufficient, for this purpose at least, that the maintenance agreement is merely *evidenced* in writing.[118] However, it need not be in a single document; an exchange of

---

[113] CSA 1991, s 4(10)(a). This provision was inserted by CSA 1995, s 18(1), but essentially re-enacted the Child Support Act 1991 (Commencement No 3 and Transitional Provisions) Order 1992 (SI 1992/2644), Sch, para 2, shorn of the phasing-in provisions.

[114] Cretney *et al*, n 1, at 452 and Bird, n 18 above, at 108.

[115] CSA 1991, ss 9(1) and 54. See also *CCS/2536/1997* (approved on this point by CA in *Brown v Chapman*, unreported, 17 April 2000), applying this definition to 'written maintenance agreement' in delegated legislation, given Interpretation Act 1978, s 11.

[116] There must accordingly—in the absence of a deed—be some consideration for the agreement, but this will not be difficult to establish in the context of an agreement to resolve competing claims: see Lowe and Douglas, n 52 above, at 750 and *Darke v Strout* [2003] EWCA Civ 176.

[117] *CCS/11052/1995.* See, in a different context, *Ahmed v Government of the Kingdom of Saudi Arabia* [1996] ICR 25 (solicitors' letter setting out opinion not a 'written agreement' for purpose of State Immunity Act 1978, s 2(2)).

[118] *CCS/15849/96* at paras 9–13, distinguishing *CCS/12767/1996* (at para 10), on the basis that the latter decision was concerned with the phasing-in provisions, in respect of which a broader interpretation was permissible.

letters may constitute a written maintenance agreement,[119] so long as the documents are more than simply evidence in writing. It must also be an enforceable legal agreement, rather than an informal understanding,[120] between the parents— and not an agreement between the non-resident parent and the qualifying child.[121] By the same token, a non-resident parent's agreement to pay sums under the social security liable relative provisions does not amount to a written maintenance agreement.[122] It is therefore arguable that a three-way agreement between the parents and a third party is not a maintenance agreement for this purpose.[123] However, an undertaking given to the court arising out of negotiations between the parties and embodied in a court order may constitute a valid written maintenance agreement.[124]

The 1991 Act also stipulates that the written maintenance agreement must be 'in force'.[125] If there is such an agreement, then the Agency's jurisdiction is effectively ousted, even if the agreement in question provides for purely nominal payments.[126] The decision on whether or not there is indeed a written maintenance agreement 'in force' is a matter for the Secretary of State which may then be challenged before an appeal tribunal.[127]

A parent with care with a pre-existing maintenance agreement who is barred from access to the Agency because of section 4(10)(a) has a number of options open to her. First, she may agree with the other party to end the maintenance agreement—but it is unlikely that such consent will be forthcoming, given that a formula-based calculation will usually produce a higher weekly amount of child support.[128] Secondly, she may be able to claim income support or income-based

---

[119] *R(CS) 7/98* at paras 19–20 *per* Mrs Commissioner Heggs, approving the guidance in the *Child Support Adjudication Guide*, App 5 para 2. This is consistent with the approach taken to the definition of a (written) maintenance agreement in Matrimonial Causes Act 1973, s 34(2): see *M H v M H* [1981] FLR 429.

[120] *CCS/12797/1996* at paras 15–17 *per* Mr Commissioner Henty. This decision concerned the meaning of 'maintenance agreement' in the context of the phasing-in provisions of reg 7(1)(a)(iii) of the Child Support (Miscellaneous Amendments and Transitional Provisions) Regulations 1994 (SI 1994/227) but the reasoning must also apply in this context.

[121] *R(CS) 7/98* at paras 20–21 *per* Mrs Commissioner Heggs.

[122] *CCS/13475/1995* at para 13, as the agreement is between the NRP and the (then) DHSS.

[123] *Young v Young* (1973) 117 Sol J 204, decided under what is now Matrimonial Causes Act 1973, s 34(2) would suggest as much. This would also be consistent with the Children Act 1989, sch 1 para 10(1)(a) which defines a maintenance agreement in terms of one 'made between the father and mother of the child'.

[124] *CCS/8328/1995* at para 18 *per* Mr Commissioner Rowland (who also decided that an undertaking could not be treated as an order: see further below).

[125] CSA 1991, s 4(10)(a); see further below in the context of court orders. It need not actually have been in force before 5 April 1993, but must have been made before that date.

[126] *CCS/12849/1996*, where the agreement provided for weekly payments of one penny (but see the criticism of this decision on another point in Jacobs and Douglas, n 109 above, at 204).

[127] *R(CS) 1/96* at para 16 *per* Mr Commissioner Rice and *R(CS) 3/97* at paras 15–17 *per* Mr Commissioner Goodman. Both decisions concerned the pre-SSA 1998 regime but the principle holds good.

[128] See R Hadwen and K Pawling, *Child support handbook* (CPAG, London, 13th edn, 2005/2006) at 47. They also suggest that the PWC may unilaterally break the agreement, but this would suggest that a party could benefit from their own wrong.

jobseeker's allowance, in which case she will be treated as having made an application for a maintenance calculation under section 6 of the 1991 Act.[129] Finally, she may apply to the court for an order varying or enforcing the maintenance element in the agreement.[130] But, with one exception, the terms of that agreement are effectively frozen so far as child maintenance is concerned. Thus, if the case is one in which the court would be prevented from making an order by virtue of section 8, the court cannot vary the agreement so as either to include a term making provision for such maintenance (where none previously existed) or to increase the amount of such maintenance.[131] However, if a private application to the Agency is barred by either section 4(10) or section 7(10)—for example, because of the existence of a pre-5 April 1993 written maintenance agreement—and the case has not become a benefit case under section 6, then the terms can be varied to the extent of increasing the level of any maintenance stipulated in the agreement (but not inserting such a term).[132] Subject to these provisos, an application to the court for variation is perhaps the most realistic in a private case in which the parent with care is dissatisfied with the level of maintenance enshrined in the maintenance agreement.[133] However, it inevitably means that she is exposed to all the difficulties associated with the court process which led to the policy decision to establish the Agency in the first place.

2 Maintenance Agreements made on or after 5 April 1993

The discussion above concerns *written* maintenance agreements which were entered into *before* the 1991 Act came into force. As we have seen, the sanctity of such arrangements is unconditional—if such a written maintenance agreement is still in force, the Agency has no jurisdiction (unless, of course, the parent with care applies for benefit, in which case the respect for private ordering is trumped by public expenditure considerations). The status of maintenance agreements made *after* the implementation of the 1991 Act is much less assured, at least south of the border. The breadth of the definition of 'maintenance agreement' in the Act is such that it may or may not be in writing, and may or may not be legally enforceable.[134] This is another reason why such agreements may not enjoy the same degree of security as their pre-5 April 1993 antecedents in writing.[135] True, the

---

[129] However, such an application will lapse if her benefit claim is refused before the Agency calculation is made: CSA 1991, s 11(3).

[130] *Ibid*, s 9(6). See also, on revocation, *B v M (Child Support: Revocation of Order)*[1994] 1 FLR 342; see p **000** below.

[131] CSA 1991, s 9(5).

[132] *Ibid*, s 9(6).

[133] See further Children Act 1989, sch 1 para 10 on the alteration of maintenance agreements.

[134] CSA 1991, s 9(1)—see above.

[135] In practice maintenance agreements are less common than was formerly the case: Lowe and Douglas, n 52 above, at 751.

legislation recognises the parties' freedom of contract by declaring that 'Nothing in this Act shall be taken to prevent any person from entering into a maintenance agreement'.[136] To that extent, the principle of private ordering is protected; moreover, any such agreement can be enforced in the courts in the same way as any other contract.[137] Indeed, as will be seen below, in private cases the courts may still make a consent order in the same terms as a maintenance agreement.[138] However, the mere existence of a post 5 April 1993 maintenance agreement cannot prevent one party from making an application to the Agency.[139] More generally, any agreement—a term not being confined to any *maintenance* agreement[140]—is barred from including a provision seeking to restrict the right of any person (in practice, the person with care[141]) to apply for a maintenance calculation.[142] As well as ensuring that an agreement cannot displace the operation of the child support scheme, this reflects the private law principle that there can be no clean break in respect of children.[143]

The position in Scotland appears to be different. In *R(CS) 3/99* it was held that a post-1993 Minute of Agreement which was registered in the Books of Council and Session (a public register of deeds) was thereby elevated to the status of being equivalent to a court 'order'. This has the effect of excluding the Agency's jurisdiction, and so a party's only remedy in such a case is to seek variation of the registered agreement, either by a supplementary agreement or through the courts.[144]

3 Court Orders made before 3 March 2003

The position of a pre-2003 court order is broadly analogous to that of a pre-1993 written maintenance agreement. Thus, section 4(10)(a) of the 1991 Act provides that, so long as the parent with care is not on benefit, the Agency has no jurisdiction to act on a private application with respect to a qualifying child or children, where:

> there is in force . . . a maintenance order made before a prescribed date in respect of that child or those children and the person who is, at that time, the non-resident parent.[145]

---

[136] CSA 1991, s 9(2).

[137] But see *ibid* s 9(5) and (6) on the court's powers to vary, discussed above.

[138] *Ibid*, s 8(5).

[139] *Ibid*, s 9(3); naturally this is subject to *ibid* ss 4(10)(a) and 7(10), dealing with pre-5 April 1993 written maintenance agreements. Conceivably in Scotland the applicant may be a child (see *ibid*, s 7).

[140] This bar therefore operates against agreements in side letters: Jacobs and Douglas, n 52 above, at 54.

[141] Again, in Scotland 'any person' might be a child of the relationship.

[142] CSA 1991, s 9(4). Similarly, a maintenance agreement may not bar access to the court: Matrimonial Causes Act 1973, s 34(1).

[143] See eg *ibid*, s 23(4) and *N v N (Consent Order: Variation)* [1993] 2 FLR 868 (CA).

[144] See further A Cubie, 'Child Support and Minutes of Agreement' (2002) *Green's Family Law Bulletin*, Issue 56, at 2. The decision in *R(CS) 3/99* was doubted (obiter) in *Woodhouse v Wright Johnston & Mackenzie* 2004 SLT 911.

[145] This provision was inserted by CSA 1995, s 18(1), but follows the Child Support Act 1991 (Commencement No 3 and Transitional Provisions) Order 1992 (SI 1992/2644), sch, para 2.

In practice pre-2003 court orders will fall into two categories. The first comprises the diminishing number of maintenance orders which were made by the courts before the 1991 Act came into force on 5 April 1993. These orders may have been made by consent or following a contested hearing. The second group consists of those court orders made after the implementation of the 1991 Act but before the 2000 Act came into force. Given the general statutory embargo in section 8(3),[146] these will usually be consent orders,[147] and are discussed in more detail below, given the complications that may arise. However, the general principles as set out in this section and in the following section apply to consent orders in the same way as to other court orders. The range of court orders promulgated before 3 March 2003, whether or not made by consent, which render the case outwith the Agency's jurisdiction is perhaps best understood by examining the meaning of each of the three key constituent terms in section 4(10)(a) of the 1991 Act, namely 'a maintenance order', which is both 'made before a prescribed date' and is 'in force'.

A Maintenance Order

The statutory definition of 'maintenance order' is the same as that which applies in the context of the provisions of section 8, discussed above.[148] The term 'order' bears its literal meaning, and so an undertaking to the court[149] which is referred to in a court order is not, of itself, a maintenance order.[150] There may be circumstances in which an undertaking has the same effect as an order,[151] but this does not of itself convert the undertaking into an order.[152] The statutory requirement that the order is one 'which requires the making or securing of periodical payments to or for the benefit of the child' has on occasion been construed relatively liberally by the Commissioners. For example, the expression has been held to include the non-resident parent's mortgage payments on the former matrimonial

---

[146] For a discussion of ways in which practitioners have sought to circumvent the bar on court orders other than by consent in child maintenance matters, see Pirrie, n 39 above, who identifies three possibilities: (1) a pre-separation order (this is unproblematic, as the Agency has no jurisdiction so s 8(3) does not bite); (2) a compensating order under s 8(10), ie an order for payments by PWC to NRP (this will only work if the NRP shares care and so can justifiably point to a need for maintenance); (3) a chain of 'Christmas orders', each of which lasts for just less than a year and so the 12 month bar on access to the Agency never expires. The last, as Pirrie admits, is patently a device and is surely an evasion rather than avoidance of the statutory rule, and hence is unlikely to survive judicial scrutiny. It has been described as an 'illegitimate artifice', see N Mostyn and R Wood, *Child's Pay* (Class Publishing, London, 3rd edn, 2002) at 142.

[147] Some will be variations of existing earlier maintenance orders.

[148] CSA 1991, ss 8(11) and 54.

[149] An undertaking is a formal and unequivocal promise to the court.

[150] *CCS/8328/1995* at paras 11–13 *per* Mr Commissioner Rowland, following *In re Hudson* [1966] ch 209; see also *R(CS) 6/99*, especially at paras 18 and 22 *per* Mr Commissioner Mesher.

[151] As was held by Mr Commissioner Howell QC in a different child support context in *R(CS) 10/99* at paras 25–32, applying *Gandolfo v Gandolfo* [1979] 1 QB 359 (CA) and *Symmons v Symmons* [1993] 1 FLR 317. On the enforceability of undertakings in matrimonial proceedings, see District Judge A Taylor, 'Promises, Promises' (2003) 100 *Law Soc Gazette* 32 (March 13, 2003).

[152] *R(CS) 6/99* at para 18 *per* Mr Commissioner Mesher.

home,[153] where such an undertaking had been given in exchange for release from any liability for child maintenance as such.[154]

Made before a Prescribed Date

The 'prescribed date' for the purpose of section 4(10)(a) of the 1991 Act is 3 March 2003.[155] A court order made before this date will shut out the Agency indefinitely, assuming the parent with care does not have to apply for benefit. For court orders made *on or after* this date, the exclusion of the Agency's jurisdiction is limited to just one year.[156]

In Force

The meaning of 'in force' has proven to be more problematic. According to one Scots authority, an order is in force so long as the order itself remains 'live', even if there is no current liability to make payments under the order. In *Cassidy v Cassidy*,[157] a decision of the Outer House of the Court of Session, a decree of divorce was granted in 1987 and custody of the three children awarded to the mother. The father was ordered to pay aliment in respect of each child until they reached the age of 16. Crucially, the order included a reservation clause enabling either party to apply for a variation at any time before the 16th birthday of the youngest child (M) in 1998. At the time the mother applied for such a variation to extend aliment to the age of 18 for the two younger children, M was still only 13 but the middle child (A) had reached the age of 16. The father did not oppose variation for M. However, he had already stopped paying aliment for A and argued that the court had no jurisdiction to order a variation in respect of her. Lord Rodger, granting the mother's application, held that the reservation clause kept the order 'in force' in respect of A, even though there was no liability to make payments of aliment for her at the time of the variation application.[158]

Conflicting views have been expressed in the Commissioners' case law on the meaning of 'in force'. In *R(CS) 4/96* the court had originally made a maintenance order in 1984, requiring the husband to pay the wife maintenance for their two young sons who were living with her. This order had been varied from time to

---

[153] For a case falling within the Agency's jurisdiction, such payments may provide grounds for seeking a variation from the standard formula: see p 382 below.

[154] *CCS/11364/1995 per* Mr Commissioner Goodman. See also *CCS/8328/1995*, at paras 15–16 *per* Mr Commissioner Rowland, in the context of a pre-existing maintenance agreement in the form of a court order and *CCS/316/1998*, para 27 *per* Mr Commissioner Jacobs, emphasising the importance of a proper interpretation of the terms of the order. An order for a lump sum, representing capitalised maintenance, is not within the ambit of the definition: *A M-S v Child Support Officer* [1998] 1 FLR 955 (CA), upholding *CCS/4741/1995*.

[155] Child Support (Applications: Prescribed Date) Regulations 2003 (SI 2003/194), reg 2.

[156] See further below at p 210.

[157] 1997 SLT 202 (OH).

[158] *Ibid*, at 206. Lord Rodger rejected the contention that it was enough for the order to remain in force as regards the youngest child (*ibid*, at 205).

time, the last occasion being in 1988. At some later date both boys went to live with their father, who subsequently applied for a maintenance assessment under the 1991 Act. The mother's argument was that the Agency had no jurisdiction, as there was a maintenance order 'in force'. Mr Commissioner Rice rejected this contention, holding that where an order was of no practical effect it was no longer 'in force', even though it had not formally been rescinded.[159] The authority of this decision, despite its status as a reported decision,[160] is questionable on at least three grounds. First, its approach is difficult to reconcile with the subsequent decision of the Outer House in *Cassidy v Cassidy*, discussed above. Secondly, the Commissioner in *R(CS) 4/96* may in any event have reached the correct conclusion for the wrong reason. This appears to have been the view of the Court of Appeal in refusing leave against that decision.[161] Simon Brown LJ concluded that the only type of order covered was 'one against a parent absent when ordered to pay maintenance and still absent when the section 4 application comes to be made under the Child Support Act'.[162] This analysis is surely accurate in the context of the statutory provision then in place.[163] That said, the insertion of the qualifying words 'at that time' in the amendment made by the 1995 Act means that the same reasoning cannot necessarily be applied now.[164] There is, however, a third and more fundamental difficulty with *R(CS) 4/96*, namely its assumption that a court order ceases to have effect simply because of a change of circumstances. Mr Commissioner Jacobs's reasoning to the contrary in *CCS/2567/1998*, notwithstanding that being an unreported decision, is more compelling in this regard.[165] The Commissioner notes that matrimonial law governing such orders makes no express provision for a maintenance order to cease to have effect consequential upon a change in the child's residence—rather, such a change of circumstances is seen as a ground for seeking a variation of the original order.

A parent with care with a pre-3 March 2003 court order who is barred from access to the Agency because of section 4(10)(a) has a number of options open to her.[166] As with pre-5 April 1993 maintenance agreements, she may apply to the

---

[159] *R(CS) 4/96*, para 13. Mr Commissioner Rice took the same approach in *CCS/3127/1995*.

[160] On the weight to be attached to Commissioners' reported and unreported decisions respectively, see p 432 below.

[161] *Kirkley v Secretary of State for Social Security and the Child Support Officer*, unreported, 15 December 1995 (refusal of leave).

[162] Cited in *CCS/2567/1998* para 11. However, this need not imply continuous absence: *ibid*, paras 21–22.

[163] This referred to there being 'in force a maintenance order . . . in respect of that qualifying child or those qualifying children and the absent parent', Child Support Act 1991 (Commencement No 3 and Transitional Provisions) Order 1992 (SI 1992/2644), sch, para 2.

[164] Thus the relevant provision (CSA 1991, s 4(10)(a)) reads 'there is in force . . . a maintenance order made before a prescribed date in respect of that child or those children and the person who is, *at that time*, the non-resident parent'.

[165] See *CCS/2567/1998* para 18 *per* Mr Commissioner Jacobs.

[166] See Hadwen and Pawling, n 128 above, at 47.

court for variation[167] or enforcement,[168] or may try and apply for benefit, so bringing her within the section 6 procedure. Alternatively, she may ask the court to revoke the order, thus enabling an application to the Agency to be made. Although the courts retain the power of revocation,[169] *B v M (Child Support: Revocation of Order)*[170] suggests that this power should not generally be exercised simply to allow access to the Agency. The court must consider all the factors specified in section 25 of the Matrimonial Causes Act 1973, which provides that the child's welfare is the first consideration. Although a formula calculation is likely to produce a higher figure, the generality of section 25 meant that it did not necessarily follow that revocation would be in the child's best interests—variation of the original order might be more appropriate.[171] However, *B v M (Child Support: Revocation of Order)* was decided in the early days of the 1991 Act,[172] at a time when it was envisaged that existing orders should remain within the court system until the end of the transitional period. That aspiration had evaporated by the time of the 1995 Act, enacted after *B v M (Child Support: Revocation of Order)*, which sanctioned the permanent exclusion from the Agency of cases involving old court orders. Arguably this might imply that the courts should now be more willing to entertain applications for revocation.[173]

4 Court Orders made on or after 3 March 2003

The position as regards court orders made on or after 3 March 2003 is the same as before that date so far as benefit cases are concerned. If the parent with care subsequently claims a relevant benefit, then the Agency automatically becomes involved by virtue of the section 6 procedure. For private cases, however, the situation is very different. Whereas court orders before that date (meaning, in practice since 1993, consent orders) provide a permanent shield against Agency intervention in cases which remain private in nature, the effect of the 2000 Act is that under the new scheme the embargo on applying to the Agency in a private case is time-limited to one year from the date of the court order.[174] Thus a parent

---

[167] CSA 1991, s 8(3A)(b) (assuming no maintenance calculation has been made). See *McGilchrist v McGilchrist* 1998 SLT (Sh Ct) 2 at 4–5. This power was to have been removed by the 2000 Act, but was reinstated following last minute lobbying by the SLFA: see Pirrie, n 15 above, at 432.

[168] If the court determines that it has no power to vary or enforce, then, since 22 January 1996, the PWC has been able to apply under CSA 1991, s 4: see Child Support (Maintenance Arrangements and Jurisdiction) Regulations 1992 (SI 1992/2645), reg 9.

[169] CSA 1991, s 8(4).

[170] [1994] 1 FLR 342.

[171] *Ibid*, at 344–45 *per* HH Judge Bryant.

[172] The case was actually decided on 25 October 25 just over six months after the 1991 Act came into force, and is any event only a county court authority.

[173] As Gillian Douglas has argued: [1998] Fam Law 510.

[174] CSA 1991, s 4(10)(aa). It seems clear that the one year runs from the date of the original order, not the date of any subsequent variation of that order: Bird, n 18 above, at 108.

with care who has agreed a consent order since 3 March 2003 but who then feels the settlement was unfair, or whose circumstances have changed, has two alternative courses of action open to her. First, and assuming that the Agency has not made a maintenance calculation (following any benefit claim made), she may apply to the court for variation of the order.[175] In principle the court always has the power to vary existing orders for financial provision.[176] In practice, however, whilst courts may be willing to entertain an application to vary an order for periodical payments in the light of changed circumstances,[177] they will be very reluctant to vary an order for a lump sum payment or a property adjustment order, given that these are designed to achieve closure in the case.[178] Secondly, she may now apply to the Agency as a private case, once a year has elapsed. This raises the prospect that a consent order may be unpicked after a year, and without the need to demonstrate any change in circumstances. The bare fact that the order has been in place for a year means that the parent with care has an absolute right to apply for a calculation. This change in policy has attracted considerable hostility from practitioners who resent the potential for the further incursion of the Agency's operations into what are fundamentally private law disputes.[179] However, it seems unlikely that significant numbers of parents with care in private cases will wish to avail themselves of this opportunity to invoke the Agency's jurisdiction. Yet the potential to do so may well influence the negotiating process between the parties, so improving the bargaining position of parents with care.

5 Consent Orders

The consent order is the mechanism by which the law reconciles the competing interests of encouraging private ordering whilst ensuring that the resulting outcomes are fair and reasonable in all the circumstances.[180] The settlement culture which dominates family law practice is such that the outcome of family litigation is much more likely to be a consent order than a court order following trial of the issues in dispute.[181] A consent order in divorce proceedings is defined, naturally enough, as 'an order in the terms applied for to which the respondent agrees'.[182] The parties' private agreement for the resolution of the outstanding issues, negotiated before or at the door of the court,[183] thus receives the imprimatur of the

---

[175] CSA 1991, s 8(3A)(a).

[176] See Matrimonial Causes Act 1973, s 31.

[177] See *ibid*, s 31(7)(a).

[178] See Cretney *et al*, n 1 above, at 390.

[179] See P Watson-Lee, 'Financial Provision on Divorce: Clarity and Fairness—Part One: The Law Society Report' [2004] 34 Fam Law 182 at 186. Pirrie warns of the risk of 'litigation pinball' as cases move between the courts and the Agency: n 39 above, at 116.

[180] Cretney *et al*, n 1 above, at 322.

[181] See DCA, *Judicial Statistics* (Cm 6565, 2005) at 76 (Table 5.7).

[182] Matrimonial Causes Act 1973, s 33A(3). See *Pounds v Pounds* [1994] 1 FLR 775 for judicial discussion of consent orders. In Scotland the equivalent is a registered minute of agreement.

[183] See generally Davis *et al*, n 4 above.

court. The court (in practice, so far as financial matters are concerned, a district judge in chambers) is presented with the draft order and a statement of information in a standard form.[184] The court may then make the consent order in the agreed terms 'unless it has reason to think that there are other circumstances into which it ought to inquire'.[185] In practice, especially where the parties are represented, the district judge will take a great deal on trust, checking merely to see that the proposed order is within the band of reasonable discretion and does not offend against any obvious principle.[186]

We have seen that the general rule under the 1991 Act is that the courts have no power to make orders for child maintenance in cases where the Agency has jurisdiction.[187] However, the Act, together with the relevant secondary legislation, provides a degree of protection for consent orders.[188] Section 8(5) is an enabling power, allowing the Lord Chancellor[189] to make an Order which provides that the general rule in section 8:

> shall not prevent a court from exercising any power which it has to make a maintenance order in relation to a child if—
>
> > (a) a written agreement (whether or not enforceable) provides for the making, or securing, by a non-resident parent of the child of periodical payments to or for the benefit of the child; and
> >
> > (b) the maintenance order which the court makes is, in all material respects, in the same terms as that agreement.

Separate provision to this effect has been made for both England and Wales[190] and Scotland.[191] The parties may therefore arrive at a private settlement, approved by the court through a consent order, even though the Secretary of State would have the jurisdiction to make a maintenance calculation were an appropriate application to be made. Neither section 8(5) nor the respective Orders qualify the court's power by reference to any cut-off date. It necessarily follows that a consent order that deals with child maintenance may be made today just as it could have been before 5 April 1993. An added attraction of a consent order, at least until the 2000 Act was implemented, was that it effectively locked out the parent with care from applying to the Agency as a private case.[192] The worst that could happen was that

---

[184] The standard form essentially includes a summary of the parties' relevant circumstances: see Family Proceedings Rules 1991 (SI 1991/1247) r 2.61 and Form M1. The procedure is less straightforward in cases involving unmarried couples brought under Children Act 1989 sch 1: see J Pirrie, 'Periodical Payments by Consent under the Children Act 1989' [1999] Fam Law 680.

[185] Matrimonial Causes Act 1973, s 33A(1).

[186] R Bird, *Ancillary Relief Handbook* (Jordans, Bristol, 5th edn, 2005) at 98.

[187] CSA 1991, s 8(3), discussed above p 187.

[188] But note that if the parties have not separated, a court order may be made even in the absence of consent.

[189] But only with the agreement of the Lord Chief Justice (or his or her delegate): see s 8(5A) and (12), inserted by Constitutional Reform Act 2005, s 15 and sch 4, para 219.

[190] Child Maintenance (Written Agreements) Order 1993 (SI 1993/620 (L4)).

[191] Child Maintenance (Written Agreements) Order 1997 (SI 1997/2943 (S188)). See also *Otto v Otto* 2002 Fam LR 95 (Sheriff Ct).

[192] CSA 1991, s 4(10)(a) and see above.

the consent order might be varied, in the same way as any other court order. What is unclear, however, is whether any such variation must also be by consent[193] or whether the court's powers are at large.[194]

The original intention was that the section 8(5) protection for consent orders would be only temporary and would ultimately be withdrawn as all cases came within the ambit of the Agency. As with other types of private case excluded from the scope of the 1991 Act, this temporary provision now has a distinct air of permanence about it. Consent orders, however, are not an absolute protection against Agency involvement. It has always been the case, since the inception of the child support scheme, that a consent order may be displaced if the parent with care claims a relevant benefit. The very act of claiming benefit transmutes a private case into a benefit case, given the mandatory nature of section 6.[195] Consequently, of course, many couples have found their previous agreements, which had been given the court's official seal of approval, effectively unpicked by the imposition of maintenance calculation.[196]

Of course, since April 1993 consent orders have necessarily been agreed in the shadow of the Agency. This is all the more so now that an order made on or after 3 March 2003 only excludes the parent with care's right to apply under section 4 of the 1991 Act for 12 months. If the Agency has already made an assessment, then the child support liability is a 'given' around which the remaining elements of ancillary relief must be packaged.[197] Whilst practitioners may find this frustrating at times, at least they are not faced with the uncertainty that exists where the Agency has yet to make a maintenance calculation. If there is no Agency assessment—either because one is pending in the system, or because the parent with care is not a benefit claimant—then how should a court order accommodate the potential child support liability? As a matter of principle the starting point should be the amount which would be payable under the 1991 Act.[198]

There is a particular difficulty in terms of formulating the order where the court is asked to approve a consent order at an early stage in ancillary relief proceedings and before the actual amount of any Agency assessment is known.[199] District Judge Segal of the Principal Registry in the Family Division developed a special type of order by way of a pragmatic short-term solution to this problem.[200] A so-called Segal order comprises an order for spousal maintenance—an area in which, of course, the courts have retained their jurisdiction—which incorporates

---

[193] The view of Professor Gillian Douglas—see [1998] Fam Law 394 and 510.

[194] The view of Nicholas Mostyn QC—see [1998] Fam Law 510 and 701, also taken by Bird, n 18 above, at 109.

[195] See below pp 212–14 on the effect of a maintenance calculation on a court order.

[196] See above pp 135–37 on clean break settlements.

[197] In divorce proceedings the NRP's known liability under the 1991 Act will obviously be a factor to be considered under Matrimonial Causes Act 1973, s 25(2)(b).

[198] See *GW v RW* [2003] EWHC 611(Fam), [2003] 2 FLR 108, at para 74 *per* Nicholas Mostyn QC.

[199] Typically this will involve an application for maintenance pending suit or interim periodical payments. If the parties are still in the same household there is no problem, as the Agency lacks jurisdiction.

[200] C Bellamy, 'Child Support Act 1991: net effect—dead or alive?' [1993] Fam Law 633.

an element of support for the children as part of the global settlement. The Segal order then provides that the spousal maintenance figure should be adjusted accordingly to reflect any sum payable by the non-resident parent for the children under a subsequent Agency calculation.[201] As the Court of Appeal commented in *Dorney-Kingdom v Dorney-Kingdom*,[202] the Segal order has an obvious utility; it is 'very convenient way for a district judge to have a form of order which will carry the parent with primary care over that interim pending the Agency's determination'.[203] However, the Court stressed that such an order could only be made by consent, given the terms of section 8(5). Moreover, given the explicit policy of section 8(3) to exclude the courts' jurisdiction, a Segal order was:

> just within the bounds of legitimacy, since it is no sort of ouster or challenge to the jurisdiction of the Agency, but merely a holding until such time as the Agency can carry out its proper function.[204]

It was therefore 'absolutely crucial that if legitimacy is to be preserved, there must be a substantial ingredient of spousal maintenance in the Segal order'.[205] Thus periodical payments for children cannot be rolled up with no or nominal spousal maintenance in order to give the court jurisdiction, as to do so 'would be the most patent evasion of the statutory prohibition on judicial assessment of child maintenance'.[206]

A Segal order may therefore provide a short-term solution to a real practical problem in some cases. However, it will not provide any assistance in a case where a clean break settlement is achieved, as by definition there will be no ongoing spousal maintenance, and/or where there is no consent. In *V v V (Child Maintenance)*[207] Wilson J, having highlighted the 'unsatisfactory interface' between the jurisdictions of the Agency and the courts, circumvented this problem by making orders for substantial lump sums for the benefit of the two children involved in order to meet the shortfall in the maintenance that would otherwise have been awarded. In doing so the judge sought to distinguish *Phillips v Peace*,[208] in which Johnson J had held that lump sum orders could not be used to disguise what was essentially periodical support for a child. The purported basis for the distinction was that in *Phillips v Peace* there had been a child support assessment, albeit a wholly inadequate one, while in *V v V* there was no Agency involvement. This reasoning is less than convincing—true, there was a difference on the facts, but *Dorney-Kingdom v Dorney-Kingdom* and *Phillips v Peace* emphasise that the courts

---

[201] As with shares, this may involve the spousal maintenance going up or down, depending on the child support assessment. See the examples given by District Judge Segal at [2002] Fam Law 923–24. The need for precise drafting in such an order is illustrated by *Warring-Davies v Secretary of State for Work and Pensions* [2005] EWHC 3011 (Admin).

[202] [2000] 2 FLR 855.

[203] *Ibid*, at para 14 *per* Thorpe LJ.

[204] *Ibid*, at para 15.

[205] *Ibid*, at para 15. On the facts of the case there was no consent and the wife's entitlement to spousal maintenance was no more than nominal.

[206] *Ibid*, at para 15.

[207] [2001] 2 FLR 799.

[208] [1996] 2 FLR 230

must respect the spirit of the section 8.[209] *V v V* is perhaps best regarded as an ingenious but essentially flawed avoidance of the exclusionary rule in section 8.[210]

The Relationship Between Maintenance Agreements, Court Orders and Maintenance Calculations

This chapter has been primarily concerned with identifying the situations in which private ordering, through the mechanisms of maintenance agreements and consent orders, is still possible in relation to child maintenance.[211] This may, however, present a rather static picture of maintenance arrangements. In real life, of course, people's circumstances are much more fluid. In particular, a parent with care may, at the point of relationship breakdown, be party to a private case. At some later date she may then claim benefit, thereby necessarily bringing in the Agency. Later still, she may leave benefit.[212] The law must therefore provide for the relationship between private ordering and an Agency maintenance calculation over time in relation to the same case, as these circumstances change. Section 10 of the 1991 Act and the related regulations[213] govern the inter-relationship between maintenance agreements, court orders and Agency maintenance calculations. These rules apply to maintenance agreements and court orders made before as well as after the 1991 Act received Royal Assent. According to a Tribunal of Commissioners, section 10 refers to 'the present effect of such orders and agreements and does not purport to act retrospectively in relation to their past operation'.[214]

Where the Agency makes a maintenance calculation with respect to a qualifying child, the basic rule is that any existing court order[215] providing for that child's maintenance:

---

[209] See to similar effect *Re L M (a minor)*, unreported, 9 July 1997 (CA).

[210] See Jacobs and Douglas, n 109 above, at 202. Certainly at least one district judge has warned against applications for child maintenance being 'dressed up to look like something else', S Gerlis, 'Read My Lips: "No Child Maintenance"' [2003] Fam Law 605. But see also the practical proposal for a child maintenance order backed by a *V v V* lump sum in J Pirrie, 'The CSA: A Practitioner Update' [2005] 35 Family Law 823 at 828.

[211] Including, for this purpose, pre-1993 court orders, which may have been made following contested hearings.

[212] But note that an application under CSA 1991, s 6 can only be terminated where the PWC leaves benefit and makes an express request to the Secretary of State to cease acting under that provision: *ibid*, s 6(9) and *CCS/5796/1997*.

[213] Child Support (Maintenance Arrangements and Jurisdiction) Regulations 1992 (SI 1992/2645). The position in Scotland is governed by the Child Support (Amendments to Primary Legislation) Scotland Order 1993 (SI 1993/660) and the Act of Sederunt (Child Support Act 1991) (Amendment of Ordinary Cause and Summary Cause) Rules 1993 (SI 1993/919). An extract copy of a minute of agreement (consent order) from the Books of Council and Session is an 'order' for these purposes: *R(CS) 3/99*, and see n 144 above.

[214] *R(CS) 1/95* (T) at para 16.

[215] Being any order made under the long list of enactments in Child Support (Maintenance Arrangements and Jurisdiction) Regulations 1992 (SI 1992/2645), reg 3(1). It is irrelevant whether the order is against the PWC or the NRP (who, of course, may have swopped roles in the meantime): *CCS/2567/1998* at paras 26–27 *per* Mr Commissioner Jacobs.

shall, so far as it relates to the making or securing of periodical payments, cease to have effect to such extent as may be determined in accordance with regulations made by the Secretary of State.[216]

The regulations made under this enabling power provide for a court order to cease to have effect on the effective date of the maintenance calculation,[217] which means two days after the calculation has been made.[218] There are three exceptions to this general rule. First, the court order naturally remains in force where it has been made in respect of special expenses associated with the child's education or disability.[219] Secondly, the order also subsists if it was made for several children, at least one of whom is not covered by the Agency's maintenance calculation, and the amount payable for each child is not separately specified.[220] Finally, but only in Scotland, a court order may cease to have effect because an Agency maintenance calculation is made, but may then be revived if the Secretary of State subsequently loses jurisdiction to act.[221] This last principle does not apply in England and Wales—if a court order from South of the border ceases to have effect, that cessation is permanent and it cannot be revived later.[222] The only exception (to this exception!) is where it is subsequently decided that the Agency calculation was made in error and no child support was in fact due.[223] In these circumstances the maintenance order is treated as still being in force and payments made under the 1991 Act are treated as if having been made under that court order.[224] But, if the original maintenance calculation assessed the non-resident parent as having a nil liability for child support purposes, this special provision is of no avail, and the original court order still ceases to have effect.[225]

In some cases a court order which is affected by these provisions will have been part of a package which also included an order for spousal maintenance. If so, either

---

[216] CSA 1991, s 10(1)(a). On the Secretary of State's obligation to notify the court, see Child Support (Maintenance Arrangements and Jurisdiction) Regulations 1992 (SI 1992/2645), reg 5.

[217] *Ibid*, reg 3(1).

[218] Child Support (Maintenance Calculation Procedure) Regulations 2000 (SI 2001/157), reg 27.

[219] Child Support (Maintenance Arrangements and Jurisdiction) Regulations 1992 (SI 1992/2645), reg 3(3), as such orders are to cover costs not met by normal child support.

[220] *Ibid*, reg 3(2)(b). In such a case the NRP could go back to court for a variation, which could be backdated to the date the maintenance calculation took effect, providing the application is made within six months: Matrimonial Causes Act 1973, s 31(11), Domestic Proceedings and Magistrates' Court Act 1978, s 20(9A) and Children Act 1989 sch 1 para 6(9).

[221] Child Support (Maintenance Arrangements and Jurisdiction) Regulations 1992 (SI 1992/2645), reg 3(4). The reason for the inclusion of this provision is a puzzle: see *CCS/2567/1998* at paras 44–46 *per* Mr Commissioner Jacobs.

[222] *Ibid*, at paras 28–30. However, where a maintenance calculation terminates or is cancelled, a court order can be backdated to that date, providing the application to court is made within six months of the Agency's assessment: Matrimonial Causes Act 1973, s 29(7), Domestic Proceedings and Magistrates' Court Act 1978, s 5(7) and Children Act 1989 sch 1 para 3(7).

[223] The Secretary of State is under no duty to notify this error to the court: *CCS/2567/1998* at para 43 *per* Mr Commissioner Jacobs.

[224] Child Support (Maintenance Arrangements and Jurisdiction) Regulations 1992 (SI 1992/2645), reg 8(1). Reg 8(2) deals with the converse situation where a court order is revoked.

[225] *Askew-Page v Page* [2001] Fam Law 794, where HH Judge Meston neatly sidestepped this difficulty by making a lump sum order to meet the costs of past maintenance.

parent can apply to the court for the variation or discharge of that spousal order. Assuming the application is made within six months of the maintenance calculation, the court can backdate any such variation or discharge to the date that the court order for child maintenance was superseded by the Agency's determination.[226]

A parallel enabling rule to that governing court orders provides that, in the event of the Agency making a maintenance calculation, any pre-existing maintenance agreement will be 'unenforceable',[227] rather than 'ceases to have effect', a distinction with important consequences. A 'maintenance agreement' for this purpose is defined in terms of the formulation used in section 9(1) of the 1991 Act.[228] Rather as with court orders, the maintenance agreement is unenforceable where the Agency determination is made which covers the same qualifying children (or, if not, the amount payable for each child is separately identified).[229] However, unlike a court order (in England and Wales at least), the maintenance agreement automatically revives if the Secretary of State subsequently loses jurisdiction.[230]

---

[226] Matrimonial Causes Act 1973, s 31(11) and Domestic Proceedings and Magistrates' Courts Act 1978 s 20(9B).

[227] CSA 1991, s 10(2).

[228] Child Support (Maintenance Arrangements and Jurisdiction) Regulations 1992 (SI 1992/2645), reg 4(1); see above p 200 on s 9(1).

[229] Child Support (Maintenance Arrangements and Jurisdiction) Regulations 1992 (SI 1992/2645), reg 4(2).

[230] *Ibid*, reg 4(3).

8

The Personal and Territorial Scope of the Child Support Act 1991

Introduction

The previous chapter examined the jurisdictional scope of the Child Support Act 1991 in terms of the relationship between the Agency and the courts. This chapter is also concerned with jurisdictional issues, but principally in terms of the personal scope of the 1991 Act. We start with a reminder of the nature of the statutory duty of child support and then examine the criteria used to define each of the three central players in any child support calculation, namely the 'qualifying child', the 'non-resident parent' and the 'person with care'. If any one of the individuals concerned fails to satisfy the relevant statutory definition, then the Agency lacks jurisdiction and the parties may be able to have resort to the courts. Finally, this chapter explores the territorial scope of the 1991 Act, which determines the geographical reach of the Agency.

The Statutory Duty of Child Support

Section 1(1) of the Child Support Act 1991 declares, with commendable clarity, that 'each parent of a qualifying child is responsible for maintaining him'. The Act makes no attempt to define 'maintenance',[1] let alone to engage with any wider meaning to be attached to the concept of the parental obligation to maintain.[2] Indeed, as we saw in chapter 1, the 1991 Act makes no attempt to expand upon the nature of the child support obligation, or to articulate the values or objectives of the statutory scheme, in contrast to child support regimes in some other common law countries. Instead, section 1(2) immediately narrows the focus of enquiry by asserting that:

---

[1] CSA 1991, s 54(1) simply defines operational terms such as 'maintenance order'. On the meaning of maintenance in other family law contexts, see p 199 above.

[2] For an unsuccessful attempt to substitute a broader version of s 1(1), see *Hansard* HL Debates vol 612 cols 1209–21 (8 May 2000).

(2) For the purposes of this Act, a non-resident parent shall be taken to have met his responsibility to maintain any qualifying child of his by making periodical payments of maintenance with respect to the child of such amount, and at such intervals, as may be determined in accordance with the provisions of this Act.

The opening section of the 1991 Act then concludes by emphasising that the duty to maintain, as defined under the legislation, is mandatory:

(3) Where a maintenance calculation made under this Act requires the making of periodical payments, it shall be the duty of the non-resident parent with respect to whom the calculation was made to make those payments.

The combined effect of these provisions is telling in terms of the social message which is being communicated. In short, non-resident parents are required to maintain their children financially. It is not a question of the rights of the child or the parent with care.[3] Where a valid maintenance calculation requires payments to be made, the sum arrived at is non-negotiable as a matter of law. Furthermore, making such payments of itself discharges the parental obligation to maintain, at least 'for the purposes of this Act'. In this way the duty to maintain is perceived as being wholly financial in nature, and measured in terms of the liabilities imposed by the legislation, thereby excluding informal support.[4] This exclusive emphasis on financial support can also 'be seen as gendered, reinforcing notions that women care and men pay'.[5] In addition, the 1991 Act stipulates that any provision in an agreement that seeks to restrict the right of a person to apply to the Agency is void.[6] It follows that parents (regardless of whether or not they are married to each other) are not able to contract out of their child support liabilities.[7]

Maintenance calculations made under the 1991 Act typically concern three key individuals: the 'qualifying child', the 'non-resident parent' and the 'person with care' (the latter is usually, but not necessarily, also a 'parent with care'). The 1991 Act provides a complex series of interlocking definitions of these terms. Before considering these definitions, one must start with the basic building blocks of the statutory lexicon. In particular, who is a 'child' and who is a 'parent' for the purposes of the legislation? Having established who is a 'child', the concept of a 'qualifying child' is relatively straightforward. Likewise, once the notion of a 'parent' is defined, the respective characteristics of the 'non-resident parent' and 'person with care' may be considered.

---

[3] See *R (Kehoe) v Secretary of State for Work and Pensions* [2005] UKHL 48; [2006] 1 AC 42 and the discussion in ch 1 above.

[4] K Clarke, G Craig and C Glendinning, 'Money Isn't Everything: Fiscal Policy and Family Policy in the Child Support Act' (1995) 29 *Social Policy and Administration* 26; see further ch 15 below.

[5] R Boden and M Childs, 'Paying for Procreation: Child support arrangements in the UK' (1996) 4 *Feminist Legal Studies* 131 at 147.

[6] CSA 1991, s 9(4); see also Matrimonial Causes Act 1973, s 34.

[7] *Evans v Amicus Healthcare Ltd (Secretary of State for Health intervening)* [2003] EWHC 2161 (Fam); [2004] 2 WLR 713 at para 253 *per* Wall J. This is consistent with earlier private law authority: see *Hyman v Hyman* [1929] AC 601, HL and *Bennett v Bennett* [1952] 1 KB 249, CA.

Children and Qualifying Children

Who is a Child?

The general rule in family law is that young people reach adulthood on their eighteenth birthday.[8] By definition, therefore, a 'child' is a young person who has not reached that age. This dividing line between the status of being a minor and that of adulthood is applicable in the absence of any other definition or the indication of a contrary intention.[9] The child support legislation, however, rejects this simple bright line definition. Instead, reflecting its origins in the welfare system, the 1991 Act adopts the traditional approach of social security law in determining who is a child (and so who in turn may potentially be a 'qualifying child'). In broad terms, child support law assumes that young persons are children if child benefit is payable in respect of them. This means that those aged under 16 are (almost invariably) children, whereas young people aged over 16 may or may not count as children, depending on their educational or other training status. Furthermore, and paradoxically, just as some 16 and 17 year olds are *not* children, eg because they are in employment, some 18 year olds (who, of course, are adults as a matter of the general law) *are* children for the purposes of both child support and social security law, eg where they are still at sixth form college.

It follows that the statutory definition of a 'child' is convoluted. First, there is a special exclusionary rule which declares that a person is *not* a child if he or she has been married, or entered into a void marriage, or into a voidable marriage which has been annulled.[10] Secondly, and subject to those rare exceptions, the 1991 Act expressly provides that a person *is* a child if he or she falls into one of three possible categories.[11] There are children aged under 16, young people aged under 19 who are in full-time education and young people aged under 18 who are available for work or training. Finally, regulations made under the Act provide for a fourth and final category which covers, albeit only for a limited period, those aged under 19 who have left full-time education. So far, the child support legislation has not

---

[8] Family Law Reform Act 1969, ss 1(1) and 9(1). Normally there is obviously no problem in ascertaining when the child reaches the age of 18 but very occasionally, in the case of children born abroad, this may give rise to a dispute: see *E (by her Litigation Friend, P W) v London Borough of X* [2005] EWHC 2811 (Admin) (age relevant for purpose of local authority's obligations under Children Act 1989).

[9] FLRA 1969, s 1(2).

[10] CSA 1991, s 55(2). So if a young person marries at 16 and is divorced a year later, he or she is not a child (at age 17) even if he or she would otherwise fall within one of the three heads set out in s 55(1).

On void and voidable marriages, see Matrimonial Causes Act 1973, ss 11 and 12. The same rule now applies to civil partnerships that are void: Civil Partnership Act 2004, s 254 and sch 24, para 3. Both the Australian and New Zealand schemes provide for liability to cease if the young person enters a de facto relationship akin to marriage: see Child Support (Assessment) Act 1989 (Cth), s 12(1)(e) and Child Support Act 1991 (NZ), s 25(1)(a)(iii) and (iv). See also *Alvey v Commissioner of Inland Revenue* [2005] NZFLR 875.

[11] CSA 1991, s 55(1).

been amended to bring it into line with the new definitions of 'child' and 'qualifying young person' which have been used in the child benefit scheme since April 2006.[12] It should also be noted that a young person who has ceased to be a 'child' for some reason may subsequently regain that status (for example if he or she leaves school at 16 but later returns to college at 17).[13]

1 Children aged under 16

A child aged under 16 will always be a 'child' for child support purposes,[14] unless affected by the special exclusionary rule concerning those who have been through a ceremony of marriage (or civil partnership). Although a marriage is void in English law if either party is under 16, as a matter of private international law such a marriage may be valid if contracted abroad.[15] It follows that a 15 year old (unmarried) teenage mother will herself remain a child for child support purposes, as well as being the parent of a baby who may also be a 'qualifying child'.

2 Young Persons aged under 19 and in Full-time Education

Young people who are aged 16, 17 or 18 are children for the purposes of the 1991 Act if they are still in (certain types of) full-time education. So, contrary to the normal family law rule, an 18 year old may remain a child for these purposes.[16] The primary legislation defines a member of this second group in the following terms:

(b) he is under the age of 19 and receiving full-time education (which is not advanced education)—

    (i) by attendance at a recognised educational establishment; or
    (ii) elsewhere, if the education is recognised by the Secretary of State.[17]

The statute thus makes a distinction between advanced and non-advanced full-time education. It then defines 'advanced education', which does not count as full-time education for these purposes, as being 'education of a prescribed description'.[18] The terminology of 'advanced education' is not particularly helpful in this context, as the expression is defined by regulations to cover any course which is itself of a standard *above* 'advanced level of the General Certificate of Education'

---

[12] See Child Benefit Act 2005 and N Wikeley, 'The Child Benefit Act 2005: one small step towards a more radical future for child benefit?' (2005) 12 *Journal of Social Security Law* 132.

[13] *CCS/2153/2004* at paras 14–25.

[14] CSA 1991, s 55(1)(a).

[15] Matrimonial Causes Act 1973, s 11(a) and see *Alhaji Mohamed v Knott* [1969] 1 QB 1.

[16] In Australia child support liability usually ceases when the child reaches 18, although payments can continue until the end of that school year (Child Support (Assessment) Act 1989 (Cth), ss 12(1)(c) and 151B). In New Zealand liability ceases (at the latest) when the young person reaches the age of 19 (Child Support Act 1991 (NZ), s 25(1)(a)(i)).

[17] CSA 1991, s 55(1)(b).

[18] *Ibid*, s 55(3).

or its equivalent.[19] So, for child support (and indeed social security) purposes, and somewhat counter-intuitively, a sixth form student studying for the 'advanced' AS and A2 examinations is pursuing a course of *non*-advanced study (and so remains a child in this context).[20] Having excluded young people under 19 who are following advanced courses, the Act stipulates that the full-time education must fall into one of two categories, being either attendance at a recognised educational establishment or education elsewhere, if recognised by the Secretary of State. These alternative categories are discussed below, as is the limited provision for interruptions in a child's education to be ignored. Finally, it should be noted that a 16–18 year old who leaves full-time education will continue to be regarded as a child for a limited period, following the model of child benefit entitlement (see category (4) below).

(i) Attendance at a Recognised Educational Establishment

The typical case involves 'attendance at a recognised educational establishment'. The starting point is that regulations treat young people as being in full-time education if they are:

> attending a course of education at a recognised educational establishment and the time spent receiving instruction or tuition, undertaking supervised study, examination of practical work or taking part in any exercise, experiment or project for which provision is made in the curriculum of the course, exceeds 12 hours per week, so however that in calculating the time spent in pursuit of the course, no account shall be taken of time occupied by meal breaks or spent on unsupervised study, whether undertaken on or off the premises of the educational establishment.[21]

This deeming provision can be broken down into three discrete requirements: (i) attending a course of education; (ii) at a recognised educational establishment; (iii) for more than 12 hours a week. This formulation follows (in all material respects) the provision traditionally used in the child benefit scheme for specifying the circumstances in which a person is to be treated as receiving full-time education.[22] It follows that the case law from the child benefit scheme may be of assistance when interpreting the child support provision.[23] Thus '*attending* a course of education' implies the physical presence of the young person at the place

---

[19] SI 2001/157, sch 1, para 2.

[20] But an 18 year old at university is in advanced education and so is not a 'child'.

[21] SI 2001/157, sch 1, para 3. The relevant enabling power is CSA 1991, s 55(5).

[22] When the child support rules were first drafted, this was to be found in the Child Benefit (General) Regulations 1976 (SI 1976/965), reg 5. Responsibility for the administration of child benefit has since been moved from the DSS (now DWP) to the Inland Revenue (now HMRC): Tax Credits Act 2002, s 50. Child Benefit (General) Regulations 2006 (SI 2006/223) now uses slightly different terms but the changes are probably not significant.

[23] As Jacobs and Douglas observe, a degree of caution needs to be exercised in applying the child benefit authorities, not least as the wording of those regulations has altered over the years: *Child Support: The Legislation* (Sweet & Maxwell, London, Edition Seven, 2005/2006) at 174.

of study, and so following a correspondence course is not sufficient.[24] A 'recognised educational establishment' is defined as one recognised by the Secretary of State 'as being, or as comparable to, a university, college or school' for these purposes.[25] The relevant Secretary of State in this context is the Secretary of State for Work and Pensions, and not the Secretary of State for Education and Skills.[26] Finally, the young person's contact hours must exceed 12 hours a week. In this context 'supervised study' presupposes that the student is in the 'presence or close proximity' of a teacher or tutor who may 'preserve order and enhance diligence', as well as providing appropriate assistance.[27]

Conceptually, the statutory provision discussed in the previous paragraph is a *deeming* rather than a *defining* measure.[28] It is not, therefore, an exhaustive definition of the concept of full-time education. It follows that, in principle at least, a young person may still be regarded as a child who is 'receiving full-time education . . . by attendance at a recognised educational establishment' even if he or she falls outside the scope of the deeming provision. This is because the Commissioners have traditionally taken the view that 'full-time education' is, in the last resort, a question of fact which must be determined according to the natural and ordinary meaning of the phrase and in the light of all the circumstances of the case.[29] In practice, however, it is unlikely that many pupils will qualify as children by this alternative route.

(ii) Other Forms of Full-time Education

The type of education discussed above presupposes that the student is attending a 'recognised educational establishment'. But a person who is under 19 may also be receiving full-time education 'elsewhere, if the education is recognised by the Secretary of State'. This enables those 16 to 18 year olds being educated at home (or 'otherwise' as it is known) to remain as children for child support purposes.[30]

---

[24] *R(F) 2/95*, para 5, *per* Mr Commissioner Skinner. The concept of 'attendance' has proven to be more problematic in the context of entitlement to carer's allowance (formerly invalid care allowance) in determining whether university students 'attend a course of education . . . for twenty-one hours or more a week', Social Security (Invalid Care Allowance) Regulations 1967 (SI 1976/409). See further *Flemming v Secretary of State for Work and Pensions* [2002] EWCA Civ 641 and *Wright-Turner v Department for Social Development* [2002] NICA 2 and the discussion by K Mullan, 'Learning to Care— Full-Time Students and Invalid Care Allowance' [2003] *Journal of Social Security Law* 86.

[25] CSA 1991, s 55(3).

[26] *R(F) 2/95*, para 6, *per* Mr Commissioner Skinner. The Commissioner was concerned with these office holders in their earlier guises as the Secretaries of State for Social Security and Education respectively, but the same principle must hold notwithstanding the change in ministerial nomenclature.

[27] *R(F) 1/93*, para 13, *per* Mr Commissioner Mitchell.

[28] See *CCS/1181/2005*, paras 7–8 *per* Mr Commissioner Jacobs.

[29] See *R(F) 4/62* (15 year old school leaver at secretarial college for mornings only not undergoing 'full-time instruction' for purposes of family allowances) and *R(F) 2/85* (T) (pupil who left school at Easter and returned solely to sit examinations not in 'full-time education' for purposes of child benefit).

[30] See Education Act 1996, s 7 and generally D Monk, 'Problematicising home education: challenging "parental rights" and "socialisation"' (2004) 24 *Legal Studies* 568.

However, this is only possible where the young person was being so educated before reaching the age of 16.[31] Essentially in this type of case it is the education which is recognised by the Secretary of State, rather than the educational establishment itself.[32]

(iii) Interruptions in a Child's Education

The 1991 Act provides that in deciding whether a young person is receiving full-time education no account is to be taken of 'prescribed' interruptions.[33] According to the regulations, any interruption of up to six months is to be disregarded 'to the extent to which it is accepted that the interruption is attributable to a cause which is reasonable in the particular circumstances of the case'.[34] The focus of the legislation is on whether the child's education has been interrupted, not whether a particular course of study has come to an end.[35] The most obvious example is where the young person's illness precludes attendance at school. Indeed, in this particular type of case the regulations allow the six months disregard to be 'extended for such further period as the Secretary of State considers reasonable in the particular circumstances of the case'.[36] But the permissible six month interruption may be caused by other factors (eg perhaps moving house and then a delay caused by having to wait for a place at the preferred new school or college to become available).[37]

3 Young Persons aged under 18 and Available for Work or Training

The third category of young people who count as 'children' for the purposes of child support law comprises those who do not fall into either of the two preceding groups, but who are under the age of 18 and in respect of whom 'prescribed conditions are satisfied'.[38] These prescribed conditions rely heavily on the notion of an 'extension period', a concept inherited from the child benefit scheme. As will be seen under the next heading, young people who leave school have traditionally been regarded as still being children for child benefit purposes until a 'terminal

---

[31] CSA 1991, s 55(4).

[32] The Secretary of State's decision on this issue in the context of child benefit entitlement is not subject to appeal: SI 1999/991, reg 27 and sch 2, para 2, but judicial review has been held to be an adequate remedy, to cure what might otherwise be a breach of Art 6 of the ECHR: *CF/3565/2001, per* Mr Commissioner Levenson. But note that the post-2006 child benefit scheme makes no provision for the benefit to be payable to children aged 16 or over who are being 'educated otherwise'.

[33] CSA 1991, s 55(6).

[34] SI 2001/157, sch 1, para 4(1).

[35] See *CCS/2621/2003.*

[36] SI 2001/157, sch 1, para 4(1).

[37] The six month dispensation does not apply where, following the period of interruption, the young person joins a work-based training scheme or receives education in connection with their employment: *ibid,* sch 1, para 4(2).

[38] CSA 1991, s 55(1)(c).

date', typically the start of the following school term.[39] Thus a child who leaves school at Easter has a terminal date of the first Monday after Easter Monday. The extension period then starts with the terminal date and ends on one of three fixed dates in January, April or July, being the start of the next school term.[40] As Jacobs and Douglas argue, the three-term assumption which underpins the broad brush nature of these arrangements has recently been undermined by the greater diversity in college provision.[41] Presumably these rules will in any event require a radical overhaul if schools and colleges move to a four (or possibly even six) term year.

The relevant prescribed criteria are fourfold.[42] First, the 16 or 17 year old in question must be registered for work or for training under a work-based training scheme for young people.[43] Secondly, he or she must not be in remunerative work[44] (other than temporary work which is due to cease before the end of the extension period). Thirdly, the extension period for the young person in question must not have expired. Fourthly, before the start of that extension period, he or she must have been a 'child' under the Act without relying on this special provision. Finally, and in addition, the regulations provide that a young person who is actually engaged in a work-based training scheme or is entitled to income support or income-based jobseeker's allowance does not count as a 'child' under these special rules.[45]

4 Young persons under 19 who have Left Full-time Education

The 1991 Act enables the Secretary of State to provide that young people who no longer fall within any of the three principal categories above may nonetheless still be treated as children (at least until they reach the age of 19) for a prescribed period.[46] This prescribed period starts from the age of 16 or the date on which the young person actually leaves school, whichever is the later. It ends with the week in which the 'terminal date' falls.[47] The terminal date is whichever of the following three dates occurs first after the young person leaves school: the first Monday

---

[39] For child benefit terminal dates, see now SI 2006/223, reg 7.

[40] SI 2001/157, sch 1, para 1(2). See Jacobs and Douglas, n 23 above, at 176–77 for the precise dates for all years from April 1993, which naturally vary according to when Easter falls.

[41] *Ibid*, at 177.

[42] SI 2001/157, sch 1, para 1(1).

[43] ie under one of the various statutory schemes referred to by *ibid*, para 6 (typically arrangements made under the Employment and Training Act 1973).

[44] Meaning work of not less than 24 hours a week: SI 2001/157, sch 1, para 6. It must be work which is done for payment or in expectation of payment, a concept borrowed from the means-tested benefits: see eg Income Support (General) Regulations 1987 (SI 1987/1967), reg 5(1) and *Chief Adjudication Officer v Ellis* (reported with *R(IS) 22/95*).

[45] CSA 1991, sch 1, para 1(3).

[46] *Ibid*, s 55(7)–(8).

[47] SI 2001/157, sch 1, para 5(1). For young people who reach the age of 19 before the terminal date, the prescribed period ends with the week including the Monday before their 19th birthday. Young persons who have not actually reached the school leaving age when they leave school are treated as having left school on their 16th birthday, and the terminal date is the next one after that date: *ibid*, para 5(2).

in January, the Monday after Easter Monday or the first Monday in September, ie the start of the next full school term.[48] A young person will not continue to count as a child for these purposes if in remunerative work, other than temporary work which is due to cease before the terminal date.[49] Those young people who return to take examinations after leaving full-time education are still children for these purposes, so long as they were entered for external examinations before leaving school or college.[50]

Who is a Qualifying Child?

The duty to maintain imposed by the 1991 Act does not apply to children as such; it relates only to a 'qualifying child', who is defined as a child in respect of whom either one or both parents is a non-resident parent.[51] A child may be a 'qualifying child' without any actual application for a maintenance calculation being made under the 1991 Act, as the term 'qualifying' means 'qualifying in relation to the scheme of the Act at large'.[52] It follows from the statutory definition that the 1991 Act has no application where the family unit remains intact. The only rationale for this can be that the state has no significant interest in determining the distribution of resources within such a family, or at least that this is not a legislative priority. However, in many families the relationship between the parents will have broken down but not quite to the extent that one parent has become a 'non-resident parent' (on the meaning of which see further below). This may be, for example, because the adults' respective resources do not enable them to set up separate homes. Yet if neither parent is, within the terms of the 1991 Act, a non-resident parent, it must follow that the child support scheme cannot bite. The parent with effective care of the child or children from the relationship will therefore have to pursue private law remedies in such a situation.[53] If, on the other hand, the non-resident parent and the parent with care, having initially separated—thereby rendering their child a 'qualifying child'—resume living together, any maintenance calculation terminates from the date of the reconciliation, as the child is no longer a qualifying child.[54]

---

[48] *Ibid*, para 5(3).

[49] *Ibid*, para 5(5).

[50] *Ibid*, para 5(6)–(8). The terminal date in such a case is then the first such date to follow their last examination.

[51] CSA 1991, s 3(1). The qualifying child must also be habitually resident: see p 250 below.

[52] *CCS/8065/1995*, para 14 (*Harper v Child Support Officer*) *per* Mrs Commissioner Heggs. This decision was reversed in relation to a different point by the Court of Appeal in *Secretary of State v Maddocks*, reported as *R(CS) 5/00*.

[53] eg under the Matrimonial Causes Act 1973, Domestic Proceedings and Magistrates' Courts Act 1978 or Children Act 1989.

[54] *R(CS) 8/99* para 16 *per* Mr Commissioner Mesher.

Parents

Who is a 'Parent'?

The 1991 Act simply defines a 'parent' in relation to a given child as 'any person who is in law the mother or father of the child'.[55] So whereas the child support legislation provides its own detailed definition of 'child', the meaning of 'parent' is left to general family law principles. This emphasises the genetic nexus between parent and child—in principle in child support law a 'parent' can only mean a natural or adoptive parent.[56] It follows that adults who exercise a parenting role without having that genetic link—for example, step-parents and foster parents—cannot be parents under the 1991 Act, and accordingly cannot face a child support liability, unless they have become an adoptive parent.[57] However, in private law proceedings married step-parents may be required to pay maintenance for their step-children, following relationship breakdown, if they have treated them as 'children of the family'.[58] Equally, another relative who may look after the child, eg a grandparent, cannot be the child's parent and so be liable under the 1991 Act, again unless and until he or she becomes an adoptive parent.[59] Such a carer may, of course, be a 'person with care' for the purpose of applying for child support.

The legal definition of 'parent' has inevitably become more complex with the scientific developments in assisted reproduction and the consequential legislative responses, first in the FLRA 1987 and now in the Human Fertilisation and Embryology Act 1990. Before the intervention of statute, a child who was born as the result of artificial insemination, using third party donor sperm, was regarded as illegitimate. Moreover the donor, and not the mother's husband, was in law the child's father. Consequently under the 1991 Act the husband (or indeed unmarried male partner) in such a case could not be liable to maintain a child conceived through artificial insemination. This was illustrated by *Re M (Child Support Act: Parentage)*,[60] in which two children had been born in such circumstances in 1981 and 1986. The Secretary of State's argument that the husband had consented to the insemination and so was estopped from denying that he was a parent was dis-

---

[55]   CSA 1991, s 54.

[56]   Adoption has the effect of extinguishing the parental responsibility of the birth parents: Adoption and Children Act 2002, s 46.

[57]   *R(CS) 6/03* paras 8–11 *per* Mr Commissioner Levenson. Similarly, in Australia, see *Tobin v Tobin* [1999] Fam CA 446.

[58]   See eg *Day v Day* [1988] 1 FLR 278.

[59]   *CCS/3128/95*, para 8, *per* Mr Commissioner Rice. Whilst this means that a grandparent in such a case cannot face any child support liability, it also means that a grandfather who was in his own right a NRP in relation to another relationship cannot claim an allowance in his exempt income under the pre-2003 scheme for a grandchild living with him as she was not a 'relevant child' of his within SI 1992/1815, reg 9(1)(g): *CCS/0736/2002, per* Mr Commissioner Jacobs.

[60]   [1997] 2 FLR 90.

missed by Bracewell J, who noted that the legislation on the consequences of assisted reproduction did not have retrospective effect.[61]

The FLRA 1987 amended the law so that, for births in such cases occurring after the legislation came into force on 4 April 1988, the mother's husband would thenceforth be regarded as the children's father, unless it could be shown that he had not consented to the insemination.[62] This proved to be merely an interim measure, and since 1 August 1991 the assignment of parentage to births involving assisted reproduction has been governed by the Human Fertilisation and Embryology Act 1990.[63] The 1990 Act provides that a woman who gives birth to a child as a result of assisted reproduction (ie by artificial insemination or by embryo or egg and sperm implantation) is to be regarded as the child's mother.[64] As regards fathers, the 1990 Act does not in so many words abolish the common law principle that, where a child is born by assisted reproduction, the donor of the sperm is the child's father. It does, however, heavily qualify that principle. As under the 1987 Act, in the case of a woman using assisted reproduction who is a member of a married couple, the husband will be the child's father, unless it is shown that he did not consent to that process.[65] Where unmarried couples are involved—a situation not covered by the 1987 Act—the male partner will be treated as the father only if the couple together received treatment licensed by the Human Fertilisation and Embryology Authority.[66] It follows that if treatment is provided to an unmarried couple by an unlicensed agency, the male partner will not be designated as the child's father;[67] likewise if the couple have separated and no longer receive treatment together.[68] In any such case the sperm donor remains in law the father, although in practice he will usually not be traceable. However, if the male partner is deemed to be the child's father by operation of the 1990 Act, then no other person—eg the sperm donor—is to be treated as the father.[69] Instead, the man treated as the father is treated as the child's father for all purposes,[70] including therefore in respect of the child support scheme. An issue which has yet to arise for decision in the United Kingdom concerns the status of a man who enters into a private arrangement with a lesbian couple to be a sperm donor for one of them. Logically, as a matter of law, he must be the resultant

---

[61] Presumably the husband might have faced liability under private law if he treated the children as 'children of the family'.

[62] Family Law Reform Act 1987, s 27.

[63] See further S Sheldon, 'Fragmenting Fatherhood: The Regulation of Reproductive Technologies' (2005) 68 *Modern Law Review* 523.

[64] Human Fertilisation and Embryology Act 1990, s 27(1). This has the effect of discouraging surrogacy; however, a married couple who commission another woman to act as surrogate mother can apply for a parental order ensuring they enjoy parental status together: *ibid*, s 30.

[65] *Ibid*, s 28(2). This carries forward the reform made by the FLRA 1987. See further *Leeds Teaching Hospital NHS Trust v A* [2003] EWHC 259 (QB); [2003] 1 FLR 1091.

[66] Human Fertilisation and Embryology Act 1990, s 28(3).

[67] As in *U v W (A-G intervening)* [1998] Fam 39, where the treatment took place abroad.

[68] *Re R (A Child) (IVF: Paternity of Child)* [2005] UKHL 33; [2005] 2 WLR 1158.

[69] Human Fertilisation and Embryology Act 1990, ss 28(4) and 29(2).

[70] Human Fertilisation and Embryology Act 1990, s 29(1).

child's father, even if it was mutually agreed by the three adult parties concerned that he should have no financial or other responsibility for the child.[71] This is because there is no scope within the 1990 legislation for the mother's lesbian partner to be designated with parental status.[72] The only way in which a lesbian partner may acquire that status is through adoption; the Civil Partnerships Act 2004 does not alter the underlying basis of liability under the Child Support Act 1991.[73]

Parentage Disputes and the Statutory Presumptions

In practice the most common problem associated with parental status is where the non-resident parent simply denies that he is the child's parent.[74] Official figures suggest that about 200,000 cases a year involve denial of paternity, but only 20,000 are subsequently subject to testing and in only 2,000 cases the denial of paternity is upheld.[75] Of course, a man subject to a potential child support liability has every incentive to deny paternity, whether he is genuinely uncertain or merely raising the issue as a delaying tactic.[76] These types of disputes were a common feature of the poor law, most notably where the mother was not married to the (alleged) father. Paternity disputes were less likely to occur in the case of married couples, given the common law presumption that the husband of a married woman is the father of her child. After 1969, the courts were able to direct the use of blood tests, but these could never strictly prove that the putative father '*is* the father but merely

---

[71] See the example reported in the press in 1994 and cited in S Millns, 'Making "social judgments that go beyond the purely medical": The Reproductive Revolution and Access to Fertility Treatment Services' in J Bridgeman and S Millns, *Law and Body Politics* (Dartmouth, Aldershot, 1995) ch 4 at 91.

[72] This issue has arisen before the Australian courts. In *B v J* (1996) FLC 92-716 a known sperm donor for a lesbian couple was held *not* to be a parent for the purposes of the child support legislation, given the relevant statutory definition of 'parent', see D Sandor, 'Children Born from Sperm Donation: Financial Support and Other Responsibilities in the Context of Discrimination' (1997) 4 *Australian Journal of Human Rights* 175. But a male friend who 'donated' semen to a female in a lesbian relationship by normal intercourse was subject to child support liability: *ND v BM* [2003] FamCA 469. Note that the Australian law on 'unofficial' inseminations is different to that in the UK. See further D Dempsey, 'Donor, Father or Parent? Conceiving Paternity in the Australian Family Court' (2004) 18 *International Journal of Law, Policy and the Family* 76. For discussion as to whether a known sperm donor is a 'parent' for the purposes of the Family Law Act 1975 (Cth), see *Re Patrick* (2002) 168 FLR 6 and *Re Mark* [2003] FamCA 822.

[73] See Adoption and Children Act 2002, s 144(4) and S Jones, 'The Civil Partnership Act 2004 and Social Security Law' (2005) 12 *Journal of Social Security Law* 119 at 130.

[74] Research suggests that the paternal discrepancy rate is in the order of 4%: see MA Bellis, K Hughes, S Hughes and JR Ashton, 'Measuring paternal discrepancy and its public health consequences' (2005) 59 *Journal of Epidemiology and Community Health* 749. But on the under-reporting of nonmarital paternity see MS Rendall, L Clarke, HE Peters, N Ranjit and G Verropoulou, 'Incomplete Reporting of Men's Fertility in the United States and Britain: A Research Note' (1999) 36 *Demography* 135.

[75] *Hansard* HL Debates vol 620 col 1094 (16 January 2001).

[76] In the USA, federal law sets requirements for in-hospital paternity acknowledgment: see R Mincy, I Garfinkel and L Nepomnyaschy, 'In-Hospital Paternity Establishment and Father Involvement in Fragile Families' (2005) 67 *Journal of Marriage and the Family* 611. For arguments in favour of mandatory genetic testing, see J Carbone and N Cahn, 'Which Ties Bind? Redefining the parent-child relationship in an age of genetic certainty' (2003) 11 *William and Mary Bill of Rights Journal* 1011.

that he *could* be the father'.[77] Yet the contemporary context of parentage disputes in the child support scheme is very different. In particular, scientific advances, and principally the advent of DNA testing, mean that it is now possible to attribute parentage to a particular individual with certainty, rather than as a matter of mere probability.[78] The child support scheme embodies a number of statutory presumptions which enable the Agency to proceed with a maintenance calculation notwithstanding denials of parentage.

The starting point is that where a man, who is alleged to be the father of a qualifying child, denies paternity, then the Secretary of State 'shall not make a maintenance calculation on the assumption that the alleged parent is one of the child's parents'.[79] However, this principle is then subject to the qualification that the Secretary of State may proceed to make an assessment if the case falls within one of nine special categories (known as 'Cases'). It follows that the Secretary of State (and, by extension, an appeal tribunal or Child Support Commissioner) may assume paternity *only* in these circumstances. The underlying purpose of this provision is to enable child support to be calculated without undue delay where a man unreasonably contests paternity. In such cases the child support liability will only cease if the non-resident parent can establish in court that he is not the child's father.[80] If there are competing presumptions, then the determination will depend on the relative weight to be attached to each in the light of the evidence.[81] If the facts do not fit within any one of these Cases discussed below, then the question of paternity must be determined through the ordinary courts,[82] and the Agency will not be able to make a calculation until that issue is resolved.[83] If paternity is accepted in respect of one child but disputed for a second child, the Secretary of State is entitled to proceed with the assessment process for the former.[84]

The nine Cases are set out in the primary legislation.[85] The original 1991 Act included just six such Cases, with a further four added and one removed by the

---

[77] Law Commission, *Family Law: Illegitimacy* (Law Com No 118, 1982) at 44.

[78] Given the developments in DNA technology, the 'paternity of any child is to be established by science and not by legal presumption or inference', *Re A and H (Paternity: Blood Tests)* [2002] 1 FLR 1145 at 1154 *per* Thorpe LJ. See R Collins and A Macleod, 'Denials of Paternity: The Impact of DNA Tests on Court Proceedings' (1991) *Journal of Social Welfare and Family Law* 209.

[79] CSA 1991, s 26(1). The provision is actually expressed in gender neutral terms but there are no recorded cases of any female NRP denying that she is the mother of the child in question.

[80] Provision for such applications to court is contained in regulations under CSA 1991, s 45: see below.

[81] See eg *Secretary of State for Work and Pensions v Jones* [2003] EWHC 2163; [2004] 1 FLR 282 (on facts presumption of legitimacy outweighed by alleged father's refusal to undergo DNA testing).

[82] CSA 1991, s 45 and Child Support Appeals (Jurisdiction of Courts) Order 1993 (SI 1993/961, L 12). See *R(CS) 13/98, Robinson v Social Security Commissioners* [1999] EWCA Civ 1184 and the discussion at pp 234–26 below. CSA 1991, s 27, discussed below, governs the procedure to be followed by the Secretary of State in such situations.

[83] There is no power to award interim child support in such cases—contrast the powers under private law in eg Matrimonial Causes Act 1973, s 22 and on the position in Scotland, see M Ross and D McKenzie, 'Financial Support for the Child in Disputed Parentage Cases' (1995) *The Juridical Review* 166.

[84] *CCS/2626/1999.*

[85] CSA 1991, s 26(2).

2000 Act.[86] The following analysis adopts the sequence of Cases as amended by the 2000 Act.[87]

Case A1

Case A1 entitles the Agency to assume that a man is the father of a child if he was married to the child's mother at any time between the date of conception and the child's birth. This represents a statutory variant of the traditional presumption in the English common law, namely that a child born to the parties whilst they are married is presumed to be legitimate.[88] It may, however, be possible to rebut the presumption.[89] As one American court has noted, the presumption of legitimacy is not intended as a 'financial prophylactic for men who have affairs with married women'.[90] Case A1 is expressed in the same terms as the presumption which operates in Scotland.[91] The legislation provides no definition of what is meant by the 'period beginning with the conception and ending with the birth of the child', but presumably in the event of any doubt both administrative and judicial notice will be taken of the usual nine months duration for a pregnancy.[92] This Case only applies where the child is habitually resident in England and Wales[93] and has not been adopted, two qualifications which also apply to Case A2.

Case A2

Case A2 allows the Agency to assume that a man who is named on the child's birth certificate in any part of the United Kingdom is the child's father, even if he was not married to the mother.[94] The mother and father of any child born in England or Wales are required to register the birth within six weeks,[95] but this does not apply to a father who is not married to the child's mother.[96] However, entry of a man's name as father on the child's birth certificate is prima facie evidence of

---

[86] CSPSSA 2000, s 15, brought into effect on 31 January 2001 (SI 2000/3354, Art 2(1)). The CSPSSA 2000 (s 85 and sch 9, pt IX) repealed Case D, which had been rendered obsolete by amendments to CSA 1991, s 27.

[87] Hence, somewhat inconsistently, Case A1 precedes Case A but Case B1 follows Case B.

[88] *Knowles v Knowles* [1962] P 161; see also Legitimacy Act 1976, s 2. For a useful discussion, see New Zealand Law Commission, *New Issues in Legal Parenthood* (Wellington, NZ, 2005) at ch 4.

[89] For example, if the husband can demonstrate that he was abroad by himself at the time when his wife must have conceived; see also *Leeds Teaching Hospital NHS Trust v A*, n 65 above.

[90] *County of Orange v Leslie B* 14 Cal App 4th 976 at 981 (1993).

[91] Law Reform (Parent and Child) (Scotland) Act 1986, s 5(1)(a).

[92] The House of Lords took judicial notice that the period is normally nine months, or 270–280 days, in *Preston-Jones v Preston-Jones* [1951] AC 391 at 401 *per* Lord Simonds. See also in Australia *OP v HM* [2003] Fam CA 454.

[93] On habitual residence, see below p 250. For Scotland, see Case E, discussed below. As to Northern Ireland, the Child Support, Pensions and Social Security Act (Northern Ireland) 2000 made the appropriate amendments to the Child Support (Northern Ireland) Order 1991 (SI 1991/2628, NI 23).

[94] As with Case A1, the child must be habitually resident in England and Wales and must not have been adopted.

[95] Births and Deaths Registration Act (BDRA) 1953, s 2.

[96] BDRA 1953, s 10(1).

paternity.[97] Case A2 applies that general principle to the specific instance of child support. This has important implications in practice, given that 40 per cent of all registered births occur outside marriage and that the father's details are included on the birth certificate in most such cases.[98] The change made by the 2000 Act has been made all the more significant by subsequent legislation[99] which provides that a man who is not married to the mother but who is (with her consent) registered as father of their child will automatically be vested with parental responsibility.[100] There is, however, no presumption of paternity simply by virtue of unmarried cohabitation, however longstanding and stable.[101] Research has demonstrated that there remains a widespread lack of awareness amongst men as to the legal consequences of fatherhood outside marriage.[102]

Case A3

Case A3 permits the Secretary of State to assume paternity if either the alleged father has refused to take a DNA test or he has submitted to such a test, which shows 'no reasonable doubt' that he is the child's parent and (implicitly) he refuses to accept the outcome. The onus will then be on the alleged parent to pursue further action in order to rebut this presumption (by applying to court for a formal declaration as to whether or not he is the father of the child, as discussed below). DNA testing is only reliable if samples are taken from all three parties—the mother, the alleged father and the child; if the parent with care declines to provide a sample, the statutory presumption does not apply. There is currently no effective sanction for non-compliance by the parent with care in such circumstances.[103]

---

[97] BDRA 1953, s 34(2); see *Brierley v Brierley and Williams* [1918] P 257 and *Jackson v Jackson and Pavan* [1964] P 25.

[98] K Kiernan and K Smith, 'Unmarried parenthood: new insights from the Millennium Cohort Study' (2003) 114 *Population Trends* 26 at 27.

[99] Adoption and Children Act 2002, s 111, amending Children Act 1989, s 4. A parallel amendment in Scotland followed in Family Law (Scotland) Act 2006, s 23.

[100] This proposal was originally contained in LCD, *Procedures for The Determination of Paternity and on The Law on Parental Responsibility for Unmarried Fathers* (1998). The mandatory nature of this proposal had been opposed by both the LCD's Advisory Board on Family Law (*Annual Report 1999*, Annex C, para 3) and the Solicitors Family Law Association (now Resolution): see J Ashley, 'Parental Responsibility—A New Deal or a Costly Exercise?' [1999] Fam Law 175.

[101] See the proposal to this effect in New Zealand Law Commission, n 88 above at para 4.35. Two US states have enacted a similar presumption: JG Dwyer, 'A Taxonomy of Children's Existing Rights in State Decision Making about their Relationships' (2003) 11 *William & Mary Bill of Rights Journal* 845 at 868 n 57.

[102] R Pickford, *Fathers, marriage and the law* (FPSC, London, 1999).

[103] CSA 1991, s 46(1)(c) (as substituted by CSPSSA 2000, s 19), which enables a reduced benefit direction to be imposed in such cases, has been in force since 3 March 2003 (SI 2003/192, Art 4). However, in practice (as at June 2006) this has procedure has not been implemented. According to CSA, *Specialist Areas: Migration & Case Conversion* (2005) at 2433: 'These cases are presently being discussed between Policy and the Magistrates Association to decide how they should be progressed'.

Case A

Case A, which covers adoptive parents, was probably included in the legislation from an abundance of caution, as an adoptive parent must be a parent of the child for child support purposes in any event.[104] The term 'adopted' is defined by reference to the Adoption Act 1976, the Adoption (Scotland) Act 1978 and the Adoption and Children Act 2002.[105]

Cases B and B1

The original Case B permitted parentage to be assumed where the alleged parent is the child's parent by virtue of a parental order under section 30 of the Human Fertilisation and Embryology Act 1990. This possibility is only open in cases of surrogacy. Case B1, which enables the Agency to presume parentage in other cases of assisted reproduction under sections 27 and 28 of the 1990 Act, is unlikely to be used in practice other than extremely rarely.[106]

Case C

Case C applies a presumption of parentage if the ordinary courts have made a formal declaration to that effect and there has been no subsequent adoption of the child in question. Section 55A of the Family Law Act 1986, inserted by the 2000 Act,[107] now provides a single mechanism for obtaining a declaration of parentage, thus replacing the two separate procedures previously contained in section 56 of the 1986 Act and in section 27 of the 1991 Act.[108] The scope of section 55A of the 1986 Act is wider than that of the original section 56 in three respects. First, in principle *any* person may make an application for a declaration of status,[109] subject to the applicant having a 'sufficient personal interest in the determination of the application'.[110] However, an applicant who is seeking an order that he or she is the parent of a named person, or that a named person is their parent, or that a named person is the other parent of their named child, has an absolute right to bring proceedings for a declaration.[111] Secondly, the application may be for a

---

[104] See the definition of 'parent' in CSA 1991, s 54, discussed above.

[105] CSA 1991, s 26(3), as amended by Adoption and Children Act 2002, s 139(1) and sch 3, para 81.

[106] See above, p 225.

[107] CSPSSA 2000, s 83. This effectively replaced the former provision for declarations of parentage under FLA 1986, s 56(1)(a) (repealed by CSPSSA 2000, s 85 and sch 9, pt IX).

[108] Hence the repeal by CSPSSA 2000 of Case D, which had applied a presumption where a declaration had been made under s 27.

[109] Only the subject of the application could apply under s 56; both parents (assuming they are alive) had to be joined as respondents (SI 1991/1247, r 3.13(3)).

[110] FLA 1986, s 55A(3). The Advisory Board on Family Law suggested that this might encompass siblings wishing to establish a right to inheritance or grandchildren. This discretion enables the court to sift out vexatious applications, eg matters which may be of (alleged) public interest, such as 'newspapers making applications to establish the paternity of public figures' (*Annual Report 1999*, Annex C, para 2(iv)).

[111] FLA 1986, s 55A(4).

declaration as to whether *or not* a named person is or was the parent of another person named in the application.[112] Thirdly, applications under section 55A may be brought in the magistrates' court as well as in the High Court or county court.[113] Section 56 of the 1986 Act remains in force, but is now confined to applications for declarations as to legitimacy or legitimation, which may only be made to the High Court or the county court.

Case E

This Case is broadly equivalent to Case A1 but applies solely to Scotland.

Case F

Case F, the last of these nine statutory presumptions, is the one that has arisen most frequently in litigation. It allows the Secretary of State to proceed with a maintenance calculation where the alleged father disputes paternity but has already been found to be the child's father in civil proceedings, so long as the child has not since been adopted. Case F can therefore have the effect of converting a purely nominal order made by a magistrates' court before the 1991 Act into a substantial obligation.[114] The requirement that the man 'has been found, or adjudged, to be the father of the child in question' does not presuppose that there had been a *contested* hearing: for example, a consent order granting the man a parental responsibility order in proceedings under the Children Act 1989 is sufficient.[115] However, a previous court order making financial provision for the 'children of the family' will not, by itself, bring the Case F presumption into play, as the issue of parentage may not have been considered by the court.[116] The significance of the Case F presumption therefore needs to be understood in the wider private law context of paternity disputes.

The Civil Evidence Act 1968 provides, assuming that there has been a court finding of paternity in whatever guise, that such a determination is admissible as

---

[112] Consequently, the former prohibition on declarations of illegitimacy in s 58(5)(b) of the 1986 Act was repealed by CSPSSA 2000. Clearly, a declaration of (non) parentage may raise ECHR issues under Arts 6 and 8: *Re L (Family Proceedings Court) (Appeal: Jurisdiction)* [2003] EWHC 1682 (Fam); [2005] 1 FLR 210.

[113] FLA 1986, s 60(5) provides for a statutory right of appeal from the magistrates' court to the High Court in respect of a decision of the former on an application for a s 55A declaration. This is in addition to the normal right of appeal by way of case stated and the possibility of seeking judicial review.

[114] *Robinson v Social Security Commissioners* [1999] EWCA Civ 1184, transcript at 6 *per* Robert Walker LJ. His Lordship accepted that the father 'may feel hard done by' in such circumstances (however, on the facts of that case, the blood tests had indicated a relative probability of paternity of 99.7%).

[115] *R v Secretary of State for Social Security and Child Support Officer ex parte W* [1999] EWHC Admin 390, Johnson J (this follows the earlier grant of leave to apply for judicial review by the CA in *R v Secretary of State for Social Security and Child Support Officer ex parte West* [1998] EWCA Civ 1821). The parties were the same as those in *R(CS) 2/98*.

[116] Given that such orders under eg MCA 1973 or DPMCA 1978 need not be confined to the parties' natural children. But the fact that the parties were married would presumably bring Case A1 into operation. If, however, the court order in divorce proceedings expressly declares that a child is *not* a child of the family, then for child support purposes that may be taken as 'conclusive for practical purposes of questions of paternity', *CCS/2626/1999* at para 20 *per* Mr Commissioner Howell QC.

evidence in any other civil litigation as proof that the man in question is indeed the father.[117] Furthermore, such a finding in earlier proceedings means that 'he shall be taken . . . to be (or have been) the father of that child, unless the contrary is proved'.[118] The prior finding of paternity must have been in 'relevant proceedings', which effectively means any proceedings under the Children Act 1989,[119] or in 'affiliation proceedings'. These latter proceedings were abolished in England and Wales with effect from 1 April 1989,[120] so there are likely to be few qualifying children who are affected today.[121]

In addition, the ordinary courts have the power, whether on application or of their own motion, to direct the use of scientific tests in any civil proceedings[122] in which parentage is in issue.[123] The courts usually take the view that it is in the child's best interests for the truth to be known, and thus will require cogent reasons for not so directing.[124] This approach reflects the right of children under the UN Convention, so far as is possible, to know their own parents.[125] Given the need to respect individual autonomy, the courts' power is confined to *directing* tests, rather than *ordering* them, and any individual involved must consent before a sample is taken.[126] However, in the event that an individual fails to comply, the court is entitled to draw 'such inferences, if any . . . as appear proper in the circumstances'.[127] In recent years, reflecting the scientific advances in paternity testing, the Court of Appeal has adopted an increasingly sceptical approach to purported explanations given for such refusals. So where a man is alleged to be a child's father but declines to comply with such a direction, the inference that he is

---

[117] Civil Evidence Act 1968, s 12(1).

[118] *Ibid*, s 12(2).

[119] *Ibid*, s 12(5), a definition section which also refers to proceedings under the Social Security Act 1986, s 26 (now SSAA 1992, s 105). 'Relevant proceedings' also include those under legislation predating the Children Act 1989, eg the Guardianship of Minors Act 1971: see *Robinson v Social Security Commissioners* [1999] EWCA Civ 1184.

[120] FLRA 1987; see Family Law Reform Act 1987 (Commencement No 2) Order 1989 (SI 1989/382).

[121] The fact that an earlier application for an affiliation order was dismissed is no bar to a subsequent application under the CSA 1991: *Re E (A Minor) (Child Support: Blood Test)* [1994] 2 FLR 548. 'Affiliation proceedings' also covers an action of affiliation and aliment in the Scottish courts: CSA 1991, s 26(3).

[122] Proceedings brought under CSA 1991, s 27 (and now FLA 1986, s 55A) are clearly 'civil proceedings' (*Re E (A Minor) (Child Support: Blood Test)* [1994] 2 FLR 548) whereas the normal processes of Agency assessment are not, unless specific proceedings under s 27 (and now FLA 1986, s 55A) are instituted (*Re H (Minors)*, unreported, CA, 13 June 1995).

[123] FLRA 1969, s 20(1). This provision used to be confined to blood tests, but its scope was widened to include eg DNA testing when s 23 of the FLRA 1987 was eventually implemented on 1 April 2001: see Family Law Reform Act 1987 (Commencement No 3) Order 2001 (SI 2001/777) and Blood Tests (Evidence of Paternity) (Amendment) Regulations 2001 (SI 2001/773).

[124] *S v S (An Infant)* [1972] AC 24; see further *Re H and A (Paternity: Blood Tests)* [2002] 1 FLR 1145. For an Australian perspective, see *TNL & CYT* [2005] FamCA 77 and *F & Z* [2005] FMCAfam 394.

[125] UN Convention on the Rights of the Child, Art 7.

[126] FLRA 1969, s 21(1). Young people aged 16 and over can consent on their own behalf: *ibid*, s 21(2). The legislation as originally enacted enabled a parent with care to veto the taking of such a sample from a younger child (*Re O; Re J (children) (blood tests: constraint)* [2000] 2 All ER 29), but amendments made by CSPSSA 2000, s 82 enable the court to provide the necessary consent in such a case.

[127] FLRA 1969, s 23(1).

indeed the father 'should be virtually inescapable'.[128] The court should accordingly only uphold 'an explanation that is objectively valid, demonstrating rationality, logicality and consistency'.[129]

There appear to be no reported cases in which the courts have found that the alleged father's explanation reaches this high threshold. There have, however, been several unreported decisions in which the High Court has reversed findings by magistrates that alleged non-resident parents had shown good grounds for declining to comply with such a direction. For example, in *R v Secretary of State for Social Security ex parte G*,[130] the President ruled that a man who had submitted to a blood test in 1981, which was inconclusive, did not have justifiable reasons for declining to provide a DNA sample 15 years later, despite his honest belief that he was not the child's father. Similarly, in *Child Support Agency v Rust*[131] the respondent denied that he had ever even met the child's mother and refused to take a DNA test, arguing that his wife was adamantly opposed. Connell J allowed the Agency's appeal by way of case stated against the magistrates' decision to accept the man's reasons. The 'virtually inescapable' inference that he was the father applied, notwithstanding that sexual intercourse had been denied, as the respondent had the means available to exclude himself and to remove the strain on his wife and family. Similarly, the fact that the mother in question was having a relationship with another man, who had not been asked to provide a DNA sample, was not, in itself, a good reason for not complying.[132] In *Child Support Agency v DF*[133] the man in question claimed that he had received intimidating anonymous telephone calls, threatening him with violence if he complied with the tests. Although this satisfied the magistrates, who also found the mother's evidence about the alleged relationship unreliable, Munby J accepted that the man's statements 'constituted a self-serving device in order to avoid the financial consequences of proof of paternity'.[134] Finally, in *F v Child Support Agency*,[135] in which an appeal against the magistrates' finding of paternity was dismissed, it was held that this inference also applies in cases where the mother is a married woman. It follows that the inference can rebut the presumption of legitimacy.[136]

---

[128] *Re A (A Minor) (Paternity: Refusal of Blood Test)* [1994] 2 FLR 463 at 473, *per* Waite LJ.

[129] *Re G (A minor)* [1997] 1 FLR 360 at 367, *per* Thorpe LJ.

[130] [1997] EWHC Admin 560, Sir Stephen Brown P.

[131] Case No CO/1223/99, QBD, 2 December 1999

[132] *R v Child Support Agency ex parte GL* CO/4491/98, QBD, 17 June 1999 (in which Owen J remitted the case for rehearing). See also, from Australia, *J & D* [2000] Fam CA 1734.

[133] Case No CO/5106/98, QBD, 26 May 2000.

[134] Para 32.

[135] CO/4600/98, QBD, 25 March 1999. In such a case the 'putative father still declines to give a blood test at his peril when ordered [sic] to do so by the court', at para 21 *per* Scott-Baker J.

[136] See also *R (on the application of Clark) v Child Support Agency* [2002] EWHC Admin 284 and *Secretary of State for Work and Pensions v Jones* [2003] EWHC 2163; [2004] 1 FLR 282.

Parentage Disputes where the Statutory Presumptions do not Apply

The nine statutory Cases are designed to enable the Agency (and tribunals and the Commissioners) to make decisions about paternity only in 'specified, clear-cut cases'.[137] If none of the statutory presumptions applies, then the usual method for establishing paternity involves DNA tests. These tests, carried out by independent testing agencies,[138] are expensive. In appropriate cases the Agency will offer an alleged non-resident father a DNA test at a discounted rate (approximately 50 per cent of the market rate).[139] The man is required to pay the testing agency direct[140] but is refunded in full by the Agency if the test establishes that he is not in fact the father.[141] If the results of the test do not exclude the man involved as being a parent, and either he does not deny paternity or a court makes a declaration of parentage (or, in Scotland, a decree of declarator of parentage), then the Agency has a statutory power to recover the cost of the test process.[142] In some cases the man concerned will only raise the issue of parentage at a later date, once a maintenance calculation has been made. This is treated as a request for a revision; in such cases the Agency will only offer DNA testing if the parent with care agrees that there may be a doubt about parentage. If she maintains that he is the father, the Agency is likely to refuse to revise and so leave the man to initiate alternative proceedings.[143]

The increased scope of the statutory presumptions as a result of the amendments made by the 2000 Act means that court proceedings to establish paternity may be rarer than in the early days of the legislation.[144] Section 27 sets out the procedure to be followed in these cases. In the 1991 Act as originally enacted, section 27 enabled either the child support officer or the person with care to refer the case to a court for a declaration of parentage. This was a freestanding provision, with the consequence that any such declaration had effect only for the purposes of child

---

[137] Jacobs and Douglas, n 23 above, at 98.

[138] More comprehensive statutory controls on such agencies were introduced by CSPSSA 2000, s 82: see N Wikeley, 'Child Support, Paternity and Parentage' (2001) 31 Fam Law 125. See new Blood Tests (Evidence of Paternity) Regulations 1971 (SI 1971/1861), reg 8A (inserted by SI 2001/773), reg 10.

[139] The official advice to staff is that they should 'only offer DNA testing if the PWC agrees there might be doubt about the identity of the father', Child Support Agency, *Specialist Areas: Welfare of the Child* (2005) at 2615.

[140] If the man says he cannot afford to pay the fee for the test in advance, the Agency may make arrangements to pay the fee on the man's undertaking to accept the outcome of the test and to pay the Agency the cost in the event that he is found to be the father: *ibid*, at 2663.

[141] The man must agree for the test results to be conveyed to the Agency and the PWC must confirm that the person she named as the father is the same man as the one photographed as attending for the purposes of the test: note that impersonation of another for the purposes of providing a sample is a criminal offence: FLRA 1969, s 24.

[142] CSA 1991, s 27A. This provision does not apply if tests have been carried out in response to a court direction or (in Scotland) a 'request'.

[143] n 139 above at 2629.

[144] 'Referrals to court by the Child Support Agency should become very few and far between', *ibid*, at 2669.

support liability.[145] Moreover, as a result of an apparent oversight, there was no statutory right of appeal against the decision of a magistrates' court to grant a declaration of parentage under the original section 27.[146] Although that omission was not remedied by the 2000 Act,[147] the amendments have to some extent side-stepped these difficulties, as seen above in the context of Case C, by introducing a single route for declarations of parentage under section 55A of the Family Law Act 1986. Consequently, the 2000 Act[148] substituted a new section 27 which is essentially a supplementary provision to the section 55A procedure discussed above. Under section 55A(3), the court should not entertain an application for a declaration of parentage unless it considers that the applicant has a 'sufficient personal interest' in the matter. Section 27, as substituted, now provides that a person with care is to be treated as having such an interest, and that this requirement of standing does not apply to the Secretary of State. This deeming rule applies where three conditions are met, namely that, the alleged parent denies paternity, the Secretary of State is not satisfied that the case falls within one of the statutory Cases and either the Secretary of State or the person with care applies under section 55A.

It follows that either the person with care or the Secretary of State (or indeed the alleged non-resident parent) may bring proceedings for a declaration of parentage. According to internal guidance, the types of cases in which the Agency might bring proceedings are those where: a parent with care on benefit refuses consent for a qualifying child to take a DNA test; the DNA evidence is inconclusive; or in cases involving fertility treatment and the alleged non-resident parent denies that he gave consent for the treatment.[149] If the decision is taken to proceed, the Agency compiles a file comprising the relevant evidence and the case is presented to the magistrates' court by a local officer.[150] If the Agency declines to take action, either the person with care or the alleged non-resident parent may bring proceedings.

Before examining the legal definition of a *non-resident* parent, there are two further matters that need to be explored in more detail. First, once an individual has either accepted or been found by a court to be the father, can that recognition or finding be reversed later when compelling evidence to the contrary emerges? This is known as disestablishing paternity. Secondly, and more generally, does the

---

[145] CSA 1991, s 27(3), as originally enacted. This limitation never applied in Scotland: see CSA 1991, s 28 and *Secretary of State for Social Security v Ainslie* [2000] SLT (Sh Ct) 35. On the original s 27, see MD Dodds and R Janson, 'Declarations of Parentage under Section 27 of the Child Support Act 1991' (1996) 160 *Justice of the Peace* 181.

[146] *T v Child Support Agency* [1997] 2 FLR 875, in which the magistrates had made a declaration at a hearing which was not attended by the alleged NRP. A subsequent DNA test established that he could not have been the father. The High Court, in the absence of a statutory right of appeal, granted a declaration under RSC Ord 15 r 16 to the effect that he was not the father of the child in question.

[147] *Re L (Family Proceedings Court) (Appeal: Jurisdiction)* [2003] EWHC 1682 (Fam); [2005] 1 FLR 210.

[148] CSPSSA 2000, sch 8, para 13.

[149] n 139 above at 2669.

[150] In Scotland cases are heard by sheriffs and are always presented on behalf of the Agency by a solicitor.

law's emphasis on genetic parenthood result in the imposition of child support liabilities in inappropriate cases—or conversely, in other cases, in a failure to require child support where it might otherwise be considered to be in the child's best interests?

Disestablishing Paternity

As we saw above in the context of the statutory presumption in Case C, it is now possible to apply to court for a declaration of non-parentage.[151] We have also noted the strong presumption in the case law that 'the truth should out', and a child should not be subject to a pretence as to her or his real identity.[152] As a result, it may be possible to 'undo' an acceptance or finding of paternity going back some years.[153] The question then arises as to whether the man may recover the child support paid in the interim and, if so, from whom. Statute provides that where a non-resident parent has overpaid child support, the Secretary of State may arrange for the man to be reimbursed (or partially reimbursed) by such payment as is considered appropriate.[154] Clearly, if the parent with care has been on benefit, the Agency should simply reimburse the 'non-father'. Indeed, in one (exceptional) case the Agency refunded £30,000 to a man who had paid child support for a child following a brief affair with a woman, only to discover seven years later, following belated DNA tests, that he was not in fact the father after all.[155] The position is more difficult where the person with care is a private client. Again, the Secretary of State has a discretion as to reimbursing the man in question, but also has a power to recover the whole or part of that refund from the parent with care.[156] The position may be complicated further where the parent with care misled the man as to the child's paternity. In such circumstances it is possible, although evidentially problematic, to bring a civil action in tort for deceit in the United Kingdom,[157] as it is in Australia[158] but not in the United States.[159] In terms of its treatment of the

---

[151] Family Law Act 1986, s 55A; see above p 230.

[152] See p 232 above.

[153] See *Dixon v Dixon* (1983) 4 FLR 99.

[154] CSA 1991, s 41B(2). As this is a discretionary provision, the welfare principle in *ibid*, s 2 applies. A nice (but as yet untested) point is whether this provision actually governs a man later proven not to be genetically related to the child at all, as he is not in law a 'non-resident parent' (although he may have been wrongly treated as such).

[155] *The Times*, 18 October 2001.

[156] CSA 1991, s 41B(3)–(5); see further Child Support (Arrears, Interest and Adjustment of Maintenance Assessments) Regulations 1992 (SI 1992/1816), regs 10A and 10B.

[157] See *P v B (Paternity: Damages for Deceit)* [2001] 1 FLR 1041, discussed by R Spon-Smith 'The man is father of the child—or is he?' [2002] Fam Law 26 and 388. See also S Sheldon, ' "Sperm bandits", birth control fraud and the battle of the sexes' (2001) 21 *Legal Studies* 460. For an example from France, see 'Husband makes cheating wife pay for time spent raising lover's child', *The Times*, 3 May 2005 at 32.

[158] See *DRP and AJL* [2004] FMCAfam 440 and *Magill v Magill* [2005] VSCA 51 (see L Young and S Shaw, '*Magill v Magill*: Families and deceit' (2005) 19 *Australian Journal of Family Law* 44).

[159] See *Wallis v Smith* 22 P 3d 682 (Court of Appeals of New Mexico, 2001)

recovery of overpayments of child support in cases in which a man is later found not to be the father, the provisions of the United Kingdom scheme are also closer to those that apply in Australia than in the United States.

In Australia there is no automatic right to the recovery of overpayments in cases where paternity is disestablished. Instead, the legislation vests the court with a broad discretion to 'make such orders as it considers just and equitable for the purpose of adjusting or giving effect to the rights of the parties and the child concerned'.[160] Any such sum is recoverable from the payee, not the Agency.[161] By way of contrast, American child support schemes are markedly less generous than their counterparts overseas to those men who are subsequently demonstrated not to be fathers. In cases of married couples, the American courts have tended to apply 'the presumption of paternity regardless of the presence of conclusive, biological evidence of non-paternity',[162] so emphasising the strong policy reasons for finality in paternity adjudications. The model statute at national level, the Uniform Parentage Act, codifying the law relating to parentage, applies a general limitation period of two years from the date of the child's birth for challenging paternity in the case of a presumed father.[163] Federal law also stipulates that where a man voluntarily acknowledges paternity, he has only 60 days to rescind such acceptance, after which rescission is subject to the provisions of state law.[164] The majority of states have adopted restrictive rules on the scope for disestablishing paternity.[165] In the rare cases where paternity is disestablished, it is very difficult for such men to recover child support erroneously paid in the past.[166]

The Nexus between Genetic Parenthood and Child Support Liabilities

The 1991 Act is premised on the fundamental principle that the genetic link between parent and the child means that a father (or mother) should be liable for

---

[160] Child Support (Assessment) Act 1989 (Cth), s 143.

[161] See further *Child Support Registrar and Z & T* [2002] FamCA 182, and *Mercer v Child Support Agency* [2004] FCA 465.

[162] BS Rogers, 'The presumption of paternity in child support cases: a triumph of law over biology' [2002] *University of Cincinnati Law Review* 1151 at 1154. For opposing views see MB Jacobs, 'When Daddy Doesn't Want to Be Daddy Anymore: An Argument Against Paternity Fraud Claims' (2004) 16 *Yale Journal of Law & Feminism* 193 and A S Epstein, 'The Parent Trap: Should a man be allowed to recoup child support payments if he discovers he is not the biological father of the child?' (2005) 42 *Brandeis Law Journal* 655.

[163] Rogers, n 162 above, at 1168 (subject to some narrow exceptions).

[164] N Myricks, 'DNA Testing and Child Support: Can the Truth Really Set You Free?' (2003) 17 *American Journal of Family Law* 31 at 35.

[165] K Santillo, 'Disestablishment of paternity and the future of child support obligations' (2003) 37 *Family Law Quarterly* 503. For a full discussion, see P Roberts, 'Truth and Consequences: Part I. Disestablishing the Paternity of Non-Marital Children' (2003) 37 *Family Law Quarterly* 35 and 'Truth and Consequences: Part II. Questioning the Paternity of Marital Children' (2003) 37 *Family Law Quarterly* 55.

[166] P Roberts, 'Truth and Consequences: Part III. Who Pays When Paternity is Disestablished?' (2003) 37 *Family Law Quarterly* 69.

child support.[167] That principle appears to command widespread public support,[168] albeit that there is considerable debate on matters such as how that support should be quantified and the procedures by which it should be assessed, collected and enforced. But does the emphasis on genetic parenthood result in 'hard cases' where the imposition of a financial liability might be thought inappropriate or even unjust? Conversely, are there other cases where the absence of any genetic (or adoptive) link means that an adult may unreasonably escape liability for child support?

First, are there any 'hard cases' in which liability is unreasonably imposed? It is important to note at the outset that neither private law nor statutory child support make any distinction between the level of support payable for a child who is the result of a casual relationship as compared with that due to a child born during a long-term marriage. As Hale J observed in *J v C (Child: Financial Provision)*, 'there is nothing in the private law provisions to distinguish between different children' on grounds that relate either to the circumstances of their birth or to the length or quality of their parents' relationship.[169] Furthermore:

> The policy of the Child Support Act 1991 was that people who had children should support them, whether or not those were wanted children. As a general proposition children should not suffer because their parents are irresponsible or uncaring towards them.[170]

To this extent, the notion of a strict liability associated with genetic parenthood appears to be widely accepted. Certainly few would have much sympathy with the man who says that the condom he used in intercourse failed.[171] Equally, a father cannot escape liability by relying on the woman's assurance that she was using contraception.[172] In addition, as we have seen, a man cannot contract out of his child support obligations,[173] even if the woman in question is prepared to enter into such an agreement.[174] Nor, of course, can the man disclaim liability if the woman declines to have an abortion.[175] Putting to one side any moral duty that

---

[167] See also ch 1 above for a discussion of the reliance on the genetic link in parentage as the basis for child support liabilities.

[168] See further ch 1.

[169] [1999] 1 FLR 152 at 154.

[170] *Ibid*, at 154.

[171] See G Douglas, 'The Intention to be a Parent and the Making of Mothers' (1994) 57 *Modern Law Review* 636 at 640, citing *Bell v Mccurdie* 1981 SLT 159 (holding that contributory negligence has no place in the law of aliment).

[172] See eg *L Pamela P v Frank S* 449 NE 2d 713 (Court of Appeals of New York, 1983) and for a discussion of the early US case law, see AM Payne, 'Parent's child support liability as affected by other parent's fraudulent misrepresentation regarding sterility or use of birth control, or refusal to abort pregnancy' (1992) 2 ALR 5th 337.

[173] n 7 above.

[174] See *Estes v Albers* 504 NW 2d 607 (Supreme Court of South Dakota, 1993) (mother's agreement that father would not be financially responsible for child, if he agreed to father child, void); see also *Straub v Todd* 645 NE 2d 597 (Supreme Court of Indiana, 1995) and *Kesler v Weniger* 744 A 2d 794 (Superior Court of Pennsylvania, 2000).

[175] For the argument that it is unjust to force responsibility on a man for choices made by the mother of his child, seem MB Kapp, 'The Father's (Lack of) Rights and Responsibilities in the Abortion Decision: An Examination of Legal-Ethical Implications' (1982) *Ohio Northern University Law Review*

may arise, the imposition of strict liability in such cases can be justified in purely instrumental terms: 'placing a support obligation on the socially unconnected biological father may deter some men from having children they do not intend to nurture, and may induce others to care about the children they are required to support'.[176] The American case law appears to stretch such strict liability to the absolute limits, so much so that where 'a man engages in an intimate sexual act resulting in his depositing of his sperm with a woman who then becomes pregnant, he is liable for child support'.[177] This principle has been applied even where the man in question did not consent to the sexual encounter because he was unconscious at the time[178] or where the woman had self-inseminated following oral sex.[179]

A rather different type of potential 'hard case' is presented by the 'under age' father. As a matter of civil law, there is no lower age limit for fatherhood. Indeed, in old-style affiliation proceedings a 13-year-old boy was held liable for the maintenance of his child.[180] Nowadays, as a matter of policy, the Agency will not normally take action against a father aged under 16.[181] In practice, once the young man reaches 16, he will be interviewed at home in the presence of an adult. Even if paternity is acknowledged or proven, it does not necessarily follow that immediate payment of child support will be required. So long as the father is himself still a child (in effect for so long as an adult receives child benefit for him), he is liable but at the nil rate.[182] Of course, once the father has an independent income, there is nothing to prevent the Agency recovering child support from him. Although the imposition of a liability in such cases is unlikely to be controversial, there may well be differences of view as to the age at which payments should be required. Is the position different, however, if the boy has become an under-age father as a result of sexual intercourse with an older woman, who has thereby herself committed a criminal offence? As a matter of strict law the young father will almost certainly be a 'non-resident parent'. However, if such a case were to arise, this might be an

---

369, EM Hiester, 'Child support statutes and the father's right not to procreate' (2004) 2 *Ave Maria Law Review* 213 and E Brake, 'Fatherhood and Child Support: Do Men Have a Right to Choose?' (2005) 22 *Journal of Applied Philosophy* 55. For a critique of such arguments, see S Sheldon, 'Unwilling Fathers and Abortion: Terminating Men's Child Support Obligations' (2003) 66 *Modern Law Review* 175.

[176] IM Ellman, 'Thinking about custody and support in ambiguous-father families' (2002) 36 *Family Law Quarterly* 49 at 71.

[177] LW Morgan, 'It's ten o'clock: do you know where your sperm are? Toward a strict liability theory of parentage' (1999) 11 *Divorce Litigation* 1.

[178] *SF v State ex rel TM* 695 So 2d 1186 (Alabama, 1996).

[179] *State of Louisiana v Frisard* 694 So 2d 1032 (1997) (the father's evidence, at 1035, was 'this woman came upon me in the [hospital] waiting room and she told me that she wanted to perform oral sex on me . . . as being any male would, I did not refuse and I wish I would have refused'). See also the case from Illinois discussed by M Berlins, *The Guardian*, 8 March 2005 (father alleged birth the result of mother's self-insemination following consensual oral sex).

[180] *L v K* [1985] Fam 144; in contrast there is an irrebuttable presumption in criminal law that a boy under the age of 14 cannot commit rape: *R v Waite* [1892] 1 QB 600; *R v Williams* [1893] 1 QB 320.

[181] n 139 above at 2714.

[182] Child Support (Maintenance Calculations and Special Cases) Regulations 2000 (SI 2001/155), reg 5(b); for old cases, see SI 1992/1815, reg 26(1)(b)(iii).

appropriate case for the Secretary of State to exercise the discretion not to take action to recover child support—not least as the father is himself a child whose welfare must accordingly be taken into account.[183] Such cases have occurred in the United States, where the courts have held that an under-age male is, in effect, strictly liable to pay child support.[184] In these cases young men who are the victims of sexual abuse have been required to pay child support 'for the child conceived during the incident of abuse'.[185] In short, 'the sexual intercourse in these cases is "factually voluntary" and thus intentional, even if it is non-consensual in the criminal sense'.[186]

Putting potential 'hard cases' of child support liability to one side, does the reliance of the child support scheme on genetic parenthood as the determining factor equally result in 'hard cases' where there is no liability for child support? Social parenthood alone cannot give rise to responsibility under the child support legislation. Most obviously, it follows that step-parents or foster parents can never be liable for child support under the 1991 Act unless they actually adopt the child in question.[187] The remedy in such cases usually lies in private law proceedings, in which step-parents and others may become liable for maintenance if they have treated the child as a 'child of the family'. Since the Civil Partnership Act 2004 came into force, this alternative avenue for securing financial support has also been available in the case of same-sex couples who are parties to a civil partnership.[188] However, the 2004 Act makes no change to the fundamental biological premise underpinning the child support legislation. Under the United Kingdom's child support scheme it remains the case, for example, that one partner in a former lesbian relationship cannot make an application under the 1991 Act against her ex-partner for support, eg for a child whom they agreed that one would bear. If the two women had entered into a registered civil partnership, then the mechanisms under the 2004 Act would be available. If, however, they had merely lived together, without formalising that relationship under the 2004 Act, then following a breakdown in their relationship the partner with care of the children has no redress against her former partner. In contrast, several United States jurisdictions have entertained the possibility of claims for child support in such

---

[183] See CSA 1991, ss 2, 4(3) and 6(3).

[184] See eg *County of San Luis Obispo v Nathaniel J* 57 Cal Rptr 2d 843 (1996); see further R Jones, 'Inequality from gender-neutral laws: why must male victims of statutory rape pay child support for children resulting from their victimization?' (2002) 36 *Georgia Law Review* 411 and D Johnson, 'Child support obligations that result from male sexual victimization: An examination of the requirement of support' (2005) 25 *Northern Illinois University Law Review* 515.

[185] E London, 'A critique of the strict liability standard for determining child support in cases of male victims of sexual assault and statutory rape' (2004) 152 *University of Pennsylvania Law Review* 1957 at 1993. London argues that 'if the male victim had been relieved of his child-support obligations, the court would have been aiding in the creation of . . . a "deviant", nonsexual mother/child family', *ibid*, at 1995.

[186] Morgan n 178 above.

[187] Note that there is a procedure under the New Zealand child support scheme whereby step-parents may become liable for child support: see Child Support Act 1991 (NZ), s 99.

[188] Civil Partnership Act 2004, s 72 and schs 5 and 6.

circumstances.[189] Using a rather different route, former lesbian partners have been held liable for child support under the New Zealand scheme in their capacity as step-parents.[190] Such cases undoubtedly present problems for any child support scheme premised on 'commonsense' notions of 'biological' parenthood. In the majority of cases, however, there will be no dispute over who are the child's parents. The question then is whether either parent is a *non-resident* parent under the statutory scheme.

Who is a Non-resident Parent?

As originally enacted, the Child Support Act 1991 used the expression 'absent parent' to denote the liable partner. This terminology understandably generated intense irritation and anger amongst separated fathers, who denied that they were 'absent' and took offence at the implication that they had abandoned their children.[191] As part of the reform process leading up to the 2000 Act, the Department explored various alternative formulations. In the end, the best term that could be devised was 'non-resident parent' as shorthand for 'the parent who is not resident with the child'. It remains at best grammatically clumsy (the liable parent will be resident somewhere) and at worst factually inaccurate (some nominally non-resident parents will be party to extensive shared care arrangements). The new expression entered the Agency's official vocabulary some time before the statutory amendments under the 2000 Act came into force.[192] The amendments made by the 2000 Act were purely semantic in nature; no change was made to the underlying legal definition of a 'non-resident parent'.

An individual will be a non-resident parent for the purposes of the child support scheme if three conditions are satisfied.[193] First, that person must be the child's parent under general family law principles, as discussed above. Secondly, that parent must not be 'living in the same household with the child'. Thirdly, and reflecting the interlocking nature of these definitions, the child in question must have 'his home with a person who is, in relation to him, a person with care'. Given

---

[189] See *LSK v HAN* 813 A 2d 872 (Superior Court of Pennsylvania, 2002) and *Kristine Renee H v Lisa Ann R* 97 P 3d 72 (Supreme Court of California, 2004), disapproving *Maria B v Superior Court* 13 Cal Rptr 3d 494 (CA, Third District, California, 2004). The US case law is reviewed in S R David, 'Turning Parental Rights into Parental Obligations—Holding same-sex, non-biological parents responsible for child support' (2005) 39 *New England Law Review* 921.

[190] See n 187 above, *T v T* [1998] NZFLR 776 and *A v R* [1999] NZFLR 249.

[191] In the debates on the original Bill, the then Lord Chancellor conceded that the expression was less than ideal; no 'pejorative effect' was intended but no feasible alternative had been identified: *Hansard* HL Debates vol 527, cols 303–4 (14 March 1991).

[192] CSPSSA 2000, sch 3 para 11(2) effected a 'search and replace' of the 1991 Act, substituting 'non-resident parent' for 'absent parent' wherever the offending phrase appeared in the original text. These changes came into force for some purposes on 31 January 2001 (SI 2000/3354, Art 2(1)(b)) and in full on 3 March 2003 (SI 2003/192, Art 3).

[193] CSA 1991, s 3(2). This definition presupposes that the individual concerned is alive, so a deceased parent is not an NRP: *R(CS) 2/03*.

that the first requirement has already been considered, and the third condition needs to be understood in the context of the definition of a 'person with care' (considered below), the focus here is on the second of these three criteria, namely that the parent concerned must not be 'living in the same household with the child'. The child support legislation provides no definition of the term 'house-hold'. However, the term is familiar from other statutory contexts, and in particular (but not exclusively) in the spheres of family law and social security law. It is perhaps a reasonable assumption that those responsible for drafting the legislation intended that the same meaning would apply as in those other jurisdictions. However, it is obviously important to bear in mind that the different statutory contexts may point to different conclusions on the facts of any given case.[194] To that extent, at least, 'household' is a protean term. However, two fundamental principles are reasonably clear.

First, a 'household' is an abstract legal concept[195] denoting a shared domestic establishment with a degree of communal living. There may, therefore, be more than one household in the same house. In practice, the smaller the property is, the more difficult it will be to find that two households co-exist.[196] The point is well illustrated in *CCS/14625/1996*, in which an estranged husband and wife continued to live in the same house with their two children. The husband was a shift worker and the couple shared care of the children, but avoided being in the house together at the same time during the day.[197] In the view of Mr Commissioner Howell QC, the question of a 'household' in the context of child support must be viewed 'in a realistic way and primarily with reference to the children themselves'.[198] The Commissioner held on the facts that the parents 'were continuing however unwill-ingly to live in the same household' and so the father could not be a non-resident parent.[199] If neither parent is a non-resident parent, it follows that the 1991 Act has no bite, even if one party is much better placed to provide financial support.[200] In such circumstances the other parent may be able to bring proceedings in the courts for child maintenance,[201] as the section 8 bar does not apply.

---

[194] See further the discussion in Jacobs and Douglas, n 23 above, at 30. See also *G v F (Non-Molestation) Order: Jurisdiction* [2000] Fam 186, in which Wall J invoked the need to give the domestic violence legislation a purposive construction.

[195] See *Santos v Santos* [1972] Fam 247 at 262 *per* Sachs LJ.

[196] There is judicial authority for the proposition that one cannot operate two households in a two-bedroom flat: *Adeoso v Adeoso* [1980] 1 WLR 1535 at 1539 *per* Ormrod LJ.

[197] He slept in the main bedroom whilst his wife slept on the floor in one of the children's bedrooms. The old divorce case law demonstrates that simply sleeping in separate bedrooms is unlikely to mean that two households have been established, if the rest of the property is shared: *Hopes v Hopes* [1949] P 227. However, see *Hollens v Hollens* (1971) 115 Sol J 327 and *Holmes v Mitchell (Inspector of Taxes)* (1991) 2 FLR 301 for examples of estranged couples living apart in separate households in the same house.

[198] *CCS/14625/1996*, para 17.

[199] *Ibid*, para 17. The Commissioner also held that these facts did not fall within the special cases provisions, discussed further below.

[200] *R(CS) 14/98*, para 21 *per* Mr Commissioner Rowland. Atypically in that case the father was the parent with care and received child benefit for his daughter.

[201] eg under Children Act 1989, sch 1.

Secondly, the decision as to whether two people are members of the same household is ultimately a question of fact and degree,[202] which focuses more on the individuals involved than the accommodation itself.[203] Being a member of a household involves 'more than a mere transitory presence, as in a friend or relative making a short visit'.[204] This requires careful fact-finding, especially in the context of a developing relationship between adults. Thus in *Kotke v Saffarini*,[205] decided under the Fatal Accidents Act 1976, the Court of Appeal drew a distinction 'between wanting and intending to live in the same household, planning to do so, and actually doing so'.[206] On the facts, the court upheld the trial judge's ruling that the claimant and her deceased partner had a shared relationship but had not actually established a joint household at the critical date, two years before the latter's death.[207] In many cases the decision will be straightforward, one way or the other. But there will be borderline cases in which different tribunals may legitimately arrive at different outcomes, depending on the weight which they attach to the relevant considerations.[208] Clearly the temporary absence of one member of the household does not bring the household itself to an end.[209] As the notion of a household is a question of fact and degree, the frequency and duration of any absences must be considered, together with the reasons for them.[210] For example, in *Gully v Dix*,[211] decided under the Inheritance (Provision for Family and Dependants) Act 1975, the claimant had started living with her partner in 1974. The relationship was characterised by temporary but short separations prompted by her partner's behaviour. In August 2001 the claimant left him again, just taking a suitcase of clothes, but three months later the partner died, having made no provision for her in his will. The Court of Appeal held that the claimant, notwithstanding her departure from the house in August 2001, satisfied the statutory requirement that she was 'living in the same household' as her partner 'during the whole of the period of two years immediately before' his death.[212] In the Court's view, one had to consider the nature and history of the relationship; on the facts it was clear that neither party viewed their relationship as at an end and so she

---

[202] *Simmons v Pizzey* [1979] AC 37 at 59 *per* Lord Hailsham, observing that there are 'no certain indicia the presence or absence of which is by itself conclusive'.

[203] *R v Birmingham Juvenile Court, ex p S (A Minor)* [1984] Fam 93 at 98 *per* Arnold P.

[204] *CCS/2318/1997*, para 14 *per* Mr Commissioner Mesher.

[205] [2005] EWCA Civ 221; [2005] 2 FLR 517, CA.

[206] *Ibid*, para 59 *per* Potter LJ.

[207] Under Fatal Accidents Act 1976, s 1(3)(b) the claimant must have been living with the deceased in the same household for two years before the latter's death. On the facts, the deceased divided his time between the claimant's house in Sheffield and his own property in Doncaster, while staying and working in London or Edinburgh during the week.

[208] *England v Secretary of State for Social Services* (1981) 3 FLR 222 at 224 *per* Woolf J.

[209] *Re M (An Infant)* [1965] 1 ch 203, at 216 *per* Buckley J, a decision turning on the phrase 'living together' in the Adoption Act 1958, s 12(3). See also *Gully v Dix*, below.

[210] Jacobs and Douglas, n 23 above, at 616–19.

[211] [2004] EWCA Civ 139, [2004] 1 FLR 918, CA.

[212] Inheritance (Provision for Family and Dependants) Act 1975, s 1(1A).

remained entitled to financial provision from his estate.[213] Yet if the claimant in *Gully v Dix* had applied for a maintenance calculation shortly before her partner died, it is difficult to imagine a decision maker or tribunal reaching any conclusion other than that they were living in separate households. One may reconcile the latter conclusion with the outcome in *Gully v Dix* on the basis that the making of an application for child support would clearly be a material difference of fact, in that it reflects a breakdown in the parties' relationship.[214] Accordingly, what constitutes a subsisting 'household' may differ according to whether one is concerned with immediate maintenance (child support) or long term financial provision (under the 1975 Act).

Similarly, it is axiomatic in social security law that a person cannot simultaneously be a member of more than one household.[215] But it is by no means self-evident that the same principle necessarily applies in the context of child support. The social security precedent was concerned with the former supplementary benefits scheme, in which entitlement to benefit was based on membership of an assessment unit, which was defined by reference to households. That legislation certainly did not envisage an individual qualifying for benefit twice by virtue of membership of two separate households at the same time.[216] It does not necessarily follow that the same considerations are relevant in the context of child support. This is exemplified by the case of a child who is the subject of a genuine shared care arrangement—in such circumstances it would be entirely reasonable to conclude that the child is a member of both households (and not simply a member of one and a visitor to the other).[217]

There is a further reason for caution in applying authorities from other areas of law. The case law from these other contexts—family law, social security law, fatal accidents cases, inheritance claims—is typically concerned with whether two adults are living in the same household. In the child support context, however, the question is rather whether the adult and the child are living in the same household. Moreover, it is not enough for a parent to be living *in* the same household as the child in order to avoid the status of being a non-resident parent. He must also live *with* the child in that household. There is authority from matrimonial law for the proposition that if two people live in the same household then it must follow, almost invariably, that they are living with each other.[218] But, as Jacobs and

---

[213] If 'the interruption is transitory, serving as a pause for reflection about the future of a relationship going through difficult times but still recognised to be subsisting, then they will be living in the same household and the claim will lie', *per* Ward LJ at para 24.

[214] 'If the circumstances show an irretrievable breakdown of the relationship, then they no longer live in the same household and the Act is not satisfied', *ibid.*

[215] *R(SB) 8/85* para 12 *per* Mr Commissioner Mitchell.

[216] *Ibid*, para 12.

[217] See *R(CS) 14/98*, para 15, *per* Mr Commissioner Rowland. However, such a case may be covered by the special rule discussed below.

[218] *Mouncer v Mouncer* [1972] 1 WLR 321 at 323 *per* Wrangham J. But see also *Fuller v Fuller* [1973] 1 WLR 730 (invalid husband, who lived as lodger with wife and her new partner, held not to be *living with each other* in the same household).

Douglas argue, it may again be that different considerations apply in the child support context, given that the legislative purpose is to encourage non-resident parents to contribute to their children's maintenance.[219] Furthermore, just because an adult and a child live *in* the same household, it does not necessarily mean that the adult lives *with* the child, especially where a couple's relationship is breaking down. Certainly the use of the expression 'lives with', rather than 'resides with', places the emphasis on the relationship between the individuals rather than their connection with the property in question.[220]

Even where a parent and child do live with each other in the same household for some of the time, in certain circumstances the regulations may still deem the parent in question to be the non-resident parent. This is one of the so-called 'special cases'.[221] The deeming rule applies where:

(a) two or more persons who do not live in the same household each provide day to day care for the same qualifying child; and

(b) at least one of those persons is a parent of the child.[222]

It is therefore a precondition for the deeming rule to apply that the adults in question live in different households (although they may possibly live in the same house).[223] The level of 'day to day care' provided by each adult is the key to determining the application of the regulation. 'Day to day care' is defined as 'care of not less than 104 nights in total during the 12 month period ending with the relevant week'.[224] The notion of 'care' itself is not defined for these purposes. Mr Commissioner Jacobs observed in *R(CS) 11/02* that the term 'care' covers a multitude of activities, from the immediate and mundane (eg when a child should go to bed) to the long-term and important (such as the child's education and religion).[225] These different aspects of care may be shared by, or divided between, different people (including the child in question, in the case of some adolescents). Moreover, the adult need not always actually be with the child in order to exercise day to day care.[226] Furthermore, the concept of day to day care does not simply mean care at some point during the day; rather, it actually means *overnight* care, the emphasis

---

[219] Jacobs and Douglas, n 23 above, at 32.

[220] See, in the context of housing law, *South Northamptonshire District Council v Power* [1987] 1 WLR 1433 at 1436 *per* Kerr LJ.

[221] See also the discussion of the shared care rules in ch 10 below.

[222] SI 2001/155, reg 8(1). A challenge to the *vires* of the predecessor provision, SI 1992/1815), reg 20 failed in *R(CS) 14/98*.

[223] Hence the pre-2003 version of this rule did not apply in *CCS/14625/1996*, see n 197 above.

[224] *Ibid*, reg 1(2). The 'relevant week' is usually the period of seven days immediately before the NRP is sent the Maintenance Enquiry Form (MEF).

[225] *R(CS) 11/02*, para 12.

[226] *R(CS) 11/02*, paras 13–17. For example, a NRP may agree to the child spending an evening with a friend, but still be exercising day to day care over that period. The significance of any separation depends on its duration and purpose, and the extent to which the parent still exercises control over and care for the child: *ibid*, para 20.

being on day *to* day care.[227] It must also be the parent who is exercising the day to day care, rather than a third party (such as a grandparent or other relative).[228]

In such dual (or even multiple) care cases, where one parent provides care 'to a lesser extent' than the other parent or adult carer, then the former is deemed to be the non-resident parent,[229] notwithstanding the fact that he is providing some day to day care. In a situation where both parents provide care to the same extent (and each provides at least as much day to day care as any other adult involved), then the parents' respective child support statuses are determined by who receives child benefit. Thus the parent not in receipt of child benefit is treated as the non-resident parent.[230] If neither parent receives child benefit, then the non-resident parent is the person who, in the Secretary of State's opinion, is not the 'principal provider of day to day care for that child'.[231] This may have capricious consequences; a parent may be more able to afford to maintain a child whose care is shared equally but be relieved of any child support obligation merely by virtue of the fact of receipt of child benefit.[232]

Applying this deeming rule requires consideration of the actual operation of the arrangements for care in practice, rather than reference to the terms of any voluntary agreement or court order.[233] Minor fluctuations in the number of nights that a child stays with either parent do not necessarily amount to a change of circumstances, given that the legislation contemplates looking back over a period of one year.[234] The regulations contemplate that there may be circumstances in which the previous year is unrepresentative of the current care arrangements.[235] In such a case the Secretary of State can select a period other than 12 months—presumably a shorter one—in which case the threshold is adjusted proportionately.[236] For example, if the previous six months, for whatever reason, provides a more representative picture than the last year, then the day to day care threshold is 52 nights.

---

[227] *CCS/499/95*, para 11 *per* Mrs Commissioner Heggs and *CCS/4840/97*, para 10 *per* Mr Commissioner Howell QC. As Mr Commissioner Jacobs noted in *R(CS) 11/02*, 'inherent in the language and the emphasis on nights is a concentration on the immediate, short-term and mundane aspects of care' (*ibid*, para 19) (in contradistinction to more fundamental issues such as choice of schooling). Given that the costs of bringing up a child are related more to such day to day issues, this approach is consistent with the purpose of the legislation (*ibid*, para 24).

[228] Thus in *R(CS) 11/02* it was held on the facts that the NRP's child was 'spending time that she could have spent in his care in the care of other relatives instead'.

[229] SI 2001/155, reg 8(2)(a).

[230] *Ibid*, reg 8(2)(b)(i).

[231] *Ibid*, reg 8(2)(b)(ii). See also *R (on application of Ford) v Board of Inland Revenue and Sayers* [2005] EWHC 1109 (Admin) (on which see N Lee (2006) 13 *Journal of Social Security Law* 119) and *CTC/2090/2004*.

[232] *R(CS) 14/98*, para 20, *per* Mr Commissioner Rowland.

[233] *CSCS/6/1995, per* Mr Commissioner Mitchell. See also below, in the context of boarders, the discussion as to the significance of residence orders made under the Children Act 1989.

[234] *CCS/11588/1995*, para 15 *per* Mr Commissioner Rowland.

[235] 'Current' in this context refers to the effective date of the maintenance calculation: *R(CS) 4/03*, para 13(3), *per* Mr Commissioner Turnbull.

[236] SI 2001/155, reg 1(2). If this approach is taken, the alternative period need not end with the relevant week: *R(CS) 4/03*, para 13, *per* Mr Commissioner Turnbull.

The cliff-edge nature of the '104 nights rule' (or its proportional equivalent) inevitably encourages disputes between parents over (typically) the number of times each year that the child has stayed overnight with the non-resident parent.[237] Typically the Agency's decision maker will be faced with conflicting and often self-serving accounts, which may be, but are more likely not to be, based on contemporaneous documentary evidence.[238] In some cases the Agency simply declines to adjudicate on these competing claims, and refers the question for determination by an appeal tribunal.[239]

The regulation also makes special provision for those especially problematic cases in which the child stays overnight temporarily with a third party, for example children who are boarders at school or hospital inpatients.[240] In this type of situation:

> the person who, but for those circumstances, would otherwise provide day to day care of the child shall be treated as providing day to day care during the periods in question.[241]

In these cases, therefore, there is no attempt to apply an arithmetical or quantitative approach to determining who provides day to day care. Instead, the Secretary of State must exercise a qualitative judgment as to who would 'otherwise provide' such care. This question is not simply determined by which parent pays the boarding school fees.[242] Rather, decision makers must take a broad brush approach, having regard to the actual pattern of contact at weekends and during holidays in deciding which parent would provide care on the hypothesis that the children were not at boarding school.[243] However, it must not simply be assumed that the division of holiday time for a child at boarding school would necessarily be replicated across term-time on the assumption that the child was not a boarder.[244]

---

[237] See eg *CCS/11588/1995* in which approximately £1,500 p/a turned on whether or not the child stayed for less than 104 nights a year with her father, prompting Mr Commissioner Rowland to point out to the parties the merits of reaching a compromise on the amount of weekly maintenance payable, 'which would enable them to escape the processes of the Child Support Agency', para 14.

[238] Diaries and calendars are often relied upon, but as Mr Commissioner Rowland realistically observed in *CCS/11588/1995*, 'arrangements for contact may be changed at the last minute without calendar entries being altered' (para 7).

[239] The Agency no longer has the power of its own initiative to refer a matter for decision by the tribunal, but the issue of shared care may be referred as part of an appeal already in process: see eg *R(CS) 4/03*, para 3.

[240] This also applies in 'other circumstances', eg 'where the child stays with a person who is not a parent of the child'. Where this provision applies, the special cases rules come into operation: SI 2001/155, reg 12.

[241] SI 2001/155, reg 1(2).

[242] *Child-Villiers v Secretary of State for Work and Pensions* [2002] EWCA Civ 1854, [2003] 1 FLR 829, *per* Potter LJ (para 25) and Chadwick LJ (para 32). See also *R(CS) 8/98*, para 19, *per* Mr Commissioner Rowland. However, payment of school fees may be treated as a payment of child support maintenance: *ibid*, para 24, regretting that the question of how the Secretary of State approached such matters was not in the public domain.

[243] *Child-Villiers v Secretary of State for Work and Pensions* [2002] EWCA Civ 1854, [2003] 1 FLR 829, para 21.

[244] *Ibid*, noting that contact patterns may be influenced by the proximity of one parent to the school. See also *CCS/37/1997*, para 34.

The terms of any residence order may be relevant to that decision but cannot be conclusive.[245] Equally, the fact that one parent has failed in an application for a shared residence order cannot be determinative of the issue.[246] Arguably, the refusal of a court to make such an order should not even be a relevant consideration.[247]

Persons with Care

An individual is a 'person with care' if three conditions are satisfied.[248] First, he or she must be the person 'with whom the child has his home'. Secondly, that person must be the one 'who usually provides day to day care for the child (whether exclusively or in conjunction with any other person)'. Thirdly, he or she must 'not fall within a prescribed category of person'. The 1991 Act expressly contemplates the possibility that there may be more than one person with care in relation to the same qualifying child,[249] even if that scenario were not implicit by virtue of the provisions of the Interpretation Act 1978.[250] It is also significant that, whereas a non-resident parent must always, by definition, be a parent, a person with care need not have that status—the person with care could be a grandparent, other relative or third party with whom the child is living. The 1991 Act does, however, employ the term 'parent with care'—meaning, unsurprisingly, a person with care who is a parent[251]—to designate a sub-set of persons with care for particular purposes. The most important of these is that only a *parent* (as opposed to *person*) with care on a relevant benefit can be deemed to have made an application for a maintenance calculation. It follows that, for example, a grandparent on income support who is caring for her grandchild does not automatically come within the Agency's remit.[252] We now examine each of the three component elements of the statutory definition in turn.

---

[245] *Child-Villiers v Secretary of State for Work and Pensions* [2002] EWCA Civ 1854, [2003] 1 FLR 829, *per* Potter LJ (para 27) and Chadwick LJ (para 34).

[246] *Ibid*, para 27 *per* Potter LJ. The reason given is that the child support regulations make no reference to any orders that may exist in family proceedings between the parties, so creating their own self-contained statutory regime.

[247] Although it is not mentioned in the Court's judgment, the 'no order' principle under Children Act 1989, s 1(5) must also mean that it is extremely unwise to read too much into a decision *not* to make any particular order.

[248] CSA 1991, s 3(3).

[249] *Ibid*, s 3(5).

[250] Interpretation Act 1978, s 6(c).

[251] CSA 1991, s 54.

[252] Although she is not deemed to have applied for child support under *ibid*, s 6, she may of course make a private application under *ibid*, s 4.

'a person . . . with whom the child has his home'

The Act does not define what is meant by 'home' in this context,[253] but a number of principles have been established in the case law. Where a person has his or her home is a question of fact which must be determined by applying ordinary common sense standards.[254] Beyond regarding the 'home' as a domestic base, it is not possible to provide a precise definition of the term. For example, a person may still have a home despite lengthy absences from it,[255] although it must be more than an occasional place of convenient resort.[256] Decision makers must also take a broad view over the course of a year, for example where arrangements differ in school holidays.[257] It is also important not to lose sight of the fact that the fundamental question is 'with whom the child has his home', and not 'where is the child's home'. Put in this way, the emphasis is clear—what matters is not the physical accommodation as such, but rather the child's relationship with the alleged person with care.[258] It follows, in principle, that a child may have his or her home with a person who is of no fixed abode.[259]

'a person . . . who usually provides day to day care for the child'

The concept of 'day to day care' has already been analysed in the context of the statutory definition of a non-resident parent, and the same principles should presumably apply here.[260]

'a person . . . who does not fall within a prescribed category of person'

This third and final condition enables the Secretary of State to exclude certain persons from the status of being a person with care even if the two previous criteria are satisfied. The prescribed categories of persons are local authorities and their foster parents.[261] If a local authority is providing part of the child's care, this counts as a special case and the non-resident parent's liability is apportioned

---

[253] Contrast SI 2001/155, reg 1(2), on which see *R(CS) 2/96.*

[254] See also the broad meaning in ECHR case law, eg *Buckley v United Kingdom* (1996) 23 EHRR 101.

[255] For example, because the child is at school or in hospital: see SI 2001/155, reg 12, which will bring into play the special cases rules.

[256] *CCS/1180/1998*, para 10 *per* Mr Commissioner Jacobs.

[257] *CCS/5818/1999*, paras 9–10 *per* Mr Commissioner Jacobs.

[258] Again, contrast SI 200/155, reg 1(2), which expressly refers to a 'dwelling'.

[259] Jacobs and Douglas, n 23 above, at 33.

[260] Above p 245; see *R(CS) 11/02*, para 24 *per* Mr Commissioner Jacobs.

[261] SI 2001/157, reg 21. The expression foster parents is used here as a shorthand for the statutory reference to 'a person with whom a child who is looked after by a local authority is placed by the authority under the provisions of the Children Act 1989' (*ibid*, para 21(1)(b); or, in Scotland, a placement under the Children (Scotland) Act 1995, s 26). So a private foster parent may be a person with care.

accordingly.[262] A local authority which is looking after a child[263] may require a parent to contribute to that child's maintenance.[264] The Secretary of State may not use this enabling power to exclude a child's parent,[265] guardian or the holder of a current residence order under section 8 of the Children Act 1989[266] from the status of being a person with care.

The Territorial Scope of the Act

The Agency cannot proceed with making a calculation simply because there is a qualifying child in respect of whom there is both a person with care and a non-resident parent. If any one of these three individuals is not habitually resident in the United Kingdom,[267] then the Secretary of State has no jurisdiction to make a maintenance calculation.[268] There are only two exceptions to this principle that all three parties must be habitually resident. The first concerns those exceptional cases in which the person with care is not an individual.[269] In this situation the habitual residence requirement applies solely to the qualifying child and to the non-resident parent. The second exception is that the Secretary of State has jurisdiction where the non-resident parent, although not habitually resident in the United Kingdom, falls into one of four categories, each of which is defined by reference to some form of employment relationship with the United Kingdom.[270] These groups comprise those non-resident parents who are: (i) employed by the Crown in the civil service (including those in the Diplomatic Service); (ii) members of the armed forces; (iii) employed by companies which are registered under legislation in the United Kingdom;[271] (iv) employed by 'a body of a prescribed

---

[262] SI 2001/155, reg 9.

[263] On which concept, see Children Act 1989, s 22.

[264] Children Act 1989, sch 2, paras 21–25. Contributions are determined according to the parent's means, not the child's needs or the local authority's expenditure: *Re C (A Minor) (Contribution Notice)* [1994] 1 FLR 111.

[265] Hence the references to placements under Children Act 1989, s 21(1)(b) expressly excludes cases where the local authority allow the child whom they are looking after to live with his or her parent under s 23(5); this becomes a special case: SI 2001/155, reg 13. The parent with whom the child is placed is then deemed to be the person with care, whether or not he or she usually provides day to day care for the child (as required by CSA 1991, s 3(3)(b)): *R(CS) 7/02* para 12 *per* Mr Commissioner Turnbull.

[266] Or its equivalent under the Children (Scotland) Act 1995, s 11.

[267] ie Great Britain and Northern Ireland (Interpretation Act 1978, s 5 and sch, 1, para 1). Thus the Channel Islands and the Isle of Man are outside this definition.

[268] CSA 1991, s 44(1).

[269] *Ibid*, s 44(2). But note that in any event local authorities (and local authority foster parents) cannot be persons with care: SI 2001/157, reg 21.

[270] CSA 1991, s 44(2A), inserted by CSPSSA 2000, s 22(3) with effect from 31 January 2001: SI 2000/3354, Art 2(1)(a).

[271] The company must be one which employs people outside the UK but makes payments in the UK, so that a deduction from earnings order (DEO) may be made under CSA 1991, s 31: see SI 1992/2645, reg 7A(1). However, the potential for abuse exists here, as an NRP living abroad may set up a UK company to receive royalties on his behalf. This would bring the case within the remit of the Agency, and so outwith the reach of the courts' private law jurisdiction. The NRP may (realistically)

description', a term which at present is defined so as to cover only local authorities and various national health service employers.[272] In this way the Act empowers the Agency to disregard the fact that such men are not habitually resident in the United Kingdom, presumably on the basis that enforcement action can be taken against them via their employers who are based in the country.[273]

These various special cases apart, all three parties must be habitually resident in the United Kingdom.[274] The term 'habitual residence' itself is defined neither in the 1991 Act nor in any child support regulations, but appears in a number of other statutory contexts, such as family law, social security law and tax law. The case law from those fields demonstrates that 'habitual residence' is more than mere presence yet cannot simply be equated with the notion of domicile.[275] Domicile is a common law concept which must be given the same meaning at all times, whereas habitual residence is a statutory expression which may carry different shades of meaning depending on the context.[276] That said, the terms 'habitual residence' and 'ordinary residence' now appear to be synonymous as a matter of law.[277] They both presuppose that two criteria are met: that the individual is resident, in the sense of having established a home within the jurisdiction, and that he or she has been so resident for an appreciable period of time.[278] So far as the former condition is concerned, whether an individual is 'resident' is a question of fact and degree, bearing in mind that the dictionary definition is 'to dwell permanently or for a considerable time, to have one's settled or usual abode, to live in or at a particular place'.[279] Yet habitual residence may not be an exclusive concept; for example, there is family law authority to the effect that a person may, as a matter of fact, be habitually resident in two jurisdictions simultaneously.[280] Moreover, an individual who is an overstayer for the purposes of UK immigration law may be habitually resident here, at least for the purposes of invoking the court's divorce jurisdiction.[281] In recent years the requirement of residence for an appreciable period of time has proved especially problematic, particularly in the context of

---

take the view that the Agency is likely to be more ineffective than the court process in recovering child support liabilities.

[272] *Ibid*, reg 7A(2).

[273] Technically, the legislation does not as such deem these fathers living abroad to be habitually resident—rather, it disapplies the habitual residence requirement.

[274] If one party is domiciled abroad, the courts may still retain jurisdiction to make a maintenance or capital order for the child: *A v A (A Minor) (Financial Provision)* [1994] 1 FLR 657.

[275] *R(U) 8/88*, Appendix 1, para 6 *per* Mr Commissioner Mitchell.

[276] *Mark v Mark* [2005] UKHL 42; [2005] 3 WLR 111 at para 37 *per* Baroness Hale.

[277] *Ibid*, at para 33, approving *Ikimi v Ikimi* [2001] EWCA Civ 873; [2002] Fam. 72, CA para 31 *per* Thorpe LJ (although the point had been left open by Lord Slynn in *Nessa v Chief Adjudication Officer* [1999] 2 FLR 1116 at 1120).

[278] *Shah v Barnet London Borough Council* [1983] 1 All ER 226.

[279] *Levene v Inland Revenue Commissioners* [1928] AC 217 at 222 *per* Viscount Cave LC. See further N Wikeley and A Ogus, *The Law of Social Security* (Butterworths, London, 5th edn, 2002) at 230–31.

[280] *Ikimi v Ikimi* and *Mark v Mark*, n 277 above. See also *C v FC (Brussels II: Free-Standing Application for Parental Responsibility)* [2004] 1 FLR 317 (at para 98).

[281] *Mark v Mark*, n 277 above.

entitlement to means-tested social security benefits.[282] It is clear that a purely temporary absence abroad is not enough to displace habitual residence, but the point
at which such an absence becomes so prolonged that this status is lost is a difficult
question of judgment.[283] If a person's habitual residence ceases, it may nevertheless be resumed relatively swiftly on returning to the jurisdiction, depending on
such factors as the reasons for the person's original departure overseas and the
subsequent return, together with the quality of the links maintained with the
United Kingdom during the period of absence.[284]

Conversely, where a person has never previously lived in the country, it will normally be some time before habitual residence is established.[285] But what is an
'appreciable period of time' is uncertain, its resolution depending on the particular circumstances of the case, including the individual's intentions. The Social
Security Commissioners' case law suggests that 'where a claimant is likely to
remain in the United Kingdom permanently or for a substantial period of time,
the conventional period that must have elapsed between his arrival and his establishing habitual residence is between one month and three months'.[286] There are
family law authorities to the effect that habitual residence cannot be acquired in a
single day, notwithstanding the relevant party's intentions.[287] It is arguable that
this principle may not necessarily apply in the context of child support.[288] One
advantage of finding that habitual residence may be established immediately on
arrival in the United Kingdom, given the requisite intent, is that such a conclusion
would avoid the problem that otherwise the habitual residence requirement may
potentially operate in a way which would be contrary to European Union law.[289]

An early authority on habitual residence in the context of child support law was
R(CS) 5/96, in which the non-resident parent, who had been born in the United
Kingdom, had been employed as a Home Office civil servant in the Immigration

---

[282] On the introduction of the habitual residence test for income support, see M Adler, 'The habitual residence test: a critical analysis' (1995) 2 *Journal of Social Security Law* 179.

[283] In *Ikimi v Ikimi*, n 277 above, the wife had homes in Nigeria and London; the Court of Appeal
held that she (just) satisfied the requirement of being habitually resident in England for the year preceding the commencement of divorce proceedings (see Domicile and Matrimonial Proceedings Act
1973, s 5(2)), having spent 161 days in London in the previous year.

[284] See joined decisions *CIS/1304/1997* and *CJSA/5394/1998*.

[285] *Nessa v Chief Adjudication Officer* n 277 above.

[286] *CIS/3280/2003, CIS/1124/2004, CIS/1840/2004* para 16 *per* Mr Commissioner Rowland, who
added that 'those are not rigid limits'.

[287] See eg *Re M (Minors) (Residence Orders: Jurisdiction)* [1993] 1 FLR 495 and the authorities discussed in Jacobs and Douglas. n 23 above, at 155.

[288] See the policy considerations referred to in *R(CS) 5/96*, discussed further below.

[289] This problem has been identified by Jacobs and Douglas, n 23 above, at 17–18. In summary, if a
French PWC follows her estranged British husband back to the UK with their child as a single parent
and takes up employment here, she will be a 'worker' for the purposes of EC Regulation 1612/68. As
such she must not be discriminated against in terms of access to social advantages, eg a child support
assessment. If 'habitual residence' cannot be established immediately on arrival, this would represent
a barrier to the free movement of labour. By analogy with C-90/97 *Swaddling v Adjudication Officer*
[1999] 2 FLR 184, it is arguable that the length of residence should not be a material consideration. This
may, of course, be an entirely academic point in that by the time the Agency issue the MEF she will be
habitually resident through the passage of time.

Department since the early 1970s. In 1992 he was posted to India, initially for 18 months, but this was later extended to five years—until 1997—with the possibility of a further one-year extension. In 1994 the Agency issued a maintenance assessment. The non-resident parent appealed successfully to a tribunal, which decided that he was not habitually resident in the United Kingdom and so the assessment should be cancelled. Mr Commissioner Rice allowed the parent with care's appeal, holding that although the non-resident parent was resident in India in 1994 he remained *habitually* resident in the United Kingdom.[290] In reaching this decision, the Commissioner highlighted a number of features of the case; the non-resident parent's strong links with the United Kingdom through birth, residence and employment; his continuing employment by the Home Office, which was subject to UK income tax;[291] and the fact that his family remained in the jurisdiction. His secondment to work in India, albeit for a substantial period of time, did not destroy his habitual residence in the United Kingdom. The case could thus be distinguished from the example from earlier times of an officer who 'went to join the Indian Army to pursue a career there throughout his working life'.[292] In reaching this decision, the Commissioner expressly relied upon the purpose of the Child Support Act 1991:

> As I understand it, the purpose underlying the child support legislation is the social need to require absent parents to maintain, or contribute to the maintenance of, their children. In determining as question of fact whether in the above context a person has ceased to be habitually resident in this country, it appears to me that emphasis should be put on factors directed to establishing the nature and degree of his past and continuing connection with this country and his intentions as to the future, albeit the original reason for his move abroad, and the nature of any work being undertaken there are also material. It is not enough merely to look at the length and continuity of the actual residence abroad.[293]

It is arguable that *R(CS) 5/96* places undue emphasis on a purposive approach to the legislation, and that, given subsequent case law in other fields, the decision failed to pay sufficient heed to the fact of the father's extended period of residence in India.[294] Either way, some caution may need to be exercised in applying the authorities on the meaning of habitual residence from other statutory regimes in the context of child support. In each case the underlying purpose of the relevant legislation needs to be considered.[295] Thus if an illegal overstayer may be habitually

---

[290] If the same facts were to arise today, there would be no dispute as to the Secretary of State's jurisdiction to make a maintenance calculation in the light of CSA 1991, s 44(2A), inserted by the 2000 Act.

[291] See also *L A v Secretary of State for Work and Pensions and T V I* 2004 SCLR 840, where the Extra Division of the Inner House held, reversing the Commissioner, that a tribunal was entitled to take the view that the fact that a Dutch national, although working for a German company in the North Sea, still paid UK income tax and national insurance was a factor pointing to continued habitual residence in Scotland.

[292] *R(CS) 5/96* at para 11.

[293] *R(CS) 5/96* at, para 9 (original emphasis).

[294] See the reservations expressed in *CCS/1229/2000* at para 16 *per* Mr Commissioner Mesher.

[295] See n 276 above.

resident for the purpose of presenting a divorce petition, arguably she should also have that same status in child support law—whereas her illegal status would preclude her from entitlement to public benefits.[296]

The case law discussed above is concerned with the habitual residence of adults and special considerations apply in the case of children. The normal rule is that children's habitual residence will be determined by that of the persons with whom they lawfully live.[297] So if the child lives with one parent by agreement, that parent's residence will be determinative. This will not apply if that parent has abducted the child, unless the other parent has acquiesced.[298] Moreover, where both parents have parental responsibility, one parent cannot unilaterally change the child's habitual residence.[299]

---

[296] *Mark v Mark* [2004] EWCA Civ 168; [2005] Fam 267 at para 45 *per* Thorpe LJ. In fact an overstayer would be barred form claiming benefits as being a 'person subject to immigration control', but the same outcome could be reached by holding that an illegal immigration status disqualified the individual from being habitually resident for benefit purposes.

[297] *Re J (A Minor) (Abduction: Custody Rights)* [1990] 2 AC 562.

[298] *Re A (Minors) (Abduction: Acquiescence)* [1992] 2 FLR 14; see further the discussion of the relevant authorities in Jacobs and Douglas, n 23 above, at 156–58.

[299] *Re N (Abduction: Habitual Residence)* [2000] 2 FLR 899.

9

Applying for Child Support

Introduction

An application for child support may start in one of three ways. First, parents with care who are in receipt of either of the two main means-tested social security benefits[1] are treated as having applied for child support under section 6 of the Child Support Act 1991. These cases, described as 'benefit cases' in the discussion that follows, formed the great bulk of the Agency's caseload in its early years.[2] Secondly, other persons with care (who are also usually, but need not be, parents with care), who are not in receipt of such benefits, have the option of applying for child support under section 4 of the 1991 Act; these are known as 'private cases'. These cases have come to form a more significant proportion of the Agency's work in recent years, not least with the change-over in October 1999 from family credit (which was subject to the section 6 requirement) to WFTC (which was not so subject).[3] The fundamental distinction is thus between those parents with care who *must* apply—indeed, since the 2000 reforms their lack of choice has been emphasised by the fact that they are automatically *treated as having applied*—and those persons with care who *may* apply (and hence, equally, may elect not to do so). Thirdly, but only in Scotland, children aged 12 or over have an independent right to make an application for child support by virtue of section 7 of the 1991 Act. These three categories will be discussed in the same order below. The chapter concludes by examining the Agency's information gathering powers and the rules relating to the disclosure of information, the role of inspectors and the ambit of

[1] Income support and income-based jobseeker's allowance.
[2] In May 1996, when there were 395,500 full assessments, 90% involved PWCs on benefit—76% of PWCs were on income support, 14% on family credit (or DWA) and just 10% 'other' (ie private cases): DSS, *Social Security Statistics 1996* (DSS, 1996) Table G2.06 at 248. By May 1999, when there were 864,000 full assessments, these proportions had shifted to 44% (income support or income-based jobseeker's allowance), 20% (family credit) and 35% (other): *Social Security Statistics 1999* (DSS, 1999) Table G2.06 at 279. By May 2004, by which time tax credits cases were outside s 6 and there were 726,400 old scheme full assessments, the proportions were 32% (benefits), 35% (tax credits) and 32% (other): DWP, *Work and Pensions Statistics 2004* (DWP, 2004) Table 5 at 196. These figures relate to the PWC status at the census date, and not at take-on date, but nonetheless indicate that benefit cases are no longer in the majority.
[3] WFTC has since been replaced by working tax credit and CTC (see Tax Credits Act 2002), neither of which are subject to the deeming rule.

the various criminal offences which may be committed under the child support legislation.

Applications under Section 6

Introduction

The mandatory nature of the child support scheme for parents with care in receipt of certain means-tested benefits has been a feature of the scheme since its inception. As will be seen later, it is also a common feature of other child support systems. Its purpose is plain: 'to prevent a parent who is in receipt of benefit from leaving financial responsibility for the child with the State instead of claiming child maintenance support from the absent parent'.[4] However, the legal framework which effectively denies parents with care on benefit any choice in respect of claiming child support has changed as a result of the 2000 reforms. Under section 6(1) of the 1991 Act, as originally enacted, parents with care on benefit were required to 'authorise the Secretary of State to take action under this Act to recover child support maintenance from the absent parent'. If they failed to comply with this requirement, the Agency had the power to impose a reduced benefit direction, cutting their benefit by a prescribed percentage and for a set period of time, unless the parent could show 'good cause' for the non-compliance. Thus under the original scheme parents with care on benefit were required to 'opt in' but could be sanctioned for failing to do so.

The reforms introduced by the 2000 Act included a new section 6(3), which now states:

(3) The Secretary of State may—

(a) treat the parent as having applied for a maintenance calculation with respect to the qualifying child and all other children of the non-resident parent in relation to whom the parent is also a person with care; and

(b) take action under this Act to recover from the non-resident parent, on the parent's behalf, the child support maintenance so determined.

It follows that the default position has changed. Parents with care on benefit, instead of having to opt in and, if they chose not to apply, having to demonstrate 'good cause' to avoid a benefit sanction, are now deemed to have opted in. Their co-operation with the Agency is not so much mandatory as assumed at the outset. That said, as we shall see, the parent with care may still elect to opt out; if so, she faces the risk of a reduced benefit decision if she cannot show 'good cause'. The meaning of 'good cause', discussed further below, has not changed as a result of the reforms in the 2000 Act, but it exists within this modified statutory framework.

---

[4] *Secretary of State of Social Security v Harmon, Carter and Cocks* [1998] 2 FLR 598, CA *per* Millett LJ at 600.

Consequently parents with care on benefit must now make a conscious decision to try and disengage from the child support scheme; inertia alone will result in their deemed agreement to making an application for child support.

The formal position is that although section 6 is, in effect, mandatory for parents with care on benefit, there is, initially at least, no corresponding duty on the Secretary of State to take action. The language of section 6(3) is clear: the Secretary of State *may* treat the parent with care as having applied and *may* take action to recover child support maintenance from the non-resident parent.[5] In principle the Agency's exercise of that discretion is governed by the welfare principle in section 2 of the Act. There is, however, no requirement that the Secretary of State consult the non-resident parent before treating the parent with care as having made an application.[6] But once the Agency's machinery has been invoked, and an effective application has been treated as made, then the Secretary of State is under a duty to process it. As section 11(1) states:

> An application for a maintenance calculation made to the Secretary of State *shall* be dealt with by him in accordance with the provision made by or under this Act. (emphasis added)

This provision imposes a duty on the Secretary of State to act, and so considerations relating to the welfare of the children are irrelevant: section 2 of the 1991 Act is simply not engaged at this stage.[7] Indeed, it therefore follows that the Secretary of State cannot, contrary to the wishes of the parent with care on benefit, refuse to make a maintenance calculation, even where officials believe that the child's welfare may be in danger.[8] Thus 'good cause' can be invoked by a parent with care as a defence but the Secretary of State cannot insist that she rely on it.

The Priority Status of a Section 6 Application

Although there are three types of application for a maintenance calculation—a benefit case, a private case and an application by a child in Scotland, under sections 4, 6 and 7 respectively—these three routes are by no means of equal status. The specific rules in the regulations governing multiple applications, discussed in

---

[5] Referring to the original version of CSA 1991, s 6, Mr Commissioner Walker QC held that the Secretary of State had a 'total discretion as to whether to take action': *CCS/12806/1996*.

[6] *R v Secretary of State for Social Security ex p Lloyd* [1995] 1 FLR 856; although decided on the basis of the original s 6, there is no reason to think this is still not sound authority; see also *R(CS) 1/98*.

[7] *CCS/14/1994* para 10 *per* Mr Commissioner Howell QC and *R(CS) 4/96* para 7 *per* Mr Commissioner Rice.

[8] See the striking case of *R(CS) 2/98* where the Agency decided, against the PWC's wishes, to take no further action against a NRP with criminal convictions for violence who had threatened to shoot the PWC. Mr Commissioner Rowland allowed the PWC's appeal; 'It is one thing for the Child Support Agency to cease action on the request of the person who has applied for child support maintenance . . . but it is entirely another matter for the Agency to cease action against the wishes of that person' (at para 18). This case subsequently went to judicial review on a separate issue relating to disputed paternity: *R v Secretary of State for Social Security ex p West* [1999] 1 FLR 1233.

detail below,[9] effectively prioritise them in the following order, namely applications under sections 6, 4 and 7 respectively. Moreover, the priority afforded to the section 6 procedure in the scheme of the 1991 Act is emphasised by three provisions in the primary legislation itself.

The first is section 6(12) of the Act:

(12) The fact that a maintenance calculation is in force with respect to a person with care does not prevent the making of a new maintenance calculation with respect to her as a result of the Secretary of State's acting under subsection (3).

This means that the Agency can treat a benefit claimant as having applied under section 6 and proceed to make a new maintenance calculation even if there is an earlier Agency assessment already in existence, for example following a previous section 4 application.[10] The converse does not apply; thus a pre-existing maintenance calculation made under section 6 precludes a subsequent private application under section 4.[11]

The second provision is section 9(3) of the Act:

(3) Subject to section 4(10)(a) and section 7(10)(a), the existence of a maintenance agreement shall not prevent any party to the agreement, or any other person, from applying for a maintenance calculation with respect to any child to or for whose benefit periodical payments are to be made or secured under the agreement.

Sections 4(10)(a) and 7(10)(a) are the provisions which preclude a private application under either of those sections where there is a pre-April 1993 written maintenance agreement (or indeed a pre-March 2003 court order) in existence.[12] But whereas such a pre-existing written maintenance agreement or court order shuts out a private application, the Agency is not debarred by section 9(3) from making a fresh assessment under section 6.

Thirdly, and finally, section 10(1) provides for a pre-existing court order to cease to have effect once a maintenance calculation is made. Given that the effect of sections 4(10) and 7(10) is that private applications to the Agency may not even be made where such an order is in existence, and the absence of any similar provision in section 6, it necessarily follows that an application under section 6 will result in a maintenance calculation which overrides a prior court order.[13] In contrast a section 4 or 7 application in otherwise similar circumstances will not even get off the ground.

---

[9] See pp 281–82 below.

[10] This principle is not affected by the rules on multiple applications, which provides that a later application 'under the *same section* of the Act' (emphasis added) for a maintenance calculation in respect of the same parties is not to be proceeded with: Child Support (Maintenance Calculation Procedure) Regulations 2000 (SI 2001/157), reg 4 and sch 2, para 4; see below p 281.

[11] CSA 1991, s 4(9). This assumes, of course, that the case is still governed by s 6: if that provision ceases to apply, the PWC may ask the Secretary of State to discontinue acting: *ibid*, s 6(9), discussed below.

[12] See further ch 7 above.

[13] See Child Support (Maintenance Arrangements and Jurisdiction) Regulations 1992 (SI 1992/2645) reg 3 and *R v Secretary of State for Social Security ex p Harris* [1999] 1 FLR 837, QBD, which remains sound law on this point.

The analysis above differs from that of Mr Commissioner Walker QC in *CCS/12806/1996*.[14] In that case, in which the parent with care was in receipt of income support, the non-resident parent argued that the Agency was barred from making an assessment under section 6 because the phasing-in rules then in operation treated applications brought under section 6 as a sub-set of those under section 4. This argument succeeded before the tribunal. Allowing the appeal by the child support officer, the Commissioner ruled that section 6 was 'essentially supplemental to section 4' which was the 'primary or general provision'.[15] However, the exclusion of applications under section 4 during the phasing-in period was confined to those cases that had entered the system by the section 4 'door', rather than via section 6. It followed that the Agency had correctly proceeded to make a maintenance assessment. Whilst that outcome was clearly correct, there are several reasons to doubt the Commissioner's conclusion on the status of applications made under sections 4 and 6 respectively. First, it is by no means self-evident that the Commissioner's decision on the impact of the phasing-in rules required the subordination of section 6 cases to section 4.[16] Secondly, the Commissioner's otherwise full and careful analysis did not take into account the statutory prioritisation described above. Thirdly, the Commissioner's decision in *CCS/12806/1996* was based on the previous version of section 6 and has been criticised elsewhere.[17] Finally, the subsequent Court of Appeal decision in *Secretary of State of Social Security v Harmon, Carter and Cocks*[18] certainly does not support the notion that section 6 is secondary to section 4.[19] Overall, therefore, the better view is that the Commissioner's reasoning in *CCS/12806/1996* was unsound and in any event has been overtaken by developments in both the case law and the legislative scheme.

The Scope of the Deeming rule

It is important to note that the mandatory section 6 route does not apply to all parents with care who receive social security benefits, even if those benefits are means-tested. The scope of the deeming rule is restricted by section 6(1):

---

[14] This was a decision by a Scottish Commissioner on an English case, reflecting the Commissioners' jurisdiction over the whole of Great Britain, irrespective of where the individual Commissioner happens to deal with the appeal.

[15] *CCS/12806/1996*, para 27.

[16] Equally in *R(CS) 10/98* Mr Commissioner Howell QC, holding that s 6 applications were not affected by the phasing-in rules, gave no indication that he regarded s 6 as supplementary to s 4: *ibid*, para 6.

[17] 'With respect to the Commissioner's detailed consideration of the arguments presented to him and his analysis of the legislation . . . there is no need for s 6 to be supplementary to s 4 or to anything else. Fortunately, the Commissioner's preferred analysis appears to be without practical significance', E Jacobs and G Douglas, *Child Support: The Legislation 1999* (Sweet & Maxwell, London, 1999) at 40.

[18] [1998] 2 FLR 598, CA.

[19] 'The two procedures are obviously mutually exclusive and exhaustive. Every case must fall into one or the other' per Millett LJ (the latter observation must be read subject to s 7, so far as Scotland is concerned).

(1) This section applies where income support, an income-based jobseeker's allowance or any other benefit of a prescribed kind is claimed by or in respect of, or paid to or in respect of, the parent of a qualifying child who is also a person with care of the child.

This provision imposes two important limitations on the applicability of section 6. The first is that it can only apply to a person with care who is also a parent of a qualifying child. Thus an aunt on income support who cares for (and claims other benefits or tax credits in respect of) her niece cannot be treated under section 6 as making an application for child support maintenance. She may, of course, elect to make a private application under section 4 (considered further below), but that is her business alone.

The second is that the rule applies solely to those parents with care who claim 'income support, an income-based jobseeker's allowance or any other benefit of a prescribed kind'.[20] Income support has been a relevant benefit for this purpose since the start of the child support scheme whereas income-based jobseeker's allowance has featured only since October 1996,[21] following the changes to benefits for unemployed people.[22] At the start of the scheme section 6 also applied to family credit, the then means-tested in-work benefit for those on low incomes; in addition, disability working allowance, a benefit based on similar principles for disabled workers on low incomes, was prescribed by regulations for these purposes. The element of compulsion for family credit claimants was removed in October 1999, when that benefit transmuted into WFTC.[23] At the same time the requirement to co-operate was abolished for claimants of the disabled person's tax credit (DPTC), the successor to DWA. The justification for this change was that as WFTC and DPTC were tax credits rather than social security benefits, it was no longer appropriate to impose such a requirement.[24] This reasoning was less than compelling at the time, given that both WFTC and DPTC involved a rebranding rather than any fundamental structural change. However, since April 2003, when working tax credit and Child Tax Credit (CTC) replaced WFTC and DPTC,[25] the government's argument has undoubtedly had more force. The net result is that section 6 now applies solely to income support and income-based jobseeker's allowance, with no other benefit currently being prescribed for these purposes.[26]

---

[20] CSA 1991, s 6(1).

[21] Jobseekers Act 1995, sch 2, para 20(2).

[22] In summary, before that date unemployed claimants could claim contributory unemployment benefit and/or (subject to the means test) income support; after 1996 they could claim contribution-based and/or income-based jobseeker's allowance. The latter is paid at the same rates as income support, which is now confined to those claimants who do not have to fulfil the labour market conditions (eg as to availability for work).

[23] Tax Credits Act 1999, s 19(4) and sch 6; see generally N Lee 'The Working Families' Tax Credit: An integration of the tax and benefits systems?' (2000) 7 *Journal of Social Security Law* 159.

[24] N Wikeley and A Ogus, *The Law of Social Security* (Butterworths, London, 5th edn, 2002) at 320.

[25] Tax Credits Act 2002; see N Lee, 'The New Tax Credits' (2003) 10 *Journal of Social Security Law* 7.

[26] In the debates on the 2000 Act, the Minister of State remarked: 'We have no plans to include any other benefit, but we cannot forecast the future', Standing Committee F, 1 February 2000, col 216, *per* Mr J Rooker MP.

Section 6 has never applied to claimants who are in receipt of the other two main means-tested benefits, housing benefit and council tax benefit,[27] in the absence of a concurrent entitlement to income support (or income-based jobseeker's allowance).

It should be noted that the section 6 deeming rule applies where one of the relevant benefits 'is claimed by or in respect of, or paid to or in respect of' a parent with care. The wording of this formulation has several ramifications. One is that if a parent with care's new partner claims a relevant benefit on her behalf, she is treated as having applied under section 6, even though she is not the claimant in respect of that application. Furthermore, the question is whether benefit has been claimed or paid, not whether it has been *lawfully* paid;[28] so, for example, an allegation by the non-resident parent that the parent with care's benefit claim is fraudulent should not delay the making of a maintenance calculation.[29] In addition, section 6 applies regardless of whether a relevant benefit is paid 'with respect to' the child (as opposed to the parent with care) in question.[30] This wording was presumably designed to deal with the admittedly unusual situation where a parent with care might have been claiming income support for herself but not for her child.[31] If so, the rationale for this provision will soon disappear with the transfer of means-tested support for children out of the benefits system and into the new CTC.[32]

Although the parent with care may initially have claimed income support (or income-based jobseeker's allowance), and so fall within the scope of section 6, her claim may have come to an end by the time that the Agency gets round to determining her deemed maintenance application. In such circumstances the Secretary of State *must* 'cease to treat that parent as having applied for a maintenance calculation'.[33] If so, and assuming that it appears that a private application could still be made,[34] the Secretary of State must inform the parent with care

---

[27] Nor does it apply to state pension credit.

[28] *Secretary of State of Social Security v Harmon, Carter and Cocks* [1998] 2 FLR 598, CA, also reported as *R(CS) 4/99*, on which see B Hodgkinson [1999] 6 *Journal of Social Security Law* 39.

[29] *Department for Social Development v MacGeagh and MacGeagh* [2005] NICA 28 (Northern Ireland).

[30] CSA 1991, s 6(6).

[31] For example, this would have applied where the child had capital in excess of £3,000 with the effect that no personal allowance would be payable for him or her.

[32] See Income Support (General) Regulations 1987 (SI 1987/1967), reg 17(1)(b), now repealed (although the complete transfer of such cases has been delayed).

[33] CSA 1991, s 11(3), reversing the effect of *R v Secretary of State for Social Security ex p Harris* [1999] 1 FLR 837, QBD, in which Scott Baker J held (at 842) that under the CSA 1991 (as originally enacted) there was no provision 'which presses the off button' once a s 6 application had been initiated. The immediate predecessor to CSA 1991, s 11(3) was s 11(1A), inserted by CSA 1995, s 19 (but since repealed by the 2000 Act). That provision, however, required the Secretary of State to discontinue action on a s 6 claim where the PWC's benefit *claim* had been 'disallowed or withdrawn'. In *R(CS) 1/02* Mr Commissioner Henty held (at para 6) that this did not cover a PWC whose benefit *award* had ceased because of remarriage, and so the PWC's s 6 assessment remained in existence. The wording of s 11(3) also reverses the effect of *R(CS) 1/02*, as it is triggered if the PWC 'has ceased to fall within section 6(1)'.

[34] ie that any private application would not be stymied by virtue of s 4(10) by the existence of a maintenance agreement or court order.

accordingly,[35] who then has a month in which to ask the Agency to treat the case as a section 4 application.[36] There is no obligation on the Secretary of State to make a parallel notification to the non-resident parent—but he will, of course, receive a MEF in the fullness of time if the parent with care elects to proceed as a private case. If for some reason a section 4 application could not be made—as where there is a pre-existing court order—the Secretary of State is required to notify both the parent with care and the non-resident parent (the latter only assuming that he was aware that the case had been treated initially as a section 6 case).[37]

The Application Process under Section 6

As a matter of law, there is no particular form that a parent with care on benefit must complete in order to make an application for child support. This is, of course, because section 6(3) of the 1991 Act enables the Secretary of State to *treat* her as making such an application. The income support claim form includes a question asking parents with care 'Do you wish to opt out of your application for child maintenance?'.[38] If the answer is in the affirmative, a Jobcentre Plus visiting officer should conduct a full interview with a view to establishing whether there is good cause for not co-operating (an issue explored further below). If, however, the parent with care does not wish to opt out, the visiting officer should interview her and record the relevant details on a 'child maintenance administration form', which is then forwarded to the Agency. This is, for all practical purposes, the maintenance application form.

Once an application has been treated as made under section 6(3)—or indeed once a private client makes an application under sections 4 or 7—the Secretary of State must, 'as soon as is reasonably practicable', notify the non-resident parent that the application has been made and 'request such information as he may require to make the maintenance calculation in such form and manner as he may specify in the particular case'.[39] The requirement that the notification be made 'as soon as is reasonably practicable' has no real bite; it is, at best, exhortatory.[40]

---

[35] The sub-section simply states that the Secretary of State 'shall notify her'—there is no statutory requirement that this be in writing.

[36] CSA 1991, s 11(4); again, there is no statutory requirement that such a request be in writing (although this is not made explicit, as it is in s 6(5)). This provision, inserted by the 2000 Act, introduces a new concept, namely a case treated as made under s 4. Elsewhere the Act simply distinguishes between (i) applications made under s 4 and (ii) applications treated as made under s 6: see E Jacobs and G Douglas, *Child Support: The Legislation* (Sweet & Maxwell, London, Edition Seven, 2005/2006) at 60.

[37] CSA 1991, s 11(5). The drafting is less than clear, as s 11(5) does not actually spell out what it is that the Secretary of State is meant to notify—presumably that no further action is being taken under s 6.

[38] Claim Form A1, pt 6, at 12.

[39] SI 2001/157, reg 5(1).

[40] Under the pre-SSA 1998 social security decision making system, the statutory requirement that claims be decided within 14 days 'so far as practicable' was at best an aspiration: see *R v Secretary of State for Social Services, ex parte Child Poverty Action Group* [1990] 2 QB 540.

Although delays have been commonplace in the system, the Agency impresses on its staff the importance of processing applications swiftly in order to ensure compliance. The notification may be 'orally or in writing',[41] and the Agency will usually seek to contact the non-resident parent by telephone.[42] Whatever form the notification takes, it must specify the effective date of the maintenance calculation and warn the non-resident parent of the Agency's power to make a default maintenance decision.[43] The Agency's practice, where possible, is to collect the necessary information over the telephone, and then to send the non-resident parent a print-out by way of confirmation. In some cases, however, a hard copy maintenance enquiry form (MEF) will be issued, for example if the non-resident parent requests a form or fails to co-operate.[44] The Agency's internal guidelines indicate that non-resident parents should be given 14 days in which to return the MEF.[45] A non-resident parent, in the same way as a parent with care, may amend any information provided so long as a maintenance calculation has not been made.[46]

The Duty to Co-operate

The statutory basis for the duty to co-operate imposed on parents with care who are benefit claimants is section 6(7) of the 1991 Act:[47]

(7) Unless she has made a request under subsection (5), the parent shall, so far as she reasonably can, comply with such regulations as may be made by the Secretary of State with a view to the Secretary of State's being provided with the information which is required to enable—

(a) the non-resident parent to be identified or traced;
(b) the amount of child support maintenance payable by him to be calculated; and
(c) that amount to be recovered from him.

Effectively identical provisions apply to private clients and child applicants in Scotland.[48] The difference lies not in the scope of the duty but in the consequences

---

[41] SI 2001/157, reg 5(1).

[42] There will clearly be circumstances where this is inappropriate (eg if the alleged NRP is unaware that he has been named as the father), in which case staff are instructed to arrange a face-to-face interview.

[43] SI 2001/157, reg 5(2). The 'effective date' is governed by *ibid*, reg 25: see *CCS/2288/2005*.

[44] The CSF 002 maintenance enquiry form can also be downloaded from the internet. Issuing a paper MEF was the standard practice before the 2000 Act reforms.

[45] R Hadwen and K Pawling, *Child Support Handbook 2005/2006* (CPAG, London, 13th edn, 2005) at 97. This is not a statutory time limit (contrast the former SI 1992/1813, reg 6(1)).

[46] SI 2001/157, reg 5(3) and (4); the parallel provisions for PWCs are reg 3(6) and (7).

[47] Unusually for legislation this provision uses the female third person form (which does, of course, reflect the reality in the great majority of cases). As Jacobs and Douglas note (n 36 above at 42), Interpretation Act 1978 s 6(a) means that formally the actual gender of the PWC is irrelevant. CSA 1991, s 6(8) applies for the s 6(7) power to be disapplied in prescribed circumstances. No such regulations have been made, but the provision has been retained 'to protect parents with care in as yet unforeseen circumstances', House of Lords Select Committee on Delegated Powers and Deregulation, *Thirteenth Report* (HL 59, Session 1999/2000) Annex 1 para 54.

[48] CSA 1991, ss 4(4) (duty on private PWC to co-operate) and 7(5) (duty on PWC, NRP and child to co-operate).

of non-compliance; a section 6 applicant who fails to co-operate runs the risk of being sanctioned with a reduced benefit decision, whereas the worst that can happen under sections 4 or 7 is simply that the Agency decides not to proceed with the assessment process.[49] Theoretically a refusal to co-operate lays the parent with care open to the risk of prosecution for failing to provide information to the Agency, but criminal proceedings are unlikely.[50]

Regulations specify at great length the various types of information which a parent with care may be required to provide. These include, for example, the name and address of the non-resident parent and his employer, details of any bank or building society accounts and, at a much more personal level, 'matters relevant for determining the parentage of a child whose parentage is in dispute'.[51] The full scope of the duty to co-operate, which affects non-resident parents and third parties (such as employers and accountants), and extends to providing evidence as well as information, is discussed in more detail later in this chapter.

Opting Out of Section 6

Parents with care have the right to opt out of section 6 in two situations, but the consequences of any such election are very different. In the first place, where a parent with care stops getting such a benefit 'she may ask the Secretary of State to cease acting under this section, but until then he may continue to do so'.[52] For example, if a parent with care who has been in receipt of benefit starts working for 16 hours a week or more, she loses her entitlement to income support (but may become eligible for working tax credit). She then faces a genuine choice: she can decide to remain within the child support system, and rely on the Agency to make assessments and, if she wishes, to arrange for collection and enforcement. Alternatively, if she is confident that maintenance can be resolved privately,[53] she has the right to request the Agency to cease acting. If she makes such a request, the Secretary of State *must* comply.[54] If matters do not work out to her satisfaction, she may of course subsequently reapply to the Agency as a private case under section 4. It is not only the parent with care who has a choice under this provision. Where the parent with care ceases to fall within the ambit of section 6(1), then unless and until she requests the Secretary of State to cease acting, 'he *may* continue to do so'. This means that in such a case the Agency has a discretion as to whether to

---

[49] See p 283 below on the withdrawal or cancellation of maintenance applications.

[50] In 2000 the DWP stated that there was no intention to prosecute non-compliant PWCs under CSA 1991, s 14A: *Thirteenth Report*, n 47 above, at Annex 1 para 53.

[51] Child Support (Information, Evidence and Disclosure) Regulations 1992 (SI 1992/1812), reg 3(2)(b), (f) and (q)).

[52] *Ibid*, s 6(9). See *ibid* s 11(3), discussed above, where the PWC leaves benefit before a maintenance calculation is actually made.

[53] Or indeed is willing to forgo child support 'for a quiet life'.

[54] CSA 1991, s 6(10).

continue acting, which must be exercised having regard to the child's welfare, in accordance with section 2 of the Act.

Secondly, any parent with care on benefit can ask the Secretary of State not to proceed under section 6(3), ie not to treat her as having applied for child support.[55] Before acting under this provision, the Secretary of State is required by law to notify the parent with care in writing of the effect of her being treated as having applied for child support, the right to opt out and the possibility of a reduced benefit decision.[56] The parent with care's request to opt out need not be in writing.[57] In principle, at least, this is an absolute rather than a conditional right; however, some of the Agency's literature might be read as implying that a parent with care can only opt out if she shows good cause.[58] In reality, of course, the parent with care's freedom is constrained by the prospect of a reduced benefit decision being made in the event that good cause is not established. The rationale for an exemption from the duty to co-operate is straightforward; there must be some limits on the state's requirement that parents with care on benefit should co-operate with the assessment, collection and enforcement of the non-resident parent's child support obligations. These limits, it is argued, are crossed if the parent or child is in some way placed at risk. The question then is where that line should be drawn. In practice, however, the existence of such an 'escape route' may prompt two quite different and competing concerns amongst policy makers and lobbying groups respectively.[59] One is that the very existence of an 'opt out' clause encourages collusion between separated parents to evade the child support system altogether.[60] The other, and opposing, concern is that given the high incidence of domestic violence, many parents with care may be putting themselves at undue risk by not requesting a good cause exemption even where they have grounds for doing so.

Next we examine how the 'good cause' rules are constructed and how they operate in the United Kingdom, before returning to these wider policy issues in considering 'good cause' provisions in other child support systems. We should note, however, that the European Court of Human Rights has ruled that the United Kingdom legislation strikes a 'fair balance' between the interest of individuals,

---

[55] *Ibid*, s 6(5).

[56] *Ibid*, s 6(4).

[57] *Ibid*, s 6(5).

[58] Hadwen and Pawling, n 45 above, at 50. For example, 'If you think that applying for child maintenance from the non-resident parent will put you or your child at risk of harm or undue distress, you can opt out of making the application. If your reasons are accepted, this is called having **good cause**', *Child support: your maintenance interview*, Agency leaflet CSL 100 (2002) at 8. This could easily be read as implying that opting out is conditional on showing good cause, which is not strictly the case. See, similarly, IS/CSA notes 02/03 *Maintenance for children* issued with the income support A1 claim form.

[59] See, from the USA, Department of Health and Human Services, Office of Inspector General *Client Cooperation with Child Support Enforcement—Use of Good Cause Exceptions* (March 2000) at 2.

[60] This concern was expressed very strongly by the House of Commons Social Security Committee in *Child Support: Good Cause and the Benefit Penalty* Fourth Report (Session 1995–96, HC 440). Fear of such collusion has been a recurrent feature of welfare discourse in Britain: see, under the poor law, p 55 above.

through the provision of a mechanism to avoid harmful disclosures, and the broader interests of the general community.[61]

The Section 46 Procedure

Section 46 of the 1991 Act deals with the consequences of a parent with care failing to co-operate with the Agency and so makes provision for a 'reduced benefit decision' (or a 'reduced benefit direction' as it was termed under the original 1991 Act) to be made on behalf of the Secretary of State.[62] The sanction under section 46 may apply in three types of case: where the parent with care on benefit has opted out but has failed to show good cause; where she has failed to comply with an information-gathering requirement; or where she has refused to take a scientific test to assist in establishing paternity.[63] The first point to note is that good cause decisions are no longer actually taken by the Agency. Since 2000 responsibility for these decisions has rested with decision makers in Jobcentre Plus,[64] the successor to the Benefits Agency. The Child Support Agency's role is to refer cases to Jobcentre Plus for investigation and decision making and to record the outcomes of such decisions. Under the procedure stipulated by section 46 and the associated regulations,[65] the first step is for the Secretary of State to serve a written notice on the parent with care asking for her reasons for making the request to opt out or for failing to comply.[66] The parent with care is given four weeks in which to provide reasons;[67] she need not do so in writing unless she is directed to do so.[68] In practice a visiting officer from Jobcentre Plus will arrange to interview the parent with care in her home shortly after the claim for benefit is made.[69] At the end of that period, the Secretary of State is required to consider whether 'there are reasonable grounds for believing that', were she to comply:

> there would be a risk of her, or of any children living with her, suffering harm or undue distress as a result of his taking such action, or her complying or taking the test.[70]

Although this provision proved to be highly controversial during the passage through Parliament of the Bill which became the 1991 Act, its scope has been the subject of very few cases before the Commissioners. This may lend some weight to

---

[61] *Stacey v United Kingdom* Application number 00040432/98 (complaint by PWC subject to s 6; application inadmissible; no breach of Arts 8 or 10).

[62] A new CSA 1991, s 46 was substituted by CSPSSA 2000, s 19.

[63] CSA 1991, s 46(1). The third type of case represented an extension made by the 2000 Act.

[64] Similarly, in Northern Ireland decision making is in the hands of the Social Security Agency.

[65] Child Support (Maintenance Calculation Procedure) Regulations 2000 (SI 2001/157) pt IV.

[66] CSA 1991, s 46(2).

[67] SI 2001/157, reg 9.

[68] CSA 1991, s 46(9).

[69] See further Agency leaflet CSL 100 (2002) and the detailed guidance in Hadwen and Pawling, n 45 above, ch 5.

[70] CSA 1991, s 46(3).

the argument that the provision is being properly applied by Agency staff.[71] There are four points which may be made on the scope of this 'good cause' exception.

First, there is no requirement that the 'harm or undue distress' actually occur. The threshold is lower, in that it is enough that there are reasonable grounds for believing there is a risk of such an eventuality. In *R(CS) 8/02* Mr Commissioner Williams, allowing the parent with care's appeal, held that:

> The safeguard requires only that it is considered that there are **reasonable grounds** to believe that there is a **risk of** harm or undue distress to the parent or child. That is a relatively easy test to meet if there is evidence suggesting either the parent or child is possibly put in some form of danger. I agree with the Commissioner in CCS/1037/1995 (at paragraph 9) that:
>
> > "Risk" is not qualified by any words such as "substantial". There must, however, in common sense be a real rather than fanciful risk.[72]

In that case the Agency had imposed a reduced benefit decision on a family credit claimant,[73] despite it being aware that she had obtained an injunction against the child's (alleged) father with a power of arrest attached. A tribunal confirmed the reduced benefit decision at a paper hearing, but without sight of relevant documentation which was in the hands of the Agency. On these facts the Commissioner had no hesitation in making his own findings of fact and substituting a decision to the effect that the reduced benefit decision should never have been made.

Secondly, there is no requirement that the risk be caused by the non-resident parent. In *R(CS) 8/02* the Commissioner held that the tribunal had erred in taking the view that threats of violence from the man she lived with, who she said was not her child's father, fell outside the scope of the exemption:

> There is no requirement that the risk arises directly from the behaviour of the person who is or may be the absent parent . . . The connecting factor in the sections is wider, namely that the anticipation of risk arises because of the Secretary of State's requirement. Of course, it may come from a person said by a mother to be the absent father. But it may come from others.[74]

Thirdly, as section 46(3) clearly refers to 'any children living with her', there is no requirement that the risk of 'harm or undue distress' be one faced by the parent with care or a *qualifying* child; the risk may be to another child, who may not even be a child of the non-resident parent.

Finally, and crucially, neither the Act nor the regulations define the expression 'harm or undue distress'. The Agency's early internal guidance advised decision makers to apply the ordinary dictionary definitions of these words; thus 'harm'

---

[71] There are, of course, other possible explanations: decision makers may be overly generous in dealing with such cases, or potential good cause cases may not enter the appeals system at all.

[72] *R(CS) 8/02*, para 12 (emphasis in the original).

[73] Since October 1999 the duty to co-operate has not been imposed on WFTC or WTC claimants (the successors to family credit—see p 260 above).

[74] *R(CS) 8/02*, paras 13 and 14.

comprises 'evil (physical or otherwise) as done or suffered, hurt, injury, damage or mischief; grief, trouble or affliction', 'undue' means 'going beyond what is appropriate, warranted or natural, excessive' and 'distress' encompasses 'severe strain or pressure'.[75] The illustrations in the guidance, although followed by a warning that they 'should not be taken as definitive or exhaustive', were all at the extreme end of the scale. For example, the guidance stated that a risk of harm may involve threats of violence; similarly decision makers 'would normally accept undue distress' where the parent with care was a rape victim, or the non-resident parent had sexually assaulted a child in her household or the child was conceived as a result of sexual abuse.[76]

The guidance then detailed a number of other scenarios in which the parent with care may claim good cause, such as where there has been no contact or where the parent with care wanted to end all links with the non-resident parent. Decision makers were advised that they *may* accept undue distress in such cases, but should consider factors such as the duty of both parents to support their children, the confidentiality system operated by the Agency and the fact that it is for the courts to determine contact issues.[77] It is arguable that the tenor of this guidance seeks to impose a higher threshold than that considered by the Commissioner to be appropriate in *R(CS) 8/02*. However, the reality is that decision makers will be alive to the potentially disastrous consequences of making a finding against a parent with care who has claimed good cause. Indeed, other official guidance encourages staff to 'err on the side of caution when making good cause decisions'.[78] To that extent the Agency's decision in *R(CS) 8/02* was atypical, which may explain why it is one of the very few which have been taken to the Commissioner on appeal. Staff are also expressly advised that they should accept the parent with care's uncorroborated evidence unless it is self-contradictory or improbable.[79] This stands in stark contrast to the position in the United States, discussed further below, where parents on welfare claiming 'good cause' are expected to provide corroboration.[80]

If the Jobcentre Plus decision maker concludes that there are no such reasonable grounds, then the Secretary of State 'may, except in prescribed circumstances, make a reduced benefit decision with respect to the parent'.[81] It follows that the decision on whether to impose a sanction is a discretionary one and so regard must be had to the children's welfare.[82] According to one unreported Commissioner's

---

[75] Child Support Agency, *Decision Makers Guide* para 2551, written at a time when Agency staff made good cause decisions. Although decisions are now taken by benefits staff working for Jobcentre Plus, there is no reason to think that the guidance is any different.

[76] *Ibid*, paras 2554 and 2555.

[77] *Ibid*, para 2555 and Table.

[78] DWP, *Income Support good cause training materials*, cited in Hadwen and Pawling, n 45 above, at 74.

[79] n 75 above, para 2553. An early study showed that PWCs provided corroboration (eg hospital or police reports) in just 4% of cases: DSS, *The Requirement to Co-operate: A Report on the Operation of the 'Good Cause' Provisions* In-house Report No 14 (1996) at 33.

[80] Department of Health and Human Services, Office of Inspector General, n 59 above, at 5.

[81] CSA 1991, s 46(5). A copy of the decision must be sent to the PWC: *ibid*, s 46(7).

[82] *Ibid*, s 2. See also *CSC2/03–04*.

decision, there must be 'some exceptional or special factor' which would suggest that a child's welfare would be adversely affected by a reduced benefit decision.[83] The prescribed circumstances, where no sanction should be applied, are where the parent with care receives a special higher rate of income support, income-based jobseeker's allowance or CTC.[84]

The Reduced Benefit Decision

The duration, amount and starting date of any reduced benefit decision are set by regulations.[85] The basic rule is that the parent with care's weekly benefit is reduced by an amount equal to 40 per cent of the full adult income support personal allowance.[86] This sanction applies for three years,[87] twice the length of the penalty under the original legislation.[88] The level and the duration of the sanction were increased by regulations in October 1996.[89] At the time ministers justified the imposition of harsher sanctions on the basis that the original system had failed to provide a sufficient incentive for parents with care on benefit to co-operate with the Agency.[90] The government also intimated that, if these measures failed to work, the possibility of making entitlement to benefit itself conditional on co-operation had not been ruled out.[91] The House of Commons Social Security Select Committee, approving these changes, advocated that consideration be given to the imposition of 'an escalating benefit penalty' if non-cooperation continued.[92] Since April 1998, however, when changes to the administrative and interviewing procedures were introduced for new benefit claims, there has been a marked increase in compliance.[93] Although the Labour government's 1998 Green Paper suggested that the definition of 'good cause' might yet be tightened, the subsequent White Paper rejected this idea, given the concerns expressed by respondents.[94] The Select

---

[83] *CCS/1037/1995 per* Mr Commissioner Sanders.

[84] This applies where the higher pensioner premium or the disability premium in the IS/income-based JSA scheme or the special disabled child rate of CTC is payable: SI 2001/157, reg 10.

[85] CSA 1991, s 46(8) and 46(10)(b) and (d).

[86] SI 2001/157, reg 11(2). In 2006/07 the reduction is £22.98 p/w.

[87] The precise starting date is determined by *ibid*, reg 11(3)–(5). The amount of the deduction is increased following the annual uprating of benefit rates: *ibid*, reg 11(7).

[88] Originally the sanction resulted in a 20% reduction for 26 weeks followed by a 10% reduction for the following 52 weeks: Child Support (Maintenance Assessment Procedure) Regulations 1992 (SI 1992/1813), reg 36 (before 1996 amendment).

[89] Child Support (Miscellaneous Amendments) 1996 (SI 1996/1945), reg 14.

[90] Incentives, in this sense, were seen in the sense of harsher sanctions rather than eg a more generous disregard of maintenance received.

[91] Whilst recognising that 'this would be a significant change in the structure of benefits in this country and would require primary legislation', *Fourth Report* n 60 above at 89.

[92] *Ibid*, at v.

[93] See p 272 below.

[94] DSS, *Children First: a new approach to child support* (Cm 3992, July 1998) at ch 3 para 22 and *A new contract for welfare: Children's Rights and Parents' Responsibilities* (Cm 4349, July 1999) at 24.

Committee also abandoned its enthusiasm for a more rigorous system and it now seems unlikely that the reduced benefit penalty will be made harsher still.[95]

Given that the reduction in benefit is set by reference to the income support rate for adults aged 25 or over, it necessarily bears more harshly on younger parents with care who are unable to show good cause—although they are paid benefit at the (lower) 18–24 rate, the reduced benefit sanction is based on the standard rate for those aged 25 and over. The amount of the deduction under the reduced benefit decision must be reduced if it would otherwise bring down the weekly amount of benefit payable to 50 pence a week or less, so as to ensure that the minimum weekly payment of income support is maintained.[96]

Regulations provide that only one reduced benefit decision may be in force in relation to a parent at any one time.[97] However, this means that a parent with care may be subject to successive reduced benefit sanctions on a back-to-back basis, although if a new decision is made with respect to the same parent with care—but a different child[98]—the existing sanction lapses and the new determination comes into force.[99] Provision is made for the suspension of a reduced benefit decision where the parent with care leaves benefit. If a further benefit claim is made within a year, the sanction is re-imposed for the remaining period. If the parent with care stays off benefit for more than one year, the sanction cannot be revived.[100] The same suspension rule applies where the parent with care remains on benefit but goes into hospital, a residential care or nursing home or a local authority home.[101] Similarly, if there is no longer a qualifying child, or the parent concerned ceases to be a person with care, the sanction is suspended for up to 52 weeks, after which it becomes ineffective.[102] The reduced benefit decision ends if the parent with care withdraws her request to opt out or otherwise complies.[103] It also terminates if the parent with care leaves benefit, subject to the one year rule.[104]

---

[95] Indeed the Select Committee adopted a very different approach to its 1996 predecessor, arguing that the penalty provisions should be suspended during the phasing-in period in order to assess whether the new incentives alone achieved higher compliance: *The 1999 Child Support White Paper*, Tenth Report (Session 1998–99, HC 798) at xxxi. The government rejected this proposal as unfair on other parents: *Reply by the Government to the Tenth Report* (Cm 4536, 1999) at 13–14.

[96] SI 2001/157, reg 12. The real significance of this is that it preserves 'passported' benefits, such as free school meals—worth considerably more than 50 pence a week—which would otherwise be lost of the family ceased to receive income support.

[97] *Ibid*, reg 11(8).

[98] ie one who was not a qualifying child at the time of the earlier decision or who has been born subsequently: *ibid*, reg 17(5).

[99] *Ibid*, regs 17 and 11(4) (any subsequent reduced benefit decision to come into force on the day after any earlier decision expires).

[100] *Ibid*, reg 13.

[101] *Ibid*, regs 14 and 15.

[102] *Ibid*, reg 18.

[103] *Ibid*, reg 16(a) and (b). Any notice of termination of a reduced benefit decision must be sent to the parent with care: *ibid*, reg 19.

[104] *Ibid*, reg 16(c); a further cause for the sanction terminating is, in Scotland only, if the qualifying child makes a successful application for child support maintenance: *ibid*, reg 16(d) and CSA 1991, s 7.

If, on the other hand, the Secretary of State takes the view that there is good cause, the Agency has no discretion in the matter; no further immediate action must be taken on the case, other than the parent with care being notified in writing of that decision.[105] Presumably then the Secretary of State can only re-open the matter subsequently by way of revision or supersession, eg if new facts come to light casting doubt on the original decision to apply the good cause exemption. The legislation, however, does provides for the Agency periodically to review the case by contacting the parent with care again to ascertain whether her decision and her reasons for maintaining her request still stand.[106]

The Operation of the Good Cause Exception in the United Kingdom

At the outset the United Kingdom child support scheme was characterised by widespread use of the 'good cause' procedure. In the Agency's first three years of operation, 'good cause' was an issue in about 15 per cent of all cases; decision makers approved exemptions in over 110,000 cases, and made about 50,000 reduced benefit directions.[107] This led to concern amongst parliamentarians and policy makers that the good cause rules were being abused, for example by parents with care claiming 'good cause' on spurious grounds, as a means of avoiding having to co-operate with the Agency. Alternatively, and more seriously, collusion was suspected in some cases, whereby the parent with care would accept the benefit penalty on the basis that the non-resident parent, freed from the prospect of intervention by the Agency, would make up the resulting shortfall in her income on an undeclared 'cash in hand' basis. Empirical evidence of such abuse was thin,[108] but the Social Security Select Committee expressed its worry that 'large numbers of PWCs appear to be able to opt out of the child support scheme. There is a real danger that co-operation with the Child Support Agency could be seen as voluntary'.[109]

These concerns were cited by the Conservative government as justification for the 1996 changes to the amount and duration of the reduced benefit penalty.[110] The Select Committee, whilst supporting the increased sanctions, identified the lack of personal contact between Agency staff and parents with care, and the delay

---

[105] *Ibid*, s 46(4).

[106] *Ibid*, s 46(6). Again, the reasons do not necessarily have to be given in writing: *ibid*, s 46(9). If the Secretary of State considers the grounds are reasonable, the sanction ceases to have effect: SI 2001/157, reg 16(c). Child Support Agency, *Procedures: Requirement to Cooperate* (2005) at 1840 advises staff that 'Past experience shows that once the RBD is imposed the PaWC is very likely to change his/her mind about opting out, because of the penalties involved'.

[107] *Fourth Report*, n 60 above, at vii.

[108] See DSS, n 79 above. Fear of such collusion was a recurrent concern for officials administering both the poor law and the subsequent liable relative rules: see eg pp 55 and 98 above.

[109] *Fourth Report*, n 60 above, at vii. Such a concern necessarily prioritises the fiscal purpose behind the child support scheme, as private clients, of course, have just such a choice.

[110] See p 269 above.

between the claim for benefit and the initial contact to arrange maintenance, as the central problem. The Select Committee's view was that 'making interviews compulsory with all PWCs drawing the relevant benefit is the key to determining co-operation by the PWC and should become an automatic part of registering for benefit'.[111] In April 1998 the Department accordingly (re)introduced face-to-face interviews with all parents with care claiming relevant benefits; the result, predictably enough, was a sharp increase in compliance. In 1997 just 30 per cent of parents with care on benefit co-operated with the Agency; by 2000 this proportion had soared to 90 per cent.[112] Moreover, as Table 9.1 shows, the number of reduced benefit directions imposed fell dramatically from 74,280 in 1997/98 to just 8,169 in 2001/02.[113] Conversely, the proportion of cases in which decision makers accepted 'good cause' increased from 22 per cent in 1998/99 to 61 per cent in 2001/02.[114] Since that time there seems to have been a slight increase in the incidence of sanctioning. In the last complete year for which statistics are available (2004/05), there were nearly 38,000 cases referred for decision, with 'good cause' being accepted in about half of those cases determined.[115]

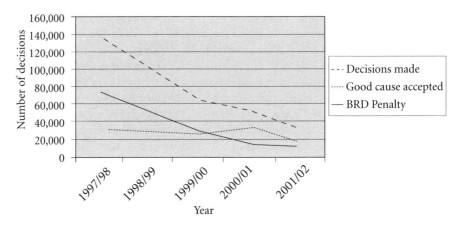

Fɪɢ 9.1 Good cause decisions 1997/98–2001/02

---

[111] *Fourth Report*, n 60 above at xii. Ironically, of course, this is precisely what the former and much maligned DHSS Liable Relative Units used to do as a matter of course.

[112] *Hansard* HC Debates vol 357 col 849W (30 November 2000).

[113] *Hansard* HC Debates vol 389 col 1548W (24 July 2002). Some of this reduction was attributable to the decision not to apply the co-operation requirement to WFTC, which replaced family credit from October 1999, but the overall trend is clear, even leaving that change aside.

[114] ie 'good cause accepted' as a proportion of 'decisions'.

[115] In 2004/05 a total of 37,907 cases were referred for decision; 'good cause' was accepted in 13,594 and rejected in 13,225, leading to 11,264 reduced benefit directions: *Hansard* HC Debates vol 436 col 2474W (12 September 2005).

Good Cause Exemptions in other Jurisdictions

United States of America

The notion of a 'good cause' exemption in the United Kingdom's child support scheme was borrowed from overseas. For many years the principal welfare programme in the United States was Aid to Families with Dependant Children (AFDC). In the post-war period AFDC became increasingly associated with poor single mothers from the black community, fuelling public concerns about the impact of illegitimacy on public finances.[116] In this climate many states sought to make a claimant's entitlement to AFDC conditional upon her co-operation with the child support authorities, but in a series of cases in the early 1970s such efforts were declared invalid by the courts.[117] However, in 1974 federal law imposed a co-operation requirement on AFDC claimants, and a year later this was modified by the inclusion of a 'good cause' exemption.[118] States were required to grant 'good cause' exemptions where the claimant or child was at risk of 'physical or emotional harm', or where the child was conceived following rape or incest, or was the subject of pending adoption proceedings.[119] Although the PRWORA 1996 replaced AFDC with Temporary Assistance for Needy Families (TANF), the legislation retained a 'good cause' proviso.[120] The 1996 Act is in one sense less prescriptive in that states can now adopt a more liberal (or indeed more restrictive) definition of 'good cause', so long as they are 'taking into account the best interests of the child'.[121] States also have some discretion as to the level of penalty which is set, provided that the minimum sanction of a 25 per cent reduction in the family's welfare payments is applied.[122] There is, however, a financial incentive for states to impose penalties, in that a failure to do so can result in a reduction in the TANF block grant paid by the federal government.[123]

Yet the US federal and state legislation only provides the framework for the good cause rules; in practice their application will be mediated through the

---

[116] SD Sugarman, '*Roe v Norton*: Coerced Maternal Cooperation' in RH Mnookin (ed), *In the Interest of Children* (New York: WH Freeman, 1985) chs 16–18, at 374; see further ch 6 above.

[117] See JM Fontana, 'Co-operation and Good Cause: Greater Sanctions and the Failure to Account for Domestic Violence' (2000) 15 *Wisconsin Women's Law Journal* 367 at 371.

[118] See Sugarman, n 116 above, for a detailed account of the development of the US case law and legislation in this period.

[119] 45 CFR 323.42, reprinted in 43 Fed Reg at 45748.

[120] PRWORA 1996 § 333; 42 USC § 654 (29) (Supp III 1997).

[121] 42 USC § 654 (29)(A)(i). See S Notar and V Turetsky, 'Models for Safe Child Support Enforcement' (2000) 8 *American Journal of Gender, Social Policy & Law* 657 at 681 for a discussion of the range of different definitions which states have adopted.

[122] 42 USC § 608(a)(2). The 25% sanction cannot be compared directly to the UK's 40% reduction, as the US penalty applies to the totality of the family's TANF payments, whereas the UK reduction applies solely to the income support adult personal allowance (there is no impact on the family premium or on CTC). Some states have applied mores stringent penalties: TL Brito, 'The Welfarization of Family Law' (2000) 48 *University of Kansas Law Review* 229 at 267 n 192.

[123] 42 USC § 609(a)(5).

operational cultures of 'street-level bureaucrats'.[124] The consequence, according to one study of the then AFDC rules, is that 'states effectively force destitute parents to chose between benefits and the privacy of their own sexual histories'.[125] Thus, as in the United Kingdom, 'non-TANF unwed mothers are spared compulsory state intrusion into these private matters and are not sanctioned for their failure to cooperate'.[126] In practice, however, American 'women almost always co-operate, but a few are excused'.[127] For example, in 2002 there were 240,920 determinations of non co-operation in the United States but only 11,412 findings of good cause (ie less than 5 per cent).[128] There are, in addition, considerable variations across states in the granting of good cause exemptions, which appear to be a function of factors such as the local demand for welfare, the values of the state bureaucracy and the political complexion of the governing party.[129] On the other hand, relatively few applications for 'good cause' exemptions are actually made in the USA; one reason may be that affected parents are simply unaware of this possibility.[130] Another factor may be that in some cases claimants' co-operation with the child support authorities is more apparent than real; one study identified a degree of 'covert non-compliance', by which mothers pretended to co-operate but failed to disclose crucial identifying information.[131] It may also be that most American parents with care who are domestic violence victims prefer to claim child support rather than plead 'good cause'.[132] This might in part reflect attitudinal and cultural views in the United States about the importance of child support. More pragmatically, the reason may be that the payment of child support takes on added importance for American parents with care in the absence of any universal tax-funded equivalent to the United Kingdom's child benefit.

Australia

The Australian child support system also operates a version of a 'good cause' exemption. A parent who receives more than the minimum rate of Family Tax Benefit[133] for a child may be required to take 'reasonable action' to obtain main-

---

[124] See LR Keiser and J Soss, 'With Good Cause: Bureaucratic Discretion and the Politics of Child Support Enforcement' (1998) 42 *Am J of Political Science* 1133 at 1138, drawing on the work of M Lipsky, *Street Level Bureaucracy: Dilemmas of the Individual in Public Services* (Russell Sage Foundation, New York, 1980).

[125] Keiser and Soss, n 124 above, at 1136.

[126] Brito, n 122 above, at 267–68.

[127] Sugarman, n 116 above, at 431.

[128] OCSE *Annual Statistical Report FY 2002* Tables 66 and 67.

[129] See Keiser and Soss, n 124 above.

[130] The official notice requirements were relaxed on the change-over from AFDC to TANF and are less onerous than in the UK. Thus in the USA 'women typically receive notice only once, buried in a TANF application packet', Notar and Turetsky, n 121 above, at 672.

[131] K Edin, 'Single Mothers and Child Support: The Possibilities and Limits of Child Support Policy' (1995) 17 *Children and Youth Services Review* 203.

[132] J Pearson, N Thoennes and EA Griswold, 'Child Support and Domestic Violence: The Victims Speak Out' (1999) 5 *Violence against Women* 427 at 440 (only 6.7% of mothers reporting domestic violence, and 2.7% of welfare recipients, said they would be interested in applying for 'good cause').

[133] In UK terms, an income support claimant.

tenance from their former partner for that child,[134] which would normally mean applying for child support. The 'reasonable action' test is not concerned solely with the reasonableness of the amount of child support paid, but also involves consideration of the reasonableness of the steps taken to secure maintenance. Thus a decision to settle for a lower amount of child support than might be fixed by the formula, but taken on professional advice, might constitute 'reasonable action', especially if the parent with care is concerned that the father might leave the country and terminate all support.[135] However, an informal agreement for a modest amount with no attempt to secure an impartial assessment of the appropriate level of maintenance was not 'reasonable action'.[136] Likewise, a parent with care who did not apply for child support because she did not wish to upset either the father's relationship with the children, or his marriage to his new partner (who was unaware that the father had had this child), failed to meet the statutory test.[137] The official guidance recognises five categories of exemption from the 'reasonable action' test: fear of violence, harmful or disruptive effect, exceptional circumstances, father's identity unknown or paternity cannot be proven.[138] Where a Centrelink[139] social worker carries out a risk assessment and concludes that it would not be reasonable to pursue child support, an exemption is granted. In all in Australia, about three per cent of parents with care are exempt from taking action under the child support scheme.[140]

New Zealand

Historically one of the most restrictive interpretations of 'good cause' has operated in New Zealand, where social security claimants are also required to apply for a formula assessment of child support.[141] Moreover, social security claimants who are lone parents are required to take 'active steps to identify who is in law the other parent'.[142] Simply naming a man as the father on an application form for benefit, where he had denied paternity, is insufficient, and the taking of active steps has to be measured objectively.[143] If the lone parent fails to co-operate with the agency,

---

[134] A New Tax System (Family Assistance) Act 1999 (Cth), sch 1, cl 10 and Child Support Assessment Act 1989 (Cth), s 151A. See further Report of the Ministerial Taskforce on Child Support, *In the Best Interests of Children—Reforming the Child Support Scheme* (May 2005) ch 11.

[135] *Re Temmen and Secretary, Department of Social Security* (1992) 28 ALD 137 (AAT), reversed on other grounds in *Re Secretary, Department of Social Security and Temmen* (1993) 17 AAR 349, (1993) 30 ALD 485 (Federal Court).

[136] *Thomas and Secretary, Department of Family and Community Services* [2004] AATA 221 (AAT).

[137] *Department of Family and Community Services and VAD* [2001] AATA 1045 (AAT).

[138] Centrelink, *Guide to the Administration of the Social Security Act*, cited in CCH, *Australian Family Law and Practice*.

[139] The Australian social security agency.

[140] Child Support Agency (Australia), *Child Support Scheme Facts and Figures 2004–05* (CSA, Canberra, 2004) at 13.

[141] Child Support Act 1991 (NZ), s 9, which covers a range of social security benefits.

[142] Social Security Act 1964 (NZ), s 70A(3)(b).

[143] *R v Chief Executive of the Department of Work and Income* [2003] 3 NZLR 319 (High Court, Christchurch).

benefit is reduced by NZ$22 for each child affected.[144] This penalty may be waived where the child was born as a result of rape or incest.[145] A further ground for non-compliance, that identifying the other parent 'would jeopardise a stable family relationship of which that person is a part', was repealed in 1992.[146] However, in 2005 the legislation was further amended to increase the benefit penalty[147] but at the same time to extend the scope of good cause to include the risk of violence.[148] Good cause may now also encompass some other 'compelling circumstance' where, even if the lone parent were to co-operate fully, 'there is no real likelihood of child support being collected in the foreseeable future from the other parent'.[149]

Applications under Section 4

Introduction

A parent with care (or indeed a person with care who is not a parent[150]) who is not in receipt of either income support or income-based jobseeker's allowance may choose whether or not to ask the Agency to assess child maintenance. Indeed, the non-resident parent also has that option.[151] According to section 4(1) of the 1991 Act:

> A person who is, in relation to any qualifying child or any qualifying children, either the person with care or the non-resident parent may apply to the Secretary of State for a maintenance calculation to be made under this Act with respect to that child, or any of those children.

People who apply under section 4 are known in the Agency as 'private clients'. Such applicants may, however, be in receipt of any number of other social security benefits or tax credits. Thus a parent with care who receives working tax credit and CTC may, but need not, apply under section 4.[152] Similarly a grandparent caring for a grandchild and in receipt of the state retirement pension may, but does not

---

[144]　Social Security Act 1964 (NZ), s 70A(2).

[145]　*Ibid*, s 70A(3)(c).

[146]　Social Security Amendment Act (No 5) 1991 (NZ), s 9, repealing Social Security Amendment Act (No 2) 1990 (NZ), s 18.

[147]　By an additional NZ$6 per claimant (not per child) after 13 weeks: Social Security Act 1964 (NZ), s 70A(5)–(8), inserted by Social Security (Social Assistance) Amendment Act 2005 (NZ), s 7.

[148]　Social Security Act 1964 (NZ), s 70A(3)(ba), inserted by Social Security (Social Assistance) Amendment Act 2005 (NZ), s 7. This represents a reversal of policy: previously the New Zealand authorities had considered extending the scope of this exemption, but had decided against, principally because 'a suitably violent liable parent could avoid liability through real or fabricated threats of violence', Head of Research and Technical Support, NZ Inland Revenue Child Support, quoted in *Fourth Report*, n 60 above, at 84.

[149]　Social Security Act 1964 (NZ), s 70A(3)(bb), inserted by Social Security (Social Assistance) Amendment Act 2005 (NZ), s 7.

[150]　Eg a grandparent or other non-parent caring for the child.

[151]　This may seem implausible, but the non-resident parent may wish to establish the extent of his financial liability to support a child.

[152]　As was seen above (p 260), family credit claimants were required to apply for child support under CSA 1991, s 6, but this obligation was removed with the advent of WFTC in 1999.

have to, apply as a private case. The drafting of section 4(1) is such that private clients, unlike those in benefit cases, have a double election at the application stage; they can choose whether to involve the Agency at all and, if so, can choose whether to request an Agency calculation for one, some or all of their qualifying children.[153]

It must be appreciated that, in the ordinary case in which the Agency would otherwise have jurisdiction, a potential private client who decides *not* to involve the Agency under section 4 cannot, with one important exception, obtain a court order for child maintenance instead.[154] The one exception is that the courts have retained their power to make consent orders for child maintenance. It follows that the courts cannot make an order determining the amount of child maintenance following a contested hearing, unless it is a case in which the Agency lacks jurisdiction in any event (eg because one of the parties is not habitually resident in the United Kingdom). In real terms, therefore, where the case is one in which the Agency has the power to make a maintenance calculation, the parent (or other person) with care effectively has a choice; either to apply to the Agency under section 4 or to reach a private agreement with the non-resident parent (with or without the court's approval through the mechanism of a consent order).

There are, however, four situations in which a parent in a private case is barred from applying under section 4. The first is that no section 4 application may be made if income support or income-based jobseeker's allowance is in payment to or in respect of the parent with care or the child(ren) in question.[155] Similarly, and secondly, the section 4 route is barred where there is already a maintenance calculation in force as a result of a prior application under section 6.[156] The third exception as seen in chapter 7 above—is where there is a pre-April 1993 written maintenance agreement or pre-March 2003 court order for child maintenance.[157] Such parents, albeit that they are a diminishing group, are necessarily still reliant, just as they were before April 1993, on either private negotiation or court proceedings to resolve disputes over maintenance. Finally, no section 4 application is possible where a post-March 2003 court order has been in force for less than a year;[158] beyond that point, however, the parent with care is free to bring in the Agency.

---

[153] Private clients can also elect whether or not to ask the Agency to collect and enforce child support; however, they have no right to be heard in enforcement proceedings: see the discussion of *Kehoe* p 448 below.

[154] The courts also retain a special jurisdiction in the exceptional cases set out in s 8; see ch. 7 above.

[155] *Ibid*, s 4(10)(b) and (11). This provision does not, as such, preclude an application under s 4 where the PWC has *claimed* income support but before her claim has been determined (and hence before she is *paid*). In such a case the actual s 4 application and the deemed s 6 application will be dealt with as a single application under s 6: see Child Support (Maintenance Calculation Procedure) Regulations 2000 (SI 2001/157), reg 4 and sch 2, para 1(2), discussed below.

[156] CSA 1991, s 4(9).

[157] *Ibid*, s 4(10)(a). To be precise, the agreement must predate 5 April 1993 and the court order 3 March 2003.

[158] *Ibid*, s 4(10)(aa).

The Application Process under Section 4

The regulations specifically provide that those who make new scheme maintenance applications under section 4 (or indeed section 7) 'need not normally do so in writing', although the Secretary of State has the power to direct that applications be made in writing.[159] In contrast, the regulations governing the original scheme stipulated that such private applicants 'shall do so on a form (a "maintenance application form") provided by the Secretary of State'.[160] The change in the statutory requirement follows the Agency's shift to telephony as the principal means of communication with its clients. It also enables a parent with care to make an application on a form downloaded from the internet.[161] An application is 'effective' if it complies with whatever formal requirements the Secretary of State decides are appropriate; the date of receipt then determines when it was made.[162] It follows that an application is effective if the form is completed and signed; doubts as to the accuracy of the information provided alone do not make it ineffective.[163] Indeed, 'ascertaining the correctness and completeness of the substantive information given on the form is what the process of assessment is all about'.[164] Assuming that the application is effective, then the non-resident parent must be notified,[165] in the same way as with a section 6 case, and the application must in due course be the subject of a decision under section 11 of the Act. Where the application is found to be ineffective, the Secretary of State may ask the applicant to provide additional information or evidence.[166]

A person who applies under section 4 is under a duty, in accordance with regulations made by the Secretary of State, to provide the Agency, so far as she reasonably can, with information enabling it to trace, assess and recover child support from the non-resident parent.[167] These requirements are set out in the Child Support (Information, Evidence and Disclosure) Regulations 1992[168] and are discussed in detail below. As we have already seen, to this extent the parent with care in a private case is required to comply with precisely the same information-gathering requirements as the parent with care on benefit. The fundamental distinction is rather that the former has an absolute right to withdraw at any point,

---

[159] SI 2001/157, reg 3(1).

[160] Child Support (Maintenance Assessment Procedure) Regulations 1992 (SI 1992/1813) reg 2(1).

[161] The relevant form is CSF 001.

[162] SI 2001/157, reg 3(2).

[163] *R(CS) 1/96* para 11 *per* Mr Commissioner Rice and *R(CS) 3/97* para 10 *per* Mr Commissioner Goodman; both cases were decided under SI 1992/1813 reg 2 but the same principle should apply to SI 2001/157, reg 3(1).

[164] *CCS/2626/1999* para 15 *per* Mr Commissioner Howell QC.

[165] SI 2001/157, reg 5.

[166] *Ibid*, reg 3(3). Where this further information is provided within 14 days (or a longer period where delay is unavoidable) the application is treated as having been made at the outset: *ibid*, reg 3(4). Otherwise the date the additional information is received determines the date of the application: *ibid*, reg 3(5).

[167] CSA 1991, s 4(4).

[168] SI 1992/1812.

whereas the latter, although she may ask the Secretary of State not to proceed, faces the risk of a reduced benefit decision if she is unable to show good cause. Thus under section 4(5) of the 1991 Act:

> Any person who has applied to the Secretary of State under this section may at any time request him to cease acting under this section.

Such a request has prospective rather than retrospective effect. It therefore does not have the effect of cancelling the maintenance calculation;[169] rather, it provides for the Secretary of State to cease acting under it. Indeed, the Secretary of State is then obliged to act upon any such request.[170] In this way a private client has an unconditional right to opt out at the outset, without even invoking the Agency, or at any later stage once the Agency has become involved.

The outcome of an application under section 4 is a maintenance calculation; the Agency may have no further involvement in the case, as the parties may be content to make private arrangements for the payment of child support (whether or not at the rate specified in the Agency's assessment). It follows that in such cases the Agency has no accurate means of estimating the extent of compliance by non-resident parents with child support maintenance calculations. However, either parent may apply to the Secretary of State for the Agency to undertake the collection and enforcement of child support.[171] If so, then the Secretary of State 'may act accordingly' where authorised 'to take steps to enforce that obligation whenever he considers it necessary to do so'.[172] In the event of any default, as we shall see, a parent with care in a private case has no standing to enforce the maintenance calculation either in her own right or on behalf of the children—only the Agency has this power.[173]

Applications under Section 7

Family law in Scotland is different in a number of important respects from that which applies in England and Wales.[174] In particular, both the civil law relating to children and the youth justice system reflect different traditions and principles. Under Scots law children aged 12 or over 'shall be presumed to be of sufficient age and maturity to form a view' on major decisions which affect the exercise of parental responsibility over them.[175] Similarly, in Scotland children are able to

---

[169] *CCS/13/1994* at para 6 *per* Mr Commissioner Goodman.

[170] CSA 1991, s 4(6). This duty is stated to be subject to any regulations made under s 4(8), but no such regulations have been made.

[171] *Ibid*, s 4(2).

[172] *Ibid*, s 4(3).

[173] See the discussion of *R (Kehoe) v Secretary of State for Work and Pensions* [2005] UKHL 48; [2006] 1 AC 42 in ch 14 below.

[174] Elsewhere in the British Isles there are also important differences in matrimonial law as between Northern Ireland and England & Wales, but these do not carry over into child support law.

[175] Children (Scotland) Act 1995, s 6(1).

make a will from the age of 12 and enjoy contractual capacity from the age of 16.[176] This distinctiveness is reflected in the structure of child support law.[177] Section 7(1) of the 1991 Act provides that:

> A qualifying child who has attained the age of 12 years and who is habitually resident in Scotland may apply to the Secretary of State for a maintenance calculation to be made with respect to him . . .

In this respect Scots law is not only different to that which apples in the rest of the United Kingdom—it appears to be unique. Certainly there is no facility in the Australian or New Zealand[178] schemes for a young person under the age of 18 to make an independent application for maintenance.

The child's right in Scotland to apply under section 7 is subject to two exceptions. The first is where either the relevant person with care or a non-resident parent has already applied; the second is where a parent with care is treated as having applied under section 6(3). It follows that the child's right to apply is subordinate to the principal application routes under sections 4 and 6 of the 1991 Act. Assuming that the child's application is not ruled out by any such prior application by an adult involved in the case, the section 7 application provides the Secretary of State with the authority to make a maintenance calculation over any other qualifying children—most obviously the applicant's younger siblings—who share the same person with care and non-resident parent.[179]

The remaining provisions of section 7 largely mirror those that apply to private cases under section 4. Thus any of the parties, including the child, may request the Agency to take over the collection and enforcement of child support payments.[180] Children who make successful applications under section 7 are also required, so far as they reasonably can, to provide information enabling the Secretary of State to trace, assess and recover child support from the non-resident parent.[181] There is also a parallel rule which precludes an application under section 7 where there is a pre-April 1993 written maintenance agreement, a pre-March 2003 court order or a post-March 2003 court order which has been in force for less than a year.[182] Under section 7 only the child concerned, but not the person with care, can request the Secretary of State to cease acting on the application.[183]

---

[176] Age of Legal Capacity (Scotland) Act 1991, s 2.

[177] The Agency produces a special leaflet *Young person's guide to applying for child maintenance in Scotland* CSL 118 (2002).

[178] *Hyde v CIR* [2000] NZFLR 385 (Family Court, Wellington).

[179] CSA 1991, s 7(2).

[180] *Ibid*, s 7(3) and (4).

[181] *Ibid*, s 7(5), representing a modern statutory warrant for the question posed in the painting by W F Yeames, 'And when did you last see your father?' (1878)—see the front cover.

[182] *Ibid*, s 7(10); see further ch 7.

[183] CSA 1991, s 7(6) and (7).

Multiple Applications

There may be circumstances in which there are competing applications for a maintenance calculation. The primary legislation encapsulates two fundamental rules for dealing with such scenarios. First, if there is more than one person with care, and not all have parental responsibility, then any person with care but *without* parental responsibility is barred from applying for a maintenance calculation.[184] For example, if a child is cared for both by her mother and a grandparent then only the former may apply for child support, assuming that the latter lacks parental responsibility.[185] The second basic rule is that 'where more than one application for a maintenance calculation is made with respect to the child concerned, only one of them may be proceeded with'.[186] Where two or more applications are made, their priority order is determined in accordance with regulations.[187] Clearly the decision on which application is processed cannot change who is liable to pay child support or the amount of the ensuing maintenance calculation. It will, however, determine who can withdraw the application or request a cancellation of such a calculation.[188]

The relevant statutory provisions distinguish between situations in which there is already a maintenance calculation in force and cases where no such determination applies. In the former case, and assuming that the new application concerns the same person with care, non-resident parent and qualifying child(ren), then the position is clear: 'that [new] application shall not be proceeded with'.[189] Instead, any change must be effected by way of revision or supersession of (or appeal against) the existing maintenance calculation.

The position is less straightforward where there are multiple applications but no extant maintenance calculation. On the assumption that the Secretary of State does not receive requests to cease acting in respect of all the applications bar one,[190] the following principles apply. In the first place, the rules differ according to whether the multiple applications are made by the same person or by different individuals. If the same person makes two applications under section 4, or alternatively two applications under section 6, then they are treated as a single application.[191] If the same person makes one application under section 4 and one

---

[184] *Ibid*, s 5(1).

[185] Grandparents, of course, do not have parental responsibility as regards their grandchildren simply by virtue of their status, however much actual care they provide. But, as with other third parties, they may acquire parental responsibility under the Children Act 1989, eg by appointment as a guardian or through obtaining a residence order.

[186] CSA 1991, s 5(2).

[187] Child Support (Maintenance Calculation Procedure) Regulations 2000 (SI 2001/157), reg 4 and sch 2, made under CSA 1991, s 5(3). Note also sch 3 which deals with multiple applications in transitional cases; see further *CCS/3868/2004*.

[188] Hadwen and Pawling, n 45 above, at 55.

[189] SI 2000/157, sch 2, para 4.

[190] *Ibid*, reg 4(2).

[191] *Ibid*, sch 2, para 1(1).

under section 6, then they are treated as a single section 6 application, assuming she still falls within that provision, failing which they will be treated as a single section 4 application.[192] Similarly, if a child in Scotland makes multiple applications under section 7 in relation to the same parents, they are again treated as a single application.[193] The statutory provisions are inevitably more complex where the applications are made by different persons.[194] The general rule is that an application for a maintenance calculation by a person with care takes priority over one made either by a non-resident parent or by a child in Scotland under section 7, and an application by a non-resident parent—in the absence of one by a person with care—takes priority over one under section 7.[195] If there are competing applications by children under section 7, the application by the elder or eldest child takes precedence.[196] If there are two non-resident parents and they both apply for a maintenance calculation, they are treated as a single application.[197]

The rules become still more convoluted where there is more than one person with care. First, the Secretary of State accords priority to a section 6 application by a parent with care in the event that a person with care with parental responsibility makes an application under section 4.[198] Secondly, if two (or more) persons with care with parental responsibility apply under section 4, then the Secretary of State will act on the application by the person with care who is not treated as the non-resident parent under the shared care rules for the purposes of making a maintenance calculation.[199] Finally, in any other circumstance involving multiple applications in a case with more than one person with care, the application from the adult who receives child benefit for the child or children takes priority. If that test does not produce an answer, the Secretary of State will act on the application from the person who is regarded as the principal provider of day to day care.[200]

If multiple applications are treated as a single application under the rules described in the previous paragraph, the relevant effective date is the date of the first such application. Moreover, the single application is to be treated as one for all the qualifying children mentioned in all the applications (even if they do not all appear in each such application).[201]

---

[192] SI 2001/157, sch 2, para 1(2).

[193] *Ibid*, para 2.

[194] See *ibid*, para 3. This all assumes no calculation has already been made in relation to any one application; if it has, then that determines the matter.

[195] *Ibid*, para 3(2)–(4). See further *CCS/3868/2004*, dealing with the parallel rule in SI 2001/157, sch 3 para 3(2).

[196] *Ibid*, para 3(5).

[197] *Ibid*, para 3(6).

[198] *Ibid*, para 3(7).

[199] *Ibid*, para 3(8).

[200] *Ibid*, para 3(9)–(11). If the same person doe s not provide the principal day to day care for all the children concerned, separate maintenance calculations are to be made: *ibid*, para 3(13). Day to day care has the same meaning as in SI 2001/155 for these purposes: *ibid*, para 3(14) and see pp 245–48.

[201] SI 2001/157, reg 4(3); see also *ibid*, sch 2, para 3(12). This is subject to the exception in para 3(13), discussed in the previous note.

Amendment, Withdrawal or Cancellation of Applications

Amendment or Withdrawal by the Applicant

A private applicant (or a child applicant in Scotland) may amend or withdraw an effective maintenance application at any time before a maintenance calculation is made.[202] Any such request need not be in writing, unless the Secretary of State so directs. Moreover, as has been described above, such an applicant can ask the Secretary of State to cease acting on an application for child support maintenance at any time (for example, as regards collection) and the Agency is bound to act on that request.[203]

There is no statutory provision for parents with care on benefit to amend their application, presumably because they are in any event deemed to make an application. They also, however, have the right to opt out, just as private clients do;[204] again, there is no requirement for such a request to be put in writing.[205] The difference, of course, is that the claimant on benefit runs the risk of being subject to a reduced benefit decision, whereas the private client can simply elect to walk away.

Withdrawal or Cancellation by the Secretary of State

There are three situations where the Secretary of State may decide to withdraw or cancel a maintenance application.

(i) Where a Private Client Fails to Provide Information

A maintenance application under either section 4 or 7 which is 'effective' within the terms of the regulations must be referred for a decision under section 11, even if that decision is not to make a maintenance calculation.[206] The mere fact that, for example, the non-resident parent has failed to provide the necessary financial information is no reason for the Agency not to act. Decision makers may seek the information elsewhere (eg from an employer) or make a reasonable estimate of income if precise figures are not available.[207] However, if the parent with care in a private case fails to provide sufficient information for the case to get beyond first base, the Agency's view seems to be that it may withdraw or cancel the application.

---

[202] SI 2001/157, reg 3(6). The PWC may, for example, wish to amend by withdrawing one child from the application (see eg *CCS/8065/1995*). Any amendment cannot relate to a change of circumstances occurring after the effective date (SI 2001/157, reg 3(7))—that would need an application for a revision or supersession.

[203] CSA 1991, ss 4(5)–(6) and 7(6)–(7).

[204] *Ibid*, s 6(5).

[205] Indeed, s 6(5) specifically states that such a request 'need not be in writing'.

[206] See the discussion above at p 278.

[207] *R(CS) 2/98* para 21 *per* Mr Commissioner Rowland.

(ii) Where a Benefit Claim is Refused or Ceases

We have already seen that if a parent with care in receipt of benefit is treated as making an application for child support by virtue of section 6(3), but that claim for benefit is refused or any award ceases before a maintenance calculation is made, then the Secretary of State must stop treating the parent as having applied.[208] Once a maintenance calculation has been made, it does not automatically end if the claimant later stops receiving benefit. She may, however, ask the Secretary of State to cease acting.[209]

(iii) Where the Qualifying Child Dies

If a maintenance application is made in respect of a single qualifying child, and that child dies before a maintenance calculation is made, the Secretary of State necessarily no longer has any jurisdiction to act.[210] He must therefore treat the application as not having been made.[211] If the application is made in respect of two or more children, it may of course proceed in respect of the remaining child or children.[212] Similarly, if the Secretary of State has already made a maintenance calculation in relation to an only child, and that child dies, the calculation ceases to have effect. Where the calculation relates to two or more children, the death of one is a ground for superseding the assessment on the basis of a change in circumstances.

Information and Evidence Gathering Powers

Introduction

We saw above that the Secretary of State has powers to make rules governing the provision of information by those applying (or treated as applying) for a maintenance calculation.[213] Such powers are confined to the provision of *information* which is required to identify or trace the non-resident parent, to calculate his liability and to recover the amount assessed.[214] The 1991 Act also vests the Secretary of State with a broad regulation-making power governing the provision of information *or evidence* which may be needed to make decisions taken under the Act.[215] The distinction between 'information' and 'evidence' is not defined under the Act

---

[208] CSA 1991, s 11(3); but the application may then be treated as a s 4 application: *ibid*, s 11(4) and p 264 above.

[209] CSA 1991, s 6(9)—see p 264 above.

[210] Given that a parent's liability under s 1(1) assumes the existence of a qualifying child.

[211] SI 2001/157, reg 6.

[212] *Ibid*, reg 6(1)(b).

[213] See p 264.

[214] CSA 1991, ss 4(4), 6(7) and 7(5).

[215] *Ibid*, s 14.

or in the regulations. In principle, the difference is straightforward: 'information is what the Secretary of State needs to know and evidence is the documentary or other proof of it'.[216] For example, 'the amount of wages is information and the wage slip that proves those wages is the evidence'.[217] The Act also makes provision for the disclosure of information *by* the Secretary of State[218] (in practice, of course, Agency staff) and for the disclosure of information held by HMRC (formerly the Inland Revenue) to the Secretary of State.[219] The principal regulations are the Child Support (Information, Evidence and Disclosure) Regulations 1992.[220]

Part II of those Regulations makes detailed provision for the furnishing of information or evidence. Regulations 2 and 3 specify, albeit by virtue of some highly convoluted drafting, both the persons under such a duty and the purposes for which such information or evidence may be required. Where such a duty applies, the person concerned must 'furnish such information or evidence' as relates to a relevant matter and 'which is in his possession or which he can reasonably be expected to acquire'.[221] Where the Secretary of State seeks such information or evidence, the request must spell out the possible consequences of a failure to comply, including details of the criminal offences of failing to provide information or providing false information.[222] Those who are asked to provide information or evidence must ensure it is 'furnished as soon as is reasonably practicable in the particular circumstances of the case'.[223] The normal court rules relating to confidentiality, inspection of documents and the disclosure of addresses are no ground for refusing to provide information to the Secretary of State; there is no need to seek the court's permission.[224]

Persons under a Duty to Provide Information or Evidence

The regulations specify ten discrete categories of potential informants (listed below). Other individuals—for example, friends, neighbours or landlords—may volunteer information to the Agency but cannot be required to do so unless they

---

[216] Jacobs and Douglas, n 36 above, at 62.

[217] *Ibid*; but as Jacobs and Douglas observe, a strict adherence to this approach may cause problems in that CSA 1991 s 50 only authorises the disclosure in certain circumstances (eg to appeal tribunals) of 'information' (but not the underlying 'evidence').

[218] CSA 1991, s 14(3).

[219] *Ibid*, s 14(4) and sch 2.

[220] SI 1992/1812. See also the Social Security (Claims and Information) Regulations 1999 (SI 1999/3108).

[221] SI 1992/1812, reg 2(1). The material must be required by the Secretary of State in order to make a decision under CSA 1991, ss 11 (maintenance calculations), 12 (default and interim decisions), 16 (revisions) or 17 (supersessions). 'Relevant persons' and court officials are under a parallel duty when the Agency is deciding about the recovery or enforcement of child support: SI 1992/1812, reg 2(1A).

[222] SI 1992/1812, reg 3A: on these criminal offences, see CSA 1991, s 14A and below p 293.

[223] SI 1992/1812, reg 5. On the meaning of 'furnish', see by analogy *Hayman v Griffiths* [1987] 3 WLR 1125 (VAT returns sent by post did not arrive—no failure to 'furnish').

[224] Family Proceedings Rules 1991 (SI 1991/1247), r 10.21A (as inserted by Family Proceedings (Amendment) Rules 1993 (SI 1993/295) r 5).

fall within one of these ten categories. The precise scope of the duty to provide information or evidence varies according to the status of the person to whom the request is made. Department for Work and Pensions investigators carrying out their general social security functions have much more extensive powers, including the ability to require information to be supplied by eg banks, credit reference agencies, mobile phone companies and utility companies.[225] The fact that these broader powers are not available to the Agency suggests that government does not attach the same priority to child support evasion as, for example, to combating benefit fraud. It may also reflect the political sensitivity of child support matters.

The assumption underlying the statutory framework governing the duty to provide information is that people will not voluntarily and willingly supply the Agency with relevant material. In many cases that assumption will be well-founded. However, the emotions generated by relationship breakdown are such that in some cases a parent (or his or her associates) will be only too eager to 'dish the dirt' on the other partner.[226] In this context it should be noted that, applying analogous social security case law, defamatory statements made to the Agency might give rise to a libel action, subject to a defence of qualified privilege.[227]

The ten categories of individuals who may be subject to a duty to provide information or evidence are as follows.

(i) Relevant Persons

'Relevant persons' include both the person with care and the non-resident parent (or a parent who is treated as a non-resident parent under the shared care rules).[228] These individuals are obviously central to the maintenance calculation process, and are accordingly subject to the widest information and evidence gathering powers.[229] The regulations set out the various purposes for which such material may be required (eg to make various decisions under the Act, to identify and trace the non-resident parent, to calculate the amount of child support

---

[225] See SSAA 1992, s 109B. The House of Commons Work and Pensions Committee recommended that utility companies be under a statutory duty to disclose NRPs' contact details: see *The Performance of the Child Support Agency*, Second Report of Session 2004–05 (HC 44-I), vol I, para 177.

[226] Any such disclosure might, in some circumstances, involve a breach of a professional code of practice, the data protection legislation or conceivably a civil contract: Hadwen and Pawling, n 45 above, at 89–90.

[227] *Purdew & Purdew v Seress-Smith* [1993] IRLR 77, QBD. Thus a plaintiff would have to prove actual malice in the production and publication of the libel. Statements made to a tribunal would be protected by absolute privilege. On the other hand, in *M v BBC* [1997] 1 FLR 51 Hale J held that the Administration of Justice Act 1960, s 12 could not be used to protect the privacy of an NRP who objected to the disclosure of his infertility by his ex-wife and an Agency official in a television documentary.

[228] And, in Scotland, a child who applies under section 7 of the 1991 Act: SI 1992/1812, reg 1(2). A maintenance application must also have been applied for (or treated as such) or be in force.

[229] *Ibid*, reg 2(2)(a).

payable, etc).[230] They also set out a non-exhaustive list of examples of the types of information or evidence which may be sought.[231] These include:

> the parties' habitual residence; their name and address and marital status; the child's name, address, date of birth and current education; the identity of those with parental responsibility over the child; matters relevant to determining paternity; the name and address of the non-resident parent's employer; the non-resident parent's earnings and other income; amounts payable under court orders or maintenance agreements; details of those living in the same household as the non-resident parent and their relationship to him; the non-resident parent's bank or building society account details.

In this way the regulations impose restrictions on the *purposes* for which information and evidence may be requested but not on the *types* of such material that may be sought.[232] It should also be noted that persons with care are under a continuing duty of disclosure in certain respects.[233] No such ongoing obligation applies to non-resident parents; for example, rather surprisingly, they are under no obligation to inform the Agency of any change in address, although the House of Commons Work and Pensions Committee has recommended that parents be under a statutory duty to inform the Agency of any such change.[234]

(ii) Alleged Fathers

Men who deny that they are the father of the child in question can only be required to provide information or evidence about their habitual residence or which is needed to identify the non-resident parent.[235] Logically this means that the Agency should not request the person's employment details unless and until parentage has been established.[236]

(iii) Employers

The non-resident parent's current or recent employer may be required to provide information or evidence for the purpose of identifying or tracing the non-resident parent, calculating or recovering his child support liability (including interest), recovering court-ordered child maintenance or deciding whether to pursue a

---

[230] *Ibid*, reg 3(1)(a)–(l).

[231] *Ibid*, reg 3(2).

[232] Hadwen and Pawling, n 45 above, at 88 (but note the considerable latitude allowed by SI 1992/1812, reg 3(1)).

[233] *Ibid*, reg 6.

[234] n 225 above, para 177. A duty to notify changes of address may be imposed in private law proceedings: see Domestic Proceedings and Magistrates' Courts Act 1978, s 32(3) and Children Act 1989, sch 1, para 12. See also, in Australia, Child Support (Registration and Collection) Act 1988 (Cth), s 111.

[235] *Ibid*, regs (2)(2)(b) (which is expressed in gender-neutral terms, but in practice applies to men) and 3(1)(b) and (d).

[236] Hadwen and Pawling, n 45 above, at 90.

liability order, charging order or garnishee proceedings.[237] The legislation provides no clue as to what is meant by a 'recent' employer but presumably a degree of common sense needs to be applied. The current or recent employer of a person alleged to be a parent may be required to provide information to identify and trace the non-resident parent.[238] The same requirements apply where the Crown is the employer.[239]

(iv) Accountants

The non-resident parent's current and any previous accountants may be required to provide information or evidence relating to his business accounts. This must be connected with either tracing him or calculating, recovering or enforcing his child support liability.[240]

(v) Companies and Partnerships

Any company or partnership for which the non-resident parent has worked on a self-employed basis can be required to disclose information or evidence to assist in tracing him or in assessing his liability.[241]

(vi) Department for Work and Pension offices

Any DWP office can pass on social security information—eg personal details held on its Departmental Central Index—to the Agency.[242] It is unclear whether this extends to information obtained by the DWP in the course of its general social security work from other sources—eg banks or credit reference agencies.

(vii) Local Authorities

Local authorities[243] can be asked to supply information or evidence to assist the Agency to determine whether there is a 'relevant person' (this could involve ascertaining a person's habitual residence or a child's educational status), to identify or trace a non-resident parent, to calculate or recover a child support liability or to

---

[237] SI 1992/1812, regs 2(2)(c) and 3(1)(d)–(f), (h), (hh) and (j).

[238] *Ibid*, regs 2(2)(ba) and 3(1)(d) and (e).

[239] *Ibid*, reg 2(2)(c) and (cd). See further below for the special case of Prison Service and DVLA employees.

[240] *Ibid*, regs 2(2)(f) and 3(e)–(f) and (h)–(hh).

[241] *Ibid*, regs 2(2)(g) and 3(e) and (f).

[242] Social Security Act 1998, s 3(1) and (2).

[243] The local authority must be one in which a 'relevant person' or alleged father either resides or has resided.

decide on further enforcement action.[244] It follows that the Agency may require a local authority to pass on details about a person's bank account if that individual is claiming housing benefit or council tax benefit.[245]

(viii) Her Majesty's Revenue and Customs (HMRC)

HMRC has a long and jealously-guarded tradition of confidentiality in its dealings with tax payers. The general principle is that information which a tax payer discloses to HMRC cannot be passed on to other government agencies. Indeed, both the staff and judiciary involved in tax matters must take an oath of secrecy.[246] However, the 1991 Act originally provided for a limited exception to this general rule where the information was required in order to trace either the current address or employer of the non-resident parent.[247] In itself, this provision did not permit HMRC to disclose other information, eg relating to the non-resident parent's income.[248] However, subsequent legislation now authorises a much more extensive flow of information from the HMRC to the Agency. To some extent these changes merely reflected the transfer of various benefit functions from the DWP (or its predecessor, the DSS) to HMRC, and so simply preserved existing information flows across the new departmental boundaries. Thus HMRC must, on request, pass on any information to the Agency which it holds relating to national insurance contributions, statutory sick pay or statutory maternity pay,[249] statutory paternity pay or statutory adoption pay,[250] or regarding a claim for a tax credit, child benefit or guardian's allowance claim.[251] The power to require the transfer of information about contributions inevitably means that the Agency can obtain the earnings information recorded on employers' end-of-year returns.[252] But, more significantly, the Agency can also now require the tax authorities to provide details on non-resident parents' self-employed incomes.[253]

---

[244] SI 1992/1812, regs 2(2)(d) and 3(1)(a), (d)–(f), (h) and (hh). The breadth of this provision probably explains the repeal of CSA 1991, sch 1 para 2 by SSA 1998, sch 7, para 49.

[245] See also SSAA 1992, s 122D, extended to include child support by SSA 1998, s 3(3).

[246] Taxes Management Act 1970, s 6 and sch 1 requires those involved in the tax system to make a declaration of confidentiality; see also Finance Act 1989, s 182 and Commissioners for Revenue and Customs Act 2005, ss 17–23.

[247] CSA 1991, s 14(4) and sch 2, para 1.

[248] Bird argues that para 1, once it applies, enables the Agency to go wider and seek information on the non-resident parent's income: R Bird, *Child Support—The New Law* (Family Law, Bristol, 5th edn, 2002) at 25. This view, however, is inconsistent with both the object of the statutory provision and the Lord Chancellor's assurance given at the Committee stage of the Bill: *Hansard* HL Debates vol 527 col 583 (19 March 1991).

[249] SSAA 1992, s 121E; this also covers information gathered under Part III of the Pension Schemes Act 1993.

[250] Employment Act 2002, s 13.

[251] Tax Credits Act 2002, sch 5, para 4. The total annual cost incurred by the Revenue in providing information to the Agency is in the order of £165,000, which the Agency reimburses: *Hansard* HC Debates vol 380 col 1034W (25 February 2002).

[252] In practice the Agency will ordinarily seek such information direct from the employer.

[253] CSA 1991, sch 2, para 1A, inserted by Welfare Reform and Pensions Act 1999, s 80.

(ix) Court Officials

Court officials[254] may be required to provide information about relevant court proceedings[255] or which may help in calculating or recovering child support maintenance.[256]

(x) Prison Service and DVLA

Prison Service officials and DVLA employees can be required to provide information to assist in tracing a non-resident parent.[257] However, the Service Level Agreement between the Agency and DVLA limits the Agency to a maximum of just 70 requests for information a month.[258]

The Consequences of Non-compliance

Neither section 14 of the 1991 Act nor the Child Support (Information, Evidence and Disclosure) Regulations 1992 includes a single portmanteau sanction for non-compliance with the duty to provide information or evidence.[259] The consequences of failing to comply depend very much on the status of the person who fails to provide the information or evidence and the attitude taken by the Agency to that failure. In general terms, the Agency may simply seek to acquire the information required from some other source, using its extensive powers described above. As was seen in the previous chapter, non-compliance by the parent with care may lead to the Agency simply abandoning any attempt to make a maintenance calculation (in a private case) or imposing a reduced benefit decision (in a section 6 case). If it is the non-resident parent who is not cooperating, the Agency may proceed to make a default maintenance decision.[260] The Agency's practice is not to draw adverse inferences from non-cooperation,[261] but appeal tribunals may well take a more robust approach. More exceptionally, and irrespective of the status of the non-compliant party, the Agency may decide in cases of more serious non-compliance to take firmer action by sending in an inspector to obtain the information and/or by bringing a prosecution under section 14A (as to both of which, see further below).[262]

---

[254] As defined by SI 1992/1812, reg 2(3). See also SI 1991/1247, r 10.21A.
[255] eg about child maintenance or parental responsibility.
[256] SI 1992/1812, regs 2(2)(e) and 3(1)(aa)–(ab), (g)–(h) and (k).
[257] *Ibid*, regs 2(2)(h) and 3(1)(e).
[258] *Hansard* HC Debates vol 441 col 1555W (19 January 2006).
[259] Jacobs and Douglas, n 36 above, at 63.
[260] CSA 1991, s 12.
[261] Jacobs and Douglas, n 36 above, at 63.
[262] *Ibid*, also noting the (largely theoretical) possibility of the Secretary of State taking enforcement action under SSAA 1992, ss 105 or 106.

Disclosure by the Agency

The previous section has considered issues relating to the provision of information and evidence *to* the Agency. But what provisions govern the disclosure of such material *by* the Agency? The general principle is that information is held by the Agency in confidence and subject to the provisions of the data protection legislation. There are, however, several more specific provisions. First, the Agency may disclose any information to a tribunal or court in relation to proceedings brought under the 1991 Act or the social security legislation.[263] Analogously, the Agency may disclose information to a court when the latter is exercising its functions in relation to a maintenance order or agreement.[264] This principle is also reflected in the data protection legislation, which exempts personal data from the non-disclosure provisions in the context of legal proceedings.[265] Secondly, the Agency has statutory authority to disclose information about one party[266] to a maintenance calculation to another party where it is necessary to do so in order to explain any one of a range of specified types of decision which it has made.[267] Indeed, 'the rules of natural justice require that the information needed to explain the end product is communicated to both parties in a maintenance assessment'.[268] However, a party's address and the identity of any third party (eg a new partner) must not be disclosed in the absence of the party's written consent.[269] Despite these provisions, the Agency has tended to adopt a much more rigid approach, typified by its insistence on 'blanking out' names, addresses and other identifying details of individuals in the case papers that are forwarded to appeal tribunals and the Commissioners.[270] Finally, unauthorised disclosure of information held by the Agency is a criminal offence (see further below).

Inspectors

The 1991 Act makes provision for child support inspectors to be appointed, typically as a means of obtaining information where other methods have proved

---

[263] SI 1992/1812, reg 8(1) and (2).

[264] *Ibid*, reg 8(3).

[265] Data Protection Act 1984, s 34 and Data Protection Act 1998, s 35.

[266] Defined to mean a 'relevant person' (see above), an appointee or a personal representative of a deceased party: SI 1992/1812, reg 9A(3).

[267] *Ibid*, reg 9A(1). These decisions relate to matters such as the making of (or decision not to make) the calculation and decisions in connection with collection and enforcement. A party may make a written application for such information (*ibid*, reg 9A(3)) although such a request is not a precondition for disclosure by the Agency.

[268] *Huxley v Child Support Commissioner* [2000] 1 FLR 898 at 906 *per* Hale LJ.

[269] SI 1992/1812, reg 9A(4).

[270] A practice which has prompted much judicial irritation, especially amongst the Commissioners: see eg *R(CS) 3/06*.

unsuccessful. During the passage of the original 1991 legislation considerable concern was expressed in Parliament at the potentially wide scope of the inspectors' powers. In practice these powers were rarely used in the first decade of the scheme's operation, principally because the 1991 Act, as originally enacted, did not permit inspectors to be appointed for an extended period; they had to be appointed 'in a particular case',[271] ie on a case-by-case basis. This made it difficult to build up a corps of trained and experienced inspectors. Amendments made by the 2000 Act now enable inspectors to be appointed 'on such terms as [the Secretary of State] thinks fit', so that appointments are no longer tied to individual cases.[272] These inspectors' powers are, in broad terms, modelled on those that apply to DWP investigators generally.[273]

The inspectors' function is 'to acquire information which the Secretary of State needs for any of the purposes of' the 1991 Act.[274] An inspector has the power to enter any premises[275] which are not solely residential and which the inspector has reasonable grounds for suspecting are premises on which the non-resident parent works as an employee or self-employed person.[276] The power of entry also extends to premises at which a third party may have information about the non-resident parent acquired in the course of the third party's own work.[277] It must also be reasonable for inspectors to require entry in order to carry out their functions.[278] Inspectors are required to produce their certificates of appointment on request.[279] Once on the premises, an inspector may question any adult found there[280] and require any such person to 'furnish . . . all such information and documents as the inspector may reasonably require'.[281] Inspectors have no powers to effect a forcible entry, to search either the premises or persons on the premises or indeed to detain people for questioning. However, those who refuse to co-operate with inspectors exercising their powers may well be committing a criminal offence.[282]

---

[271] CSA 1991, s 15(1) as originally enacted.

[272] *Ibid*, s 15(1) as amended by CSPSSA 2000, s 14(2). Tribunals may *suggest* but cannot *direct* the Secretary of State to appoint an inspector: *CCS/13988/1996* at para 7 *per* Mr Commissioner Howell QC. See also *CSC 1/99*.

[273] See generally SSAA 1992, ss 109A–109C. But, as noted above, the Agency's powers to require third parties to disclose information about NRPs is much more limited.

[274] CSA 1991, s 15(2). As Jacobs and Douglas observe (n 36 above at 66), the information/evidence confusion persists in this statutory context.

[275] As defined broadly in CSA 1991, s 15(11).

[276] *Ibid*, s 15(4)(a) and (4A)(a) and (b). So where the business is run from the kitchen table, an inspector may enter the whole premises; but if the non-resident parent lives in a flat over a shop, the inspector may enter only the shop: Jacobs and Douglas, n 36 above, at 66.

[277] CSA 1991, s 15(4A)(c). Inspectors may also enter any Crown premises for the same purposes: *ibid*, s 57(2) and (3). Quaintly, this is 'subject to Her Majesty not being in residence', SI 1992/1812, reg 7.

[278] CSA 1991, s 15(4)(b).

[279] *Ibid*, s 15(8).

[280] *Ibid*, s 15(5), subject to the right not to incriminate oneself or one's spouse: *ibid*, s 15(7).

[281] *Ibid*, s 15(6).

[282] There is protection against self-incrimination which extends to spouses and civil partners: *ibid*, s 15(7).

Criminal Offences

The 1991 Act provides for three categories of criminal offences in connection with assessing maintenance under the child support scheme.[283] These are concerned with, first, knowingly making false statements or representations (or failing to provide information); secondly, delaying, obstructing or otherwise impeding Agency inspectors; and, thirdly, the unauthorised disclosure of confidential information. The first two types of offence are directed towards the Agency's clientele and their advisers, whilst the last is a sanction for misconduct by the Agency's own staff or by those involved in the appeals process.

Knowingly Making False statements or Representations (or Failing to Provide Information)

One of the major problems faced by the Agency under the original 1991 scheme (as now) was that of non-compliance by non-resident parents in the assessment process. In particular, non-resident parents could disrupt the process by failing to supply the information required to complete a maintenance assessment, or indeed by supplying incorrect information. The Agency's response to such tactics was to impose interim maintenance assessments,[284] which normally involved fixing child support at a much higher rate than would otherwise be the case. However, this strategy rebounded on the Agency as such assessments effectively became impossible to enforce in the face of widespread non-compliance.[285] The absence of a specific criminal offence of misrepresentation in child support law, unlike in the social security jurisdiction, was identified as a weakness in the original statutory regime.[286]

Consequently, and since the implementation of the 2000 reforms,[287] it is an offence under section 14A(2) of the 1991 Act either knowingly to make a false statement or representation or to provide—or knowingly to cause or allow to be provided—a document or other information which the person knows to be false in a material particular.[288] This summary offence, which is only committed if the false statement or provision of false information is made 'pursuant to a request for information' under the relevant regulations, is modelled very closely on that of making false representations for the purposes of obtaining social security

---

[283] It is also an offence for an employer to fail to comply with a deduction of earnings order: see below p 449.

[284] Under the original CSA 1991, s 12.

[285] A new CSA 1991, s 12 has now been substituted by CSPSSA 2000, s 4.

[286] DSS Benefit Fraud Inspectorate, *Securing Child Support* (July 1999), para 4.19.

[287] These provisions came into force on 31 January 2001.

[288] This offence may only be committed by those who are required to comply with regulations made under CSA 1991, ss 4(4) or 7(5) or those who are specified in regulations made under s 14(1)(a): see s 14A(1). On 'knowingly' see *Flintshire CC v Reynolds* [2006] EWHC 195 (Admin).

benefits.[289] That being so, the provision should presumably be construed in the same way. It should therefore follow that the person's motive for making the false statement is immaterial.[290] The maximum penalty is a fine at Level 3 on the standard scale.[291] In addition, section 14A(3) provides for an offence of omission as well as commission: thus a person 'is guilty of an offence if, following such a request [for information], he fails to comply with it', subject to a defence of 'reasonable excuse',[292] a term which is not defined in the legislation.[293] Prosecutions under section 14A(3) (failing to provide information) are much more common than under section 14A(2) (making false statements).[294]

Delaying or Obstructing Agency Inspectors

The offence of intentionally delaying or obstructing an inspector mirrors a parallel provision in the social security field[295] and is triable only in the magistrates' court.[296] Similarly, it is also a summary offence, when required to do so by an inspector, to refuse or neglect to answer any question, or furnish any information, or produce any document.[297] This latter offence is again subject to a defence of 'reasonable excuse'. In relation to both types of offence the maximum penalty is a fine not exceeding Level 3 on the standard scale. As at January 2006, no prosecutions had been brought under this section since the inception of the Agency in 1993.[298]

Unauthorised Disclosure

Finally, in certain circumstances the unauthorised disclosure of information by Agency staff and others without lawful authority is an offence under the 1991 Act.[299] The maximum penalty for this offence is two years' imprisonment (following con-

---

[289] SSAA 1992, s 112. The only difference in drafting is that the SSAA 1992 offence applies where a claimant 'produces or furnishes' a false document, whereas the CSA 1991 provision refers to 'provides'. It is difficult to see that any change in meaning is intended.

[290] See *Clear v Smith* [1981] 1 WLR 399 and *Barrass v Reeve* [1980] 3 All ER 705.

[291] In contrast the social security offence under SSAA 1992 is punishable by three months' imprisonment and/or a fine not exceeding Level 5: *ibid*, s 112(2).

[292] CSA 1991, s 14A(4).

[293] In the context of investigations in the banking industry, it has been held that neither the fear of self-incrimination nor the existence of a court injunction prohibiting disclosure of the documents in question amounts to a 'reasonable excuse', *Bank of England v Riley* [1992] Ch 475, CA, and *A v B Bank (Governor and Company of Bank of England intervening)* [1992] 3 WLR 705. But see also CSA 1991, s 15(7).

[294] Between January and October 2005 there were 4 prosecutions under s 14A(2) (and 4 convictions) as against 309 under s 14A(3) (with 302 convictions): *Hansard* HC Debates vol 441 col 1366W (18 January 2006).

[295] SSAA 1992, s 111.

[296] CSA 1991, s 15(9)(a).

[297] *Ibid*, s 15(9)(b).

[298] *Hansard* HC Debates vol 441 col 1366W (18 January 2006).

[299] CSA 1991, s 50.

viction in the Crown Court) or, in the event of conviction in the magistrates' court, six months' imprisonment or a fine not exceeding the statutory maximum.[300] The categories of person who may commit this offence are specified in primary and secondary legislation. They include tribunal clerks, tribunal administrative staff and civil servants carrying out functions under the 1991 Act.[301] Regulations extend the scope of this provision to include the Comptroller and Auditor General, National Audit Office staff, the Parliamentary Commissioner for Administration (or Ombudsman), the Health Service equivalents, their various administrative staff and contractors for the Department.[302] It follows that the offence cannot be committed by a judicial member of the Appeals Service (or, of course, a Child Support Commissioner). It is not entirely clear whether the staff of the Independent Case Examiner's (ICE) office are covered by this provision. They are civil servants, but it is questionable whether they are 'carrying out . . . any functions' under the 1991 Act,[303] given that they are responsible for an extra-statutory complaints monitoring system.

The offence itself is committed where such an individual, without lawful authority, discloses any information which relates to a particular person and was acquired by him or her in the course of their employment.[304] In principle, such a disclosure will be criminal if made in any form and to any third party. However, it is expressly provided that no offence is committed where the person concerned either discloses information in summary form, such that information relating to any particular individual cannot be identified, or discloses information which has previously been disclosed to the public with lawful authority.[305] Furthermore, it is a defence for the person to show that he or she 'believed that he was making the disclosure in question with lawful authority' or 'believed that the information in question had previously been disclosed to the public with lawful authority', in both instances providing he or she 'had no reasonable cause to believe otherwise'.[306]

It follows that the concept of 'lawful authority' is central to the definition of this offence—the crime is only committed where the disclosure is without such authority and the employee has a defence where he or she believes she has lawful authority or that the information has previously been released with such authority. According to the legislation, 'a disclosure is to be regarded as made with lawful authority if, and only if, it is made' in one of the following five circumstances:[307]

---

[300] *Ibid*, s 50(4).

[301] *Ibid*, s 50(5). The statute also still refers to the Chief Child Support Officer and child support officers but these functions were abolished by SSA 1998.

[302] SI 1992/1812 reg 11, which still refers to contractors for the (now non-existent) 'Department of Social Security'—this provision was, apparently by oversight, not updated by the Secretaries of State for Education and Skills and for Work and Pensions Order 2002 (SI 2002/1397).

[303] As required by CSA 1991, s 50(5)(e).

[304] *Ibid*, s 50(1).

[305] *Ibid*, s 50(2).

[306] *Ibid*, s 50(3).

[307] *Ibid*, s 50(6).

(a) by a civil servant in accordance with his official duty

There is no legislative definition of the concept of a civil servant's 'official duty' for these purposes.[308] However, the term should not simply be read as synonymous with 'statutory duty'. In *Huxley v Child Support Commissioner*[309] the Agency imposed an interim maintenance assessment on a non-resident parent who refused to disclose his housing costs and his second wife's income in the absence of an undertaking by the Agency that it would not disclose such information to his first wife. The non-resident parent argued that the Agency's statutory obligation[310] was such that it need only disclose the outcome of the assessment to his first wife, and not these intermediate stages in that calculation. The Court of Appeal rejected this argument. Hale LJ held that the statutory provision governing notification of assessments merely specified the minimum information which had to be supplied; natural justice required more to explain the basis for an assessment.[311]

(b) by any other person either—

    (i)   for the purposes of the function in the exercise of which he holds the information and without contravening any restriction duly imposed by the responsible person; or

    (ii) to, or in accordance with an authorisation duly given by, the responsible person

The 'responsible person' in this context is a reference to the Lord Chancellor, the Secretary of State or any person authorised by them to act for these purposes.[312]

(c) in accordance with any enactment or order of a court

Neither this nor the following provision empowers a court to direct the Secretary of State or to give leave to the Agency to disclose information to an interested third party. Thus in *Re C (A Minor) (Child Support Agency: Disclosure)*[313] Ewbank J held that he could not use section 50 of the 1991 Act to order the Agency to disclose a non-resident father's address to the man's 17 year old son, who was trying to re-establish contact with his father.[314]

(d) for the purpose of instituting, or otherwise for the purposes of, any proceedings before a court or before any tribunal or other body or person mentioned in this Act

---

[308] But see *X v Commissioner of Police of the Metropolis* [1985] 1 WLR 420 on disclosure in course of 'official duties' in the context of the Rehabilitation of Offenders Act 1974, s 9.

[309] [2000] 1 FLR 898.

[310] Under the then Child Support (Maintenance Assessment Procedure) Regulations 1992 (SI 1992/1813), reg 10(2); see now SI 2001/157, reg 23.

[311] n 268 above.

[312] CSA 1991, s 50(7).

[313] [1995] 1 FLR 201.

[314] However, an alternative route was found by which the court could *request* the Secretary of State (in practice the Agency) to disclose the father's address as the son had commenced proceedings for a contact order under Children Act 1989, s 8: see further *Practice Direction (Disclosure of Addresses: 1989)* [1989] 1 FLR 307; for service personnel, see also *Practice Direction* [1995] 2 FLR 813.

The effect of this provision is that any disclosure made for the purposes of court or tribunal proceedings automatically attracts the 'lawful authority' protection. Indeed, regulations give the Secretary of State express authority to disclose information to courts or tribunals for the purposes of their proceedings.[315]

(e) with the consent of the appropriate person

The 'appropriate person' in this context is defined to mean 'the person to whom the information in question relates', or where that person is mentally incapacitated, the person exercising a power of attorney, the person's mental health appointee or other relevant individual.[316]

[315] SI 2001/1812, reg 8: see above p 291.
[316] CSA 1991, s 50(8), as amended by the Adults with Incapacity (Scotland) Act 2000 (Consequential Modifications) (England, Wales and Northern Ireland) Order 2005 (SI 2005/1790), Art 2.

10

The Child Support Formula

Introduction

This chapter examines the child support formula which applies to new cases since 3 March 2003. The main legislative provisions are to be found in Schedule 1 to the 1991 Act (as amended[1]) and in the Child Support (Maintenance Calculations and Special Cases) Regulations 2000.[2] There are four possible rates which may be used in calculating a non-resident parent's child support liability: a basic rate, a reduced rate, a flat rate and a nil rate. The basic rate is the normal or default rate, but this only applies if none of the other three rates is applicable.[3] In short, the reduced rate is for non-resident parents with weekly net incomes of between £100 and £200, the flat rate for non-resident parents on benefit or with weekly incomes of less than £100 and the nil rate applies to specific categories of non-resident parent against whom recovery of child support is regarded as unrealistic (eg prisoners). The figure produced by whichever rate is applicable—with the obvious exception of the nil rate—may be apportioned if there is more than one person with care in relation to the same non-resident parent.[4] The assessed liability may also be subject to adjustment in instances of shared care. In addition, in some cases the process of calculating the non-resident parent's liability is subject to modification by the 'special cases' rules. This chapter deals with the rules relating to the four rates, shared care and special cases. The vexed question of how the non-resident parent's income itself is calculated for the purposes of the formula is dealt with in the following chapter.

Before examining the detailed rules governing the various rates, four general points about child support calculations should be noted. First, where certain information is relevant to making a maintenance calculation—eg the number of children and whether the non-resident parent is on benefit for the purposes of the flat rate—that information is taken as it stands at the effective date.[5] Other information or amounts (such as benefit rates and earnings) have to be taken into

---

[1] By Child Support Pensions and Social Security Act (CSPSSA) 2000, s 1(3) and sch 1.
[2] SI 2001/155.
[3] CSA 1991, sch 1, para 1(1).
[4] *Ibid*, para 1(2). See further below on both apportionment and shared care.
[5] SI 2001/155, reg 2(5).

account as provided for in the regulations.[6] There is an exception to this principle in that where the Secretary of State becomes aware of a material change of circumstances, which occurs after the relevant week but before the effective date, it must be taken into account.[7] Secondly, the normal rule is that all figures in child support assessments are to be calculated on a weekly basis.[8] Thirdly, any calculations which result in a fraction of a penny are rounded up or down as appropriate.[9] An important exception to this principle is that in calculating both the normal basic rate and the reduced rate of child maintenance, all liabilities are expressed in terms of whole pounds with rounding as appropriate;[10] thus an arithmetical liability of £21.47 a week translates into a legal liability of £21, whereas one of £21.53 is rounded up to £22. The final point to note is that the definitions of 'couple' and 'partner' used in assessing child support liabilities follow those used in social security law.[11]

The Four Rates

The Basic Rate

The basic rate is payable where none of the nil, flat and reduced rates apply.[12] Given the current thresholds, this means that the basic rate applies to all non-resident parents who have a net weekly income of £200 a week or more (as determined in accordance with the principles discussed in the next chapter).[13] However, the non-resident parent's net weekly income is subject to a cap of £2,000 (or £104,000 net per annum).[14] If the non-resident parent's income exceeds this level, the parent with care may be able to apply to the court for a 'top-up' order.[15] The parent with care's income is irrelevant to the basic rate formula calculation.[16]

The basic rate is a percentage or 'slice' of the non-resident parent's weekly net income on a sliding scale depending on the number of 'qualifying children' and the number of 'relevant other children'. The basic rate percentages are enshrined in the 1991 Act rather than in regulations.[17] In itself this is not particularly

---

[6] SI 2001/155, reg 2(4).

[7] For the meaning of 'relevant week' see *ibid*, reg 1(2) and for 'effective date' see SI 2001/157, regs 25–29.

[8] SI 2001/155, reg 2(1).

[9] *Ibid*, reg 2(2).

[10] *Ibid*, reg 2(3). By definition such a rule is irrelevant in the context of the nil and flat rates.

[11] *Ibid*, reg 1(2). See also CSA 1991, sch 1, para 10C(4) and (5), as amended by Civil Partnership Act 2004, s 254 and sch 24, para 6.

[12] CSA 1991, sch 1, para 1(1).

[13] The £200 p/w threshold can be altered by regulations: *ibid*, sch 1, para 10A(1)(b).

[14] See p 332 below.

[15] See p 194 above.

[16] See p 329 below.

[17] In contrast, the reduced rate percentages appear in regulations.

significant, as the Secretary of State has the power to alter the basic rate percentages by regulations.[18] There is, however, no statutory duty on the Secretary of State to review the appropriateness of these rates.[19] The process of applying the basic rate varies according to whether or not the non-resident parent has responsibility for any children other than his 'qualifying children' who are the subject of the Agency calculation. These 'non-qualifying' children are known as 'relevant other children' and are defined as further children in respect of whom the non-resident parent (or his new partner) receives child benefit.[20] Typically these may include a non-resident parent's step-child or his child with a new partner.[21]

In the straightforward case, where the non-resident parent has no 'relevant other children', the basic rate is 15 per cent of his total net weekly income where he has one qualifying child, 20 per cent where he has two such children, and 25 per cent where he has three or more qualifying children.[22] It follows that a non-resident parent earning £400 a week net will be subject to a basic rate liability of £60 a week for one qualifying child, £80 a week for two and £100 a week for three or more. Given the cap on the net weekly income figure at £2,000, this means that the maximum weekly child support payable under the 1991 Act for new scheme cases is £300 for one child (£15,600 p/a), £400 for two children (£20,800 p/a) and £500 for three or more children (£26,000). This sliding scale has the considerable advantage of relative simplicity over the original child support formula. This is not only important for the Agency's administration of the scheme; the assumption is that if non-resident parents understand the formula and regard it as fair, they will be more disposed to comply with their obligations.[23]

What, though, is the empirical basis for the specific percentage slices of the non-resident parent's net income at 15, 20 and 25 per cent? The Government's argument was that the research evidence suggested that in broad terms an intact family with one child devotes about one third of its income to child-related expenditure, with economies of scale occurring where there were two or more children in the household.[24] Thus the White Paper argued that the new rates struck:

> the right balance between the needs of children and the other expenses non-resident parents have to meet. The proposed base rate of 15 per cent of their income is roughly half

---

[18] *Ibid*, para 10A(1)(a). Arguably, however, the fact that they appear in the primary legislation may make it politically more difficult to justify a change in the percentage rates.

[19] Contrast the position in the USA, where state legislatures are required periodically to review their child support guidelines: see p 159 above.

[20] CSA 1991, sch 1, para 10C(1) and (2); 'relevant other children' also include children of the NRP or his partner for whom child benefit would be paid but for the residency rules (SI 2001/155, reg 1(3)) and their children for whom child benefit is paid but who are cared for in part or full by a local authority: *ibid*, reg 10.

[21] In the Agency's internal parlance these are known as 'relevant non-resident children' or 'RNRCs'.

[22] CSA 1991, sch 1, para 2(1).

[23] See further ch 15.

[24] See eg S Middleton, K Ashworth and R Walker, *Small fortunes: spending on children, childhood poverty and parental sacrifice* (York: Joseph Rowntree Foundation, 1997), and the sources cited in House of Commons (HC) Social Security Select Committee, *The 1999 Child Support White Paper* (Tenth Report, Session 1998–99, HC 798) at 202.

the average that an intact family spends on a child. In larger families, research shows that less is spent on each individual child, but overall spending on children increases. The proposed higher rates for two children and three or more children (20 per cent and 25 per cent respectively) reflect this.[25]

The Government's position was that, following separation, the parent with care makes her contribution to the child's upkeep through 'housing costs, food on the table, heating, TV licence and so forth'.[26] Thus her share is provided in kind, whilst the non-resident parent's 15 per cent contribution is made by way of his cash child support liability. This argument has also been used to justify the exclusion of the parent with care's income from the assessment process, in that her financial input is already factored in by the choice of rates. The basic rate percentages are similar to those which operate in other jurisdictions, but have the distinct advantage of being more readily comprehensible as rounded figures, so making the arithmetic more straightforward. In contrast, the rates in the Australian scheme for one, two or three children respectively are 18, 27 and 32 per cent.[27] This does not necessarily mean that Australian child support liabilities are higher, given the differences between the formulas.[28]

The use of just three percentage rates for basic rate cases is, in itself, a further example of the drive for simplicity in the 2000 Act, as other jurisdictions have higher rates for four or more children. The Australian scheme, for example, currently has two extra rates for larger families: 34 per cent for four children and 36 per cent for five or more children.[29] Arguably, whilst there may be economies of scale in larger families, the omission to provide for more than three percentage rates necessarily discriminates against parents with care who have more than three children. It is true that only a small minority of parents with care in the United Kingdom may be disadvantaged by the failure to make extra provision for four or more children.[30] However, such parents with care are much more likely to be found in some ethnic minority communities.[31] The addition of a fourth or any

---

[25] DSS, *A new contract for welfare: Children's Rights and Parents' Responsibilities* (Cm 4349, 1999) at ch 2, para 5. See also HC Social Security Select Committee, *Child Support: Minutes of Evidence* (HC 1031-i, Session 1997–98) at Q10 (Baroness Hollis of Heigham).

[26] *Per* Baroness Hollis of Heigham, *Hansard* HL Debates vol 612 col 1254 (8 May 2000).

[27] Child Support (Assessment) Act 1989 (Cth), s 37. The latest review has recommended that these additional rates be repealed: Report of the Ministerial Taskforce on Child Support, *In the Best Interests of Children* (Canberra, May 2005) at 135. In New Zealand the respective rates are 18, 24 and 27% for 1, 2 or 3 children respectively but 30% for 4 or more children: Child Support Act 1991 (NZ), s 29.

[28] The Australian formula is applied to gross income, not net income as in the UK, but following the deduction of an exempt income element: see ch 6 above.

[29] Child Support (Assessment) Act 1989 (Cth), s 37.

[30] In 2003, 3.4% of divorcing couples with children had four children, and 0.9% had five or more: 'Divorces in England and Wales during 2003' (2004) *Population Trends 117*, 73, Table 4. However, these data use the MCA 1973 definition of 'child of the family', and so a direct comparison with potential CSA liabilities cannot be made. Nor, by definition, do these data reflect the size of families in which the parents were previously cohabiting. However, other surveys confirm that about 4% of all families have four or more children: M Willitts and K Swales, *Characteristics of Large Families* (DWP In-house report no 118, April 2003) at 7.

[31] *Ibid*, at 27, also noting higher levels of hardship in large families. Only 4% of white families have four or more children, as compared with 33% of Pakistani families and 42% of Bangladeshi families:

further rate would require primary legislation, as the Act only allows the three individual percentage rates to be altered.[32]

The position is a little more complicated where the non-resident parent has a step-child or a subsequent child as a result of a new relationship. In such a case the non-resident parent's net weekly income is first of all reduced by 15, 20 or 25 per cent, depending on the number of such 'relevant other children', before the appropriate slice is applied, this time depending on the number of qualifying children.[33] For example, a non-resident parent with a net weekly income of £400 who has a new child in addition to one qualifying child will be subject to a basic rate liability of £51 a week (representing 15 per cent (for the one qualifying child) of £340 (ie £400 – £60, the latter being the deduction of 15 per cent from £400 in respect of the other relevant child)). If he has two qualifying children and one new child, the basic rate liability will be £68 (that is 20 per cent—for the two qualifying children—of £340 (£400 – £60, being 15 per cent of £400 in respect of the other relevant child). The various further permutations which may arise, based on a non-resident's illustrative net weekly income of £400, are set out in Table 10.1 below.

The original child support scheme was fiercely criticised for the limited recognition it gave to second family responsibilities assumed by non-resident parents. Inevitably, therefore, the treatment of children in a non-resident parent's second family in the new child support formula was one of the more controversial aspects of the 2000 Act, reflecting the very different views in society on this issue. About two-thirds of the general public disagree with the proposition that a non-resident parent with a second family should be liable to pay less support for children of his first family.[34] However, non-resident parents are much more equivocal in their views.[35] Pragmatically, the scheme needs to recognise the social reality of serial

Table 10.1 Basic rate child support liability (£ p/w) on weekly net income of £400, according to numbers of qualifying and relevant other children

	Number of relevant other children			
Number of qualifying children	*0*	*1*	*2*	*3 or more*
1	60	51	48	45
2	80	68	64	60
3 or more	100	85	80	75

see R Penn and P Lambert, 'Attitudes towards ideal family size of different ethnic/nationality groups in Great Britain, France and Germany' (2002) *Population Trends 108*, 49 at 50.

[32] CSA 1991, sch 1, para 10A(1)(a).

[33] *Ibid*, para 2(2).

[34] See eg V Peacey and L Rainford, *Attitudes towards child support and knowledge of the Child Support Agency, 2004* (DWP Research Report No 226, London, 2004) at 14.

[35] See ch 1 above and N Wikeley *et al*, *National Survey of Child Support Agency Clients* (DWP Research Report No 152, London, 2001) at 154–55.

families as a means of encouraging better compliance. The Green Paper canvassed two options for accommodating a non-resident parent's new family responsibilities:[36] one being that adopted by the Act, the alternative being to apply the relevant percentage for all his children, in both families, to the total net weekly income and then to share the resulting amount proportionately according to the number of children in each family. The White Paper announced the government's decision to adopt the first alternative, on the basis that the scheme 'should show a slight preference to children in the first family'.[37] Although the House of Commons Select Committee, echoing the calls of several pressure groups, indicated its preference for the latter approach as ensuring equality of treatment for all children,[38] the Government pressed ahead with the option identified in the White Paper. The alternative solution was certainly more readily comprehensible. However, if it had been adopted, a father with one qualifying child and one relevant other child would have had a child support liability of just £40 p/w (being half of 20 per cent—there being two children in all—of the total of £400) rather than £51.[39] Ultimately, this choice was a question of political and policy judgment, and adopting a slight preference for children in the first family may represent a trade-off for the decision to include step-children in addition to subsequent natural children in the calculation.[40]

The application of the relevant percentage slice of income, with or without any modification for any other children as appropriate, will produce a figure which in ordinary cases is the non-resident parent's final child support liability.[41] This liability, however, may be subject to apportionment in certain cases or to adjustment in cases of shared care (or to both). The question of shared care is dealt with in more detail below, after the discussion of the other formula rates. As regards apportionment, if the non-resident parent has two or more qualifying children by different parents with care, the basic rate liability is divided up in relation to the number of qualifying children with each parent with care.[42] For example, a non-resident parent who is liable for basic rate child support of £90 a week, and who has two qualifying children by different mothers, will be liable to pay £45 per week to each mother. If he has three qualifying children by two mothers, the mother with one child should receive £30 a week (⅓ of the basic rate) and the mother with two children £60 (⅔ of that rate).

---

[36] DSS, *Children First: A new approach to child support* (Cm 3992, 1998) at ch 5 paras 13–15.

[37] DSS, n 25 above, at ch 2 para 13.

[38] *Tenth Report*, n 24 above, at paras 28–9. The worked example in para 28 of the report should have a figure of £25.50 (not £22.50) p/w as the outcome for Example B.

[39] If there are more children in the first family, the differential in outcomes as between the two methods is less significant. For example, on the same income of £400 p/w but with one new child and two qualifying children, the difference is minimal (£68 on the method adopted, £67 on the alternative method—with rounding).

[40] See HC Social Security Select Committee, n 25 above, at Q14.

[41] Subject, of course, to any phasing based on the transitional provisions or the rules governing court orders.

[42] CSA 1991, sch 1, para 6.

The Reduced Rate

The thinking behind the reduced rate is that whilst liabilities based on a fixed percentage of earnings will be appropriate in most cases, non-resident parents on low incomes will find it difficult to pay child support at those levels if they are to maintain an adequate standard of living for themselves.[43] In old scheme cases the protected income rules operate effectively by way of an afterthought to the original formula to adjust liabilities in such cases. The new scheme formula has the advantage of tackling this problem at the outset by applying a different formula rate. The reduced rate of child support is payable where neither the flat rate nor the nil rate applies and where the 'non resident parent's net weekly income is less than £200 but more than £100'.[44] The applicable reduced rate percentage depends upon the number of qualifying children and the number of 'relevant other children'[45] for the individual non-resident parent, as determined by Table 10.2.[46]

At first sight these rates seem to be *higher* than those that apply to the basic rate (15, 20 and 25 per cent of net income where there are no other children involved), but this is a misleading impression. The reason is that these reduced rates do not apply to the non-resident parent's *total* weekly income. The actual amount of reduced rate child support which is payable is calculated by applying the relevant percentage from Table 10.2 only to the amount by which the non-resident parent's income exceeds £100 and then adding that figure to the flat rate liability of £5 per week. The overall effect, therefore, is that such a non-resident parent pays child support of £5 on his first £100 of weekly income (as if he fell into the flat rate category) and then a percentage on the balance of his income over £100 a week. The underlying principle is that 'liability increases in proportion to the amount by which the net income exceeds £100'.[47]

Table 10.2 **Reduced rate percentages of child support**

Number of qualifying children of the NRP	Number of relevant other children of the NRP			
	0	*1*	*2*	*3 or more*
1	25	20.5	19	17.5
2	35	29	27	25
3	45	37.5	35	32.5

---

[43] DSS, n 36 above, at ch 5, para 10 and DSS, n 25 above, ch 2 at paras 16–18.

[44] CSA 1991, sch 1, para 3(1). These thresholds are subject to alteration: *ibid*, para 10A(1)(b).

[45] ie a child the NRP has with a new partner, or a step-child, where he or his new partner receives child benefit for that child; see n 20 above.

[46] The Table is set out (in a different format to that used here) in SI 2001/155, reg 3.

[47] CSPSSA 2000, *Explanatory Notes*, para 30.

For example, a non-resident parent with one qualifying child, and no relevant other children, who has a net weekly income of £150 will, with rounding,[48] pay £18 a week in child support (£5 p/w flat rate + £12.50 (25% × £50)). This equates to a 12 per cent rate on his total net weekly income (the standard basic rate being 15 per cent). It will be apparent from Table 10.2 that his weekly liability would be the same if he had the same income, two qualifying children but also had three relevant other children. If he had the same income, two qualifying children and no other children his child support liability would be £23 a week (£5 + £17.50 (35% × £50), when rounded), or just over 15 per cent of his total net income. The reduced rate calculation must not result in an assessment of less than £5 a week.[49]

The reduced rate, as with the flat rate, is subject to apportionment where the non-resident parent owes a child support liability to more than one parent with care,[50] and may also be adjusted in cases of shared care.[51]

The Flat Rate

The principle behind the flat rate child support liability is that 'fathers on benefit have as much of a responsibility for their children's upkeep as those with earned income'.[52] As well as its symbolic value, a flat rate liability may assist in securing long-term compliance by establishing the 'habit' of paying child support, even at a modest level, on the part of those non-resident parents on low incomes. There is widespread support for the principle amongst the general public,[53] but again non-resident parents (especially those on low incomes themselves) are much less committed to this view.[54] Overseas child support systems also impose flat rate liabilities on non-resident parents in receipt of benefits or otherwise on low incomes. For example, the Australian government introduced a minimum payment of Aus$260 a year (Aus $5 a week) in 1999,[55] and a remarkable 40 per cent of all payers are subject to this minimum liability.[56] Many United States schemes also set a minimum level for child support orders, although at a higher rate than in Australia (typically US $50 or US $100 a month).[57]

---

[48] See SI 2001/155, reg 2(3).

[49] CSA 1991, sch 1, para 3(3). Again, this rate may be altered: *ibid*, para 10A(1)(b).

[50] *Ibid*, para 6, as discussed above. Note also the curious phenomenon of the 'floating penny'. This arises because the process of apportionment and rounding may produce an aggregate child support liability which is higher than the original liability. In such cases, the Agency reduces the weekly amount due to one PWC by 1 penny; in order that no one PWC is disadvantaged, this reduction is then reallocated to the other PWC(s) from time to time: SI 2001/155, reg 6.

[51] See p 312 below.

[52] DSS, n 36 above, at ch 5 para 20.

[53] See Peacey and Rainford, n 34 above, at 15 (63% of respondents agreed that low paid NRPs or those on benefits should pay maintenance).

[54] See Wikeley *et al*, n 35 above, at 151.

[55] Child Support (Assessment) Act 1989 (Cth), s 66.

[56] Ministerial Taskforce, n 27 above, at 95.

[57] P Legler, *Low-Income Fathers and Child Support: Starting Off on the Right Track* (Policy Studies Inc, Denver, Colorado, 2003) at 25. For arguments against such an approach, see TK Cheng, 'A Call For a New Fixed Rule: Imposition of child support orders against recipients of means-tested public

Under the United Kingdom's new scheme, the flat rate, currently £5 a week,[58] serves the same purpose as the minimum contribution to child support which many non-resident parents on benefit have to pay in old scheme cases.[59] This is at present £5.80 a week, representing 10 per cent of the full adult rate income support personal allowance when rounded up.[60] The main difference is that under the old scheme non-resident parents who are either in receipt of sickness or disability benefits or are living on benefit and have a child in their new household are excused payment of child support altogether. In contrast, the exemptions for non-resident parents on benefit under the new scheme are much narrower.[61] The flat rate also represents a substantial increase on the amounts assessed before the Child Support Act 1991, when the courts typically ordered non-resident parents on means-tested benefits to pay purely nominal amounts of child maintenance (for example 5 pence a year).[62]

The flat rate applies if the nil rate is inapplicable and where one of the following three conditions applies:

(a) the non-resident parent's net weekly income is £100 or less; or
(b) he receives any benefit, pension or allowance prescribed for the purposes of this paragraph of this sub-paragraph; or
(c) he or his partner (if any) receives any benefit prescribed for the purposes of this paragraph of this sub-paragraph.[63]

As mentioned above, the principles governing the assessment of the non-resident parent's net weekly income (a factor material to head (a)) are covered in chapter 11.

The benefits prescribed for the purpose of head (b), being benefits received[64] by the non-resident parent, comprise most of the contributory and non-contributory social security benefits:

Contribution-based jobseeker's allowance, incapacity benefit, category A, B, C and D retirement pensions, bereavement allowance, widow's pension, widowed parent's allowance, widowed mother's allowance, industrial injuries benefit, carer's allowance,

---

benefits' 1995 *Annual Survey of American Law* 647 and AF Epps, 'To Pay Or Not To Pay, That Is The Question: Should SSI recipients be exempt from child support obligations?' (2002) 34 *Rutgers Law Journal* 63.

[58] This figure is subject to alteration: CSA 1991, sch 1, para 10A(1)(b).

[59] CSA 1991, s 43, the start of what Mr Commissioner Mesher has described as 'a very complicated chain' of legislation (*R(CS)5/05* at para 10). See also the same Commissioner's decision in *CCS/16904/1996*, reported on a separate point in the Court of Appeal as *R(CS)7/99* (*Dollar v Child Support Officer*).

[60] See Child Support (Maintenance Assessments and Special Cases) Regulations 1992 (SI 1992/1815), regs 13 and 28; see also Social Security (Claims and Payments) Regulations 1987 (SI 1987/1968) sch 9, para 7A.

[61] See the concerns expressed in *Tenth Report*, n 24 above, at para 27.

[62] See eg *Fletcher v Fletcher* [1985] FLR 851 and *Berry v Berry* [1986] 1 FLR 618.

[63] CSA 1991, sch 1, para 4(1).

[64] Meaning either 'paid or due to be paid', *ibid*, para 10C(3).

maternity allowance, severe disablement allowance, overseas social security benefits,[65] war disablement and war widow's pensions and training allowances.[66]

These are mainly earnings replacement benefits (industrial injuries benefit and war pensions being the principal exceptions), and so are used as a proxy for low incomes. Some recipients, however, may have much higher incomes than would normally be the case for those on benefit (eg some pensioners), but the flat rate will still apply unless a successful variation application is made.[67]

The sole benefits prescribed for the purpose of head (c), which refers to those received by either the non-resident parent or any new partner, are the three principal means-tested benefits administered by the DWP: income support, income-based jobseeker's allowance and state pension credit.[68] It follows that receipt of housing benefit or council tax benefit does not automatically passport the non-resident parent to the flat rate. However, non-resident parents receiving these local authority-administered benefits and living on the lowest incomes will presumably either also be claiming income support, income-based jobseeker's allowance or state pension credit, or have a weekly net income of less than £100. In addition, working tax credit claimants do not automatically qualify for the flat rate, although some may do so on the basis of the weekly income threshold.

The weekly flat rate of £5 is modified where the non-resident parent has a new partner who is also a non-resident parent and is subject to a maintenance calculation, and either of them receives income support, income-based jobseeker's allowance or state pension credit.[69] In such cases, the flat rate payable is £2.50 a week.[70] If the non-resident parent has two or more qualifying children by different parents with care, the flat rate is apportioned in relation to the number of qualifying children with each parent with care.[71] The flat rate may also be modified in cases of shared care.[72]

The Nil Rate

The existence of the nil rate represents a victory for pragmatism over principle in that there are some cases in which it is not feasible to collect even the flat rate child

---

[65] See the enabling power in *ibid*, para 4(3).

[66] SI 2001/155, reg 4(1). The reference to training allowances excludes those for work-based training for young people and for Skillseekers training as these fall within the nil rate: see *ibid*, reg 5(e).

[67] On variations, see ch 12 below.

[68] SI 2001/155, reg 4(2).

[69] CSA 1991, sch 1, para 4(2).

[70] SI 2001/155, reg 4(3)(a)—unless the NRP has more than one partner (presumably this is a reference to polygamous marriages) in which case the flat rate is apportioned accordingly: *ibid*, reg 4(3)(b).

[71] CSA 1991, sch 1, para 6. In the simplest case, an NRP liable for the flat rate with two qualifying children by different mothers will be liable to pay £2.50 to each. If he has three qualifying children, the mother with one child will receive ⅓ of the flat rate and the mother with two children ⅔ of that rate. In practice these amounts will be rounded to the nearest penny by virtue of SI 2001/155, reg 2(2) (ie £1.67 and £3.33 respectively).

[72] See p 312 below.

support liability. The non-resident parent is subject to the nil rate where he either has a net weekly income of less than £5[73] or he is a person 'of a prescribed description'.[74] These latter categories are defined by regulations[75] and represent those groups who 'clearly have no income or, alternatively, so few, as possibly with students, have any serious alternative income that it is not worth the hassle' of seeking to recover child support maintenance.[76] They are:

> students; children; prisoners; 16 and 17 year olds on income support or income-based jobseeker's allowance; young people receiving an allowance for work-based training (or Skillseekers training in Scotland); care home residents who receive a benefit prescribed for the purpose of the flat rate, or who have part or all of their accommodation costs met by a local authority; inpatients in hospital for more than six weeks and on income support; and hospital inpatients for more than 52 weeks and on other benefits.

These prescribed categories are similar, but by no means identical, to those groups of non-resident parents who were exempt from paying any child support under the original 1991 scheme.[77]

Obviously there is a trade-off between the principle that all non-resident parents should perhaps pay at least a token amount of child support and the administrative complications generated by having special rules for assessing and recovering child support from individuals who typically have very low incomes. The pragmatic case for a nil rate is especially compelling where there are very few non-resident parents who fall into these categories.[78] The inclusion of some categories of non-resident parents in the nil rate band—for example, non-resident parents aged under 16—has not been controversial in the United Kingdom.[79] Accordingly, younger teenage fathers are theoretically liable for child support under the 1991 Act but effectively excused payment of child support (at least during their minority), in contrast with the position in some jurisdictions in the United States.[80] However, the arguments are more finely balanced in other cases, especially where the numbers of non-resident parents involved may be rather higher and their financial circumstances more varied. These considerations may apply to both students and prisoners.[81]

Doubtless most student non-resident parents will be impecunious and not in a position to pay any child support. There is some support for this view in the

---

[73] This figure may be altered by regulations: CSA 1991, sch 1, para 10A(1)(b). See also SI 2001/155, sch, para 17.

[74] CSA 1991, sch 1, para 5.

[75] SI 2001/155, reg 5.

[76] *Per* Baroness Hollis of Heigham, *Hansard* HL Debates vol 612, col 1295 (8 May 2000).

[77] See further the discussion above in the context of the flat rate at n 61 above.

[78] For example, in 2000 there were about 40 NRPs aged 16 or 17 and claiming income support or income-based JSA and around 60 who were resident in a care home and on benefit or had at least some of their accommodation costs met from public funds: *per* Baroness Hollis of Heigham, n 76 above.

[79] *Per* Mr J Rooker, Standing Committee F, col 134 (25 January 2000).

[80] A 'child' for the purposes of the nil rate is as defined by CSA 1991, s 55—see pp 217–224 above, and on child fathers see p 239.

[81] As with other prescribed categories, the issue is the individual's status as at the effective date: see SI 2001/155, reg 2(5).

Agency's own statistical data.[82] There are, of course exceptions, and the fact that full-time students in general are 'nil rated' does not necessarily mean that individual well-to-do students will escape meeting their child support liabilities.[83] However, this depends on the person with care making an application for a variation, on the basis that the student non-resident parent possesses income or capital which justifies disapplying the nil rate rule. The possibility of applying for a variation in such circumstances appears not to be widely known, either amongst parents with care or the Agency's own staff.[84]

It is important to note that the nil rate does not apply to *all* student non-resident parents, but only to those who are full-time students within the statutory definition,[85] which follows closely that which used to apply to income support, at least up until 1995.[86] However, the child support definition has not been modified[87] to reflect the tortuous twists and turns in the amendments to the income support regulations governing the meaning of 'student' over the past decade or more.[88] The question of a student's full-time status is judged by reference to the nature of the course, not the individual's actual attendance, a task which has become more problematic with the increasing diversity and flexibility of provision in higher education courses.[89] In principle a student's status is determined by the nature of the course at its outset,[90] although some modular courses are so flexible that they cannot be classified as being full-time, even if the student's mode of attendance is actually, at the start of the course, full-time.[91] Difficulties may also arise where a student takes time out of a course, eg because of illness or exam failures. As the 'old' income support phraseology applies in the child support context, such a person is *not* a student whilst intercalating.[92]

---

[82] In August 1999 there were some 1,520 student NRPs on the Agency's books with an average weekly income of £12.86. Fewer than 10% (140) had sufficient income to make them liable for child support and less than a third of those (40 in all) were fully compliant: *per* Mr J Rooker, Standing Committee F, col 135 (25 January 2000).

[83] If an NRP is already subject to a child support liability, he will have to apply for a supersession of the maintenance calculation on becoming a student in order to be nil rated.

[84] See eg House of Commons Work and Pensions Committee, *The Performance of the Child Support Agency* (Second Report of Session 2004–05, HC 44-I, vol I) at para 20.

[85] SI 2001/155, reg 1(2).

[86] The only material difference being that the then income support definition (as now) excluded those over pensionable age from student status. For child support purposes, however, pensioners engaged in life-long learning on a full-time basis will qualify for the nil rate as students.

[87] Indeed the definition in SI 2001/155, reg 1(2) is in the same terms as its predecessor in SI 1992/1815, reg 1(2).

[88] Income Support (General) Regulations 1987 (SI 1987/1967), reg 61(1). See further N Wikeley and A Ogus, *The Law of Social Security* (Butterworths, London, 2002, 5th edn) at 288–90 and K Mullan and P McKeown, 'Supporting students in higher education—the role of social security benefits' (1999) 6 *Journal of Social Security Law* 56.

[89] See *ibid* and *CIS/152/1994* at para 7 *per* Mr Commissioner Mitchell.

[90] *O'Connor v Chief Adjudication Officer* [1999] 1 FLR 1200, CA; see K Mullan (2000) 7 *Journal of Social Security Law* 185.

[91] *Chief Adjudication Officer v Webber* [1997] 4 All ER 274, CA, also reported as *R(IS) 15/98*.

[92] *Chief Adjudication Officer v Clarke and Faul* [1995] ELR 295, CA.

Prisoners, even more so than students, usually have low or indeed non-existent incomes, which justifies their inclusion *en bloc* in the nil rate category. Again, as with students, parents with care who have reason to believe that an imprisoned non-resident parent has an income stream or substantial assets may, at least in theory, seek a variation in order to replace the nil rate with a more realistic child support liability.[93] For child support purposes, a prisoner is someone who is detained in custody either following conviction or pending trial[94] or sentencing.[95] The classification of prisoners as presumptively nil rate non-resident parents achieves the same result by a slightly different route as the old child support scheme, which disregarded prisoners' pay in assessing income[96] and which treated prisoners as special cases with no child support liability.[97]

The current Prison Service policy specifies a minimum rate of £4 a week for prisoners' pay.[98] There is an argument that a policy which imposed even a nominal deduction from this modest rate (eg 50 pence per week) might be desirable in terms both of prioritising child support and instilling the habit of regular payment of maintenance. Against that, however, there would be significant administrative costs entailed, which would almost certainly outweigh the amounts actually being transferred by way of child support. The prison authorities might also be less than keen on any change which made it more difficult to provide an incentive for inmates to engage in prison work. On the other hand, some prisoners are employed in 'normal' jobs for outside employers who must pay at least the national minimum wage. Anomalously it would appear that such prisoners are nil rated, leaving the parent with care to take the initiative and make a variation application.[99]

Other jurisdictions adopt a range of practices as regards imprisoned non-resident parents. Most states in the United States do not suspend or terminate child support liabilities for prisoners.[100] Some states impose a minimum child support obligation, whilst others assess liability based on the minimum wage or on the inmate's prior earnings.[101] On this basis a non-resident parent's child support

---

[93] A NRP who is subject to a child support liability and then imprisoned will have to apply for a supersession of the maintenance calculation in order to be nil rated.

[94] Irrespective of whether at some subsequent date the proceedings are discontinued and he is released: *R(IS) 1/94*.

[95] SI 2001/155, reg 1(2). This definition excludes those detained under the mental health legislation as well as those granted temporary home leave, who are included in the income support definition of 'prisoner', see SI 1987/1967, reg 21(3); the amendments made following *Chief Adjudication Officer v Carr*, CA, reported as *R(IS) 20/95*, were not carried over into the child support scheme.

[96] Child Support (Maintenance Assessments and Special Cases) Regulations 1992 (SI 1992/1815), reg 7(2)(c).

[97] *Ibid*, reg 26.

[98] HM Prison Service, *Prisoners' Pay* Order Number 4460 (January 2002), Annex B.

[99] The official policy states that 'if prisoners' earnings are high enough, they may be liable for contributions to the maintenance of their dependants, under the Child Support Act and social security regulations', *ibid*, para 2.9.1. However, if they are 'prisoners' under the definition in SI 2001/155, reg 1(2) they will be nil rated.

[100] KR Cavanaugh and D Pollack, 'Child support obligations of incarcerated parents' (1998) 7 *Cornell Journal of Law and Public Policy* 531; see also EA Griswold and J Pearson, 'Turning offenders into responsible parents and child support payers' (2005) 43 *Family Court Review* 358.

[101] On the assumption that imprisonment is a form of 'voluntary unemployment'.

arrears can mount up whilst he is imprisoned, leaving him with even bigger debts on his eventual release.[102] In Australia, prisoners are also not automatically excused payment. They may, however, apply for a change of assessment and are likely to be assessed at either the minimum rate or nil rate.[103] Similarly, in New Zealand, a non-resident parent who is imprisoned for 3 months or more may apply to have his child support liability suspended during his sentence, providing he has either a nil or a low income.[104] Whilst this has the advantage of putting the onus on the non-resident parent (rather than on the parent with care to make a variation application), it may result in an overly bureaucratic process in which the great majority of applications will inevitably be granted.

Shared Care

Introduction

We have already seen that the child support liability calculated by applying the basic, reduced or flat rate may be modified by either or both of the sets of rules governing apportionment and shared care. Apportionment operates where there is more than one person with care and more than one qualifying child in relation to the same non-resident parent.[105] This is a purely arithmetical matter with minimal policy implications. Shared care is a much more contested and politically controversial issue.[106] These rules apply where the non-resident parent and the person with care are both substantially involved in the care of the qualifying child or children. If both sets of rules apply, then in arriving at the final child support liability, the apportionment rules are applied first in time, followed by the shared care rules.[107]

In deciding how to treat shared care in a child support system, policy makers face two fundamental questions. The first concerns the minimum threshold that should apply before the non-resident parent qualifies for a reduction in his child support liabilities. The second issue is the methodology to be used in modifying the amount of child support payable. Under the original child support scheme, non-resident parents who shared the care of their children for fewer than two nights a week on average across the year saw no reduction in their child support liabilities. Once the threshold of 104 nights was passed, the amount of child support was reduced proportionately by the operation of a special formula.[108] The

---

[102] *Holt v Geter* (2002) 809 So.2d 68 (District Court of Appeal of Florida, First District).

[103] If they have an income of less than Aus$260 a year, they may apply to be categorised as nil rate payers.

[104] Child Support Act 1991 (NZ), s 73, inserted in 1999.

[105] CSA 1991, sch 1, para 6 and SI 2001/155, reg 6; see above p 304.

[106] As also is the relationship between child support and contact (falling short of shared care, howsoever defined), which is discussed in ch 15 below.

[107] CSA 1991, sch 1, para 1(2).

[108] SI 1992/1815, reg 20. As we will see, some overseas schemes operate a 30% threshold before shared care affects child support liabilities: 104 nights a year is equivalent to 28.4%.

scheme thus created a 'cliff-edge' effect, with the significance of the '104 nights' rule creating the potential for exacerbating conflict over contact arrangements.[109] The same phenomenon has been identified in other jurisdictions.[110] The 2000 Act has reduced the threshold for shared care to 52 nights, with increasing fractional reductions in liabilities based on broad bands of the amount of shared care, thus potentially increasing the scope for such conflict.[111] It should be noted at the outset that the impact of shared care on the amount payable under the new scheme differs according to whether the case involves the basic rate or reduced rate on the one hand or the flat rate on the other. However, before examining the details of the new arrangements, it is important to consider the policy rationale for reducing child support liabilities under the shared care rules.

The Justification for the Shared Care Rules

The parliamentary record provides few clues as to the thinking that lay behind the original '104 nights' rule. The justification given at the time was that it

> strikes the proper balance between the interests of both parents and the interests of the child, given that shared care should mean joint responsibility for all important aspects of a child's upbringing, nurture and day-to-day care and costs.[112]

In developing its proposals for the 2000 Act, the Government put forward a two-fold rationale for extending the ambit of the shared care rules. First, continued and appropriate contact between children and their non-resident parents is regarded as being in the best interests of children and so should be supported as a matter of principle. This reflects a wider phenomenon in trends in both family law and official policy, which have increasingly come to emphasise the perceived benefits of shared parenting.[113] Secondly, research demonstrates a clear correlation between regular contact and the payment of maintenance.[114] On this analysis, shared care

---

[109] In *CCS/11588/1995* some £1,500 p/a turned on whether or not the shared care was less than 104 nights or not. The old rule also used receipt of child benefit as the determining factor where shared care was equal, which could itself cause anomalous outcomes: see *R(CS) 14/98* at para 20 *per* Mr Commissioner Rowland.

[110] For example, Canada uses a 40% threshold for shared care, which, it is argued, simply invites conflict: see *Crick v Crick* 43 BCLR (3d) 251 (1997, British Columbia Supreme Court) *per* Warren J, and see nn 173–75 below.

[111] The House of Commons Select Committee, noting the possibility of unintended behavioural results from the shared care reforms, recommended that the (then) DSS jointly commission research with the DoH and the (then) LCD into the consequences for children's well-being of linking child support liabilities to overnight contact: *Tenth Report*, n 24 above, para 45. No such research appears to have been commissioned.

[112] *Hansard* HC Debates vol 210 col 763 (30 June 1992) *per* Mr A Burt.

[113] This is, of course, a theme underpinning the Children Act 1989, but has not been without its critics: see eg H Rhoades, 'The Rise and Rise of Shared Parenting Laws: A Critical Reflection' (2002) 19 *Canadian Journal of Family Law* 75 and F Kaganas and C Piper, 'Shared Parenting—A 70% Solution'? (2002) 14 *Child & Family Law Quarterly* 365.

[114] DSS, n 25 above, ch 7 and ch 15 below.

furthers children's emotional welfare whilst also improving compliance with child support liabilities.[115]

It follows that the stated objectives of the revised shared care rules are rooted in broad public policy considerations; indeed, the narrower goal of compensating non-residential parents for the costs that they incur in looking after their children is not an explicit aim.[116] There is no clear consensus on this issue in society at large.[117] Moreover, as the discussion in chapter 1 demonstrated, any attempt to base individual child support liabilities on actual child-related costs is problematic. There are, in addition, sound practical reasons why financial adjustment should not in itself be the prime purpose of the shared care rules. There would obviously be serious evidential difficulties in seeking to quantify accurately the true extra costs incurred by non-resident parents undertaking shared care, whether on an individualised or general basis. Furthermore, even though the non-resident parent may well face higher child-related expenditure if he has shared care, it does not follow that the parent with care will experience a commensurate reduction in her outgoings, as many of her expenses will be fixed costs, such as housing, with any savings being at best at the margins.[118]

From a policy point of view, therefore, the precise financial adjustment made by the shared care rules is a second order issue. Non-resident parents, however, tend to have a very different perspective; in their view the prime purpose of the shared care rules should be to reflect adequately their increased financial contribution to the care of their children by providing a discount on what would otherwise be their assessed liability.[119] This mismatch between the policy rationale and the perception of non-resident parents can only add to the potential for conflict over shared care issues. We now consider how the shared care rules operate in basic and reduced rate cases and flat rate cases respectively.

---

[115] Note that although there is some evidence from the USA that shared care is associated with higher child support awards, this probably reflects income differences between families with different types of post-separation residence arrangements: JA Seltzer, 'Legal Custody Arrangements and Children's Economic Welfare' (1991) 96 *American Journal of Sociology* 895.

[116] Although ministers also acknowledged that 'the more generous shared-care arrangements under the new scheme will ensure that the child support scheme gives proper recognition to those who take on the important job of providing day-to-day care for their children', *Hansard* HL Debates vol 620 col 1095 (16 January 2001) *per* Baroness Hollis of Heigham.

[117] Amongst the general public, about 50% agree that overnight stays should affect child support liabilities, 40% disagree and 10% believe it depends on the circumstances: D White, *Attitudes toward child support and the Child Support Agency* (DWP In-house report 100 (DWP, London, 2002) at 19; see also Peacey and Rainford, n 34 above, at 27.

[118] C Rogerson, 'Child support under the guidelines in cases of split and shared custody' (1998) 15 *Canadian Journal of Family Law* 11 at 21. Indeed, with genuinely equal shared care there will be increased costs overall because of the need to duplicate some expenses. Some overseas systems seek to accommodate this by providing for a higher exempt income allowance for NRPs engaged in shared care: see further p 322 below.

[119] See Wikeley *et al*, n 35 above, at 155–56.

Shared Care in Basic and Reduced Rate Cases

So far as the basic and reduced rates are concerned, the starting point is that, as with the old scheme, shared care is only relevant where it is such that 'the non-resident parent from time to time has care of the child overnight'.[120] According to the regulations, a night only counts for these purposes if the non-resident parent has care[121] of the qualifying child overnight *and* that child stays at the same address as the non-resident parent.[122] Accordingly, there is no specific requirement that the child stays overnight at the non-resident parent's home, providing they stay overnight at the same address.[123]

It follows that a non-resident parent who only shares day-time care of the child, or day-time care together with less than one night a week of overnight care, cannot benefit from a reduction for shared care. The pragmatic justification for this approach may be that overnight care is a useful proxy measure for demonstrating the extent of the non-resident parent's involvement in the child's life. It is also a reasonable indication that a non-resident parent has incurred costs which are higher than those ordinarily associated with contact, as overnight care will typically involve provision of an evening meal, breakfast and (possibly) school lunch as well as (possibly) higher housing costs[124]—although, of course, financial recompense is not an explicit policy goal.[125] In any event, overnight care is not a universally accurate measure for identifying those non-resident parents who have significant involvement with their children (or who incur extra child-related costs). For example, in *R (on the application of Plumb) v Secretary of State for Work and Pensions*[126]—decided under the old scheme rules—the non-resident parent was unable to avail himself of the shared care rules as his daughter stayed with him for fewer than 104 nights a year. Yet, on the actual facts of the case, he cared for her for more hours, and provided substantially more meals, than some parents who would satisfy the 104 nights test.[127] *Plumb* illustrates that the focus on

---

[120] CSA 1991, sch 1, para 7(2).

[121] This defined in terms of the NRP 'looking after the child', SI 2001/155, reg 7(2).

[122] *Ibid*, reg 7(1), made under the authority of CSA 1991, sch 1 para 9.

[123] For example, the NRP and qualifying child may stay over together at the home of the latter's grandparent. The PWC, of course, might question whether the NRP is genuinely 'looking after' the child in such a case.

[124] 'Overnight care is a very significant part of parenting involving usually two important meals, bathing, comforting, and providing calm and rest. So to that extent, night-time can be differentiated from daytime in a significant way. Seldom would the night-time custodian be merely providing a dormitory', *Thomson v Overton* [2000] NZFLR 347 at 352 *per* Ellis J.

[125] On the other hand, for judicial criticism of the Canadian 40% threshold rule, see Eberhard J in *Rosati v Dellapenta* 35 RFL (4th) 102 (1997, Ontario Court of Justice): 'This crass focus concerning the number of hours spent told me nothing whatsoever about who bears the expenses of parenting . . . Time tells me little about who arranges for the children's material needs', at para 5.

[126] [2002] EWHC Admin 1125 (HH Judge Alan Wilkie QC).

[127] This was because the NRP (who was in receipt of jobseeker's allowance) and PWC lived within a few hundred yards of each other, and his daughter spent a considerable amount of time at her father's house during daytime in addition to some overnight stays. Under the new scheme an NRP in this situation will have a nil liability so long as the 52-night rule is met; see further below. The New Zealand

overnight care may result in hard cases. It is necessarily a rough and ready measure, which makes no attempt to assess the quality of the time that the child spends with the non-resident parent.[128] However, the practical problems associated with seeking to quantify shared day-time care would be immense and probably insuperable.[129]

The next stage is that the Secretary of State has to establish the evidential base for the application of the shared care rules. This depends on the number of nights of overnight care 'which the Secretary of State determines there to have been, or expects there to be, or both during a prescribed twelve-month period'.[130] The normal approach is for the Secretary of State to look at the period of 12 months ending with the 'relevant week'.[131] The drafting of the Act and regulations implies that this assessment is a purely arithmetical exercise;[132] if this is so, no allowance should be made for the fact that the non-resident parent may, for whatever reason, have had overnight care of the child for a longer period in the preceding 12 months than would usually be the case. However, a degree of flexibility is provided where there is no pattern of frequency of overnight care in the preceding 12 months or where the Secretary of State is aware that a change in such care arrangements is intended.[133] In such situations the Agency may have regard to such lesser period as seems appropriate[134] and the number of nights scaled proportionately to arrive at a yearly figure.[135] The regulations also provide that where a child is a hospital inpatient or a boarder at school, then 'the person who, but for those circumstances, would otherwise have care of the child overnight shall be treated as providing that care during the periods in question'.[136]

---

scheme accommodates such cases by allowing shared care to be established otherwise than by the threshold of 40% of nights that usually applies: see p 321 below.

[128] Some Canadian cases have regarded this as an important factor: see eg *Dennett v Dennett* [1998] AJ No 440 (QB). This approach may be feasible in a child support system which still retains a degree of discretionary judicial input, but it is unrealistic to expect it to be operated in the UK's bureaucratic model.

[129] A concern expressed by the Independent Case Examiner: *Tenth Report*, n 24 above, para 49. See further the discussion in Rogerson, n 118 above, citing *Crick v Crick* [1997] BCJ No 2222 (SC), where the father's claim failed as he was just under the 40% threshold at 39.93% (it seems that the Canadian courts do not apply rounding in this context). Several US states use overnight stays as a measure for assessing the degree of shared care.

[130] CSA 1991, sch 1, para 7(3).

[131] SI 2001/155, reg 7(3). The 'relevant week' is typically the seven days immediately before the date on which the NRP is notified that an application for child support has been made or treated as made.

[132] E Jacobs and G Douglas, *Child Support: The Legislation* (Sweet & Maxwell, London, Edition Seven, 2005/2006) at 627.

[133] SI 2001/155, reg 7(4). Jacobs and Douglas (n 132 above) argue that this is confined to cases where recent changes demonstrate an intended change in frequency and does not include instances of changes intended for the future. The drafting of reg 7(4) in itself does not support such a restrictive interpretation, but reg 2(4) may do so. See now *CCS/2885/2005*.

[134] Such lesser period would not seem to have to end with the relevant week: see *CCS/128/2001*, decided under the old formulation but the reasoning is still applicable to the new regulation.

[135] SI 2001/155, reg 7(5). Thus 30 nights over 6 months equates to 60 nights over 12 months.

[136] *Ibid*, reg 7(6). But note that an NRP who pays boarding school fees may have grounds for applying for a variation: p 381 below.

Leaving such special cases to one side, there is clearly considerable potential for disagreement, in terms of identifying both the period over which the frequency of overnight care should be assessed and the actual number of nights involved.[137] Such conflicts in evidence should be no surprise—social surveys have consistently demonstrated marked discrepancies in the levels of contact reported by parents with care and non-resident parents respectively.[138] In principle the Secretary of State's role is inquisitorial, and so Agency staff must 'deal even-handedly with the contentions of both parents' and 'ask the parties the appropriate questions in order to elicit the requisite information'.[139] In practice the Agency is likely to be faced with competing and self-serving accounts from both parents and its staff are ill-equipped to make factual findings on such conflicting evidence. In such cases the terms of any court order setting out contact arrangements, although useful evidence, cannot be determinative; decision makers and tribunals must bear in mind that their duty is 'to deal with what the situation actually is rather than what the situation ought to have been'.[140] The official guidance advises staff that

> The decision on which of the two sets of evidence to use is the responsibility of the case-worker. The final decision to be made may be difficult and therefore the Balance of Probability may have to be considered. Evidence should not be used if it is improbable or contradictory.[141]

Agency decision makers are not lawyers and so are poorly equipped to make decisions on the basis of the evidence presented to them (typically by telephone or letter). Parents' assertions are not tested by cross-examination as would be the case in (the admittedly atypical) contested court actions over contact. The practical example given in the official guidance to staff does little to assist them in resolving difficult cases.[142]

Once the decision maker has determined the extent of the overnight care provided by the non-resident parent, his child support liability is reduced by the appropriate fraction according to Table 10.3 below.[143] There are two main

---

[137] Especially if the NRP is a shift worker: see *CCS/499/1995*.

[138] J Bradshaw, C Stimson, C Skinner and J Williams, *Absent Fathers?* (Routledge, London, 1999) at 81.

[139] *CCS/2861/2001* at para 7 *per* Mr Commissioner Rowland, applying *Payne v Payne* [2001] EWCA Civ 166, [2001] Fam 473. As such, it may not be helpful to think in terms of the burden of proof in resolving such disputes.

[140] *CSC 4/98* at para 20 *per* JAH Martin, Chief Commissioner for Northern Ireland .

[141] Child Support Agency, *Procedures: Sapphire Processes* 'PWC and NRP Supply Different Information' at 5021–22; in a similar vein, the Decision Makers Guide advised 'the DM should not presume that the evidence of the PWC is generally more reliable than that of the NRP. Both parties have a right to be believed'. This probably accounts for the perception by some tribunal chairmen that the Agency's decision makers believe whatever they were last told.

[142] Child Support Agency, *Procedures: Gather Information and Evidence*, 'Balance of Probability' at 685: 'The NRP states that he has shared care of the QC for one night p/w. However, the PWC states that there is no shared care. Despite numerous requests the NRP does not provide any evidence that he has had care of the QC. The PWC lives in Norwich and the NRP in Edinburgh. Due to the distance between the PWC/NRP the DM decides that there is no shared care'.

[143] CSA 1991, sch 1, para 7(4). These bands and fractions may be altered by regulations: *ibid*, para 10A(2)(a).

differences as compared with the approach used in old scheme cases: first, as we have already seen, the annual threshold is reduced from 104 nights to 52 nights; secondly, the new scheme employs a series of further bands, designed to make the financial impact of increasing amounts of shared care more transparent.[144] Although this avoids the 'cliff-edge' effect of the former 104 nights rule, in its place it creates a 'step-effect' with four different borderlines which will affect the calculation of child support liabilities—and so may exacerbate conflict between parents. It follows that decision makers and tribunals, notwithstanding the evidential difficulties which often arise, have no option in contested cases but to count up the number of overnight stays in a relevant period and then identify the relevant band.[145] For example, if the non-resident parent's basic rate liability is assessed at £70 a week, but on average he provides overnight care for one night a week, his weekly assessment is reduced by one-seventh to £60.

Table 10.3 Effect of shared care on basic and reduced rates

Number of nights	Fraction to subtract
52 to 103	One-seventh
104 to 155	Two-sevenths
156 to 174	Three-sevenths
175 or more	One-half

These fractional reductions are subject to three special rules. First, if the person with care is caring for two or more qualifying children with the same father, then 'the applicable decrease is the sum of the appropriate fractions in the Table divided by the number of such qualifying children'.[146] This provision enables the shared care rules to accommodate different patterns of shared care for different children. For example, if a separated couple have two children, both of whom live mainly with their mother, with one child falling in the lowest band (52–103 nights staying with father) and the other in the next band (104–155 nights), then the father's child support liability is reduced by three-fourteenths $((^1/_7 + ^2/_7) \div 2)$.[147] Secondly, if the degree of shared care is so extensive (ie it reaches 175 nights or more) that the non-resident parent qualifies for a one-half reduction in his child

---

[144] The old scheme rules require that the weekly average number of nights of shared care had to be calculated to two decimal places, which generated the figure J in the memorable equation $T = X - \{(X+Y) \times ^1/_7 \times L\}$: SI 1992/1815, reg 20(4).

[145] See *CSC 4/98*, in which the Chief Commissioner for Northern Ireland criticised a tribunal which had found shared care for one child to be 50/50 overall on a broad brush basis and had declined 'to count days and weeks' (indeed, one might add, it should have been counting overnight stays in any event).

[146] CSA 1991, sch 1, para 7(5).

[147] This makes it all the more important for a tribunal to make careful findings of fact about precisely *which* children stay *how many* nights with the NRP: see *CSC 7/94* para 9 *per* Mr Commissioner McNally.

support liability, he receives a further £7 a week reduction for each qualifying child.[148] This figure was chosen because it was approximately half of the then rate of child benefit.[149] Finally, if the effect of the shared care rules would be to reduce the non-resident parent's liability to less than £5 a week, he is subject to the fixed flat rate of £5 by way of child support.[150]

Shared Care in Flat Rate Cases

The definition of shared care is the same for the flat rate as for the basic and reduced rates,[151] but the consequences are very different. There is, understandably, no attempt to apply a graduated reduction in cases involving the £5 flat rate. If the non-resident parent pays the flat rate because of his (or his partner's) benefit status, and he has shared care for at least 52 nights a year, then his liability for child support maintenance is simply reduced to nil.[152] The justification for this is the desire to provide an incentive to all parents to engage in shared care.[153] Somewhat anomalously, this concession does not apply to those non-resident parents who are *not* on benefit but who qualify for the flat rate because their incomes are less than £100 a week.[154] It is difficult to see why this group of non-resident parents should be denied the benefit of the nil rate.[155]

Shared Care in Overseas Child Support Systems

Child support systems overseas operate a variety of different methods to deal with cases of shared care. Australia's scheme, which has adopted one of the more

---

[148] CSA 1991, sch 1, para 7(6). This is described by the Agency as 'equal shared care' which, given there are 365 nights in a year, is not entirely accurate ($2 \times 175 = 350$).

[149] DSS, n 25 above, at ch 7 para 17. Child benefit was then £14.40 p/w for an only or oldest child; the equivalent rate in 2006/07 is £17.45, so by that reasoning the reduction should now be £8.73 per child. The £7 deduction can be altered by virtue of CSA 1991, sch 1, para 10A(2)(b), but there has been no increase to date. Child benefit itself cannot be apportioned, whatever the extent of the shared care: see *Barber v Secretary of State for Work and Pensions* [2002] 2 FLR 1181. Leave to appeal was obtained from the CA but not pursued ([2002] EWCA Civ 1367). See also *R (on the application of Ford) v Board of Inland Revenue and Sayers* [2005] EWHC 1109 (Admin). For the inability to split the jobseeker's allowance personal allowance for children see *Hockenjos v Secretary of State for Social Security* [2004] EWCA Civ 1749; [2005] 1 FLR 1009.

[150] CSA 1991, sch 1, para 7(7). This is subject to apportionment under *ibid*, para 6. The £5 minimum rate can also be altered: *ibid*, para 10A(1)(b).

[151] SI 2001/155, reg 7.

[152] CSA 1991, sch 1, para 8.

[153] *Per* Ms A Eagle, Parliamentary Under-Secretary of State, Standing Committee F, col 150 (25 January 2000).

[154] CSA 1991, sch 1, para 8(1)(b) does not mention *ibid*, para 4(1)(a).

[155] The DWP point out that this omission is likely to affect only a small number of people, who may well have a second earner in the household (personal communication, 26 July 2000). But this is hardly a rational or principled justification for giving them no credit for shared care. The Agency's own staff regard the rule as anomalous: A Atkinson and S McKay, *Child Support Reform: The views and experiences of CSA staff and new clients* (DWP Research Report No 232, London, 2005) at 141–42.

complex methodologies, makes distinctions between 'shared care', 'major contact' and 'substantial contact'. 'Shared care' is where the non-resident parent has care of the child for at least 40 per cent of nights (146 nights)[156] or can otherwise demonstrate that he is sharing 'ongoing daily care of a child substantially equally' with the other parent.[157] A person enjoys 'major contact' where she is the 'principal provider of ongoing daily care' for the child but another person has 'substantial contact' with that child.[158] In turn, 'substantial contact' is where a parent cares for a child for at least 30 per cent of nights (110 nights) but less than 40 per cent of nights over a 12 month period.[159] Assuming that the non-resident reaches at least the 30 per cent threshold,[160] then:

> the child support formula treats both parents as if they were paying child support to each other and calculates an annual rate for both parents based on their relevant incomes and number of dependants. The child support that is payable by one parent to the other is the difference between those two rates.[161]

This result is achieved by ascribing to the concepts of 'substantial contact', 'shared care' and 'major contact' the values 0.35, 0.5 and 0.65 of a child respectively.[162] The usual formula rate is then adjusted according to the number of children for whom each parent is a liable parent in relation to the other.[163] For example, if a separated couple have shared care of their only child, then each is ascribed the value of 0.5 of a child. This gives rise to a modified formula rate of 12 per cent,[164] which is then applied to the formula income of each parent. If they have identical incomes, then the child support liability will be nil for each of them. More commonly, however, one will be a higher earner, in which case the lower of the two amounts (ie the mother's adjusted income amount × 12 per cent and the father's adjusted income amount × 12 per cent) is then offset against the higher to arrive at the final net liability payable by one parent.[165] Although a more complex scheme, this approach provides a more sophisticated equation for attributing the costs of different levels of combined care, especially where there are different arrangements for different children. For example, assume that a separated couple have two children, A and B, who both live with their mother and that A has only minimal contact with the father but B has substantial contact with him. On this scenario, the mother owes a child support liability to the father equivalent to 0.35 of a child (for B's substantial contact). This gives rise to a modified formula rate of

---

[156] Child Support (Assessment) Act 1989 (Cth), s 8(1).

[157] *Ibid*, s 8(2).

[158] *Ibid*, s 8(3)(a) and (c).

[159] *Ibid*, s 8(3)(b)(i) and (d)

[160] Or for less than 30% of nights but where both parents agree that there is substantial contact: *ibid*, s 8(3)(b)(ii).

[161] *N & B* [2003] FMCAfam 72 at para 23 *per* Brown FM (Federal Magistrates Court, Darwin).

[162] Child Support (Assessment) Act 1989 (Cth), s 48(1)(e).

[163] *Ibid*, s 48(1).

[164] See the Table in *ibid*, s 48(1).

[165] *Ibid*, s 49.

8 per cent which is applied to her income. The father, on the other hand, owes the mother a child support liability based on 1.65 children (for A's care and for B's major contact), a fraction which gives rise to an adjusted formula rate of 25 per cent,[166] which would then be applied to the father's income. The two resulting figures (mother's income × 8 per cent and father's income × 25 per cent) are off-set against each other to arrive at the final net liability. Notwithstanding this complexity, the Australian scheme currently makes no allowance where the level of care falls below 30 per cent of nights (110 nights) in respect of any given child,[167] a threshold which is slightly higher than the pre-2000 Act system in the United Kingdom.

The New Zealand scheme operates a pared down version of the Australian shared care rules. The threshold for shared care (or 'substantially equal sharing' as it is described in the legislation) is also fixed at a minimum of 40 per cent of nights (146 nights) in a 12 month period.[168] Again, as in the current Australian scheme, a liable parent who does not meet the 40 per cent of nights rule may still establish shared care if the circumstances are such that daily care is shared substantially equally.[169] The similarities between the two schemes stop there; as the New Zealand scheme takes no account of the parent with care's income, then the complexities of the Australian offsetting rules are avoided. So, once shared care is established (by whichever route) then the New Zealand formula rate is adjusted downwards on a straightforward sliding scale.[170] There is also no reduction in child support liabilities in circumstances where the liable parent fails to qualify under these shared care rules, but still has what the Australians would regard as substantial contact (in the sense of being above 30 per cent).

The North American jurisdictions use a range of different approaches but all appear to be premised on the assumption that the purpose of the shared care rules is to reflect the extra economic costs borne by the non-resident parent. In Canada, as in New Zealand, shared care is only taken into account once it exceeds 40 per cent of the total caring time.[171] Once this threshold is reached, the court enjoys a broad discretion to arrive at what it perceives to be an appropriate adjusted child support liability, taking into account the formula amount for each parent, the

---

[166] See *ibid*, Table—the normal formula rate for two children in 27%.

[167] Unless the couple agree that there is in fact substantial contact between the NRP and the child: see n 160 above. The Ministerial Taskforce has proposed that the Australian threshold be lowered to 14% (ie one night a week): n 27 above, at 150–54.

[168] Child Support Act 1991 (NZ), s 13(1).

[169] *Ibid*, s 13(2). This requires consideration of the various factors set out in *ibid*, s 12(b) relating to daily care, without applying an arithmetical formula: see *Johns v Commissioner of Inland Revenue* [1999] NZFLR 15 and *Andrews v Commissioner of Inland Revenue* [2003] NZFLR 193.

[170] The normal rates under the New Zealand formula, ie 18%, 24%, 27% and 30% are reduced to 12%, 18%, 21% and 24% respectively: Child Support Act 1991 (NZ), ss 29 and 35. This results in a substantial reduction in liability given that the liable parent will also gain the benefit of a higher living allowance: see the worked examples in Inland Revenue (NZ), *Helping you to understand shared care* (IR156, 2003).

[171] Section 9 of Child Support Guidelines, O Reg 391/97. Section 8 of the Guidelines deals with 'split custody' cases (ie where each parent has principal care of one child but contact with the other).

increased costs associated with shared custody and any relevant circumstances of both parents and the child(ren) concerned.[172] This can lead to bitter disputes as to how that threshold should be defined and whether or not it has been surpassed. As one Canadian judge has put it, 'the parties' inability to separate care and control issues from financial issues is exaggerated by [the shared care rule], which invites minute and perhaps not always relevant comparisons of time'.[173] As a result, 'each is scoring the children's time; each is suspicious of the other's reasons for refusing or requesting time'.[174] Similarly, Canadian child psychologists have reported that 'some parents bring calculators to discussions about quality time which indicates their true intention of ensuring a 40% or 50% split'.[175]

Most American states have lower thresholds for shared care than Canada, typically in the range of 25 to 35 per cent.[176] In some states (as in Canada) this assessment is based on a percentage of total time across the year, whilst others (as in Australia, New Zealand and the United Kingdom) only count overnight stays. The various American schemes operate a range of different methodologies for taking account of shared care above the chosen threshold. Most use some form of offset formula in which the parties' respective child support liabilities are weighed against each other with the difference being the net amount payable.[177] Several of these models increase the amount allocated to child support by both parents by a factor (eg 1.35 or 1.5) in order to reflect the added costs of shared parenting. These types of shared care models provide scope for more nuanced decisions in individual cases, but are only really feasible in a system in which the judiciary retain the final decision on the assessment of child support liability.

Arguably the broad bands adopted in the United Kingdom shared care rules reflect domestic considerations both of principle and pragmatism. The underlying purposes of the shared care rules lie not in a fruitless search for precise financial readjustment between the parents but are to be found in the broader public policy objectives discussed above. In addition, the methodology has to lend itself to being applied by relatively junior administrative staff using a legal framework (if not a computer system) designed to avoid the worst complexities of the old scheme.[178]

---

[172] See further *Contino v Leonelli-Contino* 2005 SCC 63 (Supreme Court), allowing an appeal against the decision of the Ontario Court of Appeal (232 DLR (4th) 654 (2003)), on which see GC Colman, 'Contino v Leonelli-Contino—A Critical Analysis of the Ontario Court of Appeal Interpretation of Section 9 of the Child Support Guidelines' (2004) 20 *Canadian Journal of Family Law* 291.

[173] *Penner v Penner* 135 Man R (2d) 248 (1999, Manitoba, Court of Queen's Bench) at para 10, *per* Little J.

[174] *Ibid*, at para 15. See also *Green v Green* 187 DLR (4th) 37 (British Columbia Court of Appeal) at paras 20–24.

[175] PG Jaffe, CV Crooks and GR Goodall, 'The Role of Affluence in Child Development: Implications for Child Support Guidelines in Exceptional Circumstances' (2004) 22 *Canadian Family Law Quarterly* 319 at 319.

[176] See MS Melli and PR Brown 'The economics of shared custody: developing an equitable formula for dual residence' (1994) 31 *Houston Law Review* 543 at 562.

[177] *Ibid*, at 564–68. See further MS Melli, 'Guideline Review: Child Support and Time Sharing by Parents' (1999) 33 *Family Law Quarterly* 219.

[178] See n 144 above.

That said, the very fact that the fractional reductions are based on a factor of one-seventh, when there are seven days in a week, can only reinforce in the non-resident parent's mind the perception that the prime purpose of the rules is to reflect his extra expenditure on the child.

Special Cases

The new 'simplified' child support formula does not stop at four different rates with modifications for apportionment and shared care. The regulations also make provision for a series of other 'special cases'.[179] These turn on the status of either the adult or the child in question. In the former category, there are persons providing some day to day care who are treated as non-resident parents, persons who have part-time care but who are not non-resident parents and non-resident parents who are subject to court orders to maintain other children. In the latter group there are children in local authority care (and those in care but living at home) and children who are boarders or hospital inpatients. These categories should not necessarily be regarded as mutually exclusive; indeed, there is 'no reason why two or more special cases under the [2000] Regulations should not apply simultaneously where there is no inconsistency between the cases'.[180]

Persons Providing Some Day to Day Care who are Treated as Non-resident Parents

Where two adults, at least one of whom is the child's parent, live in different households but provide day to day care for the same child, the regulations make provision for the parent providing care to a lesser extent to be deemed to be the non-resident parent. This type of special case, which will cover many cases of shared parenting across households, has already been considered in chapter 8.[181]

Persons with Part-time Care who are not Non-resident Parents

The second type of special case arises where a child's care is split between persons who live in different households[182] and neither (or conceivably none) of whom is a parent treated as a non-resident parent by the special deeming rule applicable in the preceding special case and considered in chapter 8 above.[183] The test here is

---

[179] CSA 1991, s 42 and SI 2001/155, pt III.

[180] *CCS/4451/2002*, para 25 *per* Mr Commissioner Mesher.

[181] SI 2001/155, reg 8 and see pp 245–48 above.

[182] Hence this does not apply where the parents are living largely separate lives but still, of necessity, share the same household: *CCS/14625/1996.*

[183] SI 2001/155, reg 14(1); the NRP deeming rule is *ibid*, reg 8; see p 245 above.

one of 'day to day care' as defined by the regulations, not overnight care under the shared care rules.[184] In such a case the presumption is that the person who makes the maintenance application is entitled to receive all the child support payable under the Act.[185] However, this is subject to the Secretary of State's power, on request, to arrange for the payment of an appropriate proportion to the other person(s) caring for the child, having taken into account all the circumstances of the case.[186] These include having regard to the child's interests.[187]

Non-resident Parents Liable to Pay Maintenance under a Court Order for another Child

Sometimes a non-resident parent will be liable to pay maintenance under a court order for a child who does not fall within the Agency's jurisdiction, and is then subject to a maintenance calculation for a qualifying child.[188] Typically this will arise where the former child is the subject of a consent order made by a court.[189] The problem does not arise where it is the same child who is initially the subject of a court order and subsequently comes within the ambit of the Agency, as there are separate rules to deal with such a transition.[190] Clearly it would be inequitable if the maintenance calculation for the qualifying child took no account of the court-ordered maintenance obligation to the other child. Accordingly, the regulations provide for that obligation to be reflected in the final child support liability.

This special case applies where the initial child support liability is assessed on the basis of the basic or reduced rate, or following a variation in a case which would otherwise result in either the flat or nil rate.[191] In addition, the pre-existing liability to the non-qualifying child must be under a court maintenance order, not a maintenance agreement (or informal voluntary arrangement).[192] The final liability is determined by first calculating the maintenance under the 1991 Act as though the non-qualifying child were included in the assessment and then apportioning the resulting amount between all the children involved. The child support due is the sum payable in respect of the qualifying child or children (subject to the usual modifications on the basis of the apportionment or shared care rules).[193]

---

[184] SI 2001/155, reg 1(2)—so the threshold is 104 nights, not 52 nights.

[185] *Ibid*, reg 14(2)(a).

[186] *Ibid*, reg 14(2)(b) and (c).

[187] The mention of the child's 'interests', rather than 'welfare', is not elaborated upon by the regulations.

[188] SI 2001/155, reg 11(1); this includes foreign court orders, following the Child Support (Miscellaneous Amendments) Regulations 2005 (SI 2005/785) reg 6(4).

[189] Alternatively, the courts may have jurisdiction for some other reason, eg the child is a step-child.

[190] See pp 212–14.

[191] SI 2001/155, reg 11(2).

[192] *Ibid*, reg 11(1)(b). By virtue of the Interpretation Act 1978, s 11, 'maintenance order' carries the same meaning as in CSA 1991, ss 8(11) and 54: see p 188 above.

[193] SI 2001/155, reg 11(3). In effecting this calculation, the shared care rules (both as between parents and with local authorities) are not applied to any non-qualifying child: *ibid*, reg 11(4).

Children in Local Authority Care

In a similar way to which the formula reflects the fact that separated couples may share the care of their children, special rules operate where a child's care is shared as between the person with care and a local authority.[194] These rules apply where the child 'is being looked after by the local authority'[195] within the meaning of that term in the Children Act 1989[196] and in cases involving the basic or reduced rates, or following a variation to a flat or nil rate case.[197] As with 'private law' shared care,[198] there is a minimum threshold of 52 nights in the 12 months preceding the relevant week.[199] The Secretary of State may choose a period other than the preceding year in appropriate cases.[200] Indeed, this may be a future period, where it is intended that the child will be in local authority care after the effective date.[201] Where these special rules apply, the non-resident parent's basic or reduced rate child support liability is reduced by applying the appropriate fraction in Table 10.4 below.[202]

It will be apparent that these fractional reductions are not identical to those that apply in the private law context.[203] Although the first two bands and fractions are the same, there are then three further bands with different boundaries, extending to a potential discount of five-sevenths on the overall child support liability. Whereas the rules on shared care in non-local authority cases are predominantly designed to encourage joint parenting and improved compliance, these rules are presumably designed primarily to reflect the financial contributions of the various parties. The effect is that where a child is in care five days a week and comes home to the parent with care for two nights at the weekend, the non-resident parent should only have to pay child support for two days a week as the child's maintenance is being met by the local authority for the rest of the week. The difficulty with this is that the parent with care will have fixed costs (eg as regards the provision of clothing and housing) that cannot be readily reduced in the same way as day to day expenses such as food. In this sense the non-resident parent in such a case receives

---

[194] Consequently there is no need for the NRP to share care with the local authority.

[195] SI 2001/155, reg 9(11).

[196] This phrase therefore covers both children taken compulsorily into care and those who are being accommodated by a local authority. See further Children Act 1989, s 22 and Children (Scotland) Act 1995, s 17(6). It does not cover children who are being accommodated by a local *education* authority: see *R(CS) 2/04*, decided under the old law.

[197] SI 2001/155, reg 9(1).

[198] 'Private law' is used here in the sense of there being no local authority involvement in the shared care arrangements, irrespective of the benefit status of the PWC.

[199] SI 2001/155, reg 9(2)(a).

[200] *Ibid*, reg 9(2)(b). The test is different to that which applies to private law shared care, in that the Secretary of State can choose another time-span if 'more representative of the current arrangements for the care of the qualifying child', echoing the test for departing from the usual time-frame for assessing day to day care under *ibid*, reg 1(2).

[201] *Ibid*, reg 9(1)(c); however, the drafting of reg 9(1) implies also that there must be some extant shared care between the PWC and the local authority.

[202] *Ibid*, reg 9(3)–(6).

[203] See Table 10.3, p 318 above.

Table 10.4 Effect of shared care with local authority on basic and reduced rates

Number of nights in care of local authority	Fraction to subtract
52–103	One-seventh
104–155	Two-sevenths
156–207	Three-sevenths
208–259	Four-sevenths
260–262	Five-sevenths

what may be a windfall reduction in his child support liability, as a local authority—however much actual care it provides for a child—cannot be a person with care.[204] Indeed, if the child is in care for more than five days a week on average, then in principle there can be no person with care[205] and so no child support liability arises at all. However, in such circumstances the local authority may seek to recover a contribution to the child's maintenance using its powers under the Children Act 1989.[206] The assessment method for such contributions is markedly more discretionary than under the 1991 Act.[207]

As with private law cases, the special rules are further modified for what might be called 'exceptional special cases'. So where the couple have two or more qualifying children in care, the relevant fractions are aggregated and then divided by the number of children to arrive at the appropriate fractional reduction.[208] If both the private and local authority shared care rules apply, the fractions are aggregated.[209] If the child is a hospital inpatient or boarder for any period when the local authority would normally have care, such nights are attributed to the authority.[210] Finally, if the effect of the special rules would be to reduce the child support payable to less than the flat rate, then that weekly figure is payable, as apportioned where necessary.[211]

Children in Local Authority Care but Living at Home

Only about 10 per cent of the children who are formally in care in legal terms actually live in local authority children's homes. Instead, most (some 68 per cent) are

---

[204] Child Support (Maintenance Calculation Procedure) Regulations 2000 (SI 2001/157), reg 21(1)(a).

[205] As no individual is providing day to day care for 104 nights or more: CSA 1991, s 3(3)(b) and SI 2001/155, reg 1(2).

[206] See generally Children Act 1989, sch 2, pt III.

[207] It must be 'reasonable' to recover contributions (*ibid*, para 21(2)), which cannot be sought from those on means-tested benefits or tax credits (*ibid*, para 21(4)), and are settled by agreement (*ibid*, para 22) or court order, which has regard solely to the parent's means (*ibid*, para 23(3)(a)). See further *Re C (A Minor) (Contribution Notice)* [1994] 1 FLR 111.

[208] SI 2001/155, reg 9(7).

[209] *Ibid*, reg 9(8).

[210] *Ibid*, reg 9(10).

[211] *Ibid*, reg 9(9).

placed with foster-parents, and another 10 per cent continue to live with one or both of their natural parents.[212] In the latter circumstances the definition of 'person with care' is again modified, this time to refer to 'the parent of the child with whom the local authority allow the child to live' under its statutory powers.[213]

Qualifying Children who are Boarders or Hospital Inpatients

The statutory definition of 'person with care' requires that individual to be the one 'who usually provides day to day care for the child (whether exclusively or in conjunction with another person)'.[214] If the qualifying child is a boarder or a hospital inpatient, and consequently the person who would normally be providing day to day care is arguably not doing so, then the definition is modified to refer to 'the person who would usually be providing such care'.[215] This adopts the same policy as other more specific deeming provisions to the same effect.[216] Although the reference to boarding schools might suggest this is confined to children who are educated privately, this need not be the case. The ordinary meaning of 'boarding school' covers 'any institution which is a school and which provides overnight residence for some pupils'.[217] The definition also extends to boarders whose costs are met by public funds, for example by a local authority social services department or a local education authority.[218]

---

[212] Under Children Act 1989, s 23(5) and Placement of Children with Parents etc Regulations 1991 (SI 1991/893). For statistics see DfES, *Statistics of Education: Children looked after in England 2003–2004* Issue 01/05, Table 3 (January 2005) para 2.4 and Table A.

[213] SI 2001/155, reg 13. A local authority may place the child with one parent, with the result that that parent is the PWC under reg 13, but the child may then move to live with the other parent. The other parent (or indeed other carer) may then qualify as PWC under s 3(3)—irrespective of reg 13 (see *R(CS) 7/02*).

[214] CSA 1991, s 3(3)(b).

[215] SI 2001/155, reg 12.

[216] See *ibid*, regs 1(2) ('day to day care'), 7(6) (shared care) and 9(10) (care shared with local authority).

[217] See *CCS/1324/1997* at para 11 and *R(CS) 1/04* at para 24, both *per* Mr Commissioner Mesher.

[218] See respectively *ibid*, para 24 and *R(CS) 2/0/4* at para 31 *per* Mr Commissioner Jacobs.

11

Income and the Formula

Introduction

The calculation of the non-resident parent's income is inevitably one of the most contentious areas of child support law. In this chapter we examine the general principles governing the assessment of net weekly income, as well as specific rules which deal with the earnings of employed and self-employed non-resident parents respectively. The chapter concludes with an analysis of the particular provisions which deal with tax credits, income derived from occupational or personal pension schemes and benefit income. We start, however, by addressing two more fundamental questions: first, why is it that the person with care's income is irrelevant to the formula calculation and, secondly, why is there a maximum limit, or cap, on the non-resident parent's weekly income for the purposes of the child support formula?

The Person with Care's Income

The focus throughout this chapter is on the non-resident parent's income. This reflects the fact that under the reformed child support scheme the income of the person with care is irrelevant to the calculation of any child support liability. This stands in marked contrast to the original scheme, under which the parent with care's income was, in principle at least, always factored into the formula assessment.[1] This is not to say that it necessarily had any impact on the *outcome* of the formula, given the typical incomes of parents with care.[2] Nevertheless, the policy decision to disregard the parent with care's income in the new formula was one of the more controversial aspects of the reforms and so is considered here at the outset. Intuitively it would seem only just that the formula took into account both

---

[1] If the person with care was not a parent, her (or his) income had (and indeed still has) no effect whatsoever on the formula, as from the outset only *parents'* incomes were assessed under CSA 1991, sch 1.

[2] Indeed, PWCs in receipt of income support, income-based JSA or family credit/WFTC were deemed to have a nil income: *ibid*, para 5(4) and Child Support (Maintenance Assessment and Special Cases) Regulations 1992 (SI 1992/1815), reg 10A.

parents' incomes, and this certainly appears to be the view held by the great majority of the general public.[3]

The 1999 White Paper gave three reasons for ignoring the income of the parent with care.[4] First, the percentage rates for the new formula presuppose that the parent with care is already making a contribution to the child's maintenance. This was based on the research finding that an intact household spends approximately one third of its joint income on providing for one child; this figure was then halved to produce the non-resident parent's liability.[5] Secondly, having regard to the parent with care's income would necessarily make that formula more complicated, and would prompt demands for the income of new partners to be brought into the reckoning. Finally, and pragmatically, such added complexity was unwarranted given that in 96 per cent of the cases of non-resident parents with a full assessment under the original scheme the parent with care had a net weekly income of less than £100.[6]

The counter-argument was that to disregard the parent with care's income was 'demonstrably unfair and will lead to considerable discontent'.[7] On this basis 'elementary fairness' required that the parent with care's income be taken into account. This perspective is wholly understandable given the traditional basis of assessing maintenance and property settlements in ancillary relief proceedings.[8] But does it necessarily hold good in the context of the new child support formula? For example, assume that a couple with one child separate; the mother cares for the child but both parents are in work earning £300 a week. In the absence of any special circumstances, the father will be assessed to pay £45 a week.[9] If we were to assume further that the mother (somewhat exceptionally) earns twice the father's salary, he remains liable to pay £45 a week. On one view this may not seem unreasonable, given the level of his earnings—and indeed irrespective of how much his ex-partner earns and indeed whether or not she has a new partner.

The government's decision to disregard the incomes of parents with care appears to have been driven primarily by the desire to minimise the complexity in the formula in the light of their average income levels.[10] But this invites the charge

---

[3] V Peacey and L Rainford, *Attitudes towards child support and knowledge of the Child Support Agency* (DWP Research report No 226, London) at 26. PWCs take a very different view: see N Wikeley *et al*, *National Survey of Child Support Agency Clients* (DWP Research report No 152, 2001) at 157–58.

[4] DSS, *A new contract for welfare: Children's Rights and Parents' Responsibilities* at 14 paras 32–34.

[5] See further p 301 above.

[6] At the other extreme, fewer than 6,000 PWCs had an income of more than £200 a week: see n 4 above.

[7] Put forward most forcefully by Nicholas Mostyn QC of the Family Law Bar Association: House of Commons (HC) Social Security Committee, *Tenth Report* (HC 798, Session 1998–99) at 60; see further at 63–64. Other commentators pointed out the potentially adverse impact on compliance rates: *ibid*, at xviii, para 34.

[8] See eg Matrimonial Causes Act 1973, s 25(2)(a), directing the court to have regard to the income etc of each party to the marriage.

[9] See further p 301 above.

[10] See eg the comments of Baroness Hollis, cited in HC Social Security Committee, n 7 above, at xviii, para 35.

that the proper consideration of the circumstances of individual cases is being sacrificed on the altar of bureaucratic expediency.[11] The more convincing government argument is the first of those advanced in the White Paper, namely that parents with care are in any event making (at the very least) an equal contribution in kind to the child's upkeep in the way that the percentage rates were fixed. If that is so, then by definition the parent with care's actual income must be irrelevant. That assumes, however, that one accepts the premise—which the common law has traditionally resisted—that children are entitled to a share in both parents' prosperity, right up the income scale, and not simply to needs-based maintenance.[12]

Those who do not accept that premise made various suggestions in the responses to the White Paper for accommodating the incomes of better off parents with care. One proposal was that such cases should be diverted for adjudication in the courts.[13] This idea, however, was hardly likely to find favour with a government that was committed to allowing private consent orders to be vulnerable to 'unpicking' by an Agency assessment after 12 months. The House of Commons Select Committee, influenced by the arguments associated with fairness and compliance, recommended that the formula should be adjusted to make allowance for parents with care with substantial incomes. The Committee's proposal was that a 'significant threshold' should be set 'well above average male earnings', beyond which the parent with care's income would enter into the child support calculation.[14] The government rejected this suggestion, reiterating the arguments put in the White Paper.[15]

Critics of the government's approach[16] pointed to the Australian system, which includes the parent with care's income but then disregards a sum equivalent to the state average weekly earnings figure together with social security allowances for the children in her care.[17] The effect, inevitably, is that the majority of parents with care are treated as having a nil income, but higher incomes do enter into the equation. It is true that most overseas child support systems, but by no means all, have regard to the parent with care's income.[18] The New Zealand scheme, for example, takes no account of the parent with care's income, other than as a ground for a departure. Similarly, some of the US child support schemes are based solely on the income of the non-resident parent.[19]

---

[11] See eg Mostyn, *ibid*, at 64.

[12] See further the discussion in ch 1 above.

[13] HC Social Security Committee, n 7 above, at xvii, para 33.

[14] *Ibid*, at xviii para 36.

[15] DSS, *Reply by the Government to the Tenth Report* (Cm 4536, 1999) at paras 28–30.

[16] See eg Mostyn in HC Social Security Committee, n 7 above, at 69.

[17] Child Support (Assessment) Act 1989 (Cth), ss 43–46.

[18] JT Oldham, 'Lessons from the New English and Australian Child Support Systems' (1996) 29 *Vanderbilt Journal of Transnational Law* 691 at 719.

[19] For criticisms of these schemes see LW Morgan, 'Child support and the anomalous cases of the high-income and low-income parent: the need to reconsider what constitutes "support" in the American and Canadian child support guideline models' (1996) 13 *Canadian Journal of Family Law* 161 and KM Dodd, 'Poor little rich kids: revising Wisconsin's child support system to accommodate high-income payers' (2000) 83 *Marquette Law Review* 807.

Whatever the merits of the policy decision to exclude consideration of the parent with care's income from the formula, there is no safety valve in the variations scheme, at least as presently constituted, for what may appear to be 'hard cases', involving parents with care who enjoy substantial independent incomes. The grounds for seeking variations include situations in which the parent has assets over £65,000, a lifestyle which is inconsistent with the stated income or income which has not been taken into account in the maintenance calculation.[20] However, only persons with care can bring applications based on these so-called 'additional cases'.[21] In essence, these grounds are anti-avoidance measures targeted solely at non-resident parents. This is in contrast to the previous departures scheme, under which a non-resident parent could (unless the parent with care was on benefit) seek a formula adjustment on similar grounds against a parent with care.[22]

The Statutory Cap on the Non-resident Parent's Income

Cases governed by the old scheme are subject to a maximum child support liability, the actual calculation of which is highly complex,[23] but in practical terms the effect is that the maximum weekly liability is about £120 for one child under the age of 11 and around £200 for two such children.[24] Non-resident parents on more modest incomes are subject to a lower cap, in that a non-resident parent under the old scheme cannot be required to pay more than 30 per cent of his net income.[25]

So far as the new scheme is concerned, the government's initial stance as to the desirability of an income cap was undecided.[26] By the time of the White Paper, its position had become clear:

> We have decided that there should be no maximum liability under the new scheme. Children have a right to share in the income of their parents—this applies to the children of wealthy parents as much as those whose parents have more modest incomes.[27]

[20] See Child Support (Variations) Regulations 2000 (SI 2001/156), regs 18–20.

[21] It is unclear whether this could be changed without amending primary legislation. It is arguable that a rule providing for a threshold above which the PWC's income would be taken into account might be introduced as an additional case for a variation under the enabling power in CSA 1991, sch 4B, para 4(2)(c).

[22] See Child Support Departure Direction and Consequential Amendments Regulations 1996 (SI 1996/2907), regs 9(3)(b) and 23–29.

[23] The calculation involved adding together the appropriate basic and additional elements, according to whether or nor the parent with care had any assessable income: CSA 1991, sch 1, paras 2–4 (before amendment by CSPSSA 2000) and Child Support (Maintenance Assessments and Special Cases) Regulations 1992 (SI 1992/1815), reg 6.

[24] DSS, *A new contract for welfare: Children's Rights and Parents' Responsibilities* (Cm 4349, 1999) ch 2 para 35. See further CSA 1991, s 8(6) for the possibility of an application to court where the NRP's income exceeds the statutory cap.

[25] SI 1992/1815, reg 11(6) and (6A), a provision first inserted in April 1995.

[26] The Green Paper had been silent on the point: DSS, *Children First: a new approach to child support* (Cm 3992, 1998) ch 5.

[27] White Paper, n 24 above, ch 2 at para 36.

One critic described the proposal as 'fundamentally unfair', arguing that whilst children might have an *expectation* of a share in their parents' wealth, they had no such *right*.[28] Rather, it was argued on the basis of common law principles, children only have a right to maintenance based on their reasonable needs. Fathers' groups likewise contended that if child maintenance was unlimited, then at some point it must become disguised spousal maintenance, so undermining the credibility of the new system. The Select Committee, which regarded these complaints as over-stated, were persuaded of the case for children to continue to share in their parents' wealth following separation and so declined to support a cap on net weekly income.[29]

Notwithstanding the Select Committee's support, ministers recognised that the arguments were finally balanced,[30] and the insertion of an upper limit on the amount of the non-resident parent's weekly income to be taken into account in the formula represented a last minute concession during the passage of the 2000 Act. As a result the rules governing the assessment of the non-resident parent's income in new scheme cases, discussed in this chapter, are all subject to the income cap, which provides that 'any amount of net weekly income . . . over £2,000 is to be ignored for the purposes of this Schedule'.[31] This cap was the result of a Government amendment at the Third Reading of the Bill in the House of Lords, in response to pressure from peers, and just a week before the Royal Assent. The Government acknowledged that the level of the statutory cap was 'inevitably somewhat arbitrary, but we believe that £2,000 is justifiable, reasonable and prag-matic'.[32] Arguably it is the last of these epithets that was the most appropriate, given the legislative timetable. The cap corresponds to an annual salary of just under £170,000 gross, some seven times the national average wage. According to the minister, the £2,000 cap[33] is 'sufficiently high to ensure that all children benefit from a reasonable level of maintenance, while providing that only those who are likely to have more complicated financial arrangements are affected'.[34] Official estimates suggest that this cap affects only about 50–100 parents in the Child Support Agency's caseload of 1.2 million.[35] Of course, if the non-resident parent's net weekly income exceeds £2,000 per week, the parent with care may bring an application in the courts for a top-up maintenance order.[36]

The United Kingdom scheme is unusual in setting the maximum assessable income for child support purposes at such a high level. It should also be noted that

---

[28] Nicholas Mostyn QC, 'The Green Paper on Child Support—Children First: a new approach to child support' [1999] Fam Law 95 at 98.

[29] HC Social Security Committee, n 7 above, at para 41.

[30] *Ibid*, at para 40.

[31] CSA 1991, sch 1, para 10(3).

[32] *Per* Baroness Hollis of Heigham, *Hansard*, HL vol 615, col 1083 (19 July 2000).

[33] This figure may be increased by regulations: CSA 1991, sch 1, para 10A(1)(b).

[34] *Ibid*.

[35] Under the old scheme fewer than 500 assessments were at the maximum level: DSS, n 24 above, ch 2 para 35.

[36] See p 194.

there is no consensus in society at large; the general public is equally divided between those who believe there should be no maximum to a parent's liability for child support and those in favour of an upper limit.[37] The Australian system imposes an income cap at a much lower level (2.5 times the yearly equivalent of average weekly earnings for a full-time employee).[38] Several American states have also set a cap representing a specific monthly income figure.[39] The United States case law also reflects the common law principle that the purpose of child maintenance is to meet the child's reasonable needs, and not to redistribute parental wealth. This is known in the American child support literature as the 'three pony rule', in the sense that 'no child, no matter how wealthy the parents, needs to be provided more than three ponies'.[40]

General Rules for Calculating Net Weekly Income

The non-resident's 'net weekly income' is one of the fundamental building blocks for establishing his child support liability. Thus the basic rate is 15, 20 or 25 per cent of this figure.[41] The respective criteria for the reduced, flat and nil rates all likewise refer to various bands of 'net weekly income'.[42] The 1991 Act itself provides that the calculation of net weekly income is to be determined in accordance with regulations.[43] The rules governing the assessment of the non-resident parent's net income are set out in the Child Support (Maintenance Calculations and Special Cases) Regulations 2000.[44] Subject to the £2,000 upper limit discussed above, the Schedule to the 2000 Regulations identifies five categories of net weekly income which must be taken into account in calculating a non-resident parent's child support liability. The non-resident parent's net weekly income is the aggregate of the net weekly income from these various sources.[45] These are income from employment, self-employment and tax credits along with 'other income',[46]

---

[37] Peacey and Rainford, n 3 above, at 26–27.

[38] Child Support (Assessment) Act 1989 (Cth) s 42. The annual figure for 2005 was Aus$130,767 (approx £56,000 p/a). A proposal made in the Child Support Legislation Amendment Bill (2000) (Cth) to lower this cap to 2.5 times average earnings for *all* employees was not implemented. The House of Representatives Standing Committee report *Every picture tells a story* (Canberra, December 2003) called for the cap to be lowered: recommendation 25. The Ministerial Taskforce has proposed a cap based on joint parental income: Report of the Ministerial Taskforce on Child Support, *In the Best Interests of Children* (Canberra, 2005) at 149–50.

[39] Oldham, n 18 above, at 712.

[40] *In the Marriage of Patterson* 920 P 2d 450 (Court of Appeals of Kansas, 1996) at 455. That said, the concept of the child's needs is elastic—in the extreme example of *In the Interest of Gonzalez* 993 S W 2d 147 (Court of Appeals of Texas, 1999) it included provision of a bodyguard for the child (as the wealthy father had provided bodyguards for his other children).

[41] See ch 10 and CSA 1991, sch 1, para 2(1).

[42] *Ibid*, paras 3(1), 4(1)(a) and 5(a).

[43] *Ibid*, para 10(1).

[44] SI 2001/155, sch.

[45] *Ibid*.

[46] *Ibid*, pts II–V.

that term being confined to occupational and personal pension income and similar forms of retirement benefits, and (exceptionally) some benefit income.

The fact that the Schedule refers to the five specific sources of income means that in principle any other forms of income, which do not fall into one of these categories, are *not* relevant in calculating the non-resident parent's net income.[47] It follows that various types of income which were taken into account in assessing liability under the original child support scheme no longer enter into the child support calculation for new cases as a matter of course. These include, for example, dividend income, rental income and income from capital investments. It seems that the experience under the original scheme was that few non-resident parents had investment income to such an extent that it would appreciably affect their child support liability.[48] Income from student grants and loans and from most social security benefits is likewise ignored.[49] The justification for the exclusion of such income streams is that 'there is a clear danger of a simple system of rates becoming bogged down in detailed investigations of minor sources of income for small groups of parents'.[50]

There is no all-embracing provision within the variations scheme enabling decision makers and tribunals to bring such extra sources of income back into the child support equation. Instead, further complexity has been added to the variations scheme in an *ad hoc* fashion by the introduction of amending regulations designed to address particular forms of potential injustice. Two examples illustrate this point, the first involving rental income. As we have seen, rental income was taken into account as a form of income in old scheme cases.[51] It is not recognised as an assessable form of income in the new scheme, but there is now an obscurely drafted provision in the rules governing variations which means that an application for a variation may be feasible in such cases.[52] The second example concerns the treatment of dividend income. Under the old scheme, dividend payments were taken into account as a form of 'other income'. However, there is no provision in the standard formula under the new scheme for dividend income to be taken into account. This has created a loophole that 'could be exploited by some unscrupulous non-resident parents' (for example, where the sole shareholder and employee in a 'one-man company' manipulates his income from the business).[53] Government's response has been to create a new sub-category of variation for

---

[47] Contrast the position in relation to means-tested social security benefits, for which all income is taken into account unless expressly disregarded: see eg Income Support (General) Regulations 1987 (SI 1987/1967), reg 40(1).

[48] DSS, n 24 above, Annex 2, para 8.

[49] Subject to the exception in SI 2001/155, sch, para 17: see p 361 below.

[50] DSS, n 24 above, ch 2, para 30.

[51] Subject to certain allowable deductions: see SI 1992/1815, sch 2, para 23 and *R(CS) 3/00*.

[52] SI 2001/156, reg 18(3)(d).

[53] *R(CS) 4/05* para 2 *per* Mr Commissioner Mesher.

cases in which the non-resident parent can control the amount of income he receives from a company or business.[54]

It follows that the primary focus of the 2000 Regulations—and subject to any modification in accordance with the tightly drawn constraints of the variations scheme—is on actual and not assumed income. In particular, the new child support scheme[55] contains no effective provision for imputing income to a non-resident parent.[56] In contrast, the courts dealing with ancillary relief applications must have regard not just to the parties' income but also to the 'earning capacity . . . which each of the parties to the marriage has or is likely to have in the foreseeable future'.[57] In the same way other child support schemes include provisions enabling additional income to be imputed to a parent whose income fails to reflect their true earning capacity.[58]

The Schedule to the 2000 Regulations makes provision for various sums to be ignored when calculating a non-resident parent's income. These are considered further below in the context of the rules governing the assessment of the income of employed and self-employed non-resident parents respectively. In addition, there is a general provision which expressly disregards the costs of converting payments made in currencies other than sterling and amounts payable overseas where there is a prohibition against the transfer of such funds to the United Kingdom.[59]

Finally, it is important to note that the sole focus of these rules is the non-resident parent's 'net weekly *income*' rather than his capital. As with revenue law and social security law,[60] there is no attempt in the child support legislation to define what is meant by 'income' and 'capital' respectively. The starting point is the fundamental principle of statutory interpretation that such words should be accorded their ordinary and natural meaning.[61] A Social Security Commissioner has defined income as 'money paid regularly to the recipient or to his order but

---

[54] SI 2001/156, reg 19(1A); see further N Wikeley, 'Child Support, Dividend Income and the Bertie Wooster Escape Clause' [2005] Fam Law 707.

[55] On the old scheme see SI 1992/1815, sch 1, para 27 and *CCS/4056/2004*.

[56] There is a regulation-making power in CSA 1991, sch 1, para 10B but there appears to be no current intention to use it. The Government's position is that such cases are best handled as variations to the basic rate: see House of Lords Select Committee on Delegated Powers and Deregulation, *Thirteenth Report*, (HL 59, Session 1999–2000), Annex 1 at para 49.

[57] Matrimonial Causes Act 1973, s 25(2)(a). See eg *Hardy v Hardy* [1981] 1 FLR 321.

[58] On the US case law, see L Becker 'Spousal and Child Support and the "Voluntary Reduction of Income" Doctrine' (1997) 29 *Connecticut Law Review* 647 and CM Clark, 'Imputing parental income in child support determinations: what price for a child's best interest?' (1999) 49 *Catholic University Law Review* 167. For Australia, see L Young, 'Earning capacity and child support: The fascination with motivation continues' [2004] 10 *Current Family Law* 178.

[59] SI 2001/155, sch, para 2.

[60] 'The Income Tax Acts nowhere define "income" any more than they define "capital" . . . what constitutes income they discreetly refrain from saying . . . Consequently it is to the decided cases one must go in search of light' *per* Lord Macmillan in *Van den Berghs Ltd v Clark* [1935] AC 431 at 438, cited in G Morse and DW Williams, *Davies: Principles of Tax Law* (Sweet & Maxwell, London, 4th edn, 2000), at 64.

[61] *R(IS) 4/01* para 27 *per* Mr Commissioner Angus. See also *Leeves v Chief Adjudication Officer*, reported as *R(IS) 5/99* (CA) and *Morrell v Secretary of State for Work and Pensions* [2003] EWCA Civ 526, reported as *R(IS) 6/03*, para 31 *per* Richards J.

not money which is paid and which he cannot prevent from being paid directly to a third party instead of to him'.[62] The essence of income receipts is that 'they display an element of periodic recurrence' which thereby excludes *ad hoc* payments.[63] Clearly the nature of the underlying obligation must also be taken into account, so that a capital payment made by instalments remains a capital rather than income resource.[64] Similarly, if there is an immediate obligation to repay—as may be the case with a student grant following the abandonment of a course—then such payment loses the character of being 'income'.[65] If, on the other hand, there have been regular payments with at best an uncertain and future obligation to repay, which may or may not materialise, then such payments will retain their essential character as income.[66]

In this context it is also relevant to note that the courts have traditionally been reluctant to depart from normal commercial or accountancy practices in elucidating the 'true' nature of particular payments.[67] The Social Security Commissioners have adopted the same practice.[68] As a general rule, therefore, the non-resident parent's capital holdings are not relevant to the calculation of his child support liability. The main exception to this principle is that a variation application may be made where the non-resident parent has assets in excess of £65,000, providing the strict criteria in the regulations are satisfied.[69]

Net Weekly Income of Employed Earners

As with social security legislation, child support law draws a distinction between 'employed earners' and 'self-employed earners' and adopts essentially the same definitions of these terms. An employed earner is 'a person who is gainfully

---

[62] *R(IS) 4/01* para 27 *per* Mr Commissioner Angus (holding that that part of the claimant's occupational pension which was deducted at source and paid direct to his ex-wife under an attachment of earnings order was not part of his income for income support purposes). See also *R(IS) 4/02* and *R(IS) 2/03*.

[63] *R v Supplementary Benefits Commission, ex p Singer* [1973] 1 WLR 713 at 717 *per* Bridge J. See also *R(SB) 28/95* (one-off loan made by social services department to meet claimant's arrears on hire purchase agreement held to be a capital payment).

[64] *Lillystone v Supplementary Benefits Commission* (1981) 3 FLR 52. Note that the regulation-making powers in CSA 1991, sch 1, para 10B do not permit the Secretary of State to treat income as capital and vice versa: contrast SSCBA 1992, s 136(5). Furthermore, although these powers allow the Secretary of State to treat persons as possessing income which they do not in fact have and to provide for cases of intentional deprivation of sources of income, they have not been exercised: see n 56 above.

[65] *Leeves v Chief Adjudication Officer*, reported as *R(IS) 5/99* (CA).

[66] *Morrell v Secretary of State for Work and Pensions* [2003] EWCA Civ 526, reported as *R(IS) 6/03*, para 33 *per* Richards J (regular and substantial monthly sums paid by mother to daughter to cover rent and living expenses held to be daughter's income for purposes of income support scheme).

[67] See eg *British Insulated and Helsby Cables Ltd v Atherton* [1926] AC 205, *CIR v Wattie* [1998] STC 1167 and *Smith (Herbert) (a firm) v Honour* [1999] STC 173.

[68] *R(FC) 1/91* para 38 *per* Mr Commissioner Hallett and *CIS/5481/1997* paras 14–15 *per* Mr Commissioner Williams.

[69] See p 388.

employed in Great Britain either under a contract of service, or in an office (including elective office) with general earnings'.[70] This definition is extended to include non-resident parents who are either gainfully employed in Northern Ireland or are deemed to be habitually resident in the United Kingdom because their employer is based in the jurisdiction.[71] The distinction between 'employed earners' (or employees) working under contracts of service and 'self-employed earners' (or independent contractors) operating under contracts for services is one that has bedevilled other areas of legal regulation and need not be rehearsed here.[72] In borderline cases the classification of a contract into one category or the other can be exceedingly problematic, given the uncertainty about both the criteria to be applied and the weight to be attached to individual factors.[73]

Assuming that the non-resident parent is an employee, his 'net weekly income' comprises those earnings which are calculated or estimated by reference to the relevant week, less certain deductions.[74] One must therefore consider the three issues of 'earnings', the relevant deductions and the period of assessment by which average earnings are calculated.

Earnings

Earnings are defined in general terms as 'any remuneration or profit derived from that employment'.[75] This expression is a wide one; 'derived from' in this context means 'having their origin in' the employment.[76] It is not enough simply that the payment comes from the employer; thus, where a company repays a loan made to it by one of its directors, that repayment does not constitute a profit derived from the employment in his hands.[77] This definition has also caused difficulty where an employee receives an overpayment of salary—should the excess payment be counted as earnings? The better view would appear to be that it does. This may appear unfair in that it has the effect of artificially inflating the non-resident parent's income for the period in question. However, subsequent recoveries by way of

---

[70] SI 2001/155, reg 1(2), adopting SSCBA 1992, s 2(1)(a). The reference to 'elective office' obviously brings in councillors.

[71] SI 2001/155, reg 1(2); see also CSA 1991, s 44(2A), discussed at p 250 above.

[72] Eg employment law, revenue law and the law of torts, as well as social security law. In the latter context see N Wikeley, A Ogus and E Barendt, *The Law of Social Security* (Butterworths, London, 2002, 5th edn) at 98–103.

[73] M Freedland, *The Personal Employment Contract* (Oxford University Press, Oxford, 2003), at 20–21. The task is made no easier by the unhelpful definition of 'contract of service' in SSCBA 1992, s 122(1), which by incorporation must also apply in the context of child support.

[74] SI 2001/155, sch, para 3(1)(a).

[75] *Ibid*, para 4(1).

[76] *R(SB) 21/86* para 12 *per* Mr Commissioner Rice. See also *R(SB) 2/86* (cash payment to miner in lieu of concessionary coal included within definition).

[77] *CCS/3671/2002* para 9 *per* Mr Commissioner Mesher: 'the derivation of the repayment of the loan was not the carrying out by the absent parent of his duties as an employee or as a director, but was the fact that a loan had been made by him to the company'.

deductions made by the employer through the payroll can then be construed as evidence of a contractual variation to reduce the person's salary for a later period.[78] There is, however, no requirement that the payment in question actually be made by the employer, so long as it is 'derived from' that employment. Hence where an employer becomes insolvent, and the Secretary of State makes a compensatory payment for lack of proper notice of the termination of employment, such a payment is 'derived from' that employment.[79] The regulations then specify in some detail particular types of income which are automatically regarded as being earnings, as well as listing further categories which are excluded from the statutory definition of that term.

(i) Income which is Included in the Definition of an Employee's 'Earnings'

For the avoidance of any doubt, five particular categories of income streams are expressly included within the definition of 'earnings', but subject always to the deductions considered further below.

(a) any bonus, commission, payment in respect of overtime, royalty or fees;

Each of these types of payments is in one way or another 'derived from' the employment and so is included here to preclude any argument that they do not constitute 'earnings'. Again, such payments need not be made by the employer. For example, a sales assistant in a shop who is paid a cash bonus or commission by a manufacturer receives a payment 'derived from' that employment.[80] Any bonuses or commission paid separately from the normal earnings or in respect of a longer period than those earnings are aggregated over a year and attributed on a weekly basis by dividing by 52.[81] There is no special rule for the attribution of royalty payments,[82] but in principle the same considerations as operate in respect of bonus or commission payments will apply.

Payments for working overtime are the most common form of income in this group. In practice the issue is likely to be whether the overtime is representative of the non-resident's person's earnings over a particular period. If, in the Secretary of State's opinion, the average earnings as calculated in the usual way do 'not accurately reflect the normal amount of the earnings of the person in question', then a different assessment period may be chosen.[83] In selecting an alternative period, the

---

[78] This was the analysis preferred by Mr Commissioner Mesher in *R(TC) 2/03*, who declined to follow *CCS/4378/2001*, in which Mr Commissioner Jacobs disregarded the impact of the overpayments by a different route (holding that the original excess payments were not 'derived from' the employment).

[79] Indeed, this type of payment is expressly included by virtue of SI 2001/155, Sch, para 4(1)(e).

[80] But incentives in the form of non-cash vouchers, holidays etc would not count as earnings for child support purposes as they are benefits in kind: *ibid*, para 4(2)(d), although they count for the purposes of national insurance liabilities: see SSCBA 1992, s 10ZA.

[81] SI 2001/155, sch, para 6(3) (assuming such payments were received in the 52 weeks ending with the relevant week).

[82] Contrast SI 1987/1967, reg 30(2) as regards income support.

[83] SI 2001/155, sch, para 6(4).

Secretary of State must have regard to the earnings received (or due to be received) and the duration and pattern (actual or expected) of the employment.[84]

(b) any holiday pay except any payable more than 4 weeks after termination of the employment;

Holiday pay may take the form either of pay whilst on holiday or a payment in lieu of unpaid holiday made when an employee leaves a job (subject to the 'more than four weeks after termination' exception). 'Payable' in this context means due to be paid under the contract of employment, rather than actually received or paid.[85] This provision does not itself cover a payment which is by way of compensation for the absence of any holiday entitlement,[86] but such a payment would presumably be caught as one 'derived from' that employment in the broader sense.

(c) any payment by way of a retainer;

Retainers—for example, where paid to school meals service employees during school holidays—are treated as income for social security purposes[87] and the same applies in the context of child support.

(d) any statutory sick pay under Part XI of the Contributions and Benefits Act or statutory maternity pay under Part XII of the Contributions and Benefits Act;

(dd) any statutory paternity pay under Part 12ZA of the Contributions and Benefits Act or any statutory adoption pay under Part 12ZB of that Act;

These four benefits, administered via employers, are all counted as earnings for the purposes of child support. This mirrors the position in social security law more generally; for example, such payments are treated as earnings and so subject to national insurance contributions.[88]

(e) any payment in lieu of notice, and any compensation in respect of the absence or inadequacy of any such notice, but only in so far as such payment or compensation represents loss of income.

This provision makes it clear that payments in lieu of notice and compensation for inadequate notice count as earnings, so long as they represent loss of income. On the other hand, redundancy payments, assessed principally by reference to past service, are regarded as compensation by way of a capital payment for the loss of the job itself rather than for loss of future earnings.[89] For example, in one unreported decision the Commissioner disregarded most of an 'ex gratia' payment of

---

[84] SI 2001/155, sch, para 6(4)(a) and (b).

[85] See *R(SB) 15/82*, *R(SB) 33/83* and *R(SB) 11/85*.

[86] *CIS/894/1994*. The specific disregard from earnings which applied in that context is not replicated in the child support scheme.

[87] See eg SI 1987/1967, reg 35(1)(e).

[88] SSCBA 1992, s 4(1)(a)(i)–(iv). Although statutory adoption pay and statutory paternity pay were introduced in April 2003, the child support regulations were not amended until September 2004: Child Support (Miscellaneous Amendments) Regulations 2004 (SI 2004/2415).

[89] As in social security law: see eg *R v National Insurance Commissioner, ex p Stratton* [1979] QB 361.

£10,000, negotiated through solicitors, which was in large part in settlement of a claim for a redundancy payment on the non-renewal of a contract of employment following a period of maternity leave.[90]

(ii) Income which is Excluded from the Definition of an Employee's 'Earnings'

As well as expressly specifying that the above forms of income are to be regarded as 'earnings', the regulations stipulate that the following types of payment are to be excluded from the maintenance calculation:[91]

(a) any payment in respect of expenses wholly, exclusively and necessarily incurred in the performance of the duties of the employment;

This exclusion is confined to payments in respect of expenses made *to* the employee (usually by the employer) and not made *by* the employee.[92] So a payment that an employee *receives* 'in respect of expenses wholly, exclusively and necessarily incurred in the performance of the duties of the employment' does not count as part of his earnings. This test is very similar to, but not quite identical to, the position under revenue law. Moreover, as one Commissioner has noted, this phrase 'is probably one of the most litigated phrases in income tax law, and . . . I assume its adoption into child support law is intended to carry with it the full— and, it has to be said, very restrictive—interpretation from the income tax cases'.[93]

Revenue law draws a distinction between a general rule for employees' work-related expenses and a specific provision for their travelling expenses.[94] The general rule is that expenses are deductible for tax purposes only if they were incurred 'wholly, exclusively and necessarily in the performance of the duties of the employment', and if the employee was 'obliged to incur and pay [the expenses] as holder of the employment'.[95] Travelling expenses, on the other hand, are allowable for tax purposes insofar as the employee is obliged to incur and pay them and they are 'necessarily incurred on travelling in the performance of the duties of the employment' (with no separate requirement of 'wholly and exclusively').[96] Child support law does not make this distinction: all employees' expenses, including those relating to travelling, are subject to the traditional test, namely whether they were 'wholly, exclusively and necessarily incurred'. Given these (albeit marginal) differences, decisions reached under income tax law as to the deductibility of

---

[90] *CCS/3182/1995* paras 16–19 *per* Mr Commissioner Howell QC. However, a part of that payment (some £1,400) was taken into account as it was conceded to represent a payment in lieu of notice. That decision has been criticised for failing to advert to the opening words (E Jacobs and G Douglas, *Child Support: The Legislation* (Sweet & Maxwell, London, Edition Seven, 2005/2006) at 654) but the decision is justifiable on the basis of the essentially capital-based nature of the payment.

[91] SI 2001/155, sch, para 4(2).

[92] *R(CS) 2/96* at para 15 *per* Mr Commissioner Mesher.

[93] *CCS/2561/1998*, para 21 *per* Mr Commissioner Williams.

[94] Income Tax (Earnings and Pensions) Act (ITEPA) 2003, s 336.

[95] *Ibid*, s 336(1). The latter requirement was added to ITEPA as part of the Tax Law Rewrite Project but was not designed to change the underlying legal test.

[96] *Ibid*, s 337(1).

employees' expenses are not necessarily conclusive for the purposes of child support law.

In *R(CS) 6/98* Mr Commissioner Rowland identified three further reasons why different outcomes may occur as regards the treatment of expenses under revenue law and child support law.[97] The first was that income tax legislation makes specific provision for some expenses to be deductible or for allowances to be non-taxable, independently of the 'wholly, exclusively and necessarily incurred' test.[98] Additionally, HMRC (formerly the Inland Revenue) has historically operated extra-statutory concessions which provide the taxpayer with relief even when the strict words of the legislation may not be satisfied.[99] Moreover, a decision or agreement reached as between the taxpayer and the Inspector of Taxes, in which the parent with care would not have had the opportunity of making representations, cannot bind the Secretary of State in the child support jurisdiction.[100] Thus Agency staff and appeal tribunals must reach an independent judgment in such matters, which may or may not follow HMRC's treatment of the expenses for tax purposes.[101] In doing so there is no formal burden of proof on any one party.[102] Bearing those reservations in mind, the test of deductibility of expenses for employees requires three conditions to be satisfied for the purposes of child support law.[103]

First, the expenses must be 'incurred in the performance of the duties of the employment'.[104] This requirement has invariably been strictly construed in the revenue law context. It therefore excludes expenses incurred in preparing for work or in order to be better able to carry out the work in question.[105] For example, this test would not allow the deduction of the expenses of travelling *to* work[106] (as opposed to travelling whilst *in* work) or the cost of professional subscriptions.[107] Rent or housing allowances paid to police officers have also been considered in a number of Commissioners' decisions.[108] Despite an early unreported decision to

---

[97] At para 7.

[98] For example, professional subscriptions: see n 107 below.

[99] One of the aims of the Tax Law Rewrite Project, which has led to ITEPA 2003, was to codify many of these concessions.

[100] Thus the issue is not *res judicata*.

[101] HMRC's designation will clearly be influential: *CCS/2750/1995 per* Mr Commissioner Mesher.

[102] *R(CS) 10/98* para 12 *per* Mr Commissioner Howell QC.

[103] See further the discussion in C Whitehouse *et al*, *Revenue Law—Principles and Practice* (Tottel, Haywards Heath, 23rd edn, 2005) paras 5.171–5.175.

[104] This is a narrower phrase than the equivalent for the self-employed ('for the purposes of the earner's business'), in the same way as for income tax: see Morse and Williams, n 60 above at 117.

[105] See eg *Fitzpatrick v IRC; Smith v Abbott* [1994] 1 WLR 306, HL (expenses of journalists in purchasing newspapers incurred preparatory to, rather than in the performance of, their work).

[106] *Ricketts v Colquhoun* [1926] AC 1, HL (barrister living in London with judicial appointment in Portsmouth could not deduct travelling or hotel expenses when sitting). The exclusion of commuting costs was one of the pinchpoints in the original child support scheme, and resulted in the creation under CSA 1995 of a special category of travel-to-work costs over a certain threshold: see p 134 above.

[107] *Simpson v Tate* [1925] 2 KB 214. For income tax purposes specific provision is now made for such expenses under ITEPA 2003, ss 343–345. See *CCS/3882/1997* in the child support context.

[108] The basis of these allowances has varied over the years, and they are no longer payable to new recruits: Jacobs and Douglas, n 90 above, at 632. For more detail, see *R(CS) 2/99* paras 14–18.

the contrary,[109] the better view is that such allowances are not deductible for child support purposes.[110] This would also be consistent with the approach taken in the cases involving non-resident parents in the armed services (other than those who are required to live abroad).[111]

The second requirement is that the expense must be 'necessarily' incurred in the performance of the contractual duties. Again, this condition has been construed strictly in the context of income tax. The test is an objective one, determined by whether the expense is necessary for the employment, and not simply whether the employer stipulates it as a requirement.[112] It is also clearly a narrower test than that which applies to self-employed non-resident parents, for whom the test in child support law is merely whether the expenses were 'reasonably' incurred.

Finally, the expenses must be incurred 'wholly' and 'exclusively' in the performance of the employment. These terms also apply to self-employed earners and have likewise been borrowed from the lexicon of revenue law. Again, the test is a strict one; thus a person who buys a suit solely for work purposes, even where he is required to do by his employer, cannot claim a tax-deductible expense as it is also worn to provide cover and comfort.[113] Overall, the combined effect of the requirement that the expenses be 'wholly, exclusively and necessarily incurred' imposes a very demanding threshold for the deductibility of work-related expenditure.

As we have seen, this exception applies solely to payments of expenses made *to* the employee (typically, but not necessarily, by the employer) and not *by* the employee. But what if the employee makes payments in respect of such expenses out of his own pocket but receives no recompense (whether from the employer or a third party)? A self-employed non-resident parent is clearly entitled to have certain allowable expenses set against his gross income in the process of calculating his net earnings.[114] But, in the absence of any such express statutory provision, how (if at all) can this be achieved for employees' non-reimbursed expenses?

The Agency's internal guidance acknowledges that:

> an employee may incur expenses in the performance of the work and receive no payment for these from the employer. If the expenses are incurred 'wholly exclusively and

---

[109] *CCS/12769/1996, per* Mr Commissioner Goodman.

[110] *R(CS) 10/98* (in which *CCS/12769/1996* was distinguished as exceptional on its facts), *R(CS) 2/99* (in which the Commissioner declined to follow *CCS/12769/1996*) and *CCS/2561/1998* (where the Commissioner observed that *CCS/12769/1996* had not examined the basis for the claimed tax exempt status of the allowance).

[111] The case law appears to have resulted in a distinction between home and overseas housing allowances for service personnel. For example, see *CCS/5352/1995* (UK lodging allowance paid to an army major not deductible from earnings), distinguishing *CCS/318/1995* (overseas army housing allowance deductible), and see also *CCS/4305/1995* (expenses incurred by army officer in accommodation abroad deductible).

[112] *Brown v Bullock* [1961] 3 All ER 129, CA (bank manager required by employer to be member of a club; but subscription held not necessary for the duties of the employment).

[113] *Hillyer v Leake* [1976] STC 490, and see also *Mallalieu v Drummond* [1983] 2 AC 861, HL, regarding the self-employed.

[114] SI 2001/155, sch, para 8(2)(a); see further below p 356 (the test, of course, is different).

necessarily' in the performance of the duties of the employment then they should be treated as an allowable cost to the employee.[115]

The authority cited for this proposition is *Parsons v Hogg*,[116] in which the issue was the meaning of 'gross income' for the purposes of calculating entitlement to family income supplement.[117] The claimant, a vicar, was paid a stipend comprising two elements, his taxable salary and a non-taxable allowance for heating, lighting etc. On top of this he incurred further work-related expenses which were allowed by the (then) Inland Revenue. The Court of Appeal held that in this context the 'gross amount' of the vicar's earnings meant that figure arrived at 'before the deduction of tax but after deduction of the expenses that are allowable in arriving at the taxable sum'.[118]

Parsons v Hogg was applied to the original child support scheme by Mr Commissioner Mesher in *R(CS) 2/96*.[119] The Commissioner rejected the argument that the child support regulations[120] under the old scheme provided a 'complete and unambiguous code' for the calculation of earnings. Accordingly, the non-resident parent's earnings were to be taken into account having made any *Parsons v Hogg* deduction, as well as any deductions expressly provided for by the regulations. On the facts of *R(CS) 2/96* the Commissioner confirmed, albeit with some hesitation, the appeal tribunal's findings that some of an army sergeant's expenses (eg for mess fees and dress uniform) were allowable.[121] However, the sergeant's expenses incurred in living in married quarters were held to be not deductible for child support purposes.[122] In a subsequent decision, the same Commissioner held that a non-resident parent's expenses by way of membership fees to various professional bodies were deductible from his earnings under the principle in *Parsons v Hogg*.[123] Of course, an employee's expenses will only be deductible if they were incurred 'wholly, exclusively and necessarily' in the performance of the duties of the employment.[124]

---

[115] Child Support Agency, *Procedures: Gather Information and Evidence*, 'Allowable Expenses' at 1164.

[116] [1985] 2 All ER 897 (CA), also reported as an Appendix to *R(FIS) 4/85*.

[117] A benefit for those in work on low incomes, also known as FIS, and superseded by family credit in 1988 (in turn replaced by WFTC in 1999 and WTC in 2003).

[118] [1985] 2 All ER 897 at 902 *per* Slade LJ.

[119] The *Parsons v Hogg* principle has also been applied in the contexts of family credit (*R(FC) 1/90*) and income support (*R(IS) 16/93*).

[120] At that time sch 1 to SI 1992/1815.

[121] The fact that the Inland Revenue declined to accept that such expenses were tax-deductible was not determinative of the issue: *R(CS) 2/96*, para 26.

[122] *Ibid*, para 27 *per* Mr Commissioner Mesher.

[123] But only if allowed by the Inland Revenue (now HMRC) under ICTA 1988, s 201 (now ITEPA 2003, s 343) rather than by way of extra-statutory concession: *CCS/3882/97*, para 35 *per* Mr Commissioner Mesher.

[124] See p 343 for the meaning of this expression. The Agency's own guidance cites the following (somewhat pastoral) scenario: 'The NRP was a gamekeeper who had to pay for the upkeep of two working dogs which he used solely for his gamekeeping duties. The NRP received nothing from his/her employer for these costs. It is decided to calculate weekly expenditure on the upkeep of the dogs', Child Support Agency, n 115 above, at 1336.

Whilst the applicability of *Parsons v Hogg* may be accepted by the Agency, it is less clear that this approach is legally correct. The original child support scheme stipulated that for the purpose of the formula a non-resident parent's earnings 'shall be gross earnings' less the deductions specified for income tax, national insurance and pension payments.[125] The explicit reference in this context to 'gross earnings' justifies the application of *Parsons v Hogg*. The new regulations, however, make no reference to an employed parent's 'gross earnings' at any stage. Instead, an employed non-resident parent's 'net weekly income shall be' his earnings less certain deductions, as stipulated by the legislation.[126] It must be arguable that, unlike under the original scheme, the new scheme's regulations comprise a 'complete and unambiguous code' for the calculation of employees' earnings.[127] The potential unfairness of such an approach in its respective treatment of employed and self-employed earners was evidently a factor which weighed with both the Court of Appeal in *Parsons v Hogg*[128] and with Mr Commissioner Mesher in *R(CS) 2/96*.[129] Yet there is, in any event, an element of discrimination as between these two groups in that different tests are applied for the deductibility of work-related expenses.

(b) any tax-exempt allowance made by an employer to an employee;

The regulations fail to make it clear whether a tax-exempt allowance means one exempt by virtue of the tax legislation, or whether those excluded by extra-statutory concessions are also covered. The reference to *any* such allowance implies the latter and broader construction.

(c) any gratuities paid by customers of the employer;

Although tips represent income which is 'derived from' the recipient's employment,[130] they are disregarded in calculating the non-resident parent's earnings. This represents a change from the previous system, under which tips were included as part of an employee's earnings. The reason for the new disregard is presumably part of the drive for simplification, but it clearly creates the potential for injustice where tips form a regular and substantial element in a non-resident parent's income. Moreover, the parent with care would have no obvious grounds for making an application for a variation.

(d) any payment in kind;

A payment in kind means a payment which is made otherwise than in cash or in a form which can readily be converted into cash (eg a cheque).[131] By the same token,

---

[125] SI 1992/1815, sch 1, para 1(3).

[126] SI 2001/155, sch, paras 3(1), 4 and 5.

[127] See by analogy *R(CS) 3/00* para 23 *per* Mr Commissioner Mesher; see also Jacobs and Douglas, n 90 above, at 649.

[128] See especially the concurring judgment of Griffiths LJ.

[129] Para 23.

[130] See *CCS/1992/1997*.

[131] *CCS/318/1998* para 15 *per* Mr Commissioner Williams, who also notes the distinction with 'benefit in kind', the term used in income tax law (*ibid*, para 14).

a voucher which can readily be converted into cash should not be seen as payment in kind, whereas a voucher exchangeable for goods or services should be. The provision of meals constitutes a payment in kind.[132] The exclusion of payments in kind clearly provides some scope for abuse. Under the old scheme, payments in kind, whilst disregarded in themselves, could lead to a finding of notional income against the non-resident parent.[133] The concept of notional income does not exist for new cases,[134] but a variation application on the basis of diversion of income remains a possibility.

(e) any advance of earnings or any loan made by an employer to an employee;

A payment of an advance of earnings is typically made where a new employee is awaiting the first instalment of salary, but this disregard is not confined to such cases. It is essential, however, that the advance is repayable, for example by future deductions from salary. Thus a non-repayable housing allowance paid by an employer is not an advance of earnings (or indeed a loan).[135] The most common type of loan made by employers is one to cover the cost of a season ticket for commuting, but presumably the loan may be for any purpose, whether or not work-related. To ensure consistency of treatment, the repayment of any such advance or loan is not deductible from the non-resident parent's earnings.[136]

(f) any amount received from an employer during a period when the employee has withdrawn his services by reason of a trade dispute;

Payments received from employers whilst on strike are disregarded, whereas they were taken into account for cases under the old rules. The reason for this change in policy is unclear, although it may it represent an official recognition that such payments are atypical and hence best excluded from the standard calculation process.

(g) any payment made in respect of the performance of duties as—

    (i)   an auxiliary coastguard in respect of coast rescue activities;

    (ii) a part-time fireman in a fire brigade maintained in pursuance of the Fire Services Acts 1947 to 1959;

    (iia) a part-time fire-fighter employed by a fire and rescue authority;

    (iii) a person engaged part-time in the manning or launching of a lifeboat;

    (iv) a member of any territorial or reserve force prescribed in Part I of Schedule 3 to the Social Security (Contributions) Regulations 1979;

Non-resident parents employed in these various emergency services on a part-time basis are favourably treated under the benefits system and their involvement

---

[132] *Ibid*, para 22.

[133] SI 1992/1815, sch 1, para 26.

[134] The powers under CSA 1991, sch 1, para 10B(a) and (b) not having been exercised: see n 56 above. See also the House of Commons Work and Pensions Committee, *The Performance of the Child Support Agency* (Second Report of Session 2004–05, HC 44-I), para 94.

[135] *R(CS) 6/98* para 5 *per* Mr Commissioner Rowland.

[136] *Ibid*, para 10: thus an advance is ignored both when received and when repaid.

is likewise now recognised by a complete disregard of such earnings for the purposes of the new child support scheme.[137]

(h) any payment made by a local authority to a member of that authority in respect of the performance of his duties as a member;

This is more generous treatment than under the benefits system, which ignores councillors' expenses but treats allowances for attending meetings as earnings.[138]

(i) any payment where—

(i) the employment in respect of which it was made has ceased; and
(ii) a period of the same length as the period by reference to which it was calculated has expired since that cessation but prior to the effective date;

The inter-relationship between this provision and that relating to holiday pay payable after the termination of en employment, discussed above, is perhaps less than clear.[139]

(j) where, in any week or other period which falls within the period by reference to which earnings are calculated, earnings are received both in respect of a previous employment and in respect of a subsequent employment, the earnings in respect of the previous employment.

The advantage of this provision, requiring income from a previous job to be disregarded, is that it avoids any need to invoke the rules permitting an alternative period to be taken for the purposes of assessing the 'normal amount of earnings'.[140]

Deductions

Once the employee's earnings have been established in accordance with the principles detailed above, the Secretary of State must then apply any appropriate deductions. The regulations specify just three such categories of deduction from gross earnings:[141]

(a) income tax;
(b) primary Class 1 contributions under the Contributions and Benefits Act or under the Contributions and Benefits (Northern Ireland) Act; or

---

[137] These groups qualify for the highest weekly disregard under the income support scheme (at present £20 p/w): SI 1987/1967, sch 8, para 7(1). Under the old child support scheme, only such payments relating to a period of one year or more were excluded: SI 1991/1815, sch 2, para 48B.

[138] *R(IS) 6/92.*

[139] For example, assume that an employee leaves a job and two weeks later is paid two weeks' holiday pay. This would count as earnings under SI 2001/155, sch, para 4(1)(b), but arguably should then be excluded under para 4(2)(i).

[140] *Ibid*, para 6(4). See Jacobs and Douglas, n 90 above, at 656.

[141] Curiously the expression 'gross earnings' appears in SI 2001/155, sch, para 5(1) but in none of the other provisions relating to employees.

   (c) any sums paid by the non-resident parent towards an occupational pension scheme
       or personal pension scheme or, where that scheme is intended partly to provide a
       capital sum to discharge a mortgage secured upon that parent's home, 75 per cen-
       tum of any such sums.[142]

The amount deducted in respect of income tax must be the amounts actually
deducted, including any tax in respect of payments which are not included as earnings under the foregoing rules.[143] If the non-resident parent is unable to provide
details of the relevant deductions, the Secretary of State must estimate his net earnings 'on the basis of the information available to him as to the non-resident parent's net income'.[144] These rules governing deductions are more generous than
those that apply to the assessment of earnings for the purposes of old cases—where
the standard rule, following that for the benefits system,[145] is to deduct income
tax, national insurance contributions but just half of any occupational or private
pension payments from an employee's gross earnings.[146] According to the White
Paper, the deduction of only half of the non-resident parent's occupational pension contributions introduced complexity with little gain for children.[147] If the
parent with care believes that the non-resident parent is unreasonably diverting
income into a pension scheme in order to minimise his maintenance liability, she
may apply for a variation.[148]

The three categories of income tax, national contributions and pension payments are the only permitted categories of deductions from an employed non-
resident parent's earnings.[149] It follows that there is no scope for any deductions
to be made in respect of exceptionally high contact or travel to work costs, which
might have been taken into account under the old scheme in calculating exempt
income or in a departure direction.[150] Nor—again in contrast to the old child support scheme—is there any allowance for the non-resident parent's housing costs.
The justification for the exclusion of such expenses is that this assists the goal of
simplification and that, in any event, the standard 15, 20 and 25 per cent rates are
affordable.

---

[142] SI 2001/155, sch, para 5(1).

[143] SI 2001/155, sch, para 5(2).

[144] *Ibid*, para 3(1)(b). On the detailed mechanics of dealing with deductions in estimating earnings,
see *ibid*, para 3(2).

[145] See eg SI 1987/1967, reg 36(3).

[146] Or 37.5% where the pension contributions are partly mortgage-related: SI 1992/1815, sch 1, para
1(3).

[147] DSS, n 24 above, Annex 2, para 6.

[148] SI 2001/156, reg 19; see p 391 below.

[149] This discussion assumes that *Parsons v Hogg* has no further place in the *new* child support
scheme: see p 345 above.

[150] SI 1992/1815, reg 9(1)(i) and sch 3B and SI 1996/2907, reg 13.

The Period of Assessment

The rules governing the choice of the period for calculating earnings[151] 'raise complex issues of interpretation and application'.[152] The starting point for identifying the appropriate period over which earnings are to be calculated is as follows:

> the amount of earnings to be taken into account for the purpose of calculating net income shall be calculated or estimated by reference to the average earnings at the relevant week having regard to such evidence as is available in relation to that person's earnings during such period as appears appropriate to the Secretary of State, beginning not earlier than 8 weeks before the relevant week and ending not later than the date of the calculation . . .[153]

The task is therefore to establish the non-resident parent's 'average earnings at the relevant week'.[154] This is not simply a case of accepting payslips at face value, although that may be appropriate in many cases. Rather, this provision means that the Secretary of State must potentially exercise a degree of judgment on at least four possible levels. First of all, some period must be selected for the calculation of average earnings. The Agency may use whatever period 'appears appropriate', so long as it begins 'not earlier than 8 weeks before the relevant week' and ends 'not later than the date of the calculation'.[155] Secondly, the decision maker must arrive at a figure of average earnings 'having regard to such evidence as is available'. This necessarily involves weighing different types of evidence. The non-resident parent's payslips are obviously relevant, but in some cases there may also be compelling evidence from other sources that, for example, the non-resident parent regularly receives payments on a 'cash-in-hand' basis for certain jobs. This leads us to the third type of judgment that may need to be exercised: the non-resident parent's earnings 'shall be calculated *or estimated* by reference to'[156] those average earnings. Finally, for these purposes the Secretary of State 'may consider evidence of that person's cumulative earnings' during the tax year in which the relevant week falls but before the date of the calculation.[157] The structure of the rule as a whole suggests that cumulative earnings may be used as a means of checking or corroborating the figure of average earnings already calculated or estimated.[158] All four levels of judgment require careful consideration of the evidence (rather than the assertions) in the case. District judges are well used to making such distinctions in matrimonial proceedings; Agency staff are unlikely to be as well equipped.

---

[151] SI 2001/155, sch, para 6.
[152] Jacobs and Douglas, n 90 above, at 656.
[153] SI 2001/155, sch, para 6(1).
[154] In practice the 'relevant week' will usually be the period of 7 days immediately before notification to the NRP of the child support application. See further p 300 above.
[155] SI 2001/155, sch, para 6(1). The use of separate non-consecutive weeks probably does not constitute a 'period' for this purpose: *CCS/556/1995 per* Mr Commissioner Howell QC.
[156] Emphasis added.
[157] This is the final part to SI 2001/155, sch, para 6(1), not quoted in the extract cited above.
[158] See the discussion in Jacobs and Douglas, n 90 above, at 657–58.

The degree of judgment required of a decision maker does not end there. The amount of the average earnings as assessed under the process described above is not automatically factored into the formula calculation. This is because the general rule is expressly made subject to two exceptions. The first deals with the special problem of bonus or commission payments and has already been considered.[159] The second exception addresses the possibility that the 'average earnings' arrived at by the method described above may not be truly representative and so introduces a further level of judgment. If the Secretary of State's opinion is that the standard calculation 'does not accurately reflect the normal amount of the earnings of the person in question', then an alternative assessment period may be selected to 'enable the normal weekly earnings of that person to be determined more accurately'.[160] Although this provision might appear to act simply as a back-stop, its significance is wider than this in that it confirms that the goal of these provisions as a whole is to ascertain the non-resident parent's 'normal weekly earnings',[161] a concept originally borrowed from the family credit scheme.[162] Normal is obviously a synonym for usual, as opposed to unusual,[163] abnormal or exceptional. That said, the use of the expression 'more accurately' is a statutory acknowledgement that in some cases, where there are marked fluctuations in incomes, it may be difficult to identify any 'normal' earnings.[164]

The use of such an alternative period for calculating earnings is intended to be the exception rather than the rule.[165] In deciding on a different period,[166] the Secretary of State shall have regard to:

(a) the earnings received, or due to be received from any employment in which the person in question is engaged, has been engaged or is due to be engaged; and
(b) the duration and pattern, or the expected duration and pattern, of any employment of that person.[167]

Subject to those considerations, the length of the alternative assessment period is at large, although clearly it must be based on some evidence.[168] It would obviously be appropriate to opt for a longer assessment period where the usual rule includes

---

[159] SI 2001/155, sch, para 6(3) and see p 339 above.

[160] SI 2001/155, sch, para 6(4) (made under the authority of CSA 1991, sch 1, para 10(2)).

[161] Jacobs and Douglas, n 90 above, at 659, who observe that normalcy is to be judged as at the effective date (but note that reg 2(4) may need to be applied first). Note also their argument that para 6(4) is not confined to modifying the effect of calculations under para 6(1).

[162] Family credit later became WFTC, although the underlying rules for the two benefits were not the same in all respects, and then transmogrified into WTC.

[163] *Lowe v Chief Adjudication Officer* [1985] 1 WLR 1108, CA, at 1112 *per* Griffiths LJ, also reported as an Appendix to *R(FIS) 2/85*; see also *R(FIS) 2/83* para 11(1), citing Widgery J in *Peak Trailer & Chassis Ltd. v Jackson* [1967] 1 WLR 155 at 161.

[164] *CCS/84/1998* at para 20.

[165] *CCS/11873/1996*.

[166] The Secretary of State cannot be expected to consider a longer period unless prompted to do so by one of the parties: *CCS/511/1995 per* Mr Commissioner Rowland.

[167] SI 2001/155, sch, para 6(4).

[168] See further *CCS/556/1995, CCS/11873/1996, CCS/84/1998*.

a disproportionate amount of seasonal overtime that is not available throughout the year.[169] In exercising these powers it may be helpful to bear in mind that they 'should be used as far as possible to ensure that an absent parent is able to meet future payments out of current income'.[170]

Net Weekly Income of Self-employed Earners

In the same way as for employed earners, the definition of 'self-employed earner' follows that used in social security law, so it encompasses anyone who is 'gainfully employed in Great Britain otherwise than in employed earner's employment (whether or not he is also in such employment)', with the necessary extension to Northern Ireland.[171] So the legal categories of employed earner and self-employed earner are mutually exclusive, although any individual non-resident parent may work in both roles—in which cases the two income streams will need to be aggregated.[172] In effect self-employed earners are defined by way of exclusion—they represent 'a default category of income earners who are *not* employed'.[173] This omnibus definition disguises a diverse range of different types of working practices, including sole trading, partnerships, franchise operations and sub-contractors, which make it difficult to achieve parity in terms of income measurement.[174] The calculation of self-employed non-resident parents' incomes has proven to be one of the most problematic areas in both the old and new child support schemes. The difficulties relate to issues of both principle (eg what deductions should be permissible in respect of self-employed earnings?) and practice (eg how firm is the evidential basis for decisions in particular cases?).[175] In this context it is important to bear in mind that there is no 'right' way of measuring income—accounting measures are 'social constructs' which necessarily reflect certain values and objectives.[176]

The original child support regulations adopted virtually wholesale the basis for measuring self-employed income as used in the family credit scheme,[177] even

---

[169] Eg as may be the case for seaside tourism workers over the summer or shop assistants over Christmas and New Year. As Jacobs and Douglas wryly observe, 'tribunal members will derive hours of harmless amusement from attempting to determine the normal earnings of an employment, such as that of a university canteen assistant, in respect of which there is no consistent normality' (n 90 above, at 659).

[170] *CCS/4221/1998* at para 13 per Mr Commissioner Jacobs.

[171] SI 2001/155, reg 1(2).

[172] Thus a law professor may be employed by a university but self-employed for the purpose of any book royalties, outside lecturing etc.

[173] R Boden and A Corden, *Self-employed Parents and Child Maintenance* (London: The Stationery Office, 1998), at 20.

[174] *Ibid*, at 21 and 25.

[175] There may also be particular problems in terms of enforcement where the NRP is self-employed: see ch 14 below.

[176] Boden and Corden, n 173 above, at 25.

[177] *Ibid*, at 26.

though the purposes of the two codes were very different.[178] Initially, therefore, a self-employed parent's earnings were based on the gross receipts of the business less certain allowable expenses (which did not mirror fully those permitted for tax purposes).[179] The assessment was typically based on the profit and loss account (or trading account or balance sheet) submitted by the self-employed person.[180] The rules were amended in October 1999 so as to allow self-employed parents to provide the Agency with the figures they supplied to the Inland Revenue (now HMRC) for self-assessment of their earnings for tax purposes. This change was designed to introduce a 'simpler and more effective basis for getting maintenance flowing'.[181] Consequently, the self-assessment income tax return became the standard basis for calculating earnings for child support purposes.[182] At the same time, an amendment to the primary legislation enabled the Agency to obtain information on non-resident parents' self-employed earnings direct from HMRC.[183]

The new scheme likewise starts from the premise that the figures submitted to HMRC should be used. It is only if both the self-assessment return or the subsequent tax calculation notice are for some reason unavailable, or unrepresentative, that the decision maker reverts to the original but now alternative method of calculating earnings by reference to gross receipts less allowable deductions. The principles governing these two different approaches are discussed in more detail below. As a preliminary point, it should be noted that both sets of rules are subject to a special provision which applies where a self-employed non-resident parent provides board and lodging. If this is his 'only or main source of income',[184] then the board and lodging payments should be included as self-employed earnings in the usual way.[185] If, however, any such payments are merely a subsidiary source of income, they are now disregarded altogether.[186] This concession offers the self-employed non-resident parent with a spare room in his house an entirely legitimate way of maximising his income whilst at the same time not increasing his child support liability.[187]

---

[178] The aim of income measurement for family credit was to calculate how much benefit the self-employed earner should *receive*, whereas for child support the goal was to assess how much he should *pay out*: *ibid*, at 1.

[179] SI 1992/1815, sch 1, para 3.

[180] *Ibid*, para 5.

[181] Ms A Eagle MP *Hansard* HC Debates vol 327 col 51w (8 March 1999); see Child Support (Miscellaneous Amendments) Regulations 1999 (SI 1999/977).

[182] SI 1992/1815, sch 1, paras 2A and 5A, as amended by SI 1999/977.

[183] CSA 1991, sch 2, para 1A inserted by WRPA 1999, s 80: see p 289 below. In the year to March 2001 the Agency made 9,121 such requests; in the year to March 2002 this increased to 19,182 enquiries: *Hansard* HC Debates vol 389 col 116W (15 July 2002).

[184] By analogy with the case law on capital gains tax, 'main' means 'principal' or 'most important' and is ultimately a question of fact and degree: *Frost (Inspector of Taxes) v Feltham* [1981] 1 WLR 452 at 455G per Nourse J; see also *R (Williams) v Horsham District Council* [2004] 1 WLR 1137, CA.

[185] SI 2001/155, sch, para 10.

[186] A secondary income stream from board and lodging payments would be included as 'other income' under the old cases rules: SI 1992/1815, sch 1, para 10.

[187] In doing so he can—within limits—also avoid liability for income tax, as the HMRC operates a 'rent a room' tax exemption under which the first £4,250 of rent received is tax-free: see Finance (No 2) Act 1992, s 59 and sch 10 and the Income Tax (Furnished Accommodation) (Basic Amount) Order 1996 (SI 1996/2953).

The Normal Method: Figures Submitted to HMRC

The standard way of determining a self-employed non-resident's parent net weekly income is to make certain prescribed deductions from the gross earnings calculated by reference to *either* his 'total taxable profits' as returned to HMRC on the self-assessment form *or* the self-employed income as set out in the subsequent tax calculation notice (or revised notice).[188] This method may only be used if the earnings relate to a period which ended not more than two years before the relevant week.[189] The choice of whether to use the self-assessment form or the tax notice is a matter for the Secretary of State.[190]

The expression 'total taxable profits' itself is not defined in the legislation and has caused immense difficulty. On one view ('Basis A') it means the annual trading profit net of allowable revenue expenses, or in other words the profit chargeable to income tax under what used to be Schedule D. The alternative view is that it is that sum less also any relevant capital allowances, being the net figure used to calculate the individual's final tax liability ('Basis B'). The two approaches may result in wildly divergent outcomes. For example, in *Smith v Secretary of State for Work and Pensions*[191] the non-resident parent operated a business leasing specially adapted vehicles to driving schools. The turnover of his business was in excess of £¼ million but necessarily involved a high rate of depreciation and replacement. His business accounts for the relevant year showed a total trading profit of nearly £170,000 (Basis A); but once capital allowances were deducted, his net taxable income was just over £20,000 (Basis B). The Commissioner adopted Basis A as the proper construction of the term 'total taxable profits',[192] holding that capital allowances, although quite properly deducted for income tax purposes, were not deductible in the context of the child support scheme.[193] The Court of Appeal disagreed, although the rigour of its reasoning is open to question.[194] The parent with care's appeal in *Smith* was heard by the House of Lords in May 2006.

---

[188] SI 2001/155, sch, para 7(1). For definitions, see *ibid*, para 7(7).

[189] *Ibid*, para 7(6). The original scheme required accounts which ended within the previous 12 months, a condition that proved too burdensome, being replaced in April 1995 by the two year rule: Boden and Corden, n 173 above, at 28. Under the old rules the period covered by the self-assessment return also had to be for a minimum of 6 months but not more than 15 months, as well as ending in the 24 months period prior to the relevant week; this is the only significant difference between the old and new scheme rules governing the assessment of self-employed earnings.

[190] Moreover, if, for example, the NRP produces the self-assessment return, the Agency can require the tax notice to be produced (or vice versa): *ibid*, para 7(2). Any such request must specify the possible consequences of non-compliance (eg the commission of an offence under CSA 1991, s 14A: SI 2001/155, sch, para 7(8)).

[191] [2004] EWCA Civ 1318; [2005] 1 WLR 1319.

[192] *CCS/2858/2002 per* Mr Commissioner Howell QC.

[193] The principal reason for his conclusion was that there was no evidence that the change in 1999, enabling self-assessment returns to be used, was designed to alter the substantive principles governing the assessment of self-employed individuals' incomes: *ibid*, para 26.

[194] N Wikeley and L Young, '*Smith v Secretary of State for Work and Pensions*: child support, the self-employed and the meaning of "total taxable profits"—total confusion reigns' (2005) 17 *Child and Family Law Quarterly* 267.

The regulations then provide for only three types of deductions to be made from the gross earnings, as with employed earners. The first permissible deduction is for income tax.[195] The amount to be deducted is not the actual amount paid or payable by the self-employed parent in respect of that year, which may of course include HMRC adjustments for under- or overpayments of tax in previous years. Instead, the regulations provide for an amount equivalent to any relevant personal allowance to be disregarded[196] and then for the deduction for income tax to be calculated on the remaining earnings for child support purposes.[197] Secondly, an amount is deducted from the gross earnings for a self-employed earner's Class 2 and/or Class 4 national insurance contributions.[198] Finally, deductions may be made for any premiums the non-resident parent pays into a personal pension scheme or under a retirement annuity contract.[199] No other deductions are permissible.

The Alternative Method: Gross Receipts Less Deductions

There are three situations in which the Agency should not simply adopt HMRC figures (subject to the deductions stipulated above). These are where the statutory precondition for using such data is not satisfied,[200] or where the Secretary of State either accepts that it is not reasonably practicable for the person concerned to provide such information or believes that the self-assessment return (or tax notice) does not accurately reflect the individual's normal weekly earnings. If any of these circumstances apply, then the Agency should calculate the person's earnings by reference to the gross receipts from the self-employment less specified deductions.[201] In doing so, the net weekly income is determined by reference to the average earnings in the 52 weeks ending with the relevant week (assuming that the non-resident parent has been self-employed for 52 weeks or more).[202] There are two exceptions to this principle. If the non-resident parent has been in business for less than 52 weeks, then the net weekly income is judged by reference to the average earnings in the period for which he has been in business. If, as is often the case, the ratio of expenses to receipts is higher in such a case than for a more established business, then the resulting assessment will be low. However, as also applies to figures submitted to HMRC, there is a further provision enabling the Secretary of

---

[195] SI 2001/155, sch para 7(3)(a).

[196] Based on the yearly rate applicable at the effective date and adjusted *pro rata* if the figures relate to a period other than one year: *ibid*, para 7(4)(a) and (d). Para 7(4)(a) was amended by SI 2005/785, reg 6(5) to reverse the effect of *R(CS) 1/05*.

[197] Again, based on the rate at the effective date and adjusted according to the period in question: SI 2001/155, sch, para 7(4)(b) and (c).

[198] Again, based on the rates applicable at the effective date: *ibid*, paras 7(3)(b) and (5).

[199] *Ibid*, para 7(3)(c) and see *R(CS) 3/00*; the allowable deduction is limited to 75% of the premium if the scheme is mortgage-related.

[200] ie the figures relate to a period which ended more than two years ago.

[201] SI 2001/155, sch, para 8(1). See also *CCS/3405/2002* under the old scheme rules.

[202] SI 2001/155, sch, para 9(2)(a).

State to choose an alternative period if the assessment under the normal rules 'does not accurately reflect the normal weekly income of the non-resident parent in question'.[203] Even so, the mere fact that self-employed earnings fluctuate is not in itself sufficient reason to depart from the normal assessment period.[204]

Gross Receipts

If, for whatever reason, the normal method of relying on the self-assessment return or tax notice is not used, the alternative starting point is to identify the self-employed person's 'gross receipts'. This raises a conceptual problem which has bedevilled the means-tested benefits schemes for some years.[205] The case law from that jurisdiction demonstrates that the expression 'gross receipts' refers solely to income receipts.[206] Accordingly capital receipts, the proceeds of the sale of business assets and start-up loans[207] are all to be excluded. In this respect any determination made by HMRC as to the character of particular payments, whilst not conclusive, should be taken into account.[208]

In practice, the more common problem is not one of identifying the legal character of particular receipts, but rather that of establishing the true amount of a self-employed person's earnings. The same problem, of course, may also arise in the context of the figures presented to HMRC under the self-assessment system.[209] The typical problem is where the parent with care alleges that her ex-partner's self-employed earnings have been artificially depressed for the purposes of his income tax and child support liabilities. It may be that she was previously employed in his business (eg as a bookkeeper), in which case her evidence may be persuasive.[210] But in many cases such an allegation will be more by way of assertion than based on any firm evidence. In principle the Agency has a number of avenues to pursue when faced with an obstructive self-employed non-resident parent.[211] As well as acquiring information from HMRC, its officers may seek information from the self-employed person's accountants and companies or partnerships for which he has supplied services.[212] The extent to which the Agency is prepared to take such

---

[203] *Ibid*, para 9(3).

[204] *CCS/3182/1995* at para 11 and *CCS/6145/1995* paras 9–13, both *per* Mr Commissioner Howell QC.

[205] Particularly in the context of what was family credit and later WFTC, now WTC.

[206] *R(FC) 1/97* paras 29–33 *per* Mr Deputy Commissioner Hallett; see also *R 2/92 (FC)* from Northern Ireland.

[207] But not Business Start Up Scheme payments (formerly enterprise allowance payments), which count as income and are non-deductible: SI 2001/155, sch, para 8(3)(b)(iv).

[208] *R(CS) 2/96* para 26 *per* Mr Commissioner Mesher.

[209] The presumption, however, appears to be that the earnings figures in the self-assessment or tax notice are to be accepted, unless, in the opinion of the Secretary of State, that information does not 'accurately reflect' the self-employed NRP's normal weekly earnings: SI 2001/155, sch, para 8(1)(c).

[210] See also *CCS/7966/1995*, in which the PWC produced documentary evidence (relating to previous court proceedings in which the NRP had claimed for loss of earnings) at the tribunal hearing.

[211] Leaving aside, for example, the use of an inspector or the institution of criminal proceedings under CSA 1991, s 14A.

[212] Child Support (Information, Evidence and Disclosure) Regulations 1992 (SI 1992/1812), reg 2(2)(f) and (g)—see further ch 9 above.

steps is open to question, given the complaints received from parents with care whose ex-partners are self-employed.[213] The problems of dealing with non-compliant self-employed non-resident parents may well seem to be intractable, but decision makers and tribunals have been advised that they would be:

> justified in proceeding, in the absence of anything better, on the best evidence they are able to obtain of the estimated level of earnings in a particular locality of a person carrying on a self-employed sub-contracting business of the kind being conducted by the children's father, for which figures are no doubt available from the Inland Revenue and Contributions Agency Departments concerned with similar sub-contractors without the need for disclosure of a particular individual's own figures.[214]

An alternative source for relevant comparators is the official data on pay levels included in the periodic New Earnings Survey.[215]

Deductions

The deductions allowed from gross receipts include the provisions parallel to those for self-assessment cases to take account of income tax, national insurance contributions and personal pension or similar premiums.[216] The deductions for tax and national insurance are again based on an assumed rather than actual basis. Before these three deductions are made, however, the regulations also provide for two other prescribed categories of allowable deductions.[217] These are for any excess VAT paid in the period in question[218] and for self-employed expenses. The latter type of deduction requires particular attention.

The first question is what types of expenditure may count as 'expenses' for a self-employed non-resident parent. There is no statutory definition of the term 'expenses'. One must therefore have recourse to normal accounting conventions; it follows that items of an income or revenue nature are included, but not capital outlays.[219] The underlying principle is that to qualify as an 'expense' the item in question must involve expenditure.[220] Thus expenditure on a trader's stock is clearly an expense.[221] Applying the same principle, taxes paid in the course of

---

[213] For example, in *CCS/13988/1996* at para 4 Mr Commissioner Howell QC noted that the earnings figures supplied by the NRP were 'barely credible' yet accepted by Agency staff without further scrutiny.

[214] *CCS/13988/1996*, at para 8.

[215] *CCS/2901/2002* at para 12 *per* Mr Commissioner Jacobs.

[216] *Ibid*, para 8(2)(c)–(e) and 8(4).

[217] There is no need to make provision for these in relation to HMRC self-assessments or tax notices as these two categories will be excluded from such figures in any event.

[218] ie any VAT paid out which is in excess of VAT received during the period: *ibid*, para 8(2)(b).

[219] See *CCS/15949/1996* paras 5–6 *per* Mr Commissioner Howell QC (interest on loan to acquire share in partnership not allowable, but interest on a further loan to purchase new business premises deductible). See also *R(FC) 1/91*, para 38 *per* Mr Commissioner Hallett. The distinction between revenue and capital payments may be problematic: 'Indeed, in many cases it is almost true to say that the spin of a coin would decide the matter almost as satisfactorily as an attempt to find reasons' *per* Sir Wilfred Greene MR in *British Salmson Aero Engines Ltd v IRC* [1938] 2 KB 482, CA, at 498.

[220] Jacobs and Douglas, n 90 above, at 630.

[221] The correct approach being to aggregate the opening stock figure and the amount spent on stock during the accounting period and then subtract from that total the closing stock figure: *R(FC) 1/96* and *R 1/99(FC)*.

earning self-employed profits are deductible (eg council tax) whereas income tax itself is not, as such, an expense of the self-employment.[222] Similarly, depreciation of a capital asset is not an expense in this sense.[223] Moreover, in contrast to revenue law, there is no provision to claim capital allowances in lieu of depreciation, which adds to the perceived unfairness of the child support rules in the eyes of those self-employed non-resident parents who are subject to this regime.[224] However, this rule only applies in cases dealt with on the 'gross receipts' basis; if the self-assessment figures are used, then *Smith*[225] is authority for the proposition that capital allowances should be deducted when computing 'total taxable profits'.

The next question is whether such expenses are allowable for child support purposes. The statutory test for deductibility is whether the expenses were 'reasonably incurred and are wholly and exclusively defrayed for the purposes of the earner's business'. This test is different to that which applies to expenses incurred by employed non-resident parents[226] in two fundamental respects. First, the expenses only have to be 'reasonably' as opposed to 'necessarily' incurred, and what is (or is not) 'reasonable' is left undefined by the legislation. Secondly, an employee's expenses must meet the strict test of being 'incurred *in the performance of* the duties of the employment', whereas for a self-employed person it is sufficient if they are 'defrayed *for the purposes of* the earner's business'.[227] Again, this test imposes a lower threshold for deductibility. This test for deductibility is closer to, but still not identical with, the test that applies to a self-employed person's expenses for income tax purposes. The tax rules apply the 'wholly and exclusively' test, but have no separate requirement that the expenses in question be 'reasonably incurred'. The child support regulations also stipulate that certain categories of expenses are included, but others excluded, from the ambit of the rule, but the list is not the same as for tax purposes.[228] Under the child support rules, the repayment of capital on any loan taken out to replace or repair a business asset is a deductible expense (subject to sums paid under an insurance policy for repair).[229] Similarly, income spent on repairing an existing business asset (again, subject to insurance policy payments) and interest payments on business loans may be

---

[222] The reasoning being that income tax is an expense incurred after profits have been earned, not one incurred whilst earning the profits: see *Ashton Gas Company v Attorney-General* [1906] AC 10 (HL), applied in the child support context in *CCS/15949/1996* (para 10). There is, of course, a standard allowable deduction for income tax under the regulations once the gross profits have been established.

[223] Indeed, depreciation is expressly excluded as an allowable expense by SI 2001/155, sch, para 2(3)(b)(iii).

[224] There is some evidence that the failure of the child support scheme to take account of depreciation may also cause some self-employed non-resident parents serious financial difficulties: Boden and Corden, n 173 above, at 33–35.

[225] See n 191 above.

[226] See SI 2001/155, sch, para 4(2)(a) and the discussion above.

[227] Emphasis added in both cases.

[228] ICTA 1988, ss 74 and 577.

[229] SI 2001/155, sch, para 8(3)(a)(i). This provides some scope for creative accountancy to manipulate the measurement of self-employed income: see Boden and Corden, n 173 above, at 37.

deducted from gross receipts as expenses in self-employment.[230] Inevitably the list of self-employed expenses which are non-deductible for child support purposes is longer: other repayments of capital; capital expenditure; depreciation of capital assets;[231] sums used in setting up business; losses relating to earlier accounting periods; business entertainment expenses; losses incurred in other types of self-employment.[232] This list of excluded expenses mirrors that which used to apply for the purposes of calculating a self-employed person's income for family credit purposes.[233] As indicated above, it does not sit easily with the income tax rules.

A common issue in practice is whether it is proper to apportion expenses to business and personal uses respectively and, if so, in what measure. The income tax position is that a single expense which has a dual use, both business and personal, is not deductible as it fails the 'wholly and exclusively' test.[234] Thus the cost of lunch is non-apportionable.[235] In other cases, however, it may be possible to apportion expenditure into business and private usage (eg with transport or telephone costs) so that the former element is deductible.[236] There are no specific statutory provisions for apportionment of expenses in the child support context and, although a decision by HMRC to accept apportionment is not determinative,[237] in practice it may well be followed.

Income from Tax Credits

The system of tax credits has undergone a dramatic transformation in recent years. 'True' tax credits in the sense of allowances against tax are a well-established feature of the income tax system but are not relevant in this context.[238] In October 1999 the existing family credit and disability working allowance, both in-work social security benefits for the low paid, were reconfigured and re-launched as WFTC and DPTC respectively.[239] Although described as 'tax credits', both the eligibility criteria and the essential features of WFTC and DPTC remained the same

---

[230] SI 2001/155, sch, para 8(3)(a)(ii) and (iii). As regards the latter, the interest must be on a loan 'taken out for the purposes of the business', not for the purposes of *acquiring a share in* the business: see *CCS/15949/96* para 7 *per* Mr Commissioner Howell QC.

[231] But see the discussion of *Smith* in the context of 'total taxable profits' at p 353 above.

[232] SI 2001/155, sch, para 8(3)(b)(i)–(vii). There is also no provision for setting off a trading loss in a self-employed business against employed earnings: *R 1/96 (CSC)*.

[233] Family Credit (General) Regulations 1987 (SI 1987/1973), reg 22(5) and (11). On the inability to offset losses from one form of self-employment to another, see *R(FC) 1/93*.

[234] Eg *Prince v Mapp* [1970] 1 All ER 519 (guitarist could not deduct cost of operation on finger, as played guitar both for business and pleasure).

[235] *Caillebotte v Quinn* [1975] 1 WLR 731 *per* Templeman J, a principle applied in the child support context in *CCS/15949/1996* (at para 11).

[236] See the detailed analysis of Mr Commissioner Hallett in *R(FC) 1/91* paras 26–35. See also *CCS/2153/2004* (at paras 53–62), decided under the old scheme rules.

[237] See *ibid*, para 39 and *R(CS) 6/98* para 7 *per* Mr Commissioner Rowland.

[238] Eg tax credits related to dividends from UK companies.

[239] Tax Credits Act 1999, s 1(1).

as their predecessor, social security benefits.[240] In April 2001 the government introduced a children's tax credit, a reduction of income tax, as a partial replacement for the abolished married couple's allowance.[241] These were, however, merely transitional measures, as a more fundamental recasting took place under the Tax Credits Act 2002.[242] WFTC, DPTC and the short-lived children's tax credit were all swept away as part of these reforms. In their stead, since April 2003 the Inland Revenue (now HMRC) has been responsible for administering working tax credit[243] and CTC.[244] Working tax credit is a new-style tax credit, replacing the adult elements of WFTC and DPTC, which brings together the main credits and allowances paid to people in work on low incomes, irrespective of whether or not they have children. CTC is arguably more radical still, in that it replaces the children's tax credit and the child elements of WFTC and DPTC, as well as the child-related allowances and additions that were previously paid with both means-tested and national insurance benefits. CTC is paid in addition to the universal child benefit and, unlike working tax credit, is available to middle-income groups as well as to the low-paid.

In assessing the non-resident parent's income, any working tax credit (WTC) payable to him is taken into account at the rate payable at the effective date, assuming that he has qualified for the tax credit on the basis of being in work.[245] It follows that if the non-resident parent's new partner qualifies for WTC because of *her* work, but he stays at home as the principal child-carer, then the WTC coming into his new household is *not* part of his net income for child support purposes.[246] Where WTC is payable because both the non-resident parent and his new partner are in work,[247] a relatively crude attribution rule operates. If the non-resident parent's earnings exceed those of his new partner, the WTC is attributed in full to him as his income for child support purposes. In the perhaps uncommon event that

---

[240] N Lee, 'The Working Families' Tax Credit: An integration of the tax and benefit systems?' (2000) 7 *Journal of Social Security Law* 159.

[241] Income and Corporation Taxes Act 1988, s 257A and sch 13B. The *children's* tax credit (a temporary feature of the income tax system) must be distinguished from the *child* tax credit under the Tax Credits Act 2002.

[242] See N Lee, 'The New Tax Credits' (2003) 10 *Journal of Social Security Law* 7 and for the annotated legislation N Wikeley and D Williams, *Tax Credits and Employer-Paid Social Security Benefits, Social Security Legislation 2005*, vol IV (London: Sweet & Maxwell, 2005).

[243] Tax Credits Act 2002, ss 10–12 and Working Tax Credit (Entitlement and Maximum Rate) Regulations 2002 (SI 2002/2005).

[244] Tax Credits Act 2002, ss 8 and 9 and Child Tax Credit Regulations 2002 (SI 2002/2007).

[245] SI 2001/155, sch, para 11(1). Rather confusingly this still refers to the NRP's 'engagement in, and normal engagement in, remunerative work', the test that previously applied to WFTC (SSCBA 1992, s 128(1)(b)) but which does not appear in quite the same terms in the WTC legislation.

[246] This is despite the fact that a couple, married or unmarried, can only make a claim for WTC together: Tax Credits Act 2002, s 3(3). Moreover, as seen above, there is no notional income or deprivation of income rule in the new child support scheme.

[247] The couple may qualify for WTC so long as at least one of them is working a minimum of 16 hours a week: SI 2002/2005, reg 4. Childless WTC claimants must be aged at least 25 and work a minimum of 30 hours a week.

their earnings[248] for WTC purposes are equal,[249] he is regarded as having half of the WTC income, whereas if his earnings are less than his partner's, none of the WTC is regarded as his income for the child support calculation.[250] A parallel provision was enacted for DPTC but subsequently repealed, with the consequence that DPTC is always disregarded in full.[251]

Payments of CTC are included in full as the non-resident parent's income, whether payable to him or to his new partner.[252] In one sense this is not unreasonable, given that CTC, in the same way as WTC, has to be claimed jointly by a couple,[253] and entitlement is based on a household means-test. On the other hand, entitlement to CTC follows eligibility for child benefit, and the child in question, in respect of whom CTC is payable, is almost certainly not the qualifying child. Moreover, to compound the perceived sense of injustice, the parent with care's receipt of CTC for the qualifying child (or children) is irrelevant to the child support formula calculation.

Part IV of the Schedule also stipulates that any employment credits still payable are to be taken into account as the non-resident parent's income.[254]

Other Forms of Income

The three main categories of income discussed above—from employment, self-employment and tax credits—will cover most non-resident parents' sources of income. The regulations make limited provision for other forms of income to be taken into account. These include:

> any periodic payment of pension or other benefit under an occupational or personal pension scheme or a retirement annuity contract or other such scheme for the provision of income in retirement whether or not approved by the Inland Revenue.[255]

A non-resident parent's income includes the aggregate of such occupational or private pension benefits or other retirement income, net of any income tax deducted.[256] Assuming that such payments have been received throughout the six

---

[248] This refers to employment and self-employment income; no account is taken of other forms of income (eg pension income and investment income) which may be relevant to a WTC calculation: SI 2001/155, sch, para 11(2A).

[249] This may arise, however, where the NRP and his new partner have 50:50 shares in a business partnership.

[250] SI 2001/155, sch, para 11(2).

[251] *Ibid*, para 13, as substituted by SI 2002/1204, reg 7(3) but then removed by SI 2003/328, reg 8(4)(d).

[252] SI 2001/155, sch, para 13A. CTC is taken into account at the rate payable at the effective date.

[253] Tax Credits Act 2002, s 3(3); thus where an NRP and his new partner are living together, she can not claim CTC alone for her own child(ren) from a previous relationship living with them (ie the NRP's step-child(ren)).

[254] SI 2001/155, sch, para 12. This can only apply to a handful of old New Deal 50 Plus cases, as the employment credit has now been subsumed within WTC.

[255] *Ibid*, para 15.

[256] *Ibid*, para 14.

months ending with the end of the relevant week, the weekly amount of such other income is calculated by simply dividing the total amount by 26.[257] If the payments have only been received for part of that period, the aggregate amount is divided by the number of complete weeks in respect of which payments were received in order to arrive at the appropriate weekly amount.[258] If the Secretary of State forms the view that this method of calculation produces a figure which 'does not accurately reflect the normal amount of the other income of the non-resident parent in question', then an alternative assessment period may be selected, having regard 'to the nature and pattern of receipt of such income'.[259] This is, of course, subject to the general rule that where the Secretary of State 'becomes aware of a material change of circumstances occurring after [the relevant week], but before the effective date, he shall take that change of circumstances into account'.[260]

Benefits Pensions and Allowances

The general rule is that social security benefits do not count as 'income' for child support purposes. This is subject to one exception—in determining whether a non-resident parent is liable for the nil rate, on the basis of having a net weekly income of less than £5, then benefits which are prescribed for the purposes of the flat rate liability and which are payable to the non-resident parent or his partner are taken into account.[261] In principle, any *other* income streams which the non-resident parent enjoys, which do not fall within this or any of the preceding provisions, are not taken into account in establishing his net weekly income.[262]

---

[257] *Ibid*, para 16(1)(a).
[258] *Ibid*, para 16(1)(b).
[259] *Ibid*, para 16(2).
[260] *Ibid*, reg 2(4).
[261] *Ibid*, sch, para 17.
[262] See p 335 above.

12

Variations on the Formula

Introduction

The policy underpinning the Child Support Act 1991 was that liability should be assessed according to the statutory formula in all cases, save for those exceptional matters reserved to the courts. This, it was argued, would deliver the objectives of consistency, fairness and predictability which had been so noticeably absent from the previous court-based arrangements for determining child maintenance.[1] As we have seen, it was slightly misleading to refer to '*the* formula', as the 1991 Act did not, contrary to popular mythology, adopt a 'one size fits all' philosophy. True, it was certainly assumed that the great majority of cases would be accommodated by the standard formula. However, from the beginning the legislation made provision for various 'special cases',[2] for example where both parents were non-resident parents or where the person with care had children with more than one non-resident parent. Yet the common characteristic of these 'special cases' was that the status of either the family (as above) or the child (for example, being a child in local authority care) was in some way atypical. The particular financial circumstances of the non-resident parent did not amount to a 'special case'. To that extent it was true to say that there was no discretion in the assessment of child support under the 1991 legislation as originally enacted.

The United Kingdom system was unusual in making no provision from the outset for handling cases outside the constraints of the formula. In both Australia and New Zealand the original child support schemes included a 'departures scheme'. In Australia applications for departures, known as changes of circumstances, are now dealt with by special case officers following a 'conference' with each parent separately.[3] The officer's decision may then be reviewed internally, following which there is a right of appeal to the Family Court, although this avenue is rarely pursued in practice. In New Zealand the Inland Revenue make decisions on child support liability, but the legislation originally provided for either parent to apply

---

[1] DSS, *Children Come First* (Cm 1264-I, 1990), chs 2 and 4.

[2] CSA 1991, s 42 and Child Support (Maintenance and Special Cases) Regulations 1992 (SI 1992/1815), pt III.

[3] See generally Child Support (Assessment) Act 1989 (Cth), pt 6A. Some special case officers are employed full-time by the Agency in Australia, whilst others work in this role part-time.

to the Family Court for a departure from the formula.[4] These arrangements were later modified to allow the Revenue to make a departure without requiring the parties to apply to court. As was seen in chapter 6, the American system accommodates discretion in a rather different way. State judges are expected to apply the relevant child support guidelines, but can give reasons for departing from those guidelines where they see fit.

The attempt to impose an entirely formula-driven system of child support in the United Kingdom did not last long. As was seen in chapter 5, the vociferous campaigning of non-resident parents resulted in a series of amendments to the regulations in April 1995 which introduced extra allowances (within the confines of the formula) for particular types of costs incurred by non-resident parents (such as high costs relating to contact or travel to work). These changes were merely a prelude to the Child Support Act 1995, which introduced the system of departure directions, designed 'to reach the parts that formula assessment could not reach'.[5] In this way the government recognised the need to 'introduce a degree of flexibility so as to address certain special costs which it would be neither right nor realistic to include in the universal formula'.[6] Yet the policy intention remained that 'formula assessment should continue to be the norm; that the standard formula assessment should be the starting point even when a departure is allowed; and that departures should not be common'.[7]

The 1995 Act amended the 1991 Act to provide for certain 'gateways' to the departures system; in so far as these grounds related to travel-to-work costs and the effect of capital and property settlements, they built on the April 1995 adjustments to the formula. The 1995 Act also introduced further grounds for departures, which had not foreshadowed by the April 1995 amendments to the regulations.[8] An application for a departure could only succeed if both the 'gateway' ground was established and the Secretary of State (or tribunal) considered it 'just and equitable' to make such an order. The departures system was piloted from April 1996,[9] but only came into force fully in December of that year. The available statistics demonstrate that, in keeping with the policy of the 1995 Act, a departure from the formula was very much the exception rather than the rule.[10]

---

[4] Child Support Act 1991 (NZ), s 104 ff.

[5] *CCS/8/2000* para 6 *per* Mr Commissioner Jacobs, citing counsel's 'catchy phrase'. The UK system was modelled on the first two elements of the three-fold antipodean test—(1) statutory grounds for departures; (2) a 'just and equitable' test; (3) the making of an order being 'otherwise proper'; Child Support (Assessment) Act 1989 (Cth), s 98C and Child Support Act 1991 (NZ), s 105.

[6] *Per* Mr A Burt, Under-Secretary of State for Social Security, Standing Committee E, col 3, (28 March 1995).

[7] DSS, *Improving Child Support* (Cm 2745, 1995) at para 2.4.

[8] See generally J Priest, 'Departure directions in the Child Support scheme' (1998) 5 *Journal of Social Security Law* 118.

[9] Child Support Agency, *Departure Directions Pilot Evaluation Report* (September 1996).

[10] In 1999 about 4% of cases in the Agency's yearly intake applied for departures, less than half of which were successful: *per* Ms A Eagle, Standing Committee F, cols 72 (20 January 2000) and 278 (1 February 2000).

This policy was continued with the reforms made by the 2000 Act which included the introduction of the variations scheme as the successor to the system of departures. The rules governing the variations scheme for cases assessed under the new child support scheme are contained in the Child Support Act 1991[11] (as amended by the 2000 Act[12]) and in the Child Support (Variations) Regulations 2000.[13] The overall legislative structure of the previous departures scheme has been retained. The primary legislation is mostly concerned with procedural matters relating to applications for variations. An outline of the substantive grounds upon which variations can be directed is contained in Schedule 4B to the 1991 Act, but the detailed rules for these 'gateways' are contained in the Variations Regulations 2000. The main difference between (old scheme) departures and (new scheme) variations is that the grounds on which a variation may be sought are somewhat narrower.[14] Most notably, there is no provision in the variations scheme for a non-resident parent to apply for an adjustment to the formula because of his high travel-to-work costs or the special costs associated with his illness or disability. The justification for the narrowing of the available grounds is that the basis for a variation on the formula should in some way be related to the child, rather than the non-resident parent's own particular circumstances. Critics of the new scheme have argued that the broad brush nature of the new formula is such that the grounds for variations should be relaxed rather than tightened further.[15] The counter-argument is that, in the main, the new formula generates reasonable outcomes in terms of child support liabilities and consequently there is less of a need to accommodate so-called exceptional cases.

Procedural Provisions for Variation Applications

Any party involved in an application for a maintenance calculation may apply to the Secretary of State for 'the rules by which the calculation is to be made to be varied *in accordance with this Act*'.[16] The italicised phrase highlights the limitations of the variations scheme; if they are to succeed, applications must be made in the

---

[11] CSA 1991, ss 28A–28G and schs 4A and 4B.

[12] CSPSSA 2000, ss 5–7 and sch 2.

[13] SI 2001/156, made under the authority of CSA 1991, sch 4B, para 5(1). Reg 33 of SI 2001/156 deals with the transition of cases from the old to new schemes.

[14] The other significant difference is that an application for a variation may be made even before a maintenance calculation has been made, whereas a departure could be applied for only once a maintenance assessment had been undertaken; see n 19 below.

[15] See eg House of Commons (HC) Social Security Committee, *The 1999 Child Support White Paper* (Tenth Report, Session 1998–99, HC 798) at 61 (N Mostyn QC).

[16] CSA 1991, s 28A(1), emphasis added. Thus an application may be made by a PWC, NRP or (in Scotland) a child applicant. The formal name for such a request is an 'application for a variation' (*ibid*, s 28A(2)). If a maintenance calculation has already been made, s 28A is modified by SI 2000/3173, reg 3; see further n 20 below.

stipulated manner[17] and must fall within one of a number of narrowly prescribed grounds.[18]

An application for a variation may be made at any time either before[19] or after[20] the Secretary of State has reached a decision on the maintenance calculation. The applicant must state the grounds for the application but need not apply in writing unless specifically directed to do so.[21] This reflects the Agency's increasing emphasis on communicating with parents by telephone rather than by post. The date on which the applicant notifies the Agency that he or she wishes to make an application is treated as the date of the application itself.[22] A variation application may be amended or withdrawn at any time before a decision is made on it; again such a request need not be in writing, unless the Secretary of State so directs.[23] The Secretary of State may also request the applicant to provide further evidence or information in order to make the decision.[24]

The next step is for the Agency to undertake an initial sift—known in the legislation as the 'preliminary consideration of applications'—in order to establish that there is at least an arguable case for a variation decision to be made.[25] Accordingly, the Secretary of State may reject the application if any one of three circumstances applies.[26] The first is that 'there are no grounds on which he could agree to a variation'—for example, the non-resident parent makes an application on the basis that the maintenance calculation is too high because he has substantial work-related expenses which were not accommodated under the standard formula.[27] The second is that the Agency has insufficient information to make a decision on

---

[17] The relevant procedural rules are made under the enabling powers in CSA 1991, sch 4A (modified, where relevant, by SI 2000/3173, reg 8).

[18] The regulations governing the substantive grounds are made under the enabling powers in CSA 1991, sch 4B (again, as modified where appropriate).

[19] *Ibid*, s 28A(3); contrast *ibid*, s 28A(1) before amendment by the 2000 Act.

[20] CSA 1991, s 28G(1); in which case see the modifications to *ibid*, ss 28A–28F and schs 4A and 4B made by the Child Support (Variations) (Modification of Statutory Provisions) Regulations 2000 (SI 2000/3173). These regulations are needed as the provisions in the CSA 1991 are premised on the variation application being made in advance of the maintenance calculation.

[21] CSA 1991, s 28A(4). If the Secretary of State directs that the application be made in writing, it may be on an official form or in such other written form as the Agency accepts as sufficient: SI 2001/156, reg 4(1). Assuming s 28A(4) and any further procedural requirements are satisfied, the application is treated as 'duly made', SI 2001/156, reg 4(6).

[22] *Ibid*, reg 4(2). For the rules governing the date of application for written requests, see *ibid*, reg 4(3)–(5). For the general rules governing the date of receipt of documents, see *ibid*, reg 2.

[23] *Ibid*, reg 5(1). However, an amendment cannot relate to any change of circumstances occurring after the effective date of the variation decision: *ibid*, reg 5(2).

[24] *Ibid*, reg 8(1), made under CSA 1991, sch 4A, para 4 and modelled on Social Security (Claims and Payments) Regulations 1987 (SI 1987/1968), reg 7(1), on which see *R(IS) 4/93* and *Kerr v Department for Social Development* [2004] UKHL 23; [2004] 1 WLR 1372. If the evidence or information is not forthcoming within one month, or such longer period as the Secretary of State thinks reasonable, then the Agency can proceed to determine the application regardless (SI 2001/156 reg 8(2)—which may, of course, result in its rejection on the initial sift; see *ibid*, reg 6(2)(c)).

[25] CSA 1991, s 28B(1) and sch 4A, para 3.

[26] *Ibid*, s 28B(2) (modified, where appropriate, by SI 2000/3173, reg 4). This is not, as such, a determination of the application: *R(CS) 2/06* at para 33 *per* Mr Commissioner Jacobs.

[27] This qualifies as a ground for departure but not for a variation.

the maintenance application itself, and so intends to make an interim mainten-ance calculation.[28] The third and more diverse category is where one of a number of prescribed circumstances applies. Some of these are procedural or evidential grounds—for example, the applicant has failed to respond to a request for further information[29] or where there is no basis for concluding that the case falls within of the substantive grounds for a variation decision.[30] Others are what might be described as 'threshold tests', namely where the applicant's evidence, even if accepted, would not bring the case above the minimum threshold—for example, as regards the level of special expenses—required for the application of one of the substantive grounds.[31] Finally, in cases where a maintenance calculation is already in place, an application may be rejected on the initial sift in a range of circum-stances in which its acceptance would be either inappropriate (eg because there is a default maintenance decision in force as a result of the non-resident parent's non-compliance) or pointless (eg because the application is made by a non-resident parent who is, in any event, liable only to pay the nil rate).[32]

The purpose of the initial sift is to weed out cases which stand no prospect of success, and to do so in such a way as not to trouble the other party. If the appli-cation survives this preliminary consideration, the other parent will normally be asked for his or her views on the matter. It is then that the application becomes, in the Agency's parlance, a 'contest'. At this point the Secretary of State is required to notify the other party of the application and the grounds on which it is made, and to invite representations (orally or in writing) on the application.[33] In doing so the other parent must be informed about any evidence or information supplied by the applicant.[34] The Agency's duty to disclose such matters is subject to a number of exceptions based on considerations of confidentiality, either on medical grounds or relating to a person's address (where there is a risk of harm or undue distress).[35] There are a number of circumstances in which the other parent's representations on the application need not be sought, such as where the Secretary of State decides to reinstate an existing variation following a supersession decision.[36] The Secretary of State also has the power to treat an application made on one ground as having been made on an alternative ground.[37] Once any such representations have been

---

[28] See CSA 1991, s 12.

[29] SI 2001/156, regs 6(2)(c) and 8.

[30] *Ibid*, reg 6(2)(d).

[31] *Ibid*, reg 6(2)(b)(i)–(iii).

[32] *Ibid*, regs 6(2)(a); and see *ibid*, reg 7 (made under CSA 1991, s 28G(3)) for the detailed grounds.

[33] SI 2001/156, reg 9(1).

[34] Where the applicant sends in further evidence or information after the notification to the other parent, this *may* be sent out for comment: *ibid*, reg 9(7).

[35] *Ibid*, reg 9(2). On the non-disclosure of medical evidence, see the parallel provision in Social Security and Child Support (Decisions and Appeals) Regulations 1999 (SI 1999/991), reg 42 and *R(A) 4/89*, *CSDLA/5/1995* and *CDLA/1347/1999*. See further L Lundy and G McKeever 'Withholding harm-ful medical evidence' (1997) 4 *Journal of Social Security Law* 71.

[36] SI 2001/156, reg 9(3).

[37] *Ibid*, reg 9(8); if so, this must be made clear in the notifications to the parents. The Secretary of State may also consolidate two or more variation applications made in respect of the same maintenance calculation: *ibid*, reg 9(9).

received, then the Secretary of State may—'if he considers it reasonable to do so'—send a copy of such observations to the applicant, inviting his or her comments within 14 days (or such longer period as seems reasonable).[38] On the expiry of that time limit, the Secretary of State may then proceed to determine the variation application,[39] obviously taking into account any representations received.[40] There are, however, two further procedural steps which may be taken before a decision is taken on an application for a variation, namely the imposition of an interim maintenance decision and a regular payments condition.

The 'interim maintenance decision', despite its similar terminology, should not be confused with the 'interim maintenance assessment' under the original child support regime. Interim maintenance assessments were penal assessments imposed in cases of non-compliance. In contrast, an interim maintenance decision is a calculation put in place as a temporary measure where a variation application is made but before the maintenance calculation itself is carried out.[41] The amount of maintenance under an interim maintenance decision is calculated in the same way as for an ordinary maintenance calculation;[42] effectively it is a form of statutory child maintenance pending suit, albeit governed by exactly the same formula as the standard application for child support. An interim maintenance decision may itself be revised[43] and in any event is automatically replaced by a subsequent maintenance calculation in the case.[44]

The policy behind the new scheme assumes that an interim maintenance decision will usually be accompanied by the imposition of a regular payments condition. The Secretary of State may impose such a condition where a non-resident parent makes an application for a variation which has survived the initial sift and in respect of which an interim maintenance decision is made.[45] Such a condition requires the non-resident parent to pay the appropriate amount of child support under that interim decision, or such lesser amount as the Secretary of State agrees to, pending the outcome of the case.[46] In effect, the non-resident parent is required to pay some child support on account as a token of good faith. If the non-resident parent fails to comply with the condition,[47] the Secretary of State may refuse to consider the variation application and may simply proceed with the decision on the

---

[38] *Ibid*, reg 9(4). This is obviously subject to the same confidentiality exceptions as listed in *ibid*, reg 9(2).

[39] *Ibid*, reg 9(5).

[40] *Ibid*, reg 9(6). See also CSA 1991, s 28E(3).

[41] CSA 1991, s 12(2).

[42] *Ibid*, s 12(3).

[43] SI 1999/991, reg 3A(4).

[44] CSA 1991, s 28F(5), with the consequence that any appeal against the interim maintenance decision lapses.

[45] *Ibid*, s 28C(1). Section 28C is modified by SI 2000/3173, reg 5 for cases where the variation application is made once a maintenance calculation is already in force. The imposition of such a condition must be notified to all the parties: CSA 1991, s 28C(3).

[46] *Ibid*, s 28C(2). The lesser amount is not negotiable—it is the amount of the interim maintenance decision adjusted by the variation, based on the assumption that the NRP's application is successful: SI 2001/156, reg 31(1). The decision on whether to impose the normal amount or the varied amount is one for the discretion of the Secretary of State.

[47] The NRP is typically to be given one month's grace to make up the payments: *ibid*, reg 31(2) and (3).

maintenance calculation itself.[48] The decision on whether or not the non-resident parent is in breach of the regular payments condition is one for the Secretary of State, who must notify the parties.[49] The regular payments condition only ceases to have effect once a maintenance calculation is made (with or without any variation) or if the variation application is withdrawn.[50] The language of the primary legislation makes it plain that the decision as to whether to impose a regular payments condition and, if so, at what rate, is a discretionary one for the Secretary of State, who must therefore consider the children's welfare.[51] There is no right of appeal against such a decision,[52] although in principle judicial review must remain a possibility. That said, the Agency's computer system, at the outset of the new scheme at least, was unable to accommodate the imposition of regular payments conditions.[53]

Once these various procedural steps have been complied with,[54] an application for a variation is ready for determination. The Secretary of State then has three options: he or she can agree to the variation, refuse the application or refer it to a tribunal for it to determine whether or not to agree to the variation.[55] If the Secretary of State decides to agree (or not) to the variation, the Agency must also proceed to make a maintenance calculation (or a default maintenance decision if relevant information is missing).[56] The third option of referring the matter to a tribunal for decision is a unique power in the child support jurisdiction.[57] On such a referral the tribunal has the same powers and duties as the Secretary of State at first instance.[58] The tribunal may also consider a different basis for a variation to the ground cited in the original application.[59] This is subject, of course, to the dictates of natural justice and to the Convention rights of the parties to the case.[60]

---

[48] CSA 1991, s 28C(5).

[49] *Ibid*, s 28C(6) and (7).

[50] *Ibid*, s 28C(4).

[51] *Ibid*, s 2.

[52] There is no reference to s 28C in either *ibid*, s 20 or in SI 1999/991, reg 30A.

[53] 'The functionality for setting a Regular Payment Condition (RPC) will not be available until Release 2. Until then, whilst it is possible for an RPC to be considered, it is **not advisable** to impose one . . .', Child Support Agency, *Procedure: Arrears Management*, 'Regular Payments Condition' at 5842.

[54] In other words, the application has not 'failed' in the sense of being withdrawn or rejected on the initial sift, and assuming its consideration has not been refused for non-compliance with a regular payments condition: CSA 1991, s 28D(1) and (2).

[55] *Ibid*, s 28D(1). See further pp 401–03 below on the implementation of variation decisions.

[56] CSA 1991, s 28D(1)(a). If there is already a maintenance calculation in place, then the Agency must implement a revision or supersession decision as appropriate: SI 2000/3173, reg 6(1), modifying CSA 1991, s 28D(1)(a).

[57] *Ibid*, s 28D(1)(b). The same facility applied to departure directions. The option of a direct referral to a tribunal was adopted from the previous arrangements for social security appeals (SSAA 1992, s 21(2)), but the power was abolished in that jurisdiction by SSA 1998.

[58] CSA 1991, s 28D(3). The tribunal may hear a referral alongside an appeal under s 20 against an interim maintenance decision (*ibid*, sch 4A, para 5(3)); it may also hear two or more variation applications together: SI 1999/991, reg 45. The tribunal's decision on a referral is subject to the revision or supersession procedures: CSA 1991, ss 16(1A)(c) and 17(1)(d).

[59] *R(CS) 3/01* at para 50 *per* Mr Commissioner Jacobs, referring to the parties' power to amend an application (now SI 2001/156, reg 5).

[60] E Jacobs and G Douglas, *Child Support: The Legislation* (Sweet & Maxwell, London, Edition Seven, 2005/2006) at 112.

The original proposal in the Green Paper was that all variation applications would be referred for decision by tribunals, but this idea was later abandoned as unworkable.[61] The justification for the power of referral is that it enables especially problematic or complicated cases to be sent direct for determination by a tribunal with the appropriate expertise and independent judgment.[62] The Secretary of State's internal guidance currently states that 'novel or particularly contentious cases are to be passed to the Appeals Service for referral to tribunal'.[63] In practice, however, there are complaints from the tribunal judiciary that the Agency routinely uses the power of referral to avoid having to institute more detailed inquiries into the circumstances of the case.[64] The result is that cases may come on for hearing at a tribunal without the Agency having undertaken all the necessary prior investigations.[65]

The Substantive Grounds for Variation Applications

Assuming that the necessary procedural steps have all been satisfied, the Secretary of State may agree to a variation application, but only if two conditions are met.[66] The first is that he or she is satisfied that the circumstances fall within one or more of the particular cases specified in the legislation as a ground for a variation.[67] These various cases fall into three general categories: special expenses, property or capital transfers and additional cases.[68] The particular criteria for each of the cases are considered in more detail below. If the circumstances do not fall within one of these cases, no variation can be allowed—there is no general 'discretion' to permit variations.[69] The second requirement is that, in the Secretary of State's opinion, and 'in all the circumstances of the case, it would be just and equitable to agree to a variation'.[70] Again, the effect of this provision is analysed more fully below.

Before doing so, however, it is important to note that the legislation also stipulates that certain general principles must be observed in deciding whether or not to agree to a variation.[71] These principles 'infuse all stages of the determination';[72]

---

[61] DSS, *A new contract for welfare: Children's Rights and Parents' Responsibilities* (Cm 4349, 1999) ch 6, para 16.

[62] *Ibid*, at 42, para 18.

[63] Child Support Agency, *Procedure: Specialist Areas*, 'Novel or Particularly Contentious Applications' at 2955.

[64] See eg K Mullan, 'Supersession—the one true interpretation?' (2004) 11 *Journal of Social Security Law* 148 at 155, referring to this phenomenon as 'a complete abrogation of responsibility by the Agency'.

[65] See eg *CCS/4503/2003*.

[66] CSA 1991, s 28F(1).

[67] *Ibid*, s 28D(1)(a).

[68] *Ibid*, sch 4B, pt I.

[69] *Ibid*, sch 4B, para 5(2). See also *CCS/2357/2003* at para 50 *per* Mr Commissioner Mesher.

[70] CSA 1991, s 28D(1)(b).

[71] *Ibid*, s 28E(1) and (2). The 1991 Act also specifies various other matters which must either be taken into account or wholly disregarded in making such a decision: see *ibid*, s 28E(3) and (4) and below.

[72] Jacobs and Douglas, n 60 above, at 114.

accordingly they must be taken into account in making judgments both as to whether the criteria for a particular ground for a variation are made out and as to whether it is 'just and equitable' to agree to the variation. It necessarily follows that these principles must be applied by a tribunal dealing with a referral on a variation application[73] (or on appeal) as well as by Agency staff involved in determining such cases at first instance. The 1991 Act lays down two such general principles to which the Secretary of State and tribunals must pay regard when deciding whether or not to agree to variation.[74]

The first general principle is that 'parents should be responsible for maintaining their children whenever they can afford to do so'.[75] In one sense this merely reaffirms the principle of parental responsibility for the maintenance of children which is fundamental to the 1991 Act.[76] However, the qualifying phrase 'whenever they can afford to do so' arguably represents a softening of the absolute principle of responsibility stated in section 1 of the Act. Doubtless one explanation for this is that its inclusion in section 1 would have been surplusage—policy makers would argue that the new child support formula was designed in such a way that it accommodated issues of affordability from the outset. Yet the use of this qualifying phrase in the context of variations demonstrates that, at the margins at least, questions of affordability may become pertinent when dealing with such applications. Moreover, it should not be assumed that this statutory injunction will necessarily operate to the advantage of a parent seeking to reduce his child support liability. On the contrary, the initial income assessment may be unrealistically low, owing either to the limitations of the formula or the deficiencies of the Agency's evidence-gathering procedures. In that event the question of affordability may take on a rather different complexion, with the consequence that liability is increased, rather than decreased, on an application for a variation.

The second general principle is that:

> where a parent has more than one child, his obligation to maintain any one of them should be no less of an obligation than his obligation to maintain any other of them.[77]

This means that a non-resident parent's responsibility to his children with whom he lives cannot override his responsibility to his other children from his first

---

[73] CSA 1991, s 28D(3).

[74] The 1991 Act (s 28E(1)) also provides that regard must be had 'to such other considerations as may be prescribed'; to date no such further provisions have been specified. When this provision was first enacted in CSA 1995, the Government's stated intention was to use this power only if it became necessary to do so in order to ensure that discretion was used consistently in dealing with applications (*per* Lord Mackay of Ardbrecknish, *Hansard* HL Debates vol 565 col 63, 19 June 1995). One possibility canvassed at the time was that regulations might provide that the Secretary of State, in considering a departure in a case where there was a court order before an assessment was made under the 1991 Act, should have regard to the level of the court order in deciding whether a departure direction was appropriate (HL Select Committee on the Scrutiny of Delegated Powers, *10th Report* (Session 1994–95) Appendix I, para 16).

[75] CSA 1991, s 28E(2)(a).

[76] *Ibid*, s 1(1).

[77] *Ibid*, s 28E(2)(b).

family. The notion of an equal liability to support all one's children represents a subtle shift from the philosophy underlying the original 1991 Act. The 1990 White Paper contained no explicit acceptance of the principle that a parent was under an *equal* obligation to support all his children. Rather, it declared that where a parent had formed a second family, 'he is liable to maintain all his own children. A fair and reasonable balance has to be struck between the interests of the children of a first family and the children of a second'. [78] Indeed, the practical effect of the original formula was to prioritise the children of the first family. The assertion by the 1995 Act of a general principle of equal support, if only in the context of departures directions (and now variation applications), indicated a greater degree of sensitivity on behalf of policy makers to the complexity of separated parents' new circumstances.[79] That said, the extent of this recognition in the context of decisions on applications for variations remains somewhat muted. This general principle is still phrased in terms of parents' financial obligations to support *their own* children. Step-parents, foster parents or others who treat a child as their own do not qualify for the status of 'parent' in this context.[80] It follows that the underlying principle for the purpose of variation applications remains that a parent's primary responsibilities are to his natural children.[81] The official position at the time of the 1995 Act was that, so far as step-children were concerned, a natural father would usually be liable to provide maintenance, and so as a general rule it would be inappropriate to have regard to the assumption of support by step-parents in the context of departure directions.[82] Accordingly, it was only possible to obtain a departure direction for a step-child in very limited circumstances.[83] However, the 2000 Act has elevated both the new natural children and also the new step-children of a non-resident parent to the status of 'relevant other children' for the purposes of the revised formula, and so their presence in the equation will affect the initial calculation of the child support liability.[84] Consequently, the variations scheme makes no general provision for any children supported by the non-resident parent who are not 'qualifying children' under the Act.[85]

In addition to these general principles, the 1991 Act requires the Secretary of State to take into account any representations made by the parties on the application for a variation.[86] In determining an application for a variation the Secretary of State must also disregard the fact that the parent with care depends to some

---

[78] DSS, n 1 above, at para 2.1.

[79] As discussed below, this trend has continued with the 2000 Act, which has amended the standard formula itself to take account of the existence of a second family: see also pp 303–04 above.

[80] CSA 1991, s 54(1).

[81] And to those who are effectively deemed to be natural children, eg adoptive children.

[82] Mr A Burt, Parliamentary Under-Secretary of State for Social Security, Standing Committee E, col 74 (30 March 1995).

[83] SI 1996/2907, reg 18.

[84] CSA 1991, sch 1, para 10C(2); see p 304 above.

[85] An exception is made for disabled 'relevant other children'; see SI 2001/156, reg 11.

[86] CSA 1991, s 28E(3), as modified by SI 2000/3173, reg 6(2) for applications made where the calculation has already been made. See further SI 2001/156, reg 9, discussed at p 367 above.

extent on one of the means-tested social security benefits[87] (or would do so if the application were granted).[88] This provision was inserted to protect the interests of the taxpayer:

> by countering the risk that, if the person with care is on benefit, any reduction in maintenance might be seen as justified regardless of wider considerations since benefit will increase to compensate in full or in part for the shortfall.[89]

By the same token, the fact that any child support payable as a result of the variation application being approved might be taken into account in assessing entitlement to one of these benefits must also be ignored.[90] The justification for this provision has been put in terms of respecting the wishes of a parent with care who applies for increased child support, irrespective of the fact that her benefit income may be reduced, and so to prevent the Secretary of State from second-guessing that decision.[91]

The following sections analyse the specific types of cases in which variations may be agreed, before returning to the question of whether it is 'just and equitable' to make a variation.[92]

Special Expenses

Introduction

The first point to note is that only a non-resident parent can apply for special expenses to be considered.[93] It follows that a parent with care with extra expenses in terms of high child care costs cannot ask for the formula assessment to be varied upwards, although she may be eligible for assistance via the tax credits scheme.[94] In Australia a parent with care can apply for a change of assessment (effectively a variation) where her child care costs are more than 5 per cent of her income.[95]

---

[87] ie income support, income-based jobseeker's allowance, housing benefit or council tax benefit: see SI 2001/156, reg 32, made under CSA 1991, s 28E(5). Note that the list has not been amended to include state pension credit: it is unclear whether this was a deliberate omission or an oversight.

[88] *Ibid*, s 28E(4)(a).

[89] *Tenth Report*, n 15 above, Appendix I, para 15.

[90] CSA 1991, s 28E(4)(b).

[91] 'I believe that [the PWC] is likely to apply only if she wishes to receive an increased level of maintenance. Therefore, it seems illogical to then give the Secretary of State power to deny her that increase because of what he considers to be in her best interests' *per* Lord Mackay of Ardbrecknish, *Hansard* HL Debates vol 565 col 67, 19 June 1995.

[92] See *R (Qazi) v Secretary of State* [2004] EWHC 1331 (Admin), reported as *R(CS) 5/04*, holding that the parallel 'just and equitable' requirement in the departures scheme was not triggered unless a valid ground was made out: at para 32 *per* Charles J.

[93] CSA 1991, sch 4B, para 2(1). In Australia either parent may apply for a change of assessment: Child Support (Assessment) Act 1989 (Cth), s 98B.

[94] If she is in work and on a low income, she may qualify for help with child care costs through WTC: see Tax Credits Act 2002, s 12 and Working Tax Credit (Entitlement and Maximum Rate) Regulations 2002 (SI 202/2005), regs 13–16. If she earns too much to qualify for WTC, she may be better off trying to negotiate a private maintenance arrangement.

[95] Child Support (Assessment) Act 1989 (Cth), s 117(2)(b)(i)(C).

There are five categories of special expenses which non-resident parents may use as the basis for an application for a variation.[96] Consideration of such costs is subject to two financial constraints. The first rule provides for relatively trifling[97] amounts of extra expenditure to be disregarded. In order to be taken into account, any such special expenses (with the exception of costs incurred because of a relevant other child's illness or disability) must exceed a minimum threshold of £15 a week (or £10 per week if the non-resident parent's net weekly income is less than £200).[98] If the non-resident parent has special expenses under more than one category, then the £15 (or £10) a week minimum threshold applies to the aggregate of all such costs. The second financial constraint is an anti-abuse provision and applies to all categories of special expenses. This enables the Secretary of State, where it is considered that the non-resident's parent's special expenses are 'unreasonably high or to have been unreasonably incurred', to substitute some lower figure (which may be below the relevant threshold amount or be nil).[99] This might apply, for example, where the non-resident parent's claimed contact costs include an overnight stay 'at an expensive hotel when more reasonably priced accommodation was available' or an overnight stay 'where there is no valid justification for one'.[100]

Contact Costs

The failure of the original child support scheme to take any account of contact costs was a frequent source of complaint by a minority of non-resident parents.[101] The departures scheme, introduced under the 1995 Act, made some limited allowance for such costs,[102] although the High Court has expressed concern that those rules might act as a disincentive to non-resident parents maintaining contact.[103] In a similar way, various forms of expenditure incurred for the purpose of maintaining contact with a qualifying child—either by the non-resident parent himself or by the child at his expense—may also form the basis for a variation application under the new scheme.[104] The regulations list in considerable detail the types of contact-

---

[96] It is open to the Secretary of State to prescribe further categories (see CSA 1991, sch 4B, para 2(3)), but as yet there have been no additions to these five categories of special expenses.

[97] In other words, in pre-Woolf legalese, a *de minimis* rule. If the threshold is not exceeded, the case may be dismissed on the initial sift: see SI 2001/156, reg 6(2)(b)(i).

[98] *Ibid*, reg 15(1). 'Net weekly income' means that which would be taken into account under the formula, ignoring any variation: *ibid*, reg 15(4).

[99] *Ibid*, reg 15(2).

[100] Child Support Agency, *CS2 Help and Guidance*, 'Reasonable Costs'.

[101] This was one of the grounds for the unsuccessful ECHR application in *Logan v United Kingdom*, App. No 24875/94. Note that under the old scheme, some 44% of NRPs lived within 5 km of the PWC and a total of 72% within 20km: Child Support Agency, *Child Support Agency Quarterly Summary Statistics: May 2005*, Table 3.4.

[102] SI 1996/2907, reg 14.

[103] *Qazi (R(CS) 5/04)*, n 92 above, at para 37 *per* Charles J, who also recognised the force of the applicant's argument that his ineligibility for a departure direction was not fair, or just and equitable: *ibid*, at para 39.

[104] CSA 1991, sch 4B, para 2(2)(a) and SI 2001/156, reg 10.

related costs which may qualify for this purpose,[105] namely those relating to the purchase of travel tickets,[106] fuel,[107] taxi fares,[108] car hire,[109] overnight stays[110] and minor incidental costs.[111] Such special expenses can also include the cost of a travelling companion for either the non-resident parent or the child, but only if the Secretary of State is satisfied that such a chaperone is 'necessary'.[112] This includes, but is not confined to, cases where either the non-resident parent or the child has a disability or long-term illness[113] or the child is too young to travel alone.[114] These rules are more generous in a number of respects than those that apply to the equivalent head for a departure direction.[115] However, the statutory list of allowable expenses is exhaustive, and so no account is taken of other expenditure incurred by non-resident parents, either in the actual exercise of contact or in other related costs (eg telephone charges, meals out with the children, pocket money[116] or treats, cinema tickets, general car maintenance costs etc). Moreover, there can only be limited scope for argument as to what constitute 'minor incidental costs' in the final 'catch all' category of allowable expenditures.[117]

Given the disputes which typically may arise over the extent of contact, the calculation of contact-related costs may be problematic. The regulations provide that there must either be an established or an intended set pattern as to the frequency of contact.[118] If the former, the actual costs incurred in exercising contact over the preceding 12 months (or a shorter period if appropriate) are averaged out to arrive

---

[105] *Ibid*, reg 10(1)(a)–(f).

[106] There are no restrictions on the form of travel: air fares are thus allowable, assuming they are less than a reasonable alternative by coach or train (*ibid*, reg 15(2) may be invoked if the travel costs are unreasonably high).

[107] Agency submissions to tribunals typically rely on petrol costs as cited by the AA for the average family car.

[108] But only if disability or long-term illness (as defined by reg 11(2)(a) and (c)—see further below) makes other forms of transport impracticable: *ibid*, reg 10(1)(c).

[109] But only if cheaper than the cost of public transport and/or taxis: *ibid*, reg 10(1)(d).

[110] But only if a return journey on the same day is impracticable, or contact includes two or more consecutive days: *ibid*, reg 10(1)(e).

[111] Such as road or bridge toll fees, or breakfast where an overnight stay is involved: *ibid*, reg 10(1)(f).

[112] *Ibid*, reg 10(2).

[113] See *ibid*, reg 11(2)(a) and (c).

[114] For example, a court order may stipulate supervised contact.

[115] The departure directions rules made no provision for car hire or B & B contact-related costs: see SI 1996/2907, reg 13. In *Qazi (R(CS) 5/04)*, n 92 above, the Court of Appeal, whilst expressing sympathy for the NRP, held that these rules were human rights compliant.

[116] If authority for the proposition that the ordinary formula takes no account of pocket money is needed, see *R(CS) 9/98* para 8 *per* Mr Commissioner Rice.

[117] The examples given in SI 2001/156, reg 10(1)(f)—see n 111 above—suggest that the provision will be strictly construed. It should surely cover a credit card booking fee or a seat reservation charge, although Jacobs and Douglas, n 60 above, at 675, imply that the latter would not be included. They also raise the nice point as to whether sleeper or cabin charges qualify; these are almost certainly not a 'minor incidental cost' but could be 'accommodation' or even regarded as an intrinsic element of the travel cost. After all, if it is unreasonable, then SI 2001/156, reg 15(2) applies. See also *CCS/2816/2004*, paras 30–33, decided under the old scheme.

[118] SI 2006/156 reg 10(3)(a).

at a weekly amount.[119] If the latter, the intended pattern must have been agreed by both parents, so a unilateral intention as to future contact on the part of the non-resident parent is insufficient. The allowable special expenses are then calculated according to the anticipated costs.[120] If the parents agree a pattern of contact and the non-resident parent is granted a variation on that basis, but he then fails to maintain contact, the parent with care could apply for a supersession of the variation decision on the basis of a change in circumstances. If, on the other hand, the parent with care obstructs contact, the non-resident parent will have no grounds for seeking a variation as he will, by definition, have incurred no allowable costs.[121] Moreover, the question of whether particular contact arrangements are being adhered to is a matter which must be ignored in deciding whether it is 'just and equitable' to agree to a variation.[122]

The non-resident parent cannot invoke the benefit of these rules where he is already receiving credit under the shared care provisions.[123] This prevents double recovery and is designed to discourage parents with care from withdrawing from shared care on the ground that they would face a double penalty. In all variation decisions relating to contact costs the fact that there may be a court order for contact in existence is, in itself, of no relevance,[124] with one exception. If the Secretary of State reduces the amount allowable by way of contact costs on the basis that the figure claimed is either unreasonably high or unreasonably incurred, then the lower figure must not render impossible the continuance of contact at the frequency specified in the court order.[125] However, this provision offers no relief to the non-resident parent who claims that the ordinary formula assessment itself makes it impossible for him to exercise contact in accordance with the court order.

---

[119] SI 2001/156, reg 10(3)(b)(i); if contact has already ceased, see *ibid*, reg 10(3)(b)(ii).

[120] *Ibid*, reg 10(3)(b)(iii).

[121] However, assume that an NRP living in London has a court order for monthly contact with his child living with the PWC in Glasgow. Arguably if he makes regular visits with a view to exercising contact, but on arrival the PWC prevents contact on each occasion, then his travel etc costs should be allowed (unless they have been 'unreasonably incurred' under reg 15(2)—but surely the NRP is being reasonable in seeking to exercise contact under the court order?). The test in reg 10(1) is *not* whether the costs are incurred in relation to *actual* contact, but whether they are incurred 'for the purpose of *maintaining* contact'. Clearly, however, legal costs incurred in seeking to enforce contact are not an allowable expense under the regulations, however meritorious the NRP's case. Legal costs in enforcing contact are allowable in Australia, if necessarily incurred: see L Young, 'Child Support: A Practical Approach to the Change of Assessment Process' (2002) 8 *Current Family Law* 45 at 49.

[122] SI 2001/156 reg 21(2)(d); see p 396 below.

[123] SI 2001/156, reg 10(4). Additionally, if he receives financial help with contact costs from a third party, it is only the balance of his own expenditure that is allowable: *ibid*, reg 10(5).

[124] Thus under *ibid*, reg 10(3)(a) what matters is the established contact pattern or the agreed intended pattern, irrespective of what the court may have ordered.

[125] SI 2001/156, reg 15(3). This is subject to the requirement that the NRP 'is maintaining contact at that frequency'—but, if the NRP is doing so, how can it be 'impossible' for him to do so (Jacobs and Douglas, n 60 above, at 669). Perhaps SI 2001/156, reg 15(3) should be read to mean 'impossible in the absence of severe financial hardship or debt'.

The allowable weekly contact costs must, of course, exceed the relevant threshold for the non-resident parent of £15 or £10 a week.[126] (The Australian scheme operates a different approach: contact costs must exceed 5 per cent of the liable parent's income for child support purposes for a change of assessment to be considered).[127] If a variation is agreed under the United Kingdom arrangements, then the weekly amount of contact expenses is deducted from the non-resident parent's net weekly income.[128] Special rules apply where the non-resident parent's income is the 'capped amount', ie the maximum net weekly income for the purposes of the formula (currently £2,000 p/w).[129] The 'just and equitable' test, discussed further below, is relevant both to the issue of whether to agree a variation at all and to the amount of the contact expenses to be deducted.[130]

Costs in Respect of Relevant other Child with Disability or Long-term Illness

As we saw in the previous chapter, the standard child support formula now takes account of 'relevant other children', typically the non-resident parent's children from a new relationship or step-children,[131] by providing for a deduction of 15, 20 or 25 per cent from his net weekly income before the child support liability is calculated.[132] These are necessarily broad brush allowances which do not factor in any special needs the other child may have. Accordingly, a variation may be applied for where the 'relevant other child' has a disability or long-term illness such that the non-resident parent necessarily incurs extra expenses.[133]

A person[134] is disabled for this purpose if any rate of DLA or attendance allowance[135] is in payment[136] or he or she is registered blind.[137] The use of such proxy definitions is, from an administrative point of view, simpler to apply than the more open-ended definition used under the departures regulations.[138] A 'long-term illness' is one which will last for at least a year (or the remainder of the

---

[126] Thus in *Qazi* (n 92 above) the London-based NRP's application was rejected as his contact costs averaged out at £14.38 p/w, there being no allowance under the old scheme rules for his stays in a guest house in Wrexham near his children.

[127] Child Support (Assessment) Act 1989 (Cth), s 117(3).

[128] SI 2001/156, reg 23(1). 'Net weekly income' means as assessed under SI 2001/155: SI 2001/156, reg 27(7).

[129] *Ibid*, reg 23(2).

[130] See *CCS/3151/1999* paras 19–23 *per* Mr Commissioner Jacobs, dealing with SI 1996/2907, reg 37(1). Thus the mandatory language of SI 2001/156, reg 23(1) ('effect shall be given') cannot displace consideration of the 'just and equitable' test.

[131] See SI 2001/156, reg 11(2)(d) and CSA 1991, sch 1, para 10C(1).

[132] *Ibid*, sch 1, para 2(2).

[133] *Ibid*, sch 4B, para 2(3)(b) and SI 2001/156, reg 11.

[134] The definition refers to 'person' rather than 'child' as this definition also applies for the purposes of reg 10.

[135] Or a mobility supplement under any of the various war pension schemes: *ibid*, reg 11(2)(a)(i).

[136] Or would be were s/he not a patient: *ibid*, reg 11(2)(a)(ii).

[137] Or treated as blind under the income support rules (ie for 28 weeks following removal from the register): SI 1987/1967, sch 2, para 12(1)(a)(iii) and (2).

[138] SI 1996/2907, reg 15(6)(a), echoing CSA 1991, s 8(9), and on which see *CCS/7522/1999*, paras 20–24 *per* Mr Commissioner Jacobs.

person's life, if less).[139] The regulations include a list of allowable items of expenditure,[140] such as costs relating to care needs, mobility, domestic help, heating, laundry, diet,[141] day care and respite care. There are a number of restrictions on such special expenses; they must appear on the statutory list, they must be 'necessarily incurred . . . due to' the disability or illness and they must not fall foul of the 'unreasonably high' or 'unreasonably incurred' rule. The costs must also be incurred in respect of the child by the non-resident parent (and not, for example, his partner). There is, however, no threshold amount.[142] As with contact costs, where financial assistance is forthcoming from a third party (or DLA is payable for the child), it is only the non-resident parent's net special expenses which can be taken into account.[143]

It follows that the rules make no provision for the formula amount to be adjusted where the special costs are incurred by the non-resident parent in respect of his own disability or long-term illness. The explanation for this omission is presumably that these are not *child*-related costs and the assistance provided through general disability benefits is regarded as sufficient. These rules are also inapplicable where it is the parent with care who incurs extra costs because of a qualifying child's health condition. However, this is one of those special cases in which the courts retain their jurisdiction to make top-up orders.[144] As with contact costs, a variation for a relevant other child's special expenses is given effect by deducting the appropriate weekly amount from the non-resident parent's net weekly income.[145]

Prior Debts of the Relationship

Settlements on the breakdown of a relationship are not simply about splitting the parties' assets—there may well be debts which need to be divided. Non-resident parents who took on sole responsibility for such debts understandably felt aggrieved at the failure of the original child support formula to accommodate such liabilities. The 1995 Act enabled non-resident parents to apply for a departure direction in relation to debts incurred before the breakdown of the relationship.[146] The variations scheme now makes virtually identical provision,[147] subject to the

---

[139] SI 2001/156, reg 11(2)(c). See further *CCS/7522/1999*, paras 16–19.

[140] SI 2001/156, reg 11(1)(a)–(m).

[141] The diet must be recommended by a 'medical practitioner', a term which stands undefined here; see, however, Interpretation Act 1978, sch 1 and the commentary in Jacobs and Douglas, n 60 above, at 677–79. On assessing allowable dietary costs, see further *CCS/7522/1999*.

[142] SI 2001/156, reg 15(1) deliberately omits any reference to reg 11.

[143] *Ibid*, reg 11(3). 'Financial assistance' in this context includes eg voluntary/charitable donations and payments under an insurance policy, but not social security benefits: *R(CS) 2/02*.

[144] CSA 1991, s 8(8).

[145] SI 2001/156, reg 23(1), with the special rule for 'capped amount' cases: *ibid*, reg 23(2).

[146] SI 1996/2907, reg 16.

[147] CSA 1991, sch 4B, para 2(2)(c) and SI 2001/156, reg 12. The only drafting difference of any significance seems to lie in the new variation reg 12(2)(d) and (e), replacing the former departure reg 16(1)(d), but the new provisions are not without their problems: see further below.

rules governing thresholds and unreasonable costs.[148] The 1995 Act also permitted a departure from the formula where the non-resident parent was subject to other pre-April 1993 financial commitments from which it was either impossible or unreasonable to withdraw.[149] This head has not been replicated in the variations scheme, presumably as any such allowances (for example, in respect of car loans) would not be directly related to the children and, in event, are likely to occur very rarely in practice, given the passage of time since 1993.

Repayments can be taken into account only if the debts concerned meet the restrictive statutory conditions. First, the debts must have been incurred before the non-resident parent acquired that status in relation to the qualifying child and at a time when the parents were still a couple.[150] Secondly, the debts in question must have been for the benefit of one of the particular prescribed categories of individuals.[151] These rules differ depending on whether the beneficiary is an adult or a child.

As regards adults, the prescribed categories are the couple jointly, the parent with care alone (where the non-resident parent is subject to a legal liability to repay in part or in full) and a person who was a child living with both parties at the time the debt was taken on and was the child of at least one of them.[152] For example, subject to the exclusions discussed below, a loan taken out in happier times to pay for a family holiday or for home improvements might be covered by a variation on this ground.

The rules governing beneficiaries who are still children are more complex and indeed problematic. Debts incurred in respect of either a qualifying child or a child who was the parent with care's own child and the non-resident parent's step-child also qualify for inclusion.[153] For example, a Jewish couple might take out a large loan in order to pay for their son's Bar Mitzvah celebrations. This could qualify for inclusion irrespective of whether the boy is still a child,[154] or is now over 18,[155] or even if, regardless of his age now, he was the non-resident parent's step-son.[156] Yet not all children are covered. For example, the regulation is drafted in such a way that where the boy in question is the non-resident parent's natural son, but a

---

[148] SI 2001/156, reg 15.

[149] SI 1996/2907, reg 17; one of the pre-conditions was that there had been a court order or maintenance agreement in place.

[150] SI 2001/156, reg 12(1). A 'couple' means a married couple, an unmarried couple or civil partners (or two same sex individuals living together as civil partners) living in the same household: *ibid*, reg 1(2) and CSA 1991, sch 1, para 10C(5) as amended by Civil Partnership Act 2005, s 254 and sch 24 para 6. The statutory definition may require some careful fact-finding; see eg *R(CS) 3/02* para 10 *per* Mr Commissioner Levenson.

[151] SI 2001/156, reg 12(2)(a)–(c).

[152] Thus a debt incurred on behalf of an adult who was previously the NRP's step-child in a former relationship would qualify, where there was also a qualifying child from that relationship.

[153] SI 2001/156, reg 12(2)(d)–(e).

[154] In which case *ibid*, reg 12(2)(d) would apply. 'Child' is not defined by SI 2001/156, reg 1(2), but the definition in CSA 1991, s 55(1) (see p 217 above) should apply, given Interpretation Act 1978, s 11.

[155] In which case SI 2001/156, reg 12(2)(c) would apply.

[156] *Ibid*, reg 12(2)(e) applies if the NRP's step-son is still under 18, while reg 12(2)(c) applies if he is now an adult.

step-son of the parent with care,[157] and now lives with the non-resident parent and is still aged *under* 18, then the debt cannot be taken into account.[158] Such a scenario, whilst perhaps a little strained, is hardly implausible and demonstrates the problems inherent in the convoluted style of drafting typically adopted in the child support regulations. Even more perversely, the costs of such a loan to pay for a Bar Mitzvah could be included if the non-resident parent's son in question is now *over* 18, even where he is not the parent with care's child.[159]

Even if these tests relating to both the timing of the debt and the relevant beneficiaries are satisfied, the repayments must not relate to any one of a number of excluded debts.[160] The list of non-qualifying debts includes: debts in relation to any assets retained by the non-resident parent; trade or business debts; gambling debts, fines; unpaid legal costs; credit card debts;[161] and bank overdrafts (unless for a specified amount repayable over a specified period). Loans in general are excluded[162] unless they were obtained from a qualifying lender,[163] typically a bank or building society, or from the non-resident parent's former or current employer.[164] Special rules relate to mortgage loans; these qualify as prior debts only if they were taken out 'to facilitate the purchase of, or to pay for repairs or improvements to' the current home of the parent with care and qualifying child.[165] Repayments under insurance policies (such as endowment premiums) are also excluded unless they are related to a mortgage or charge.[166] This means that there is no recognition for repayments made in settlement of the negative equity in the former matrimonial home, assuming that the parent with care is no longer living in the property.[167] Moreover, unless these special rules apply, debts are in general excluded where the non-resident parent assumed responsibility for them as part of a financial settlement or under a court order.[168] The Secretary of

---

[157] This assumes, for the sake of this example, that the boy is the NRP's son from a previous relationship, and that the NRP and the PWC had at least one qualifying child together who now lives with the PWC.

[158] SI 2001/156, reg 12(2)(c) does not apply as the boy is not yet an adult; reg 12(2)(d) cannot apply as he is not a qualifying child in this sense (see also reg 12(1)(a)); and reg 12(2)(e) cannot apply as the PWC is not one of his parents.

[159] As *ibid*, reg 12(2)(c) would then apply.

[160] *Ibid*, reg 12(3).

[161] Jacobs and Douglas, n 60 above, at 682 argue that this exclusion does not affect debit cards or charge cards (as opposed to credit cards).

[162] SI 2001/156, reg 12(3)(k).

[163] In the income tax sense of that term: *ibid*, reg 12(6)(a) and see the discussion in Jacobs and Douglas, n 60 above, at 683.

[164] An 'employer' carries its normal meaning of a person who employs another under a contract of service. A person who engages the NRP as an independent contractor is not an 'employer', *R(CS) 3/03* para 8 *per* Mr Commissioner Turnbull.

[165] SI 2001/156 reg 12(3)(h). The statutory definition of 'repairs and improvements' (*ibid*, reg 12(6)(b)) follows the old income support rules, rather than the more restrictive rules introduced in 1995, on which see N Wikeley, 'Income support and mortgage interest: the new rules' [1995] 2 *Journal of Social Security Law* 168 at 173–74.

[166] SI 2001/156, reg 12(3)(i).

[167] *R(CS) 5/03*.

[168] SI 2001/156, reg 12(4); such debts, however, may qualify for consideration as part of a property or capital transfer under CSA 1991, sch 4B, para 3 and SI 2001/156, reg 16.

State also has a general power to exclude any other debt where satisfied that it is reasonable to do so.[169] That said, the exclusions are 'all fairly tightly and specifically defined'.[170] The common theme is that it is the 'extraordinary items of expenditure which are candidates for exclusion'; it follows that 'it is reasonable to exclude debts which were incurred to provide an extravagant lifestyle or to purchase items not reasonably required'.[171] Thus the general power should not be used to disregard a debt incurred in relation to the payment of day-to-day living expenses. It should be noted that any debt which is taken out to repay an earlier debt which would itself have qualified as a prior debt for these purposes will count as a special expense.[172] As with contact and disability costs, a variation for special expenses in relation to prior debts is given effect by deducting the appropriate weekly amount from the non-resident parent's net weekly income.[173]

Boarding School Fees

The failure of the original child support scheme to take any account of the payment of boarding school fees, even after the introduction of the departures scheme, led to complaints voiced by some of the Agency's better-off non-resident parents.[174] Under the new child support scheme, a non-resident parent may apply for a variation where he incurs (or reasonably expects to incur) boarding school fees[175] for a qualifying child.[176] It follows that the non-resident parent can receive no credit for boarding school fees paid in relation to other children[177] or for private school fees generally.[178] Only the 'maintenance element' of such fees may be taken into

---

[169] *Ibid*, reg 12(3)(m). Debts for which credit was previously given under an earlier variation but which remain unpaid are likewise excluded: *ibid*, reg 12(3)(l).

[170] *R(CS) 3/02* para 8 *per* Mr Commissioner Levenson.

[171] *Ibid*.

[172] SI 2001/156, reg 12(5). This applies whether the new debt is taken out to replace the old debt in part or in full: *R(CS) 3/03* para 17 *per* Mr Commissioner Turnbull. However, the loan must still have been made by a qualifying lender: *ibid*, para 19.

[173] SI 2001/156, reg 23(1), with the special rule for 'capped amount' cases: *ibid*, reg 23(2).

[174] Note that the mere fact that the NRP pays school fees does not automatically mean that he is providing 'day to day care' to the exclusion of the PWC: *Child-Villiers v Secretary of State for Work and Pensions* [2002] EWCA Civ 1854. Moreover, in general terms the original 1991 Act (as amended by CSA 1995) made no provision for taking the payment of school fees into account in the *assessment* of child support liabilities. The extent to which the Secretary of State took account of such payments in practice, in dealing with *collection* and *enforcement*, was unclear: see *R(CS) 8/98* para 24 *per* Mr Commissioner Rowland. However, school fees paid in pursuance of an undertaking incorporated into a court order could be taken into account in assessing a NRP's protected income under the pre-2000 scheme: *R(CS) 10/99*.

[175] As defined by SI 2001/156, reg 13(5)—see also CSA 1991, sch 4B, para 2(5).

[176] *Ibid*, para 2(3)(d) and SI 2001/156, reg 13.

[177] For example, those of a previous or subsequent relationship.

[178] This is one area in which the courts retain a potential jurisdiction: see CSA 1991, s 8(7) and p 196 above. Note that in Australia the equivalent ground refers to the child being 'educated or trained in the manner that was expected' by the parents, so covering private education generally: Child Support (Assessment) Act 1989 (Cth), s 117(2)(b)(ii). However, the pressure for recognition of such costs will be much higher as some 30% of Australian pupils are in private (predominantly Church) schools.

account as special expenses.[179] If the non-resident parent receives help with the
cost of the fees from any source (such as a charitable trust) or part of the fees are
paid direct by a third party, then his proportionate share of the maintenance element of the fees may qualify as special expenses.[180] The usual weekly threshold and
the 'unreasonably high' or 'unreasonably incurred' rules apply. In addition, the
effect of any allowance for boarding school fees cannot reduce the non-resident's
assessed income by more than 50 per cent.[181] As with other types of special
expenses, a variation for boarding school fees is given effect by deducting the
appropriate weekly amount from the non-resident parent's net weekly income.[182]

Mortgages, Loans and Insurance Policies

In some cases, as part of the package agreed on separation or divorce, the non-
resident parent will continue to pay the housing costs on the former matrimonial
home. The failure of the original scheme to make allowance for such expenditure
was a persistent source of grievance for some non-resident parents. It also resulted
in tribunals occasionally engaging in some manipulation of the rules in order to
ensure that the non-resident parent should not be disadvantaged.[183] The departures scheme omitted to make any special provision for such cases. However, for
the purposes of the variations scheme, the payment of mortgages, loans and insurance policies on the former matrimonial home may now qualify as a special
expense, irrespective of whether such payments are made to the person with care
or direct to the lender.[184] There are, however, a series of restrictive conditions to
be satisfied. Although the payments may relate to a mortgage for the purchase of
the property, or to a loan for repairs or improvements, that mortgage or loan must
have been taken out by a person other than the non-resident parent (typically the
parent with care).[185] It follows that this category of special expense will not apply
if the non-resident parent remains on the mortgage (for example because the
mortgagee will not agree to his release).[186] The property in question must also
have been the parties' home when they were a couple and must remain the home
of the parent with care and a qualifying child.[187] Crucially, however, the
non-resident parent must have no legal or beneficial interest in or charge over the

---

[179] SI 2001/156 reg 13(1). If such costs cannot be isolated 'with reasonable certainty', the Secretary
of State may apportion fees into 'maintenance costs' and 'other costs' (eg tuition costs), subject to the
former not exceeding 35% of the total: *ibid*, reg 13(2).

[180] *Ibid*, reg 13(3).

[181] *Ibid*, reg 13(4).

[182] SI 2001/156, reg 23(1), with the special rule for 'capped amount' cases: *ibid*, reg 23(2).

[183] See eg G Davis, N Wikeley and R Young, *Child Support in Action* (Hart Publishing, Oxford, 1998)
at 30.

[184] CSA 1991, sch 4B, para 2(3)(e) and SI 2001/156, reg 14.

[185] *Ibid*, reg 14(2)(a)(i). See also *ibid*, reg 14(2)(a)(ii), excluding payments made under a debt
incurred by, or any other legal liability of, the NRP.

[186] Jacobs and Douglas, n 60 above, at 686.

[187] *Ibid*, reg 14(2)(a)(iii). Thus the (admittedly less common) scenario in which the NRP remains
in the former matrimonial home but pays towards the mortgage on a new home for the PWC and QC
is not covered.

property.[188] Similarly, this ground cannot be relied upon where the non-resident parent remains a beneficiary under an endowment policy in respect of which he is paying the premiums.[189]

Although these rules are a partial improvement on the pre-2000 position so far as non-resident parents are concerned, they still illustrate a lack of 'fit' between the child support and social security legislation. This is because a mortgage or loan arrangement which meets the criteria specified for special expenses in the child support scheme may well disadvantage the parent with care so far as her own income support entitlement is concerned. If the original mortgage on the matrimonial home predates October 1995 and still subsists, she would start receiving some help with her mortgage costs eight weeks after first claiming benefit. However, a remortgage after that date (at least in the terms recognised by the special expenses rules for a variation under the child support scheme) may result in no assistance with housing costs for the first 39 weeks of an income support claim.[190] In addition, the general rule is that a claimant on income support who increases the size of her mortgage is not entitled to help with the extra amount of interest which becomes payable.[191] Although there are some limited exceptions to this principle, these do not include remortgaging following relationship breakdown or divorce.[192] If the parent with care is self-supporting, obviously these particular difficulties will not arise.

As with other types of special expenses, a variation for payments in respect of mortgage, loan or insurance policy payments is given effect by deducting the appropriate weekly amount from the non-resident parent's net weekly income.[193]

Property or Capital Transfers

An application for a variation based on a property or capital transfer may be brought by either parent,[194] although in practice parents with care are unlikely to make such a request. Such an application may result in a variation from the formula if two sets of conditions are satisfied, relating to the timing and nature of the prior settlement on the one hand and its consequences on the other.

First, there must have been either a relevant court order or agreement in place before 5 April 1993.[195] A court order qualifies for this purpose if it relates to the non-resident parent and either the person with care or any qualifying child. It

---

[188] *Ibid*, reg 14(2)(a)(iv).

[189] *Ibid*, reg 14(2)(b).

[190] Income Support (General) Regulations 1987 (SI 1987/1967), sch 3, paras 6 and 8.

[191] *Ibid*, sch 3, para 4(2).

[192] Contrary to the recommendation of the Social Security Advisory Committee: *Income Support (General) Amendment Regulations 1994* Cm 2537 (1994) paras 45–50.

[193] SI 2001/156, reg 23(1), with the special rule for 'capped amount' cases: *ibid*, reg 23(2).

[194] For the background to these provisions reflecting 'clean break' settlements, see ch 5 above.

[195] CSA 1991, sch 4B, para 3(1). Thus the actual transfer may have taken place after 5 April 1993, so long as the order/agreement was already in place.

must also be a 'qualifying transfer'—in the sense defined below—under any of the specified matrimonial jurisdictions.[196] An agreement without the court's approval will suffice if it is a written agreement made between such parties in connection with a qualifying transfer.[197] In order to qualify, the non-resident parent must have transferred his beneficial interest in any asset to the person with care or the qualifying child (or to trustees, providing that at least one of the objects of the trust is the provision of maintenance).[198] The transfer of property in question must be valued at £5,000 or more.[199] The reference in the regulations to the transfer of 'any asset' demonstrates that the provision is not confined to settlements in relation to the matrimonial home.[200] Strictly, there is no requirement that the transfer actually take place under the court order or agreement,[201] although this will almost invariably be the case.

Secondly, the consequence of the transfer(s) valued at or above £5,000 must be that either the non-resident parent was not required to pay any maintenance, or the amount of such maintenance 'was less than would have been the case had that transfer or those transfers not been made'.[202] In this context, 'maintenance' means periodical payments for normal day to day living expenses in respect of the qualifying child, otherwise than under the 1991 Act.[203] It follows that if the transfer was wholly in lieu of spousal maintenance then no variation can be allowed. Equally, if the basis for the nil or low payments of child maintenance was the straightened financial circumstances of the non-resident parent, rather than because of any property transfer, then no variation is permissible.[204] In the typical case, involving a transfer under a consent order, the terms of the order itself must be scrutinised. The reasons for the order may be discernible from contemporary correspondence, although a Commissioner has warned that the parties' letters may be self-serving.[205] Establishing the causal link between the transfer and the level of maintenance ordered or agreed may be a matter of inference, bearing in mind the factors which judges must take into account in decisions on ancillary relief

---

[196] *Ibid*, para 3(1)(a) and SI 2001/156, reg 16(1)(a); for the full list of such jurisdictions, see CSA 1991, s 8(11) and Child Support (Maintenance Arrangements and Jurisdiction) Regulations 1992 (SI 1992/2645, reg 2).

[197] CSA 1991, sch 4B, para 3(1)(b) and SI 2001/156, reg 16(1)(b). The agreement may be relatively informal; for example, there is no need for it to be signed—see, by analogy, *CCS/3151/1999* paras 4–6.

[198] SI 2001/156, reg 16(2).

[199] Or the aggregate of several transfers; *ibid*, reg 16(4), defining the threshold at £4,999.99. Note also *ibid*, reg 16(3) dealing with the special case where an initial transfer would not have qualified but a subsequent transfer brings the settlement within the ambit of reg 16.

[200] An 'asset' in this context is not confined by the narrow definition in *ibid*, reg 18(2).

[201] *R(CS) 4/00* para 18 *per* Mr Commissioner Jacobs.

[202] CSA 1991, sch 4B, para 3(2).

[203] *Ibid*, para 3(3) and SI 2001/156, reg 17(4). Thus the transfer of an interest in the matrimonial home, to provide a stable base for the children, cannot itself amount to 'maintenance' within this definition: *R(CS) 4/00* para 16.

[204] As was the case in *R(CS) 4/00*: see para 40.

[205] The best evidence, but in practice rarely available, would be the reasons given in any judgment, as evidenced by a lawyer's note: *ibid*, para 21.

claims.[206] The simple passage of time between the making of the transfer and the maintenance order respectively may not be fatal to proving such a connection.[207]

Assuming that the above conditions are satisfied, the regulations then provide for the calculation of an 'equivalent weekly value' to reflect the value of the transfer of property in question. This need not be the total transfer value; a variation is only permitted in respect of 'that part of the transfer . . . which the Secretary of State is satisfied is in lieu of periodical payments of maintenance'.[208] In making this decision, the Secretary of State is required by statute to operate on the assumption that the couple had equal beneficial interests in the asset before the order or agreement.[209] It follows that in the admittedly less common situation nowadays, where the matrimonial home was in the man's sole name in terms of both the legal and equitable estates, the man will receive credit for at best 50 per cent of the transfer value. This provision represents an interesting, if limited, statutory recognition of the principle of equal division of property rights on divorce, albeit in the narrow context of child support variation applications. In the case of a married couple, the further assumption must be made that half the value of the transfer was for the benefit of the parent with care (and *not* the qualifying child). This assumption may be rebutted by the terms of the court order or agreement.[210] If the parents were not married to each other, then the regulations assume, in line with the normal principles of family law,[211] that none of the value of the transfer was for the benefit of the parent with care.[212] The 'equivalent weekly value' is then calculated in accordance with a Table contained in the Schedule to the regulations (see Table 12.1).[213] This requires the sum representing the value of the property or capital transfer to be multiplied by the appropriate fraction listed in the Table.[214] The choice of the appropriate faction is determined by the 'number of years of liability'[215] and the 'statutory rate' of interest.[216] For example, the appropriate fraction for a case with 18 years of liability in which the statutory rate was 11 per cent[217] is 0.00250; thus if the value of the transfer was £10,000, the 'equivalent weekly value' is £25 (£10,000 × 0.00250). As the duration of the liability gets

---

[206] *Ibid*, paras 22, 26 and 27.

[207] *Ibid*, paras 30 and 38.

[208] SI 2001/156, reg 17(1). Any transfer made by the PWC to the NRP must be deducted to arrive at the net transfer figure.

[209] *Ibid*, reg 17(2)(a).

[210] As to the difficulties of which see *R(CS) 4/00*.

[211] Namely that unmarried cohabitants do not owe each other any duty of maintenance.

[212] SI 2001/156, reg 17(2)(b) and (c).

[213] *Ibid*, reg 17(3) and sch.

[214] *Ibid*, sch, para 1(1) and (2).

[215] ie the number of years from the date of the order/agreement to either its expiry date or the date on which the youngest child attains the age of 18: *ibid*, sch, para 1(3)(a). Periods of six months or more are rounded up to one year, whilst shorter periods are disregarded.

[216] Meaning the standard judgment debt rate of interest at the time of the order/agreement: *ibid*, sch, para 1(3)(b); Jacobs and Douglas (n 60 above at 714) helpfully contains the relevant rates and time periods.

[217] As was the case in Scotland from 7 January 1975 to 5 April 1983: see *ibid*.

Table 12.1 Equivalent weekly value of a transfer of property

Number of years of liability	Statutory Rate							
	7.0%	8.0%	10.0%	11.0%	12.0%	12.5%	14.0%	15.0%
1.	.02058	.02077	.02115	.02135	.02154	.02163	.02192	.02212
2.	.01064	.01078	.01108	.01123	.01138	.01145	.01168	.01183
3.	.00733	.00746	.00773	.00787	.00801	.00808	.00828	.00842
4.	.00568	.00581	.00607	.00620	.00633	.00640	.00660	.00674
5.	.00469	.00482	.00507	.00520	.00533	.00540	.00560	.00574
6.	.00403	.00416	.00442	.00455	.00468	.00474	.00495	.00508
7.	.00357	.00369	.00395	.00408	.00421	.00428	.00448	.00462
8.	.00322	.00335	.00360	.00374	.00387	.00394	.00415	.00429
9.	.00295	.00308	.00334	.00347	.00361	.00368	.00389	.00403
10.	.00274	.00287	.00313	.00327	.00340	.00347	.00369	.00383
11.	.00256	.00269	.00296	.00310	.00324	.00331	.00353	.00367
12.	.00242	.00255	.00282	.00296	.00310	.00318	.00340	.00355
13.	.00230	.00243	.00271	.00285	.00299	.00307	.00329	.00344
14.	.00220	.00233	.00261	.00275	.00290	.00298	.00320	.00336
15.	.00211	.00225	.00253	.00267	.00282	.00290	.00313	.00329
16.	.00204	.00217	.00246	.00261	.00276	.00283	.00307	.00323
17.	.00197	.00211	.00240	.00255	.00270	.00278	.00302	.00318
18.	.00191	.00205	.00234	.00250	.00265	.00273	.00297	.00314

longer, so the appropriate fraction diminishes, as in effect the value of the transfer is apportioned over the entirety of the period in question.

The 'equivalent weekly value' is then deducted from the normal formula amount of child support payable by the non-resident parent.[218] This principle is subject to the qualification that the resulting weekly figure must not be lower than the amount of maintenance payable under the court order or agreement which has given rise to the variation.[219] If this is the case, the equivalent weekly value can be reduced accordingly. If adjustments are needed for other variations or for shared care, these are applied before the equivalent weekly value is deducted.[220] Any variation agreed under these rules will cease to have effect at the end of the liability period specified in the court order or agreement in question.[221]

[218] SI 2001/156, reg 24.
[219] *Ibid*, sch, para 3.
[220] *Ibid*, reg 27(5).
[221] *Ibid*, reg 17(5).

Additional Cases

Introduction

The regulations provide for four types of 'additional cases' as potential grounds for a variation application.[222] The common theme is that these all represent situations in which the 'person with care considers that she is being "short-changed" by the normal rule' of the standard formula.[223] These are: (i) where the non-resident parent has assets which exceed £65,000; (ii) where his life-style is inconsistent with his income; (iii) where he has income which is not taken into account in the standard formula; or (iv) where he has unreasonably reduced his income.[224] The primary legislation is phrased in such a way that, with the exception of the first category outlined above, it appears that either parent may apply for a variation on the basis of one of these additional cases. In practice, however, the regulations only permit the person with care to be the applicant, presumably because her resources are regarded as wholly irrelevant to the child support formula. It is open to the Secretary of State to prescribe further additional cases in the regulations, although this power has not been exercised to date.[225] For example, this power might be exercised if the government changes its policy and decides to make special provision by way of a variation for cases in which the parent with care, rather than the non-resident parent, has an income above a certain threshold.[226]

If a variation is agreed on the basis of one of these additional cases, the effect is to increase the non-resident parent's net weekly income[227] by the weekly amount concerned, as determined in accordance with the rules governing the additional case in issue.[228] However, special rules apply to non-resident parents at either end of the income scale. If the non-resident parent's net weekly income, including the additional case income, would exceed the 'capped amount' of £2,000 a week, then it is that maximum figure which is factored into the maintenance calculation. If, on the other hand, the non-resident parent would otherwise be liable for the flat-rate,[229] then the non-resident parent's liability is the *lesser* of two weekly figures, which for the purposes of exposition will be described as Figure A and Figure B.[230] Figure A is the aggregate of the flat-rate payment (currently £5 p/w) and the outcome of applying the formula to the additional income, less any benefit, pension or allowance which is prescribed for the purpose of the flat-rate liability. Figure B

---

[222] CSA 1991, sch 4B, para 4(2).

[223] House of Lords Select Committee on Delegated Powers and Deregulation, *Thirteenth Report* (HL 598, Session 1999–2000), Annex 1 at para 74.

[224] These various grounds are discussed below in the order in which they appear in the regulations rather than in the primary enabling legislation.

[225] CSA 1991, sch 4B, para 4(1).

[226] See also the discussion in ch 11.

[227] As assessed under SI 2001/155: SI 2001/156, reg 27(7).

[228] *Ibid*, reg 25.

[229] Or would be but for the operation of the shared care rules or but for the fact that he is subject to the nil rate as a member of a prescribed category of NRP.

[230] SI 2001/156, reg 26. This is known in the Agency's parlance as the 'better buy provision'.

is simply the result of applying the formula to the additional income identified by the variation.

Non-resident Parent has Assets over £65,000

A fundamental principle of the 1991 Act is that a non-resident parent's liability is calculated on the basis of his income rather than his capital. This stands in stark contrast to the position in ancillary relief proceedings on divorce, when the courts (and solicitors in negotiations) take into account both the parties' income and capital resources. This additional case represents the one significant exception to the usual approach in child support law. It provides that where the non-resident parent's capital assets exceed a set figure, then it will be assumed that those assets generate a weekly income at an appropriate level.[231]

The first point to note is that this ground has no application if the non-resident parent's aggregate net assets are less than £65,000 in value.[232] Moreover, any interest received on capital investments below this level is also ignored.[233] As the £65,000 threshold is laid down in regulations, rather than in the primary legislation, it may be altered relatively easily.[234] For this purpose an asset is defined as money, whether in cash or on deposit, a legal estate or beneficial interest in land,[235] shares, stocks and unit trusts, gilt-edged securities and other similar financial instruments.[236] The definition of 'asset' also encompasses 'choses in action' (enforceable debts), providing the Secretary of State is satisfied enforcement would be reasonable.[237] Assets held outside Great Britain are also included.[238] The statutory definition is exhaustive,[239] and so a car is not an 'asset' for this purpose.[240] For the same reason, neither is a milk quota held by a farmer, although the monies realised by its sale would be.[241] Various types of asset are specifically disregarded[242] (in addition to the general £65,000 threshold): any property which is

---

[231] CSA 1991, sch 4B, para 4(2)(a).

[232] SI 2001/156, reg 18(3)(a). Thus any sum owing under a mortgage or charge must be deducted first, as must the value of any asset taken into account under *ibid*, reg 19(1A).

[233] Investment income is not regarded as income for the purposes of the formula assessment under the Schedule to SI 2001/155. A NRP with £60,000 in savings at an interest rate of say 5% will therefore receive £3,000 p/a (over £57 p/w) before tax which does not enter into the child support maintenance calculation.

[234] Under the departures scheme for old cases the equivalent threshold is just £10,000: see SI 1996/2907, reg 23(2)(a).

[235] Including rights in or over land.

[236] SI 2001/156, reg 18(2)(a)–(c). See *CSCS/1/2005*.

[237] SI 2001/156, reg 18(2)(d). In Scotland 'monies due or an obligation owed' are included as 'money' within reg 18(1)(a); on the similar provision under the departures scheme, see *CSCS/14/2003*, paras 31–41 *per* Mrs Commissioner Parker.

[238] SI 2001/156, reg 18(2). There are no special rules on valuation of such assets; contrast SI 1987/1967, reg 50.

[239] *CCS/8/2000* paras 17–22 *per* Mr Commissioner Jacobs. However, ownership of an expensive car or cars may be evidence for the inconsistent life-style ground (see below).

[240] *R(CS) 4/00* para 11 *per* Mr Commissioner Jacobs. A car may, however, be an 'asset' for the purpose of a property or capital transfer under SI 2001/156, reg 16.

[241] *R 1/03(CS)* at paras 40 and 45 *per* Mrs Commissioner Brown.

[242] SI 2001/156, reg 18(3)(b)–(e).

the non-resident parent's home,[243] or the home of any of his children; any asset used in his trade or business;[244] any personal injury compensation; payments from the MacFarlane Fund, the Independent Living Fund or similar trusts;[245] and any asset which is being retained by the non-resident parent 'for a purpose which the Secretary of State considers reasonable in all the circumstances of the case'.[246] The non-resident parent must also enjoy the requisite degree of ownership or control of the asset for this additional ground to be invoked by the person with care. In this context, the regulations provide for three types of case.

The first situation is where the non-resident parent either has the beneficial interest in[247] or has the ability to control the asset.[248] The concept of an 'ability to control' is left undefined, and its application is likely to prove problematic in practice. One example would be a shadow director's control over company shares.[249] It may be, of course, that the non-resident parent is a joint rather than a sole owner of the asset in question. In those circumstances, the Secretary of State must assume, in the absence of contrary evidence, 'that the asset is held by them in equal shares'.[250] This does *not* mean that the net value of the asset is apportioned equally; rather, the non-resident parent is assumed to have an equal share which must then be valued in its own right. If the non-resident parent is unable to obtain the other co-owner's consent or to force a sale, then it may be that his 'equal share' will be worth 'nothing or next to nothing'.[251]

The second possibility is an anti-avoidance provision, which covers the case where the non-resident parent transfers the asset to trustees, under a trust of which he is a beneficiary, with the aim of reducing the amount of assets which would otherwise be taken into account.[252] It is unclear whether that objective must be the sole, predominant or merely an operative reason for the transfer.

[243] This exception is confined to the NRP's normal or principal home: see *ibid*, reg 1(2) and SI 2001/155, reg 1(2) for the meaning of 'home'.

[244] Unless it comprises land producing income which does not form part of the NRP's formula-based net weekly income (eg rental income).

[245] As listed in SI 1987/1967, sch 10, paras 22 and 64.

[246] Child Support Agency, *Child Support: A Technical Guide* (CSL 109, 2005) gives the following example (at 108): 'money which has been obtained from the sale of a home if it is clear that the intention is to use the money shortly to buy a new home'. On this basis, the Schedule of capital disregards which applies to income support claimants may provide some guidance, although clearly it cannot be binding: SI 1987/1967, sch 10.

[247] Thus, in principle, if the NRP holds the legal estate in land on bare trust for another who has the sole beneficial interest, this additional case cannot be used (unless in practice the NRP has the ability to control that third party). As Mr Commissioner Jacobs observes in *CCS/8/2000* para 24, the drafting of reg 18(1)(a) and 18(2)(c), taken together, results in the nonsensical reading that reg 18 applies where 'there is [a beneficial interest in land] in which the non-resident parent has a beneficial interest'.

[248] SI 2001/156, reg 18(1)(a).

[249] *CCS/8/2000* para 28. The concept of 'ability to control' is also used in SI 2001/156, reg 19(4)(a), on which see *CCS/741/2002*, in which Mr Commissioner Williams adopted the company law definition of a shadow director, applying *Secretary of State for Trade and Industry v Deverell* [2001] Ch 340, CA.

[250] SI 2001/156, reg 18(4).

[251] See *CCS/8/2000* para 59 *per* Mr Commissioner Jacobs (and the discussion at paras 32–37 and 54–59). See further, in the social security context, N Wikeley, 'Co-ownership of property and entitlement to means-tested benefits' (2001) 8 *Journal of Social Security Law* 95.

[252] SI 2001/156, reg 18(1)(b).

Thirdly, assets are also covered where they have become subject to a trust 'created by legal implication' of which the non-resident parent is a beneficiary.[253] This would presumably include cases where the legal title to property may be in the non-resident parent's name but where a constructive trust has arisen.

If the person with care succeeds in her application for a variation on the basis of this additional case, the non-resident parent is assumed to be in receipt of additional income derived from the assets in question. That income is equivalent to the weekly value of those assets, calculated by applying the statutory rate of interest to the value of the assets and dividing by 52.[254] These provisions have the potential to create a harsh cliff-edge effect; a non-resident parent with assets of £60,000 faces a child support liability calculated without any reference to either his capital or any actual or potential investment income, while such a parent with £70,000 has an additional income imputed to him on the basis of all his net assets, not merely the balance above £65,000.

Non-resident Parent has Income not taken into Account

The person with care may, in certain circumstances, apply for a variation on the basis that her ex-partner has income which is not taken into account in the standard child support formula.[255] This additional case only applies if the income excluded from the formula assessment exceeds £100 a week.[256] As a result of amendments made in 2005,[257] there are now two ways in which this ground might be made out.

The original 'income not taken into account' ground required that two further conditions be satisfied. First, the non-resident parent's child support liability, on the standard formula, must be either the nil rate, based on the non-resident parent's status as a member of a prescribed category (eg prisoners or students[258]), or the flat rate, based on his status as a recipient of a prescribed benefit other than income support, income-based jobseeker's allowance and state pension credit (including cases where it is less than the flat rate owing to the operation of the shared care rules).[259] Secondly, the Secretary of State must be satisfied that the non-resident parent is in receipt of income which would otherwise be taken into account, had he not been subject to the nil rate or the flat rate in the circumstances outlined above.

The cumulative effect of these conditions is to narrow the potential scope of this first ground for this additional case very significantly. It cannot be used where the

---

[253]   *Ibid*, reg 18(1)(c).

[254]   *Ibid*, regs 18(5) and 25. The 'statutory rate of interest' is defined by reg 18(6). The wording of reg 18(5) is not quite the same as its predecessor, SI 1996/2907, reg 40(2), on which see the divergent views in *CCS/2357/2003* and *CSCS/14/2003*.

[255]   CSA 1991, sch 4B, para 4(2)(c).

[256]   SI 2001/156, reg 19(2).

[257]   Child Support (Miscellaneous Amendments) Regulations 2005 (SI 2005/785), reg 8(5).

[258]   See the special rule in SI 2001/156, reg 19(3) regarding the calculation of a student's income.

[259]   *Ibid*, reg 19(1)(a).

non-resident parent is subject to a basic rate or reduced rate liability, even if he also has substantial investment income, or indeed any other form of income that falls outside the normal formula.[260] This additional case is also inapplicable to non-resident parents who are subject to the nil rate because their assessable income (under the formula) is less than £5 a week or who are liable to the flat rate on some other basis (namely having an assessable income of less than £100 or owing to their receipt of income support, income-based jobseeker's allowance or state pension credit). Again, the person with care can have no recourse to this type of additional case in the admittedly unlikely event that such a non-resident parent has a significant non-formula source of income.

However, the 2005 amendments have created a second basis for this additional case, subject again to two requirements.[261] First, the non-resident parent must have 'the ability to control the amount of income he receives from a company or business'[262] (whether via employment or self-employment). Secondly, the Secretary of State must be satisfied that the non-resident parent is receiving such income 'which would not otherwise fall to be taken into account' under the standard rules for the assessment of income. This provision was designed to deal with the problem of non-resident parents who, through their control of 'one-man' or other small companies, are able to pay themselves in dividends.[263] One weakness of this approach is that it relies on a departure application being made, rather than allowing decision makers or tribunals to take such income into account under the formula itself.

In cases in which either of these routes is satisfied, the non-resident parent is attributed with the whole of the income which would otherwise have been taken into account under the formula, along with any benefits, pensions or allowances which he receives.[264]

Diversion of Income by Non-resident Parent

Statute also enables a variation to be applied for on the basis of an additional case where a person has 'unreasonably reduced' the income taken into account in the standard calculation.[265] The regulations pose a two-fold test. First, the non-resident parent must have the 'ability to control the amount of income he receives',[266] as in the case of a shadow director.[267] Secondly, the Secretary of State must be satisfied that the non-resident parent has 'unreasonably reduced' his assessable income 'by

---

[260] We have seen in ch 11 that the NRP's 'net weekly income' is effectively confined to earnings, tax credits and certain pension income.

[261] SI 2001/156, reg 19(1A).

[262] A formulation borrowed from the diversion ground; see further below.

[263] HC Work and Pensions Committee, *The Child Support Agency: Government Response to the Committee's 2nd Report of Session 2004–05* (1st Special Report of Session 2004–05), HC 477, para 9. See p 335 above.

[264] SI 2001/156, regs 19(5)(a) and 25; reg 26 specifies benefits etc to be disregarded.

[265] CSA 1991, sch 4B, para 4(2)(d).

[266] SI 2001/156, reg 19(4)(a); see further *CSCS/1/2005*.

[267] See *CCS/741/2002*.

diverting it to other persons or for purposes other than the provision of such income for himself'.[268] This is patently an anti-avoidance provision.[269] The Agency's internal guidance gives the following illustration:

> Non-resident parents can set themselves up as a limited company, paying themselves a small salary whilst concurrently paying a third party a much larger salary from which they themselves benefit.
>
> Probably the most common practice is where a new partner is paid a high salary for a purely token position they hold, such as a director or company executive which is in name only. Diversion of income by this method is likely to involve someone with whom the parent has a close relationship, most commonly a new partner, but it could be a family member or even a friend.[270]

The notion of 'diversion' would seem to require some sort of positive conduct to deflect income; inaction alone should be insufficient.[271] If the non-resident parent is a partner in a business, this ground cannot be used to bring back into the equation income which has already been allocated to another partner, for example under the normal rule that partners take an equal share in profits.[272] However, if a partner decides to take his share in the profits by way of a benefit in kind (eg a company car) rather than cash, then the diversion ground might bite.[273] In cases in which this additional case applies, the non-resident parent is imputed to have the whole of the amount by which it is decided that his income has been unreasonably reduced.[274]

Non-resident Parent's Life-style is Inconsistent with Declared Income

The last of the four additional cases has probably caused the most difficulty in practice.[275] This ground applies where the non-resident parent's life-style is inconsistent with his declared income.[276] Whilst this is an easy allegation for parents with care to put forward, it may be rather more difficult to make out a

---

[268] SI 2001/156, reg 19(4)(b). These are 'wide words', see *CCS/114/2005* at para 20 *per* Mr Commissioner Williams (decided under the old scheme). Note the repeal of the caveat 'in order to reduce his ability to pay child support maintenance' (by SI 2005/785, reg 8(5)(c)(ii)).

[269] Child Support Agency, *Procedures: Specialist Areas*, 'Diversion of Income' at 3006 advises staff that 'Before any contact is made with the NRP a check for fraud involvement should be made. This is because if there is a CSA Investigations involvement, any communication with the NRP may interfere with an ongoing investigation and also jeopardise a prosecution'.

[270] *Ibid*, 'Example of Diversion to a Third Party' at 3006.

[271] *CSCS/14/2003* at para 27 *per* Mrs Commissioner Parker (decided under departures regime). See also *CCS/1813/2004*: claiming unwarranted business expenses does not divert income. Instead, it is a ground for revision or supersession of the underlying assessment rather than a basis for a departure.

[272] *CCS/1246/2002* at para 7 *per* Mr Commissioner Mesher (an old scheme case). This might be a case for a variation under other provisions.

[273] *R(CS)6/05*.

[274] SI 2001/156, regs 19(5)(b) and 25.

[275] This was also the most commonly cited ground in the 1996 pilot project for departures directions (18% of all application): Child Support Agency, n 9 above, para 10.

[276] CSA 1991, sch 4B, para 4(2)(b) and SI 2001/156, reg 20.

case under the somewhat tortuous regulations. It is 'not enough merely to point to suspicions'; rather decision makers and tribunals 'must be given something concrete if it is to justify giving a direction'.[277] According to the Agency's internal guidance:

> This ground for Variations, is usually intended to deal with cases where NRPs are self-employed. Their business accounts may show low, or only modest levels of income, because income is being offset against business expenses. Or it may be suspected that the NRP has undeclared income, for example, by working in the black economy.[278]

There is, however, a strong argument that that there is no need to have such an additional case in the variations scheme at all. If there is an obvious disparity between the non-resident parent's declared income under the standard formula and his life-style, then—absent some other plausible explanation (for example, that the life-style is funded from capital or by a partner)—one might reasonably infer that his *actual* income is considerably higher. That higher income could then simply be factored into the ordinary maintenance application, bearing in mind that income may be 'calculated' or 'estimated',[279] without any need for a variation to be agreed. In practice, however, the Agency's approach is often to rely simply on the bald income figures declared by the non-resident parent,[280] and to eschew any investigative role which might lead to an inference that the actual (undeclared) income is higher.[281]

Indeed, contrary to the example given in the Agency's internal guidance, this additional case is not premised on the existence of undeclared income.[282] Rather, 'it is expressed in terms of an unexplained mismatch between the income on which the formal calculation was based and the non-applicant's overall lifestyle'.[283] Two conditions must be satisfied if this ground is to apply. The first is that the non-resident parent's child support liability is (or would be if assessed) at one of the basic, reduced, flat or nil rates.[284] The second, and typically more contentious point, is that the Secretary of State must be satisfied:

---

[277] *CCS/3331/1999* at para 11 *per* Mr Commissioner Jacobs.

[278] Child Support Agency, n 269 above, 'Lifestyle Inconsistent with Declared Income' at 3001.

[279] See further ch 11.

[280] Eg wage slips, P60s and accounts (see *R(CS) 3/01* para 26).

[281] As Mr Commissioner Rowland observes in *CCS/6282/1999*, para 9, the Agency's staff 'have not understood how to draw inferences and have not appreciated that it is legitimate to make estimates as a way of calculating actual income, with the result that they have been very reluctant to find facts where there has been neither an admission nor documentary evidence', a problem exacerbated by the fact that the Agency conducts decision making on the papers. See, to similar effect, *CCS/2623/1999* para 13, *CCS/7411/1999*, para 12 and *CSC 6/03-04(T)*, paras 43–45.

[282] It is not, therefore, tantamount to a fraud enquiry: *CCS/2623/1999* para 12 *per* Mr Commissioner Jacobs.

[283] *Ibid*, para 13.

[284] SI 2001/156, reg 20(1)(a)(i)–(vi) and (2); somewhat confusingly two different provisions apply to the various categories of flat rate and nil rate, but this is because they are subject to varying exceptions: see *ibid*, reg 20(3) and (4).

that the income which has been, or would be, taken into account for the purposes of the maintenance calculation is substantially lower than the level of income required to support the overall life-style of the non-resident parent.[285]

The 'inconsistent life-style' additional case is inapplicable if the Secretary of State is satisfied that the non-resident parent's life-style is met from any one (or more) of a number of specified alternative sources. These include income which is either disregarded under the formula assessment or is covered by the rules governing the diversion of income (so as to avoid double counting).[286] There is a further exception where the non-resident parent's life-style is paid for from 'assets as defined for the purposes of regulation 18, or income derived from those assets'.[287] In addition, the regulations exclude cases in which the non-resident parent's life-style is paid for from his partner's income or assets, 'except where the non-resident parent is able to influence or control' that partner's income or assets.[288] In respect of some categories of non-resident parents liable for the flat rate or nil rate, there are further exemptions where the life-style is met from a net weekly income of less than £100 or from income which is imputed on the basis of the additional cases relating to income not taken into account or diverted income.[289]

The applicability or otherwise of these exemptions requires careful fact-finding. For example, the non-resident parent may claim that his life-style is supported by his new partner. That may well be the case where she has an independent income. If she works in and is being paid a salary by the non-resident parent's own business, then it will be important to determine whether the non-resident parent can 'influence or control' the amount of that income. If he is the owner or dominant business partner then such influence or control may be readily inferred. However, it does not follow necessarily that the non-resident parent will be subject to a variation. Even if he cannot plead this exemption, it may not be 'just and equitable' to agree a variation; for example, the evidence may point to the conclusion that the non-resident parent's partner is simply receiving the normal rate for the job, rather than an artificially inflated salary. Moreover—leaving aside cases in which influence or control is exercised—the exemption only applies where the partner pays for the *entirety* of the difference between the non-resident parent's formula income and the level of income needed to support his life-style.[290] If she does, no

---

[285] *Ibid*, reg 20(1)(b); a parallel provision applies under reg 20(2) for certain categories of flat rate and nil rate NRPs.

[286] *Ibid*, reg 20(3)(a)–(b). The meaning of 'disregard' in this context is unclear. It may mean any income not covered by the usual formula rules, such as investment income (see *CCS/0029/2005* at para 13). Or it may mean income which is subject to the special disregard rule in SI 2001/155, sch, para 2.

[287] SI 2001/156, reg 20(3)(c). The drafting is less than ideal; it might have been preferable for the cross-reference to have been made specifically to *ibid*, reg 18(2) to avoid confusion, given that reg 18(3) contains some exceptions.

[288] *Ibid*, reg 20(3)(d) and (e). For the meaning of 'partner' see CSA 1991, sch 1, para 10C(4): SI 2001/156, reg 1(2) and see *CCS/2230/2001* under the old scheme.

[289] SI 2001/156, reg 20(4).

[290] *R(CS) 6/02* para 15(1) *per* Mr Commissioner Turnbull.

variation is possible. If she does not, then a variation may be agreed if it is 'just and equitable' to do so. If a variation is agreed, but the partner makes some contribution to the life-style in question, that amount of income should presumably not be attributed to the non-resident parent.[291]

There may be another explanation for the disparity between the non-resident parent's income and life-style which, if accepted, would mean that a variation is inappropriate.[292] For example, the non-resident parent may be able to support his life-style by careful budgeting[293] or the use of credit facilities.[294] The burden of proof is initially on the person with care to demonstrate that the non-resident parent's life-style cannot be supported by his formula income.[295] This might include evidence of the non-resident parent's ability to service loans and to engage in ventures which generate receipts not included in the declared income.[296] If she makes out a case, the burden then shifts to the non-resident parent to account for the disparity identified.[297] In both situations the normal civil standard of proof applies. The calculation of the income to be attributed in 'life-style' cases also needs to be undertaken with some care.[298] It is not simply a case of assessing the non-resident parent's total income.[299] Rather, the legislation requires decision makers and tribunals to add to the non-resident parent's formula income 'the difference between the income which the Secretary of State is satisfied the non-resident parent requires to support his overall life-style' and the income which has been taken into account under the standard formula.[300] It follows that the evidence available to decision makers and tribunals will be crucial. As we have seen, the Agency rarely takes the initiative in such cases. According to one official report, 'it was never the [policy] intention that the CSA would investigate any applications made on the grounds of an ex-partner's lifestyle or diversion of income'.[301] Tribunals, with their more inquisitorial approach, may be more pro-active; indeed, it is standard practice for all variation cases to be referred to a District Chairman for directions to be given to the parties on the production of evidence.[302] Tribunals may also be

---

[291] This was certainly the case under the departures scheme: *ibid*, paras 15(4) and 16.

[292] Thus the statutory list of such circumstances is not exhaustive.

[293] 'It would not be enough for the applicant to show, for example, that the NRP pursued one extravagant activity, such as regularly going on expensive foreign holidays, since it is quite possible that he may do this because he has an otherwise self denying existence', Child Support Agency, n 278 above, 'Lifestyle Inconsistent with Declared Income' at 3001.

[294] *R(CS) 3/01* paras 22–24 *per* Mr Commissioner Jacobs.

[295] This much is implicit in *CCS/3331/1999*, even though this is supposed to be an inquisitorial jurisdiction.

[296] See eg *CSC 6/03-04(T)*, paras 46–50.

[297] *CCS/2623/1999* paras 31–3; *CSC 6/03-04(T)*, para 73.

[298] Although, as Mr Commissioner Jacobs acknowledges in *CCS/3927/1999*, para 19 and *CSCS/4242/2002* para 13, this is not something that can be done with precision.

[299] *Ibid*, para 15, *CCS/2623/1999* paras 29–30 and *CCS/1840/1999* para 12. See also *CCS/2152/2004*.

[300] Or the income which would have been taken into account but for the operation of CSA 1991, sch 1, para 4(1)(b) or 5(a) on flat and nil rates; see SI 2001/156, regs. 20(5) and 25. See also *CCS/1840/1999* paras 8 and 12 *per* Mr Commissioner Angus.

[301] M Chetwynd *et al*, *The Departures Pilot Scheme* (DSS In-house report 33, 1997) at 38.

[302] See *CCS/2623/1999* para 27 and SI 1999/991, reg 38(2).

more inclined to draw adverse inferences[303] where a party fails to comply with such directions and (assuming the party in question attends an oral hearing) where they have the opportunity to test that evidence.[304]

The 'Just and Equitable' Requirement

An application for a variation will only succeed if, in addition to it falling within any one (or more) of the various cases considered above, the Secretary of State is of the opinion that it is 'just and equitable' to agree to a variation.[305] This legislative requirement first appeared in the context of departures directions. It undoubtedly provides the potential for a more sensitive balancing of interests than the alternative test, one of hardship to the non-resident parent, which the 1995 White Paper had originally suggested would be a precondition for eligibility for such a direction.[306] The case law on the meaning of the 'just and equitable' test in other statutory contexts would suggest, at least at first sight, that it offers decision makers and tribunals considerable scope for the exercise of discretionary judgment. For example, the Court of Appeal has held that the phrase 'just and equitable' is a term which is not 'capable of precise definition'. Rather, 'the words should be interpreted broadly to mean just what they say'.[307] The same phraseology is also used in the Law Reform (Married Women and Tortfeasors) Act 1935 where, according to one High Court judge, it means that 'exercising a judicial discretion in the matter I am intended to do that which I think is right between the parties'.[308] As a matter of principle this means that a generalised 'just and equitable' test cannot be reduced to an exhaustive list of relevant considerations.[309]

There is, however, an important difference between the operation of the 'just and equitable' test in these other statutory contexts and in the child support jurisdiction. Elsewhere, the expression typically vests judges with an entirely untrammelled discretion to take into account such matters as they see fit in order to achieve a fair outcome in the case concerned. The 1991 Act, on the other hand, does not leave the 'just and equitable' test to stand alone without further definition. First, the legislation requires the Secretary of State to have regard to 'the

---

[303]   On which see *R(CS)6/05*.

[304]   Although 'the chairman's position means that the questioning will always lack the rigor [sic] of a hostile cross-examination by opposing advocates', *CCS/2623/1999* para 16 *per* Mr Commissioner Jacobs.

[305]   CSA 1991, s 28F(1).

[306]   DSS, n 7 above, para 2.5.

[307]   *Hanning v Maitland (No 2)* [1970] 1 QB 580 at 591 *per* Salmon LJ (recovery of costs from legally-aided plaintiff). Similarly, the expression was considered by the Court of Appeal to be 'of very wide import' in the context of possession proceedings under the Rent Act 1977: *Bradshaw v Baldwin-Wiseman* (1985) 49 P & CR 382 at 388 *per* Griffiths LJ.

[308]   *Daniel v Rickett, Cockerell & Co. Ltd. and Raymond* [1938] 2 KB 322 at 326 *per* Hilbery J.

[309]   Thus, in the context of company winding up applications, Lord Wilberforce warned against 'a tendency to create categories or headings under which cases must be brought if the clause is to apply. This is wrong. Illustrations may be used, but general words should remain general and not be reduced to the sum of particular instances', *Ebrahimi v Westbourne Galleries Ltd* [1973] AC 360 at 374–75.

welfare of any child likely to be affected if he did agree to a variation'.[310] This is something of a belt and braces provision, given that the legislation in any event requires regard to be had to this factor when considering any discretionary power conferred by the Act.[311] As with section 2, it is the welfare of *any child likely to be affected* which must be taken into account, not just that of a qualifying child.[312] However, whatever the legislation may say, it is by no means clear that the children's welfare is routinely considered in practice.[313] Arguably, the statutory reminder to have regard to children's welfare in no way affects the generality of the 'just and equitable' test. Yet the legislation also provides that the Secretary of State 'must, or as the case may be must not, take any prescribed factors into account, or must take them into account (or not) in prescribed circumstances'.[314] Thus the notions of justice and equity are carefully circumscribed by regulations.

The regulations set out two general factors which must be taken into consideration in deciding whether it is just and equitable to agree to a variation. The first is whether the effect of making a variation 'would be likely to result in a relevant person ceasing paid employment'.[315] A threat by a non-resident parent to give up work is thus a factor to take into account, but is not decisive, and Jacobs and Douglas warn that this provision should not become 'a blackmailer's charter'.[316] The second general consideration is the extent (if any) of the non-resident parent's liability to pay maintenance under any earlier court order or agreement.[317] In addition, if the application falls within one of the special cases, regard must be had to whether the non-resident parent could have arranged his finances so as to meet the expenses without a variation, or whether he has other resources at his disposal, not used for his essential needs, which could be deployed to meet those costs.[318] The following example was given during the debates on the 1995 Act:

---

[310] CSA 1991, s 28F(2)(a).

[311] *Ibid*, s 2. Jacobs and Douglas, n 60 above, at 116 suggest an alternative reason for the inclusion of this provision, namely that the 'just and equitable' test does not strictly involve the exercise of a discretion for the purposes of s 2 (by analogy with *George Mitchell (Chesterhall) Ltd. v Finney Lock* [1983] 2 AC 803 at 815 *per* Lord Bridge, on the 'fair and reasonable' test under UCTA 1977). However, the government's view at the time of the passage of CSA 1995 was clearly that consideration of a departure application involved the exercise of a discretionary power: *Hansard* HL Debates vol 565 col. 67 (19 June 1995) *per* Lord Mackay of Ardbrecknish.

[312] As Jacobs and Douglas observe (n 60 above, at 116), technically the wording of s 28F(2)(a) excludes consideration of the effect on a child if a variation is *not* agreed, but this would fall within the generality of the 'just and equitable' test.

[313] 'Astonishingly, the Secretary of State's submissions in departures cases regularly make no mention at all of the qualifying children', *R(CS) 3/01* para 46 *per* Mr Commissioner Jacobs (in that case the only child affected was a qualifying child). See also the same Commissioner's strictures in *CCS/7522/1999* at para 1.3.

[314] CSA 1991, s 28F(2)(b).

[315] SI 2001/156, reg 21(1)(a)(i).

[316] n 60 above, at 702. The weight to be attached to this factor is for a tribunal to determine: *CSCS/16/03*, para 11 *per* Sir Crispin Agnew of Lochnaw Bt QC. In practice, although NRPs may commonly make such threats, it appears that they are rarely carried out.

[317] SI 2001/156, reg 21(1)(a)(ii). This only applies if the applicant is the NRP. Note that in this context the regulation refers to a prior 'agreement', not a prior 'written maintenance agreement'. It could therefore presumably include a purely informal agreement to pay maintenance.

[318] *Ibid*, reg 21(1)(b)(i) and (ii).

Let us suppose that an absent parent has requested a departure because he has a debt which costs him £25 a week to repay. It is clear that the debt is a reasonable one, that he has not been able to reschedule it and that he therefore has to meet the payments. On the face of it, he may qualify for a departure. However, perhaps we may suppose that he is horse-racing enthusiast, a car enthusiast or something similar and has a part share in a racehorse which costs him £2,500 a year . . . The Secretary of State may consider that, in view of the circumstances of the case, it would not be just and equitable to allow a debt to reduce support for the absent parent's own child, when he is spending much more on an expensive hobby.[319]

On the other hand, the government stated that there was no intention that the just and equitable test would result in 'routine refusal of departures' solely on the ground that the non-resident parent's income was higher than that of the parent with care: 'The purpose is to make sure that the case is looked at in the round and that all relevant factors relating to the individual circumstances of the parties involved are taken into account'.[320]

As well as these factors which must be considered, the potential scope of the 'just and equitable' test is significantly cut back by a further list of factors which must *not* be taken into account:

(a) the fact that the conception of the qualifying child was not planned by one or both of the parents;

(b) whether the non-resident parent or the person with care of the qualifying child was responsible for the breakdown of the relationship between them;

(c) the fact that the non-resident parent or the person with care of the qualifying child has formed a new relationship with a person who is not a parent of that child;

(d) the existence of particular arrangements for contact with the qualifying child, including whether any arrangements made are being adhered to;

(e) the income or assets of any person other than the non-resident parent, other than the income or assets of a partner of the non-resident parent taken into account under regulation 20(3);

(f) the failure by a non-resident parent to make payments of child support maintenance, or to make payments under a maintenance order or a written maintenance agreement; or

(g) representations made by persons other than the relevant persons.[321]

The first four factors (sub-paragraphs (a) to (d)) all concern the parties' conduct either during their relationship or since their separation.[322] Given the fraught nature of such questions, which inevitably involve apportioning blame, the government's desire to exclude the consideration of such issues in the context of variations is wholly understandable. According to the minister, 'it would be wrong

---

[319] *Per* Lord Mackay of Ardbrecknish, *Hansard* HL Debates vol 565, col 83 (19 June 1995).

[320] *Per* Mr A Burt, Parliamentary Under-Secretary of State for Social Security, Standing Committee E, col 80, 30 March 1995.

[321] SI 2001/156 reg 21(2).

[322] On *ibid*, reg 21(2)(a) see also Hale J's comment that 'The policy of the Child Support Act 1991 was that people who had children should support them, whether or not those were wanted children', *J v C (Child: Financial Provision)* [1999] 1 FLR 152.

to be influenced, in what is essentially a decision about financial circumstances, by the moral rights or wrongs of a couple's separation'.[323] Whilst this approach is consistent with the trend towards no-fault divorce, it sits uneasily with the views of separating parents themselves who typically 'use a vocabulary of personal responsibility' to interpret failed relationships, and so are often keen to attribute blame.[324] It follows that there is a significant risk that many of the Agency's clients will perceive the system as inherently *un*just and *in*equitable precisely because they are effectively precluded from raising such issues at any stage in the child support process.[325]

The drafting of the fifth consideration (sub-paragraph (e)), requiring any third party's income or assets to be disregarded, is worthy of special note. This is the only factor which has been added to the list of such matters since the 2000 Act.[326] It ensures that a non-resident parent's application for a variation cannot be prejudiced by the fact that his new partner may have considerable financial resources of her own.[327] It also means that the wealth of the non-resident parent's immediate or wider family, for example his parents,[328] is irrelevant to the determination. In addition, it means that the parent with care's own financial position is to be disregarded in deciding whether it is just and equitable to agree to a variation.[329] This reflects the changed nature of the child support obligation following the 2000 Act. As amended in 1995, the 1991 Act[330] provided that, in dealing with departure directions, both parties' 'financial circumstances' had to be considered alongside the children's welfare in determining the 'just and equitable' issue. Now, however, the relevant primary legislation makes no explicit reference to the parties' financial circumstances. Thus, just as the parent with care's income is ignored for the purpose of the standard maintenance calculation, so also is it irrelevant when deciding whether it is 'just and equitable' to agree to a variation. This reaffirms that the primary goal of the new scheme is to ensure that the child in question benefits from a share of the non-resident parent's income, rather than merely that the costs of raising children are in some way equitably apportioned between the parents.

The drafting of the sixth matter (sub-paragraph (f)) which cannot affect the operation of the 'just and equitable' test is problematic. This precludes consideration of the non-resident parent's failure to comply with a child support maintenance assessment or an earlier court order or written maintenance agreement. At one level

---

[323] *Per* Mr A Burt, Parliamentary Under-Secretary of State for Social Security, Standing Committee E, col 80, 30 March 1995.

[324] A Sarat and WF Felstiner, *Divorce Lawyers and their Clients* (Oxford University Press, New York, 1995) at 37.

[325] Indeed, these disregards relate to the 'acrimonious issues in the break up of a relationship', *CSCS/16/03*, para 17 *per* Sir Crispin Agnew of Lochnaw Bt QC.

[326] Sub-paras (a)–(d), (f) and (g) have all been re-enacted in SI 2001/156, reg 21 having previously appeared in SI 1996/2907, reg 30(2).

[327] This is necessarily subject to the exceptional case which falls within the 'inconsistent life-style' case under SI 2001/156, reg 20(3).

[328] And the qualifying children's grandparents.

[329] See *CCS/1129/2005* at para 9 *per* Mr Commissioner Howell QC.

[330] CSA 1991, s 28F(2).

this exclusion is unsurprising—this is another 'conduct' issue, and the case will presumably not have reached this stage if the non-resident parent had failed to comply with a regular payments condition.[331] It is also perhaps reasonable that a non-resident parent should not be able to rely on his own past non-compliance as evidence of financial hardship. However, the provision is worded in such a way that previous failure to pay is *always* to be disregarded. Arguably this is an unwarranted fetter on the exercise of the discretion of the Secretary of State and tribunals. For example, one might envisage a case where, on the facts, a non-resident parent may have a very strong case for a variation based on his present financial circumstances. Although the history of the case may demonstrate a persistent refusal to meet his child maintenance liabilities in the past, the regulations mean that a record of non-compliance cannot be taken into account in deciding whether it is 'just and equitable' to agree to a variation. One principled justification for this approach is that the remedy for serious arrears in the past period is proper enforcement of the liability for that period, whereas the variations scheme is designed to be forward-looking. However, this distinction may not be consistent with everyone's concept of either justice or equity.[332] As one Commissioner has noted, 'there may be cases in which some element of punishment for a deliberate attempt to evade the child support legislation is appropriate'.[333]

The final factor to be excluded from the reckoning (sub-paragraph (g)) is an anti-busy body provision. It simply ensures that the Secretary of State need not take into account any comments on the variation application received from a third party, such as a new partner or a relative of one of the parents.[334]

Although the legislation lists these various factors above as matters which must either be taken into account or excluded in deciding whether it is 'just and equitable' to agree to a variation, both decision makers and tribunals need to remind themselves that these considerations are not exhaustive.[335] Subject to those particular rules, the overriding requirement is to have regard to 'all the circumstances of the case'.[336] Given that the test necessarily requires a consideration of the respective formula outcomes with and without the variation being agreed, a tribunal will usually need to know what impact an assessment would have on the standard formula assessment.[337] In some cases, for example where there is a

---

[331] See CSA 1991, s 28C(5).

[332] See eg Lord Cross's observation (in the very different context of an application to court to wind up a company) that 'a petitioner who relies on the "just and equitable" clause must come to court with clean hands', *Ebrahimi v Westbourne Galleries Ltd* [1973] AC 360 at 387.

[333] *CCS/2357/2003* para 44 *per* Mr Commissioner Mesher.

[334] As Jacobs and Douglas observe, n 60 above, at 703, this complements CSA 1991, s 28E(3) but does not preclude the Secretary of State from making submissions to a tribunal!

[335] The Secretary of State's internal guidance reminds staff, when making discretionary decisions, to 'use discretion with sensitivity and imagination . . . [do] not prejudge the possible relevance of factors that may seem to be beyond the scope of existing guidance . . . consider all circumstances of a case and [ensure] that each case is determined on its own merits' Child Support Agency, n 269 above, 'Discretion' at 2840.

[336] CSA 1991, s 28F(1)(b).

[337] *R(CS) 3/01* para 43 *per* Mr Commissioner Jacobs.

significant disparity between the declared income and the income required to support the life-style, this is unnecessary.[338] There is no formal burden of proof on any party in deciding whether or not it is 'just and equitable' to agree to a variation.[339]

Implementing a Variation and Jurisdictional Issues

The interaction between maintenance calculations and variation applications can be problematic and may generate some thorny jurisdictional issues. We have already seen that an application for a variation may be made before or after a decision is taken on the maintenance calculation.[340] Obviously, whenever the application for a variation is made, it must be determined by the Secretary of State in accordance with the regulations analysed in this chapter.[341]

If the variation application predates the decision on the maintenance calculation, there are three situations in which the Secretary of State must not agree to a variation. The first is where he or she is satisfied that there is 'insufficient information' to make a decision in respect of the maintenance calculation (and so a default maintenance decision would be made).[342] The second is where the circumstances are such that the case would be bound to fail on the initial sift.[343] Lastly, and most obviously, the Secretary of State must not agree to a variation if it would not be just and equitable to do so, having regard to the factors identified in the regulations.[344]

If, on the other hand, the Secretary of State decides to agree to a variation, he or she must decide how this impacts on the normal formula assessment and then make a decision on the maintenance application accordingly.[345] That decision, incorporating the variation decision, then carries the normal appeal rights.[346] The decision is also susceptible to revision or supersession.[347] Where the application

---

[338] *CSC 6/03-04*, paras 69–71.

[339] *Ibid*, para 44, citing Sedley LJ in *Karanakaran v Secretary of State for the Home Department* [2000] 3 All ER 449. According to Sedley LJ, 'The civil standard of proof, which treats anything which probably happened as having definitely happened, is part of a pragmatic legal fiction. It has no logical bearing on the assessment of the likelihood of future events or (by parity of reasoning) the quality of past ones' (at 477D)—nor, necessarily, on the *quality* of *future* events, ie what would be just and equitable.

[340] CSA 1991, ss 28A(3) and 28G(1) respectively.

[341] *Ibid*, s 28F(6). Or, of course, referred to a tribunal.

[342] CSA 1991, s 28F(3)(a). Parents are given one month to supply such further information: SI 2001/156, reg 8.

[343] CSA 1991, s 28F(3)(b) and SI 2001/156, reg 30(a).

[344] CSA 1991, s 28F(3)(b) and SI 2001/156, reg 30(b).

[345] CSA 1991, s 28F(4). If an interim maintenance decision has been made under *ibid*, s 12(2), that decision is replaced by the new s 11 decision and any appeal against the earlier decision automatically lapses: *ibid*, s 28F(5).

[346] CSA 1991, s 20(1)(a). This is different from the departures system, under which the departure decision generated separate appeal rights: CSA 1991, sch 4C, para 3 (before amendment by CSPSSA 2000) and see *R(CS) 9/02* para 10 *per* Mr Commissioner Jacobs.

[347] SI 1999/991, reg 15B, which prescribes a procedure analogous to SI 2001/156, reg 9.

for a variation is made before the Secretary of State makes a maintenance calculation or a default maintenance decision, the general rule is that the effective date of the variation is the same as that of the maintenance calculation. If, however, the ground giving rise to the variation arose after that date, then the effective date is the first day of the maintenance period in which the change occurred.[348] Obviously, if the basis for the variation has already ceased to exist by the time the Secretary of State makes the maintenance calculation, then the variation is time-limited to the last day of the maintenance period in question.[349]

If a maintenance calculation is already in place when the application for a variation is made, the request for a variation is treated as either an application for a revision or supersession as appropriate.[350] Again the Secretary of State must not agree to a variation if it would not be just and equitable to do so.[351] If, however, the decision is to agree to the variation, the Secretary of State must similarly determine the effect on the maintenance calculation and revise or supersede that decision as appropriate.[352] As before, this carries with it the normal rights governing appeals, revisions and supersessions.[353] The effective date of the decision will be in accordance with the rules governing revisions and supersessions.[354]

If the non-resident parent's child support liability is subject to a variation, whenever the application was made, the adjusted liability is itself subject to the normal rules on shared care in basic and reduced rate cases.[355] A variation cannot reduce the amount of child support payable to less than the flat rate.[356] Moreover, if a variation is agreed but then any of the circumstances arise which would have enabled an application to be rejected on the initial sift, as being inappropriate or pointless, then the effect of the variation is suspended for the period that those circumstances apply.[357]

Decision makers may be faced with more than one variation application in relation to the same maintenance calculation. If so, the applications can be consolidated and considered together.[358] If more than one ground for a variation is found to apply in relation to the same period, then the effects are aggregated.[359] These

---

[348] SI 2001/156, reg 22(1). If the NRP has made voluntary payments under CSA 1991, s 28J in relation to prior debts or mortgage or related expenses (SI 2001/156, regs 12 and 14), then the effective date is the first day of the maintenance period after the NRP has been notified of the amount of his child support liability: *ibid*, reg 22(2).

[349] *Ibid*, reg 22(3).

[350] SI 1999/991, regs 3A(1)(a)(ii) and 6A(6).

[351] CSA 1991, s 28F(3) as substituted by SI 2000/3173, reg 7(a). The first two grounds specified in the preceding paragraph are inapplicable in this situation.

[352] CSA 1991, s 28F(4) as substituted by SI 2000/3173, reg 7(b)–(c).

[353] CSA 1991, s 20(1)(a) and SI 1999/991, reg 15B.

[354] See SI 1999/991, regs 5A and 7B(6).

[355] SI 2001/156, reg 27(2), modifying CSA 1991, sch 1, para 7(2) accordingly, and SI 2001/156, reg 27(3) (which also applies where care is shared with a local authority).

[356] *Ibid*, reg 27(5). Curiously this caveat does not appear to apply to special cases departures.

[357] *Ibid*, reg 27(6). See further *ibid*, reg 7 for the detailed circumstances. If those circumstances later cease to apply, the variation should automatically be applied without need for a new application. See also *ibid*, reg 29.

[358] CSA 1991, sch 4A, para 5(1) and SI 2001/156, reg 9(9).

[359] *Ibid*, reg 27(1).

effects may, of course, point in different directions; a variation based on special expenses will reduce the non-resident parent's net weekly income whilst one based on one of the additional cases will cause it to increase, requiring offsetting in order to arrive at the net effect.[360]

Tribunals have the express statutory power to consider a referral in respect of a variation application at the same time as an appeal against an interim maintenance decision.[361] Tribunals may also hear two or more referrals in respect of variation applications together.[362] Subject to any natural justice considerations, an appellant is entitled to ask a tribunal to consider an alternative ground for a variation to the one specified in the original application.[363] More generally, legally qualified panel members have the power to issue directions for the 'just, effective and efficient conduct of the proceedings',[364] which might involve listing appeals to be heard together and orders for the production of documents.

---

[360] These are known by the Agency as 'concurrent variations'. Where the same effective date applies, Agency policy is to apply the additional case variation first in order to determine the correct amount of income to use for the special expense threshold.

[361] CSA 1991, sch 4A, para 5(3).

[362] SI 1999/991, reg 45.

[363] *R(CS) 3/01* para 50 *per* Mr Commissioner Jacobs.

[364] SI 1999/991 reg 38(2).

13

Complaints, Reviews and Appeals

Introduction

The focus of this chapter is how the Agency's decisions, as well as its actions (and indeed inaction) can be challenged through both legal and other channels. The first section summarises the Agency's internal complaints procedure and the possibility of further investigation of complaints by the Independent Case Examiner (ICE) and by the Ombudsman, as well as the Agency's arrangements for compensation payments. The second section examines the complex provisions governing revisions and supersessions, two internal review procedures which may be invoked to change an existing decision. The third section deals with the right of appeal to an independent tribunal, whilst the fourth part is concerned with the further right of appeal from a tribunal to a Child Support Commissioner. The fifth section deals with appeals thereafter to the Court of Appeal and (in Scotland) the Court of Session (and to the House of Lords). The final section summarises the various ways in which child support issues may still fall for determination by the ordinary courts.

It should not be assumed from this sequential exposition that a dissatisfied client must pursue each of these stages in turn. In short, the complaints procedure is an appropriate avenue to follow when a parent is unhappy with the level of service provided by the Agency; in itself, the complaints procedure cannot result in a decision made under the child support legislation being altered, although it may result in the payment of compensation. A substantive decision in a case can be changed only through the formal routes of revision, supersession or appeal, but there is no requirement that either of the first two steps be undertaken before an appeal is lodged.[1] However, an appeal cannot be taken to the Child Support Commissioner unless the case has first been heard by an appeal tribunal. There is, accordingly, a hierarchy of decision making; initial decisions are taken by Agency officers, acting on behalf of the Secretary of State, whilst tribunals and Commissioners provide two levels of appellate scrutiny. This specialist regime means that the ordinary courts are largely bypassed. As we see in the final section to this chapter, their residual role is largely confined to dealing with parentage

---

[1] This was a requirement under the original 1991 Act, but was abolished by SSA 1998.

disputes (in the magistrates' court), enforcement matters (typically magistrates' courts and county courts), applications for judicial review (in the Administrative Court, part of the High Court) and hearing appeals from decisions of the Child Support Commissioners (in the Court of Appeal).

Complaints

The Internal Complaints Procedure

The very nature of the Agency's work is bound to generate complaints. The Agency operates a three-fold internal system for handling complaints.[2] First, complaints are considered by a complaints resolution officer in the relevant Agency office. Secondly, if the individual concerned remains dissatisfied, the complaint may be referred to the Agency's area manager. Finally, if the matter is still not resolved satisfactorily, a parent may complain to the Agency's Chief Executive. If one starts with the premise that the goal of an internal complaints system is 'to turn dissatisfied clients into satisfied clients',[3] then the Agency's own scheme is a dismal failure. In one study a significant proportion of the Agency's customers reported having made some sort of complaint, with non-resident parents being more inclined to do so.[4] Over 70 per cent of those using the Agency's complaints procedures were 'very dissatisfied' with the way in which their complaint was handled.[5] Complaints were predominantly about poor customer service rather than the substantive provisions of child support law itself.[6] There appear to be particular problems with the first stage of the complaints procedure, as about 25 per cent of complaints proceed to the next stage.[7] Overall, however, very few complainants pursue their grievance as far as the Chief Executive or beyond to the ICE.

---

[2] See generally Child Support Agency, *How do you complain?* (CSL 119, January 2005).

[3] Commonwealth Ombudsman, *Review of the Child Support Agency's Complaint Service* (Canberra, July 2001) at 10.

[4] Thus 40% of NRPs and 28% of PWCs reported that they had telephoned with a complaint, and 29% of NRPs and 15% of PWCs had written with one: N Wikeley *et al*, *National Survey of Child Support Agency Clients* (DWP Research Report No 152, 2001) at 88.

[5] *Ibid*, at 88.

[6] *Ibid*, at 89.

[7] HC Work and Pensions Committee, *The Performance of the Child Support Agency* (HC 44-II, Session 2004–05) Evidence of Ms Jodi Berg, ICE, at Ev 2: "they are simply not resolving as many as they should be solving as soon as people come to them with a problem . . . that is probably because people in the teams at first point of contact do not do enough to help [complaints resolution officers] sort out the problems'. In contrast, the Australian Agency's Complaints Service was found to have 'effectively and efficiently resolved' the great majority of complaints, although customer awareness of the availability of the procedure remained low: Commonwealth Ombudsman, n 3 above, at 17 and 23.

The Independent Case Examiner

The ICE has no statutory basis. The office was established by the Agency in 1997, effectively as a type of internal specialist ombudsman.[8] As the first ICE explained, her role is to act 'as an impartial referee where people feel they have been badly treated by the Child Support Agency'.[9] The ICE will investigate complaints about the way in which the Agency has handled a case (but not grievances about the child support legislation itself), providing that: (i) the complainant has exhausted the Agency's three-stage internal complaints procedure; (ii) the complaint is made within six months of the Chief Executive's response; and (iii) the Parliamentary Commissioner for Administration (the Ombudsman) is not involved in the case.[10] Complaints that are accepted as suitable for review by the ICE are then investigated by her office, initially with a view to seeing if the matter can be settled. If this is not possible, the ICE makes a formal report with recommendations, which the Agency will usually (but not always) accept. Most of the common themes underlying complaints about the Agency, identified in the ICE's first annual report, have recurred in subsequent reports—typically delays, errors and poor communications, and problems with obtaining maintenance from self-employed parents and with complaints handling itself. Complainants who have used the ICE's services appear to be more satisfied than those who have only had resort to the Agency's internal procedures, although awareness of the role of the ICE amongst the Agency's clientele is low.[11]

The Ombudsman

The role of the Parliamentary Commissioner for Administration (or Ombudsman) is to investigate complaints of maladministration made against government departments. Citizens cannot make a complaint direct to the Ombudsman; rather, complaints must be referred by an individual's Member of Parliament. Notwithstanding this filtering arrangement, the contentious nature of the Agency's work has inevitably generated a considerable caseload for the Ombudsman. Indeed, in August 1994, when the scheme was not even 18 months old, the Ombudsman took the unusual step of declining to take on the investigation of any new complaints against the Agency, unless they involved some new issue or the

[8] This followed a proposal by the Parliamentary Commissioner for Administration (the Ombudsman), first made in May 1995.

[9] ICE, *Annual Report 1997/98* (1998) at 7. The first ICE (August 2001) was Anne Parker; since then the post has been held by Jodi Berg.

[10] ICE, *The Independent Case Examiner's Office: our service and standards* (ICE, Chester, September 2005).

[11] About a quarter of NRPs and a half of PWCs described themselves as 'very satisfied' or 'fairly satisfied' with the ICE's handling of their complaint, but only 10% of all Agency customers had heard of the ICE: Wikeley *et al*, n 4 above, at 91. The ICE's own customer satisfaction surveys reports much higher satisfaction rates (83% or more): *Annual Report 2004/05* (2005) at 16.

complainant had suffered actual financial loss. In 1995 the Ombudsman issued a special report on the customer service problems experienced by the Agency's clientele, which included cases of mistaken identity, inadequate procedures, incorrect or misleading advice and, of course, delays at all stages of the maintenance process.[12] The Agency's subsequent decision to establish the office of ICE was a somewhat belated response to one of the Ombudsman's recommendations. Although there is no formal bar on a complaint being made to the Ombudsman without having used the ICE procedure, in practice complainants will be encouraged to try the ICE route first.

Compensation Arrangements

The Child Support Agency operates two main types of compensation arrangements—'special payments' and a 'temporary compensation scheme'. Special payments are a form of compensation for various forms of Agency maladministration, and fall into three categories. *Ex gratia* special payments may cover actual financial loss, compensation for delay and so-called 'consolatory payments' (where Agency maladministration has caused gross inconvenience or severe distress). Extra-statutory payments may be made where the law is defective and fails to reflect the policy intention, so causing loss to a particular individual. Finally, advance payments may be made to compensate parents with care where arrears of more than £100 have built up because of Agency delay or error, and it would take more than six months for the non-resident parent to pay off the arrears at the agreed rate.[13] The levels of special payments vary considerably, according to the circumstances—for example, the parent with care in *R (Kehoe) v Secretary of State for Work and Pensions* received an *ex gratia* payment of over £10,000 to compensate her for financial loss caused by the Agency's maladministration, whereas the 'going rate' for consolatory payments is £100.

Whereas special payments are dealt with entirely outside the legislation, the temporary compensation scheme now has a statutory basis.[14] The purpose of this latter scheme was to provide some incentive to non-resident parents to clear arrears of child support and so to improve compliance. The scheme applied where a non-resident parent had more than six months' worth of arrears, of which at least three months were due to the Agency's unreasonable delay, had no other maintenance arrears and was paying child support regularly through the Agency.[15]

---

[12] Parliamentary Commissioner for Administration, *Investigation of complaints against the Child Support Agency* (Third Report, Session 1994–95, HC 135).

[13] The Agency's Standards Committee has identified serious problems with decision making in this area (in a small sample, 35% of such decisions were found to be inadequate, although this is a better performance than in previous years): *2004/2005 Annual Report: Final report* (Child Support Agency, 2005) at 11–12.

[14] CSPSSA 2000, s 27. But note this scheme has now expired: see n 16 below.

[15] Child Support (Temporary Compensation Payment Scheme) Regulations 2000 (SI 2000/3174), reg 4.

In such cases the Secretary of State could then agree with the non-resident parent to remit part of the arrears,[16] and that no recovery action would be taken so long as the agreement was maintained.[17] If the agreement was indeed fulfilled, the payer's liability for any outstanding arrears ceased but the Secretary of State could reimburse the parent with care for her lost maintenance (known as 'deferred debt compensation').[18] If the agreement was broken, then the non-resident parent became liable to pay the full arrears.[19]

Changing Decisions: Revisions and Supersessions

From Adjudication to Decision-Making and Appeals

The Child Support Act 1991 adopted the then social security model of adjudication for deciding matters of entitlement and resolving disputes, in which decisions of adjudication officers (nominally independent of the Secretary of State) were subject to review, with a right of appeal to a social security appeal tribunal. So child support officers made decisions about child support liabilities, which could be changed through various review procedures and challenged on appeal before a child support appeal tribunal. The main difference was that a child support appeal tribunal could not hear an appeal unless it had already been the subject of an internal 'second-tier review'.[20] The legislation also provided for periodic reviews and for reviews initiated either by the parties or by a child support officer, resulting in a complex and cumbersome statutory machinery which struggled to keep up with the often rapidly changing circumstances of the parties.[21] 'In short, the adjudication procedures have produced institutionalised delay and uncertainty'.[22] A case which was then taken further on appeal might literally take years to resolve.[23]

The social security adjudication machinery was overhauled by the SSA 1998, which implemented the then DSS's so-called 'DMA' (decision making and appeals) reforms. The merits of these changes have been debated elsewhere;[24] it is

---

[16] Initially such agreements had to be made before 1 April 2002 and expire before 1 April 2003 (CSPSSA 2000, s 27(5)); this was later extended to agreements made before 1 April 2005 and ending before 1 April 2006 (Child Support (Temporary Compensation Payment Scheme) (Modification and Amendment) Regulations 2002 (SI 2002/1854)).

[17] CSPSSA 2000, s 27(3) and (6).

[18] *Ibid*, s 27(7).

[19] *Ibid*, s 27(8).

[20] In social security appeals, the mandatory internal review procedure applied only to DLA and attendance allowance cases. It has since been abolished in that jurisdiction too.

[21] G Davis, N Wikeley and R Young, *Child Support in Action* (Hart Publishing, Oxford, 1998), ch 6.

[22] *CCS/1535/1997* para 23 *per* Mr Commissioner Jacobs.

[23] See eg *Secretary of State for Social Security v Foster* [2001] 1 FLR 376—MAF in August 1993 leading ultimately to a Court of Appeal hearing in December 2000, by which time the elder 'child' was 23.

[24] See eg N Wikeley, 'Decision making and appeals under the Social Security Act 1998' (1998) 5 *Journal of Social Security Law* 104

sufficient to note for present purposes that the changes were, for the most part, mapped on to the child support system virtually by default. There was certainly little discussion of the consequential child support changes either in the consultation process or during the parliamentary debates on the 1998 Act.[25] Moreover, despite these modifications, 'there is still plenty of scope for parents to find themselves going round in circles' in the adjudication process.[26]

At the level of Agency decision making, the principal effects of the 1998 Act were two-fold. First, the role of child support officer was abolished, so that all decisions are now taken in the name of the Secretary of State. This had limited impact in terms of how child support decisions were actually made;[27] perhaps of greater significance was the loss of the independent office of the Chief Child Support Officer (CCSO), whose annual reports had highlighted problems with the quality of first instance decision making.[28] Secondly, the 1998 Act swept away the various different review mechanisms established under the 1991 Act and replaced them with two new procedures—revision and supersession.[29] In principle, the fundamental difference between the two regimes is simple; revision is a means of changing an initial decision which is wrong, with effect from the date of that original decision, whereas supersession is a means of substituting a new decision with effect from some later date, for example because of a subsequent change in circumstances.[30] The legislation, however, is just as complex, if not more so, than the pre-1998 statutory provisions, as evidenced by the series of cases in which the Social Security Commissioners have sought to unravel the consequences of the DMA regulations.[31] Allied with errors in first tier decision making, the result can be a jurisdictional morass in which the parties and tribunals alike are left floundering.[32] As one Commissioner observed in the early years of the scheme, it is a matter of regret that there is:

> no power allowing a tribunal or Commissioner to pull together all outstanding disputes and make one overall decision. The legislation encourages the proliferation of separate

---

[25] See eg DSS, *Improving decision making and appeals in Social Security* (Cm 3328, 1996), the consultation paper preceding SSA 1998, which merely mentions child support adjudication in passing.

[26] *R(CS) 3/01* para 31 *per* Mr Commissioner Jacobs. See also *R (Clark) v Child Support Agency* [2002] EWHC 284 (27 hearings in civil courts on the same parentage dispute).

[27] One advantage was the removal of some confusion over nomenclature, given that before the 1998 Act some decisions were taken by child support officers and some by the same officers in a different guise as Secretary of State.

[28] The annual reports of the Agency's Standards Committee, whilst informative, are much less comprehensive than those of the CCSO—and receive much less publicity (they are buried in the Agency's website).

[29] In doing so it also abolished the mandatory second-tier review process.

[30] A supersession may not take place where a revision can be carried out: Social Security and Child Support (Decisions and Appeals) Regulations 1999 (SI 1999/991), reg 6A(7).

[31] See especially the decision of the Tribunal of Commissioners in *R(IB) 2/04*, 'whose exceptional length and complexity bears witness to the difficulties caused by the 1998 Act' *per* Mr Commissioner Howell QC in *CCS/2330/2003* at para 14.

[32] See eg *CCS/2330/2003*, in which the Commissioner identified 'an assessment decision, a supersession, a revision, another revision, and finally a revision of the second revision', with the result that the Agency was 'constantly chasing a moving target', *ibid*, para 4. See also the multiple appeals in *CCS/0185/2005* and related appeals.

decisions, even though they may all be concerned with a single underlying area of dispute.[33]

Revisions

The Secretary of State has the power to revise any of the following:

— a decision in respect of a maintenance calculation or a default or interim maintenance decision;
— a supersession decision;
— a reduced benefit decision;
— a decision to impose a penalty payment;
— a decision to require payment of a fee;
— a decision to adjust the amount of child support payable (or to cancel an adjustment) because of voluntary payments or overpayments of child support;
— an appeal tribunal decision on a referral of a variation application.[34]

This list covers most, if perhaps not all, of the types of disputes that are likely to arise on a child support maintenance application.

The decision to revise may be in response to an application for a revision or may be taken on the initiative of the Secretary of State.[35] The normal rule is that a person may apply for a revision within one month—known by the Agency as the 'dispute period'—of the date of notification of the original decision.[36] In such circumstances, there is no need to show any specific ground for revision. The process is intended to provide a quick and straightforward means of correcting a decision without undue procedural complications.[37] In the absence of any specific rules governing the manner of an application, it follows that the request may be made by telephone. Likewise, there is no need for a wholesale reconsideration of the original decision[38] and the basis for the revision may be a question of fact or law, or even the exercise of a discretion on the existing facts and law.[39] A late application to revise can also be accepted, outside the usual one month time limit, if it is reasonable to do so, so long as the application has merit and there were 'special circumstances' rendering it not practicable for the application to have been lodged

---

[33] Mr Commissioner Howell QC in *CCS/11588/1995* at para 13.

[34] CSA 1991, s 16(1)–(1A) and SI 1999/991, reg 3A(6). At present the Agency is not imposing penalty payments or fees.

[35] CSA 1991, s 16(1)(b).

[36] SI 1999/991, reg 3A(1)(a).

[37] A revision may likewise take place if the application is initially rejected because the Agency has not been provided with the requisite information or evidence, but a further application is made within another month (or such longer period as is deemed reasonable) which contains sufficient material: *ibid*, reg 3A(1)(b).

[38] CSA 1991, s 16(2).

[39] E Jacobs and G Douglas, *Child Support: The Legislation* (Sweet & Maxwell, London, Edition Seven 2005/2006) at 410.

in time. Any late application must be brought within an absolute time limit of 13 months from the original notification.[40]

Additionally, the Secretary of State may take the initiative by starting revision proceedings within one month of the notification of the original decision without showing any particular grounds.[41] Again, this procedure is meant to enable simple mistakes to be identified and corrected with the minimum of formality. A revision may also take place where the Secretary of State is satisfied that the original decision was wrong because of a misrepresentation or failure to disclose a material fact[42] and as result was more advantageous to the person at fault than would otherwise have been the case.[43] Furthermore, the Secretary of State may effect a revision in response to a pending appeal.[44] In all the above circumstances, the Secretary of State is prevented from effecting a revision where the purported ground is a change of circumstances which either post-dated the date on which the original decision took effect or is one which is expected to occur.[45] Finally, the Secretary of State may at any time revise an earlier decision which 'arose from an official error', as that term is rather narrowly defined,[46] or where the alleged non-resident parent transpires not to have been the child's parent after all.[47]

As the purpose of a revision is to replace an earlier decision which was wrong, the normal rule is that the revised decision takes effect from the operative date for the original decision.[48] If there is an outstanding appeal against the original decision, that appeal lapses unless the new decision is less advantageous to the appellant.[49]

Supersessions

It has to be said that the statutory provisions governing revisions, complex as they are, are a model of clarity when compared with those dealing with supersessions.[50] The Secretary of State has the power to supersede any of the following:

---

[40] SI 1999/991, reg 4. By analogy with *R(CS) 4/04* (*Denson v Secretary of State for Work and Pensions*) this is presumably ECHR compliant.

[41] SI 1999/991, reg 3A(1)(d).

[42] On which see *CCS/15846/1996*; there is a formidable body of case law on the meaning of 'misrepresentation' and 'failure to disclose' in the context of overpayments of social security benefits.

[43] SI 1991/991, reg 3A(1)(c). There is no time limit in this particular type of case.

[44] *Ibid*, reg 3A(1)(cc).

[45] *Ibid*, reg 3A(2). Such situations are more appropriately dealt with by way of a supersession.

[46] *Ibid*, reg 3A(1)(e); an 'official error' is one made by a departmental officer to which no third party contributed, and excludes any error of law which comes to light as a result of a later decision of a Commissioner or court: *ibid*, reg 1(3) and see *R(CS) 3/04*.

[47] *Ibid*, reg 3A(1)(f); see ch 8 above on disestablishing paternity.

[48] CSA 1991, s 16(3). Special rules apply where the effective date of the original decision was wrong or where a default maintenance decision is revised: *ibid*, s 16(4) and SI 1999/991, reg 5A. In addition, for the purpose of appeal time limits the revised decision is regarded as having been made on the date of revision: CSA 1991, s 16(5); see also SI 1999/991, reg 31(2).

[49] CSA 1991, s 16(6) and SI 1999/991, reg 30. As a result a tribunal which hears such an 'appeal' is acting outside its jurisdiction: *CCS/2357/2003* paras 9–10 *per* Mr Commissioner Mesher.

[50] Supersessions have been identified as a long-running problem area for the Agency's decision makers: see Standards Committee, n 13 above, at 8.

— a decision in respect of a maintenance calculation or a default or interim maintenance decision or a supersession decision, whether as originally made or as revised;
— a reduced benefit decision;
— a decision to adjust the amount of child support payable (or to cancel an adjustment) because of voluntary payments or overpayments of child support;
— an appeal tribunal decision on a referral of a variation application or on an appeal;
— a Child Support Commissioner's decision.[51]

However, a decision to refuse an application for a maintenance calculation is not susceptible to supersession[52]—it can be changed only by revision, assuming that the criteria for that procedure are met. A decision to supersede may be taken either on the initiative of the Secretary of State or in response to an application from one of the parties.[53] The regulations provide for five types of circumstances in which a decision may be superseded. First, the Secretary of State may act on his or her own initiative to supersede a decision where there has been a relevant change of circumstances or where the original decision was made in ignorance of, or based on a mistake as to, a material fact.[54] Secondly, a party may likewise apply for a supersession of the original decision on the ground of a relevant change of circumstances (actual or impending) at any time, and not just within the first month 'dispute period'.[55] However, in such a party-initiated application, as a general rule the original decision will only be superseded if the resulting difference in the non resident parent's net income is at least 5 per cent (known as the tolerance rule).[56] This provision is designed to avoid the administrative complications caused by having to make large numbers of adjustments to maintenance calculations in response to relatively minor changes in a parent's income. Thirdly, and likewise in response to an application, the Secretary of State again has the power to supersede a decision made in ignorance of, or based on a mistake as to, a material fact.[57] Fourthly, acting either independently or in response to an application, the Secretary of State may supersede a decision—other than one taken on appeal—for error of law.[58] Finally, the Secretary of State may supersede in response to an application for a variation of a maintenance calculation.[59]

---

[51] CSA 1991, s 17(1) and SI 1999/991, reg 9A(9).

[52] *Ibid*, reg 6A(8).

[53] CSA 1991, s 17(1). If the Secretary of State intends to take the initiative, the parties potentially affected must be notified: SI 1999/991, regs 7B(7)–(8) and 7C.

[54] *Ibid*, reg 6A(2).

[55] *Ibid*, reg 6A(3).

[56] *Ibid*, reg 6B(1); *ibid*, reg 6B(3) provides that the tolerance rule is not applied if the original decision is superseded for a non-income change (eg a change in the number of children). For further exceptions where the superseding decision takes effect even though the tolerance rule is not breached, see *ibid*, reg 6B(4).

[57] *Ibid*, reg 6A(4).

[58] SI 1999/991, reg 6A(5). It follows that tribunal and Commissioner decisions may be superseded only on other grounds, eg a change of circumstances.

[59] *Ibid*, reg 6A(6).

The categories of revision and supersession are mutually exclusive in that a supersession may not be effected where a revision is feasible.[60] However, as with revisions, the reconsideration process does not necessitate a review of all the circumstances of the case, enabling decision makers to focus on the particular issue(s) raised.[61] Although administratively convenient, this rule has the potential to cause injustice, not least as a party applying for a supersession is under no obligation to inform the Agency of other changes which may harm his or her case (and indeed which may be unknown to any other party).[62] As a general rule—but subject to various exceptions set out in some utterly impenetrable regulations—the new decision takes effect from the beginning of the maintenance period in which it was made (or in which the application was made).[63]

First Tier Appeals: The Tribunals

Why Tribunals?

The White Paper preceding the 1991 Act accepted that there had to be a right of appeal against decisions on child support matters, but indicated that the government was undecided as to whether that should lie to a court or rather to a tribunal.[64] It declared that the final decision would be made in the light of several considerations, including ease of access, avoiding double handling and waste and ensuring that arrangements for children were part of an integrated package.[65] The original Bill kept all options open, by providing for a right of appeal against the child support officer's appeal to the Secretary of State, with a further right of appeal to the court,[66] although 'court' was defined as 'such court or tribunal as the Lord Chancellor may . . . by order specify'.[67] In the early debates on the Bill the Lord Chancellor, whilst accepting that it was a 'finely balanced question', indicated a preference for appeals to be heard by a tribunal modelled on the social security appeal tribunal.[68] He acknowledged, however, that as the family justice system developed, it might be 'more appropriate that such appeals should be dealt with by the court'.[69] By the Report stage of the Bill, the government's position had firmed up and amendments were introduced establishing child support appeal tribunals.

---

[60] *Ibid,* reg 6A(7).

[61] CSA 1991, s 17(2).

[62] On the limited duty to inform the Agency of changes of circumstances, see p 287 above.

[63] CSA 1991, s 17(3); for 'maintenance period' see *ibid* s 17(4). For the exceptions, see SI 1991/991, reg 7B, usefully tabulated in R Hawden and K Pawling, *Child support handbook* (CPAG, London, 13th edn, 2005/2006) at 417–19.

[64] DSS, *Children Come First* (Cm 1264-I, 1990), paras 3.40–3.46.

[65] CSA 1991, para 3.46.

[66] Child Support Bill 1991 (HL Bill 29, 14 February 1991), cls 17 and 18.

[67] *Ibid,* (cl 18(7)).

[68] *Hansard* HL Debates vol 527 col 615 (19 March 1991).

[69] *Ibid.*

The principal justification for this decision was to draw on the expertise of social security appeal tribunals, as their role was to be very similar, namely 'to apply to a set of facts a formula set out in the statute and in regulations'.[70] In addition, the family courts at that time had 'their hands full in implementing the Children Act'.[71] This decision was also consistent with the concern to rein in public expenditure, as generally legal aid is not available for representation before tribunals.[72] The new tribunals, as in the social security jurisdiction, would consist of a lawyer and two lay persons and 'thus combine legal and technical expertise with local knowledge'.[73] Again, as with the existing tribunals, the new tribunals within the umbrella of the then Independent Tribunal Service (now the Appeals Service) were to include members of both sexes, in order to minimise perceptions of bias from users.[74] Once the appeal tribunals were in place, then the example of the social security model led inevitably to the creation of a further tier of appeal in the Child Support Commissioners.[75] However, the 1991 Act reserves the power to the Lord Chancellor[76] to redirect cases away from tribunals and back to the courts, either in all types of dispute or only in specific categories of appeal.[77] To date this power has been exercised solely for the purpose of ensuring that parentage disputes in child support appeals are heard by the magistrates' courts.[78]

The composition of child support tribunals was radically altered by the SSA 1998, the prime focus of which was inevitably the much larger social security appeals system.[79] The government's concern to increase efficiency and cut delays in hearing such appeals led, in a somewhat confused fashion, to the decision to abolish the long standing role of lay members in social security and related tribunals.[80] This proved highly controversial, crowding out any wider discussion of the implications of this change for the much lower volume of appeals heard in the

[70] *Hansard* HL Debates vol 528 col 1816 (16 May 1991).

[71] *Hansard* HL Debates vol 528 col 553 (29 April 1991).

[72] See now Access to Justice Act 1999, s 6(6) and sch 2.

[73] *Hansard* HL Debates vol 528 col 553 (29 April 1991).

[74] *Ibid*, cols 555 and 563–64. Indeed, the original CSA 1991 was more prescriptive in this regard than its social security counterpart: sch 3, para 2(2) provided that the three tribunal members 'must not all be of the same sex'. The parallel social security rule (now repealed) was merely that 'If practicable, at least one of the members of the tribunal hearing a case shall be of the same sex as the claimant', Social Security Act 1975, sch 10, para 1(8).

[75] Not without some adverse comment; see eg Lord Simon of Glaisdale's complaint about the 'fragmentation of our system of judicature in order to provide additional specialisation', *Hansard* HL Debates vol 528 col 1810 (16 May 1991).

[76] Now presumably the Secretary of State for Constitutional Affairs; this is not a 'protected function' of the Lord Chancellor within Constitutional Reform Act 2005, s 19 and sch 7.

[77] CSA 1991, s 45(1).

[78] See pp 226–36 above and p 435 below.

[79] The DSS consultation paper reported that the Independent Tribunal Service received a total of 216,754 appeals in the previous year, of which just 7,947 (less than 4%) were child support appeals: n 25 above, at 62. This proportion has since fallen to less than 2%: DWP *Work and Pensions Statistics 2004* at 213, Table 3.

[80] See further N Wikeley, 'Burying Bell: Managing the Judicialisation of Social Security Tribunals' (2000) 63 *Modern Law Review* 475.

child support system.[81] There was likewise little attention devoted to child support appeals in the parliamentary debates.[82] Formally the 1998 Act created 'unified appeal tribunals' from the merger of the various tribunals (including child support appeal tribunals) within the remit of what is now known as the Appeals Service.[83] Regulations made under the 1998 Act subsequently provided that the default position is that appeal tribunals should consist of a legally qualified panel member sitting alone.[84] Thus, by a side-wind, three-person child support appeal tribunals with both legal and lay membership became appeal tribunals usually consisting of a lawyer sitting alone, much in the way a county court district judge does—but without the latter's broad discretion in family matters. The need to reflect both sexes in the composition of the tribunal, regarded as so important in 1991, had apparently become readily dispensable by 1998.

The Composition of the Appeal Tribunal

It follows that the appeal tribunal which hears a child support appeal will normally comprise a single legally qualified panel member. These lawyer members are either salaried full-time judicial office holders (known within the Appeals Service as District Chairmen) or part-time chairmen, typically local practitioners.[85] The lawyer member will not always sit alone; he or she may be joined as part of the tribunal by a financially qualified panel member (ie an accountant).[86] The regulations provide that such a two-person tribunal should sit to hear child support appeals raising 'issues which are, in the opinion of the President, difficult' and which relate to matters such as the interpretation of accounts.[87] In practice, of course, the President does not exercise this judgment on an individual case-by-case basis; instead, District Chairmen typically give directions in appropriate appeals for the case to be listed before a tribunal which includes a financially qualified member.[88] The Child Support Commissioners have also emphasised the

---

[81] See eg *Annual Report of the Council on Tribunals for 1997/98* (Session 1998/99, HC 45) paras 1.2–1.20 on SSA 1998, which does not mention the child support issue.

[82] The only substantive (and very short) debates on SSA 1998, s 42 (on child support appeals) were at Standing Committee B, cols 315–19 (11 November 1997) and *Hansard* HL Debates vol 588 col 433 (2 April 1998).

[83] SSA 1998, s 4. The introduction of the 'unified appeal tribunal' was really a semantic change: to this day there are separate tribunal lists for different types of appeal (eg general social security, DLA, child support) and not all chairmen are appointed to sit in all jurisdictions.

[84] SI 1999/991, reg 36(1). In practice the bulk of appeals concern incapacity or disability benefits, which are heard by two or three member tribunals respectively: *ibid*, reg 36(2) and (6); see also SSA 1998, s 7(1).

[85] See *ibid*, ss 6 and 7(2) for the qualifying criteria for appointment.

[86] Exceptionally a further member may be appointed, eg for the purposes of judicial induction: SI 1999/991, reg 36(5).

[87] *Ibid*, reg 36(3)(b).

[88] A rather different approach has been adopted in Northern Ireland since 2004, where the President of the Appeals Service has taken a deliberate policy decision to include accountant members in all tribunals hearing child support appeals.

value of having the tribunal constituted in this fashion, especially in cases involving the interpretation of a self-employed non-resident parent's accounts.[89]

The Right of Appeal to a Tribunal

Only a 'qualifying person', usually a person with care or a non-resident parent, enjoys the right of appeal to a tribunal.[90] The right of appeal exists in relation to the following decisions of the Secretary of State:[91]

— to make a maintenance calculation or a default or interim maintenance decision, whether as originally taken or following a revision or supersession;[92]
— not to make a maintenance calculation or not to supersede a decision;
— to make a reduced benefit decision;[93]
— to impose penalty payments or fees;[94]
— to adjust amounts payable under a maintenance calculation in the light of voluntary payments or overpayments of child support.[95]

This list covers most important decisions taken by the Agency's staff. Decisions relating to variation applications are not included as they are an integral part of the decision on the maintenance calculation, and so an independent right of appeal is unnecessary.[96] If the decision in question is not appealable, for example a refusal to revise, it may still be possible to lodge a late appeal against an earlier decision. In principle, if not readily in practice, judicial review may be available in respect of non-appealable decisions. The tribunal's jurisdiction is defined by these statutory provisions, and so the parties can neither extend nor restrict the tribunal's jurisdiction, whether by agreement between or amongst themselves or unilaterally.[97] Similarly, the tribunal has no jurisdiction over questions of enforcement—these are for the Secretary of State and the courts.[98]

Those with the right of appeal must be given notice both of the decision in question and of that right.[99] The appeal must be submitted in writing, either on

---

[89] *CCS/872/2000.*

[90] CSA 1991, s 20(1); the term 'qualifying person' also includes children in Scotland applying under *ibid*, s 7, and certain others affected by appealable decisions: *ibid*, s 20(2).

[91] *Ibid*, s 20(1)(a)–(e).

[92] See also SI 1999/991, reg 30A.

[93] The reduced benefit decision must have taken effect: CSA 1991, s 20(6).

[94] At present the Agency is not imposing penalty payments or fees.

[95] SI 1999/991, reg 30A.

[96] Departure decisions, on the other hand, required an independent right of appeal: see CSA 1991, sch 4C, para 3 (now repealed) and *R(CS) 9/02.*

[97] *R(SB) 15/87* paras 10–11 (Tribunal of Commissioners), *CCS/449/1995* para 5 *per* Mrs Commissioner Heggs and *CCS/2083/2004* para 10 *per* Mr Commissioner Jacobs. See further on jurisdictional issues, Jacobs and Douglas, n 39 above, at 71–72.

[98] *R(CS) 5/98* para 6 *per* Mr Commissioner Rowland.

[99] CSA 1991, s 20(3) and SI 1999/991, reg 15C (*ibid*, reg 28 is in pt IV, ch I which expressly excludes child support appeals). The extent to which this happens in practice is a matter of some dispute.

the official appeal form or in some other form accepted by the Secretary of State, citing the decision being challenged and giving grounds for the appeal, and must be sent to an office of the Agency.[100] Any appeal must be lodged within one month of the notification of the decision being challenged.[101] In practice this gives appellants rather less than one month in which to act, as time starts to run from the date the decision is sent out, whereas the appeal must actually be received within the time limit.[102] The Agency itself may admit a late appeal, but only if this is regarded as being 'in the interests of justice', as defined by the regulations.[103] An Appeals Service legally qualified panel member has a slightly wider discretion to admit a late appeal, either in the 'interests of justice' or alternatively where there are 'reasonable prospects that the appeal will be successful', in both instances again as defined by the regulations.[104] No appeal may be brought more than one year after the expiry of the normal one month limit.[105] Overall, these provisions on admitting late appeals are less generous than those that apply to appeals from the tribunals themselves to a Child Support Commissioner.

Although the focus in this section is on the tribunal's appellate jurisdiction, it should not be overlooked that tribunals may also make initial decisions on applications for a variation from the formula in those cases which are referred to them by the Secretary of State for this purpose.[106] However, the Secretary of State has no power to refer an application for a supersession of an existing departure direction, and so the tribunal lacks jurisdiction to hear any such 'referral'.[107]

Before the Tribunal Hearing

The Agency's offices forward appeals to the Central Appeals Unit at Lytham St Annes, which in turn sends the appeal on to the relevant Appeals Service regional office with a submission on behalf of the Agency. The submission should include a copy of the decision in issue with an explanation as to how it was reached, supported by relevant evidence (copies of Agency calculations, correspondence from the parties and evidence submitted).[108] In preparing the submission, the Agency

---

[100] SI 1999/991, reg 33.

[101] Or, where a statement of reasons has been requested, within a further 14 days: *ibid*, reg 31(1). If the original decision has been revised or superseded, the time limit runs from the notification of the new decision: *ibid*, reg 31(2).

[102] *Ibid*, reg 2; for a discussion as to whether this rule infringes ECHR Art 6, see *CDLA/5413/1999* and see also *CCS/6302/1999*.

[103] SI 1999/991, reg 32(4)(b); on the 'interests of justice', see *ibid* reg 32(5)–(8).

[104] *Ibid*, reg 32(4).

[105] *Ibid*, reg 32(1) (or the longer period otherwise permitted under reg 31). The 13 month absolute limit was held to be human rights compliant in *Denson v Secretary of State for Work and Pensions*, reported as *R(CS) 4/04*.

[106] CSA 1991, s 28D(1)(b). For criticism of this provision, see p 370 above. An application for a variation may be amended to include another ground: see *R(CS) 3/01*.

[107] *CSC 3/04-05*.

[108] *R(CS) 1/99* para 8 *per* Mr Commissioner Mesher.

will ask the parties whether they wish their addresses or any other information 'which could reasonably be expected to lead' to them being located to be withheld from the appeal papers.[109] In practice the Agency can be over zealous in seeking to protect parties' confidentiality, with the result that all sorts of relevant material may be excised from the papers (eg the name and address of one party's lawyer or accountant).[110] Subject to the confidentiality rule, and the special rule relating to potentially harmful medical evidence,[111] any relevant evidence must be made available to all parties.[112]

A number of interlocutory steps may be taken before the appeal comes on for hearing.[113] The regulations provide that the procedure for the consideration and determination of an appeal is a matter for a legally qualified panel member.[114] In particular, he or she may give such directions as are 'necessary or desirable for the just, effective and efficient conduct of the proceedings', either of his or her own initiative or in response to a party's application.[115] For example, where both parents have appealed against the same decision, their appeals should be heard together.[116] This also includes the power to direct parties to provide such details or produce such documents as may reasonably be required. Used appropriately, this may be a means of encouraging an otherwise non co-operative party to produce relevant evidence. Tribunal chairmen frequently issue such directions with the warning that if the party in question fails to comply, without good reason, then the tribunal will draw such inferences as it thinks fit.[117] Tribunals lack any other effective sanctions to deal with breach; for example, they have no power to punish for contempt.[118] If an oral hearing is to take place, tribunal chairmen may also summon witnesses to attend 'to answer any question or produce any documents'.[119] This might include, for example, an official from a bank with whom a party holds an account.[120] However, again the regulations provide for no effective

---

[109] SI 1999/991, reg 44.

[110] See the discussion in *R(CS) 3/06*, where the law governing disclosure was described as 'a bewildering hotchpotch' at para 19 *per* Mr Commissioner Jacobs.

[111] SI 1999/991, reg 44.

[112] See *CCS/1925/2002* (hearing unfair when evidence sent by NRP to Appeals Service but not disclosed to PWC until a few minutes before the hearing over two months later), which also notes that CSA 1991, s 2 may be relevant to issues of disclosure.

[113] For an early account, when these matters were handled centrally by ITS, see S Pinder, 'Interlocutory decisions in Child Support Appeal Tribunals' (1996) 3 *Journal of Social Security Law* 36.

[114] SI 1999/991, reg 38(1).

[115] *Ibid*, reg 38(2). Tribunal clerks have a much more limited power to issue directions: *ibid*, reg 38(3).

[116] *R(CS) 4/98*.

[117] See *CCS/2061/2000* and *CCS/3757/2004*.

[118] It is arguable that the courts have the power to punish for such contempt, if a tribunal is a 'court' within Contempt of Court Act 1991, s 19, as to which 'a case can be made', see CJ Miller, *Contempt of Court* (Oxford University Press, Oxford, 2000, 3rd edn), para 3.22.

[119] SI 1999/991, reg 43(1). This is subject to the normal court rules on compellability: *ibid*, reg 38(2).

[120] This was used to good effect by the tribunal at first instance in *CSC 6/03-04(T)*.

remedy in the event of breach[121]—although the tribunal is entitled to proceed without such testimony.[122]

There are three circumstances in which an appeal may come to an end without going before a tribunal.[123] First, as has already been seen, if the Agency decides to revise the decision as a result of its reconsideration while preparing the submission on the case, the appeal will lapse unless the revised decision is no more favourable to the appellant.[124] Secondly, the appellant has the right to withdraw an appeal at any time before it is determined; such a withdrawal request may be made either before the hearing (in which case it must be in writing) or at the oral hearing itself.[125] This is an absolute right; there is no requirement that the tribunal (let alone another party) consents.[126] Finally, the regulations provide for certain types of appeal to be struck out. A tribunal clerk may strike out an appeal for want of prosecution or for failure to comply with any directions.[127] An appellant may make representations to the clerk or to a legally qualified panel member for such an appeal to be reinstated.[128] The further statutory power for legally qualified panel members or tribunals to strike out appeals on the basis that they were 'misconceived' has now been repealed.[129] The regulations make no express provision for dealing with appeals which are outside the tribunal's jurisdiction.[130]

The Tribunal Hearing

Before the changes to the social security appeals system in the late 1990s, the holding of an oral hearing was an automatic part of the process. This is no longer the case; instead, parties must 'opt in' for an oral hearing. Appellants and other parties to the proceedings[131] must indicate on the prescribed form whether they

---

[121] In principle the High Court may issue a subpoena to support a tribunal, although the Appeals Service lacks the administrative machinery for such a process: see Jacobs and Douglas, n 39 above, at 451. However, on at least one occasion Order 38 r 19 of the Supreme Court Rules has been invoked to order a bank to comply with a tribunal's direction: Hadwen and Pawling, n 63 above, at 433.

[122] *Denson v Stevenson*, reported as *R(CS) 2/01*.

[123] If a party dies, the Secretary of State may appoint someone to continue with the appeal: SI 1999/991, reg 34.

[124] CSA 1991, s 16(6) and SI 1991/991, reg 30.

[125] *Ibid*, reg 40. The Secretary of State enjoys a parallel power to withdraw a referral of a variation application.

[126] Similarly, if a maintenance application is withdrawn, the tribunal has no jurisdiction: *CCS/2910/2001*.

[127] SI 1991/991, reg 46.

[128] *Ibid*, reg 47.

[129] See *R(CS) 5/02* and Social Security, Child Support and Tax Credits (Decisions and Appeals) Amendment Regulations 2004 (SI 2004/3368), reg 2(8), repealing SI 1999/991 reg 48.

[130] See Jacobs and Douglas, n 39 above, at 456. Thus it would seem that whereas out of jurisdiction social security appeals can be struck out by a clerk, only a tribunal can strike out an out of jurisdiction child support appeal.

[131] For the definition of 'party to the proceedings', see SI 1999/991, reg 1(3); the term includes the Secretary of State.

want an oral hearing or are content for a hearing 'on the papers'.[132] If the clerk receives a request for an oral hearing within the requisite time limit, then the tribunal must proceed to hold such a hearing.[133] If no oral hearing is requested, the tribunal will proceed to hear the case as a 'paper appeal', either as part of a normal session of oral hearings or in a special 'paper list'.[134] However, a tribunal chairman always has the option of directing an oral hearing if satisfied that this is necessary to enable the tribunal to reach a decision.[135] A failure by the appellant to respond at all may result in the appeal being struck out.[136]

Parties must be given 14 days notice of the time and place of an oral hearing.[137] Clerks and legally qualified panel members have the power to agree to a postponement request made in advance of the hearing, or to decide to postpone an appeal of their own initiative, and tribunals have the power to adjourn a hearing once it has been opened.[138] However, in a series of decisions the Commissioners have held that tribunals are entitled to take a robust line in dealing with parties who fail to attend either with no explanation or for no credible reason. According to Mr Commissioner Jacobs:

> The proceedings before an appeal tribunal and a Commissioner are legal proceedings. They are not a game. If the absent parent is not prepared to participate properly in the proceedings, he must take the consequences. In particular, the tribunal will have to decide whether the circumstances of his refusal to make evidence properly available entitled it to draw adverse inference about his income and other circumstances.[139]

So, if a party who has been given the appropriate notice fails to attend an oral hearing, the tribunal may decide to go ahead in his or her absence, having regard to all the circumstances.[140] This might include, for example, disbelieving a party's statement that he is unable to attend for medical reasons, and so refusing a postponement or adjournment.[141] On the other hand, there will always be cases in which an adjournment is inevitable, typically to obtain further evidence.[142]

As a matter of principle, oral hearings must be in public, although the chairman may decide to hold the hearing in private, for example 'for the protection of the

---

[132] *Ibid*, reg 39(1).

[133] *Ibid*, reg 39(3) and (4).

[134] The regulations make no specific provision for the procedure to be adopted for paper hearings, but see Jacobs and Douglas, n 39 above, at 442–43.

[135] SI 1999/991, reg 39(5).

[136] *Ibid*, regs 39(2) and 46(1)(c) and (d). Responses are subject to a 14 day time limit: *ibid*, reg 39(3).

[137] *Ibid*, reg 49(2); a party may waive this right: *ibid*, reg 49(3).

[138] *Ibid*, reg 51.

[139] *CCS/2901/2002* para 15. See further *CCS/3757/2004* on the drawing of adverse inferences.

[140] SI 1999/991, reg 49(4); the tribunal may not simply dismiss the appeal on the ground of non-attendance: *R(CS) 1/95*. See also SI 1999/991, reg 49(5).

[141] See eg *Denson v Stevenson*, reported as *R(CS) 2/01*, where Simon Brown LJ ruled that the NRP might 'properly be adjudged to be a scheming parent playing the system'.

[142] About one in five child support appeals are adjourned: Appeals Service, *Report by the President of Appeal Tribunals on the standards of decision-making by the Secretary of State 2004–2005* (Appeals Service, London, 2005) at 49. On the principles governing adjournments generally, see N Harris, 'Adjournments in social security tribunals' (1996) 3 *Journal of Social Security Law* 11.

private or family life of one or more parties to the proceedings'.[143] In practice it is extremely unusual for members of the public (other than those connected with the parties) to attend. Any party has the right to be present and to be heard, and may be accompanied by a representative, whether or not he or she is professionally qualified.[144] Whilst this is elementary in terms of the principles of natural justice, this may result in considerable tension at the hearing, for example where one parent insists on being accompanied and represented by a new partner. Parties (and their representatives) may also address the tribunal, give evidence, call witnesses and question any other witnesses.[145] Subject to such specific requirements, the general rule is that the procedure at the hearing is a matter for the chairman to determine.[146] Especially in the child support jurisdiction, the chairman may feel compelled to intervene 'to curtail repetitious or irrelevant submissions'.[147] The chairman also has the power to administer the oath,[148] although views differ amongst tribunals as to the value of this procedure.[149] The formal rules of evidence do not apply.[150] The chairman's tasks include keeping a record of the proceedings by way of a note of the evidence, the submissions made and any other relevant matters (such as an adjournment in the course of the hearing). Any party can apply for a copy of the record of proceedings within the following six months.[151]

The Secretary of State, in the same way as any other 'party to the proceedings', has the right to be present and to be heard, and the Agency may send a 'presenting officer' to the hearing. The role of 'presenting officer' was developed in the social security jurisdiction, with such staff being expected to act as a type of lay 'amicus curiae',[152] so as to assist the tribunal in arriving at the correct decision. This has proven to be a problematic role in social security appeals, given that presenting officers are departmental staff, but they face further difficulties in a child support appeal in that they may feel obliged to explain and defend the Agency's decision in

---

[143] SI 1991/991, reg 49(6)(b). Prior to 2002, although the presumption was that hearings were in public, a party had an absolute right to request a private hearing.

[144] *Ibid*, reg 49(7)(a) and (8); see *ibid* reg 49(9) for other persons who are entitled to be present at a hearing, whether in public or private. A person may be 'present' by a live television link: *ibid*, reg 49(7)(b) and (13).

[145] *Ibid*, reg 49(8) and (11).

[146] *Ibid*, reg 49(1).

[147] Jacobs and Douglas, n 39 above, at 482. See Davis, Wikeley and Young, n 21 above, at 142–45. This may well require the chairman to keep 'a discrete eye on the clock', *CCS/252/2000* at para 6 *per* Mr Commissioner Jacobs.

[148] SI 1999/991, reg 43(5).

[149] See Jacobs and Douglas, n 39 above, at 485–87.

[150] For a full analysis, *see ibid*, at 465–76. On the admissibility and weight to be attached to judgments and documentation from earlier court proceedings, see *R(CS) 4/00*, *CCS/4438/2001*, *CCS/3749/2003* and *CCS/1495/2005*.

[151] SI 1999/991, reg 55.

[152] Or 'friend of the court'; see further N Wikeley and R Young, 'Presenting Officers in Social Security Appeal Tribunals: The Theory and Practice of the Curious Amici' (1991) 18 *Journal of Law and Society* 464.

front of two warring parents.[153] The Commissioners have emphasised the importance of presenting officers attending tribunal hearings, given 'the tripartite nature of child support proceedings and the need for the tribunal to take account of every possible consideration that may affect the children themselves'.[154] In recent years, much to the chagrin of both the Appeals Service and the Commissioners,[155] the norm has been for the Department to fail to send a presenting officer to hearings of social security appeals, and non-attendance now appears to be a serious problem in child support tribunals as well. However, when such officers do attend, Appeals Service chairmen have specifically commended the standard of presentation in child support cases.[156]

Are Appeal Tribunals Inquisitorial or Adversarial?

Social security appeal tribunals have traditionally espoused an inquisitorial approach, with an 'investigative function [that] has as its object the ascertainment of the facts and the determination of the truth'. The tribunal 'is not restricted, as in ordinary litigation where there are proceedings between the parties, to accepting or rejecting the respective contentions' of the claimant and the Department.[157] Allied with the 'enabling role' identified by early researchers as a goal for such tribunals,[158] this became part of the corporate judicial philosophy of the Independent Tribunal Service and later the Appeals Service.[159] Subsequent researchers demonstrated that tribunal practice often fell some way short of the ideal; despite the apparent informality of tribunals, 'procedures remain inherently "adversarial" and often legalistic'.[160] Yet, given the common organisational structure and personnel, it was perhaps inevitable that the child support tribunals would adopt the same rhetoric (if not always the reality) of the inquisitorial philosophy. The Commissioners were quick to reinforce this approach. In one of the earliest appeals to that level, the Commissioner held, echoing the social security

---

[153] Or, literally, *between* two warring parents, as the presenting officer will typically sit facing the tribunal and between the two other parties.

[154] *CCS/2618/1995* para 11 *per* Mr Commissioner Howell QC. This should include taking 'an active role in challenging the case put forward by the parties attending the appeal, and drawing attention to possible opposing arguments or interpretations of the facts'.

[155] And also the Council on Tribunals: see *Annual Report 2003/2004* (Session 2003–04, HC 750) at 23.

[156] Appeals Service President's Report, n 142 above, at 36.

[157] *R(S) 4/82* para 25 *per* Tribunal of Commissioners. This approach has consistently been approved by the higher courts; see eg *R v Deputy Industrial Injuries Commissioner, ex p Moore* [1965] 1 QB 456 at 486ff.

[158] See especially K Bell, *Research Study on Supplementary Benefit Appeal Tribunals* (DHSS, London, 1975).

[159] See generally Wikeley, n 80 above, at 494–95.

[160] H Genn, 'Tribunals and Informal Justice' (1993) 56 *Modern Law Review* 393 at 398. See also J Baldwin, N Wikeley and R Young, *Judging Social Security* (Clarendon Press, Oxford, 1992), ch 4 and H Genn, B Lever and L Gray, *Tribunals for diverse users* (DCA research report 1/2006 (DCA, London, 2006).

case law, that the new tribunals were 'under a general duty to inquire into all material issues to which a case before them gives rise'. Furthermore, they were 'there to determine the true entitlements and obligations of the people involved in the cases before them, and are not limited by the opposing contentions made to them'.[161]

In principle, at their inception, child support tribunals had the potential to be more inquisitorial than their social security counterparts, in that they were given powers to summon witnesses and to order the production of documents, which originally had no parallel in the arena of social security.[162] Early research, however, found that tribunals were reluctant to use these powers.[163] There is, moreover, a fundamental difficulty with applying the social security model of an inquisitorial procedure to child support appeals. In short, social security appeals are 'state v citizen' disputes whereas many child support appeals are, by their very nature, tripartite and often bitterly contested.[164] In this context, Baroness Hale's characterisation of the social security inquisitorial approach as 'a co-operative process of investigation in which both the claimant and the department play their part'[165] has little resonance. In effect, child support matters are a hybrid form of process: 'the proceedings may be adversarial as between the two parents but the role of the Secretary of State in child support cases is investigatory. Tribunals, too, "form part of the statutory machinery for investigating claims" '.[166] Given the weaknesses of the Agency in investigating cases at first instance, this may put tribunals in an impossible position. They must somehow reconcile a commitment to an inquisitorial approach, and so judicially 'determine the true entitlements and obligations of the people involved in the cases before them',[167] whilst striving to avoid the perceptions of bias that will inevitably arise if they appear to be doing the Agency's job for it.[168]

Changes made by the SSA 1998 have limited further the extent to which tribunals hearing child support appeals may be regarded as truly inquisitorial.[169] The legislation now provides that tribunals 'need not consider any issue that is not raised by the appeal',[170] although it is unclear whether this provision merely codifies the previous law and practice or whether it seeks to limit the tribunal's inquisitorial approach.[171] A more serious constraint is the statutory stipulation

---

[161] *CCS/12/1994*, para 46, *per* Mr Commissioner Howell QC.

[162] The powers in SI 1991/991, regs 38 and 43 are now of general application.

[163] See Davis, Wikeley and Young, n 21 above, at 148–52.

[164] This was reflected in *CCS/2/1994*, where the Commissioner advised tribunals to adopt a primarily inquisitorial approach to issues between the PWC/NRP and the Agency, but a primarily adversarial approach to disputes between the PWC and NRP.

[165] *Kerr v Department for Social Development* [2004] UKHL 23; [2004] 1 WLR 1372 at para 62.

[166] *CCS/2861/2001* para 7 *per* Mr Commissioner Rowland.

[167] n 161 above.

[168] See Mr Commissioner Powell's warnings in *CCS/61/2003*, para 8 and *CCS/4503/2003*, para 12.

[169] For criticism of these changes in the field of social security, see Wikeley, n 80 above, at 495–98.

[170] CSA 1991, s 20(7)(a); see *R(CS) 1/03*.

[171] The NI Court of Appeal has held that the former is the case; the parallel provision in the social security context demands that tribunals adopt 'a more proactive approach', *Mongan v Department for Social Development* [2005] NICA 16.

that tribunals 'shall not take into account any circumstances not obtaining at the time when the Secretary of State made the decision'.[172] This prevents tribunals from considering the prospective effect of any changes of circumstances after the date of the Agency's decision. Tribunals and Commissioners have shown some ingenuity in applying this limit on a tribunal's powers; thus the rule does not preclude a tribunal relying on evidence which, although occurring after the date of the Agency's decision, refers back to some earlier period (eg business accounts produced after the Agency's decision may justify a finding that income has changed before that decision). Yet this approach may only assist at the margins. The fact remains that a party who believes, not unreasonably from a lay point of view, that the tribunal will be able to make relevant findings of fact and resolve all disputes 'down to the date of the hearing' will be sorely disappointed. Rather, a change of circumstances that post-dates the Agency's decision will need to be the subject of a separate application for a supersession (which in turn will carry its own appeal rights). The consequence is inevitably a fragmentation of, and further delay in, the proceedings and a sense of deep frustration on the part of those disadvantaged by this restriction on the tribunal's jurisdiction. This is a long way from the traditional approach of the courts to roll matters up to date.

The Tribunal's Decision

Typically, as we have seen, a tribunal will comprise a legally qualified panel member sitting alone, and so the decision of the tribunal will be the decision of that individual. Where the tribunal sits with a financially qualified panel member, the lawyer member is the chairman and, in the event of any disagreement, has the casting vote.[173] The tribunal may dismiss the appeal, in which case the Agency's decision stands, or it may allow the appeal; in the latter eventuality it may either make such decision as it considers appropriate or remit the case to the Secretary of State with directions as necessary.[174] About half of all appeals relating to child support assessments are successful.[175]

The regulations require the chairman to record the tribunal's decision in summary form on a standard template.[176] The normal practice is to announce the decision orally at the end of the hearing, with or without having had a recess for

---

[172] CSA 1991, s 20(7)(b).

[173] SSA 1998, s 7(3). In practice it is very unusual to have majority decisions in tribunals, at least in the social security jurisdiction: see Baldwin, Wikeley and Young, n 21 above, at 147. If there is a dissenting view, this must be recorded on the decision notice and the reasons explained in any statement of reasons: SI 1999/991, reg 53(5).

[174] CSA 1991, s 20(8). The 1991 Act originally required tribunals to remit allowed appeals to the Secretary of State (CSA 1991, s 20(3), as first enacted). This was replaced with the current broader power in 1998—but there has been little difference, and in practice tribunals must give decisions in the form of directions 'setting out findings and principles by reference to which the absent parent's liability for child support maintenance is to be determined', *CCS/284/1999*, para 25 *per* Mr Commissioner Jacobs.

[175] DWP, n 79 above, at 213, Table 3.

[176] SI 1999/991, reg 53(1)–(2). The decision need not actually be signed: *CCS/14/1994*.

deliberations,[177] and to hand the summary decision notice to the parties.[178] The summary notice, by definition, includes only the tribunal's decision and possibly a brief outline of its findings and reasons on the main points in dispute.[179] Depending on the circumstances, the tribunal's decision notice may well not specify the actual amount of child support payable. Given the complexity of the scheme, tribunals simply lack the time and resources to undertake the necessary calculations. Usually the tribunal's role is confined to deciding the points in dispute (eg the level of the non-resident parent's income, the amount of shared care, etc) and so the matter is then remitted to the Secretary of State for the necessary further calculations.[180] It is incumbent upon the Agency to implement the tribunal's decision and to comply with its directions.[181] The parties (including the Secretary of State) may apply for a statement of reasons, commonly known as a 'full statement', within one month of receipt of the summary notice.[182] A chairman may extend this time limit to a maximum of three months from the date of the original notification, if it is 'in the interests of justice' (as that term is narrowly defined in the regulations) to grant such a late application.[183] There are also powers to correct accidental errors in decisions (and presumably in full statements) and to set decisions aside on procedural grounds, such as where a party failed to receive notification of the hearing or copies of relevant papers.[184]

The Right of Appeal to a Child Support Commissioner

There is a right of appeal from a tribunal's decision[185] to a Child Support Commissioner, which may be exercised by either the Secretary of State or 'any person who is aggrieved' by its decision.[186] There is no statutory definition of an 'aggrieved person' for child support purposes,[187] but in practice it will mean one

[177] See SI 1999/991, reg 49(12).

[178] *Ibid*, reg 53(3). Parties are also given a note explaining their rights to seek a statement of reasons and to appeal. A tribunal may decide to communicate its decision by post eg in a particularly complex matter or where there are concerns as to how one or more parties will react to the decision. Obviously if a party fails to attend, the decision notice and explanatory note are sent on by post. Decision notices may also be sent by e-mail: *ibid*, reg 57AA.

[179] There is no statutory requirement to give reasons in the summary notice, but some chairmen adopt this practice, no doubt partly to assist the parties but also partly in the hope that this might head off a request for a (time-consuming) full statement.

[180] *CCS/5310/1995* paras 14–15 and *CCS/4741/1995* paras 20–21. As Jacobs and Douglas, n 39 above, at 496 observe, there should be liberty to restore the matter to the tribunal in the event of any dispute as to the consequences of the tribunal's decision.

[181] *R(CS) 3/98* para 15.

[182] SI 1991/991, reg 53(4).

[183] *Ibid*, reg 54.

[184] *Ibid*, regs 56 and 57; and see reg 53(4A) on time limits in such cases.

[185] On the scope of the term 'decision' in this context see the discussion in Jacobs and Douglas, n 39 above, at 79–82.

[186] CSA 1991, s 24(1).

[187] A PWC who had taken no earlier part in the proceedings was held to be an aggrieved person in *R(CS)15/98*.

or other parent.[188] Indeed, individual parents bring the vast majority of appeals to the Commissioner; the Secretary of State is only likely to lodge an appeal if the Agency believes that an authoritative ruling is required on a particular point. Whoever brings the appeal, it must involve 'a question of law'.[189] The Commissioners' jurisprudence from the social security jurisdiction has identified the following main heads as being errors of law on the part of an appeal tribunal: misinterpreting or misapplying the law; reaching a decision for which there is no evidence (or which no reasonable tribunal could have reached on the available evidence); breaching the rules of natural justice; and failing to make proper findings of fact or to give adequate reasons for its decision.[190]

The Secretary of State or 'aggrieved person' must first apply to the tribunal chairman[191] for leave to appeal within one month of being sent the tribunal's full statement of reasons.[192] This period can be extended by up to one year if the tribunal chairman accepts that there are 'special reasons' for admitting the late application.[193] The term 'special reasons' is left undefined by the legislation and so is potentially a much wider concept than the restricted grounds on which a late appeal to a tribunal can be admitted.[194] Originally the chairman's decision was a simple binary one, either to grant or to refuse leave. Chairmen now have a third option; if they take the view that the tribunal's decision is wrong in law, they can set it aside and order a rehearing.[195] The great advantage of this procedure is that it avoids the need for the full panoply of an appeal to a Commissioner in a case which would in any event be sent back for rehearing. If the tribunal chairman refuses leave,[196] the applicant may renew the application by applying to a Child Support Commissioner for leave.[197] The application to the Commissioner must normally be made within one month of the tribunal's refusal of leave, but again the Commissioner may allow an out-of-time application where there are 'special reasons', providing no more than a year has elapsed.[198] Whether the application

---

[188] In Scotland, a child applicant under the 1991 Act could clearly be a 'person aggrieved'; whether a parent's new partner could be a 'person aggrieved' has not to date arisen for determination.

[189] CSA 1991, s 24(1).

[190] *R(A) 1/72, R(SB) 11/83, R(IS) 11/99.* For a comprehensive analysis, see Jacobs and Douglas, n 39 above, at 82–91.

[191] CSA 1991, s 24(6)(a) and SI 1999/1305, reg 10(6).

[192] Child Support Commissioners (Procedure) Regulations 1999 (SI 1999/1305), reg 10(1). If (but only if) the applicant for leave is the Secretary of State, the other parties must be informed and be given the opportunity to comment on the application: ibdi, reg 10(2)–(3). But see on late applications for leave *CCS/2064/1999.*

[193] *Ibid,* reg 10(5). Note also the special rule in reg 10(7), which seems designed to deal with *CCS/2884/2003,* holding that SI 1999/991, reg 57A was ultra vires so far as the child support legislation is concerned.

[194] See p 418 above and on 'special reasons' see Jacobs and Douglas, n 39 above, at 527–28.

[195] CSA 1991, s 23A. In the unlikely event that all parties agree on the tribunal being in error of law, the chairman *must* set aside the decision and direct a rehearing: *ibid,* s 23A(3).

[196] In theory the tribunal chairman's refusal of leave may be open to judicial review, but only in the plainest of cases. In practice it is far simpler to seek leave direct from a Commissioner.

[197] SI 1999/1305, reg 10(1), which makes it clear that an application must first be made to the tribunal chairman.

[198] SI 1999/1305, reg 10.

for leave is made to the tribunal chairman or to a Commissioner, the regulations specify certain details and other procedural requirements which must be met.[199] There are similar requirements for a notice of appeal proper.[200] There is no right of appeal against the Commissioner's determination on an application for leave, although judicial review remains a possibility.[201]

Second Tier Appeals: The Child Support Commissioners

The Child Support Commissioners

The judicial office of Child Support Commissioner was first established by the 1991 Act, although in practice the jurisdiction was bolted on to the existing jurisdiction of the Social Security Commissioners,[202] in the same way as the Independent Tribunal Service (now the Appeals Service) assumed responsibility for first tier appeals. As a result the judge who is the Chief Social Security Commissioner is also the Chief Child Support Commissioner, and other Social Security Commissioners are likewise Child Support Commissioners.[203] The combination of roles was probably inevitable once the decision had been taken to route first tier appeals away from the courts and to the appeal tribunals. This arrangement has also enabled the Commissioners to bring their expertise in interpreting complex social security regulations to the equally dense undergrowth of child support law. Furthermore, the relatively low caseload of second tier appeals could hardly have justified the establishment of an entirely new second tier appellate machinery.[204] The Commissioners, who are essentially specialist social security judges, tend to be recruited from three sources: from practice, typically but not necessarily at the Bar; from the ranks of Appeals Service district chairmen; and from academia.[205] There are also a number of Deputy Child Support Commissioners who sit on a part-time basis.[206]

---

[199] SI 1999/1305, reg 11.

[200] *Ibid*, regs 14–15. With the parties' consent, a Commissioner may treat an application for leave to appeal as an appeal proper, thereby avoiding any further delay in the matter: *ibid*, reg 13(3).

[201] *Bland v Chief Supplementary Benefit Officer* [1983] 1 WLR 262 (also reported as *R(SB) 12/83*). See also *CSC 1/05-06* on the Commissioner's inherent power to set aside a refusal of a late application for leave to appeal.

[202] On the history of the Commissioners' jurisdiction, see D Bonner, 'From whence the Social Security Commissioners? The creation of the National Insurance Commissioner and the Industrial Injuries Commissioner' (2002) 9 *Journal of Social Security Law* 11. See further T Buck, D Bonner and R Sainsbury, *Making Social Security Law* (Ashgate, Aldershot, 2005).

[203] The qualifications for appointment are the same: see CSA 1991, s 22 and sch 4 (*ibid*, s 23 and sch 4, para 8 for Northern Ireland) and SSA 1998, s 14(12) and sch 4. See further the Commissioners' website: http://www.osscsc.gov.uk/.

[204] Indeed, the current trend in the wake of the Leggatt Report is towards amalgamating such second tier appellate systems (with the launch of the Tribunals Service in April 2006).

[205] Several Commissioners, of course, have experience in more than one of these fields.

[206] CSA 1991, sch 4, para 4—but, unlike their full-time equivalents, not all Deputy Social Security Commissioners are necessarily appointed as Deputy Child Support Commissioners.

Procedure before the Child Support Commissioner

Once leave to appeal has been granted and a notice of appeal lodged, the Commissioner may give directions on the appeal (eg, where a parent appeals, for the Secretary of State to forward a written submission on the appeal and the respective parties be given the opportunity to make further representations in the light of that submission).[207] In the same way as in the social security jurisdiction, the Child Support Commissioners see their role as being inquisitorial, so the directions on the case may specifically direct that submissions address a particular point identified by the Commissioner (but which may not have been raised by the parties). Parties are at liberty either to conduct an appeal by themselves or with the assistance of any representative, whether or not he or she is legally qualified.[208] Legal aid, however, is not available for proceedings before a Child Support Commissioner, despite appeals being confined to points of law.[209]

An appeal to a Child Support Commissioner does not necessarily involve an oral hearing of the case. Indeed, this tends to be the exception rather than the rule, as the Child Support Commissioners have adopted the same law and practice as applies in the parallel social security appellate jurisdiction. The default position is that a Commissioner may, and usually does, dispose of an appeal without a hearing.[210] Although any party may request a hearing, the regulations stipulate only that the Commissioner 'shall grant the request unless he is satisfied that the proceedings can properly be determined without a hearing'.[211] As one Commissioner has noted, an oral hearing 'is not an opportunity to ask questions about the fairness of the child support scheme or about the facts of the case or the circumstances of the parties'.[212] In the event that an oral hearing is directed, the procedure is the same as before a Social Security Commissioner,[213] and typically involves rather more formality than the average appeal tribunal hearing at first instance.[214] The absence of an oral hearing in most cases may be justified on a number of grounds:

---

[207] SI 1999/1305, regs 18–19. For the Commissioners' general procedural powers, see *ibid* reg 5. To assist with the expeditious transaction of business, some of these powers may be delegated to the Commissioners' legal officers (CSA 1991, sch 4, para 4A and SI 1999/1305, reg 7). There are confidentiality provisions in *ibid*, reg 9.

[208] *Ibid*, reg 17.

[209] Access to Justice Act 1999, s 6(6) and sch 2; however, in exceptional cases funding may be authorised—see *ibid* s 6(8).

[210] SI 1999/1305, reg 21(1). About 4% of all Commissioners' appeals are the subject of oral hearings: Council on Tribunals, n 155 above, at 66–67.

[211] SI 1999/1305, reg 21(2).

[212] *R(CS) 9/02*, para 5 *per* Mr Commissioner Jacobs, and the same Commissioner's comment in *CCS/2128/2001*, para 6, that the Commissioners 'have no general powers or responsibility to investigate or oversee the work of the Child Support Agency'.

[213] SI 1999/1305, reg 22.

[214] The fundamental difference is that at a Commissioner's oral hearing the parties are asked to stand as the Commissioner enters the room, usually to sit at a raised dais, whereas at an appeal tribunal hearing the parties are ushered in to sit down across the table from the tribunal chairman, who is already seated. Beyond that, of course, the conduct of the hearing depends for a large part on the personality and style of the chairman or Commissioner concerned.

appeals are confined to points of law, and so an appeal to the Commissioner is not an opportunity to introduce new evidence; the procedure is inquisitorial, with directions being used to identify and isolate the central arguments in written submissions; furthermore, in many cases a rehearing before a first tier tribunal may be inevitable, and so the case may be more swiftly disposed of at the Commissioner level without a hearing. However, the advent of the Human Rights Act 1998 may have resulted in a tendency to direct oral hearings more readily than was previously the case.

The great majority of appeals are dealt with by a single Commissioner, although the Chief Child Support Commissioner has the power to direct that a case involving 'a question of law of special difficulty' should be considered by a Tribunal of three Commissioners.[215] Given this precondition, an oral hearing would normally be directed in such a case. To date only a handful of such Tribunals of Commissioners have been convened to consider child support appeals.[216]

The Child Support Commissioner's Decision

A Child Support Commissioner has a range of options open to him or her in deciding a case.[217] If the tribunal's decision is found to be correct as a matter of law, then obviously it stands. If, however, the decision is wrong in law, the tribunal's decision *must* be set aside; the Commissioner *may* then *either* give the decision which the tribunal should have done,[218] if this is possible on the available evidence and findings of fact,[219] *or* refer the case back for rehearing by an appeal tribunal.[220] If the latter, the usual practice is for the rehearing to be in front of a differently-constituted tribunal.[221] This raises the possibility, in particularly intractable cases, that the appeal may see-saw to and fro between the two tiers, as each tribunal decision is found wanting in law and a new rehearing ordered. The Commissioner has the power to correct accidental errors in his or her decision and to set aside for a procedural irregularity.[222] Otherwise, and subject to the right of appeal to the Court of Appeal, the decision of a Child Support Commissioner is final.[223]

As is evident from this book, the decisions of the Child Support Commissioners serve as important precedents within the system of child support law. Few cases

---

[215] CSA 1991, sch 4, para 5. See also in the social security jurisdiction, SSA 1998, s 16(7).

[216] See *R(CS) 2/95* and *CCS/2725/2004* in Great Britain and *CSC 6/03-04(T)* and *CSC 7/03-04(T)* in Northern Ireland.

[217] The procedural requirements for a decision are set out in SI 1999/1305, reg 26.

[218] This may, depending on the circumstances, be exactly the same as the tribunal's decision.

[219] Commissioners may find facts for themselves but if the facts are disputed, and the tribunal's findings inadequate, a reference back for a rehearing is more likely.

[220] CSA 1991 s 24(2) and (3); in some cases a reference back to the Secretary of State may be appropriate; *ibid*, s 24(3)(d).

[221] *Ibid*, s 24(4).

[222] SI 1999/1305, regs 27 and 28; there is no right of appeal against such decisions: *ibid*, reg 29(2).

[223] CSA 1991, sch 4, para 6.

will reach the Court of Appeal, and so the Commissioners' decisions on questions of law perform a vital role in the development of this body of law. All appeals to the Commissioners are allotted a file number when they are received by their office; for example, *CCS/1371/2003* was the 1371st case received in the year 2003, and the prefix CCS represents 'Commissioner Child Support'.[224] The file references for Scottish cases employ an extra 'S' in the prefix, for example *CSCS/14/03*. Northern Ireland decisions now have a slightly different form of citation which includes the tax year, eg *CSC 6/03–04*.[225] The Commissioner's decision is then issued to the parties with this file number as its formal reference. The majority of child support decisions at Commissioner level will receive no wider circulation.

However, individual Commissioners may nominate their decisions for inclusion in the database of publicly accessible decisions on the Commissioners' website, if they consider that they may be of wider significance.[226] The Editorial Board of the Commissioners, chaired by the Chief Commissioner and including one Northern Ireland Commissioner, then considers these decisions, and any others drawn to its attention, for 'highlighting'. The Commissioners as a whole are invited to comment on the suitability of such highlighted decisions for formal reporting, and lists of such decisions are likewise periodically circulated to users for their views.[227] Following such consultation, the Editorial Board selects particular highlighted decisions for reporting if they command the support of at least a majority of Commissioners, so as to ensure a reasonable degree of consistency.

Once selected, the decision in question is accorded a new number beginning with an 'R': thus *CCS/1371/2003* has been reported as *R(CS) 1/05*.[228] These reported decisions are published quarterly in loose-leaf format by the DWP and by The Stationery Office in bound volumes every two years.[229] The previous arrangements for reporting Commissioners decisions in the social security jurisdiction were the subject of considerable criticism by the House of Commons Select Committee in 2000,[230] and the problems identified by the Committee account for

---

[224] As opposed, for example to CIS (income support) or CJSA (jobseeker's allowance).

[225] The mode of citation before 2001–02 was eg *CSC 1/94*.

[226] See http://www.osscsc.gov.uk. This allows decisions to be searched eg by subject matter. Northern Ireland decisions are available at http://www.dsdni.gov.uk/index/law_and_legislation/ nidoc_database.htm.

[227] These are available at http://www.osscsc.gov.uk/decisions/highlighted.htm. To confuse matters further, between 1987 and 2001 some selected decisions were subject to a similar process known as starring, and given a different reference number: for example, *CCS/7334/1999* became known as *Starred Decision No 75/01*, and was then later reported as *R(CS) 7/02*. The starring practice has now been discontinued, and this book does not use references to the old starred numbers.

[228] Until 1999, the final digits identified the year in which the decision was selected for reporting. Since 2000, they have indicated the year in which the decision was published by the DSS or (now) DWP. Scottish decisions are not expressly identified as such. Northern Ireland's reported decisions are cited as eg *R 1/03 (CSC)*.

[229] As well as being accessible on the Commissioners' own website, they can also be found on line at the DWP site: http://www.dwp.gov.uk/advisers/docs/commdecs/.

[230] It was a 'chaotic and almost laughable situation', redolent of 'typically British, amateur, worst practice', HC Select Committee on Social Security, *Social Security and Child Support Commissioners*, Fourth Report (Session 1999–2000, HC 263), paras 31–41.

the difficulty in accessing some decisions of the Child Support Commissioners from the mid to late 1990s.[231]

The principles governing the precedent value of decisions of the Child Support Commissioners follow those that apply in the field of social security. Thus Commissioners' decisions, so far as their legal principles are concerned, must be followed by appeal tribunals and decision makers; reported Commissioners' decisions must be given more weight than unreported ones; and, in the event of conflict, a decision of a Tribunal of Commissioners must be followed in preference to the ruling of a single Commissioner.[232] Commissioners' decisions are also 'of high persuasive effect on other Commissioners',[233] and so previous decisions are likely to be followed unless there are very good reasons for taking an alternative view.[234] Constitutionally, Great Britain and Northern Ireland are separate jurisdictions, but in practice Commissioners will pay equal heed to relevant decisions in the neighbouring jurisdiction.[235]

Third Tier Appeals: The Court of Appeal and the Court of Session

There is a further right of appeal from the decision of the Child Support Commissioner to the Court of Appeal (or, in Scotland, to the Court of Session).[236] This right of appeal, as with that from an appeal tribunal to a Commissioner, is confined to 'a question of law'.[237] Similarly, there is also a requirement that leave to appeal be obtained. Only the Secretary of State or a person who was a party to the original (tribunal) decision or the appeal decision may apply for permission to appeal.[238] In the first instance the dissatisfied party must apply to the Child Support Commissioner for leave.[239] The application must be in writing, stating the grounds for applying for leave, and be made within three months of the date the applicant was sent the Commissioner's decision.[240] In practice, applications for leave are considered by the Commissioner who made the decision under appeal. A Commissioner is only likely to grant leave to appeal if satisfied that there

---

[231] Commissioner Howell QC's own website at http://www.hywels.clara.co.uk/commrs/cases.htm provides an invaluable resource for tracking down many of these decisions.

[232] *R(I) 12/75.*

[233] *R(CS) 2/97*, para 16 *per* Mr Commissioner Goodman.

[234] But individual Commissioners may on occasion depart from decisions of Tribunals of Commissioners: see eg *R(CS) 3/04.*

[235] There has perhaps been a degree of convergence in recent years as the arrangements for training and for reporting decisions have become more cross-jurisdictional within the UK. In addition, several full-time Commissioners in GB and Northern Ireland respectively have been appointed to serve as Deputy Commissioners in the 'other' jurisdiction.

[236] CSA 1991, s 25(1) and (3A).

[237] *Ibid,* s 25(1) and see above p 427 on what is a point of law.

[238] CSA 1991, s 25(3). The Act (s 25(3)(c)) allows any other person authorised by regulations made by the Lord Chancellor to apply for leave, but no such regulations have been enacted.

[239] *Ibid,* s 25(2)(a).

[240] SI 1999/1305, reg 30(1).

is clearly an important point of principle at stake; Commissioners incline to the view that it is for the Court of Appeal to determine which types of cases it hears.[241] Furthermore, the Commissioner's determination on leave is not susceptible to appeal, as it is not itself a 'decision' which determines a person's rights for the purposes of the legislation.[242] However, if the Commissioner refuses leave to appeal, the applicant may apply direct to the Court of Appeal (or Court of Session) for permission.[243]

The principles governing the granting of leave to appeal by the Court of Appeal in social security cases were considered in *Cooke v Secretary of State for Social Security*.[244] Hale LJ indicated that the Court 'should take an appropriately modest view, especially when it has heard only one side of the argument, of how likely it is that the Commissioner will have got it wrong',[245] given that the Commissioners are 'a highly expert and specialized legally qualified body', that this is a very technical area of law and that there is an independent two-tier appellate structure in place.[246] Accordingly, although formally the strict test for granting of leave to appeal in the Administration of Justice Act does not apply, the Court of Appeal 'should approach such cases with an appropriate degree of caution' and should adopt 'a robust attitude to the prospect of success criterion'.[247] The combined effect of the attitude towards the granting of leave by the Commissioners and by the Court of Appeal means that in practice few cases will proceed any further than the Child Support Commissioner. This is likely to be all the more so when the costs and delays involved in taking proceedings in the courts and the difficulties in securing legal aid are taken into account. Given the nature of law reporting in this jurisdiction, and the inadequacy of official statistics, it is impossible to be certain as to the precise number of child support appeals which have been heard by the Court of Appeal. However, by the end of 2005—after the scheme had been in force more than a decade—the Court of Appeal appeared to have dealt with at most a total of about 20 cases on appeal from the Child Support Commissioners.[248]

There is a further right of appeal from the Court of Appeal (or the Court of Session) to the House of Lords. There are no specific provisions under the child

---

[241] The general rule (but see below) in the civil courts is that the Court of Appeal should only grant leave if satisfied that there is an important point of principle or practice raised by the case or there is 'some other compelling reason' why the Court should hear the appeal: Administration of Justice Act 1999, s 55(1).

[242] See, by analogy, *Bland v Chief Supplementary Benefit Officer* [1983] 1 All ER 537.

[243] CSA 1991, s 25(2)(b).

[244] [2001] EWCA Civ 734; although this decision was in relation to leave to appeal from the decision of a Social Security Commissioner, the same principles apply to leave to appeal from a Child Support Commissioner: *Baggs v Secretary of State for Work and Pensions* [2005] EWCA Civ 23.

[245] [2001] EWCA Civ 734, para 17.

[246] *Ibid*, para 15.

[247] *Ibid*, paras 16 and 17. On the AJA 1999 s 55 test, see n 241 above.

[248] This figure has been calculated from the author's own library of reported and unreported Court of Appeal decisions made under CSA 1991 up until the end of 2005. This search has identified 14 substantive appeals and 5 other applications for leave. Obviously this total omits cases which have progressed to the Court of Appeal through other routes (eg by way of judicial review), but these account for only a handful of cases (6 have been identified).

support legislation which apply to such further appeals, and so the normal principles governing civil appeals apply. It follows that leave to appeal should in the first place be sought from the Court of Appeal, although in practice the Court—in the same way as the Commissioner at the stage below—adopts a very sparing approach to the granting of leave, taking the view that this is a matter for the House of Lords itself to determine. Assuming the Court of Appeal refuses leave to appeal, the applicant must apply direct to the House of Lords,[249] which will grant leave to appeal only if there is 'a point of law of general public importance' involved. The position is different in Scotland—as a general rule, leave to appeal from the Court of Session to the House of Lords is not required in civil cases.[250] Although this might suggest a differential degree of access to the highest court in the United Kingdom for appellants in child support cases, it does not appear to have had any impact in practice. Indeed, the first occasion on which the House of Lords was called upon to determine a matter of child support law was more than ten years after the inception of the scheme.[251]

The Residual Role of the Courts in Child Support Appeals

It is axiomatic that one of the fundamental purposes of the child support legislation was to oust the role of the courts in deciding most matters relating to child maintenance.[252] However, child support issues still fall to be resolved by the courts in five sets of circumstances. First, as we have already seen, there are those exceptional cases where the courts retain jurisdiction to assess the actual quantum of child maintenance payable.[253] Secondly, and as described in the preceding section, the courts have a role in construing the child support legislation when hearing appeals on points of law from the Child Support Commissioners in cases which have worked their way through the specialised adjudicative machinery established by the 1991 Act. Thirdly, the appeal tribunals and Commissioners have no jurisdiction to determine parentage disputes; such appeals must be commenced in the magistrates' court or, in Scotland, the sheriff's court.[254] The magistrates and sheriffs also have a limited role in hearing appeals relating to deduction of earnings orders.[255] Fourthly, and more generally, the Agency may resort to the courts for

---

[249] Applications (or petitions as they are known at this stage) for leave to appeal are considered by an Appeals Committee of three law lords.

[250] Court of Session Act 1988, s 40. There have, however, been no such appeals from Scotland in the field of child support to date.

[251] *R (on the application of Kehoe) v Secretary of State for Work and Pensions* [2005] UKHL 48; [2006] 1 AC 42.

[252] See generally ch 7.

[253] *Ibid*, pp 190–98.

[254] CSA 1991, s 45 and Child Support Appeals (Jurisdiction of Courts) Order 2002 (SI 2002/1915) and Child Support Appeals (Jurisdiction of Courts) (Scotland) Order 2003 (SSI 2003/96). Such cases may be transferred up the hierarchy of civil courts hearing family matters. See also *R(CS) 13/98*.

[255] P 450 below.

the purposes of enforcing its assessments, for example through a liability order, driving disqualification order or ultimately committal for non-payment of child support.[256] Finally, Agency decisions which may not be challenged through these various statutory routes within the child support legislation—for example, as regards enforcement—may be susceptible to judicial review. In certain circumstances decisions by Child Support Commissioners (such as the decision on whether to grant leave to appeal) or by appeal tribunals may also be open to judicial review. An applicant for judicial review must establish illegality, irrationality or some procedural impropriety on the part of the Secretary of State, appeal tribunal or Commissioner. Applications for judicial review must be heard by the High Court; if successful, the court will set aside the decision and direct that it be reconsidered in an appropriate and lawful fashion. It is inherent in the very nature of judicial review that the High Court has no power to substitute its own decision on the merits for that under challenge. Moreover, as Baroness Hale memorably remarked in her dissenting opinion in *Kehoe*:

> A promise that the Agency is doing its best is not enough. Nor is the threat or reality of judicial review. Most people simply do not have access to the Administrative Court in the way that they used to have access to their local magistrates' court. Judicial review may produce some action from the Agency, but what is needed is money from the absent parent. Action from the Agency will not replace the money which has been irretrievably lost as a result of its failure to act in time.[257]

---

[256] Pp 453–460 below.
[257] *R (Kehoe) v Secretary of State for Work and Pensions* [2005] UKHL 48 at para 72.

14

Collection, Arrears and Enforcement

Introduction

Difficulties in enforcing child maintenance liabilities have been a persistent feature of both public and private law for many years.[1] As Beatrice and Sidney Webb remarked of the old poor law, 'It was easy to get an order made against a putative father for a weekly contribution; but unless he was a man of property or position, its enforcement was quite another matter'.[2] In the second half of the twentieth century, the extent to which the Department pursued liable relatives for financial contributions towards the support of their dependents who were reliant on means-tested benefits varied according to official priorities at the time. Moreover, in explicitly recognising a man's financial support for his new partner and second family as a relevant factor in determining the level of any contribution payable to his first family, social security policy eschewed an overtly ideological approach. That pragmatic realism ended with the advent of the Child Support Act 1991 which was also, in part at least, a response to both the real and perceived failings of the private law system of assessing and enforcing child maintenance. In this chapter we explore the current legislation as regards collecting payments due under child support orders made under the 1991 Act, dealing with arrears and enforcing maintenance calculations against defaulters. In doing so comparisons are made with how these matters—especially the collection and enforcement issues—are handled in other jurisdictions, and in particular in Australia and in the United States of America.

Collection

The Benefit Case / Private Case Distinction

The fundamental distinction in child support law between benefit cases and private cases remains significant in the context of collection procedures. Where the parent with care is in receipt of a relevant benefit, the Secretary of State is entitled

---

[1] See chs 2–5 above.

[2] S Webb and B Webb, *English Poor Law History—Part 1: The Old Poor Law* (Longmans, Green & Co, London, 1927, repr Frank Cass & Co Ltd, 1963) at 309.

to proceed to recover payments of child support from the non-resident parent.[3] This power derives from the parent with care's benefit status; there is no additional requirement for her to authorise the Secretary of State to proceed with such action. The legislation stipulates that the Secretary of State '*may* . . . take action under the Act to recover from the non-resident parent, on the parent's behalf, the child support maintenance so determined',[4] and so in principle the child's welfare must be considered.[5] In practice this appears to be assumed and the normal expectation is that collection action will follow automatically.[6] In private cases, however, the Secretary of State can only so act if the parent with care expressly requests the minister to proceed with collection and/or enforcement.[7] There is no requirement for such authorisation to be made at the time of the application for the maintenance calculation. A private client may ask the Agency simply to make an assessment, and not to become involved in collection, in the expectation or hope that the non-resident parent will comply with the outcome. If payments are not forthcoming, she can request the Agency to undertake collection at some later stage. Moreover, in private cases the parent with care 'may at any time request [the Secretary of State] to cease acting under this section'.[8] It follows that parents with care in private cases enjoy a series of choices denied to those in benefit cases; they can decide whether or not to apply for a formula-based maintenance calculation in the first place, they can elect whether to ask the Agency also to arrange for collection or enforcement or to arrange payment privately and they can, at a later stage, request the Secretary of State to desist from pursuing the matter.

The Secretary of State's own powers as regards the collection of maintenance fall into two categories, depending on whether the maintenance in question has been determined under the 1991 Act or through the ordinary courts.

Collection of Child Support Maintenance

The Secretary of State's powers to collect payments of child support maintenance derive from section 29 of the 1991 Act. This provision entitles the Secretary of State to arrange for the collection of any child support maintenance payable as a result of a maintenance calculation in a benefit or a private case.[9] It also provides that payments of child support maintenance 'shall be made' in accordance with regulations made by the Secretary of State.[10] It follows that this latter provision applies to all cases, and not simply to those in which the Secretary of State is

---

[3] CSA 1991, s 6(1)–(3).
[4] *Ibid*, s 6(3)(b).
[5] *Ibid*, s 2.
[6] Child Support Agency, *Procedures: Specialist Areas*, 'When to Consider Welfare of the Child' at 2507 cites various examples of specific discretionary collection decisions (eg whether to impose a DEO) but makes no mention of the initial s 6(3)(b) decision.
[7] CSA 1991, s 4(2). As regards children's independent rights in Scotland, see *ibid* s 7(3).
[8] *Ibid*, s 4(5). For the parallel provision for children in Scotland, see *ibid* s 7(6).
[9] *Ibid*, s 29(1).
[10] *Ibid*, s 29(2).

arranging collection. Therefore, in theory at least, non-resident parents in private cases, where the parties have made their own arrangements for payment, are still bound to comply with the regulations governing collection procedures. It is not obvious what sanctions apply in the case of non-compliance, other than the parent with care's right at any stage to return to the Agency and to ask it to take over responsibility for collection. The remainder of section 29 merely gives an indication as to the types of issues which can be covered in the regulations.[11]

The relevant regulations are contained in Part II of the Child Support (Collection and Enforcement) Regulations 1992.[12] These regulations provide that the Secretary of State may direct the liable person to make payments to the person caring for the child[13] or to or through the Secretary of State or his or her nominee.[14] As a matter of policy, the Agency's preferred method of payment in private cases is 'maintenance direct' (ie direct to the parent with care) rather than 'non maintenance direct' (ie via the Agency).[15] In benefit cases the official position is now neutral,[16] whereas previously it pressed parties to arrange for payment through the Agency.[17] The regulations depart from the standard usage of 'person with care' or 'parent with care' and instead refer to 'the person caring for the child or children in question'. This enables the Agency to specify that payment of child support maintenance should be made to someone who is temporarily looking after the child, rather than the formal person with care.[18] The Secretary of State may also specify whichever of the following mechanisms is regarded 'as appropriate in the circumstances', namely standing order, direct debit or analogous arrangements, cheque, postal order, debit card or cash.[19] Where the Agency is responsible for collection, it prefers automated methods, namely direct debits, standing orders and what it describes as 'voluntary DEOs'.[20] The other payment methods are 'acceptable, but not encouraged'.[21] The Secretary of State must also

---

[11] *Ibid*, s 29(3).

[12] SI 1992/1989.

[13] Or, in Scotland, directly to the child, where the application has been made under CSA 1991, s 7.

[14] SI 1992/1989, reg 2(1). The 'liable person' is, unsurprisingly, 'a person liable to make payments of child support maintenance', *ibid*, reg 2(2). If the method ordered is via the Secretary of State or his or her nominee, onward payment to the person entitled to receive the payment may be by credit transfer, cheque, girocheque, other payable order or cash: *ibid*, reg 5(1).

[15] Child Support Agency, *Procedures: Collection*, 'Methods of Collection Available to the NRP' at 16.

[16] 'Maintenance direct should not be encouraged or discouraged', *ibid*.

[17] The previous advice was: 'Direct payments [in benefit cases] are allowed but should not be encouraged in order to minimise the risk of fraud', Child Support Agency, CS2 *Help and Guidance*, 'MoPs Available to PWC'.

[18] *R(CS) 14/98*, para 18, *per* Mr Commissioner Rowland.

[19] SI 1992/1989, reg 3(1). There is also an odd provision enabling the Secretary of State to direct that a liable person take all reasonable steps to open an account from which such payments may be made: *ibid*, reg 3(2) and see E Jacobs and G Douglas, *Child Support: The Legislation* (Sweet & Maxwell, London, Seventh Edition, 2005/2006) at 296 for some of the potential difficulties associated with this provision. The courts have a similar power under Maintenance Enforcement Act 1991, s 1(6).

[20] Child Support Agency, *Procedures: Collection*, 'Non maintenance direct' at 21. DEOs are usually only used against defaulting NRPs: see below p 449.

[21] Because they are non-automated and increase the risk of late/non-payment and are less secure: Child Support Agency, n 20 above. Payment to the Agency via internet banking is currently not available.

specify the day for payment and the intervals between payments, taking into account such matters as whether the liable person is paid weekly or monthly, his preferences as to the appropriate interval and the time taken to clear payments through the banking system.[22] Before making directions under these various provisions, the Secretary of State is required to give the respective parties the right to make representations on matters such as the method and intervals for payments.[23] Finally, the Secretary of State must send the liable person a notice setting out the amount payable, the person to whom it must be paid, the method, day and intervals for payment and a statement of any outstanding arrears.[24]

There is one obvious omission from the prescribed statutory modes of paying child support—direct deduction from salary. True, the Agency *may* impose a DEO, but this is regarded as an *enforcement* mechanism rather than a *collection* method. The United Kingdom approach is in stark contrast to the position in both Australia and the United States, where regular deduction from salary is one of the standard methods for collecting child support.[25]

Collection of Maintenance other than Child Support

The Secretary of State also has the power to collect payments of maintenance other than child support by virtue of section 30 of the 1991 Act. This enables the Secretary of State to collect 'periodical payments, or secured periodical payments, of a prescribed kind which are payable to or for the benefit of any person who falls within a prescribed category' alongside any payments of child support maintenance.[26] The relevant regulations prescribe three categories of such 'other' payments of maintenance.[27] These are: payments under a court maintenance order by virtue of one of the special provisions in section 8 of the 1991 Act;[28] periodical payments under a court order[29] for spousal maintenance;[30] and periodical payments under a court order for maintenance of a former child of the family.[31]

---

[22] SI 1992/1989, reg 4. The explicit reference to considering the 'needs of the person entitled to receive payment' was repealed as part of the April 1995 changes, but this could still come into play as 'any other matter' which is regarded as relevant in the circumstances of the case.

[23] *Ibid*, reg 6.

[24] *Ibid*, reg 7(1). The notice must be sent as soon as is reasonably practicable after the maintenance calculation is made or any change in the collection requirements is effected: *ibid*, reg 7(2).

[25] See further p 452 below.

[26] CSA 1991, s 30(1); *ibid* s 30(2), which provides for the Secretary of State to collect other payments even where child support is not involved, has not been brought into force as yet.

[27] Child Support (Collection and Enforcement of Other Forms of Maintenance) Regulations 1992 (SI 1992/2643), reg 2.

[28] ie top up maintenance, or maintenance to cover education or disability costs: CSA 1991, s 8(6)–(8).

[29] So a maintenance agreement is not included (although registered minutes of agreement in Scotland are within the scope of this provision).

[30] The spouse or former spouse in question must be the PWC of a qualifying child in respect of whom a maintenance calculation has been made and collection arranged under CSA 1991, s 29.

[31] On the meaning of 'child of the family', see Matrimonial Causes Act 1973, s 52(1).

There may be cases in which the Secretary of State arranges for the collection of different payments from the same non-resident parent, but the amount paid to the Agency is less than the total amount due. In this event the Secretary of State can apportion such payments as he or she sees fit amongst those entitled, unless the liable person has stipulated how the sum paid is to be allocated as between the different creditors.[32] Where the Secretary of State arranges for collection of non-child support maintenance under section 30, the normal range of enforcement provisions which apply to payments of child support maintenance under section 29 is also available.[33]

The purpose of section 30 is clear; so far as possible, the Agency's procedures should be available to collect both maintenance assessed under the 1991 Act and maintenance ordered by a court, providing a 'joined-up' service. In principle it should be to the benefit of parents with care if the Agency collects both types of maintenance, thus relieving them of the need to invoke the court's enforcement machinery. Where benefit cases are concerned, this facility may also be of direct financial benefit to the state. Magistrates' courts also have the power, when making orders for other types of maintenance, to direct that such orders be met via the Agency's collection procedure where that system is already in use for a maintenance calculation under the 1991 Act.[34] However, somewhat incongruously, this power is only available to the magistrates' courts, and not to the county courts or to the High Court, which in practice would be the more likely forum for a top-up maintenance order.[35]

Fees

The policy intention at the outset was that those parents who could afford to do so would pay the Agency an appropriate fee for the service provided.[36] Accordingly, the 1991 Act enabled the Secretary of State to make provision for fees to be charged.[37] Both parents in private cases and the non-resident parent in benefit cases were made liable for such fees.[38] The Agency's catastrophic performance at the beginning of the scheme made it politically impossible to pursue clients for

[32] CSA 1991, s 30(3). It seems odd that the non-resident parent should apparently have the power to direct eg that preference should be accorded to spousal over child support maintenance, although such a scenario is difficult to envisage occurring in practice.

[33] See CSA 1991, s 30(4) and (5); see also SI 1992/2643, reg 3 (England and Wales) and reg 4 (Scotland). These powers are subject to notice under *ibid*, reg 5.

[34] See Child Support Act 1991 (Consequential Amendments Order) 1994 (SI 1994/731), which inserted a new Magistrates' Courts Act 1980, s 59(3)(cc) and (3A).

[35] See Jacobs and Douglas (n 19 above at 323), observing that the creditor would first have to have the order from the higher court registered in the magistrates' court under the Maintenance Orders Act 1958.

[36] DSS, *Children Come First* (Cm 1264-I, 1991) at para 5.28.

[37] CSA 1991, s 47.

[38] The assessment fee was £44 and the collection fee £34 (both annual figures), subject to exemptions for various categories of parents: Child Support Fees Regulations 1992 (SI 1992/3094).

fees, and in 1995 the government announced that fees would be suspended until April 1997, when they would be reintroduced.[39] This proved to be hopelessly optimistic, and the payment of fees was further suspended until April 1999, and then yet again to April 2001. Even this target proved to be unrealistic, and the relevant regulations were repealed in 2000.[40] The new government reaffirmed its commitment to the principle of charging fees—in the absence of the Agency, parents would be paying court and legal fees—but acknowledged that this was not feasible so long as the Agency's service 'is not of an acceptable standard'.[41]

Arrears

The Problem of Initial Arrears

Problems associated with arrears have bedevilled the child support system since its inception in 1993.[42] One reason for this is that the structure of the scheme is such that some arrears are virtually inevitable at the outset of a case, let alone at any later date. This is because the maintenance calculation is necessarily made after the effective date, with the result that arrears usually build up in the meantime.[43] This problem has been compounded by the serious delays in making both old scheme maintenance assessments and new scheme calculations. The initial notification of the maintenance calculation will separately itemise any sum outstanding by way of arrears.[44] The Agency's internal guidance advises staff to start from the presumption that any initial arrears should be paid off as a lump sum,[45] but this is subject to negotiation, which may typically lead to payment of arrears by instalments. The guidance continues by emphasising the psychological importance of such negotiations: 'Never accept the NRP's first offer (unless it is for the full amount) . . . The harder the NRP has to work to obtain a lower payment arrangement the more the NRP will feel they have negotiated a good deal'.[46]

What if the non-resident parent has voluntarily made payments 'on account', either to the Agency or directly to the parent with care, pending the outcome of the Agency's assessment process? Previously the Agency operated internal policy

---

[39] DSS, *Improving Child Support* (Cm 2745, 1995) at para 6.11.

[40] Child Support (Collection and Enforcement and Miscellaneous Amendments) Regulations 2000 (SI 2001/162), reg 4 repealed SI 1992/3094.

[41] DSS, *A new contract for welfare: Children's Rights and Parents' Responsibilities* (Cm 4349, 1999) at ch 4 para 36.

[42] In fairness, of course, the court system's failure adequately to deal with arrears was one of the motivations behind the introduction of the 1991 Act.

[43] The principal exception is where there is a court order in force, as in such cases the effective date is two days after the maintenance calculation is made: see p 213.

[44] SI 1992/1989, reg 7(1)(e).

[45] Child Support Agency, *Procedures: Arrears Management*, 'Re-establishing Collections' at 5837.

[46] Child Support Agency, *Procedures: Sapphire Processes*, 'Arrears Negotiation' at 5046.

guidelines that defined the types of voluntary payments which could be set off against the initial arrears of child support. The government's view was that a discretionary scheme for recognising voluntary payments lacked transparency and failed to act as a sufficient incentive for non-resident parents to begin payments of at least some child support. Accordingly, the 2000 Act inserted a new provision into the 1991 Act, providing for a degree of statutory recognition for certain voluntary payments of child support.

There are three preliminary requirements for the recognition of voluntary payments.[47] First, there must have been either an actual application for child maintenance by a private client (or, in Scotland, a child) or a deemed application from a parent with care on benefit. Secondly, that application must be awaiting a decision by the Secretary of State. Thirdly, the non-resident parent must have made a 'voluntary payment', defined by the Act as one which is made on account of an anticipated liability (whether based on any estimate provided by the Secretary of State or on the individual's own estimate) and which is made before the actual calculation is notified to the non-resident parent.[48] The voluntary payment must be made either to the Secretary of State or, with the Agency's agreement, to the person with care or a third party where appropriate.[49]

The concept of a 'voluntary payment' is then further defined by regulations[50]— it must meet the statutory preconditions and be made after the effective date of the maintenance calculation. The Agency may also require verification of payments, either by way of a bank statement or receipt or on the basis of the person with care's confirmatory evidence.[51] There is plenty of scope for disputes to arise in this context, given the empirical evidence of disagreements about the receipt of child support payments.[52] Any such payments must also be one of a defined type; in this regard the regulations stipulate that it must only be for specific purposes (eg by way of child support maintenance, or the parent with care's costs for housing, utilities or essential repairs etc) and made by one of a number of different prescribed methods.[53] The regulations make no provision for payments in kind, that is, where the non-resident parent spends money on other items for the child, for example essentials such as clothing or 'luxuries' such as treats on contact visits, to be taken into account.[54] This is in contrast to the Australian scheme, which permits

---

[47] CSA 1991, s 28J(1).

[48] Or before the Secretary of State has notified him that he has declined to accept the application: see *ibid*, s 28J(2).

[49] *Ibid*, s 28J(4). See also SI 1992/1989, reg 5A.

[50] Child Support (Voluntary Payments) Regulations 2000 (SI 2000/3177), reg 2.

[51] *Ibid*, reg 4.

[52] See eg N Wikeley *et al*, *National Survey of Child Support Agency Clients* (DWP Research Report No 152, 2001) at 95–99. Child Support Agency, *Procedures: Collections*, 'Conflicting evidence' at 93 gives this advice: 'Where there is a dispute over payments, the burden of proof lies with the NRP to prove payment. If the NRP can prove payment, the burden of proof then moves to the PWC to prove that payment has not been received'.

[53] eg cash, cheque, postal order, standing order, debit card etc; see SI 2000/3177, reg 3.

[54] See *R(CS) 9/98* (payment of regular pocket money not relevant to formula assessment).

non-resident parents to make provision in kind for a certain proportion of their child support liabilities.[55]

Assuming the non-resident parent's payments qualify under these rules as voluntary payments, and the other criteria discussed above are satisfied, then those payments are offset against any arrears of child support, either under any previous maintenance calculation or under the current assessment.[56] In the event that the total of the non-resident parent's voluntary payments exceeds the initial arrears due under the maintenance calculation, the balance is treated as overpaid child support maintenance and is remitted to the payer in one form or another.[57]

Accumulated Arrears

The problem of initial arrears, discussed above, is one that is endogenous to the child support scheme. The far more serious and intractable problem is where arrears build up as a result of non-compliance on the part of the non-resident parent. If the Agency's collection service is not being used,[58] then it is for the parties to resolve any disputes over arrears between themselves (which might, of course, result in the parent with care asking the Agency to assume responsibility for collection). Where the Agency is responsible for collecting child support, and at least one payment has been missed, then the Agency's first formal step is to issue an 'arrears notice' to the non-resident parent.[59] The arrears notice must itemise the outstanding payments, summarise the legal provisions relating to arrears and request payment of the arrears due.[60] These notices are generated automatically by the Agency's computer system, which will also flag up late or missed payments for staff to investigate, typically by making telephone contact.[61]

Normally the Agency will seek to establish an 'arrears agreement' with the defaulting non-resident parent, under which the latter agrees 'to pay all outstanding arrears by making payments on agreed dates of agreed amounts'.[62] As with initial arrears, the terms on which arrears are to be paid off is a matter for negotiation, bearing in mind that the objective 'is to make the best possible payment arrangement on behalf of the PWC that the NRP can afford to pay',[63] whilst

---

[55] In certain circumstances a liable parent may meet up to 25% of his child support liability by way of payments in kind, known as non agency payments (NAPs), even without the payee's consent: Child Support (Registration and Collection) Act 1988 (Cth), ss 71, and 71A–71D. NAPs might cover eg school fees or medical expenses.

[56] Child Support (Arrears, Interest and Adjustment of Maintenance Assessments) Regulations 1992 (SI 1992/1816), reg 10(3A).

[57] CSA 1991, s 41B(1A).

[58] The collection service is in principle now optional in all cases: see above, p 439.

[59] CSA 1991, s 41(1) and SI 1992/1816, reg 2.

[60] *Ibid*, reg 2(3). Further non-payment does not automatically trigger a new arrears notice: a subsequent missed payment will not result in another arrears notice unless payments have been made in full for an intervening period of 12 weeks or more (*ibid*, reg 2(4)).

[61] See R Hadwen and K Pawling, *Child support handbook* (CPAG, 13th edn, 2005/2006), at 464.

[62] SI 1992/1816, reg 5(1).

[63] Child Support Agency, n 46 above.

not jeopardising the current flow of maintenance. Although the Agency's initial request is invariably for immediate payment of the full arrears, this is essentially a negotiating tactic and payment by instalments is often agreed. In reaching such agreement, staff are advised to take into account the needs of both the non-resident parent (and any new family he may have) and the parent with care and qualifying child(ren), and any representations from the payer about hardship.[64] As a starting point, the Agency's computer system will calculate a timetable for the payment of arrears based on a maximum of 5 per cent of the non-resident parent's net income.[65] Once an arrears agreement is reached, the Agency prepares an arrears schedule to confirm the timetable for repayment.[66] Inevitably such schedules will not always be adhered to, and so the Secretary of State is explicitly given the power to renegotiate arrears agreements.[67] If the non-resident parent receives one of a number of non-means-tested benefits, a standard contribution of £1 per week is deducted in respect of arrears, together with the flat rate deduction.[68]

Where payments of child support arrears are made, the Agency retains that element of the arrears payments which would not have been passed on to the person with care had the payment been made when it was actually due.[69] This effectively gives the Secretary of State the first call on any payments of arrears which are received where the parent with care is on benefit. The Secretary of State also has a general power to attribute any payment of child support to a current liability or to arrears 'as he thinks fit'.[70]

If the non-resident parent fails to comply with an arrears agreement, there are a number of possible consequences, depending on the circumstances of the case and the view taken by the Agency. One possibility is that the Agency and the non-resident parent negotiate a revised arrears agreement. Another is that the Agency may decide temporarily to suspend action where the non-resident parent's position is such that it would either be insensitive or unusually difficult to enforce recovery, for example where he is in hospital or in prison.[71] But the Agency may decide to use other mechanisms both to secure recovery of arrears and encourage compliance for the future; these include imposing penalty payments and the use of enforcement tools such as DEOs or court-based remedies. These are discussed in turn below.

[64] *Ibid*, 'Arrears Amount'.
[65] *Ibid*.
[66] SI 1992/1816, reg 5(3).
[67] *Ibid*, reg 5(5).
[68] Social Security (Claims and Payments) Regulations 1987 (SI 1987/1968), sch 9B, para 3.
[69] CSA 1991, s 41(2) and (2A) and SI 1992/1816, reg 8. Any sums so received are paid into the Consolidated Fund: CSA 1991, s 41(6).
[70] SI 1992/1816, reg 9, which must be subject to CSA 1991, s 2.
[71] Child Support Agency, *Procedures: Arrears Management*, 'Suspending debt' at 5897.

Penalty Payments

The new section 41A of the 1991 Act, inserted by the 2000 Act,[72] makes provision for the levying of penalty payments. This provision is the third such attempt in the relatively short life of the child support scheme to devise an effective 'stick' with which to encourage compliance.[73] The 1991 Act originally envisaged that interest charges would be imposed where arrears of child support maintenance built up.[74] These arrangements proved to be extremely difficult both to administer and to explain to the Agency's clients and were subsequently abandoned. Instead, the 1995 Act inserted the original section 41A,[75] which provided for an alternative scheme under which financial penalties for late payments of child support maintenance could be imposed as an alternative to interest charges. However, that provision was never brought into force and was replaced by the new section 41A in the 2000 Act.

The new section 41A itself is essentially an enabling provision. The regulations provide that the Secretary of State can levy a penalty payment in two types of case.[76] The first is where outstanding arrears are not received within seven days of the Agency sending the non-resident parent an appropriate notice; the second is where the non-resident parent defaults on an arrears agreement. In either case the non-resident parent is required to pay the penalty payment within 14 days.[77] The primary legislation imposes a ceiling on such penalty payments of 25 per cent of the amount of child support payable in any given week.[78] Subject to that maximum, the actual level of any penalty payment is a matter for the Agency's judgment.[79]

The new penalty scheme differs from the earlier attempts to introduce such arrangements in three main respects. First, penalty payments are not imposed automatically on child support defaulters; the Secretary of State is vested with a discretion as to whether to levy such a payment.[80] Secondly, although the financial penalty may be charged in respect of each week of unpaid maintenance, these liabilities are not compounded.[81] Thirdly, penalty payments do not form part of the child support owed to the other parent and hence are not payable to the parent with care.[82] Moreover, the imposition of a penalty has no effect on the non-resident parent's liability to pay the relevant arrears.[83] In practice it seems that

---

[72] CSPSSA 2000, s 18(2).

[73] A system of financial penalties for those who are slow to discharge their liabilities is standard practice in other contexts (eg in filing income tax returns and meeting tax demands).

[74] CSA 1991, s 41(3)–(5).

[75] See CSA 1995, s 22.

[76] SI 1992/1989, reg 7(1)(e) and 7A(2) and (3).

[77] *Ibid*, reg 7A(4).

[78] CSA 1991, s 41A(2).

[79] See Hadwen and Pawling, n 61 above, at 465–67.

[80] SI 1992/1989, reg 7A(3): CSA 1991, s 2 applies.

[81] This was a major practical difficulty in operating the original 1991 scheme.

[82] See CSA 1991, s 41A(6), which provides for receipts to be transferred to the Consolidated Fund.

[83] *Ibid*, s 41A(3).

penalty payments will be rarely levied; rather, the official policy appears to be that their prime purpose is to provide a further bargaining tool to aid compliance.[84] Indeed, as at June 2006 it seemed that the Agency's computer system was still unable to generate penalty payment decisions.[85]

Enforcement

Introduction

Sections 31 to 41B of the 1991 Act provide the Secretary of State with a range of powers to enforce payment of child support maintenance in the event of non-compliance by the non-resident parent. In order of increasing severity, these methods are: a deduction from earnings order (DEO), distress, enforcement in the county courts, disqualification from driving and imprisonment. The first of these mechanisms, the DEO, is an administrative act by the Secretary of State, which does not require prior approval by a court. Only the court, however, can make an order for one of the other enforcement remedies, and an essential prerequisite for any such action is that the Secretary of State has previously applied for, and obtained, a liability order from the magistrates' court. Accordingly, this procedure will be discussed below immediately after the treatment of DEOs. The statutory insistence on a judicial gateway to the more draconian forms of enforcement stands in contrast to the position in the USA, where in some states administrative agencies have much wider powers, for example to revoke licences without prior court intervention.[86] The House of Commons Work and Pensions Select Committee has recommended that the Agency be accorded greater administrative powers to recover maintenance, albeit with appropriate safeguards by way of appeal rights.[87]

Before examining the various remedies available in detail, it should be noted that the powers contained in sections 31 to 41B of the 1991 Act and discussed below are a comprehensive code for the purposes of enforcement of child support liabilities. This has two important consequences.

The first is that the Secretary of State can only rely on one of these specific statutory mechanisms. The Agency cannot, therefore, apply for a freezing order[88] to restrain a non-resident parent with substantial child support debts from disposing

---

[84] According to the Minister, the aim of the Agency's negotiations with the NRP 'will be to ensure that maintenance is paid promptly, rather than to impose a penalty', *per* Mr J Rooker, Minister of State, Standing Committee F, col 341 (3 February 2000). Similarly, the *Explanatory Notes* to the 2000 Act indicated that 'it is envisaged that the penalty will rarely need to be applied, but that it will provide a useful incentive for persuading non-resident parents to meet their responsibilities' (para 229).

[85] Child Support Agency, *Procedures: Arrears Management*, at 5865.

[86] See further p 462 below.

[87] House of Commons (HC) Work and Pensions Select Committee, *The Performance of the Child Support Agency* (Second Report of Session 2004–05, HC 44-I), paras 161–67.

[88] Formerly a *Mareva* injunction.

of capital assets before an application for a liability order is made.[89] In contrast, the Australian Agency is not confined to using its powers under the child support legislation; it may also bring enforcement proceedings in the general family law jurisdiction or for the recovery of child support as an ordinary civil debt.[90] This means that ultimately the Australian Agency (unlike its counterpart in the United Kingdom) can bring bankruptcy proceedings against a defaulting parent.

The second consequence of the statutory framework is that the power to take enforcement proceedings under the 1991 Act lies exclusively with the Secretary of State. This was confirmed by the decision of the House of Lords in *R (Kehoe) v Secretary of State for Work and Pensions*.[91] The majority of the House held that the exclusion of the parent with care from any role in the enforcement process involved no breach of Article 6 of the ECHR as she had no 'civil right' under the 1991 Act to the payment of child support. This outcome is less than satisfactory, not least where the parent with care is a private client and the Secretary of State has no direct interest in whether or not child support is actually paid.[92] Again, overseas child support systems do not operate such a total bar on the parent with care's involvement in enforcement proceedings.[93]

Deduction from Earnings Order

The Secretary of State is entitled to make a DEO against a liable person to secure the payment of child support maintenance.[94] As this is a discretionary power, it follows that the welfare of any children who might be affected (not just qualifying children) must be considered[95] and indeed may be a factor of 'considerable weight'.[96] There are no 'grounds' as such for making a DEO: indeed, somewhat bizarrely, neither the 1991 Act nor the regulations give any indication of the circumstances in which the imposition of a DEO may be appropriate. The primary legislation simply provides that a DEO may apply to the recovery of past or future child support liabilities, or to both together.[97] There is therefore no formal bar to the Secretary of State proceeding to make a DEO in the absence of any arrears. The Agency's internal guidance suggests that DEOs should be considered where, for

---

[89] *Department of Social Security v Butler* [1996] 1 FLR 65, CA.

[90] Child Support (Registration and Collection) Act 1988 (Cth), ss 104, 105 and 113.

[91] [2005] UKHL 48; [2006] 1 AC 42.

[92] For criticism of this decision, see N Wikeley, 'A duty but not a right: child support after *R (Kehoe) v Secretary of State for Work and Pensions*' (2006) 18 *Child and Family Law Quarterly*, 287.

[93] See, in the context of the CA decision, N Wikeley, '*R (Kehoe) v Secretary of State for Work and Pensions*: no redress when the Child Support Agency fails to deliver' (2005) 17 *Child and Family Law Quarterly* 113.

[94] CSA 1991, s 31(2).

[95] *Ibid*, s 2 and *R v Secretary of State for Social Security, ex parte Biggin* [1995] 1 FLR 851; see also *R v Secretary of State for Social Security ex parte Anderson* (CO/2131/99) (QBD, 19 July 2000).

[96] *ex parte Biggin*, n 95 above, at 855 *per* Thorpe J. However, the only way to challenge the weight given to this factor is by way of judicial review: see below, p 451.

[97] CSA 1991, s 31(3).

example, other payment methods have proven to be ineffective and late or missing payments have occurred, or where the non-resident parent fails to respond to warning letters. The guidance also indicates that a non-resident parent may voluntarily request payment direct from his earnings.[98] In practice, however, the Agency views making a DEO as a last resort—or, at least, as a last internal resort before an application to the courts is made—and so such an order is unlikely to be made unless attempts to secure payment by agreement have failed.[99] Certainly parents with care complain that the Agency is slow to make DEOs.[100]

Once made by the Agency, the DEO operates as an instruction[101] to the liable person's employer to make deductions from that individual's earnings and to pay such sums to the Secretary of State as from the specified date. The DEO must be served on both the employer and the liable person himself. Once the order has been made and served on the employer, it becomes the employer's duty to comply with its requirements.[102] Indeed, it is a criminal offence to fail to comply with the requirements of a DEO, or with various of the statutory duties imposed under the regulations discussed below.[103]

The DEO is modelled on the attachment of earnings order, one of the standard ways of recovering civil debts and outstanding fines. The most important distinction is that the issue of a DEO by the Secretary of State is an administrative act, whereas only the court can make an attachment of earnings order. However, the procedural provisions governing DEOs, contained in Part III of the Child Support (Collection and Enforcement) Regulations 1992,[104] are very similar to those which apply to attachment of earnings orders.[105] The DEO must therefore specify a normal deduction rate, typically the weekly or monthly amount to be deducted from the non-resident parent's earnings,[106] and a protected earnings proportion, being the level below which the debtor's earnings must not be allowed to fall.[107] For these purposes 'earnings' are defined as sums payable by way of wages or salary (including overtime, bonuses, commission payments and fees), and include pension payments and statutory sick pay.[108] Working tax credit, social security

---

[98] Child Support Agency, *Procedures: Arrears Management* at 5869.

[99] See DSS, *The Child Support, Pensions and Social Security Bill: Regulatory Impact Assessment* at 6 (DSS, 2000).

[100] Hadwen and Pawling, n 61 above, at 469 and see generally R Moorhead, M Sefton and G Douglas, *The Advice Needs of Lone Parents* (One Parent Families, London, 2004) at 47.

[101] CSA 1991, s 31(4) and (5).

[102] *Ibid*, s 31(6), effectively giving employers seven days' grace to comply.

[103] *Ibid*, s 32(8)–(11) and SI 1992/1989, reg 25.

[104] SI 1992/1989. CSA 1991, s 32 is the relevant enabling power.

[105] One difference is that the Secretary of State does not have power to summons a NRP to attend to give his employment and income details: contrast the powers of the Australian Child Support Registrar under Child Support (Registration and Collection) Act 1988 (Cth), s 120.

[106] SI 1992/1989, regs 8(1) and 10.

[107] SI 1992/1989, reg 11. This used to be known as the protected earnings *rate* and was calculated by reference to income support rates. It was changed in 2000 to the protected earnings *proportion*, being 60% of the liable person's net earnings (as defined by *ibid*, reg 8(5)). The new definition has the advantage of involving both an easier calculation and a more individualised approach.

[108] *Ibid*, reg 8(3).

benefits and disablement pensions are excluded from the definition,[109] as are pay and allowances for members of HM Forces (excepting reservists).[110]

The normal deduction rate and protected earnings proportion, along with personal details enabling the defaulting parent to be identified, must be specified in the DEO.[111] The employer must then make regular deductions from earnings at the normal deduction rate, or if necessary such lesser amount so that the liable person's earnings do not fall below the threshold represented by the protected earnings proportion.[112] Employers must also notify the liable person in writing of the deduction[113] and pay over such amounts deducted to the Secretary of State.[114] The Agency must review a DEO if there is a change in the amount of the maintenance calculation or if arrears or penalty charges payable under the order are paid off.[115] The Secretary of State also has the power to discharge a DEO in certain circumstances (eg where no further payments are due under it).[116] The regulations additionally make special provision for cases in which the liable person is subject both to a DEO and to one or more attachment of earnings orders (or, in Scotland, diligences against earnings).[117] DEOs can be made against Crown employees, but special provisions apply.[118]

Given that the making of a DEO is a purely administrative act, the means of challenging such an action take on a greater significance. Leaving aside the option of pursuing the matter as a complaint within the Agency (and then to the ICE), there are two formal legal routes by which a DEO may be challenged. The first is by an appeal to the magistrates' court (or, in Scotland, to the sheriff).[119] The 1991

---

[109] *Ibid*, reg 8(4).

[110] There are, however, parallel provisions which enable deductions to be made for child support maintenance from the pay of serving members of the armed forces: Child Support Act 1991 (Consequential Amendments) Order 1993 (SI 1993/785), amending the Army Act 1955, Air Force Act 1955 and Naval Forces (Enforcement of Maintenance Liabilities) Act 1947. The origins of these powers are of some antiquity—see p 47 above.

[111] eg name and address, national insurance number, payroll number etc: SI 1992/1989, reg 9. The liable person is obliged to provide such information on request by the Secretary of State: *ibid*, reg 15. Employers' duties to notify the Secretary of State (eg as to a liable person leaving their employment, on which see also reg 21) are contained in reg 16.

[112] *Ibid*, reg 12(1) and (2); in doing so the employer is entitled to make a deduction of £1 for administrative costs: *ibid*, reg 12(6).

[113] *Ibid*, reg 13. But note quite independently the duty on employers under Employment Rights Act 1996, ss 8 and 9 to provide itemised pay statements and standing statements of fixed deductions, and the employee's right to refer breaches to an employment tribunal: *ibid*, ss 11 and 12.

[114] SI 1992/1989, reg 14. Transfers must be made by the 19th of the month following the month in which the deduction was made.

[115] *Ibid*, reg 17; see regs 18 and 19 on the subsequent variation of a DEO.

[116] *Ibid*, reg 20. DEOs also lapse automatically where the liable person leaves the employment in question: *ibid*, reg 21.

[117] *Ibid*, reg 24. In England and Wales DEOs take priority over AEOs for civil debts, but DEOs and AEOs for other purposes, eg payment of court fines, are dealt with in date order. In Scotland DEOs always take priority over diligences against earnings.

[118] CSA 1991, s 57(4) and SI 1992/1989, reg 23.

[119] The appeal must be by way of complaint for an order (or, in Scotland, by way of application) within 28 days of the DEO being made: SI 1992/1989, reg 22(2). In Scotland the form of the application is set out in the Act of Sederunt (Child Support Rules) 1993 (SI 1993/920, S 127)), r 5 and Form

Act suggests that this right of appeal may potentially be rather broad, in that it enables regulations to provide for an appeal by a liable person aggrieved by the making of an order, or the terms of an order, or where there is a dispute as to whether payments constitute earnings or about any other prescribed matter.[120] The regulations, however, confine this right of appeal to two grounds only, namely that the DEO itself is defective or that the payments in question are not earnings.[121] A 'defective' DEO is one which fails to comply with the technical requirements relating to notification of relevant details, including the normal deduction rate and the protected earnings proportion, such that it is impracticable for the employer to comply with their obligations.[122] It follows that the magistrates' court (or sheriff) has no power to question the underlying maintenance calculation: any challenge to the assessment itself must be under the appeals machinery established by the Act.[123] If the court or sheriff decides to allow the appeal, their powers are limited to quashing the order (if defective) or specifying which payments (if any) do not constitute earnings.[124] Magistrates and sheriffs have no power to order the repayment of sums deducted under a defective DEO,[125] so this has to be achieved through administrative action by the Agency.[126]

The second way in which a DEO may be challenged is by way of judicial review under normal administrative law principles. Although such an action is not confined to the narrow grounds available in an appeal to the magistrates' court or the sheriff, the broader merits of the case cannot be questioned on judicial review. Thus in one reported case the Secretary of State's decision to make a DEO in respect of arrears of child support, without taking into account earlier voluntary overpayments of child maintenance, was upheld.[127] Judicial review is also the only way in which to challenge the weight attached by the Secretary of State to the welfare principle in deciding whether or not to make a DEO.[128]

There are, undoubtedly, a number of weaknesses in the system of DEOs. The very nature of a DEO is such that it cannot be used as a measure to secure compliance by a self-employed liable parent. Furthermore, as currently constituted, DEOs are of limited practical value when dealing with non-resident parents who change jobs regularly—precisely those who are perhaps more prone to

---

6. There is no such prescribed form for England and Wales, but see the suggestion for modifying the Scots version in Hadwen and Pawling, n 61 above, at 475.

[120] CSA 1991, s 32(5).

[121] SI 1992/1989, reg 22(3).

[122] *Ibid*, reg 8(1)—but note that only the liable person, and not the employer, has the right of appeal under *ibid*, reg 22(1). This definition of 'defective' puts the decision in *R v Secretary of State for Social Security, ex parte Biggin* [1995] 1 FLR 851 on a statutory footing in this respect.

[123] CSA 1991, s 32(6) and *Secretary of State for Social Security v Shotton and others* [1996] 2 FLR 241.

[124] SI 1992/1989, reg 22(4).

[125] *Secretary of State for Social Security v Shotton and others*, n 123 above.

[126] See CSA 1991, s 41B (repayment) and SI 1992/1816, reg 10 (adjustment).

[127] *R v Secretary of State for Social Security, ex parte Newmarch Singh* [2000] 2 FLR 664.

[128] *R v Secretary of State for Social Security, ex parte Biggin*, n 95 above, at 855 *per* Thorpe J.

non-compliance.[129] There is, however, evidence from overseas that more active use of such mechanisms can assist in improving collection rates. In both Australia and the USA, payment of child support liabilities by deduction from salary is seen as a standard collection method rather than as an enforcement measure. In Australia, the Agency is required to collect registered maintenance liabilities by deductions from the payer's wage or salary if it is practicable to do so in a procedure known as 'employer withholding'.[130] Other methods of payment apply only if the payer so elects and the Agency 'is satisfied that the payer is likely to make timely payments'.[131] In 2005 the Australian Agency recovered 41 per cent of liabilities in cases in which it was responsible for collection via employer withholding.[132] The equivalent proportion in the United Kingdom is 22 per cent.[133]

In the United States, legislative reforms in the 1980s have made automatic deduction from salary (known in the USA as 'income withholding') the standard method of collecting child support.[134] Research has indicated that income withholding has helped to improve compliance.[135] This system has been reinforced by the PRWORA 1996. This legislation requires all employers to report the details of new employees to the state authorities, and all such data is entered on a National Directory of New Hires (designed to deal with the particular problem of inter-state child support liabilities). In the 2002 financial year, income withholding accounted for over US$15 billion out of a total of nearly US$24 billion of child support liabilities collected.[136] Collection rates in the USA have apparently more than doubled since 1996,[137] although it should be noted that the 1996 Act brought in a range of other measures designed to improve compliance.

The traditional arguments against using payroll deductions as a routine collection measure in the United Kingdom have included concerns about protecting the privacy of individual employees and not increasing the administrative burden on employers. The Select Committee has recommended that DEOs should be the standard method of payment for employed non-resident parents who default on more than two payments in any rolling 12 month period, and has asked the

---

[129] However, the simple fact that a liable person's earnings in one job fluctuate should not be a reason for declining to impose a DEO, by analogy with attachment of earnings orders: *R v York Magistrates' Court, ex parte Grimes* [1997] EWHC Admin 461.

[130] According to the heading to the Child Support (Registration and Collection) Act 1988 (Cth), s 43, this is the 'General rule of collection by automatic withholding in case of employees'.

[131] *Ibid*, s 44.

[132] Child Support Agency, *Child Support Scheme: Facts and Figures 2004–05* (Canberra, CSA, October 2004) at 40.

[133] DWP, *Child Support Agency Quarterly Summary Statistics: December 2005* (2005), Table 9.

[134] Child Support Enforcement Amendments 1984 and the Family Support Act 1988.

[135] See I Garfinkel and MM Klawitter, 'The Effect of Routine Income Withholding of Child Support Collections' (1990) 9 *Journal of Policy Analysis and Management* 155 and DR Meyer and J Bartfeld, 'Compliance with Child Support Orders in Divorce Cases' (1996) 58 *Journal of Marriage and the Family* 201.

[136] Office of Child Support Enforcement, *Financial Year 2002 Annual Statistical Report* (US Government Administration for Children and Families, Washington DC, 2003), Table 16.

[137] V Turetsky, 'Child Support Trends' (May 2003, conference presentation).

Department to investigate the feasibility of making such orders automatically transferable to new employers.[138] Greater emphasis on the option of making payments of child support by deduction from salary is arguably the one reform that would have the most positive impact on improving the compliance rate of non-resident parents with child support assessments.

Liability Order

If the Agency decides to institute any of the other available enforcement mechanisms, it must first seek a liability order. A liability order is thus a necessary procedural step rather than an enforcement method itself.[139] The statutory provisions governing liability orders have been held by the High Court to be compliant with the ECHR.[140] The power to make a liability order arises only where the liable person has failed to make one or more payments of child support and where it appears to the Secretary of State that either it is inappropriate to make a DEO (for example, because the non-resident parent is self-employed) or such an order has been made but has proven to be ineffective.[141] The Secretary of State may apply to the magistrates' court or, in Scotland, the sheriff for a liability order.[142] Applications cannot be made in respect of arrears which have been outstanding for more than six years.[143] The six year period runs from the date of the notification of the maintenance calculation to the non-resident parent, as being the date 'on which payment of the amount in question became due', rather than the date the maintenance enquiry form was sent out.[144] As the decision to make such an

---

[138] n 87 above, paras 153–57. Interestingly, the Government's response emphasised the practical difficulties rather than any principled objection to greater use of DEOs: HC Work and Pensions Committee, *The Child Support Agency: Government Response to the Committee's 2nd Report of Session 2004–05* (1st Special Report of Session 2004–05, HC 477) paras 20–21.

[139] Just as DEOs were modelled on attachment of earnings orders, so liability orders under the 1991 Act are based on liability orders for unpaid council tax.

[140] On the basis that Art 8 is not engaged or, if it is, any interference with the liable person's Art 8 rights is both justified and proportionate: *R (on the application of Denson) v Child Support Agency* [2002] 1 FLR 938 at paras 45–46, *per* Munby J.

[141] CSA 1991, s 33(1).

[142] *Ibid*, s 33(2). The relevant procedural rules are made under *ibid*, ss 34 (England and Wales) and 37 (Scotland). The Agency must give the liable person at least seven days' notice: SI 1992/1989, reg 27. The application may be signed by an Agency litigation officer rather than a solicitor: *Secretary of State for Social Security v Love* 1996 SLT (Sh Ct) 78. It should be made to the court having jurisdiction in the area in which the liable person resides: *ibid*, reg 28(1). On the enforcement of orders in the different jurisdictions in the UK, see CSA 1991, s 39, SI 1992/1989, reg 29(2)–(4) and also the Child Support (Northern Ireland Reciprocal Arrangements) Regulations 1993 (SI 1993/584).

[143] SI 1992/1989, reg 28(2). In principle such debts might still be recovered by a DEO, but that method will presumably have already been tried, where appropriate. There is a clear incentive here for the non-compliant self-employed non-resident parent to string out proceedings for as long as possible. The Secretary of State has indicated the Government's intention to abolish the six-year time limit: HC Work and Pensions Committee, *Minutes of Evidence*, HC 920-i (15 February 2006) at Q18.

[144] *R (on the application of Sutherland) v Secretary of State for Work and Pensions* [2004] EWHC 800 (Admin), Collins J. See also *R(CS) 10/02* (process of making application under CSA 1991 not within Limitation Act 1980).

application is a discretionary one, the children's welfare must be considered;[145] accordingly, in principle at least, the Secretary of State's decision so to proceed (or not) is susceptible to judicial review. The fact that the liable parent may have lodged an appeal against the maintenance calculation does not suspend his liability to pay child support, or indeed prevent the Secretary of State from applying for a liability order.[146]

Once an application for a liability order has been made by the Secretary of State, the court must make the order sought 'if satisfied that the payments in question have become payable by the liable person and have not been paid'.[147] Furthermore, the legislation expressly bars the court from going behind the application to question the maintenance calculation in respect of which the non-compliance has arisen.[148] It follows, for example, that the liable parent cannot use the court hearing to dispute the finding that he was habitually resident and so challenge the Agency's jurisdiction to make such a calculation.[149] Equally, the court has no power to apply any offset in respect of overpayments of maintenance paid under a pre-existing court order[150] or to investigate the wider merits of the case.[151] Once the liability order is obtained, the Secretary of State may proceed down three routes.[152] First, the Agency may levy distress without instituting any further court action. Secondly, the Secretary of State may designate the liability order under the Act so that it is treated as a judgment which will appear in the county court register of judgments and debts,[153] so jeopardising the liable person's credit rating. Finally, obtaining a liability order opens up the possibility of the Agency taking further enforcement action, either in the county court (third party debt order or charging order) or through the magistrates' court (driving disqualification or imprisonment).

[145] CSA 1991, s 2.

[146] *Secretary of State for Social Security v Nicol (No 2)* 1997 SLT 572.

[147] CSA 1991, s 33(3). The liability order must be in the form set out in sch 1 to SI 1992/1989.

[148] CSA 1991, s 33(4). See also *Secretary of State for Social Security v Shotton and others*, n 123 above. Thus a challenge to the underlying assessment must be via the statutory appeals route to a tribunal and thence the Commissioner. However, the Court of Appeal has held that the magistrates' court has a wider jurisdiction: see *Farley v Child Support Agency and Secretary of State for Work and Pensions* [2005] EWCA Civ 778 and 869, under appeal to the House of Lords at the time of writing.

[149] *R (on the application of Clark) v Child Support Agency* [2002] EWHC Admin 284 at para 17 *per* Wilson J and *R (on the application of J) v Reading Magistrates' Court* [2002] EWHC Admin 950. Of course, the habitual residence finding may be challenged through the child support appeals machinery.

[150] *Secretary of State for Social Security v Thomson* 1997 SLT 610.

[151] *Secretary of State for Social Security v Nicol (No 2)* n 146 above, at 574 *per* Lord Clyde.

[152] *R (on the application of Denson) v Child Support Agency* n 140 above at para 34, *per* Munby J.

[153] CSA 1991, s 33(5) and Register of County Court Judgments Regulations 1985 (SI 1985/1807), regs 1A and 6A, inserted by the Register of County Court Judgments (Amendments) Regulations 1996 (SI 1996/1177).

Distress

Distress is an ancient means of enforcing judgments that involves the seizure and sale of a person's belongings to pay debts.[154] Where a liability order has been obtained, the Secretary of State 'may levy the appropriate amount by distress and sale of the liable person's goods'.[155] There are, however, limits on what can be seized. Distress may not be levied against the liable person's cash, nor against his clothing, furniture, household equipment and such other items as are 'necessary for satisfying his basic domestic needs'.[156] The liable person's tools, vehicles and other items used for the purposes of employment are also exempt from seizure.[157] The breadth of these exemptions may be one reason why distress is rarely successful—apparently distraint on goods is effective in less than 10 per cent of cases.[158] Regulations set out the procedures which must be adopted when levying distress.[159] If the liable person pays the appropriate amount before the goods are seized and/or sold, the distress must not be proceeded with.[160]

A person who is aggrieved by the levying of distress—which need not be the liable person—has the right of appeal by way of complaint to the magistrates' court.[161] The court, if satisfied that the distress was irregular, may order the return of the goods seized or make an equivalent award of compensation.[162] The term 'irregular' is not defined in the legislation.[163] The High Court has held that there was a clear irregularity where the Agency had failed to inform both the bailiffs and, on the hearing of the liable person's complaint, the magistrates' court, that the amount in arrears had been recalculated and substantially reduced since the liability order had originally been granted.[164] Commentators disagree as to whether the term 'irregular' is confined to procedural defects,[165] or might include disputes over the

---

[154] The discussion that follows applies only to England and Wales: see CSA 1991, s 58(9). For the provisions relating to Scotland see *ibid*, s 38. Note that poinding and sale in Scotland was abolished with effect from 31 December 2002: Abolition of Poindings and Warrant Sales Act 2001 (Sc).

[155] CSA 1991, s 35(1). 'The appropriate amount' is the aggregate of the child support debt together with the charges connected with the distress: *ibid*, s 35(2). On the charges, see SI 1992/1989, reg 32 and sch 2.

[156] CSA 1991, s 35(3). Domestic needs include those of any member of his family with whom he resides: *ibid*, s 35(4).

[157] *Ibid*, s 35(3)(a)(i).

[158] Baroness Hollis, *Hansard*, HL Debates, vol 612 col 1349 (8 May 2000).

[159] CSA 1991, s 35(7) and (8). Thus bailiffs must carry written authorisation and hand to or leave at the premises copies of various documents: SI 1992/1989, reg 30(2).

[160] *Ibid*, reg 30(4) and (5).

[161] *Ibid*, reg 31(1) and (2).

[162] *Ibid*, reg 31(3).

[163] But note that distress is not rendered 'unlawful' merely because of a defect in the liability order: *ibid*, reg 30(3).

[164] *R (on the application of Marsh) v Lincoln District Magistrates Court and Secretary of State for Work and Pensions* [2003] EWHC 956 (Admin). The disparity here was considerable: the liability order was for a debt of £3,389.30, but the arrears were later reassessed at £2,101.39. Thus there was a clear injustice on the facts of this case: *quaere* whether the outcome would have been the same if the arrears had only been marginally reduced.

[165] R Bird, *Child Support—The New Law* (Family Law, Bristol, 5th edn, 2002), at 100.

ownership of the goods seized.[166] The latter view is surely the preferable one, given the potential impact on third party rights. However, the court is entitled, when faced with a complex factual or legal dispute about the ownership of goods seized, to leave the appellant to seek his remedy in the higher courts under civil law.[167]

Enforcement in the County Courts

Assuming that the liability order has been registered, and arrears remain outstanding, the Secretary of State can enforce the debt through the county court (but not the High Court) by means either of a third party debt order[168] or a charging order.[169] A third party debt order is used to require a third party, typically a bank with which the liable person has an account in surplus, to pay the money owing. A charging order secures the payment of arrears from property or other funds belonging to the liable person. This enables the Secretary of State to seek a charging order on the liable person's home, which may then in the last resort be enforced by an application to court for an order for sale. Applications for both types of order are governed by the County Court Rules,[170] rather than any rules specific to the child support jurisdiction.

Disqualification from Driving

The sanction of withdrawing the non-resident parent's driving licence for persistent non-payment of child support liabilities was first used in the United States in the mid-1990s. This option was only introduced in the United Kingdom in April 2001, following amendments made by the 2000 Act.[171] The proposal emerged for public debate here in the 1999 White Paper,[172] not having been mentioned in the preceding Green Paper, but had in fact been an option under consideration by policy makers for some time.[173] A limited precedent had been set by criminal justice legislation in 1997, which provides that the Crown Court or magistrates' court may disqualify an offender from driving on conviction for any offence, either in addition to or instead of any other sentence.[174] The extension of this type of

---

[166] K Puttick, *Child Support Law* (Emis Professional Publishing, 2003), at 322.

[167] Jacobs and Douglas, n 19 above, at 315, citing *R v Basildon Justices, ex parte Holding and Barnes plc* [1994] RA 157.

[168] Formerly a garnishee order.

[169] CSA 1991, s 36(1).

[170] SI 1981/1687, Ord 30 (third party debt order) and Ord 31 (charging order); on the latter, see also Charging Orders Act 1979 and the discussion in Jacobs and Douglas, n 165 above, at 136 and Bird, n 165 above, at 100–1.

[171] CSA 1991, s 39A, inserted by CSPSSA 2000, s 16(1) (see SI 2000/3354, Art 2(3)).

[172] DSS, n 41 above, at ch 8 para 16.

[173] For example, there is a (currently closed) PRO file (JB 3/106) from 1996 entitled 'Child support policy: simplifications and proposals to ban absent parents in maintenance arrears from driving'.

[174] Crime (Sentences) Act 1997, s 39; see now Powers of Criminal Courts (Sentencing) Act 2000, s 146. By the time Parliament was considering the 2000 Bill, pilot schemes under the 1997 Act suggested

penalty to the realm of child support prompted a range of reactions in Parliament. Lord Stoddart described the provision as 'a nasty, discriminatory, extremist and authoritarian clause'.[175] The Conservative Opposition in the House of Commons somewhat mischievously proposed that non-compliant non-resident parents should alternatively face the possibility of a benefit penalty, a home detention curfew under the Crime and Disorder Act 1998 or a community service order.[176] The White Paper also raised the possibility of removing passports from child support defaulters, but this idea was not subsequently pursued.[177]

The 1991 Act now provides that the Secretary of State may apply to the court where he has either sought to levy distress or to recover the sum owing through enforcement in the county court (or, in either case, via the parallel Scottish procedure) and that sum (or part of it) remains unpaid.[178] The court in question is either the magistrates' court or, in Scotland, the sheriff.[179] The court then has the power either to issue a warrant committing the liable person to prison (which is discussed further below) or to make a driving disqualification order.[180] The court may make whichever order it considers appropriate in all the circumstances of the case,[181] and both the Secretary of State and the liable person are entitled to make representations on the point.[182] In considering such an application, the court must, in the presence of the liable person, inquire as to his means.[183] The case law on committal to prison for non-payment of rates (now council tax) demonstrates that magistrates must conduct a detailed means enquiry, or any subsequent order may be quashed.[184] Although the hearing of the application can only proceed in the presence of the liable person, there are measures available to deal with those who fail to attend.[185] The court must also consider whether the liable person needs a driving licence to earn his living.[186] A 'driving licence' is

---

that courts would rarely use the power to disqualify: out of a total of 84,000 fines issued, 155 fine defaulters had received driving disqualifications (*per* Baroness Hollis, *Hansard*, HL Debates vol 614 col 498 (22 June 2000).

[175] *Hansard*, HL Debates vol 612 col 1347 (8 May 2000).

[176] Standing Committee F, cols 321–31 (3 February 2000). This may, of course, simply have been a probing amendment.

[177] See further below.

[178] CSA 1991, s 39A(1).

[179] *Ibid*, s 39A(6).

[180] *Ibid*, s 39A(2).

[181] It may not issue a warrant for committal and make a driving disqualification order: *ibid*, s 40B(2).

[182] *Ibid*, s 39A(4).

[183] *Ibid*, s 39A(3)(b). A signed statement from the employer detailing wages paid 'shall be evidence of the facts there stated', SI 1992/1989, reg 35(2). Note that if the NRP attends the court may order him to be searched and any money found on his person may be used to satisfy the debt. This is because Magistrates' Courts Act 1980, s 80 is applied by virtue of CSA 1991, s 40B(10).

[184] See eg *R v Richmond Justices, ex parte Atkins* [1983] RVR 148 (magistrates wrongly assumed debtor could borrow further funds from bank).

[185] A magistrate can issue a summons requiring the liable person to attend (with his driving licence), and a warrant for arrest may be issued in the event of non-attendance: SI 1992/1989, reg 35(1).

[186] CSA 1991, s 39A(3)(a).

defined by reference to domestic legislation[187] and so excludes those issued by the authorities in other countries.[188]

Most importantly, the court may only make a driving disqualification order if it is satisfied that there has been 'wilful refusal or culpable neglect' on the debtor's part.[189] This statutory formula is of considerable vintage in the context of committal to prison for non-payment of maintenance and other civil debts.[190] The expression connotes deliberate defiance or reckless disregard; mere dilatoriness or improvidence is not enough.[191] Such a degree of blameworthiness must be established either on the criminal standard of proof or at least a high civil standard.[192] If satisfied that this ground has been made out, the court then has a discretion to make an order disqualifying the liable person for up to two years from holding or obtaining a driving licence.[193] Alternatively, the court may make such an order but suspend its operation for such period and on such terms as it thinks just. The disqualification order must state the amount owing in both arrears and the Secretary of State's costs.[194] The legislation provides for the court to require the liable person to surrender his driving licence and for the court to send it to the Secretary of State.[195] Given that the purpose of this sanction is to provide the defaulting non-resident parent with a final opportunity to comply, the 1991 Act also enables either the liable person or the Secretary of State to apply for the order to be revoked, or for a shorter period of disqualification to be imposed, if all or part of the arrears are paid.[196] If the court decides not to make an order, the Secretary of State may later renew the application on the basis that the liable person's circumstances have changed.[197]

So far, the Agency has made relatively little use of its powers to apply for driving disqualification orders.[198] The Select Committee has suggested that the govern-

---

[187] *Ibid*, s 39A(5) refers to a licence granted under pt III of the Road Traffic Act 1988. HGV licences are issued under pt IV of the 1988 Act, but it is a prerequisite that the driver has a valid ordinary licence.

[188] There is very limited cross-border recognition of driving disqualification orders. Even within the UK itself, driving bans in GB and Northern Ireland respectively were not recognised in the other jurisdiction until October 2004 (Crime (International Co-operation) Act 2003, s 76). A scheme for cross-border recognition between the UK and the Republic of Ireland was announced in February 2006 (DoT press release 9 February 2006). The EU Convention on Driving Disqualification (98/C 216/01) is not yet in force and would not cover child support- related bans in any event.

[189] CSA 1991, ss 39A(3)(c) and 40B(1).

[190] The terminology 'wilful refuses or neglects' appears in the Bankrupts Act 1731 s XIX and Vagrancy Act 1824, s 3; on the latter see *Lewisham Union Guardians v Nice* [1924] 1 KB 618.

[191] *R v Luton Magistrates' Court, ex parte Sullivan* [1992] 2 FLR 196.

[192] *R v South Tyneside Justices, ex parte Martin* (1995) *Independent*, 20 September.

[193] CSA 1991, s 40B(1). The order must be in the format set out in SI 1992/1989, sch 4 (see also reg 35(4)).

[194] CSA 1991, s 40B(3). As to costs, see SI 1992/1989, reg 35(5).

[195] CSA 1991, s 40B(4), (8) and (9). In practice it is then sent to the DVLA. If the liable person fails to produce the licence, see SI 1992/1989, reg 35(6) and (7).

[196] CSA 1991, s 40B(5) and (6).

[197] SI 1992/1989, reg 35(3).

[198] In the first five years since CSPSSA 2000, just 11 driving licences had been removed and 63 suspended disqualification orders made: *Hansard* HC Debates vol 442 col 864W (6 February 2006).

ment investigate the feasibility of making driving licence removal an administrative rather than judicial process.[199]

Imprisonment

The ultimate sanction of imprisonment for non-payment of child support has been part of the scheme since its inception in 1993. But this was nothing new; in adopting this option, the state scheme followed the approach of both the poor law and private law, as imprisonment has long been the final resort in cases of non-payment of maintenance.[200] The initial procedure is governed by the same statutory provision that applies in the context of driving disqualification orders.[201] The Secretary of State may apply to court[202] only where he has either sought to levy distress or to recover the sum owing by a third party debt order or a charging order (or, in either case, via the parallel Scottish procedures) and that sum (or part of it) remains unpaid.[203] The court then has the power either to issue a warrant committing the liable person to prison or to make a driving disqualification order.[204] The same procedure applies as regards conducting a means enquiry and requiring the court both to determine whether there has been 'wilful refusal or culpable neglect' and to listen to representations from the parties.[205]

If satisfied that the case is made out, the magistrates' court must then exercise its discretion to decide whether the issue of a warrant or a driving disqualification order is 'appropriate in all the circumstances',[206] bearing in mind that committal to prison and disqualification orders are mutually exclusive.[207] The court may issue an immediate warrant of commitment or fix a term of imprisonment but postpone the issue of the warrant on such terms as it considers just.[208] It is normal practice to suspend the warrant to give the defaulting liable parent one last chance.[209] Any such warrant must specify the sum outstanding (including costs)[210] and the maximum period of imprisonment must not exceed six weeks.[211]

Plainly the decision to commit the liable person to prison is an extremely serious matter. The mere fact that the court disbelieves the liable person's evidence does not necessarily mean that committal is appropriate; it must examine whether he

---

[199] n 87 above, para 172. This approach would follow that used in many American jurisdictions.
[200] See chs 2–4 above and see now Magistrates' Courts Act 1980, s 76.
[201] CSA 1991, s 39A.
[202] For procedure on such an application, see SI 1992/1989, reg 33.
[203] CSA 1991, s 39A(1).
[204] *Ibid*, s 39A(2).
[205] *Ibid*, s 39A(3) and (4).
[206] *Ibid*, s 39A(2).
[207] *Ibid*, s 40B(2). Committal warrants may not be issued against liable persons under the age of 18; *ibid*, s 40(5).
[208] *Ibid*, s 40(3). The form of the warrant is specified by SI 1992/1989, sch 3.
[209] See also SI 1992/1989, reg 34(5) and (6) on the effect of part payment.
[210] CSA 1991, s 40(4).
[211] *Ibid*, s 40(6) and (7).

has the means to pay before concluding that there has been 'wilful refusal or cul-pable neglect'.[212] The High Court held in *ex parte Sullivan*,[213] involving arrears due under a court order for maintenance, that committal is a 'power of extreme sever-ity . . . Parliament has made it plain that the power is to be exercised sparingly and only as a last resort'.[214] Thus it was not appropriate on the facts of that case, in which arrears had built up as a result of the debtor's ill-health and redundancy, and in which the magistrates had made a committal order following his failure to attend a means enquiry without considering possible alternative measures. Equally, even the power to make a suspended order for such a civil debt 'is one to be exercised with great caution and only if there is no other practical alternative'.[215]

The particular statutory provisions discussed above do not apply to Scotland,[216] but there are analogous rules with the necessary modifications for that juris-diction.[217]

Is there a Case for Additional Enforcement Measures?

Some of the weaknesses with the existing legislative framework have been discussed in the context of particular enforcement tools. A more fundamental question is whether there is a case to be made for the introduction of additional enforcement measures, such as banning child support defaulters from overseas travel. As explained in more detail below, the US authorities have the power both to refuse applications for passports and to revoke current passports in such cases. We have already seen that the possibility of a statutory power to withdraw a defaulter's pass-port was canvassed in the White Paper preceding the 2000 Act, but that this option was not pursued at the time. The issue (and withdrawal) of a British passport is a matter for the royal prerogative, and decisions relating to passports are subject to judicial review. The most common reason for refusing, revoking or withholding a passport is because of a risk that the individual will leave the country in order to evade justice.[218] So it remains the case that, at least as far as statute is concerned, it is only British football hooligans, rather than child support defaulters, who may be prevented (albeit temporarily) from travelling abroad.[219]

---

[212] *S N v S T* [1995] 1 FLR 868. See also *Ellis v Ellis* [2005] EWCA Civ 853 and *Rundell v Rundell* [2005] EWCA Civ 1764.

[213] *R v Luton Magistrates' Court, ex parte Sullivan*, n 191 above.

[214] *Ibid*, at 201 per Waite J.

[215] *Daddi v Marshall, Clerk to the Justices on behalf of Karen Buckenham* CO/430/99, *per* Keene J.

[216] CSA 1991, s 40(12).

[217] *Ibid*, s 40A and the Child Support (Civil Imprisonment) (Scotland) Regulations 2001 (SI 2001/1236 (S3)).

[218] Hansard HC Debates (5th Series) vol 746 col 183 (13 May 1968), cited in *Halsbury's Laws of England* vol 18(2) 4th Edition Reissue (2000) para 612.

[219] Convicted football hooligans may be made subject to a banning order under s 14B of the Football Spectators Act 1989 (inserted by Football (Disorder) Act 2000, s 1 and sch 1), which may include a condition requiring the (temporary) surrender of a UK passport (see s 22A) before a game to be played overseas (s 14E(3)); see also the summary powers under ss 21A–21C. These powers were renewed for a further five years by the Football (Disorder) (Amendment) Act 2002.

There may yet be a case for including withdrawal of a non-resident parent's passport as a potential weapon in the Agency's enforcement armoury. This would certainly be welcomed by those parents with care who seek a departure direction on the basis of their ex-partner's lifestyle being inconsistent with his declared income, pointing to his expensive holidays abroad.[220] Non-resident parents would doubtless argue that the refusal or withdrawal of a passport would constitute an unwarranted breach of the father's human rights, but a court might well conclude that, in appropriate cases, it was a proportionate response to the problem of enforcing child support liabilities.[221] However, the Select Committee has recommended that the Department examine the use of travel bans and passport withdrawal as an enforcement tool for non-resident parents who persistently default on their child support commitments.[222] It is therefore relevant to consider the enforcement mechanisms available in comparable jurisdictions, and especially in the United States of America and Australia.

Enforcement Measures in the United States

The Development of Child Support Enforcement Measures in the USA

The child support authorities in the United States enjoy access to a wider range of enforcement tools and sanctions to secure payment of child support than their counterparts in the United Kingdom. In part this simply reflects the fact that enforcement of child support liabilities has long been accorded a higher political priority in the United States. A further explanation lies in the fact that the state-based nature of the child support jurisdiction in the USA has encouraged local initiative in developing new enforcement methods. States were required to establish child support enforcement agencies by legislation in 1974.[223] Subsequent legislation in 1981 enabled the federal tax authorities to withhold tax refunds from child support debtors and states to recoup child support liabilities from unemployment benefits.[224] Further amendments in the 1980s provided for wage withholding and state tax intercepts.[225] Non-payment of child support in interstate cases was criminalised by the Child Support Recovery Act 1992.[226] Similarly, the American

---

[220] M Chetwynd *et al*, *The Departures Pilot Scheme* (DSS In-house report 33, London, 1997) at 32.

[221] The Court of Appeal has held that football banning orders do not contravene either the right to a fair trial under Art 6 of the ECHR or the right to freedom of movement: *Gough v Chief Constable of the Derbyshire Constabulary* [2002] EWCA Civ 351, [2002] 2 All ER 985.

[222] n 87 above at para 192.

[223] Child Support Enforcement Act 1974; see also ch 6 above.

[224] Omnibus Budget Reconciliation Act 1981.

[225] Child Support Enforcement Amendments of 1984; see also Family Support Act 1988.

[226] See further above, p 153.

authorities tend to make more use of imprisonment as a penalty for non-payment of child support than is the case today in the United Kingdom.[227]

Typically, the traditional tools for enforcing civil orders in the USA, such as wage attachment, liens against property and levying and execution against property, required case by case action, initiated by the parent with care.[228] However, several US states developed licence suspension programmes in the early 1990s, which were designed to provide a more systematic approach to dealing with non-compliance, with proceedings instigated by administrative rather than individual action. These initiatives were given greater impetus by the passage of the PRWORA 1996.[229] The 1996 Act required employers to report details of all new employees they hired to a central registry in order to facilitate the process of tracing child support debtors. It also made provision for the refusal or suspension of licences and passports to those in arrears.

Licence Denial and Suspension Programmes

In 1990 Arizona and Vermont introduced novel procedures under which business, professional or trade licences could be suspended for non-payment of child support.[230] By 1995 a total of 19 states had instituted licence suspension schemes. These were primarily concerned with occupational licences; only seven states extended these arrangements to drivers' licences, possibly reflecting state legislators' concerns not to interfere with debtors' continuing employment.[231] The PRWORA 1996 required state-level child support agencies to put in place arrangements for withholding, suspending or restricting drivers' and occupational licences for child maintenance debtors.[232] Failure to do so jeopardises federal funding for state child support agencies. The actual details of such licence suspension arrangements were left to the discretion of states.

Consequently there is considerable diversity of practice across states in both the scope and the execution of licence suspension arrangements. According to one

---

[227] The argument that imprisonment improves compliance is supported by D Chambers, *Making fathers pay: the enforcement of child support* (University of Chicago Press, Chicago, 1979), discussed by RH Moonkin, 'Review: Using Jail for Child Support Enforcement' (1981) 48 *University of Chicago Law Review* 338 and more recently by DA Swank 'Incarceration's Impact on Child Support Compliance' [2001] *International Family Law* 131.

[228] MR Fondacaro and DP Stolle, 'Revoking motor vehicle and professional licenses for purposes of child support enforcement: constitutional challenges and policy implications' (1996) 5 *Cornell Journal of Law & Public Policy* 355 at 359.

[229] Canada followed suit with federal legislation in 1997; by 2001 nine of the 14 jurisdictions operated some form of licence denial and suspension programme: S Moyer, *Licence Suspension and Denial: Overview of a New Mechanism for Child Support Enforcement* (Department of Justice, Canada, 2001) at iii.

[230] *Ibid*, at 5.

[231] *Ibid*, at 6.

[232] The 1996 Act also stipulated that applicants for various types of licences had to provide their social security number (SSN, the US equivalent to a NINo) on applications; this obviously facilitates computerised checking of databases for defaulters.

study,[233] all 52 US states and territories make provision for the suspension of professional licences, whereas the number of jurisdictions which apply such schemes to occupational and/or trade licences and to business licences is 44 and 25 respectively. Some 39 states and territories are able to suspend recreational licences, eg fishing and hunting permits.[234] The 'trigger point' at which suspension action is taken also varies; typically two months' arrears (11 states) or three months' arrears (21 states) are required before proceedings are instituted.[235] Some states also set a threshold in terms of a dollar amount of arrears (typically US$1,000) which must have accumulated before licences can be suspended.[236] States also differ as to whether licence suspension is a judicial or administrative process, or a combination of the two, typically administrative action to implement licence suspension with the opportunity of judicial review.[237] Whilst administrative suspension processes may well be less sensitive to individual circumstances, the American experience suggests that they have the advantage over court-based procedures in terms of speed, efficiency and improved collection rates.[238]

Indeed, considerable claims as to the success of such initiatives have been made across the United States. It is argued that drivers' licence suspension programmes are effective in improving child support compliance, especially in private cases involving self-employed non-resident parents.[239] In California the authorities claimed to have generated the payment of US$14 million in child support arrears through licence revocation procedures between 1992 and 1995, during which period 27,000 state-issued business and professional licences were revoked.[240] However, the methodology underlying such assertions has been questioned, and there are difficulties in accurately measuring the impact of such procedures.[241] That said, the objective of such legislation may be as much about general behaviour modification—in terms of ensuring that a higher priority is attached in society to child support liabilities than traditionally has been the case—as with encouraging payment in particularly intractable cases of arrears.[242]

---

[233] Moyer, n 229 above, at 8.

[234] There are practical problems in suspending such licences, given that they are typically sold at small retail outlets and in the absence of any centralised database of permit holders: *ibid*, at 12.

[235] *Ibid*, at 14. Exceptionally Florida has no minimum amount or period of arrears, although its law states that occupational licences cannot be suspended until other remedies have been exhausted: *ibid* at 13.

[236] *Ibid*, at 13–14.

[237] *Ibid*, at 14–15.

[238] *Ibid*, at 17. Texas deals with licence suspensions in welfare cases by administrative means and judicially in the enforcement of private maintenance liabilities: *ibid*, at 14.

[239] DA Swank, 'The National Child Non-Support Epidemic' (2003) *Michigan State DCL Law Review* 357 at 371.

[240] AM Rotondo, 'Helping families help themselves: using child support enforcement to reform our welfare system' (1997) 33 *Californian Western Law Review* 281 at 294.

[241] Moyer, n 229 above, at 19–22. In particular, there are difficulties in identifying the extent to which arrears are paid specifically in response to licence revocations.

[242] CV Piersol, 'Child support enforcement in South Dakota: a practitioner's guide' (1995) 40 *South Dakota Law Review* 393 at 396.

To date the courts in the United States have upheld legislation providing for the revocation and suspension of licences, as commentators predicted would be the case, notwithstanding several challenges on constitutional grounds.[243] For example, in California the withdrawal of drivers' licences has been held to be rationally related to the legitimate government purpose of enforcing child support liabilities.[244] Similarly, the Supreme Court of Montana, upholding its state's licence suspension laws, ruled that the child support liability was a 'social obligation that a parent owes not only to their children but to the state as well'.[245]

Withdrawal of Passports

The American federal authorities have the power to refuse or withdraw passports as a result of amendments made by the PRWORA 1996.[246] Where a non-resident parent owes more than US$5,000 in child support arrears, the authorities are required to notify the Secretary of State,[247] who *must* then refuse an application for a passport and *may* 'revoke, restrict, or limit a passport issued previously to such individual'.[248] In the fiscal year 2000, more than US$6.5 million in lump sum child support payments was collected through this means, and currently about 60 passports daily are denied to child support debtors.[249] The American courts have rejected arguments that such action constitutes a violation of an individual's constitutional rights; according to the US Court of Appeals Ninth Circuit, this sanction 'passes rational basis review with flying colors'.[250] The court in that case observed that the non-resident parent, a (female) lawyer with arrears in excess of US$20,000, 'is free to be a worker in the vineyards of the law, or to be a worker in another field . . . but the Constitution does not require that she be given a passport at this time'.[251]

---

[243] Fondacaro and Stolle, n 228 above, at 398–99.

[244] See eg *Tolces v Trask* (1999) 76 Cal App 4th 285, 90 Cal Rptr 2d 294 (4th District). See also *Thompson v Ellenbecker* 935 F Supp 1037 (1995) (District Court, Sth Dakota).

[245] *Hopper v Hopper* (1999) 297 Mont 225, 991 P2d 960 at 237 *per* Hunt J. It was thus irrelevant that the youngest child in question had already passed the age of majority when licence suspension proceedings were instituted.

[246] PRWORA 1996 § 370(a)(1), inserting 42 USC § 652(k).

[247] A state's entitlement to federal funds depends on appropriate procedures being in place: § 654(31).

[248] *Ibid*, § 652(k)(2). It is planned to lower the threshold for arrears to US$2,500 from 1 October 2006.

[249] US House of Representatives, Committee on Ways and Means, *2004 Green Book* at 8-40. In practice revocations only take place where an individual applies to renew a passport: see *Weinstein v Albright* (2001) 261 F 3d 127 at 138.

[250] *Eunique v Powell* (2002) 302 F 3d 971 at 975, *per* Fernandez J (but see the strong dissent by Kleinfeld J). A due process challenge to the absence of a federal hearing before refusal or revocation of a passport failed in *Weinstein v Albright* (2001) 261 F 3d 127 given the opportunity to contest the arrears determination at state level.

[251] *Eunique v Powell* (2002) 302 F 3d 971 at 976, *per* Fernandez J. There is similar legislation in Canada permitting the revocation of federal passports and licences (Family Orders and Agreements Enforcement Assistance Act 1985, pt III, as amended in 1997), which is currently under challenge in *Caruso v Attorney-General of Canada* (Superior Court of Québec, 2006).

Other Enforcement Mechanisms

The diversity of the US child support system has spawned a range of other enforcement techniques.[252] For example, some state agencies issue 'Wanted' posters in an attempt to track down child support evaders.[253] In 1997 Virginia pioneered the use of wheel clamping as a 'last resort' child support enforcement tool, a procedure now adopted in several other jurisdictions.[254] As with the use of 'Wanted' posters, wheel clamping in Virginia is consciously designed to shame defaulters in a highly visible fashion—the wheel clamps are pink where the arrears relate to a daughter and blue for a son, along with fluorescent windscreen stickers explaining the reason for the clamping.[255] It is a nice question as to whether public opinion in the United Kingdom would ever be receptive to such an avowedly public process of 'naming and shaming' child support defaulters.

Enforcement Measures in Australia

An Overview of Child Support Enforcement Measures in Australia

The Australian Child Support Agency, as with its United Kingdom counterpart, has a strong preference for arrangements for the payment of child support to be negotiated, either privately between the parties or between the Agency and the liable parent. If voluntary payments are not forthcoming, the Registrar has a range of administrative enforcement powers available. Some of these are comparable to those which exist in the United Kingdom scheme; for example, the Agency may make deductions from Centrelink payments of social security benefits and may require employers to make deductions direct from salary. In other respects, the Registrar's powers are more extensive: for example, the Australian Agency may intercept income tax refunds and also collect child support arrears from third parties by administrative action, eg by accessing funds in savings accounts or superannuation funds.[256] The Agency in Australia may also impose a departure

---

[252] Not including more imaginative proposals which have yet to be put into practice: see eg JS Schepler, 'Prosecuting child support frauds: a novel application of the federal mail fraud statute to the wilful avoidance of child support' (1999) 51 *Baylor Law Review* 581.

[253] Eg South Dakota: see Piersol n 242 above at 394–95. There are a number of examples available on the www. See, for instance, http://www.mostwanted.dshs.wa.gov/ with 'mugshots' of those in Washington 'Wanted for Non-Payment of Child Support'.

[254] Or, as the procedure is known in the USA, 'booting', after 'the Denver Boot'. See Swank, n 239 above, at 372–75 and see generally DA Swank, 'Das Boot! A national survey of booting programs' impact on child support compliance' (2002) 4 *Journal of Law and Family Studies* 265.

[255] *Ibid*, at 268.

[256] Child Support (Registration and Collection) Act 1988 (Cth), s 72A. A Parliamentary Committee has proposed that the Australian Agency be granted additional enforcement powers: see House of Representatives Standing Committee on Family and Community Affairs, *Every picture tells a story* (Canberra, AGPS, December 2003), recommendation 25. See also Report of the Ministerial Taskforce on Child Support, *In the Best Interests of Children* (Canberra, May 2005) ch 10.

prohibition order, which is discussed further below, to prevent the liable parent from leaving the country. If administrative action is unsuccessful or inappropriate, the Registrar may initiate court action to enforce a child support liability, for example to seek orders for the sale of assets. In addition, the Registrar may apply to court for an order setting aside a particular transaction made to defeat or reduce the liable parent's ability to pay child support.[257] This type of anti-avoidance provision exists in matrimonial proceedings in the United Kingdom, but not in the child support jurisdiction here.[258] Furthermore, whereas the United Kingdom Agency's court-based enforcement powers are confined to those set out in the 1991 Act,[259] the Registrar may enforce the child support debt either as an ordinary civil debt or through the family law jurisdiction.[260] However, the success of a child support agency cannot be judged by the severity of the sanctions available to it—neither driving disqualification orders nor imprisonment are open to the Australian authorities as penalties.[261]

Departure Prohibition Orders

Since 2001 the Australian Agency has been able to impose departure prohibition orders on child support debtors, based on an enforcement tool used by the ATO for tax defaulters.[262] The Child Support Registrar has the power to make a departure prohibition order (DPO) if four conditions are satisfied. The first three are that the parent in question must have a child support liability, must not have made satisfactory arrangements to discharge that liability and must have 'persistently and without reasonable grounds' failed to pay his child support debts . Finally, the Agency must believe that it is desirable to make such an order to ensure that he does not leave Australia without meeting his liabilities in full or making satisfactory arrangements to do so.[263] The effect of a DPO is that a liable parent in arrears is ordered 'to pay up or stay put',[264] although he may move freely within the country.[265] Although a draconian measure, the making of a DPO is a purely

---

[257] Child Support (Registration and Collection) Act 1988 (Cth), s 72C.

[258] Matrimonial Causes Act 1973, s 37.

[259] See p 448 above.

[260] N Harden, 'Child Support Enforcement' (2003) 16 *Australian Family Lawyer* 13 at 15.

[261] The Standing Committee suggested that driving licence revocation be considered in Australia: n 256 above, but this was rejected by the ministerial Taskforce: n 256 above at 173. Note also that the issue of driving licences in Australia is a state rather than federal responsibility.

[262] Child Support (Registration and Collection) Act 1988 (Cth), pt VA; see also Taxation Administration Act 1953 (Cth), s 14S and *Re: Edelsten and Seberry and the Deputy Commissioner of Taxation* (1992) 108 ALR 195.

[263] Child Support (Registration and Collection) Act 1988 (Cth), s 72D.

[264] 'Parents ordered to pay up or stay put', *The Age* (Melbourne), 25 August 2003. For an illustration of a DPO having the desired effect, see *A & A & Y* [2004] FMCAfam 209: the liable parent, 'clearly shocked' by the imposition of a DPO, undertook to pay Aus$29,000 to the payee.

[265] A phenomenon referred to anecdotally by some Agency staff in Western Australia as 'disappearing over in Queensland'.

administrative act by the Agency. The DPO remains in force until either the Registrar revokes it or a court sets it aside.[266]

In practice the Australian Agency uses DPOs as a last resort enforcement tool, typically where there is evidence that a liable parent has a propensity for overseas travel and where other administrative enforcement activities have not proved successful. The Agency has used DPOs to collect Aus\$6.98 million in child support dents in a total of 773 cases between 1 July 1999 and January 2006.[267] This is in stark contrast to the limited use of driving licence disqualification orders in the United Kingdom. As yet there has been no systematic comparative study of the United States and Australian experiences with overseas travel-based enforcement tools. The Australian sanction appears to have the wider reach in two respects, precisely because it is a DPO rather than a process for withdrawing or revoking passports.[268] First, it can take effect immediately (DPOs are copied to the federal police, customs and immigration services) without any need physically to impound individuals' passports. Secondly, and equally importantly given the multicultural nature of modern Australian society, there is no requirement that the subject of a DPO be an Australian citizen.[269]

---

[266] Child Support (Registration and Collection) Act 1988 (Cth), s 72H. A person subject to a DPO can apply for a Departure Authorisation Certificate or DAC (*ibid*, s 72F), and the Registrar's refusal to issue a DAC, or to revoke a DPO, can be reviewed by the Administrative Appeals Tribunal (AAT): *ibid*, s 72T. The decision to make a DPO in the first place may be appealed to the Federal Court: *ibid*, ss 72Q–72S.

[267] Australian Child Support Agency, personal communication.

[268] The New Zealand scheme operates a different approach still—there is no power to revoke passports, or to issue a DPO as such, but the authorities have the power to issue an arrest warrant if they believe a child support debtor is about to leave the country: Child Support Act 1991 (NZ) s 199; and see *Commissioner of Inland Revenue v Karika* [1999] NZFLR 409 and *Commissioner of Inland Revenue v C* [2004] NZFLR 1019.

[269] Indeed, in one of the few reported court decisions on DPOs, the Australian liable parent subject to a DPO was a Czech national: *T & G v Child Support Registrar* [2003] FMCA fam 197.

Part III

15

Conclusion: Child Support Compliance and Reform

Introduction

This concluding chapter addresses one of the most important and pressing questions facing social policy makers today: in short, does the United Kingdom's child support system have a future and, if so, what might that future look like? In doing so, the discussion draws on this book's analysis of the principles underpinning child support law,[1] the less than glorious history of child maintenance arrangements before the Child Support Act 1991 in the realms of both public and private law,[2] the experience of formula-based schemes in overseas jurisdictions,[3] and the highly complex legal framework of today's United Kingdom child support scheme.[4] This discussion is set against the backdrop of the Labour government's current 'root and branch' review of child support arrangements. In February 2006 the Secretary of State for Work and Pensions conceded that 'neither the agency nor the policy is fit for purpose'[5] and announced a two-stage strategy for reform. First, the Agency launched yet another plan designed to stabilise and improve its lamentable operational performance.[6] Secondly, Sir David Henshaw[7] was appointed to oversee a redesign of the child support scheme with a view to producing a report for ministers by the summer of 2006 containing recommendations for the longer term policy and delivery arrangements for child support.[8]

At the outset, however, it is important to recognise the limitations of both the law and the legal process. We know that in practice there are considerable difficulties in enforcing judgments in the ordinary civil courts. Indeed, in general terms 'obtaining the court judgment is the easy part of civil litigation: enforcing it is the

---

[1] Ch 1 above.
[2] Chs 2–5 above.
[3] See especially ch 6 above.
[4] Chs 7–14 above.
[5] Rt Hon John Hutton, *Hansard* HC Debates vol 442 col 1020 (9 February 2006).
[6] Child Support Agency, *Operational Improvement Plan 2006–2009* (February 2006).
[7] Formerly Chief Executive of Liverpool City Council.
[8] See further N Wikeley, 'Child Support—Back to the Drawing Board' (2006) 36 *Family Law* 312 and 'Child Support—Looking to the Future' (2006) 36 *Family Law* 360.

real problem'.[9] Studies of debt enforcement in the wider civil justice field likewise demonstrate that 'whether people pay their creditors is dependent on two factors: their *ability* to pay and their *commitment* to doing so'.[10] Logic dictates that if there are serious problems in enforcing orders which are issued with the full majesty of the court process,[11] then these difficulties may be all the more acute when child support liability orders are generated by a government agency, at least if that organisation lacks either the appropriate enforcement tools or the corporate will to tackle non-compliance effectively. These problems are further compounded by the depth of emotional conflict and trauma which is often associated with relationship breakdown. Indeed, one pessimistic view of family law is that it is 'inherently unenforceable in the traditional sense since it attempts to regulate intimate human relationships'.[12] This is notoriously so in the case of some intractable disputes over children's residence and contact arrangements.[13] It follows that compliance with child support obligations, even more so than with 'ordinary' civil debts, is inextricably linked to both ability and willingness to pay.[14] Much of the media criticism of the performance of the Agency fails to acknowledge this fundamental feature of its work.[15]

Doing nothing, however, is not a realistic policy option. For a start, as a matter of principle, there is the compelling argument that children enjoy a right to child support and it is therefore incumbent on government to ensure that this right is effective and not merely aspirational.[16] Furthermore, the United Kingdom's international treaty obligations require it to have in place a scheme for ensuring that child maintenance obligations are enforced.[17] In addition, in the domestic sphere, one of the current Government's central commitments is the halving of child poverty by 2010 and its eradication by 2020.[18] The attainment of this goal will only

---

[9] J Baldwin, *Evaluating the Effectiveness of Enforcement Procedures in Undefended Claims in the Civil Courts* (LCD Research series, Report No 3/03, London, 2003) at 5.

[10] N Dominy and E Kempson, *Can't Pay or Won't Pay? A review of creditor and debtor approaches to the non-payment of bills* (LCD Research Series, Report No 4/03, London, 2003) at v (original emphasis).

[11] Although admittedly 'the full majesty of the court process' may now simply be a county court default judgment obtained via Money Claim Online.

[12] A Bainham, 'Changing Families and Changing Concepts: Reforming the Language of Family Law' in J Eekelaar and T Nhalpo (eds), *The Changing Family: International Perspectives on the Family and Family Law* (Hart Publishing, Oxford, 1998), ch 10 at 154.

[13] See, eg *A v A* [2004] 1 FLR 1195 at para 23, where Wall J cites with approval from the guardian's report noting that the parents had been in 'a virtual state of war . . . for over 5 years . . . The bundle of case papers I was sent at the start of this case was so large it could be measured with a ruler . . . reading the bundle was a sad testimony that two intelligent people had lost all perspective and common sense in their hatred of each other and their need to battle and win over their ex-partner'. See now the Children and Adoption Bill 2006.

[14] A Atkinson and S McKay, *Investigating the compliance of Child Support Agency clients* (DWP Research Report No 285, London, 2005) at 35.

[15] For a notable exception, see D Aaronovitch, 'What did you expect? The CSA can't solve a million domestic mini-Balkans', *The Times*, 29 November 2005.

[16] See the discussion in ch 1 above.

[17] See eg United Nations Convention on the Rights of the Child, art 27(4) and see p 28 above.

[18] See further HM Treasury, *Child Poverty Review* (HM Treasury, London, 2004) and DWP, *Making a difference: tackling poverty—a progress report* (DWP, London, March 2006).

be hampered in the absence of proper child support arrangements. Moreover, the Public Service Agreement targets set for the Department for Work and Pensions include the ambitious aim of doubling the proportion of parents with care on income support or income-based jobseeker's allowance who receive child maintenance to 60 per cent by March 2006 and to 65 per cent by March 2008.[19] In the 2002 Spending Review this was listed separately as an independent objective,[20] but by the 2004 Spending Review it had been incorporated within the overall goal of abolishing child poverty.[21] This helps to reinforce the message that the target is driven by the objective of seeking to ensure the best start in life for children, rather than a narrower concern for controlling public expenditure.[22]

An effective child support system may also serve a number of other social policy objectives. The research evidence demonstrates that, on average, women and children still face greater financial hardship than men in the wake of relationship breakdown,[23] although the position will be more complex for men in new relationships with new children. To some extent child support payments have a potential redistributive effect in terms of redressing this imbalance.[24] In addition, the receipt of maintenance is positively associated with moving off welfare and into work, especially for lone parents.[25] Higher child support liabilities may have a beneficial impact on children's post-separation cognitive development[26] and may also reduce the risk of couples separating in the first place,[27] in itself generally regarded as a socially desirable goal.[28] Similarly, there is some evidence that increased emphasis on the enforcement of child support liabilities may reduce

---

[19] On the likely failure to meet this target, see p 507 below.

[20] HM Treasury, *Opportunity and Security for All* (Cm 5570, 2002) at 120.

[21] HM Treasury, *2004 Spending Review: Public Service Agreements 2005–2008* (Cm 6238, 2004) at 37.

[22] DWP, *Department for Work and Pensions: Departmental Report* (Cm 6539, 2005) at 16. The new child maintenance premium will result in the Treasury foregoing child support receipts from non-resident parents: see further below at p 506.

[23] J Eekelaar and M Maclean, *Maintenance after Divorce* (Clarendon Press, Oxford, 1986) and M Maclean and J Eekelaar, *The Parental Obligation* (Hart Publishing, Oxford, 1997); see also J Bartfeld, 'Child Support and the Postdivorce Economic Well-Being of Mothers, Fathers, and Children (2000) 37 *Demography* 203.

[24] The difficulty, of course, given the typical post-separation residence arrangements, is that higher levels of child support will be seen by some as thinly disguised spousal or ex-partner support. In addition, in many cases both parents will be in relatively poor financial circumstances.

[25] See eg J Bradshaw and J Millar, *Lone Parent Families in the UK* (DSS Research Report No 6, London, 1991) at 38 and A Marsh and S Vegeris, *The British Lone Parent Cohort and their Children 1991 to 2001* (DWP Research Report No 209, 2004) at 62.

[26] Although this may well depend on the quality of the parents' subsequent relationship: eg LM Argys, E Peters, J Brooks-Gunn and JR Smith, 'The Impact of Child Support on Cognitive Outcomes of Young Children' (1998) 35 *Demography* 159. See further SE Mayer, *The Influence of Parental Income on Children's Outcomes* (NZ Ministry of Social Development, Wellington, 2002) at 61–64.

[27] See I Walker and Y Zhu, *Child Support Liability and Partnership Dissolution* (IFS WP04/18, London, 2004), arguing that the UK divorce rate would have been 15% higher were it not for the introduction of the child support formula.

[28] Although there will be cases involving violence where separation is in the best interests of both parents and children.

divorce and separation rates.[29] These findings need to be seen in the context of the well-established link between parental divorce and subsequent disadvantage for the children concerned.[30] Finally, stronger child support enforcement may reduce teenage pregnancy rates. Put simply, 'if adolescent males realize that fathering a child incurs a financial obligation that lasts for up to 18 years, they are more likely to restrain their sexual activity and take more responsibility for contraception'.[31] It is a mistake, therefore, to see the potential beneficial outcomes of child support policy purely in financial terms.

This chapter starts by exploring the reach of the existing child support arrangements in practice and reviewing the Agency's performance in terms of securing payment of assessed liabilities. It then examines the factors which appear to increase the likelihood of non-resident parents meeting their child support obligations and how these considerations might inform a model for improving compliance rates. In the light of these findings, the discussion then considers three broad policy options which are open to government. First, what are the advantages and disadvantages of a guaranteed maintenance scheme? Secondly, is the return of some or all of the work involved in assessing, collecting and enforcing child maintenance to the courts (and, in practice, to private negotiation) a viable option? Thirdly, if the decision is taken to retain a formula-based administrative child support system, what are the main aspects of the current child support legislation that need to be revisited? These include controversial issues such as the role of a child support disregard for parents with care on benefit and the range of enforcement powers open to the Agency.

The Coverage of the Current Child Support Arrangements in Practice

Socio-legal scholars have long emphasised the importance of the distinction (and often the divergence) between the 'law in books' and the 'law in action'. This is especially evident in the context of child maintenance. The existence of the combined machinery of the 1991 Act and the various residual private law remedies might suggest that, one way or another, child support law and practice will impinge on most families where children live apart from one or other of their

---

[29] LA Nixon, 'The Effect of Child Support Enforcement on Marital Dissolution' (1997) 32 *Journal of Human Resources* 159; but, for a contrary view, see BT Heim, 'Does Child Support Enforcement Reduce Divorce Rates? A Reexamination' (2003) 38 *Journal of Human Resources* 773.

[30] See eg W Sigle-Rushton, J Hobcraft and K Kiernan, 'Parental Divorce and Subsequent Disadvantage: A Cross-Cohort Comparison' (2005) 42 *Demography* 427.

[31] C-C Huang and W-J Han, 'Perceptions of child support and sexual activity of adolescent males' (2004) 27 *Journal of Adolescence* 731. See also RD Plotnick, I Garfinkel, SS McLanahan and I Ku, 'Better Child Support Enforcement: Can It Reduce Teenage Premarital Childbearing?' (2004) 25 *Journal of Family Issues* 634 and C-C Huang, 'Pregnancy Intention from Men's Perspectives: Does Child Support Enforcement Matter?' (2005) 37 *Perspectives on Sexual and Reproductive Health* 119.

genetic parents. The reality, however, is very different. According to the 2004 Families and Children Study (FACS), nearly half (49 per cent) of all families in which children live apart from one of their parents have neither an Agency assessment, nor a court order, nor a private agreement for child support.[32] Obviously there will be a range of reasons for the absence of any such provision, which will not always be a matter of choice for the parent with care.[33] Amongst other families, where there is some sort of arrangement in place, 43 per cent have a voluntary agreement, 38 per cent have an Agency assessment, 8 per cent have a court order and 10 per cent have a combined award.[34] In general terms, child maintenance arrangements are more commonly found amongst couple families than lone parent families, and amongst those working 16 hours or more a week, whether couple or lone parent families, than those who are either not working or are working below that threshold.[35] Moreover, those working more than 16 hours a week are much more likely to have a voluntary agreement than an Agency assessment, whereas those who are not in employment, or are working for less than 16 hours a week, are much more likely to rely on an Agency assessment than a private agreement.[36] This reflects the fact that those parents with care in the latter category are effectively conscripts rather than volunteers.[37] Indeed, the fact that a significant proportion of the Agency's caseload comprises parents with care who are on benefit is in stark contrast to the more universal child support schemes that operate in both Australia and the United States.[38] Private clients in the United Kingdom, on the other hand, may readily opt out and reach their own agreement (or, as FACS demonstrates, no arrangement at all, whether through choice or otherwise[39]). The result is that the Agency has not replaced the courts, as was anticipated in 1991—rather, private ordering has superseded the role of the courts.[40] This is confirmed by studies which suggest that, where possible, many lone parents will try to resolve child maintenance issues without resort to the Agency.[41]

---

[32] N Lyon, M Barnes and D Sweiry, FACS (DWP Research Report No 340, 2006), ch 15 at 313.

[33] Bradshaw and Millar's 1991 study revealed that although 20% of lone parents who were not in receipt of child maintenance said that they did not want payments, most had little option (15% said the absent parent was unemployed, 14% that he could not afford to pay, 11% that he refused to pay and 14% did not know where he was): n 25 above at 80. Note that this survey focussed on lone parents, and there may be other reasons for the absence of child support arrangements where the PWC has a new partner.

[34] Lyon *et al*, n 32 above, at 315.

[35] *Ibid*, at 313.

[36] *Ibid*, at 315.

[37] Contrast CSA 1991 ss 4 and 6.

[38] See further below p 496.

[39] There appears to be no recent UK research on why a significant proportion of parents with care do not have any child support arrangement at all in place (see n 33 above); see by contrast C-C Huang and H Pouncy, 'Why Doesn't She Have a Child Support Order?: Personal Choice or Objective Constraint' (2005) 54 *Family Relations* 547. For a US perspective on the difficulties experienced by PWCs on benefit in securing child support orders, see J Bartfeld, 'Falling Through The Cracks: Gaps in Child Support Among Welfare Recipients' (2003) 65 *Journal of Marriage and Family* 72.

[40] Contrast the 2004 FACS data with the study by Bradshaw *et al* (see n 43 below) at 134–36. I am grateful to Stephen McKay for this insight.

[41] R Moorhead, M Sefton and G Douglas, *The Advice Needs of Lone Parents* (One Parent Families, London, 2004) at 21.

We now turn to consider what is known about both the levels of child support awards in practice, focussing in particular on that subset of cases in which the Agency is directly involved, and also the compliance rates in such cases. It is evident from FACS that this group represents a minority—about one in five[42]—of all families in which children live apart from one of their genetic parents.[43] Common sense dictates that this caseload, as well as including a large number of benefits cases, is likely to include a higher proportion of other cases in which relations between parents are strained, as compared with those subject to voluntary arrangements.[44]

Levels of Child Support Awards

Court orders for child maintenance before the advent of the 1991 Act were typically for modest, and occasionally insulting, amounts.[45] In some cases, but by no means all, these awards were part of an overall settlement brokered by the parties' respective legal advisers, designed to provide the parent with care with a secure home and the non-resident parent with a complete or virtual 'clean break' in financial terms. But low child maintenance orders also reflected the failure by the legal system to acknowledge the true costs of child-raising[46]—or, to put it another way, its greater willingness to prioritise the financial concerns of non-resident parents over the interests of other family members.[47]

In cash terms, the 1990 White Paper reported that the 'going rate' for child maintenance orders at that time was about £18 a week for one dependent child.[48] In all those cases in which child maintenance was actually in payment, regardless of the number of children involved, the mean weekly payment was £24. The then Government's expectation was that the introduction of the child support formula would result in average assessments (across all such cases) of about £40 a week.[49] As we saw in chapter 5,[50] this was arguably the one accurate assumption behind

---

[42] The 'one in five' estimate is based on there being some arrangement in place for just 51% of eligible children, in 38% of which cases there was an Agency assessment: see above.

[43] In one leading study (completed in 1996) only 16% of NRPs were subject to an Agency assessment: J Bradshaw, C Stimson, C Skinner and J Williams, *Absent Fathers?* (Routledge, London, 1999) at 136.

[44] See Argys *et al*, n 26 above, at 167.

[45] See chs 4 and 5 above.

[46] In the broadest possible sense, so including opportunity costs.

[47] For an econometric analysis of this phenomenon, see D Del Boca, 'Mothers, fathers and children after divorce: The role of institutions' (2003) 16 *Journal of Population Economics* 399. See also D Del Boca and CJ Flinn, 'Rationalizing Child-Support Decisions' (1995) 85 *The American Economic Review* 1241.

[48] See p 132 above. The county court average was £20 whereas both magistrates' courts and DSS liable relative orders averaged at £15 p/w per child: DSS, *Children Come First* (Cm 1264-II, 1990) at para 4.1.1.

[49] See p 132 above.

[50] See p 133 above.

the 1991 Act: in June 1994, a little over a year into the scheme, the average full maintenance assessment for non-resident parents who were not on benefit was precisely £40.14. However, despite rising real incomes, there was little change in the value of assessments over the following decade. By May 2004 the average assessment for employed non-resident parents under the old scheme was £39.31 a week, whilst the average liability for the self-employed was just £23.09.[51] It is helpful to benchmark the Agency's average awards with what is known about the typical levels of child maintenance actually received across the board, taking into account all types of arrangements. In 2004 the mean amount of child support in payment across all families with eligible children—whether through an Agency assessment, a voluntary agreement, a court order or some combination of these arrangements—was £60 a week.[52] This higher figure over all cases suggests that the Agency is dealing with a disproportionate number of non-resident parents on low incomes.

Following the introduction of the reforms in the 2000 Act, average liabilities according to the child support formula under the new scheme were expected to fall to £30.50 a week,[53] although there were expected to be both winners and losers.[54] Overall, the government's strategy was clear—'the new simpler rules, tougher sanctions and better enforcement of maintenance will mean that at least 80 per cent of maintenance due will be paid under the new scheme'.[55] This was the essence of the deal for parents with care: average awards would come down but, to compensate for these reductions, compliance would go up (and, for parents with care on benefit, the child maintenance premium would provide a real boost to incomes).[56] Yet it is important to appreciate that the 80 per cent figure was not an *estimate* of future compliance but rather a *target* driven by the need for the reforms to be cost-neutral in public expenditure terms; indeed, it was 'not, in any way, founded on concrete empirical evidence concerning the determinants of compliance'.[57] In overall terms the new child support formula has in one sense at least delivered lower liabilities: in 2004–05 the average child support liability per case (and so irrespective of the number of children), and excluding those cases with a nil assessment, was £43.23 a week under the old scheme but only £28.67 under the new scheme. Looking at it another way, the amount assessed per child was £30.22

---

[51] DWP, *Work and Pension Statistics 2004* (DWP, 2004) at 198, Table 7.

[52] Lyon *et al*, n 32 above, at 317; the median figure was £46 p/w. Note that these figures relate only to families where some form of child maintenance was in payment.

[53] DWP, *A new contract for welfare: Children's Rights and Parents' Responsibilities* (Cm 4349, 1999) at ch 2 para 23.

[54] House of Commons (HC) Social Security Committee, *The 1999 Child Support White Paper* (Tenth Report, Session 1998–99, HC 798) at paras 22–26.

[55] DWP, n 53 above, at ch 2 para 24.

[56] On the child maintenance premium, see p 506 below.

[57] G Paull, I Walker and Y Zhu, 'Child Support Reform: Some Analysis of the 1999 White Paper' (2000) 21 *Fiscal Studies* 105 at 137. There was also a lack of clarity as to the meaning of the 80% figure: it might assume that 80% paid in full, and 20% not at all; or everyone paid 80% of their liability: *ibid.* at 120.

in old scheme cases but just £19.54 under the new scheme.[58] But it would be a serious mistake to assume that *all* child support liabilities have come down. It is true that nearly 80 per cent of the total of all assessments under both schemes fall in the range between nil and £40 a week and there is little change in the distribution of awards above that level. However, a closer analysis of the weekly maintenance liabilities under the old and new schemes respectively as at March 2006 reveals two marked differences in the levels of assessments (see Figure 15.1).[59]

First, more than half of the old scheme cases (57 per cent) are currently assessed as having a nil liability, as against just over one in eight cases (13 per cent) in the new scheme. This reflects the impact of the policy decision under the 2000 Act to remove most of the exemptions that apply to the requirement that non-resident parents on benefit should pay a nominal weekly amount by way of child support.[60] This phenomenon reinforces the strong linkage between the child support and social security systems. The futility of a child support system which assesses more than half its cases at a nil liability speaks for itself.

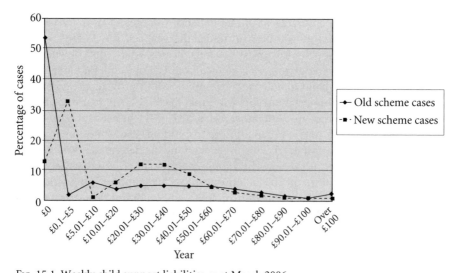

Fig. 15.1 Weekly child support liabilities as at March 2006

---

[58] HC Work and Pensions Committee, *The Child Support Agency: Government Response to the Committee's Second Report of Session 2004-05* (First Special Report of Session 2004-05, HC 477) at 9.

[59] This graph is based on data in DWP, *Child Support Agency Quarterly Summary Statistics: March 2006* (2006) at Table 15.

[60] As a result 32% of cases under the new scheme are assessed at between £0.01 and £5, most (if not all) of which will be at the £5 rate. Note that in Australia 40% of all NRPs are assessed at the minimum rate (Aus$260 p/a, or Aus$5 p/w) or less, although by no means all are on benefits: Ministerial Taskforce on Child Support, *In the Best Interests of Children—Reforming the Child Support Scheme* (FACS, Canberra, 2005) at 95.

Secondly, there has been a marked shift in the internal distribution of the value of assessments for those cases in which the non-resident parent is not on benefit. This is demonstrated by the divergence in the number of assessments in the bands between £20 and £40p/w, which account for nearly one in four (24 per cent) of all liabilities under the new scheme in contrast with just 10 per cent of those under the old scheme (although 24 per cent of old scheme cases are spread fairly evenly between £10 and £60 a week). This presumably reflects the 'broad brush' nature of the new scheme formula which pays no regard to housing costs or other outgoings considered under the old scheme.

This double effect—the abolition of most of the nil rate cases and the clustering effect between £20 and £40 a week in the new scheme—is the main reason why, although the average child support assessment (*excluding* nil liability cases) has dropped with the arrival of a large number of fixed rate £5 assessments, the mean liability across all cases (*including* the now smaller proportion of nil liability cases) has actually risen by a third from £18 (old scheme) to £24 (new scheme).[61]

These levels of Agency-ordered child support need to be seen in context. There is no escaping the fact that, in its own way, the implementation of the new child support formula under the 2000 Act has been just as difficult as the introduction of its predecessor under the 1991 Act. Child support awards clearly have to be both accurate and timely. The ministerial target for the Agency's accuracy rate[62] in new scheme cases is 90 per cent; the performance has been rather lower to date at 82 per cent in 2003–04 and 75 per cent in 2004–05.[63] Inaccuracy, of course, may work both ways; however, the National Audit Office's estimate is that in overall terms in 2004–05 non-resident parents underpaid almost three times as much in child support (£13.4 million) as they overpaid (£4.7 million).[64] Although the Agency's failure to meet the accuracy target has been criticised by the House of Commons Work and Pensions Select Committee,[65] this needs to be seen in perspective: the Agency's performance on accuracy in the first years of the original scheme (from April 1993) was much worse.[66]

The problem, however, is not just one of (in)accuracy; there have also been serious delays in issuing maintenance calculations, which impacts on subsequent compliance. It was anticipated by government that under the new scheme 'maintenance will be flowing in four to six weeks, rather than six months or more, as

---

[61] DWP, n 59 above.

[62] This is defined in terms of accuracy to the nearest penny in the last decision made on all maintenance calculations that are checked in the relevant year.

[63] Child Support Agency Standards Committee, *2004/05 Annual Report* at 6. There was a similar drop in accuracy of last decisions in old scheme cases, from 86% (2003–04) to 78% (2004–05). By September 2005 accuracy had picked up again slightly to 80% (old scheme) and 83% (new scheme): *Hansard* HC Debates vol 440 col 710W (1 December 2005).

[64] Child Support Agency, *Annual Report and Accounts 2004–05* (HC 256, Session 2005–06) at 74.

[65] HC Work and Pensions Select Committee, *The Performance of the Child Support Agency* (Second Report, HC 44-I, Session 2004–05) at paras 83–85.

[66] The proportion of maintenance assessments that were definitely correct in cash terms rose slowly from 25% in 1993–94 to 62% in 1996–97: Central Adjudication Services, *Annual Report of the Chief Child Support Officer 1996–1997* (TSO, 1997) at 2.

now'.[67] The reality is that there has been little if any improvement: the six-week ministerial target for calculating maintenance was dropped in 2004–05, and by March 2006 only about one in four new scheme cases were being cleared within this timescale.[68] Sadly, this has simply reinforced the poor public perception of the Agency, and reaffirmed its reputation as 'a byword for administrative incompetence'.[69] As a result, parents with care and non-resident parents alike feel disenfranchised by the Agency.[70] Of course, issuing child support assessments is one thing; ensuring that the relevant payments are made is quite another. By February 2006 the total amount in child support debt not collected by the Agency stood at over £3 billion,[71] much of which it believes is now simply irrecoverable.[72] We must therefore consider the Agency's compliance targets and the extent to which child support liabilities under the 1991 Act are actually met in practice.

Child Support Agency Compliance Targets and Outcomes

The Agency is subject to two official compliance measures. The first is 'case compliance', which measures the proportion of those cases in which the non-resident parent makes some payment. The second is 'cash compliance', which quantifies the amounts paid by non-resident parents against the total sum of assessed maintenance due.[73] It is important to note that neither measure covers the Agency's full caseload: both are based solely on those cases which use the official collection service—there is no formal target (or measure) of compliance in maintenance direct (or private collection) cases.[74] There are, however, serious practical problems in quantifying compliance in the latter type of case with any precision, not least because of the disparity between what non-resident parents report as having paid and what parents with care declare as having been received.[75] More generally, whether dealing with payments made either through the Agency or directly between parents, it is important to appreciate that any compliance measures are

---

[67] n 53 above at 5.

[68] DWP, n 59 above, Table 4. See further n 65 above at paras 74–82.

[69] H Davies and H Joshi, 'Who has borne the cost of Britain's children in the 1990s? in K Vleminckx and TM Smeeding (eds), *Child Well-Being, Child Poverty and Child Policy in Modern Nations* (Policy Press, Bristol, 2001) ch 12 at 303. See further ch 5 above on the migration of old cases to the new scheme.

[70] Moorhead *et al*, n 41 above, at 47 ('a pervading sense of fatalism on the part of lone parents') and Atkinson and McKay, n 14 above, at 56 (NRPs sometimes felt 'they were being treated like criminals').

[71] *Hansard* HC Debates vol 442 col 1019 (9 February 2006).

[72] Likely reasons include the age of the debt, problems in locating non-resident parents and difficulties in enforcing punitive interim maintenance assessments under the old scheme.

[73] n 65 above at para 96.

[74] Maintenance direct accounts for 18% of old scheme cases and 14% of the new scheme caseload: DWP, n 59 above, at Table 9b. See further A Bell, A Kazimirski and I La Valle, *An investigation of CSA Maintenance Direct Payments: Qualitative study*, DWP Research Report No 327 (DWP, London, 2006).

[75] For one of several studies which suggests that NRPs are prone to over-report having paid child support, see NC Schaeffer, J Seltzer and M Klawitter, 'Estimating Non response and response bias' (1991) 20 *Sociological Methods and Research* 30.

no more than snapshots. In practice the compliance status of a non-resident parent is not static, there being a degree of mobility in both directions. For example, a significant proportion of non-resident parents begin as nil compliant but become partially or fully compliant, whereas conversely large numbers of others who start as fully compliant become less (or nil) compliant over time.[76]

Initially, following the implementation of the 2000 Act, there were different targets for old and new scheme cases respectively, some of which were laid down internally and some of which were set by ministers. For example, the Agency's own internal targets for old scheme cases in 2004–05 were 75 per cent for case compliance and 68 per cent for cash compliance.[77] On the face of it, the Agency managed reasonably well, in that by March 2006 it had achieved a compliance rate of 75 per cent in both case and cash terms in old scheme cases.[78] However, case compliance measures simply whether any payment has been made, and so the actual rate of full compliance will be lower. Indeed, it is customary to categorise compliance by non-resident parents in three ways as full, partial or nil.[79] On this basis, in 2005, 46 per cent of non-resident parents were fully compliant, 24 per cent partially compliant and 30 per cent nil compliant.[80]

The ministerial targets for new scheme cases for 2004–05 were rather more demanding, at 78 per cent for case compliance and 75 per cent for cash compliance. One might have anticipated that the compliance rates would have improved with the new, simpler formula. In fact, the Agency's actual performance that year fell a considerable way short of the targets, at 66 per cent and 61 per cent respectively.[81] This reflects the well documented and chronic problems in implementing the child support reforms and in particular the difficulties associated with the new computer system.[82] For 2005–06 onwards ministers have set a case compliance target of 78 per cent and a cash compliance target of 75 per cent for new scheme cases using the Agency's collection service.[83] By March 2006, the Agency had achieved case and cash compliance rates of just 67 per cent and 63 per cent respectively on the new scheme,[84] indicating that to date there had been no real improvement on the 2004–05 outturn.

---

[76] HE Peters, LM Argys, EM Maccoby and RH Mnookin, 'Enforcing Divorce Settlements: Evidence from Child Support Compliance and Award Modifications' (1993) 30 *Demography* 719 at 726. See also, in the UK context, Marsh and Vegeris, n 25 above, at 45.

[77] HC Work and Pensions Select Committee, n 58 above, at para 10.

[78] DWP, n 59 above, Tables 7.1 and 11.

[79] Strictly speaking, such terminology is inaccurate, as 'partial' compliance, where the child support award is not honoured in full, is actually a form of non-compliance: the NRP 'is not complying with the order, no matter how small the difference between the payment and the ordered amount': Del Boca and Flinn, n 47 above, at 1246.

[80] *Hansard* HC Debates vol 441 col 696W (11 January 2006).

[81] Child Support Agency, n 64 above, at 11.

[82] This was, however, some improvement on the Agency's truly disastrous performance in the first year of the new scheme (2003–04) for both case compliance (target 78%, outturn 50%) and cash compliance (target 75%, outturn 43%).

[83] DWP, *DWP Autumn Performance Report 2005* (Cm 6715, 2005) at 85–6.

[84] DWP, n 59 above, at Tables 7.1 and 11.

These compliance rates need to be understood in the wider context. In broad terms, across the whole spectrum of child maintenance arrangements—whether organised by the Agency, the courts or privately—two out of three families with some type of order or agreement (65 per cent) have actually received child support payments. Within that global group of recipients, about the same proportion (63 per cent) have received the full sum due on time, whilst almost one in four (24 per cent) have received the correct sum owing but not on time.[85] Unsurprisingly, full and timely compliance was best with voluntary agreements (68 per cent); the corresponding rate for court orders was 60 per cent, but for Agency assessments was just 47 per cent.[86] At first sight this might imply that the Agency's performance in terms of compliance rates is even worse than that of the courts. However, compliance with court orders might be anticipated to be better as these awards are likely to be either for lower amounts (for pre-1993 cases) or to have been made in cases where (after 1993) the parties have agreed a consent order. The apparent disparity may also be in part a function of the methodology used.[87] Whatever the explanation, it is plain that the current rate of compliance with Agency assessments is very unsatisfactory. But it is equally clear that, before the 1991 Act, maintenance obligations in both private law and public law were as much honoured in the breach as the observance.[88] The question then is to identify those factors which influence compliance and how these might inform a theoretical model of compliance.

The Research Evidence on Compliance

The most important point to emerge from the international literature on the case characteristics which influence compliance with child support liabilities is that 'receipt of child support is determined by multiple factors, only some of which are under governmental control'.[89] For example, the decline in the real value of child support payments in the United States in the 1970s and early 1980s, when enforcement of liabilities was largely a matter of private initiative, has been attributed to a combination of high inflation, increases in non-marital childbearing, reductions in the earning power of low-skilled men and the passage of no-fault divorce laws.[90] Since the mid-1980s, however, more proactive enforcement strategies have seen

---

[85] Lyon *et al*, n 32 above, at 318.

[86] *Ibid*, at 319–21. The published figure of 63% at 319 for court orders is incorrect (DWP, personal communication, 27 April 2006).

[87] The sample size for Agency cases (unweighted base 190) is much smaller than that for court orders (773) or voluntary agreements (577), so exaggerating any effect.

[88] See chs 2–4 above.

[89] AC Case, I-F Lin and SS McLanahan, 'Explaining Trends in Child Support: Economic, Demographic, and Policy Effects' (2003) 40 *Demography* 171 at 187.

[90] *Ibid*, at 187. See also J Bartfeld and DR Meyer, 'The Changing Role of Child Support Among Never-Married Mothers' in LL Wu and B Wolfe (eds), *Out of Wedlock: Causes and Consequences of Nonmarital Fertility* (Russell Sage Foundation, New York, 2001), ch 7.

child support payments rise in the United States, despite continued downward pressure from the increasing rate of non-marital births. In effect, the higher proportion of today's American parents with care that fall into the 'never married' category means that 'child support enforcement efforts are "swimming upstream", and the picture would look much worse in the absence of these policy changes'.[91] Three particular policies have been associated with increases in child support receipts in the United States since the 1980s: genetic testing, legislative guidelines and universal wage withholding.[92] Of these tools, the United Kingdom has embraced only legislative guidelines (in the shape of the child support formula).

Just as in the United States, there are a range of socio-economic and demographic factors which affect compliance rates in the United Kingdom but which are completely outside the control of the Agency.[93] Non-resident parents who pay child support tend to be older and better educated, and are more likely to be owner-occupiers and to be economically active.[94] Non-resident parents on higher earnings also tend to be more compliant.[95] One reason for this may be that for better-off parents 'it is difficult or more costly to avoid enforcement by changing jobs or moving to the underground economy',[96] although they may also be more likely to stay engaged in the lives of their children. Conversely, the poorest parents with care are the least likely to receive child support.[97] To some extent, therefore, child support compliance is a function of a phenomenon known by social scientists as 'assortative mating'—in simple terms, individuals tend to marry or cohabit with partners who share similar economic and social backgrounds.[98]

The legal status of the parents' prior relationship is also an important factor. It is clear, for example, that compliance is much higher for parents who are divorced or separated rather than those who have never married (or never cohabited).[99] In the same way, men who were both present at the child's birth and named on the

[91] J Kunz, P Villeneuve and I Garfinkel, 'Child support among selected OECD countries: a comparative analysis' in Vleminckx and Smeeding, n 69 above, ch 19 at 497. See also TL Hanson, I Garfinkel, SS McLanahan and CK Miller, 'Trends in Child Support Outcomes' (1996) 33 *Demography* 483.

[92] Case *et al*, n 89 above, at 188—obviously genetic testing is a more important factor for never-married mothers, whereas guidelines and wage withholding are more significant for mothers who are or have been married (as they are more likely to have an award in the first place).

[93] Some of these factors may be affected by wider government policies, but child support considerations may not be high on the relevant political agenda.

[94] Bradshaw *et al*, n 43 above, at 127–29. See also Atkinson and McKay, n 14 above, at ch 5.

[95] N Wikeley *et al*, *National Survey of Child Support Agency Clients* (DWP Research Report No 152, London, 2001) at 108.

[96] LM Argys and HE Peters, 'Can adequate child support be legislated? Responses to guidelines and enforcement' (2003) 41 *Economic Inquiry* 463 at 477. See further LM Rich, 'Regular and Irregular Earnings of Unwed Fathers: Implications for Child Support Practices' (2001) 23 *Children and Youth Services Review* 353.

[97] Bradshaw *et al*, n 43 above, at 131. Where PWCs were not on benefit, the odds of receiving maintenance increased more than five-fold: *ibid.*, at 137.

[98] See J Silvey and B Birrell, 'Financial Outcomes for Parents After Separation' (2004) 12 *People and Place* 46, demonstrating that Australian NRPs are disproportionately men on low incomes.

[99] See Wikeley *et al*, n 95 above, at 108: NRPs who had been married to or cohabited with the PWC were 5 and 3 times respectively more likely to comply than those who had been in more casual relationships.

birth certificate are much more likely to pay child maintenance.[100] As a result, child support compliance is positively associated with longer-term rather than casual or fleeting relationships.[101] Similarly, the parties' subsequent relationship status may be significant. If the parent with care has a new partner, receipt of child support is much less likely, as shown by a study which tracked a cohort of lone parents from 1991 through to 2001. One third of this group stated in 2001 that they had been in receipt of child maintenance in 1991, but the overall proportion within the cohort still in receipt of child support in 2001 had virtually halved to 17 per cent. However, this fall masked a more important finding—the proportion of those continuing to receive child maintenance in 2001 remained (relatively) firm at 26 per cent for those who were still lone parents, but had plummeted to just 10 per cent for those who were lone parents in 1991 but who were cohabiting with new partners by 2001.[102] Clearly, the arrival of a new partner for the parent with care may make the child's father less willing to provide support[103] or the mother less inclined to pursue maintenance from her former partner—or both. There is no doubt that non-resident parents are inclined to use their own perception of financial equity across different households 'to rationalise their reluctance to pay maintenance'.[104] Similarly, if non-resident parents remarry or acquire a new partner, they are much less likely to pay child support.[105] If both parents are living with new partners, we may assume that the chances of child support being paid diminish still further.

But compliance with child support liabilities is not determined simply by the parties' socio-economic and demographic status. Inevitably the quality of the post-separation relationship between the parents will impact on compliance. For example, non-resident parents who do not attribute fault following separation, and so presumably have a reasonably amicable relationship with their ex-partner, are three times more likely to comply with child support obligations.[106] According to the leading qualitative study of non-resident parents, 'all the enforced payers and non-payers were hurt, confused, frustrated and/or angry' about their past relationships.[107] The intense hostility that some of these men felt towards their former partners was such that 'demonising mothers was the only way these fathers could make sense of their lack of involvement in their children's lives'.[108] They refused to accept the legitimacy of the maintenance obligation in their particular

---

[100] K Kiernan, *Non-residential Fatherhood and Child Involvement: Evidence from the Millennium Cohort Study* (CASEpaper 100, LSE, 2005) at 12–13.

[101] Bradshaw *et al*, n 43 above, at 133.

[102] Marsh and Vegeris, n 25 above, at 45. However, 47% of lone parents had received child support at some point between 1991 and 2001, again demonstrating that compliance is not a static phenomenon.

[103] It is not just that payment of child support is less likely; amounts in payment will be lower: Bradshaw *et al*, n 43 above, at 147. See generally ch 1 at p 19 above.

[104] Bradshaw *et al*, n 43 above, at 197.

[105] Wikeley *et al*, n 95 above, at 108 and 181: NRPs who were now married to or cohabiting with a new partner were 4 and 2 times respectively less likely to comply.

[106] *Ibid*, at 181.

[107] Bradshaw *et al*, n 43 above, at 198.

[108] *Ibid*, at 201.

circumstances, having decided 'that the mother and children did not need it, or that the mother did not deserve it as she had obstructed contact, or that she could not be trusted to spend it only on the children'.[109] For these men, child support responsibilities were inherently conditional; in contrast, the willing payers regarded paying maintenance as their 'duty'.[110] There is, of course, ample empirical evidence that non-resident parents who see their children frequently tend to demonstrate better compliance with child support orders.[111] Whilst establishing the cause and effect of these relationships is distinctly more problematic,[112] there is no doubt that many men regard rights to contact and child support as linked through a 'process of balanced reciprocity'.[113] Many parents with care likewise find it difficult to understand the law's insistence on separating contact and child support: from their perspective, if fathers fail to provide financial support, they have forfeited any claim to contact.[114] Thus for many parents questions of contact and child support are 'a combined moral obligation, not a disaggregated bureaucratic one'.[115]

The nature (and, perhaps more importantly, the perception) of the child support scheme itself and the way it is administered will also impact on compliance. As Mandell has argued, 'the man tends to develop the perception that bad laws and a depersonalised bureaucracy, rather than his own behaviour, have made him a "bad guy"'.[116] According to one major quantitative survey, non-resident parents who believe that the assessment is fair are twice as likely to be compliant.[117] This should come as no surprise: for example, we know that people are more likely to comply with the law if they perceive themselves as being treated fairly by the criminal justice system.[118] Perceptions of fairness are, in turn, strongly influenced by three indicators of the quality of contact between liable parents and the Agency: ease of understanding Agency correspondence, access to the 'right' member of staff and a belief that the assessment was calculated correctly.[119] The comprehensibility of the scheme in general is also a factor in compliance. To this extent, the

---

[109] *Ibid*, at 222; see also at 204.

[110] *Ibid*, at 190; see also Atkinson and McKay, n 14 above at 47.

[111] See eg JA Seltzer, 'Relationships between Fathers and Children Who Live Apart: The Father's Role after Separation' (1991) 53 *Journal of Marriage and the Family* 79 and Bradshaw *et al*, n 43 above, at 134. For an econometric analysis, see D Del Boca and R Ribero, 'Visitations and Transfers After Divorce' (2003) 1 *Review of Economics of the Household* 187.

[112] Bradshaw *et al*, n 43 above, at 87 and 98.

[113] *Ibid*, at 208–9. However, this issue was not raised by NRPs in the sample studied in Atkinson and McKay, n 14 above (at 46). See further J Herring, 'Connecting Contact: Contact in a Private Law Context' in A Bainham, B Lindley, M Richards and L Trinder, *Children and Their Families: Contact, Rights and Welfare* (Hart Publishing, Oxford, 2003) at 106–11.

[114] C Smart, V May, A Wade and C Furniss, *Residence and Contact Disputes in Court: Volume I* (DCA Research Series 6/03 (DCA, London, 2003) at 81–85.

[115] *Ibid*, at 21.

[116] D Mandell, *'Deadbeat Dads': Subjectivity and Social Construction* (University of Toronto Press, Toronto, 2002) at 24.

[117] Wikeley *et al*, n 95 above, at 109 and 181.

[118] TR Tyler, *Why People Obey the Law* (Yale University Press, New Haven, 1990).

[119] *Ibid*, at 74, 109 and 177–78.

transparency of the new child support formula may encourage separating parents to reach their own private agreements where possible. As we have seen, the complexity of the original formula is such that this is simply not feasible in old scheme cases. However, it seems that under the new scheme significant numbers of people are using the Agency's website to calculate the child support payable in their case.[120] The sheer size of the Agency and the scope of its operations may in certain circumstances have an adverse impact on compliance. American research suggests that 'the larger the caseload, the less the bureaucracy collects, which makes sense given that higher caseloads mean caseworkers have less time to spend on each case'.[121] On the other hand, the Australian experience would imply that there may be certain economies of scale for the right type of mass child support system.[122]

All this statistical evidence on compliance is informative, but of itself it does not help with devising practical solutions to assist in ensuring that child support obligations are observed. The question then is how to create a robust compliance model which can inform policy decisions.

Building a Compliance Model

There has been relatively little theoretical work in the United Kingdom on building models of child support compliance. One exception is the Baseline Survey conducted on behalf of the Department for Work and Pensions before the ill-fated implementation of the new child support reforms.[123] Using multivariate statistical analysis, this report developed a framework to explain compliance (see Figure 15.2).[124] The resulting model is consistent with the findings from the range of studies discussed in the previous section. The model demonstrates that compliance is affected by a non-resident parent's perception of the fairness of the assessment and by the quality of contact with the child or children. Fairness and contact are in turn influenced by the socio-demographic characteristics of both parents, their current relationship with each other and any new relationships they may have experienced since the breakdown of their relationship with their original partner; these latter factors also affect compliance behaviour directly.[125] In addition, non-resident parents' experiences of dealings with the Agency and issues of comprehensibility, accessibility and responsiveness, as well as their general attitudes to the principle of child support, feed into compliance, either directly or indirectly through percep-

---

[120] 28,000 'hits' in April 2005: DWP, *Opportunity for all: Seventh Annual Report 2005* (Cm 6673, 2005) at 101.

[121] VM Wilkins and LR Keiser, 'Linking Passive and Active Representation by Gender: The Case of Child Support Agencies' (2006) 16 *Journal of Public Administration Research and Theory* 87 at 97. See also D Chambers, *Making Fathers Pay* (University of Chicago Press, Chicago, 1979) at 86, 91 and 97.

[122] See ch 6 above.

[123] Wikeley *et al*, n 95 above.

[124] *Ibid*, at 49.

[125] See further Bradshaw *et al*, n 43 above, ch 12, emphasising NRPs' perceptions of reciprocity and the need for a process of negotiation involved in setting child support liabilities.

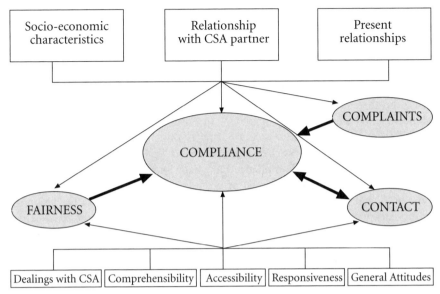

Fig. 15.2 A model of child support compliance

tions of fairness or through participation in the complaints process.[126] Further analysis in the Baseline Survey, involving simulations of future changes, suggested that although improving comprehensibility and accessibility would assist in increasing perceptions of fairness, it was better responsiveness on the part of the Agency which had the most impact. This resonates with the procedural justice literature: according to Tyler, 'the legitimacy of authorities is closely intertwined with the procedures they use when dealing with the public'.[127] In practice, the Agency's correspondence is sometimes 'written in language that is highly unlikely to elicit cooperation from parents'.[128] The Baseline Survey modelling showed that improvements in all these areas would improve compliance rates overall, although the data did not enable specific categories of non-resident parents who are more likely to respond to such changes to be identified.[129]

In stark contrast to the position in the United Kingdom, there is a rich literature in the United States discussing models of child support compliance, which have been developed to identify why child support is not paid and how collection rates might be improved. The early econometric studies proceeded on the assumption that divorcing parents are unable to reach cooperative agreements. In particular,

---

[126] It is a mistake to associate complainants with non-compliance: in fact NRPs who understood the system and complained are twice as likely to comply: *ibid*, at 109.

[127] Tyler, n 118 above, at 165.

[128] *Hansard* HC Debates vol 441 col 751 (17 January 2006), Mr M Hunter MP, who continued: 'Many parents face a CSA that acts as a judge, jury and executioner in its dealings with them'.

[129] Wikeley *et al*, n 95 above at 110–11.

Weiss and Willis emphasised that within marriage a combination of 'mutual trust, altruism, and proximity . . . will prevent ex post opportunistic behavior' and ensure that 'child expenditures are treated as a public or collective good'.[130] On divorce, however, the non-resident parent cannot monitor or verify the parent with care's allocation of resources. So, 'if, for instance, the wife has custody, then the husband is unable to determine whether the custodian spends a dollar on herself or on the children. She in turn treats all sources of her income (ie, earnings, alimony, child support) as fungible'.[131] In economic terms, as the parties are unable to reach a cooperative solution, this asymmetry leads to inefficient outcomes—in other words, less child support is paid. Several subsequent economic analyses of child support compliance have likewise tended to assume this predominantly non cooperative model of post-separation human relationships.[132] On this view of the world, the answer to non-compliance is legislative action to ensure stronger and more effective enforcement, including greater reliance on routinised administrative collection methods and, in the last resort, more aggressive criminal sanctions against defaulters.[133]

More recently, however, further studies have sought to develop cooperative models of child support compliance. For example, Flinn models both cooperative and non cooperative behaviour between parents in relation to child support payments and questions the assumption that increased enforcement activity necessarily results in higher compliance rates in all types of case.[134] Rather, he argues, compliance occurs where the gains in cooperation exceed the value of non cooperation for both parents, the policy implication being that child support authorities should devote greater attention to encouraging post-separation cooperative behaviour. Similarly, Argys and Peters contend that formulaic guidelines and stricter enforcement can increase payments when awards are court-ordered— where, by definition, the parties do not cooperate—but may not increase, and may even reduce, payments where some transfers would have taken place voluntarily. In other words, 'the characteristics of self-enforcing settlements will be different from those associated with court-imposed settlements'.[135] They conclude that 'policies encouraging involvement of [non-resident parents] and reducing antag-

---

[130] Y Weiss and RJ Willis, 'Children as Collective Goods and Divorce Settlements' (1985) 3 *Journal of Labor Economics* 268 at 272. See also JD Teachman, 'Who Pays? Receipt of Child Support in the United States' (1991) 53 *Journal of Marriage and the Family* 759 at 760: 'In a two-parent family, propinquity generally acts to maximise the investment of both parents in their children'.

[131] Weiss and Willis, n 130 above, at 272. For a more recent analysis by one of these authors, see RJ Willis, 'Child support and the problem of economic incentives' in WS Comanor (ed), *The Law and Economics of Child Support Payments* (Edward Elgar, Cheltenham, 2004), ch 2.

[132] See eg Del Boca and Flinn, n 47 above.

[133] See eg Chambers, n 121 above, and KJ Beron, 'Applying the Economic Model of Crime to Child Support Enforcement: A Theoretical and Empirical Analysis' (1988) 70 *The Review of Economics and Statistics* 382.

[134] CJ Flinn, 'Modes of Interaction between Divorced Parents' (2000) 41 *International Economic Review* 545.

[135] Argys and Peters, n 96 above, at 471.

onism during the divorce process can simultaneously increase the well-being of children and their divorced parents'.[136]

Social statisticians in the United States have also developed more nuanced theoretical frameworks for understanding child support compliance. Lin identifies three approaches for ensuring that laws are observed: these she describes as deterrence-based, compliance-based and consensus-based strategies.[137] In the child support context, a deterrence-based approach involves stricter enforcement with harsher sanctions for defaulters. A compliance-based strategy seeks to establish norms and regulate compliance behaviour before any breach takes place, and so includes measures such as universal and automatic deduction from salary. A consensus-based approach assumes that compliance occurs when the individual's personal norms coincide with social or legal norms, and works by trying to change those norms (for example by the use of formulaic guidelines in settling child support liabilities). The particular value of Lin's analysis is that she compares empirically non-resident fathers' perceptions of the fairness of child support awards with their compliance rates. The results indicate that 'both perceived fairness and routine income withholding have positive effects on compliance';[138] moreover, routine deduction from salary resulted in higher compliance rates amongst fathers who thought that their assessed liabilities were unfair.[139] Lin usefully identifies the practical implications for child support policy: in particular, a dual strategy of simultaneously seeking both to improve perceptions of fairness and to promote automatic income withholding is likely to improve overall compliance. Her conclusions also offer a counterweight to the persistent arguments from those calling for a shift back to a more discretionary scheme:

> If the child support system employed more uniform guidelines to determine support orders and if fewer exceptions were made, a compliance 'climate' or 'norm' might develop, similar to that in the social security and income tax systems.[140]

Equally, however, she counsels against over-reliance on deterrence-based strategies; whilst these might operate effectively where breaches of the law are relatively rare and readily identified, they start to lose their effect where the incidence of law-breaking increases and breaches pass unnoticed. In such circumstances, 'a more proactive form of social control—a compliance-based approach—may be a better tool for inducing public compliance'.[141]

Lin's work has been taken forward by Bartfield and Meyer, who differentiate between those they label as 'discretionary' or 'nondiscretionary' child support obligors amongst those non-resident fathers who have children in another household

---

[136] *Ibid*, at 478.
[137] I-F Lin, 'Perceived Fairness and Compliance With Child Support Obligations' (2000) 62 *Journal of Marriage and the Family* 388 at 389.
[138] *Ibid*, at 395.
[139] *Ibid*, at 396.
[140] *Ibid*, at 396.
[141] *Ibid*, at 397.

reliant on welfare.[142] The 'discretionary' obligors are those fathers who are beyond the reach of routine bureaucratic enforcement methods (typically, but not exclusively, the self-employed) and for whom child support payments depend largely on voluntary cooperation. The nondiscretionary obligors are those subject to routine enforcement mechanisms such as automatic income withholding. Bartfield and Meyer then test compliance rates for both groups against a range of variables, namely non-resident fathers' ability and willingness to pay and their incentives to cooperate, as well as the effectiveness of enforcement systems. Their analysis suggests that different factors influence the compliance patterns of discretionary and nondiscretionary obligors respectively. For example, ability to pay is linked to compliance for both groups of fathers, but the association is much stronger for discretionary obligors. In addition, 'the impact of the enforcement system appears greater for nondiscretionary obligors, whereas the impact of individual preferences appears greater for discretionary obligors'.[143] In policy terms, these findings confirm that enforcement strategies linked to formal employment will have little impact on those discretionary obligors not currently paying child support. They also emphasise the importance of developing policies to avoid the accumulation of large levels of arrears, possibly including 'carefully designed amnesty policies' as a means of encouraging future compliance.[144]

Of course, economists and social statisticians have developed such models in the context of the various United States child support schemes, and their findings may not apply with equal force in a different jurisdiction. However, the wider literature provides strong support for a more sophisticated child support enforcement strategy that responds to different categories of non-resident parent in a more nuanced way. Most notably, Ayres and Braithwaite have developed the notion of 'responsive regulation', contending that 'governments should be responsive to the conduct of those they seek to regulate in deciding whether a more or less interventionist response is needed'.[145] Similarly, Julian Le Grand has argued that British social policy reforms have traditionally assumed that individuals were either 'knights' (public spirited altruists) or 'pawns' (passive recipients of state largesse), whereas the contemporary assumption is increasingly that they are 'knaves' (self-interested actors).[146] On this basis the child support system might be characterised as a coercive mechanism to stop 'fathers knavishly ducking their duties'.[147] Le Grand's contention is that we need to develop welfare policies 'that allow for the possibility of different kinds of human motivation and hence

---

[142] J Bartfield and DR Meyer, 'Child Support Compliance among Discretionary and Non-discretionary Obligors' (2003) 77 *Social Service Review* 347.

[143] *Ibid*, at 364.

[144] *Ibid*, at 365.

[145] J Braithwaite, *Restorative Justice and Responsive Regulation* (Oxford University Press, Oxford, 2002) at 29; see further I Ayres and J Braithwaite, *Responsive Regulation: Transcending the Deregulation Debate* (Oxford University Press, New York, 1992).

[146] J Le Grand, 'Knights, Knaves or Pawns? Human Behaviour and Social Policy' (1997) 26 *Journal of Social Policy* 149.

[147] *Ibid*, at 159.

have the potential for more successful outcomes'.[148] Certainly, the Australian Agency has shown that different enforcement methods will work best for different client groups of parents with substantial child support arrears.[149] It follows that the child support system should not be predicated solely on coercion. Rather, Le Grand argues, 'by indicating through the legal system social disapproval of the practices concerned' (such as non-compliance with child support responsibilities), the regulatory system can 'help internalise that disapproval within individuals, thus helping convert the knave into the knight'.[150] We have already seen, on the empirical evidence, that social attitudes are an important predictor of compliance. Le Grand's framework has been applied in a stimulating critique of child support policy in New Zealand by Uttley, who argues that the assumption that non-resident parents will always act as knaves means that 'despite 150 years of attempts to locate absent parents and collect money from them, the end result is one of extremely limited effectiveness'.[151]

The question then is how, in the light of this empirical evidence and theoretical work, one might best improve compliance rates with child support obligations. The next three sections explore the arguments for and against three broad options for reform of child support law and policy. These are a guaranteed maintenance scheme (described here as option 1), a partial or full return to the courts (option 2) and reform of the current child support system (option 3). These three avenues of reform are categorised in this way solely for the purposes of exposition; it may be possible, for example, to envisage a package of measures that combines, for example, elements of all three options.

Reform Option 1: A Guaranteed Maintenance Scheme?

The United Kingdom's decision in 1991 to follow its common law cousins in Australia and (to a lesser extent) the United States of America in implementing a national, formula-based administrative scheme for assessing, collecting and enforcing private child support liabilities means that we have taken a very different path from our North European neighbours.[152] Guaranteed maintenance

---

[148] *Ibid*, at 150.

[149] A Shephard, 'The Australian Child Support Agency: Debt Study and Follow-Up on Intensive Debt Collection Process' (2005) 43 *Family Court Review* 387.

[150] Le Grand n 146 above at 163. For further elaboration of the wider arguments, see J Le Grand, *Motivation, agency and public policy: of knights and knaves, pawns and queens* (Oxford University Press, Oxford, 2003).

[151] S Uttley, 'Child Support: The Limits of Social Policy Based on Assumptions of Knavery' (1999) 33 *Social Policy and Administration* 552 at 558.

[152] This reflects, of course, the very different traditions of the 'Anglo-Saxon' as compared with 'Scandinavian' models of the welfare state: see J Millar, 'Mothers, workers and wives: comparing policy approaches to supporting lone mothers' in E Bortolaia Silva (ed), *Good enough mothering? Feminist perspectives on lone motherhood* (Routledge, London, 1996), ch 5. See also, comparing France and the UK, eg C Martin, 'Father, Mother and the Welfare State: Family and social transfers after marital breakdown' (1995) 5 *Journal of European Social Policy* 43.

schemes operate in at least eight countries[153] and their adoption has been urged by the Council of Europe.[154] In such schemes, a public authority, typically the social security office, makes advance payments of child support where the non-resident parent either does not pay, or cannot pay, and then assumes responsibility for collecting and offsetting contributions from the defaulting parent.[155] The precise details of the arrangements vary; support is guaranteed in some states regardless of the income of the parent with care,[156] whereas in others it is assured only for those on low incomes or those in financial difficulties.[157] Similarly, in some countries a parent with care may apply for guaranteed maintenance as soon as any payments are missed, whereas in other states further conditions may apply (eg as regards the period in arrears or the unsuccessful use of court procedures).[158]

The option of a guaranteed maintenance scheme has attracted some interest in the United Kingdom from voluntary sector organisations working with lone parents.[159] The principal argument is that, as private child support is an inherently unreliable source of income, guaranteed child support would provide greater security, especially for low income families not claiming benefit, and would operate as a further incentive for lone parents on welfare to move into paid work.[160] In this way guaranteed child support would also contribute to the task of tackling child poverty. To date, however, such proposals have received only limited political support. In 1999 the House of Commons Social Security Select Committee agreed with ministerial objections and concluded that such a scheme would remove the incentive to comply with the Agency.[161] In 2005 its successor Select Committee was less dismissive of the idea, and called on the Department to undertake more research on the potential benefits and costs of a system of guaranteed child maintenance.[162] The Department, however, restated its objections, arguing that guaranteed child support would simply become an additional benefit payment and there was a real risk that compliance with the Agency would diminish still further.[163] The disincentive effect might be countered by the state matching child support payments made by non-resident parents up to a certain level,[164] but

---

[153] Austria, Denmark, Finland, Germany, Luxembourg, Norway and Sweden: see J Bradshaw and N Finch, *A comparison of Child Benefit packages in 22 countries* (DWP Research Report No 174, London, 2002) at 55.

[154] Council of Europe, Recommendation No R(82)2 (4 February 1982).

[155] H Barnes, P Day and N Cronin, *Trial and error: a review of UK child support policy* (Family Policy Studies Centre, 1998) at 43.

[156] Bradshaw and Finch, n 153 above (Denmark, Finland and Norway).

[157] *Ibid*, (Luxembourg and Sweden).

[158] A Corden, *Making child maintenance regimes work* (Family Policy Studies Centre, 1999) at 42–43 (probably the most comprehensive comparison of such schemes to date).

[159] One Parent Families have argued for the introduction of such a scheme. See also A Garnham and E Knights, *Putting the Treasury First: The truth about child support* (CPAG, Poverty Publication 88, 1994) at 137.

[160] Corden, n 158 above, at 42.

[161] HC Social Security Select Committee, n 54 above, at para 71.

[162] HC Work and Pensions Select Committee, n 65 above, at paras 143–52.

[163] HC Work and Pensions Select Committee, n 58 above, at para 19.

[164] Although the history of the child maintenance bonus is unhelpful in this respect.

this would of course have public expenditure implications. In truth, so far as lone parents on welfare are concerned, the United Kingdom already operates a guaranteed maintenance scheme—it is just called income support.[165] Of course, a comprehensive guaranteed child support system would bring within its scope those parents with care on low or modest incomes who are not currently on benefit.

The underlying issue here is the appropriate balance between public and private support for children who live apart from one (or indeed sometimes both) of their genetic parents.[166] In this context it is hard to envisage that there will be much of a political appetite for any initiative involving a significant further increase in public expenditure on state support for children. The Treasury would argue that the public purse has already made a significant contribution to the cause of combating child poverty, both by improvements in the real value of child benefit and means-tested out-of-work benefits for children and through the extension and generosity of the new tax credits scheme, which has channelled more resources to those in work on low or modest incomes who have children.[167] Indeed, in contrast to the experience in the United States, welfare reform in the United Kingdom since 1997 has involved more 'carrot' than 'stick', and the employment rate of single mothers 'increased from a very low base of 40 per cent in the early 1990s to about 50 per cent by the end of the decade'.[168] On this analysis, the continuing problems of child support need to be addressed by reinforcing, rather than undermining, private responsibility for the financial support of children. If this is right, is the Agency, rather than the courts, the mechanism for doing so?

Reform Option 2: A Return to the Courts and More Private Ordering?

In the last resort, disputes about the quantification and enforcement of civil liabilities may be pursued through the courts. The dismal performance of the Agency in recent years should not disguise the fact that it was the inability of the courts to provide an effective child maintenance system that was one of the prime reasons for the adoption of the 1991 Act. We have seen that the courts have retained a largely residual role under the current child support legislation.[169] In summary, where the parent with care is in receipt of income support or income-based jobseeker's allowance, she is treated as having applied for child support.[170] The Agency's maintenance calculation will then override any pre-existing court order

---

[165] Corden, n 158 above, at 45–46.

[166] See the discussion in ch 1 at p 22.

[167] See generally J Hills and K Stewart (eds), *A More Equal Society?* (Policy Press, Bristol, 2005).

[168] R Dickens and DT Ellwood, 'Child Poverty in Britain and the United States' (2003) 113 *The Economic Journal* F219 at F236; see also H Sutherland and D Piachaud, 'Reducing Child Poverty in Britain: An Assessment of Government Policy 1997–2001' (2001) 111 *The Economic Journal* F85.

[169] See ch 7 above.

[170] Unless, of course, she can establish 'good cause'.

or agreement. If the parent with care is not claiming one or other of those benefits, then she may reach a private agreement with the non-resident parent about child support. The parties concerned may also embody that agreement in a consent order by the court, although such a consent order now only bars an application to the Agency for a period of 12 months.[171]

A number of organisations have argued that the courts should be granted a greater role in child support issues.[172] The most far-reaching proposal is that the Agency should be abolished and all its functions returned to the courts. The obvious difficulty with this option is that there was 'no golden age of child maintenance before the CSA was set up';[173] this suggestion also ignores the substantial volume of cases previously dealt with by liable relative officers within the benefits system. There are, however, a number of other ways in which the courts might be given a greater role in child support matters. In organisational terms, one might characterise a potential redrawing of the division of responsibility between the courts and the Agency in terms of either child support functions or child support client categories.[174]

At an operational level, the most radical option would be to return the assessment of child support payments to the courts but to leave the enforcement of such liabilities to the Agency. If this route is taken, one would then have to determine how far the courts should be bound by the current (or any future) legislative formula for child support. The argument in favour, as Maclean observes, is that:

> there remains a choice between devoting considerable resources, whether public or private, to negotiating finely tuned individualized arrangements, or accepting the blunter instrument of a formula-based arrangement which should be less costly per case and could be designed to achieve a broader measure of social justice.[175]

Bradshaw and his colleagues, on the other hand, advocate that the formula should be abandoned: their view is that this area of policy 'calls for a degree of flexible, individualised justice that probably cannot be handled within the disciplines and culture of social security'.[176] Yet dispensing with the formula and reverting to discretion to determine child support liabilities on the basis of the intrinsic merits of the case would generate its own problems. It is important to bear in mind that the highly discretionary legislative framework for resolving ancillary relief claims on divorce (for example for capital orders or, in rare cases, spousal support) has itself

---

[171] CSA 1991, s 4(10)(aa); in old scheme cases, however, a consent order may lock out a parent with care from the Agency indefinitely: *ibid*, s 4(10)(a).

[172] eg Resolution (formerly the Solicitors' Family Law Association).

[173] *Hansard* HC Debates vol 441 col 718 (17 January 2006), Mr J Plaskitt MP (Parliamentary Under Secretary of State).

[174] There are, of course, variants which combine such categorisations.

[175] M Maclean, 'Delegalized Family Obligations' in J Kurczewski and M Maclean (eds), *Family Law and Family Policy in the New Europe* (Dartmouth, Aldershot, 1997) ch 7 at 136.

[176] Bradshaw *et al*, n 43 above, at 229. They envisage the Agency's role being confined to collection and enforcement: *ibid*, at 230.

been the subject of much criticism.[177] The unpredictability of outcomes has led Douglas and Perry to describe it as not so much 'bargaining in the shadow of the law' as 'operating in a vacuum'.[178] Moreover, in some areas of family law, such as residence and contact disputes, the courts hold out the promise of individualised justice but actually deliver—at considerable private and public expense—what parents perceive to be a standard formula-based package.[179] To that extent 'flexible, individualised justice' is perhaps the preserve of the very rich.[180]

An alternative approach would be to redefine the boundaries between the courts and the Agency in terms of their respective client categories. In its crudest form, this might mean that the Agency would retain responsibility for assessing, collecting and enforcing child support liabilities for parents with care on welfare, whilst all other cases would return to the courts.[181] This solution is sometimes advocated by those who argue that the state has no interest in the determination of child support liabilities unless there are consequences for public expenditure, typically in the extra costs borne by the social security budget. There is certainly an argument that, in order to avoid the duplication of proceedings, courts should have the power to determine child support liabilities, subject to the legislative formula, in cases which are already in the courts for the determination of ancillary relief matters. There are, however, at least three compelling sets of reasons, based on both principle and pragmatism, which suggest that a broader restructuring on this basis is undesirable.

In the first place, this type of approach assumes that the primary goal of a child support system is to protect the public purse. This was, obviously, a major concern for the Conservative administration which introduced the Agency. Chapter 1 of this book, on the other hand, has argued that child support schemes should be premised on an acknowledgement of children's moral right to support. In that context, it is simply irrelevant whether or not the parent caring for the child is claiming a means-tested benefit.[182]

Secondly, the history of the welfare state demonstrates that a system designed for the poor often becomes a poor service. Conversely, one of the reasons for the

---

[177] See eg P Watson-Lee, 'Financial Provision on Divorce: Clarity and Fairness' [2004] 34 *Family Law* 182 and 348.

[178] G Douglas and A Perry, 'How parents cope financially on separation and divorce—implications for the future of ancillary relief' (2001) 13 *Child and Family Law Quarterly* 67 at 76, echoing the seminal paper by R Mnookin and L Kornhauser, 'Bargaining in the shadow of the law' (1979) 88 *Yale Law Journal* 950.

[179] Smart *et al*, n 115 above, at 28.

[180] But see J Eekelaar, 'Shared Income After Divorce: A Step Too Far' (2005) 121 *Law Quarterly Review* 1 and 'Miller v Miller: The Descent into Chaos' (2005) 35 *Family Law* 870, arguing that 'discretion must be centred on firm principle and policy'.

[181] But see n 174 above. So, for example, one might envisage a system in which the responsibility for assessment rested with the courts in private cases and with the Agency in benefits cases, but the Agency had sole powers of enforcement.

[182] Moreover the logical corollary of arguments based on saving public expenditure is that all parents in receipt of other means-tested benefits (eg housing benefit and council tax benefit) and child or working tax credits should be deemed to have applied for child support.

relative success of the Australian child support scheme is arguably its very universality: all separated parents are within the ambit of the Agency and 94 per cent of those eligible to register do so[183] (although many then opt for private collect and have no further contact with the Agency, other than for an annual reassessment). Even in the United States, about 60 per cent of eligible families participate in state child support programmes. Moreover, although there are marked disparities in the composition of caseloads across different American states, over 80 per cent of child support recipients are *not* currently on welfare.[184] Indeed, Crowley has argued that the American child support system has been transformed from one exclusively for those on welfare to one for all parents with care, with the result that 'the child support enforcement program is one of the most popular social policy initiatives in the United States'.[185] As a result the American and Australian systems avoid the stigmatisation associated with what is effectively a two-tier system in place in the United Kingdom.

Thirdly, and more pragmatically, this type of realignment would face serious operational problems, as parents' status as a 'private' or 'benefit' case is not fixed and immutable—in particular, parents with care typically move on and off benefit, depending on their circumstances at any one time. There is a real danger that a system which categorised parents with care in this way would simply reinvent the problem identified by the Finer Report with the arrangements in place before the diversion procedure was introduced, when women who were owed maintenance were buffeted from pillar (the magistrates' court) to post (the National Assistance Board office) and back again.[186]

In fact, to present the policy issue as a binary choice between the courts and the Agency is misleading. In practice, the real choice is between private ordering in the broadest sense (with the courts being involved as an absolute last resort) and the Agency. We have seen already that voluntary child support agreements tend to result in higher payments and better compliance. However, it is by no means self-evident that the interests of parents with care and children will always be best served by child support being negotiated privately between the respective parties, especially in the absence of clear rules as to the basis for quantifying support obligations. Research in the context of ancillary relief proceedings demonstrates that many parents will feel under intense pressure to compromise on unsatisfactory terms in order to avoid further stress or conflict.[187] In some cases there will also be real doubts as to the parties' true financial positions, making it difficult to

---

[183] Ministerial Taskforce, n 60 above, at 77.

[184] V Turetsky, 'What If All The Money Came Home? Welfare Cost Recovery in the Child Support Program' (2005) 43 *Family Court Review* 402 at 403–4. This may, of course, reflect in part the inadequacy of US social welfare programmes.

[185] JE Crowley, 'The Gentrification of Child Support Enforcement Services, 1950–1984' (2003) *Social Service Review* 585 at 585; see further JE Crowley, *The Politics of Child Support in America* (Cambridge University Press, Cambridge, 2003).

[186] See ch 4 at p 95 above.

[187] F Wasoff, 'Mutual Consent: Separation Agreements and the Outcome of Private Ordering in Divorce' (2005) 27 *Journal of Social Welfare and Family Law* 237 at 245.

gauge whether a negotiated settlement is fair.[188] There are, in addition, very real concerns about the extent to which separated parents will have access to independent and expert advice on child support issues.[189] So private ordering may not involve individual empowerment; rather, such settlements may be characterised by a sense of 'reluctance, duress [and] perceived absence of reasonable alternatives'.[190] Indeed, some lawyers concede that female lone parents 'think they just have to struggle on whatever their income is and whatever the husband agrees to pay them'.[191]

Reform Option 3: Changes to Child Support Law?

There may be insufficient political support for the introduction of a guaranteed maintenance scheme on the model of other North European welfare states. There are also, as we have seen, real practical problems with returning child maintenance business wholesale to the courts. Since 1991 there has in any event already been a significant shift towards private ordering, as parents in private cases have voted with their feet and entered into voluntary agreements (with or without the backing of a consent order) rather than approach the Agency. In the last resort, however, the need for some sort of state intervention to resolve child support disputes will remain. The final strategy for reform might involve retaining the existing framework for child support law and policy but identifying necessary modifications to those arrangements. This section accordingly considers some of the key issues that remain in relation to the three broad areas of critical importance in any child support scheme: assessment, collection and enforcement.

Assessment

There is little doubt that the new scheme formula has several advantages over its predecessor; in particular, its relative simplicity and transparency has the potential to encourage greater compliance with child support orders in the longer term. There are, however, at least five areas which might be revisited in terms of further reform; these are recognition of informal child support, the allowance for contact and shared care, the burden on low-income non-resident parents, the basis for income assessments and the relationship with the tax system.

The first is whether the child support system should recognise informal child support. Both the old and the new schemes assume that child support is measurable only in direct cash terms.[192] The legislative characterisation of child support

---

[188] *Ibid*, at 248. See further eg J Eekelaar, M Maclean and S Beinart, *Family Lawyers: The Divorce Work of Solicitors* (Hart Publishing, Oxford, 2000) at 162–66.

[189] See generallly Moorhead *et al*, n 41 above.

[190] Wasoff, n 187 above, at 247. See also Douglas and Perry, n 178 above, at 78.

[191] Moorhead *et al*, n 41 above, at 19.

[192] CSA 1991, s 1: see p 216 above.

in exclusively financial terms means that some non-resident parents are less willing to provide more informal support, whether through the purchase of goods or through the provision of assistance in kind (such as child care).[193] In particular, there is a risk that policies designed 'to promote the financial involvement of low-income single fathers can discourage their paternal involvement altogether'.[194] A number of researchers in the United States have challenged the popular perception that poorer non-resident parents are 'deadbeat dads', arguing that many are in fact actively engaged in their children's lives.[195] In the United Kingdom, Bradshaw points to the fundamental difference between formal and informal child support—in particular, the latter renders the non-resident parent's status as the payer visible as well as ensuring that the money is spent only on the children.[196] Atkinson and McKay also show how non-resident parents resent their lack of control over how child support is spent, and argue that this could be addressed by diverting payments to a savings account or to a child trust fund.[197] One obvious difficulty with this proposal is that child support is intended to provide an income stream today, not an asset to be unlocked in the future. This criticism might be addressed by allowing child support payments above a certain level to be directed towards a savings account.[198] An alternative approach might be to permit a certain proportion of any child support liability to be met in kind, as the Australian scheme allows through so-called 'non-agency payments'. This would be consistent with the drive to establish a more responsive child support regime which encourages individual responsibility and private collection methods, although it would be at the price of simplicity. The inevitable difficulties in monitoring such arrangements might suggest that these should only be credited against child support liabilities where both parties agree. The risk remains that one parent will seek to exploit the potential these agreements offer to exercise continuing control over the other, even though the relationship between the adults is over.

The second and related area concerns a specific type of informal child support, namely the relationship between child support and contact or shared care. Policy makers and the courts have always affirmed the conceptual distinction between the two issues of the payment of child support for a child and contact with that child, although many parents regard them as inherently inter-connected.[199] Putting to one side the questions of principle, there are obvious practical reasons

[193] Bradshaw *et al*, n 43 above, at 172 and 174.

[194] K Roy, 'Low-Income Single Fathers in an African American Community and the Requirements of Welfare Reform' (1999) 20 *Journal of Family Issues* 432 at 433.

[195] See eg *ibid*, and S McLanahan, I Garfinkel, NE Reichman and JO Teitler, 'Unwed Parents or Fragile Families? Implications for Welfare and Child Support Policy' in Wu and Wolfe, n 90 above, ch 7. But see A Rangarajan and P Gleason, 'Young Unwed Fathers of AFDC Children: Do They Provide Support?' (1998) 35 *Demography* 175.

[196] Bradshaw *et al*, n 43 above, at 217.

[197] n 14 above at 49.

[198] This would be consistent with the view that child support serves a dual function, as discussed in ch 1—to provide for basic needs but also to ensure that the child shares in any higher standard of living enjoyed by both parents.

[199] See n 114 above.

for any child support scheme to disregard minimal levels of contact in assessing child maintenance liabilities. It is, however, important that the public perceive courts and state agencies to be equally firm with parents who deny contact unreasonably as with parents who refuse to pay child support.[200] This is because, as we have seen, wider perceptions of fairness are fundamental to improving compliance with child support responsibilities.

The relationship between child support and shared care is more problematic. As we saw in chapter 10, where there is shared care of children then child support liabilities will be reduced, providing the degree of co-parenting exceeds a certain threshold.[201] Experience both here and overseas indicates that disputes may well arise between parents over the true level of shared care and its impact on child support liabilities. So far as possible, child support schemes need to be designed to limit the scope for such disagreements occurring, which implies imposing a higher rather than lower threshold.[202] In this context policy makers need to be clearer about the underlying rationale for making adjustments to assessments on the basis of shared care. If the purpose of the statutory scheme is to ensure that children receive a basic level of support and also share in both parents' standard of living, then we need to abandon the notion that the purpose of the shared care rules is simply to compensate non-resident parents who provide shared care for the expenditure they incur when the children live with them. Rather, if the state's policy is to encourage the provision of shared care as—by and large—a worthwhile enterprise for children whose parents live apart, then we need to be explicit about that objective, and not the reimbursement of financial outlays, as being the reason for reducing child support liabilities.

A third area of controversy concerns the way in which low income non-resident parents are treated by the child support system. Across the Atlantic, the changes to American child support systems in the 1980s assumed that the fundamental problem was one of awards being both too low and not properly enforced. This has been associated in popular discourse with the notion of the 'deadbeat dad' who wilfully fails to fulfil his parental responsibilities. Certainly early research suggested that non-resident parents in the United States could afford to pay more by way of child support than was the case under typical state guidelines.[203] Moreover, simply because non-resident parents may start off on low incomes does not mean that they remain poor thereafter.[204] Subsequent studies, however, have highlighted the diversity of non-custodial fathers' financial circumstances. For example, Mincy and Sorenson drew a distinction between 'deadbeats' and 'turnips',

---

[200] See now the measures in the Children and Adoption Bill 2006.

[201] Effectively two nights a week under the old scheme or one night a week under the new scheme.

[202] A higher threshold would also reflect the fact that the parent with care's fixed costs are unlikely to change much.

[203] I Garfinkel and D Oellerich, 'Noncustodial Fathers' Ability to Pay Child Support' (1989) 26 *Demography* 219.

[204] E Phillips and I Garfinkel, 'Income Growth among Nonresident Fathers: Evidence from Wisconsin' (1993) 30 *Demography* 227.

estimating that as many as a third of young absent fathers simply could not afford to pay child support.[205] There is, therefore, a growing recognition in the United States that low income fathers are routinely required to pay too much by way of child support.[206] However, several of the reasons cited—such as regressive child support guidelines and imputed incomes being higher than actual incomes—do not apply in the United Kingdom context.

In contrast to the extensive literature in the United States, there has been relatively little research in the United Kingdom on the extent to which non-resident parents, and especially those on low incomes, are able to meet their child support liabilities. Before the 1991 Act, Bradshaw and Millar reported that only about one third of lone parents who were not receiving maintenance believed that the non-resident parent could pay more.[207] Later work by Bradshaw and others estimate that nearly two-thirds of those non-resident parents not paying child support have no potential to do so because of their other commitments.[208] However, that study's definition of 'ability to pay' may be unduly broad, not least given what is known about the correspondingly worse levels of poverty experienced by many parents with care.[209] It must also be remembered that, although the new child support scheme has led to a significant increase in the proportion of non-resident parents liable for the fixed £5 a week assessment, it has also built in reduced rates for those on low earnings.[210] To that extent one can argue that the new scheme in the United Kingdom avoids the worst and most regressive features of some American child support systems. In addition, it may be that the failure of the existing system to be responsive to changes in incomes means that some non-resident parents' improved circumstances are not being picked up.[211]

This leads on to the fourth issue, which is the periodic basis for income assessments and reviews using the formula. A government bureaucracy simply could not operate the type of open-ended and highly discretionary system in use in the courts for setting maintenance awards. Yet the decision to base the original formula on the model of the main means-tested social security scheme necessarily introduced the very same complexities that bedevil the welfare system.[212] Moreover, in any child support scheme there will always be trade-offs between the

---

[205] RB Mincy and EJ Sorensen, 'Deadbeats and Turnips in Child Support Reform' (1998) 17 *Journal of Policy Analysis and Management* 44; in the UK we might say 'stones' rather than 'turnips', as the label is based on the American saying that 'You can't get blood from a turnip'.

[206] See eg M Cancian and DR Meyer, 'Fathers of Children Receiving Welfare: Can They Provide More Child Support?' (2004) 78 *Social Service Review* 179 and C-C Huang, RB Mincy and I Garfinkel, 'Child Support Obligations and Low-Income Fathers' (2005) 67 *Journal of Marriage and Family* 1213.

[207] Bradshaw and Millar, n 25 above, at 83.

[208] Bradshaw *et al*, n 43 above, at 141.

[209] H Barnes, L Clarke, G Paull and I Walker, *Child Support Reform and Low Income Families* (FPSC Working paper 10, FPSC, London, 2000) at 30.

[210] See ch 10 above.

[211] For example, note that although 55% of child support liabilities across both the new and old schemes are for £5 or less, only 28% of NRPs are currently on benefit: compare DWP, n 59 above, Tables 13.2 and 15a.

[212] See further NAO, *Dealing with the complexity of the benefits system* (HC 592, Session 2005–06).

simplicity of the rules and their sensitivity to the circumstances of individual cases.[213] The complexity of the child support scheme was exacerbated by the incremental changes in the mid 1990s, designed to accommodate non-resident parents' complaints about the rigidity of the original formula.[214] Most notably, the system of departures (now variations), intended to provide a degree of flexibility in the application of the basic formula, has only added to the complexity of both the old and new schemes. The question then is where any element of discretion should be introduced and how this should be best managed to ensure consistency.[215]

To date, the Agency's continuing administrative difficulties, not least with its new computer system, have clearly not delivered the improvements expected of the new scheme. These problems will not be solved by designing an IT system which is fit for purpose. True, the new child support formula no longer shadows the social security system in the same way as the old scheme formula. But although substantive child support law now eschews such a close relationship with the benefits system, the procedural provisions underpinning the 1991 Act continue to mirror social security law and practice, creating serious problems for the decision making and appeals processes. In particular, the child support scheme continues to operate on the 'week by week' mentality of the benefits system. Allied with the cumbersome adjudicatory machinery of revisions and supersessions, the result is that many cases may go round and round in ever decreasing (or perhaps increasing) circles without any realistic prospect of resolution.[216]

A radical approach to this problem would be to move to a system which determines child support liabilities on a longer term basis, such as the previous year's taxable income, either as it stands or as adjusted for child support purposes, as happens in the Australian scheme. There are undoubtedly potential difficulties with this type of reform, as has been demonstrated by the problems associated with the introduction of the new tax credits scheme from April 2003, not least in reconciling provisional awards with the final end of year tax data and the risk of overpayments. These difficulties also include uncertainties over the reliability of income figures declared to the tax authorities, especially by some self-employed parents. There would, in addition, have to be a means of accommodating subsequent changes in circumstances that avoided the worst excesses of the departures and variations schemes. However, such a reform offers the prospect of bringing a greater degree of operational stability to the whole assessment process.

Lastly, any such reforms of the basis of income assessments inevitably raise the wider question of the relationship between the child support and tax systems. In

---

[213] See eg N Wikeley, 'Child Support, Dividend Income and the Bertie Wooster Escape Clause' (2005) 35 *Family Law* 707 on the differing treatment of dividend income under the old and new schemes respectively.

[214] See generally ch 5 above.

[215] See N Wikeley and L Young, '*Smith v Secretary of State for Work and Pensions*: child support, the self-employed and the meaning of "total taxable profits"—total confusion reigns' (2005) 17 *Child & Family Law Quarterly* 267.

[216] See ch 14 above.

particular, is administrative reorganisation part of the answer to the problems of
child support? The discussion above of Option 2 contemplated the reallocation of
functions as between the Agency and the courts. Option 3 might involve the
wholesale transfer of the Agency to Her Majesty's Revenue and Customs (HMRC),
formerly the Inland Revenue. An alternative strategy would be to leave the Agency
in charge of the assessment of liabilities but to reassign its collection and enforcement functions to HMRC. The official justification for locating the Agency within
the then DSS, rather than constituting it as part of the Inland Revenue, were
explored in chapter 5.[217] Successive administrations have reaffirmed that the DSS,
now the DWP, remains the optimum location for the Agency.[218] It is true that,
under the Blair governments, the tax authorities have assumed a significant role in
the delivery of state-funded financial support to children—today HMRC has
responsibility for the payment of child benefit and child tax credits, as well as for
the administration of the child trust fund scheme.[219] On that basis it would be
logical to include child support within HMRC's remit. This would also help to
remove the stigma of association with the benefits system which currently sur-
rounds the Agency.

There are, however, several reasons why HMRC may not be the natural home for
the Agency.[220] First, child support is as much about private as public support for
children. Secondly, the Agency has to deal with many parents with care and non-
resident parents who are also benefits claimants, emphasising the need for efficient
liaison with other parts of the DWP (not least in ensuring that the child maintenance premium operates effectively). Thirdly, HMRC's well-publicised problems in
implementing the tax credits scheme since 2003 suggest that from an operational
point of view, at least in the short term, there may now be little to be gained in
transferring the Agency or any part of its functions from the DWP to HMRC.
Finally, there is the very real and wider concern that transferring responsibility for
child support to HMRC would jeopardise the integrity of the tax base. Certainly
there is some evidence from Australia that putting the revenue authorities in charge
of collecting child support increases non-compliance in relation to tax liabilities—
eg through under-declaring income or over-claiming deductions.[221]

Ultimately, however, the location of the Agency within the overall organisational framework of government is a question of process, not principle. A more
fruitful immediate avenue for reform might be to explore ways in which the
Agency might have readier access to data held by HMRC. At the present, the flow

---

[217] See p 127 above.
[218] See eg HC Social Security Committee, *Child Support: Good Cause and the Benefit Penalty, Fourth
Report* (HC 440, Session 1995–96) Minutes of Evidence at 55–56 and *Child Support*, Minutes of
Evidence (HC 1031-I, Session 1997–98) at 18.
[219] See N Wikeley, 'Child Trust Funds—asset-based welfare or a recipe for increased inequality?'
(2004) 11 *Journal of Social Security Law* 189.
[220] We might note that the Australian Agency, originally part of the ATO, has since been moved out
of the tax system, although there remain strong operational links: see p 170 above.
[221] E Ahmed and V Braithwaite, 'When Tax Collectors Become Collectors for Child Support and
Student Loans: Jeopardizing the Revenue Base?' (2004) 57 *Kyklos* 303.

of information between the Agency and HMRC is subject a number of restrictions, in terms of both the law and practice.[222] There are also significant barriers to the transfer of information across other organisational interfaces,[223] so further hindering Agency attempts to trace and assess non-resident parents.

Collection

Once child support liabilities are assessed, there obviously need to be effective collection systems in place. But ensuring that payment methods are easy to use and efficient is just one part of improving collection rates. The discussion earlier in this chapter has identified the wide range of factors which may impinge on compliance, including the Agency's own responsiveness. Compliance is also affected by the position of the parent with care, and so in this context the new child maintenance disregard is considered.

As regards collection methods, the fundamental question is the balance to be struck between private arrangements and official channels respectively for the payment of child support. The United Kingdom scheme is relatively unusual for its heavy reliance on the use of the Agency as an intermediary for the collection of child support. Only about one in six cases on the Agency's books involve 'maintenance direct', or private arrangements for the payment of Agency-assessed child support.[224] In Australia, by contrast, the balance is nearly 50:50.[225] To a large extent this difference reflects the high proportion of benefits cases within the United Kingdom system. On any basis, reliable private arrangements for child support transfers are to be preferred over Agency involvement, although there will clearly be cases where the Agency can serve a valuable function as a buffer between parents in a difficult relationship.

Where the Agency is responsible for collection, its workload will necessarily increase, a problem exacerbated by the methods of collection typically used. Convenience is one of the best determinants of compliance, yet at present payment of child support is not even possible by debit card or credit card.[226] The most common collection method across the whole of the Agency's caseload is 'manual', ie where a non-resident parent pays by cheque, bank giro credit or Transcash.[227] Obviously these methods mean that the liable parent must take positive action to make each payment—and the authorities must then follow up non-payments. Historically, the Agency has used DEOs primarily as an enforcement mechanism,

---

[222] See p 289 above.

[223] eg in relation to DVLA: see p 290 above.

[224] DWP, n 59 above, Table 9a (16%). The proportion is actually higher in old scheme (18%) than new scheme (14%) cases: see *ibid* Table 9b.

[225] CSA collect 47.8% and private collect 52.2%: Australian Child Support Agency, *Child Support Scheme: Facts and Figures 2004–05* (Canberra, 2006) Table 3.2 at 17.

[226] There are plans to introduce these methods of payment: see Child Support Agency, n 6 above at 8.

[227] These manual methods still account for 24% of all cases (down from 37% in 1995): DWP, n 59 above, Table 9a.

rather than as a standard collection tool; just 22 per cent of the Agency's total case-load is subject to DEOs or analogous requests.[228] DEOs will not be suitable for all cases, especially where the parent concerned changes job frequently. However, if DEOs were more common,[229] they might avoid the stigma of default with which they are currently associated. Research in the United States suggests that deduction of payments at source from wages has a positive effect on compliance.[230] In Australia 'employer withholding' is used in just over 40 per cent of Agency collect cases.[231]

Convenient and effective collection methods then need to be backed up by a comprehensive debt enforcement strategy that ensures timely compliance. This is standard practice in any large commercial organisation: for example, utility customers are first encouraged (often with discounts) to opt for payment by direct debit; those who remain on manual methods are periodically billed and any non-payment prompts the red demand notice and/or a telephone call. This type of action is not the monopoly of the private sector, as any self-employed person who has been late in submitting accounts or paying instalments of tax to HMRC knows. The Agency, unlike the court system, was supposed to monitor non-payment frequently and deal promptly with cases of non-payment.[232] The reality, of course, has been very different. The Agency's lack of responsiveness to dealing with parents' changes in circumstances has been matched only by its failure to tackle child support arrears at an early stage in the life of its caseload. There has also been little sign in the past that the Agency has appreciated the importance of risk-profiling to ensure that the right techniques are used for different categories of non-resident parents who are in arrears.[233] There are now indications that the Agency has belatedly appreciated the importance of learning lessons on debt enforcement strategies from other private and public sector organisations.[234]

The remaining issue to be addressed in this section is the potential for a child support disregard (now introduced in the form of the 'child maintenance premium') to improve collection rates. A child support disregard allows parents with care on income support to receive a certain amount of child maintenance without it affecting their entitlement to benefit. A disregard, it is argued, increases the likelihood of

---

[228] DWP, n 59 above, Table 9a.

[229] As is promised in the Agency's 2006 Operational Improvement Plan: see n 6 above at 8.

[230] See eg I Garfinkel and M Klawitter, 'The Effect of Routine Income Withholding on Child Support Collections' (1990) 9 *Journal of Policy Analysis and Management* 155 and AC Case, I-F Lin and SS McLanahan, n 89 above, at 184. But, for a more cautious view on this point, see JH Cassetty and R Hutson, 'Effectiveness of federal incentives in shaping child support enforcement outcomes' (2004) 27 *Children and Youth Services Review* 271 at 286.

[231] Australian Child Support Agency, n 225 above, Table 5.7 at 40. This figure is not directly comparable to the UK DEO rate of 22%, as the Australian figure refers solely to Agency collect cases, whereas the UK figure refers to the total Agency caseload. The comparable UK statistic (as a percentage of cases in which the Agency is responsible for collection of child support) is 26%.

[232] DSS, *Children Come First* (Cm 1264-I, 1991) at paras 5.17–5.19.

[233] See further n 65 above at paras 116–24.

[234] See Child Support Agency, n 6 above at 10.

compliance,[235] as non-resident parents see (some or all of) their payments going directly to support the child, rather than the Treasury.[236] (This assumes, of course, a reasonably amicable relationship between the now separated parents).[237] In turn, a disregard encourages parents with care on benefit to cooperate with the Agency, so minimising the risk of collusion between parents in the form of undeclared cash payments.[238] In addition, such an initiative would assist in the task of effectively tackling child poverty. Overseas experience is mixed: Australia has always operated a form of disregard for parents with care on welfare,[239] whereas the United States withdrew the federal requirement for a disregard in 1996.[240]

Historically there has been little enthusiasm in official circles in the United Kingdom for such a measure. The Conservative government which introduced the 1991 Act consistently rejected calls for a child support disregard, arguing that it would act as a disincentive for parents with care to enter the labour market[241] and would not represent good value for money.[242] A generous disregard would also raise issues of equity between the beneficiaries of such a policy and those parents on benefit who, for whatever reason, do not receive any child maintenance.[243] The Conservative government's grudging response to continuing demands for a child support disregard was to introduce under the 1995 Act the largely ineffective child maintenance bonus, which still operates as a delayed and very limited disregard in old scheme cases.[244] Meanwhile, successive governments have made the child support disregard for means-tested *in work* benefits and tax credits, as opposed to

---

[235] For empirical support for this proposition, at least in the context of the US schemes, see Cassetty and Hutson, n 230 above.

[236] In one US ethnographic study, NRPs regarded child support payments which defrayed welfare costs 'as a responsibility to keep the state off their backs, not as a responsibility toward their children': see Roy n 194 above at 445.

[237] The potential incentive effect of a disregard on NRPs will be much reduced where the relationship is fraught, given some NRPs' unwillingness or inability to trust PWCs to use child support appropriately: see above p 484.

[238] An ever-present official concern, dating back in one form or another to the poor law, has been that, in return for the PWC not passing their details to the Agency, NRPs will pay maintenance informally which the PWC on benefit fails to declare to the social security office. The existence of a (relatively generous) disregard would make such an option much less attractive for the PWC.

[239] Known as the 'maintenance income test': see ch 6 above at n 204.

[240] Federal law required states to operate a welfare disregard or 'pass through' of US$50 a month as from 1984 (Deficit Reduction Act), but this condition was abolished by the Personal Responsibility and Work Opportunity Reconciliation Act 1996. The pass through is now a matter for states' discretion, most of which have withdrawn it: see further D Kurz and A Hirsch, 'Welfare Reform and Child Support Policy in the United States' (2003) 10 *Social Politics* 397 at 400.

[241] As they would need to earn a higher salary in order to be better off in work than on benefit: DSS, n 232 above, at para 6.6. See also DSS, *Improving Child Support* (Cm 2745, 1995) at para 5.4.

[242] DSS, *Child Support: Reply by the Government to the Second and Third Reports from the Select Committee on Social Security Session 1990–91* (Cm 1691, 1991) at paras 5 and 6.

[243] L Burghes, *One-parent families: Policy options for the 1990s* (FPSC/Joseph Rowntree Foundation, York, 1993) at 13. One might argue that these concerns have become less pressing with the advent of more generous public support for children through increased child benefit and child tax credit.

[244] CSA 1995, s 10 and Social Security (Child Maintenance Bonus) Regulations 1996 (SI 1996/3195) and see ch 5 n 121 above. Any tribunal chairman who has dealt with appeals under the tortuous 1996 regulations might be forgiven for wondering whether the objective was really to see that the bonus was easy to claim.

out of work benefits such as income support, much more generous. Initially, in April 1992, the Conservatives implemented a £15 a week maintenance disregard for family credit and housing benefit.[245] Then, in October 1999, when working families' tax credit replaced family credit, the new Labour government introduced a total maintenance disregard for tax credit claimants.[246] Accordingly, there is now an even greater incentive for lone parents to work 16 hours or more a week (and so qualify for working tax credit) rather than just 15 hours a week (in which case they remain eligible for income support).[247]

Subsequently, and as part of the package of measures associated with the introduction of the new child support scheme in 2003, the government implemented a genuine child support disregard, although this is confusingly described as a 'child maintenance *premium*'.[248] The premium means that parents with care on income support who are receiving child support under the new scheme qualify for a maximum £10 a week disregard.[249] Both the scope and timing of this initiative were negotiated on a cost neutral basis with the Treasury.[250] As a result, the premium has two obvious weaknesses. The first is that there is no guarantee that its value will be increased over time to match inflation.[251] The second is that it is not available to parents with care who remain subject to the old scheme.[252] The Select Committee's recommendation in 2005 that the benefit of the premium be extended to old scheme cases has been rejected by government on grounds of operational efficiency rather than principle.[253] In practice, and to compound these weaknesses, the benefits of the child maintenance premium have yet to reach the majority of parents with care who are eligible under the new scheme, as a result of operational problems in its implementation and poor compliance. As at March

[245] And for their then companion benefits, disability working allowance (now part of WTC) and community charge benefit (now council tax benefit). See further P Bingley, E Symons and I Walker, 'Child Support, Income Support and Lone Mothers' (1994) 15 *Fiscal Studies* 81 and P Bingley, G Lanot, E Symons and I Walker, 'Child Support Reform and the Labor Supply of Lone Mothers in the United Kingdom' (1995) 30 *Journal of Human Resources* 256 at 268–73.

[246] This remains the case for WTC, introduced in April 2003. Housing benefit remains subject to the £15 disregard, which has now not been uprated for more than ten years.

[247] One possible reason for some parents with care preferring to remain on income support is that this benefit covers mortgage costs, unlike WTC.

[248] Strictly a premium is a component element of the income support applicable amount (see Income Support (General) Regulations 1987 (SI 1987/1967), reg 17 and sch 2), whereas the child maintenance premium operates as a standard income disregard.

[249] *Ibid*, reg 60B and sch 9, para 73. For some of the technical difficulties with this provision, see P Wood *et al*, *Social Security Legislation 2005, Vol II: Income Support, Jobseeker's Allowance, State Pension Credit and the Social Fund* (Sweet & Maxwell, 2005) at 635–36.

[250] HC Social Security Select Committee, n 54 above, at para 67. The estimated cost of disregarding all child support payments for the purpose of all benefits is some £230 million: *Hansard* HC Debates vol 440 col 422W (29 November 2005).

[251] The Government 'is committed to reviewing the value of the premium from time to time' (DSS, *The 1999 Child Support White Paper* (Cm 4536, 1999)), but see the history of the housing benefit disregard, n 246 above. A higher disregard will cause child poverty to fall further, assuming compliance increases: see Paull, Walker and Zhu, n 57 above, at 128.

[252] See further N Wikeley, 'Compliance, Enforcement and Child Support' (2000) 30 *Family Law* 888 at 888–89.

[253] See n 162 above, paras 133–42, and n 163 above, paras 16–18.

2006 there were just 42,000 new scheme parents with care receiving the benefit of the child maintenance premium, although 139,000 of such parents are on benefit.[254] Equally, the Agency has fallen a long way short of the 2002 Spending Review target of doubling the proportion of parents with care on benefit[255] who receive child support to 60 per cent by March 2006. By November 2005 the relevant proportion overall was just 25 per cent (but a more promising 38 per cent under the new scheme).[256] There will, in any event, always be limits in practice to the value of such a disregard to many parents with care on benefit, given the low incomes (and hence low assessments) of their former partners.[257]

Enforcement

The Agency already enjoys wide-ranging powers under the 1991 Act for enforcing child support liabilities. It is noteworthy that the most punitive measures available for dealing with especially recalcitrant non-resident parents—driving disqualification orders and imprisonment—are not replicated in the armoury of the Australian agency, which appears to have a much better record on compliance.[258] At present non-resident parents in the United Kingdom, on the basis of the official track record to date and its negative portrayal in the media, simply do not believe that the Agency will enforce payment, 'a worrying situation for an organisation seeking to enforce compliance'.[259] On this basis, it is entirely reasonable to argue that the Agency should simply use its existing powers promptly and efficiently in order to maximise compliance.[260]

The Agency's own internal review, carried out by the incoming Chief Executive in 2005,[261] identified two new sanctions that might be added to its portfolio of enforcement options: curfew orders and the revocation of passports. Both of these measures would necessarily require primary legislation, and so ministers have deferred a final decision on these possible sanctions until the recommendations of the Henshaw Report are known.[262] The potential advantages of passport revocation in cases where there has been serious and persistent default on child support liabilities have already been explored in chapter 14.[263] It is less clear that the imposition of curfew orders would be a helpful addition to the Agency's range of enforcement

---

[254] DWP, n 59 above, Tables 13.2 and 14.

[255] Income support or income-based jobseeker's allowance.

[256] DWP, n 59 above, Table 13.1.

[257] In March 2006 46% of NRPs under the new scheme had an assessed liability of £5 a week or less: DWP, n 59 above, at Table 15.

[258] See ch 6 above.

[259] Atkinson and McKay, n 14 above, at 60.

[260] There are signs that the Agency is putting more effort into its enforcement activity. A dedicated enforcement directorate was established in April 2005 and has already had an impact: see DWP, n 59 above, Table 20.

[261] Child Support Agency, *Summary of the CSA Strategic Plan* (November 2005), available on its website.

[262] *Hansard* HC Debates vol 442 col 1021 (9 February 2006).

[263] See pp 460–61 above.

options. The purpose of curfew orders would presumably be to provide an alternative to imprisonment by confining the child support defaulter to his home address during certain hours, thereby both restricting his liberty of movement and curtailing his opportunity to spend his income on his own leisure pursuits.[264]

Any such changes to the enforcement system will need to be handled with great care. Child support compliance will not be improved simply by waving big sticks. As Ayres and Braithwaite's model of responsive regulation implies, we need a regulatory pyramid; the presumption should be to start at the bottom, but 'as we move up the pyramid, more and more demanding and punitive interventions in peoples' lives are involved'.[265] Moreover, given the typical media portrayal of child support issues, there is a clear risk that increased sanctions alone, and especially the introduction of punitive measures such as curfew orders, will reinforce both the perception of non-resident parents as 'deadbeat dads' and the negative associations of any involvement with the Agency. Mandell argues that non-payers 'frame withholding of support as a means of self-empowerment, a way to regain the control they perceive they have lost'. She concludes that non-payment 'is an expression of resistance to identities that the system imposes on them'.[266] Issues of legitimacy and procedural justice are therefore crucial; if these values are not effectively promoted, then increased sanctions may actually reduce compliance.[267] In a similar vein, McLanahan and others in the United States have argued that 'the most fundamental problem with the public child support system is that it does almost nothing to help fathers'.[268] The Australian Agency appears to have learnt this lesson and has introduced a number of initiatives designed to provide guidance and support for non-resident parents.[269]

Finally, the Agency's effective monopoly over enforcement proceedings may need to be revisited. There are certainly arguments for the Agency to have the lead role in enforcing child support debts,[270] but it is debateable whether the total exclusion of parents with care from the enforcement process, even where they are private clients, is justified. There is an obvious danger that private cases, especially those involving non-resident parents with complex financial affairs, will be neglected in a system which is dominated by benefits cases, and in which securing public expenditure savings has so far been a central mission.[271] The present

---

[264] Or, as was reported by the *Daily Mirror*, 'Dodgy Dads To Be Tagged' (7 November 2005).

[265] Braithwaite, n 145 above, at 30.

[266] n 116 above, at 222 and 226.

[267] K Murphy, 'Regulating More Effectively: The Relationship between Procedural Justice, Legitimacy and Tax Non-compliance' (2005) 32 *Journal of Law and Society* 562; see further Tyler, n 118 above.

[268] McLanahan *et al*, n 195 above, at 223.

[269] See A Burgess, 'Bringing fathers back in: Child support in Australia' (2005) 12 *Public Policy Research* 49.

[270] eg in encouraging consistency of approach and 'reducing adversarial heat in fraught cases of parental separation' (*R (Kehoe) v Secretary of State for Work and Pensions* [2004] EWCA Civ 225; [2004] QB 1378 at para 90 per Ward LJ).

[271] According to one US study, 'child support bureaucracies with few TANF [welfare] cases do a much better job collecting for their non-TANF clients than those with caseloads dominated by TANF': Wilkins and Keiser, n 121 above, at 11.

arrangements have survived scrutiny from the House of Lords but may yet face a challenge before the ECHR.[272] In this context the Australian Ministerial Taskforce has recommended that parents with care be granted concurrent enforcement powers, so long as this does not conflict with action instigated by the Agency.[273]

Conclusion

Child support policy will always be contentious, as 'it stands at the juncture of the public and private domains, and must operate across the spheres of welfare policy and family law in a highly charged and emotional area'.[274] Indeed, there is no doubt that some parents 'can be pathologically hostile, obsessively controlling, manipulative, negligent and spiteful'.[275] It is therefore easy to conclude that the Agency has been given 'an impossible job'.[276] This view was reflected in the Prime Minister's comment in November 2005 that the Agency was 'not properly suited' to the task of enforcing parental obligations towards children. He added that it was 'extremely difficult to make this operation cost-effective when the agency is the investigating, adjudicating and enforcing authority'.[277] Yet this need not be the case: HMRC combine those three functions in relation to the assessment and recovery of tax revenues. Furthermore, child support policy is as controversial in Australia as it is in the United Kingdom (if not more so) but, for the reasons explored in this book, the Australians have developed a workable scheme with 80 per cent of the Agency's clients there describing themselves as 'satisfied' or 'very satisfied' with the service provided.[278] In this way, despite a less than auspicious start, the Australian scheme has recently been described as 'a success in a great many ways' and as having 'certainly led to a cultural change in community attitudes about the responsibility of both parents to provide for and support their children regardless of their relationship with each other'.[279]

In contrast, the early years of the United Kingdom's agency were simply disastrous, with the policy decision to apply the 1991 Act to existing as well as new cases resulting in public hostility and catastrophic administrative failings. The result was that in 1997 Labour 'inherited a child support system that many reckoned had put the whole cause back a generation'.[280] There was a widespread perception at the

---

[272] See *R (Kehoe) v Secretary of State for Work and Pensions* [2005] UKHL 48; [2006] 1 AC 42 and N Wikeley (2006) 18 *Child & Family Law Quarterly* 287.

[273] n 60 above at 173–74.

[274] Smart *et al*, n 115 above, at 82.

[275] *Ibid*, at 90.

[276] The assessment is that of one of the key players in process leading up to the 1991 Act: H Barnes *et al*, n 155 above, at 80.

[277] *Hansard* HC Debates vol 439 col 964 (16 November 2005).

[278] Burgess, n 269 above, at 50.

[279] Ministerial Taskforce, n 60 above, at 76.

[280] J Lewis, 'Women, Men and the Family' in A Seldon, *The Blair Effect* (Little, Brown, London, 2001), ch 22 at 497.

time that the reforms embodied in the 2000 Act represented the 'last chance saloon' for the Agency.[281] The further operational debacle associated with the implementation of the new scheme has only emphasised the importance of designing a child support system that is capable of effective delivery. On receipt of the Henshaw Report, the Government will therefore be faced with a number of pressing policy decisions. For example, the experience to date suggests that any redesigned scheme should not apply to the entirety of the Agency's existing case load. Rather, a pragmatic decision may have to be taken to write off certain categories of arrears so that the Agency is not saddled with an impossible debt mountain. If that line is taken, there would be a compelling case for proper compensation payments for parents with care who have been deprived of child support due to the Agency's past failures. Important though these decisions are, they must be based on a principled approach to child support which addresses the issues posed in the opening chapter to this book. These include, most significantly, the proper balance between private and public support for children and the theoretical basis underpinning the parental responsibility for child support. In particular, is that responsibility limited to meeting the child's economic needs, or does the child have a right to a share in parental income? So far, in the United Kingdom, both Parliament and the courts have singularly failed to conceptualise child support as an issue of children's rights rather than simply parental obligations.

---

[281] The phrase appears to have originated with Iain Duncan-Smith (*Hansard* HC Debates vol 719 col 744, 6 July 1998) but was echoed later by both One Parent Families and James Pirrie in their evidence to the HC Social Security Select Committee: *The 1999 Child Support White Paper* (HC 798, Tenth Report, Minutes of Evidence) at 32 and 97.

INDEX